Lecture Notes in Computer Science 15257

Founding Editors

Gerhard Goos
Juris Hartmanis

AF167465

The series Lecture Notes in Computer Science (LNCS), including its subseries Lecture Notes in Artificial Intelligence (LNAI) and Lecture Notes in Bioinformatics (LNBI), has established itself as a medium for the publication of new developments in computer science and information technology research, teaching, and education.

LNCS enjoys close cooperation with the computer science R & D community, the series counts many renowned academics among its volume editors and paper authors, and collaborates with prestigious societies. Its mission is to serve this international community by providing an invaluable service, mainly focused on the publication of conference and workshop proceedings and postproceedings. LNCS commenced publication in 1973.

Nicky Mouha · Nick Nikiforakis
Editors

Information Security

27th International Conference, ISC 2024
Arlington, VA, USA, October 23–25, 2024
Proceedings, Part I

 Springer

Editors
Nicky Mouha 🆔
Strativia, NIST Associate
Largo, MD, USA

Nick Nikiforakis 🆔
Stony Brook University
Stony Brook, NY, USA

ISSN 0302-9743   ISSN 1611-3349 (electronic)
Lecture Notes in Computer Science
ISBN 978-3-031-75756-3   ISBN 978-3-031-75757-0 (eBook)
https://doi.org/10.1007/978-3-031-75757-0

This Springer imprint is published by the registered company Springer Nature Switzerland AG
The registered company address is: Gewerbestrasse 11, 6330 Cham, Switzerland

If disposing of this product, please recycle the paper.

Preface

The 27th Information Security Conference (ISC 2024) was held on October 23–25, 2024 at George Mason University in Arlington, Virginia.

We had the honor as program co-chairs to handle the reviewing process, and we are extremely grateful to the authors, the reviewers, the steering committee, and the organizing committee who made it all possible. Special thanks go to the General Chair (Qiang Zeng), the Publications Chair (Anomadarshi Barua), the Publicity Chair (Billy Tsouvalas), and the Web Chair (Xiaokuan Zhang). We also thank the publisher, Springer, for sponsoring the Best Paper award.

The program co-chairs of ISC 2023 had significantly expanded the size of the program committee from 23 to 41 members, and they advised us to expand the size of the program committee even further. Following their suggestion, we expanded the committee to 73 members. This was excellent advice, as the number of submissions increased from 98 to 120. This made the overall reviewing load manageable, as every PC member was assigned four or five papers, with papers receiving on average three reviews and the vast majority of reviewers successfully completing their assigned reviews. We accepted 33 out of 120 papers, which corresponds to an acceptance rate of 28%. This is in line with previous ISC events. A new addition to this year's ISC was a rebuttal phase, which the authors and the reviewers found very helpful. We also encouraged the reviewers to ask questions to the authors when this seemed helpful. This communication was proxied by us to ensure a double-blind review process.

We encourage the program co-chairs of ISC 2025 to consider expanding the size of the program committee even further, as we found it significantly easier to invite program committee members when we explained that the expected review load would be manageable and close to their area of research. We had no difficulty matching papers to reviewers who submitted a positive bid to review them. A significant number of junior researchers were invited, and we provided them with additional support if this was their first experience on a program committee. We tried to find a balance between different areas of expertise, and focused on diversity in various other aspects as well, including geographic region, gender, ethnicity, and type of affiliation (academic vs. industry). Prospective program committee members received a form on which they could recommend another person if they declined the invitation. We automatically invited the person who was recommended, and hope that this strategy can help to ensure that overlooked researchers will also receive program committee invitations.

October 2024

Nicky Mouha
Nick Nikiforakis

Preface

Organization

General Chair

Qiang Zeng   George Mason University, USA

Program Chairs

Nicky Mouha   Strativia, NIST Associate, USA
Nick Nikiforakis   Stony Brook University, USA

Steering Committee

Zhiqiang Lin   Ohio State University, USA
Javier Lopez   University of Málaga, Spain
Masahiro Mambo   Kanazawa University, Japan
Bart Mennink   Radboud University Nijmegen, Netherlands
Eiji Okamoto   University of Tsukuba, Japan
Michalis Polychronakis   Stony Brook University, USA
Willy Susilo   University of Wollongong, Australia
Jianying Zhou   Singapore University of Technology and Design, Singapore

Publications Chair

Anomadarshi Barua   George Mason University, USA

Publicity Chair

Billy Tsouvalas   Stony Brook University, USA

Program Committee

Mohamed Ahmed Abdelraheem   Entrust, USA
Gunes Acar   Radboud University, Netherlands

Web Chair

Xiaokuan Zhang　　　　　　　　George Mason University, USA

Local Organization Team

Lannan Luo　　　　　　　　　　George Mason University, USA
Minghao Hu　　　　　　　　　　George Mason University, USA
Xiaoyue Ma　　　　　　　　　　George Mason University, USA
Ying Meng　　　　　　　　　　George Mason University, USA
Chuxiong Wu　　　　　　　　　George Mason University, USA

Additional Reviewers

Murat Ak
Daniel Apon
Jules Baudrin
Hao Cheng
Daniel Collins
Nicolas David
Julien Devevey
Ruoyu Ding
Raphael Heitjohann
Andreas Hellenbrand
Hans Heum
Aissa Houdjedj
Orhun Kara
Anıl Kayan
Changjiang Li
Mary Loubele

Tamer Mour
Misato Nakabayashi
Tao Ni
Tabitha Ogilvie
Fatih Özkaynak
Ray Perlner
Maxime Romeas
Caroline Sandsbråten
Zülfükar Saygı
Johnny So
Chris Tsoukaladelis
Billy Tsouvalas
Weijia Wang
Ricardo Yaben
Derui Zhu
Floyd Zweydinger

Contents – Part I

Software Security

Multi-Party Computation

Contents – Part II

Web Security

Intrusion Detection

Blockchain

The Formal Verification of Aptos Coin

Kundu Chen[1,2], Jie Luo[1]([✉]), Yi Lu[2], Zhongyun Zhang[3], Wenbo Zhang[3], Xudong Wang[4], Pan Li[2], and Jun Zhao[2]

[1] State Key Laboratory of Complex & Critical Software Environment, School of Computer Science and Engineering, Beihang University (BUAA), Beijing 100191, People's Republic of China
luojie@nlsde.buaa.edu.cn
[2] BitsLab, Singapore, Singapore
[3] College of Information Technology, Shanghai Ocean University, Shanghai 200000, People's Republic of China
[4] Department of Computing, The Hong Kong Polytechnic University, Hong Kong, China

Abstract. The fungible contract tokens encounter numerous security challenges due to the vulnerabilities in contract languages; while Move, a novel and secure contract language, is designed to mitigate these vulnerabilities theoretically. To verify the security of the Move-based contract coin, this paper employs formal methods to model the Aptos coin, a leading Move-based token, and assess its high-level properties. Firstly, we examined Aptos Coin's contract code and integrated the Move's characteristics to construct a bottom-up model. Subsequently, we specified the necessary high-level properties that the model should possess. Finally, we utilize the Move Prover, a model-checking tool to verify the essential secure properties of Aptos coin. The results demonstrate that the Aptos coin can satisfy the properties with few prerequisite conditions.

Keywords: Smart Contract · Move Language · Formal Verification · Fungible Token

1 Introduction

The evolution of public blockchains has given rise to the concept of cryptocurrency, simply *tokens*, which are awarded to blockchain nodes for their role in data storage and computation upon the successful mining of a valid block. These tokens, characterized by their interchangeable nature, are named *fungible tokens*. Initially, blockchain protocols generated and allocated these fungible tokens, focusing predominantly on security with relatively constrained functionality [16].

As blockchain applications are raised, the primary fungible tokens have become insufficient for the requirements of blockchain ecosystems. In various blockchains that are capable of executing smart contracts, like Ethereum, a new paradigm known as *contract tokens* has emerged. These are facilitated through

N. Mouha and N. Nikiforakis (Eds.): ISC 2024, LNCS 15257, pp. 3–22, 2025.
https://doi.org/10.1007/978-3-031-75757-0_1

the intricate design of smart contracts, enabling the formation of a contract module analogous to fungible tokens [12]. Unlike the primary token, contract tokens boast the ability to customize their functions and policies, thereby offering a more versatile economic framework.

Obviously, the establishment of contract tokens necessitates a comprehensive set of guidelines and procedures, collectively referred to as a *token standard*. A prime example of such standards is *ERC-20*, which restricted the implementation of specific functions within the smart contract. Token standards delineate the functional attributes of tokens and build the foundation for their preliminary economic and operational frameworks [2].

However, token standards are not rigid in their requirements, leaving the specifics of function implementations largely undefined. This flexibility permits extensive customization of contract tokens but also introduces a series of vulnerabilities. These vulnerabilities include infinite loops, access control breaches, and arithmetic anomalies such as underflows and overflows, each posing significant risks to the integrity of the smart contract [6].

1.1   Move Language Based Token

In an ideal scenario, a token should be considered a resource, not just a key of numerical value. Its transfer, creation, and destruction should be conducted under restriction. Regards physical currency: although users primarily focus on its value during transactions, physical currency must be processed integrally, and its value can not be changed arbitrarily. as shown in Fig. 1:

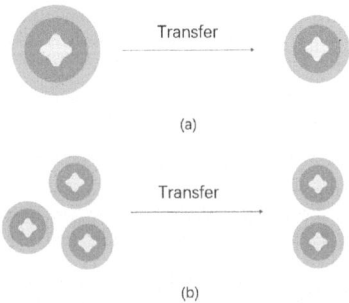

Fig. 1. The ideal contract token. (a) When a transfer occurs, only the value of the token changes. This is the current approach of most contract tokens. (b) The token is integrally moved/removed after the transfer. The Move contract token is the approach to the ideal scheme.

The ideal token does not encounter the issues prevalent in contract tokens, such as unauthorized transfers and double-spending. For most financial applications, it is evident that they desire the token attributes within smart contracts to closely approximate the ideal token. The *Move* language, is an innovative and secure contract language designed to meet these stringent requirements. The move has undergone significant enhancements aimed at resolving security concerns. The subsequent sections will explore the intriguing features of the Move language in depth. Fundamentally, Move accentuates the rarity of data, treating data as *resources* under specific conditions. These resources are cohesive, strictly regulated data entities, transformable exclusively between states that align with their inherent properties.

1.2   Our Contribution

To model the Move-based token, a specific token must be selected for analysis. Among the principal Move-Based tokens are the *Sui token* and *Aptos coin* (APT). The APT, built based on Aptos-Move, extends from the original Move framework without compromising its fundamental structure. Meanwhile, APT has widespread recognition and has relatively mature implementation [10]. Conversely, the Sui token is based on Sui-Move, incorporates certain modifications to Move, and introduces an object model [17]. To preserve the integrity of the Move's properties, our study will concentrate on APT as the focal point of our research.

This paper selects APT as the typical Move-based token to analyze and verify its security properties. Our goal is to specify the APT model simply and clearly. However, due to the presence of numerous interesting features in Move, modeling and verifying APT can become quite challenging. In the mentioned work, formalism and symbols were extensively used to model Move's resource and syntax features. Employing a similar approach for describing Move-based tokens would not only make it too complex to grasp the characteristics of APT but also introduce unnecessary redundancy into the analysis.

Hence, we adopts the finite state machine (FSM) approach to model and analyze APT in a simplified way. We found that for contract token, its essence revolves around the *states* of the user's address and their corresponding *state transitions* (e.g. the quantity of tokens owned by an address is the state, any functions capable of changing the token quantity is a state transition). Clearly, by ensuring that there are no anomalies in all state transitions, we can guarantee the securety of APT. In summary, our work carried out in this paper includes the following aspects:

- **Modeling APT**: We constructed a straightforward and lucid model to describe APT. We define and analyze APT from the structs, functions, and interface implementations, and gather them into a formal model.
- **Summarization of APT's Properties**: Based on the APT model and the functionalities that contract tokens should possess, we summarize the properties that APT should contain, including enforced properties and local properties.
- **Formal Verification of APT**: We specify the properties of APT using the Move specification language (MSL) and verified by the *Move Prover*. We demonstrate that APT can satisfy most of the specified properties after solving minor deficiencies.

The rest of the paper is arranged as follows: In Sect. 2, we introduce the background and essence of the Move language and the Move Prover. In Sect. 3, we demonstrate and analyze the model of APT using a down-top scheme. In Sect. 4, we derive the properties of the APT model and give the specification of each property. In Sect. 5, we employ the Move Prover to formally verify the APT model, and evaluate its performance. Finally, we summarize the related works and conclusion in the Sects. 6 and 7.

2   The Move Language

Move is a language developed by Libra, designed primarily for smart contract development. Its creation was to address the security issues associated with the deflecting of existing contract language [3]. Compared to other contract languages, Move has tons of interesting characteristics. For simplicity, we will not go through all of them, as has been described in existing work [4]. In this case, we introduce only its key aspects, which are *Ability, Resource, Address and Generic*.

Ability: In Move, the type system of variable includes *primitive types* and *struct*, where primitive types include integer, bool, etc.; struct is closed to the concept in other languages like C. *Ability* indicate the operations that can be performed on a type, which include *copy, drop, key*, and *store*, as shown in **Code-I**:

Code I: Struct and Ability

```
1  // struct and its ability
2  struct k has copy, drop {
3      u: u64; // field
4  }
5  fun main() {
6      let x: k = k { u:1 };
7      let x1 = x;   \\ copy x;
8      let x2 = &x;  \\ also copy x;
9  }
```

Specifically, copy indicates whether data can be copied, and drop indicates whether data can be destroyed. Almost all of the primitive types employ copy and drop. Copy is more complex under the hood. Move adopts the concept of *ownership regulation*, inspired by languages like Rust, which enforces borrowing when using variables. In this case, any reference of a variable is, in fact, leverages the copy ability.

Resources: However, scarce data like contract tokens, should not be copyable or arbitrarily erased. Therefore, the struct without copy and drop ability is named *resources*. A resource must at least possess one of the key and store abilities, where key indicates the struct can be retrieved in an address, and store indicates the struct is kept in global storage.

Obviously, resources have no copy ability, and according to the ownership regulation, they can't be accessed directly. It has to operate *move_to* and *move_from* to migrate resources between address, as shown in **Code-II**:

Code-II: Resources Operation

```
1  struct k has key, store {}
2  fun main(a: address, b: &signer) {
3  \\ get k from a
4  let r = move_from<k>(a);
5  \\ give r to b
6  move_to<k>(b,r)
7  }
```

Address and Generic: In the **Code-II**, the concept of address and generic has been introduced. The resources in Move are actually stored inside the address. In addition, *Signer* is a special type that is used to represent the authorization of an address (Simply, it can be regarded as an address too).

Generics are used to define functions and structures over different input data types. For instance, *move_from<k>(a)*, generic k enforces the operation to get resources k from a. The overall demonstration is illustrated in Fig. 2:

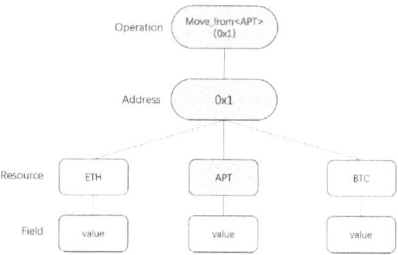

Fig. 2. The workflow of Move, the yellow section highlighted the path of execution. In this case, the operation extracts APT from the address 0×1 (Color figure online)

Through these features, Move enables the manipulation of data like the management of real-world resources. After understanding the features of the Move language, the next step is to discuss how to formally verify code built in the Move language.

The Move Prover: The Move Prover was developed to facilitate accurate verification of the Move code. The Move Prover is a comprehensive verification framework that uses a specialized language named Move Specification Language (MSL) to describe the Move code while utilizing z3 to verify the desired specifications [18]. The workflow is illustrated in Fig. 3:

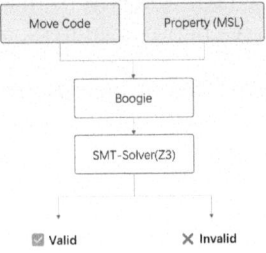

Fig. 3. The workflow of the Move Prover, the yellow section highlighted the input. (Color figure online)

Most of the Move Prover's processes are automated, but manual intervention is required to specify the desired properties [5].

3   Modeling Aptos Coin

In this section, we first present a high-level overview of the APT, and subsequently, adopt a bottom-up approach to analyze APT's resources, functions, and interfaces, and finally derive a comprehensive model for APT.

3.1   Overview

Modeling APT becomes more challenging compared to other contract tokens, considering the interesting feature introduced by Move. Specifically, while APT is a contract token, the functions executing APT also form a token standard through the address-resources scheme and generics. We will provide a detailed explanation of this concept in the following subsections.

Furthermore, besides the language level, the design of APT is significantly different from other contract tokens. Ideally, each token would operate independently, yet this would significantly impair token efficiency. As a trade off, APT requires inter-APT operations for any function modifying an APT's value, as depicted in Fig. 4.

Specifically, each APT possesses a mutable value. This value is readable but cannot be directly modified. To modify an APT's value, operations must be conducted as follows: to increase an APT's value, a user must merge it with another APT, thus augmenting the former's value. Conversely, to decrease an APT's value, a user must split the APT into two distinct entities.

In the following subsection, we will describe the specifics of its implementation from resources to workflow.

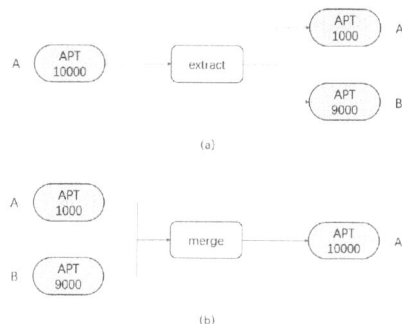

Fig. 4. The transfer of APT. (a) When A intends to decrease the value of APT tokens it possesses, it must do so by using the "extract" function to split APT into two parts. (b) When A intends to increase the value of APT tokens it possesses, it must use the "merge" function to combine its APT tokens with those of another APT.

3.2 Resources

The representation of APT, struct *AptosCoin*, is merely an empty struct with only *key* ability. APT, as well as any other Move contract token, is generally implemented through generics. For instance, *Coin<AptosCoin>* and *Coin<ETH>* are distinct tokens. Therefore, the generics make the resources and functions related to APT a token and a token standard simultaneously, we use *CoinType* as the sign of generics. In this case, we apply *AptosCoin* to *Coin*, *CoinStore*, and *CoinInfo*:

- **Coin**: Represents a specific token, and its token type is denoted by generics. In this case, *Coin < AptosCoin >* represents an APT token, with its sole parameter being the value of the APT. As Coin does not have key ability, it can't be accessed directly.
- **CoinStore**: Represents the collection of APT that are stored under an address. The frozen field is used to determine whether the address is allowed to conduct transactions. There are two additional terms within *CoinStore*, which are *deposit_ events* and *withdraw_ events*. However, they are used to record transactions for subsequent querying, and they have minimal impact on the security of the model, so we won't include them in the APT model.
- **CoinInfo**: holds metadata information corresponding to APT, including its name, symbol, precision, and supply.

Among these resources, *Coin* and *CoinStore* are crucial for the operation of APT, whereas *CoinInfo* primarily records metadata of APT and can be disregarded.

3.3 Functions and Roles

After analyzing the resources associated with APT, we proceed to examine the corresponding functions. We focus solely on functions capable of modifying the aforementioned resources, as only functions capable of altering the address state fall within the APT model. Additionally, we do not consider functions with similar or duplicate functionality, nor do we delve into interface functions. We have summarized all the functions that meet these criteria:

– **Initialize**: This function initializes the APT *CoinType*. It creates a *CoinInfo* and returns three special permissions to the calling address: *FreezeCapability*, *MintCapability*, and *BurnCapability*. Only addresses with these capabilities can invoke the *Mint, Burn, Freeze* functions.
– **Mint, Burn**: When called by a user with *BurnCapability/ MintCapability*, this function destroys/create a specific APT, and updates the supply in the *CoinInfo*.
– **Freeze, Unfreeze**: When Freeze is called by a user with *FreezeCapability*, sets the *CoinStore.Frozen* at the specified address to true. Consequently, the address is unable to transfer or receive APT. On the contract, Unfreeze set *CoinStore.Frozen* to false and allow the transfer of APT.
– **Extract**: This function splits an APT, it deducts amounts from the value of the input APT and returns a new APT with a value of amount. Noticed that the extracted coin should be sent to another address before the end of the function through another operation.
– **Merge**: This function combines two distinct APTs. It extracts the entire value from *source_coin* and appends it to the value of *dst_coin*.

From the functions, we observed the *Initial, Freeze, Mint, Burn* functions involved with special capability, which is not available for normal APT owners. The addresses possessing these capabilities are referred to as *Administrator*. The address invoking the Initialize function serves as the administrator of APT. Apart from the administrator, all other addresses have uniform permissions, referred to as *Users*. Clearly, while the administrator has its privileges, it also has access to the functionalities that users can execute.

3.4 Interface

Interface functions are necessary, due to resources lacking the *key* ability, and becomes impossible to modify them directly through internal functions. For instance, the *merge* function requires Coin as input, which does not possess the key ability. Consequently, an address cannot directly access its possessed Coin. To address this issue, APT has introduced several interface functions:

– **Deposit**: This function adds APT into the *CoinStore* of an address.
– **Withdraw**: This function retrieves APT from the *CoinStore* of an address. Same as the extract, the withdrawn coin should be sent to another address before the end of the function through another operation.
– **Transfer**: This function takes APT from the *CoinStore* of from_address to the *CoinStore* of to_address.
– **Register**: This function creates *CoinStore* for an address. If the address already has *CoinStore*, it shall do nothing.

- **Burn_from**: This function required the *BurnCapability* to operate, it destroys a certain amount of APT from the *CoinStore* of an address.
- **Destroy_Capability**: It is actually the simplified description of three different functions, which required the corresponding *Capability* to operate, it destroys the *Capability* of an address. After destruction, the *Capability* cannot be recovered.

As introduced before, some functions required capability, including burn, burn_from, destroy_capability, mint, freeze, and unfreeze. We named these *authorized functions*.

3.5   Model

As mentioned, the APT model essentially comprises the state from the perspective of an address and its corresponding transition functions. It can be conceptualized as a finite state machine. By aggregating all resources, functions, and interfaces, we can consider all resources under an address as states and functions as state transitions.

However, different addresses may have variations in their finite state machines due to the presence of access control of resources and functions. We refer to these different address types as roles. As mentioned, there are two types of roles, which are the *Users* and *Administrator*. The state difference between user and administrator is illustrated in Fig. 5:

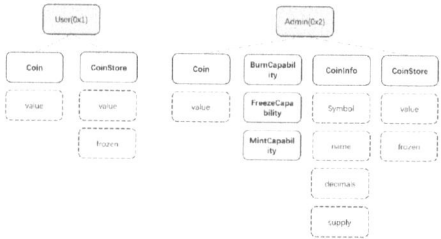

Fig. 5. The state of APT. The left is the state of the user, and the right is the state of the administrator. The yellow section is the address, the white solid section is the struct, and the white dashed section is the field of the struct. (Color figure online)

From the figure, the user is simply a restricted administrator. It shall not be able to call the initialize function, therefore, the resources it contains are lesser than the administrator, which only includes *Coin* and *CoinStore*, while the administrator has *Capabilities* and *CoinInfo* additionally. To obtain an accurate APT model, we need to examine these roles separately.

User Model: Firstly we inspect the user. Let s_n be the state, and S_u be the user's set of state, it consists of the following state (1):

$$S_u = \{s_{null}, s_{user}, s_{increase}, s_{decrease}, s_{frzoen}\} \tag{1}$$

The s_{null} is the base state of the address, after an address operates the register function, it becomes the user of APT, and transits to s_{user}. $s_{increase}$ indicate the $CoinStore.Coin.value$ is transited and increased, where $s_{decrease}$ is the opposite. The freeze function can modify $CoinStore.frozen$ to true, and transits any other state to s_{frozen}. Meanwhile, the unfreeze function can modify $CoinStore.frozen$ to false and transits s_{frozen} to base state s_{user}. The model of the S_u is illustrated in the Fig. 6:

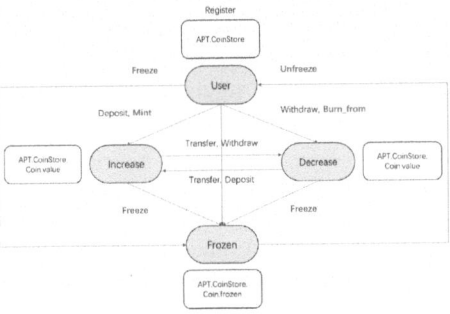

Fig. 6. The user's APT model. The yellow section is the state of address, the white section is the field that transits, the line is the state transition and related functions, and the red function requires the capability to operate.

Let the state transition from s_n to s_m be the s_m^n, and denoted the transit function as t_n from the figure, it can be described as 1:

Algorithm 1. State and transit of S_u

1: $t_{withdraw}(s, coin) \rightarrow s_{dec}$
2: $s_{user}^{null} = \{t_{register}\}$
3: $s_{increase}^{user} = \{t_{deposit}, t_{transfer}, t_{mint}\}$
4: $s_{decrease}^{user} = \{t_{withdraw}, t_{transfer}, t_{burn\_from}\}$
5: $s_{decrease}^{increase} = \{t_{transfer}, t_{withdraw}\}$
6: $s_{increase}^{decrease} = \{t_{transfer}, t_{deposit}\}$
7: $s_{frozen}^{increase}, t_{frozen}^{decrease}, t_{frozen}^{user} = \{t_{freeze}\}$
8: $s_{user}^{frozen} = \{t_{unfreeze}\}$

We noticed that $Coin$ has no key ability, therefore, the state transition is only associated with $CoinStore$. Moreover, the extract and merge function modified only $Coin$ resources, so they need to rely on the interface function to operate. Therefore, the transition only includes the interface.

Administrator Model: The user model is a subset of the administrator model, where the administrator has *Capability* and *CoinInfo* resources. Let S_a be the administrator's set of states, it consists of the following state (2):

$$S_a = \{S_u, s_{admin}, s_{increase\_supply}, s_{decrease\_supply}\} \tag{2}$$

For simplicity, we won't go through the state and transition that have been described in S_u. For *CoinInfo*, besides *supply*, other fields are unchangeable. In this case, the mint functions can transit state to $s_{increase\_supply}$, and burn, burn_from can transit state to $s_{decrease\_supply}$. For *Capability*, they can used to operate authorized functions. However, when the destory_capability function is used, the Administrator cannot operate the authorized functions, which transit the s_{admin} to the s_{user}. The model of the S_u is illustrated in the Fig. 7:

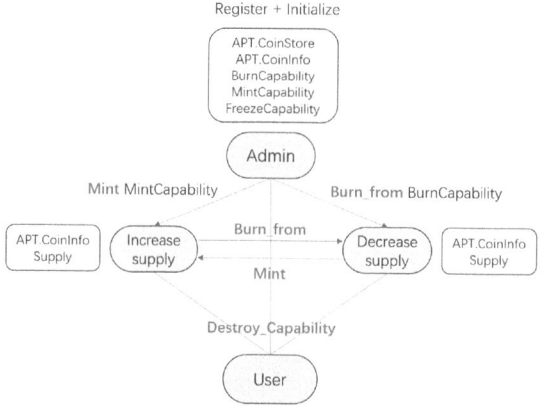

Fig. 7. The additional administrator's APT model. The yellow section is the state of address, the white section is the field that transits, the line is the state transition and related functions, and the red function requires the capability to operate.

Subsequently, we need to specify the state transit from the figure, it can be described as 2:

Noticed that when transit s_{null} to s_{admin}, both $t_{register}$ and $t_{intialize}$ are needed. Meanwhile, when s_{admin} transit to s_{user}, there is no transit to make it back.

4   Secure Properties

In this section, we analyzed the APT model and summarize its secure-related properties. Identifying which properties are necessary is a challenging task. To verify the security of APT, we need to guarantee the correctness of all state transitions. Therefore, the properties of APT are essentially the expected state outcomes of state transitions. for simplicity, we denoted $s_{increase\_supply}$ as s_{incsup}, $s_{decrease\_supply}$ as s_{decsup}, $s_{increase}$ as s_{inc}, $s_{decrease}$ as s_{dec}.

Algorithm 2. State and transit of S_a

1: $t_{withdraw}(s, coin) \rightarrow s_{dec}$
2: $s_{admin}^{null} = \{t_{register}\ \&\ t_{intialize}\}$
3: $s_{increase\_supply}^{admin} = \{t_{mint}\}$
4: $s_{decrease\_supply}^{admin} = \{t_{burn\_from}\}$
5: $s_{decrease\_supply}^{increase\_supply} = \{t_{burn\_from}\}$
6: $s_{increase\_supply}^{decrease\_supply} = \{t_{mint}\}$
7: $s_{user}^{admin} = \{t_{destroy\_capability}\}$

Property 1. It should always be possible to determine if a coin exists and determine if a user registered a coin. If a coin exists, it should always be possible to request the name, symbol, and supply.

Specification. On the one hand, When *CoinInfo* and *CoinStore* have key ability, it can be retrieved from the address. Specifically, it can be examined by *exists<APT>(address)* operation. On the other hand, if APT does not exist, or an address hasn't been registered, the address has no *CoinStore* and *CoinInfo* resources. Therefore, their corresponding field cannot be accessed as well.

Property 2. Coin operations may only be done on coins of the same type.

Specification. This requirement indicated that functions should abort when operating on coins of different types. Apparently, the generic system enforced the coin with different types cannot be operated. For instance, *transfer<APT>(from, to, amount)* does only receive APT. It is impossible to assign more than one generic in a function. Therefore, the property is enforced.

Property 3. The supply of APT is only affected by burn, burn_from, and mint operations. [mint, burn, burn_from]

Specification. For most of the functions, the supply of APT should remain unchanged. We could specify it by employing a post-condition, that checks if the total supply in the pre-executed stage is equal to the total supply in the post-executed stage. In the burn_from and mint functions, the post supply should be the initial supply add/minor the amount of change. In the burn function, the amount should be the value of the coin. It can be specify as 3:

Property 4. During the coin operations, the sum value of the coin should remain unchanged. [transfer, deposit, withdraw]

Algorithm 3. Supply Scope

Data: Transition t, State s

Require: $s \in \{S_a\}$

1: $t_{mint}(s, amount, cap) \rightarrow s_{incsup}$
2: $s.coininfo.supply = s_{incsup}.coininfo.supply \text{ - } amount$
3: $t_{burn_from}(s, address, amount, cap) \rightarrow s_{decsup}$
4: $s.coininfo.supply = s_{decsup}.coininfo.supply + amount$
5: $t_{burn}(s, coin, cap) \rightarrow s_{decsup}$
6: $s.coininfo.supply = s_{decsup}.coininfo.supply + coin.value$

Specification. This property requires that when performing operations on an APT, its value should not unexpectedly increase or decrease. Since all interface functions are composed of basic functions, we only regard the interfaces. For the operation of merging coins, the value of the merged coin equals the sum of the values of the coins before merging. Conversely, for the operation that involves extracting coins, the value of the coin before splitting equals the sum of the values of the coins after extraction. It can be specify as 4:

Algorithm 4. Unchanged Coin Operation

Data: Transition t, State s

Require: $s \notin \{s_{null}, s_{frozen}\}$

1: $t_{withdraw}(s, coin) \rightarrow s_{dec}$
2: $s.coinstore.coin.value = s_{dec}.coinstore.coin.value + coin.value$
3: $t_{deposit}(s, coin) \rightarrow s_{inc}$
4: $s.coinstore.coin.value = s_{inc}.coinstore.coin.value \text{ - } coin.value$
5: $t_{transfer}(s^{from}, amount) \rightarrow s_{dec}^{from}$
6: $t_{transfer}(s^{to}, amount) \rightarrow s_{inc}^{to}$
7: $s^{to}.coinstore.coin.value = s_{inc}^a.coinstore.coin.value \text{ - } amount$
8: $s^{from}.coinstore.coin.value = s_{dec}^a.coinstore.coin.value + amount$

Property 5. Only the owner of a coin may mint, burn or freeze coins. [mint, burn, burn_from, freeze, unfreeze].

Specification. This requirement specifies that only the administrator should be able to invoke the mint, freeze, and burn functions. It is equivalent to requiring that the caller must possess the corresponding capability when calling these functions. To check if a resource exists, we can examine if the state s contains the desired capability. It can be specify as 5:

Property 6. Coin operations should fail if the user's CoinStore is frozen. [transfer, deposit, withdraw].

Algorithm 5. Capability Restriction

Data: Transition t, State s

Require: $s \in \{S_a\}$

  1: $t_{mint}(s, amount) \rightarrow s_{incsup}$
  2: $mintcapability \in s$
  3: $t_{burn}(s, coin) \rightarrow s_{decsup}$
  4: $burncapability \in s$
  5: $t_{burn\_from}(s, coin) \rightarrow s_{decsup}$
  6: $burncapability \in s$
  7: $t_{freeze}(s, amount) \rightarrow s_{freeze}$
  8: $freezecapability \in s$
  9: $t_{unfreeze}(s, amount) \rightarrow s_{admin}$
10: $freezecapability \in s$

Specification. This requirement stipulates that no operations on a coin can be carried out from an address when *addres.coinstore.frozen == true*. Since *CoinStore* and addresses are related, only interface functions are affected. We can verify this by implementing $\neg t_n(s_m)$, indicating the transition t_n will not happen at state s_m. It can be specify as 6:

Algorithm 6. Frozen Restriction

Data: Transition t, State s

Require: $s = \{s_{freeze}\}$

  1: $\neg\ t_{transfer}(s_{freeze})$
  2: $\neg\ t_{deposit}(s_{freeze})$
  3: $\neg\ t_{withdraw}(s_{freeze})$

In the actual process of writing MSL, there will be many tedious implementation considerations. Therefore, the MSL specification should be more complex than the description above. To save space, we add the link to the specification in the appendix.

5 Evaluation

In this section, we validate the APT model described using MSL and assess its performance. Verification is conducted via the Move Prover, yielding three potential outcomes: (1) The APT Model fulfills all predefined properties and successfully passes verification. (2) The APT Model does not meet certain properties, leading to verification failure, with the solver pinpointing the specific unmet issues. (3) The solver's solving process consumes excessive time, resulting in a timeout.

A paramount concern during verification is whether the verification can proceed successfully. The intricate nature of the APT model's specification can

Table 1. The time cost of each function.

Function	Con.	build time	verify time	Sum
global	4	1.355 s	2.883 s	4.238 s
initial	7	1.313 s	1.262 s	2.575 s
mint	4	1.328 s	1.134 s	2.462 s
burn	12	1.323 s	1.363 s	2.686 s
burn_from	9	1.311 s	1.302 s	2.686 s
freeze	3	1.307 s	1.112 s	2.419 s
unfreeze	3	1.333 s	1.243 s	2.419 s
extract	3	1.296 s	1.056 s	2.352 s
merge	1	1.288 s	1.034 s	2.322 s
deposit	4	1.325 s	1.213 s	2.538 s
withdraw	6	1.316 s	1.049 s	2.365 s
transfer	8	1.341 s	1.287 s	2.628 s
overall	74	1.677 s	6.342 s	8.019 s

lead to solver timeouts. To minimize the probability of timeouts, we adopted a function-specific testing methodology. We conduct isolated tests for different functions and document the duration of each test. Furthermore, to curtail prolonged verification periods, we have imposed a 60-second timeout limit for each function. The outcomes of these tests are depicted in Table 1:

In the table, the term *global* indicates the configurations and essential settings at the module level. The results clearly demonstrate that overall verification consumes less time than the function-by-function approach. The verification of local properties for various functions exhibits relatively consistent time consumption, except for the *burn, burn_from, initial, deposit,* and *transfer* functions, which each take slightly over 1.2 s to verify. Nonetheless, every function is verified within a reasonable timeframe.

After guaranteeing the effectiveness of the verification process, we examine the results of the verification. All predefined properties have been successfully verified. However, certain functions required minor modifications, as outlined in the Table 2:

The table reveals that the *mint, extract, burn_from,* and *transfer* functions required modifications to pass verification. Specifically:

Amount Not Zero: Functions that involve a numerical amount, should check the amount is not zero. In this case, the state shall not transit and potentially violate Property 4 (No coin operation happened). We introduced additional assertions to validate the amount, thereby addressing this issue.

Table 2. The verification result.

Function	Passed	Fixed	Related
global	✓	×	–
initial	✓	×	–
mint	×	✓	Property 4
burn	✓	×	–
burn_from	×	✓	Property 4
freeze	✓	×	–
unfreeze	✓	×	–
extract	×	✓	Property 4
merge	✓	×	–
deposit	✓	×	–
withdraw	✓	×	–
transfer	×	✓	Property 4

Duplicate Address: The transfer function necessitates that the *from* address and the *to* address must be different; otherwise, it would violate Property 4. We add a pre-condition that ensures $addr_{from} \neq addr_{to}$ to solve this issue.

After making these adjustments, the APT model successfully satisfied all the properties. The result shows that all of the states and the corresponding transitions of APT are operated as expected, indicating the security of the APT model.

Comparison: To further ensure the correctness of the result, we leverage a traditional state-of-the-art vulnerability detection tool for the Move language, the MoveScan [13]. It is capable of finding the error in the code level. We using the MoveScan to testify the entry function in *coin, aptos_coin* module, the result is shown as follows 3:

Table 3. The comparison of result.

Function	Formal	MoveScan	Comment
initial	✓	✓	–
mint	×	✓	Property 4
burn	✓	×	Unused Constant
deposit	✓	✓	–
withdraw	✓	✓	–
transfer	×	✓	Property 4

From the result, we can discover that our formal verification has found the potential issue in the mint and transfer function, where the MoveScan has been ignored. As for burn, the MoveScan has found an unused *U64* constant, which is a minor issue that merely affects the safety of Aptos coin. Overall, the result of the formal verification is promising.

6   Related Work

In this section, we presented several notable works in the vulnerability detection and formal verification of smart contracts [11,14].

6.1   Vulnerability Type

Common smart contracts often exhibit similar types of vulnerabilities, and these vulnerabilities may exist across different contract languages. Some typical vulnerabilities include:

Re-entrancy: This vulnerability occurs when a contract makes an external call to another contract before completing its internal state changes. An attacker can exploit this to re-enter the contract and perform malicious actions [7].

Unhandled Exceptions: Failing to properly handle exceptions or errors in a contract can lead to unexpected behavior and potential vulnerabilities. Exception handling is critical for maintaining the contract's security [15].

Transaction Order Dependency: Vulnerabilities related to the order of transactions can occur when a contract's behavior depends on the sequence of incoming transactions. Attackers can exploit this to manipulate the contract's state.

Integer Overflow: Integer overflow vulnerabilities occur when mathematical operations result in values exceeding the data type's maximum limit, leading to unintended behavior. secureguarding against integer overflows is crucial.

Unrestricted Action: Contracts may lack proper access control mechanisms, allowing unauthorized users to perform actions that should be restricted. Implementing proper access controls is vital to prevent unrestricted actions.

Addressing these common vulnerabilities is essential for the security and integrity of smart contracts across various contract languages. Proper auditing, testing, and code review practices can help identify and mitigate these issues before they lead to exploitation.

6.2   Formal Method

To further enhance the security of smart contracts beyond vulnerability detection, some researchers have introduced formal methods for verification and validation. These methods can be primarily categorized into two approaches: theorem proving and model checking.

Theorem Proving: Theorem proving involves using formal logic and mathematical proofs to demonstrate that a smart contract adheres to specified properties and invariants. Developers express the desired properties and invariants using a formal specification language. It defines what the contract should achieve and under what conditions. Notable work includes using the Isabelle/HOL theorem prover to check the security of smart contracts [1]. In this approach, the target smart contract is divided into basic blocks and instructions. Each instruction is individually modeled using Isabelle, and Hoare logic is employed to verify whether the entire sequence of instructions satisfies specific conditions. However, it requires significant manual intervention and expertise in using theorem provers.

Model Checking: Model checking is an automated technique used to verify whether a smart contract meets specific properties by exhaustively exploring its state space. It involves constructing a formal model of the contract and systematically checking all possible states. Using model checkers like NuSMV and SPIN for formal verification of smart contracts is a noteworthy approach [8] [9]. These tools typically involve the transformation of smart contracts into a specification language, followed by the verification of properties using underlying SMT solvers. This process helps ensure the correctness and security of smart contracts. However, these approaches do not support all the features and syntax of Solidity.

7   Conclusions

In summary, this paper utilizes a formal method to verify the security of the fungible token construct by the Move language. We selected APT, one of the most representative move-based tokens to analyze, and review its code and framework to derive its formal model. Subsequently, we specify the enforced and local properties that APT should possess. Finally, we converted the properties to MSL and verified them using the Move Prover. The results confirmed that APT satisfies all the specified properties.

However, our work does have limitations. While the model-checking process is automated, property specification still relies on manual review. Furthermore, since other token protocols may not be implemented using the Move language, this paper does not offer a comparison of different token standards. It could be the main challenge of our future work.

Appendix

The specification of this paper can be found in the Aptos repository, at https://github.com/aptos-labs/aptos-core/tree/main/aptos-move/framework/aptos-framework, including *Coin* and *AptosCoin* module.

References

1. Amani, S., Bégel, M., Bortin, M., Staples, M.: Towards verifying ethereum smart contract bytecode in Isabelle/HOL. In: Proceedings of the 7th ACM SIGPLAN International Conference on Certified Programs and Proofs, pp. 66–77 (2018)
2. Bauer, D.P.: ERC-20: fungible tokens. In: Getting Started with Ethereum: A Step-by-Step Guide to Becoming a Blockchain Developer, pp. 17–48. Apress, Berkeley, CA (2022). https://doi.org/10.1007/978-1-4842-8045-4_3
3. Blackshear, S., et al.: Move: a language with programmable resources. Libra Assoc., 1 (2019)
4. Diem.: The move book (2024)
5. Dill, D., Grieskamp, W., Park, J., Qadeer, S., Xu, M., Zhong, E.: Fast and reliable formal verification of smart contracts with the move prover. In: TACAS 2022. LNCS, vol. 13243, pp. 183–200. Springer, Cham (2022). https://doi.org/10.1007/978-3-030-99524-9_10
6. He, D., Deng, Z., Zhang, Y., Chan, S., Cheng, Y., Guizani, N.: Smart contract vulnerability analysis and security audit. IEEE Netw. **34**(5), 276–282 (2020)
7. Luu, L., Chu, D. H., Olickel, H., Saxena, P., Hobor, A.: Making smart contracts smarter. In: Proceedings of the 2016 ACM SIGSAC Conference on Computer and Communications Security, pp. 254–269 (2016)
8. Nehai, Z., Piriou, P.Y., Daumas, F.: Model-checking of smart contracts. In: 2018 IEEE International Conference on Internet of Things (iThings) and IEEE Green Computing and Communications (GreenCom) and IEEE Cyber, Physical and Social Computing (CPSCom) and IEEE Smart Data (SmartData), pp. 980–987. IEEE (2018)
9. Osterland, T., Rose, T.: Model checking smart contracts for ethereum. Pervasive Mob. Comput. **63**, 101129 (2020)
10. Pierro, G.A., Ibba, G., Tonelli, R.: A study on diem and Aptos distributed ledger technology. Int. J. Parallel Emergent Distrib. Syst., 1–17 (2023)
11. Qian, P., Liu, Z., He, Q., Huang, B., Tian, D., Wang, X.: Smart contract vulnerability detection technique: a survey. arXiv preprint arXiv:2209.05872 (2022)
12. Shirole, M., Darisi, M., Bhirud, S.: Cryptocurrency token: an overview. In: Patel, D., et al. (eds.) IC-BCT 2019. BT, pp. 133–140. Springer, Singapore (2020). https://doi.org/10.1007/978-981-15-4542-9_12
13. Shuwei, S., et al.: Sui Move: modern blockchain programming with objects (2024)
14. Singh, A., Parizi, R.M., Zhang, Q., Choo, K.K.R., Dehghantanha, A.: Blockchain smart contracts formalization: approaches and challenges to address vulnerabilities. Comput. Secur. **88**, 101654 (2020)
15. Tikhomirov, S., Voskresenskaya, E., Ivanitskiy, I., Takhaviev, R., Marchenko, E., Alexandrov, Y.: SmartCheck: static analysis of ethereum smart contracts. In: Proceedings of the 1st International Workshop on Emerging Trends in Software Engineering for Blockchain, pp. 9–16 (2018)

16. Wang, G., Nixon, M.: SoK: tokenization on blockchain. In: Proceedings of the 14th IEEE/ACM International Conference on Utility and Cloud Computing Companion, pp. 1–9 (2021)
17. Welc, A., Blackshear, S.: Sui Move: modern blockchain programming with objects. In: Companion Proceedings of the 2023 ACM SIGPLAN International Conference on Systems, Programming, Languages, and Applications: Software for Humanity, pp. 53–55 (2023)
18. Zhong, J.E., et al.: The move prover. In: Lahiri, S.K., Wang, C. (eds.) CAV 2020. LNCS, vol. 12224, pp. 137–150. Springer, Cham (2020). https://doi.org/10.1007/978-3-030-53288-8_7

Anonymous, Timed and Revocable Proxy Signatures

Ghada Almashaqbeh[1][(✉)] and Anca Nitulescu[2]

[1] University of Connecticut, Storrs, CT, USA
ghada@uconn.edu
[2] IOG, Paris, France
anca.nitulescu@iohk.io

Abstract. A proxy signature enables a party to delegate her signing power to another. This is useful in practice to achieve goals related to robustness, crowd-sourcing, and workload sharing. Such applications, especially in the blockchain model, usually require delegation to satisfy several properties, including time bounds, anonymity, revocability, and policy enforcement. Despite the large amount of work on proxy signatures in the literature, none of the existing schemes satisfy all these properties; even there is no unified formal notion that captures them.

In this work, we close this gap and propose RelaySchnorr, an anonymous, timed, and revocable proxy signature scheme. We achieve this in two steps: First, we introduce a tokenizable digital signature based on Schnorr signature allowing for secure distribution of signing tokens. Second, we utilize a public bulletin board, instantiated as a blockchain, and timelock encryption to support: (1) one-time usage of the signing tokens by tracking tokens used so far based on unique values associated to them, (2) timed delegation so that a proxy signer cannot sign outside a given period, and (3) delegation revocation allowing the original signer to end a delegation earlier than provisioned. All of these are done in a decentralized and anonymous way so that no one can tell that someone else signed on behalf of the original signer or even that a delegation took place. We define a formal notion for proxy signatures capturing all these properties, and prove that our construction realizes this notion. We also discuss several design considerations addressing issues related to deployment in practice.

1 Introduction

Proxy signatures allow one user (the original signer) to delegate their signing right to another party (the proxy signer). The proxy signer can generate signatures that are verified using the original signer's certified public key.[1] Proxy signatures are useful in many applications related to distributed systems, e-cash using smart cards, grid computing, and workload sharing [16,31,33,38]. For example, Alice can let her assistant (Bob) reply to (and sign) emails on her

---

[1] This is not to be confused with proxy re-signatures [3,7], in which Alice gives a trusted third party a secret key $sk_{b \to a}$ that is used to transform Bob's signature into Alice's signature. Our focus in this work is on signature delegation.

N. Mouha and N. Nikiforakis (Eds.): ISC 2024, LNCS 15257, pp. 23–43, 2025.
https://doi.org/10.1007/978-3-031-75757-0_2

behalf while on a vacation, or simply she can share the workload of handling emails with Bob. Anonymous delegation guarantees that no one can tell that the task was delegated. Alice may further limit the delegation rights to a certain task or period of time, and may retain the ability to revoke the delegation at any moment of her choice.

The concept of proxy signatures was first introduced in [30], where several types of delegation were presented: full delegation—the original and proxy signers share the same secret key, partial delegation—the original signer generates a delegation key for the proxy signer to use, and delegation by warrant—the original signer specifies a policy that restricts which messages the proxy signer can sign. Since then, a large number of followup works emerged analyzing security and efficiency of older schemes, and devising new constructions, e.g., [4,14,23–25,31,39]. Other foundational works focused on formulating and unifying the security requirements of proxy signatures, and strengthening the adversary model [9,29,35]. Furthermore, several works focused on extending proxy signatures to handle different settings and support new features, such as threshold proxy signatures [22,37], blind proxy signatures [42], and anonymous proxy signatures [17].

Motivation. Our motivation stems from recent advances in distributed systems and Web 3.0 applications, and their need for delegation of signing rights. The continuous emergence of such applications raises the question of whether we can realize many of the robustness, user-control, and flexible-configuration features (facilitated by trusted banks/financial institutions) in the trustless blockchain model. This model also introduced new needs that did not exist before, such as managing hot and old wallets and targeted attacks against consensus. Having cryptographic schemes that cover various properties is valuable as these can always become off-the-shelf solutions for new needs arising in this active area. In this work, we identify the properties and capabilities that decentralized applications require from signature delegation, and how to realize them. Towards this, we discuss two motivating applications, and we explain how existing solutions are not suitable as there is no single scheme that supports *all* the required properties.

Application 1: Decentralized Finance (DeFi) and Wallet Management. In DeFi, blockchains are used to facilitate financial services. There is always the question of whether DeFi can replace traditional banking systems. For example, can Alice allow a family member to spend currency from her Ethereum account in a controlled way without giving away her secret key? (in a similar way to issuing a credit card to a family member while the original account owner controls the credit limit and activation period of the new card.) Delegated signatures can easily enable that: Alice delegates signing rights to her sister Eve, under a *policy* ensuring that, e.g., only transactions with capped values can be issued, and that delegation is valid only for a *given period*. Alice can also end, or *revoke*, the delegation earlier if desired. Given the decentralized nature of blockchains, Alice wants to do all of that in a *decentralized* way.

Another use case is related to cold and hot cryptocurrency wallets. Cold wallets are used to store most of the funds and are not connected to the Internet. It happens that the hot wallet (e.g., a mobile application) may need more funds for a particular activity than what was originally anticipated. Transferring funds between the two wallets requires the cold wallet to be connected to the network, which is risky. By delegating the signing capability to the hot wallet, it can *non-interactively* transfer funds out of the cold wallet, reducing security risks.

Application 2: System Robustness. Another important application is related to system robustness and addressing targeted attacks. Take Byzantine agreement-based consensus as an example. For each round, a committee will agree on the next block. A party, say Alice, can designate a few other parties as backups to sign on her behalf. If Alice's machine is down, Bob can sign on Alice's behalf after a preset timeout. So, even if Alice is a victim of a targeted attack, Bob will do the work until she recovers. Here *anonymity* is a key; backups must be anonymous to avoid targeted attacks against them as part of attacking Alice. The same analogy can be applied to any system in which designated parties must be available to perform particular functionalities.

These applications outline several desired properties. *Delegation anonymity* hides that a delegation took place and the identities of the proxies, ensuring that to an outsider everything appears to be done by the original signer. Also, delegation should be of an *ephemeral nature* so it can be exercised during a preset time period. Another feature is *revocability*, which could be automatic when the delegation period is over, or on-demand due to unforeseen circumstances. Moreover, *policy enforcement* allows restricting the proxy signer's power, e.g., signing messages that belong to a certain class. Furthermore, *decentralization and non-interactivity* are important features especially for large-scale distributed systems. That is, all delegation information are generated by the original signer and can be sent to the proxy signer in one shot; no further interaction with the original signer and no trusted third party are needed when the proxy generates signatures. This promotes scalability and agrees with the spirit of delegation— the original signer can go offline once the delegation is created.

Despite the large amount of work around signature delegation, there is no single proxy signature scheme that achieves all the properties mentioned above, and there is no formal notion that covers all these properties. Full delegation, by giving away the signing key, offers anonymity but at the price of losing control over the delegation. Many schemes allow some fine-grained control [14,20,30], but violate anonymity. Others [4,17] support controlled and anonymous delegation, but without any revocation capability or timed notion. At the same time, schemes that support timed delegation and/or revocation [27,28,36,41] either do not offer anonymity, require interaction between the original and proxy signers, rely on trusted/semi-trusted third party, or do not have formal security analysis.

These observations raise the following question: *Can we construct a decentralized and non-interactive proxy signature scheme that is anonymous, timed and revocable? and how to formally define its security?*

1.1 Contributions

In this paper, we answer this question in the affirmative by defining a formal notion for anonymous, timed and revocable proxy signatures, and constructing a proxy signature scheme, called RelaySchnorr, that satisfies all the properties discussed above.

Formal Modeling. Our notion builds on previous proxy signature definitions [9,17,29] and defines the additional properties that we require. We generalize the notion to produce generic delegation information instead of restricting these to be tokens or delegation keys. We also introduce a revocation algorithm covering automatic and on-demand revocability. For policy enforcement, we view it as two parts: a policy over time encapsulating the delegation period, and a policy over the message specifying which messages can be signed. To support delegation anonymity, verification of all signatures is done under the original signer's public key without involving the proxy signers' identities. We formally define correctness and security, where the latter covers unforgeability under chosen message attacks, anonymity, revocability, and policy enforcement. We note that none of the existing definitions covered all these properties at once, and none of them defined a time policy or revocation.

Construction. We introduce a new proxy signature scheme, RelaySchnorr, that realizes our notion. RelaySchnorr combines Schnorr signature, timelock encryption, and a public bulletin board to support token-based delegation that is anonymous and revocable, and enforces time and message policies.[2] We introduce a *one-time tokenizable digital signature scheme* based on Schnorr signatures. This is done via a *two-layered approach*: the first layer produces a token, while the second layer produces a signature over the intended message using this token. The original signer can produce tokens on her own and communicate them securely to the proxy signer. Signature verification is done against the public key of the original signer, and the signature structure is identical whether it is generated by the original or proxy signer. In terms of size, a signature consists of four field elements and one group element, so the cost of delegation consists of one group element and two field elements compared to original Schnorr signatures.

We enforce *one-time use* of a token by publishing its unique value (i.e., a unique random element k) on the bulletin board. Any signature with an already published k value will be rejected, and upon accepting a valid signature, the verifier publishes the corresponding k value on the board, preventing the proxy signer from reusing a token. This differs from conventional one-time signatures, where if a signer signs more than one message her signing key will be revealed. A proxy signer would attempt to reveal the original signer's signing key, and hence the conventional notion does not work in our setting. Our approach does not reveal the key even if a proxy signer (locally) uses a token to sign several messages, and still only one of these signatures will be accepted. As noted, verifiers are trusted to publish the k values of the signatures they accept. In blockchain applications (our main target) signed transactions are verified by the miners/validators, so consensus honest majority guarantees this behavior.

---

[2] We assume a secure bulletin board that is an append-only, publicly-accessible log instantiated in a decentralized way as a blockchain maintained by a set of miners (we refer to the miners as validators). Any secure bulletin board (that satisfies persistence and liveness) can be used whether it is based on proof-of-work, proof-of-stake, etc.

For the *timed delegation*, we achieve that in a decentralized way without involving a time server or public warrants that compromise anonymity. We utilize the bulletin board along with timelock encryption [19]. In timelock encryption, a ciphertext is locked to a time ρ so that when time ρ comes, some public information will become available allowing for decryption. To enforce a proxy signer to exercise the delegation within a time period $[\rho_a, \rho_b]$, where ρ is a round number from the board, the original signer encrypts the delegation tokens locked to time ρ_a and privately sends them to the proxy signer. Only at time ρ_a the proxy signer can access the tokens. To enforce the end of the period, or *automatic revocation of delegation*, the original signer encrypts all unique k values of these tokens in another ciphertext locked to time ρ_b and publishes that on the board. When time ρ_b comes, the board validators will decrypt and publish all unused k values preventing the proxy signer from using any unused tokens after ρ_b.

For *on-demand revocation*, we do that in a similar way to automatic revocation. The difference is that the original signer publishes the unused k values of the delegated tokens before time ρ_b. To the best of our knowledge, we are the first to support revocability and the timed notion in an anonymous and decentralized way. For *policy enforcement over messages*, we follow generic approaches [17,20] for two cases: public policy (using the warrant approach) and private one (using non-interactive zero knowledge proofs—NIZKs).

A few challenges arise when deploying our scheme in practice. Examples include synchronization issues of the board, denial of service (DoS) attacks, and anonymity concerns related to mass publication of k values during revocation. We discuss these and other challenges, along with solutions, in our construction.

Security. We formally prove security of RelaySchnorr based on our notion. Unforgeability relies on the unforgeability of Schnorr signatures in the random oracle model [34], and the Schnorr knowledge of exponent assumption [5,12]. Anonymity is achieved by having identical signature structure and behavior (i.e., with respect to any information published on the board) for the original and proxy signers. Revocability relies on the security of timelock encryption and the bulletin board. Policy enforcement relies on the security of digital signatures (for public warrants) or NIZKs (for private policies), as well as security of timelock encryption and the bulletin board.

Lastly, we note that the techniques we devise to support the timed/revocability notion could be of independent interest; they could be used to support these features for other cryptographic functionalities. Furthermore, the reliance on Schnorr signature, which is a widely studied and used cryptographic primitive, favors construction simplicity. This could also make it easier for our construction to be adopted in practice by systems that use Schnorr signatures (e.g., Bitcoin is awaiting the adoption of Schnorr signatures as proposed in BIP 340 [40]).

1.2   Related Work

We review existing proxy signature schemes showing that none of them support all the properties we aim to achieve. In the full version [2], we further review works on relevant notions and position our work with respect to these efforts.

Anonymity. Anonymity is usually not supported since the proxy signer's key is public and needed for verification, e.g., [30]. Fuchsbauer et al. [17,18] address this issue by unifying the notion of proxy and group signatures, and they consider traceability with a trusted authority holding a trapdoor that can compromise anonymity if needed. Beside introducing a centralized entity, this scheme does not support revocation or timed delegation. Functional signatures [11] allow deriving a secret key sk_f, from the original signer's key, so a proxy signer can sign a message m only if $f(m) = 1$ (where f represents the policy). Delegatable functional signatures [4] utilize signature malleability to allow delegation. Both notions support anonymity but not timed or revocable delegation.

Time-Bounded Delegation. The few works on timed notion for delegation are limited. Lu et al. [28] add the delegation period to the public warrant, and relies on a trusted server to issue a timestamp for each signature a proxy signer wants to generate. Sun et al. [36] adopt an interactive delegation process; a verifier asks the proxy signer to sign a message, and one of these parties generates a timestamp that the other verifies. Beside being interactive and involving a trusted server, these schemes violate anonymity and do not have formal security.

Revocation. Techniques for revoking delegation rights [30,41] are based on changing the original signer's key so all delegated signatures will be rejected, or on creating a public list of revoked proxy signers' keys. The scheme in [41] uses revocation epochs, where for each signature, the proxy signer generates a proof that her key is not on the epoch revocation list, so anonymity is not supported. Others [13,27,28] rely on a (semi-)trusted server, where the proxy signer must contact this server when generating a signature: the original signer updates the server with all revoked proxy signers to deny their requests. This approach introduces centralization and trust issues, which we avoid in our scheme.

Policy Enforcement. Warrants are used to enforce a policy over delegation, and are usually public—a verifier rejects any signature over a message that violates the warrant [9,29]. Private warrant approaches either rely on NIZKs to show that a signed message belongs to a hidden (committed) set of messages [21], on polynomial commitments to restrict the proxy signer to sign messages following a specific template [20], or on anonymous non-interactive credentials [14]. However, none of these schemes offer anonymity. Functional (delegatable) signatures [4,11] and traceable policy-based signatures [1] support private policy and proxy anonymity using NIZKs, but without any timed notion for the delegation (and the latter requires interaction between the proxy and the tracing authority). In terms of message policy enforcement, we use these generic approaches, while we leave traceability for future work as we do not to involve a trusted entity.

2   Preliminaries

We provide an overview of timelock encryption (TLE) that we utilize in our construction. More about the correctness, security, and candidate constructions of TLE, and an overview of Schnorr signatures (where we adopt the formulation from [32] that mitigates related key attacks), can be found in the full version [2].

Notation. We denote the natural numbers by $\mathbb{N}$, the integers by $\mathbb{Z}$, and the integers modulo some q by $\mathbb{Z}_q$. Elements of $\mathbb{Z}_q$ are lowercase, and elements of a multiplicative group $\mathbb{G}$ of order q generated by generator $G \in \mathbb{G}$ are uppercase. λ denotes the security parameter, pp denotes the public parameters, $\mathsf{negl}(\lambda)$ denotes a function negligible in λ, and PPT stands for probabilistic polynomial time.

Timelock Encryption (TLE). TLE enables encrypting messages towards a time ρ (which is a round number from the bulletin board) such that they can be decrypted only after that time. Thus, for each ρ, a round-related information π_ρ is published on the board to enable decryption. We adopt the definition in [19] with a more generalized time information production algorithm as shown below.

Definition 1 (Timelock Encryption (TLE)). *A Timelock encryption scheme $\mathcal{E}$ is a tuple of five PPT algorithms defined as follows:*

TLE.Setup(1^λ) $\rightarrow$ (pp, s): *Takes as input the security parameter λ, and outputs public parameters pp and a private key s.*[3]
TLE.RoundBroadcast(s, ρ) $\rightarrow \pi_\rho$: *Takes as input the round number ρ and a private key s, and outputs the round-related decryption information π_ρ.*
TLE.Enc(ρ, m) $\rightarrow$ (ct_ρ, τ): *Takes as input the round number ρ and a message m, and outputs a round-encrypted ciphertext ct_ρ, and trapdoor τ for pre-opening.*
TLE.Dec($\pi_\rho, \mathsf{ct}_\rho$) $\rightarrow m'$: *Takes as input the round-related decryption information π_ρ and a ciphertext ct_ρ, and outputs a message m'.*
TLE.PreOpen(ct_ρ, τ) $\rightarrow m'$: *Takes as input a ciphertext ct_ρ and a trapdoor τ, and outputs a message m'.*

We use TLE in a blackbox way by invoking the algorithms defined above. We leave any details of, e.g., model and security of the blockchain and time information, to the concrete instantiation (which we require to be fully decentralized and publicly verifiable). We briefly discuss TLE correctness and security, and TLE instantiations in the full version [2].

3 Definitions

In this section, we formulate a notion for anonymous, timed and revocable proxy signature scheme. We build on previous definitions for proxy signatures [9,17,29] and extend them to cover the additional properties we require.

Definition 2. *An anonymous, timed and revocable proxy signature scheme Σ is a tuple of seven PPT algorithms defined as follows:*

Setup(1^λ) $\rightarrow$ pp: *Takes the security parameter λ as input, and outputs a set of public parameters pp.*[3]
KeyGen(1^λ) $\rightarrow$ (sk, vk): *Takes the security parameter λ as input, and outputs a signing key sk and a verification key vk.*
Sign(sk, m, policy) $\rightarrow \sigma$: *Takes the signing key sk, a message m, and a policy policy as inputs, and outputs a signature σ over m.*

---

[3] The public parameters pp are implicitly input to all subsequent algorithms.

Delegate(sk, vk, degspec) → (degInfo, rk): *Takes as inputs the signing and verification keys* (sk, vk), *and delegation specifications* degspec *(i.e., any auxiliary information and the policies over the time period and the messages that can be signed). It outputs delegation information* degInfo *and a revocation key* rk.

DegSign(m, degInfo) → σ: *Takes a message* m *and the delegation information* degInfo *as inputs. It outputs a signature* σ *over* m.

Revoke(degInfo, rk, revState[vk]) → revState[vk]': *Takes* degInfo, *the revocation key* rk, *and the revocation state associated to* vk *as inputs, and outputs an updated revocation state* revState[vk]'.

Verify(vk, m, σ, revState[vk]) → 1/0: *Takes as inputs the verification key* vk, *a message* m, *a signature* σ *over* m, *and the revocation state* revState *of* vk. *It outputs 1 if the signature is accepted, and 0 otherwise.*

We require the scheme Σ *to satisfy the following properties: correctness, existential unforgeability under chosen message attacks, anonymity, revocability, and policy enforcement, which we define below.*

As shown above, the inputs for Sign include the policy, which we view to be composed of two sub-policies: $policy_m$ determines which messages can be signed, and $policy_t$ determines the time period so that a signature produced and verified outside this period will be rejected. Although the latter is needed for the timed delegation but we include it here to satisfy anonymity. That is, all signatures whether produced by the original or proxy signer will have the same structure. The term policy is general and could be extended to include additional polices if desired. Also, policy is configured by the original signer; the proxy signer cannot change it. For delegation, Delegate takes as input the delegation specifications degspec, which includes all auxiliary information needed for delegation configuration, such as number of signing tokens in token-based schemes, and the policy policy to be enforced. The produced degInfo that will be sent to the proxy signer will include the same policy found in degspec and all information a proxy signer needs to sign.

Our definition contains one verify algorithm used for all signatures whether produced by the original or proxy signer. Verify will reject any signature that does not satisfy the policy, and checks that the signature is not revoked (based on the revocation state revState associated with vk that is publicly available).[4]

Lastly, note that when Revoke is invoked, it updates the revocation state of vk to which the delegation is associated. This update is simply a concatenation operation that appends the new revocation information. Furthermore, this is a revocation of a delegation so the proxy signature cannot exercise the delegation anymore. It is not about revoking signatures that were already accepted.

---

[4] In our construction, Verify takes the current revocation state of vk (retrieved from the bulletin board) as input; it uses this state to check the freshness of the signature and then updates this state to include the unique value of the accepted signature to enforce one-time usage. One may argue that the definition of Verify should output an updated state revState to reflect that. However, we did not incorporate that to keep the definition general so it can be used by future constructions that may not rely on a bulletin board to enforce the one-time property.

Now we define the properties listed in Definition 2. We use code-based games [6] to formulate our security notions; an experiment $\mathsf{Exp}^{\mathsf{sec}}_{\Sigma,\mathcal{A}}$ is played with respect to a security notion sec and an adversary $\mathcal{A}$ against a scheme Σ. Furthermore, and similar to [8], we define the following helper functions that are not available in the actual scheme, but only for the challenger in the experiments.

SimSetup(1^λ) $\rightarrow$ (pp, td): Receives the security parameter λ, and outputs the public parameters pp which distribution is computationally indistinguishable from what is produced by Setup, and a trapdoor td.

ExtDeg(td, σ, {degInfo}) $\rightarrow$ 1/0: Receives a trapdoor td, a valid signature σ, and a set of delegation information {degInfo}. It returns 1 if any of the degInfo in this set was used to generate σ, and 0 otherwise.

As shown, ExtDeg determines if a forgery signature was generated via a delegation based on hidden values in the signature. We resort to the use of such help function, as in [8], since this check cannot be performed on the available public signature values without a special extractor, since that would break the anonymity property of the scheme.

Correctness. Informally, correctness implies that a signer holding a valid secret key or delegation information can always produce a valid signature σ over a message m such that Verify will accept that signature if: the signature verifies correctly against vk; it is not revoked based on the latest version of revState[vk]; and that it does not violate the specified policy.

For all λ, all $m \in \{0,1\}^*$, any policy policy = (policy$_m$, policy$_t$) such that m satisfies policy$_m$ and the time of signing/verification is within policy$_t$, any delegation specifications degspec and delegation information for this specifications degInfo such that policy = degspec.policy = degInfo.policy, and the latest public revocation state revState based on which the signature σ is not revoked, the following probability is 1:

$$
\Pr\left[\mathsf{Verify}(\mathsf{vk}, m, \sigma, \mathsf{revState}[\mathsf{vk}]) = 1 \;\middle|\; \begin{array}{c} \mathsf{pp} \leftarrow \mathsf{Setup}(1^\lambda) \\ (\mathsf{sk}, \mathsf{vk}) \leftarrow \mathsf{KeyGen}(1^\lambda) \\ (\mathsf{degInfo}, \mathsf{rk}) \leftarrow \mathsf{Delegate}(\mathsf{sk}, \mathsf{vk}, \mathsf{degspec}) \\ \sigma \leftarrow \mathsf{Sign}(\mathsf{sk}, m, \mathsf{policy}) \;\vee \\ \sigma \leftarrow \mathsf{DegSign}(m, \mathsf{degInfo}) \end{array} \right]
$$

Existential Unforgeability. This property states that no adversary can produce a valid signature without the knowledge of the signing key sk or a delegation information degInfo created with respect to (sk, vk). Formally, for all λ, all $m \in \{0,1\}^*$, and any PPT adversary $\mathcal{A}$, there exists a negligible function negl such that $\Pr[\mathsf{Exp}^{\mathsf{ProxyEUF\text{-}CMA}}_{\Sigma,\mathcal{A}}(\lambda) = 1] \leq \mathsf{negl}(\lambda)$, where $\mathsf{Exp}^{\mathsf{ProxyEUF\text{-}CMA}}_{\Sigma,\mathcal{A}}$ is the experiment of existential unforgeability under chosen message attacks defined in Fig. 1, and the probability is taken over all randomness used in the experiment.

We note the following in the description of $\mathsf{Exp}^{\mathsf{ProxyEUF\text{-}CMA}}_{\Sigma,\mathcal{A}}$. Checking if the forged signature has been produced using a delegation obtained through ODelegate is done by invoking ExtDeg over the signature and L$_{\mathsf{deleg}}$ (with the

$\mathsf{Exp}_{\Sigma,\mathcal{A}}^{\mathsf{ProxyEUF\text{-}CMA}}(\lambda)$	$O\mathsf{Sign}(m, \mathsf{policy})$
1 : $\mathsf{L_{sign}} \leftarrow \varnothing, \mathsf{L_{deleg}} \leftarrow \varnothing$	1 : $\sigma \leftarrow \mathsf{Sign}(\mathsf{sk}, m, \mathsf{policy})$
2 : $(\mathsf{pp}, \mathsf{td}) \leftarrow \mathsf{SimSetup}(1^\lambda)$	2 : $\mathsf{L_{sign}} \leftarrow \mathsf{L_{sign}} \cup \{m\}$
3 : $(\mathsf{sk}, \mathsf{vk}) \leftarrow \mathsf{KeyGen}(1^\lambda)$	3 : **return** σ
4 : $O \leftarrow \{O\mathsf{Sign}, O\mathsf{Delegate}\}$	$O\mathsf{Delegate}(\mathsf{vk}, \mathsf{degspec})$
5 : $(m^*, \sigma^*) \leftarrow \mathcal{A}^O(\mathsf{vk})$	1 : $(\mathsf{degInfo}, \mathsf{rk}) \leftarrow$
6 : **if** $m^* \in \mathsf{L_{sign}} \ \vee \ \mathsf{ExtDeg}(\mathsf{td}, \sigma^*, \mathsf{L_{deleg}}) = 1$	$\mathsf{Delegate}(\mathsf{sk}, \mathsf{vk}, \mathsf{degspec})$
7 : **return** 0	2 : $\mathsf{L_{deleg}} \leftarrow \mathsf{L_{deleg}} \cup \{\mathsf{degInfo}\}$
8 : **if** $\mathsf{Verify}(\mathsf{vk}, m^*, \sigma^*, \mathsf{revState[vk]}) = 0$	3 : **return** $(\mathsf{degInfo}, \mathsf{rk})$
9 : **return** 0	
10 : **return** 1	

Fig. 1. Existential unforgeability under chosen message attacks.

$\mathsf{Exp}_{\Sigma,\mathcal{A}}^{\mathsf{DegAnon}}(\lambda)$	$\mathsf{Chal}_b(m^*, \mathsf{degspec})$
1 : $b \xleftarrow{\$} \{0,1\}$	1 : **if** $b = 0$
2 : $\mathsf{pp} \leftarrow \mathsf{Setup}(1^\lambda)$	2 : $\sigma_0 \leftarrow \mathsf{Sign}(\mathsf{sk}, m^*, \mathsf{degspec.policy})$
3 : $(\mathsf{sk}, \mathsf{vk}) \leftarrow \mathsf{KeyGen}(1^\lambda)$	3 : **if** $b = 1$
4 : $O \leftarrow \{O\mathsf{Delegate}, O\mathsf{Sign}\}$	4 : $(\mathsf{degInfo}, \mathsf{rk}) \leftarrow \mathsf{Delegate}(\mathsf{sk}, \mathsf{vk}, \mathsf{degspec})$
5 : $(m^*, \mathsf{degspec}) \leftarrow \mathcal{A}^O(\mathsf{vk})$	5 : $\sigma_1 \leftarrow \mathsf{DegSign}(m^*, \mathsf{degInfo})$
6 : $\bar{\sigma} \leftarrow \mathsf{Chal}_b(m^*, \mathsf{degspec})$	6 : **return** σ_b
7 : $b^* \leftarrow \mathcal{A}^O(\bar{\sigma})$	
8 : **if** $b^* = b$	
9 : **return** 1	
10 : **return** 0	

Fig. 2. Anonymity for delegation ($O\mathsf{Sign}$ and $O\mathsf{Delegate}$ are as defined in Fig. 1).

trapdoor τ) which will decide if this signature was produced using any of the degInfo in $\mathsf{L_{deleg}}$. Note that this helper function is not part of the actual scheme, and that τ is secret. Thus, seeing a signature does not reveal that a signature was produced by the original or proxy signer, thus compromising anonymity.

Delegation Anonymity. This implies that the verifier, or any adversary, will not be able to infer any information about a delegation (one that he does not know its degInfo). That is, all signatures will appear as if they were produced by the original signer—they do not reveal anything about the identity of the proxy signers or even that there are delegations in the first place. Thus, all signatures are indistinguishable (in terms of structure and behavior) and all are verified against the original signer's verification key vk. Also, the produced degInfo is

$$\text{Exp}_{\Sigma,\mathcal{A}}^{\text{DegRev}}(\lambda)$$

1 : $(\text{pp}, \text{td}) \leftarrow \text{SimSetup}(1^\lambda), (\text{sk}, \text{vk}) \leftarrow \text{KeyGen}(1^\lambda)$

2 : $O \leftarrow \{O\text{Sign}, O\text{Delegate}\}$

3 : $\text{degspec} \leftarrow \mathcal{A}^O(\text{vk})$

4 : $(\text{degInfo}, \text{rk}) \leftarrow \text{Delegate}(\text{sk}, \text{vk}, \text{degspec})$

5 : $\text{revState}[\text{vk}]' \leftarrow \text{Revoke}(\text{degInfo}, \text{rk}, \text{revState}[\text{vk}])$

6 : $(m^*, \sigma^*) \leftarrow \mathcal{A}^O(\text{vk}, \text{degInfo})$

7 : **if** $\text{ExtDeg}(\text{td}, \sigma^*, \text{degInfo}) = 1 \ \wedge \ \text{Verify}(\text{vk}, m^*, \sigma^*, \text{revState}[\text{vk}]') = 1$

8 : **return** 1

9 : **return** 0

Fig. 3. Delegation revocation (OSign and ODelegate are as defined in Fig. 1).

transmitted to the proxy signer over a secure channel, thus outside these two parties, no one will be able to tell that such information was produced.

Formally, for all λ, all $m \in \{0,1\}^*$, and any PPT adversary $\mathcal{A}$, there exists a negligible function negl such that $\Pr[\text{Exp}_{\Sigma,\mathcal{A}}^{\text{DegAnon}}(\lambda) = 1] \leq \frac{1}{2} + \text{negl}(\lambda)$, where $\text{Exp}_{\Sigma,\mathcal{A}}^{\text{DegAnon}}$ is the experiment of delegation anonymity defined in Fig. 2, and the probability is taken over all randomness used in the experiment.

As shown in the figure, the adversary $\mathcal{A}$ will choose a message m^* and delegation specifications degspec (where the latter includes a policy policy). The challenger, based on the value of b, signs m^* using either delegation information degInfo generated based on degspec, or the signing key sk (hence, no delegation) and returns the signature to $\mathcal{A}$. The adversary $\mathcal{A}$ is challenged to tell which method was used for signing.

Revocability. This implies that an adversary $\mathcal{A}$ cannot produce a valid signature that will convince the verifier using a revoked delegation. Formally, for all λ, all $m \in \{0,1\}^*$, and any PPT adversary $\mathcal{A}$, there exists a negligible function negl such that $\Pr[\text{Exp}_{\Sigma,\mathcal{A}}^{\text{DegRev}}(\lambda) = 1] \leq \text{negl}(\lambda)$, where $\text{Exp}_{\Sigma,\mathcal{A}}^{\text{DegRev}}$ is the experiment of delegation revocation defined in Fig. 3, and the probability is taken over all randomness used in the experiment.

As shown in the figure, $\mathcal{A}$ is challenged to produce a valid signature (that will be accepted) using the revoked delegation. Thus, the game checks that indeed the signature σ^* is produced using the revoked degInfo as done before. This check is needed to rule out the following trivial attack: $\mathcal{A}$, who has access to ODelegate, can produce a valid signature that verifies under vk using a different delegation from the one in the challenge that is not revoked, thus always winning the game.

Policy Enforcement. Informally, this implies that an adversary holding a valid delegation cannot produce a signature, that will be accepted, such that policy is not satisfied. This covers violating the policy over the message or the time.

$\mathsf{Exp}_{\Sigma,\mathcal{A}}^{\mathsf{DegPolicy}}(\lambda)$

---

1 : $\mathsf{pp} \leftarrow \mathsf{Setup}(1^\lambda), (\mathsf{sk}, \mathsf{vk}) \leftarrow \mathsf{KeyGen}(1^\lambda)$

2 : $O \leftarrow \{O\mathsf{Sign}, O\mathsf{Delegate}\}$

3 : $\mathsf{degspec} \leftarrow \mathcal{A}^O(\mathsf{vk})$

4 : $(\mathsf{degInfo}, \mathsf{rk}) \leftarrow \mathsf{Delegate}(\mathsf{sk}, \mathsf{vk}, \mathsf{degspec})$

5 : $(m^*, \sigma^*) \leftarrow \mathcal{A}^O(\mathsf{vk}, \mathsf{degInfo})$

6 :   Parse $\mathsf{degspec.policy}$ as $(\mathsf{policy}_m, \mathsf{policy}_t)$

7 :   **if** $\mathsf{Verify}(\mathsf{vk}, m^*, \sigma^*, \mathsf{revState}[\mathsf{vk}]) = 1 \;\wedge\; (m^* \notin \mathsf{policy}_m \vee \mathsf{now} \notin \mathsf{policy}_t)$

8 :   **return** 1

9 :   **return** 0

Fig. 4. Policy enforcement ($O\mathsf{Sign}$ and $O\mathsf{Delegate}$ are as defined in Fig. 1).

Formally, for all λ, all $m \in \{0,1\}^*$, and any PPT adversary $\mathcal{A}$, there exists a negligible function negl such that $\Pr[\mathsf{Exp}_{\Sigma,\mathcal{A}}^{\mathsf{DegPolicy}}(\lambda) = 1] \leq \mathsf{negl}(\lambda)$, where $\mathsf{Exp}_{\Sigma,\mathcal{A}}^{\mathsf{DegPolicy}}$ is the experiment of delegation policy enforcement defined in Fig. 4, and the probability is taken over all randomness used in the experiment. As shown in the figure, we use the variable now to refer to the current time, which is publicly accessible in the system. Thus, to check that the time policy is violated we check that now is outside the time period specified in policy_t. Also, the notion $m^* \notin \mathsf{policy}_m$ represents checking that m^* does not satisfy policy_m.

4   Construction

We present RelaySchnorr, an anonymous, timed and revocable proxy signature scheme that realizes the notion defined in the previous section. It relies on distributing one-time signing tokens to the proxy signers. Towards that, we introduce a tokenizable version of Schnorr signature, and employ a public bulletin board (an immutable, append-only log maintained by a set of validators with an honest majority, which can be instantiated as a blockchain), and timelock encryption to enforce the one-time use of signing tokens as well as the timed and revocable properties. The full construction is shown in Figs. 5 and 6. To simplify the discussion, we present our scheme with only the time policy, and we assume full synchrony with the bulletin board (i.e., any message that is sent appears immediately there). Toward the end of the section, we discuss enforcing a policy over the messages and handling synchrony of the board, as well as issues related to reducing the storage and information lookup on this board.

As mentioned before, the board state state is public and accessible by all parties. The time notion we use is in term of rounds derived from this board (in a similar way as done in blockchains). That is, a round is a block index from the board, which we denote as $\mathsf{state.round}$. We also use the notation $\mathsf{state}[\mathsf{vk}]$ to access the revocation state associated with vk, and state.roundInfo(ρ) to access the TLE decryption information published on the board for round ρ.

One-Time Tokenizable Signature Scheme. This is based on Schnorr signatures, and done via a two-layered approach; layer 1 produces a token, while layer 2 produces a signature over m using the token.

For the signing algorithm, as shown in Fig. 5, we first generate a token using the signing key sk $= x$, that is actually a Schnorr signature over a random element k with a secret randomness r. In particular, the signature requires computing $w = \mathsf{H}(k, X, R)$, where $R = G^r$. Looking ahead, the tuple (z, w, k) will be the token given to the proxy signer. To sign a message m, the original signer uses z as a secret key and produces another Schnorr signature over m with randomness e (note that the value z is also a random element in $\mathbb{Z}_p$). So this signature will be over the value $c = \mathsf{H}(m, Z, E)$, where $Z = G^z$. The output signature is $\sigma = (w, c, s, k, Z)$. The verification algorithm uses the public key vk $= X$ to verify a signature by verifying the two layers of the Schnorr signature. As shown in Fig. 6, this is done by computing the randomness R and E and then verifying that the signed hashes, w and c, are indeed correct hashes based on the computed randomness.

The one-time property is enforced as follows. Each new signature contains a unique, freshly generated value k. When receiving a valid signature, the verifier checks that k is not on the board state associated to vk, namely state[vk], and if so, the signature will be accepted and the verifier posts the k value on the board to be appended to state[vk].[5] Any signature with an already-published k will be rejected. Looking ahead, this will enable one-time use of delegated tokens. As noted, verifiers are trusted to behave as prescribed by publishing the k values of the signatures they accept. In blockchain applications (our main target) signed transactions are verified by the miners who publish valid signed transactions (that include the k values) on the blockchain, so consensus honest majority guarantees this behavior (hence, it is not a trust in a single entity). Also, as shown, due to the reliance on the updated bulletin board state to enforce the one-time property, our construction is stateful (in practice, updating the state is done automatically in blockchain applications since accepting a valid transaction means that this transaction and its signature—including k—will be published on the board).[6]

To preserve delegation anonymity, the original signer must mimic the behavior of signatures produced by delegation (which we will see shortly). As shown in Fig. 5, every now and then the original signer will publish on the board a TLE ciphertext of a list of fresh and previously-used k values (locked to a future time). This is done to mimic having ct_b associated with a delegation (and so the automatic revocation). Also, every now and then, the original signer will gener-

---

[5] The verifier sends k to the board validators who will update the state state[vk] when publishing a new block.

[6] Having a bulletin board does not introduce direct interaction between the original and proxy signers; an original signer produces degInfo and sends it in one shot to the proxy signer who can exercise delegation without any help from the original signer.

Let λ be a security parameter, S be the original signer, P be the proxy signer, and TLE be a timelock encryption scheme as defined in Definition 1. Construct an anonymous, timed and revocable proxy signature scheme $\Sigma = $ (Setup, KeyGen, Sign, Delegate, DegSign, Revoke, Verify) as follows:

Setup(1^λ): On input the security parameter λ, set $\mathbb{G}$ to be a cyclic group of a prime order q with a generator $G \in \mathbb{G}$ and hash function $H : \{0,1\}^* \times \mathbb{G}^2 \to \mathbb{Z}_q$, initialize state $= \{\}$, and invoke TLE.Setup(1^λ). Output pp $= $ (TLE.pp, H, $\mathbb{G}$, G, q, state).

KeyGen(1^λ): On input the security parameter λ, choose uniform $x \in \mathbb{Z}_q$, then compute $X = G^x$. Output the signing key sk $= x$ and the verification key vk $= X$.

Sign(sk, m): On input the signing key sk $= x$ and some message m, do:
1. Choose uniform $k, r, e \in \mathbb{Z}_q$, compute $R = G^r$, $E = G^e$
2. Compute $w = H(k, X, R)$, $z = (r + wx) \bmod q$, and $Z = G^z$
3. Compute $c = H(m, Z, E)$ and $s = (e + cz) \bmod q$ (if $z = 0$ or $s = 0$ start again with fresh r and e)
4. Output the signature $\sigma = (w, c, s, k, Z)$

Every now and then, S either (1) populates a set klist from the stored k values and fresh ones, encrypts it as $(ct_b, \tau_b) = $ TLE.Enc(klist, ρ_b), where ρ_b is some future round number, and posts (ρ_b, ct_b) on the board (resulting in state'[vk] $= $ state[vk]$\|(\rho_b, ct_b)$), or (2) posts a fresh klist on the board (resulting in state'[vk] $= $ state[vk] $\|$ klist).

Delegate(sk, vk, degspec): On input the keypair (sk $= x$, vk $= X$) and delegation specifications degspec $= (u, [\rho_a, \rho_b])$, where $u \in \mathbb{N}$ and $[\rho_a, \rho_b]$ is the delegation period, do the following:
1. Set klist $= \{\}$
2. Do the following for $i \in \{1, \ldots, u\}$:
   (a) Choose uniform $k_i, r_i \in \mathbb{Z}_q$
   (b) Compute $R_i = G^{r_i}$ and $w_i = H(k_i, X, R_i)$
   (c) Compute $z_i = (r_i + w_i x) \bmod q$ (if $z_i = 0$ start again with fresh r_i)
   (d) Set $t_i = (z_i, w_i, k_i)$ and klist $= $ klist $\cup \{k_i\}$
3. Compute two ciphertexts: $(ct_a, \tau_a) = $ TLE.Enc($t_1 \| \cdots \| t_u, \rho_a$) and $(ct_b, \tau_b) = $ TLE.Enc(klist, ρ_b) (where τ_b is the revocation key rk).
4. Set degInfo $= (\rho_a, \rho_b, ct_a)$
5. Output (degInfo, $ct_b \| \tau_b$)

S stores ciphertext ct_b and trapdoor τ_b to be used for revocation if needed (τ_a is dropped as it is not needed), posts (ρ_b, ct_b) on the board (resulting in state'[vk] $= $ state[vk] $\| (\rho_b, ct_b)$), and sends degInfo to P.

Fig. 5. RelaySchnorr—continued in Fig. 6.

ate a fresh list of k values and publish the list itself on the board. This is done to mimic the mass publishing of k values associated with on-demand revocation.

Timed Delegation. To delegate signing, i.e., the Delegate algorithm in Fig. 5, the original signer chooses the delegation specifications including the number of signing tokens and the delegation period. The original signer uses her signing key sk $= x$ to generate u fresh signing tokens, denoted as $t_1, \ldots, t_u$. Each of

DegSign(m, degInfo): On input a message m and delegation information degInfo, P does the following (let $\rho_{now} =$ state.round be the current round number):

1. If $\rho_{now} < \rho_a$ or $\rho_{now} > \rho_b$, then do nothing
2. If $\rho_a \leq \rho_{now} \leq \rho_b$, then:
   (a) If degInfo $= (\rho_a, \rho_b, \mathsf{ct}_a)$, then retrieve π_{ρ_a} from the board ($\pi_{\rho_a} =$ state.roundInfo(ρ_a)) and set degInfo $= (\rho_a, \rho_b, \mathsf{TLE.Dec}(\pi_{\rho_a}, \mathsf{ct}_a))$
   (b) Pick an unused signing token $t = (z, w, k)$ from degInfo
   (c) Compute $Z = G^z$
   (d) Choose uniform $e \in \mathbb{Z}_q$ and compute $E = G^e$
   (e) Compute $c = \mathsf{H}(m, Z, E)$, and $s = e + cz \mod q$ (if $s = 0$ start again with a fresh e)
   (f) Output the signature $\sigma = (w, c, s, k, Z)$

Revoke(degInfo, rk, state[vk]): On input degInfo $= (\rho_b, \mathsf{ct}_b)$, revocation key rk, and revocation state state[vk], do (let $\rho_{now} =$ state.round be the current round number):

1. If $\rho_{now} \geq \rho_b$, then retrieve π_{ρ_b} from the board ($\pi_{\rho_b} =$ state.roundInfo(ρ_b)) and compute klist $= \mathsf{TLE.Dec}(\pi_{\rho_b}, \mathsf{ct}_b)$
2. If $\rho_{now} < \rho_b$, then use rk $= \tau_b$ to compute klist $= \mathsf{TLE.PreOpen}(\mathsf{ct}_b, \tau_b)$
3. Add all k values such that $k \in$ klist $\wedge$ $k \notin$ state[vk] to the board state state[vk] associated with vk resulting in an updated state state[vk]$'$.

Verify(vk, m, $\sigma = (w, c, s, k, Z)$, revState $=$ state[vk]): On input the verification key vk $= X$, the message m, signature $\sigma = (w, c, s, k, Z)$ over m, and the revocation state state[vk], if $k \in$ state[vk], then output 0. Else, add k to state[vk] (resulting in state$'$[vk] $=$ state[vk] $\| k$) and do the following:

1. Compute $R = Z \cdot X^{-w}$ and $E = G^s \cdot Z^{-c}$
2. Output 1 if and only if $w = \mathsf{H}(k, X, R) \wedge c = \mathsf{H}(m, Z, E)$.

Fig. 6. RelaySchnorr (cont.).

these tokens contains z (first layer Schnorr signature over a fresh k), and the corresponding w and k values.

Our goal is to enforce a time period over the delegation in a decentralized way and without violating anonymity. To do that, we utilize a recent notion of timelock encryption TLE (defined in Sect. 2) in the blockchain model (again, we view the bulletin board as a blockchain). We represent the time period $[a, b]$ in terms of block indices, or rounds, covering the intended period. That is, this period will be $[\rho_a, \rho_b]$, where ρ_a (respectively ρ_b) is the round number during which the block with index a (respectively index b) is mined. To force a proxy signer to use the signing tokens only during $[\rho_a, \rho_b]$, we propose the following. The original signer uses TLE to encrypt the tokens in a ciphertext ct_a such that when ρ_a comes, and so the decryption information π_{ρ_a} becomes publicly available, the proxy signer can decrypt ct_a to retrieve the tokens. To enforce the end of the period, recall that any signature with a k value that appears on the board state state will be rejected. Thus, the original signer uses TLE to produce another ciphertext ct_b for time ρ_b encrypting klist (the list of k values of the delegated tokens) and posts ct_b on the board. When time ρ_b comes, and so π_{ρ_b}

becomes publicly available, the board validators will decrypt ct_b and publish all unused k values in klist on the board (this is included under Revoke in Fig. 6). This will prevent the proxy signer from using the unused tokens after time ρ_b.

The original signer stores ct_b and its secret trapdoor τ_b that can be used for early revocation (if needed) as we explain shortly. He then sends the delegation information deglnfo $= (\rho_a, \rho_b, ct_a)$ to the proxy signer over a secure channel since this is secret information, and posts (ρ_b, ct_b) on the board.

Delegated Signing. As shown in Fig. 6, at time ρ_a, the proxy signer decrypts ct_a using the decryption information π_{ρ_a} that will become available on the board at that time. This will reveal deglnfo containing the signing tokens. The proxy signer can use any of these tokens to sign a message m as follows: it chooses a random e and computes a signature using any of the unused (k, w, z) in deglnfo, which produces the second layer Schnorr signature. This signature has the same structure as the signatures that the original signer would produce, and will be verified using the same Verify algorithm against the original signer's verification key vk $= X$, thus preserving anonymity of the proxy signer.

Revocation. We support decentralized and anonymous two types of revocation: automatic, when the delegation period is over enforced by the timed property discussed above, and on-demand allowing the original signer to end the delegation before time ρ_b. Both are done by decrypting ct_b and publishing all unused k values on the board, preventing the proxy signer from using the tokens tied to them. The difference is that for automatic revocation, decryption is done using π_{ρ_b} that will become publicly available at time ρ_b. While for on-demand revocation, that only the original signer can execute, the trapdoor τ_b of deglnfo (in particular ct_b) is used to PreOpen ct_b.

As mentioned in Sect. 2, we employ a decentralized TLE scheme in our construction. The decryption information is produced using RoundBroadcast for each round (either by relying on a period random beacon as in [19] or a committee that will be elected at round ρ as in [15]). This information will be published on the board. For the decryption of ct_b and publishing all unused k values, we piggyback that on the tasks that the board validators do. Thus, the validators keep a record of all ct_b for each round ρ, and when π_ρ becomes available, they decrypt ct_b and post all unused k values on the board. Furthermore, RoundBroadcast as defined in Definition 1 involves a secret value s that is used to produce the round decryption information. This value (and whether it is needed) is based on the concrete instantiation of the TLE scheme (e.g., using the scheme in [19], s will be shared among the producers of the threshold random beacon).

As noted, during revocation or when the delegation period ends, multiple k values will be published on the board. One may argue that such mass production, or even the existence of ct_b, may violate delegation anonymity. However, this is not the case since: (1) this information does not contain anything about the identity of the proxy signer or which delegation it is tied to, and (2) the original signer will mimic a similar behavior (i.e., periodic publishing of multiple k values and ct_b) for her own signatures as outlined in the Sign algorithm in Fig. 5.

Policy Enforcement. The construction above enforces only a time policy. To restrict the proxy signer to sign messages that satisfy certain policy policy_m, we can adopt two generic approaches from the literature [17, 20].

Public Policy. If policy_m is public, we use the warrant approach. The original signer encodes the conditions that message m must satisfy in policy_m, and signs it using a separate signing key (to prevent a proxy signer from using one of the signing tokens to sign any policy she wishes). Any secure signature scheme can be used to sign policy_m; no need to be a proxy scheme. Thus, an original signer will be known using two public keys: the one used for signing the policy and the one used for the proxy signature. The original signer sends the signed policy as part of $\mathsf{deglnfo}$ as discussed previously. For Sign, the original signer can pick any policy_m. Both Sign and $\mathsf{DegSign}$ will output policy_m as part of output signature structure σ. Verifying a signature now additionally includes verifying that policy_m is signed by the original signer, and that m satisfies this policy.

Private Policy. For private policy policy_m, we employ a NIZK proof system, so that a signature includes a proof π attesting that m satisfies policy_m and that this private policy is signed by the original signer as above. policy_m is basically encoded as a function f (or a circuit that encodes the required conditions). Also, the public parameters of the system will include any public parameters needed for the NIZK proof system. In terms of signing, σ will be computed over $m \parallel \pi$ to preserve the proof integrity. Verifying a signature will involve verifying π to ensure that the private policy_m is satisfied.

Denial of Service (DoS) Attacks Against Signers. A signature will be directly rejected if its k value is already published on the board. Earlier we state that the k values are either published by the verifiers (after accepting a valid signature), by the original signer (when executing an early revocation), or by the board validators (when a delegation period ends after decrypting ct_b). However, in practice an attacker may perform a DoS attack against the original or proxy signers by intercepting a signature (before being verified) and publishing its k value on the board to invalidate the signature.

We can address this attack as follows: instead of just logging only the k value of a signature, we publish *the whole signature and the hash of the signed message.* Thus, a signature will be rejected if another valid signature (with the same k value) over a *different message* is already on the board. This also means that ct_b will contain valid signatures over random hashes using the tokens instead of just a list of the k values of these tokens. Thus, when we say a k value, we implicitly refer to a valid signature tied to this k value and the component c in the signature (based on construction) is computed over the hash of m rather than m itself. In blockchain applications, our main target, this is not an issue; either way transactions are already published on the chain with their signatures, which will prevent DoS attacks against signers.

Remark 1 (Validity of Accepted Signatures Outside the Delegation Period). A valid signature produced during the delegation period will stay valid outside that period since the verifier can easily check that it is for the same message in hand and can be verified as many times as desired. A signature over a different message means a reuse of a token and either way will be rejected.

Bulletin Board Synchronization and Off-Chain Processing Issues. In presenting our construction earlier, we assumed that the board is instantly synced. That is, any information sent to the board will appear directly and all parties will see the updated board state instantly. However, this is not the case in practice; propagation delays and other factors may prevent that. So a verifier might be checking an old state that does not contain the updated list of k values/signatures, which allows a proxy signer to use a token several times (with several verifiers) during this period. Furthermore, our scheme is similar to off-chain processing in blockchains. That is, a signature is handed directly to verifiers who rely on the current state of the board during verification. Similar to the concept of double spending in off-chain payments, a malicious proxy signer may reuse a token to generate several valid signatures each of which is handed to a different verifier at the same time. All these verifiers will accept these signatures since none of these signatures is published on the board yet.

We handle both issues by introducing the concept of *delayed signature acceptance*. A verifier will verify the signature as before, then publish it on the board as above, but will not take any action based on this valid signature—which is basically based on the content of the signed message—until later, e.g., a few rounds later. If at that time this verifier finds out that more than one valid signature (over different messages than what she has) using the same k value appeared on the board, they will reject the signature. Note that in blockchain applications, the signature is destined to the board validators, e.g., it is a signature over transactions to be posted on the board. Hence, this issue is resolved by consensus itself. That is, only one valid signature associated with a given k value will be accepted and parties act based on the confirmed state of the blockchain.

Reducing Information Lookup Time. As noted, a verifier has to check that the k value (or basically the signature) is not already published on the board (under state[vk]) before accepting a valid signature. The cost of information lookup grows linearly with the number of signatures produced under a given vk. This cost can be reduced by using, e.g., universal accumulators [10,26] that are dynamic and allow for non-membership proofs. For each vk, the board validators compute an accumulator of the associated k values and they update it as more k values are published. A signature will be accompanied with a non-membership proof proving that its k value is not in the accumulator. Thus, a verifier just needs to verify the validity of this proof.

5   Security

In the full version [2], we prove the following theorem (where schnorr-koe is the Schnorr knowledge of exponent assumption [5,12]).

Theorem 1. *Assuming EUF-CMA security of Schnorr signatures, the* schnorr-koe *assumption, a secure bulletin board, a CCA-secure TLE scheme, an EUF-CMA secure signature scheme, and a secure NIZK proof system,* RelaySchnorr *is an anonymous, timed and revocable proxy signature scheme (cf. Definition 2).*

Acknowledgements. We thank Yolan Romailler for insightful discussions about timelock encryption and drand. The work of G.A. is supported by Protocol Labs grant program RFP-013: Cryptonet network grants, and in part by NSF Grant No. CNS-2226932.

References

1. Afia, I., AlTawy, R.: Traceable policy-based signatures with delegation. In: Deng, J., Kolesnikov, V., Schwarzmann, A.A. (eds.) CANS 2023. LNCS, vol. 14342, pp. 51–72. Springer, Singapore (2023). https://doi.org/10.1007/978-981-99-7563-1_3
2. Almashaqbeh, G., Nitulescu, A.: Anonymous, timed and revocable proxy signatures. Cryptology ePrint Archive (2023). https://eprint.iacr.org/2023/833
3. Ateniese, G., Hohenberger, S.: Proxy re-signatures: new definitions, algorithms, and applications. In: CCS (2005)
4. Backes, M., Meiser, S., Schröder, D.: Delegatable functional signatures. In: Cheng, C.-M., Chung, K.-M., Persiano, G., Yang, B.-Y. (eds.) PKC 2016. LNCS, vol. 9614, pp. 357–386. Springer, Heidelberg (2016). https://doi.org/10.1007/978-3-662-49384-7_14
5. Bellare, M., Crites, E., Komlo, C., Maller, M., Tessaro, S., Zhu, C.: Better than advertised security for non-interactive threshold signatures. In: Dodis, Y., Shrimpton, T. (eds.) CRYPTO 2022. LNCS, vol. 13510, pp. 517–550. Springer, Cham (2022). https://doi.org/10.1007/978-3-031-15985-5_18
6. Bellare, M., Rogaway, P.: The security of triple encryption and a framework for code-based game-playing proofs. In: Vaudenay, S. (ed.) EUROCRYPT 2006. LNCS, vol. 4004, pp. 409–426. Springer, Heidelberg (2006). https://doi.org/10.1007/11761679_25
7. Blaze, M., Bleumer, G., Strauss, M.: Divertible protocols and atomic proxy cryptography. In: Nyberg, K. (ed.) EUROCRYPT 1998. LNCS, vol. 1403, pp. 127–144. Springer, Heidelberg (1998). https://doi.org/10.1007/bfb0054122
8. Bobolz, J., Diaz, J., Kohlweiss, M.: Foundations of anonymous signatures: Formal definitions, simplified requirements, and a construction based on general assumptions. In: Financial Cryptography and Data Security (2024)
9. Boldyreva, A., Palacio, A., Warinschi, B.: Secure proxy signature schemes for delegation of signing rights. J. Cryptol. **25**(1), 57–115 (2012)
10. Boneh, D., Bünz, B., Fisch, B.: Batching techniques for accumulators with applications to IOPs and stateless blockchains. In: Boldyreva, A., Micciancio, D. (eds.) CRYPTO 2019. LNCS, vol. 11692, pp. 561–586. Springer, Cham (2019). https://doi.org/10.1007/978-3-030-26948-7_20
11. Boyle, E., Goldwasser, S., Ivan, I.: Functional signatures and pseudorandom functions. In: Krawczyk, H. (ed.) PKC 2014. LNCS, vol. 8383, p. Boyle, E., Goldwasser, S., Ivan, I.: Functional signatures and pseudorandom functions. In: PKC (2014)-519. Springer, Heidelberg (2014). https://doi.org/10.1007/978-3-642-54631-0_29

12. Crites, E., Komlo, C., Maller, M.: How to prove Schnorr assuming Schnorr: security of multi-and threshold signatures. Cryptology ePrint Archive (2021)
13. Das, M.L., Saxena, A., Gulati, V.P.: An efficient proxy signature scheme with revocation. Informatica **15**(4), 455–464 (2004)
14. Derler, D., Hanser, C., Slamanig, D.: Privacy-enhancing proxy signatures from non-interactive anonymous credentials. In: Atluri, V., Pernul, G. (eds.) DBSec 2014. LNCS, vol. 8566, pp. 49–65. Springer, Heidelberg (2014). https://doi.org/10.1007/978-3-662-43936-4_4
15. Döttling, N., Hanzlik, L., Magri, B., Wohnig, S.: McFly: verifiable encryption to the future made practical. In: Baldimtsi, F., Cachin, C. (eds.) FC 2023. LNCS, vol. 13950, pp. 252–269. Springer, Cham. (2023). https://doi.org/10.1007/978-3-031-47754-6_15
16. Foster, I., Kesselman, C., Tsudik, G., Tuecke, S.: A security architecture for computational grids. In: CCS (1998)
17. Fuchsbauer, G., Pointcheval, D.: Anonymous proxy signatures. In: Ostrovsky, R., De Prisco, R., Visconti, I. (eds.) SCN 2008. LNCS, vol. 5229, pp. 201–217. Springer, Heidelberg (2008). https://doi.org/10.1007/978-3-540-85855-3_14
18. Fuchsbauer, G., Pointcheval, D.: Anonymous consecutive delegation of signing rights: unifying group and proxy signatures. In: Cortier, V., Kirchner, C., Okada, M., Sakurada, H. (eds.) Formal to Practical Security. LNCS, vol. 5458, pp. 95–115. Springer, Heidelberg (2009). https://doi.org/10.1007/978-3-642-02002-5_6
19. Gailly, N., Melissaris, K., Romailler, Y.: tlock: Practical timelock encryption from threshold BLS. Cryptology ePrint Archive, Paper 2023/189 (2023)
20. Hanser, C., Slamanig, D.: Blank digital signatures. In: ASIA CCS (2013)
21. Hanser, C., Slamanig, D.: Warrant-hiding delegation-by-certificate proxy signature schemes. In: Paul, G., Vaudenay, S. (eds.) INDOCRYPT 2013. LNCS, vol. 8250, pp. 60–77. Springer, Cham (2013). https://doi.org/10.1007/978-3-319-03515-4_5
22. Herranz, J., Sáez, G.: Verifiable secret sharing for general access structures, with application to fully distributed proxy signatures. In: Wright, R.N. (ed.) FC 2003. LNCS, vol. 2742, pp. 286–302. Springer, Heidelberg (2003). https://doi.org/10.1007/978-3-540-45126-6_21
23. Kim, S., Park, S., Won, D.: Proxy signatures, revisited. In: Han, Y., Okamoto, T., Qing, S. (eds.) ICICS 1997. LNCS, vol. 1334, pp. 223–232. Springer, Heidelberg (1997). https://doi.org/10.1007/bfb0028478
24. Lee, B., Kim, H., Kim, K.: Strong proxy signature and its applications. In: Proceedings of SCIS, vol. 2001, pp. 603–608 (2001)
25. Lee, J.Y., Cheon, J.H., Kim, S.: An analysis of proxy signatures: Is a secure channel necessary? In: Joye, M. (ed.) CT-RSA 2003. LNCS, vol. 2612, pp. 68–79. Springer, Heidelberg (2003). https://doi.org/10.1007/3-540-36563-x_5
26. Li, J., Li, N., Xue, R.: Universal accumulators with efficient nonmembership proofs. In: Katz, J., Yung, M. (eds.) ACNS 2007. LNCS, vol. 4521, pp. 253–269. Springer, Heidelberg (2007). https://doi.org/10.1007/978-3-540-72738-5_17
27. Liu, Z., Hu, Y., Zhang, X., Ma, H.: Provably secure multi-proxy signature scheme with revocation in the standard model. Comput. Commun. **34**(3), 494–501 (2011)
28. Lu, E.J.L., Hwang, M.S., Huang, C.J.: A new proxy signature scheme with revocation. Appl. Math. Comput. **161**(3), 799–806 (2005)

29. Malkin, T., Obana, S., Yung, M.: The hierarchy of key evolving signatures and a characterization of proxy signatures. In: Cachin, C., Camenisch, J.L. (eds.) EURO-CRYPT 2004. LNCS, vol. 3027, p. Malkin, T., Obana, S., Yung, M.: The hierarchy of key evolving signatures and a characterization of proxy signatures. In: EURO-CRYPT (2004)-322. Springer, Heidelberg (2004). https://doi.org/10.1007/978-3-540-24676-3_19

30. Mambo, M., Usuda, K., Okamoto, E.: Proxy signatures for delegating signing operation. In: CCS (1996)

31. Okamoto, T., Tada, M., Okamoto, E.: Extended proxy signatures for smart cards. In: ISW 1999. LNCS, vol. 1729, pp. 247–258. Springer, Heidelberg (1999). https://doi.org/10.1007/3-540-47790-X_21

32. Morita, H., Schuldt, J.C.N., Matsuda, T., Hanaoka, G., Iwata, T.: On the security of the Schnorr signature scheme and DSA against related-key attacks. In: Kwon, S., Yun, A. (eds.) ICISC 2015. LNCS, vol. 9558, pp. 20–35. Springer, Cham (2016). https://doi.org/10.1007/978-3-319-30840-1_2

33. Neuman, B.: Proxy-based authorization and accounting for distributed systems. In: International Conference on Distributed Computing Systems (1993)

34. Pointcheval, D., Stern, J.: Security arguments for digital signatures and blind signatures. J. Cryptol. **13**(3), 361–396 (2000)

35. Schuldt, J.C.N., Matsuura, K., Paterson, K.G.: Proxy signatures secure against proxy key exposure. In: Cramer, R. (ed.) PKC 2008. LNCS, vol. 4939, pp. 141–161. Springer, Heidelberg (2008). https://doi.org/10.1007/978-3-540-78440-1_9

36. Sun, H.M.: Design of time-stamped proxy signatures with traceable receivers. IEE Proc.-Comput. Digit. Tech. **147**(6), 462–466 (2000)

37. Sun, H.M., Lee, N.Y., Hwang, T.: Threshold proxy signatures. IEE Proc.-Comput. Digit. Tech. **146**(5), 259–263 (1999)

38. Varadharajan, V., Allen, P., Black, S.: An analysis of the proxy problem in distributed systems. In: IEEE Computer Society Symposium on Research in Security and Privacy (1991)

39. Wang, H., Pieprzyk, J.: Efficient one-time proxy signatures. In: Laih, C.-S. (ed.) ASIACRYPT 2003. LNCS, vol. 2894, pp. 507–522. Springer, Heidelberg (2003). https://doi.org/10.1007/978-3-540-40061-5_32

40. Wuille, P., Nick, J., Ruffing, T.: Schnorr signatures for secp256k1. Bitcoin Improvement Proposal 340 (2020)

41. Xu, S., Yang, G., Mu, Y., Ma, S.: Proxy signature with revocation. In: Liu, J.K., Steinfeld, R. (eds.) ACISP 2016. LNCS, vol. 9723, pp. 21–36. Springer, Cham (2016). https://doi.org/10.1007/978-3-319-40367-0_2

42. Zhang, F., Kim, K.: Efficient ID-based blind signature and proxy signature from bilinear pairings. In: Safavi-Naini, R., Seberry, J. (eds.) ACISP 2003. LNCS, vol. 2727, pp. 312–323. Springer, Heidelberg (2003). https://doi.org/10.1007/3-540-45067-X_27

Symmetric-Key Cryptography

MILP/MIQCP-Based Differential-Linear Cryptanalysis on CHAM-64/128

Yong Liu[1] , Zejun Xiang[2](✉) , Shasha Zhang[2] , and Xiangyong Zeng[1]

[1] Faculty of Mathematics and Statistics, Hubei Key Laboratory of Applied Mathematics, Hubei University, Wuhan, China
`liuyong_crypto@163.com, xzeng@hubu.edu.cn`
[2] School of Cyber Science and Technology, Hubei University, Wuhan, China
`xiangzejun@hubu.edu.cn, amushasha@163.com`

Abstract. Differential-linear (DL) cryptanalysis decomposes a cipher E into three parts, that is the differential part E_1, the middle part E_m, and the linear part E_2. The exact correlation of a DL distinguisher is the sum of the correlations of all DL trails, which needs to exhaust the output difference of E_1 and the input mask of E_2. However, the DL distinguishers that searched by existing automated models only consist of a single high-correlation DL trail. In addition, these models are challenging to search for certain DL distinguishers that involve a large number of rounds, due to limitations in computing resources. In this paper, we propose an automated tool based on a `divide-and-conquer` strategy to consider both the number of rounds and the accuracy of the correlation. Specifically, we first prepare a large number of r_d-round differential characteristics and r_l-round linear trails, whose probabilities and correlations fall within specific ranges. Then, by considering all combinations of the aforementioned differential characteristics and linear trails, and connecting them through an r_m-round middle part, we derive $(r_d + r_m + r_l)$-round DL trails and preserve the input difference and output mask pairs (Δ, Γ) of the trails with competitive correlations. Finally, the correlations of multiple DL trails are clustered to more accurately evaluate the correlation of the candidate distinguishers, and the distinguisher with the highest correlation is selected. We apply our automated tools to search for DL distinguishers of CHAM-64/128. As a result, we find DL distinguishers covering from 9 to 41 rounds. To the best of our knowledge, our 41-round distinguisher is the longest distinguisher for CHAM-64/128 in the single-key scenario. Furthermore, we present a 45-round DL attack on CHAM-64/128 based on eight 41-round distinguishers. The data and time complexities of our attack are $2^{60.2}$ and $2^{117.71}$, respectively.

Keywords: Differential-linear Cryptanalysis · Differential-linear Trail · CHAM-64/128

1 Introduction

Nowadays, the Internet of Things (IoT) is developing rapidly and involves increasingly sensitive user data. At the same time, IoT devices face limitations

N. Mouha and N. Nikiforakis (Eds.): ISC 2024, LNCS 15257, pp. 47–66, 2025.
https://doi.org/10.1007/978-3-031-75757-0_3

such as smaller memory and lower power consumption compared to a typical PC or laptop. Therefore, cryptographic primitives, as a crucial technology to ensure data security, must take into account both efficiency and security when applied to IoT devices. From the perspective of designing cryptographic primitives, an increasing number of research works have been dedicated to developing lightweight methods for efficiently encrypting data. For example, the National Institute of Standards and Technology has initiated a process to solicit, evaluate, and standardize lightweight ciphers. Addition-Rotation-XOR (ARX), as one of the nonlinear structures, is preferred by many lightweight cipher designs, such as HIGHT [15], SPECK [2], LEA [14], SPARX [12], CHAM [24], etc.

The security of symmetric primitives is evaluated as their resistance against known attacks. Differential cryptanalysis [6] and linear cryptanalysis [22] are two main classes of cryptanalysis techniques that have been used to launch the most well-known attacks on numerous block ciphers. In differential cryptanalysis (resp. linear cryptanalysis), one needs to search for high-probability differentials (resp. high-bias linear approximations) with as many rounds as possible. Limited by computing resources, the adversary often uses the probability of the best differential characteristic (resp. the correlation of the best linear trail) to approximate the probability of the best differential (resp. the correlation of the best linear approximation). Until now, the absence of a long-round differential distinguisher with a high-probability or a long-round linear distinguisher with a high-correlation has remained a central criterion in the block cipher design. In fact, there are many effective cryptanalysis techniques that are extended by differential and linear cryptanalysis, such as impossible differential cryptanalysis [4,19], zero-correlation linear cryptanalysis [10], multiple linear cryptanalysis [7], boomerang cryptanalysis [25], rotational cryptanalysis [18], differential-linear cryptanalysis [20], etc.

Differential-linear (DL) cryptanalysis [20] creates a long-round distinguisher by merging a high-probability short-round differential with a high-correlation short-round linear approximation. Specifically, one first decomposes the n-bit target cipher E into two subciphers $E = E_2 \circ E_1$, and then searches for a differential $\Delta_{in} \xrightarrow{p} \Delta_m$ for E_1 and a linear approximation $\Gamma_m \xrightarrow{q} \Gamma_{out}$ for E_2 with a probability p and a correlation q, respectively. In [20], Langford and Hellman fixed the differential probability p at 1 and succeeded in analyzing up to 8-round reduced variants of DES [23]. Then, Biham et al. relaxed the constraint on the probability p of the differential part being 1 and proposed an extension of DL cryptanalysis in which p is smaller than 1 [5]. The overall correlation of DL distinguisher ($\Delta_{in} \rightarrow \Gamma_{out}$) can be estimated with the piling-up lemma as pq^2 under two statistical assumptions, that is, E_1 and E_2 are independent and the output difference Δ_{out} of E_1 exhibits a certain randomness when Δ_{out} is not equal to Δ_m. In fact, Biham et al. have noted that the second assumption above may fail in many cases and suggested to check the overall bias of the approximation experimentally. Then, Blondeau et al. [9] provided an exact expression of the correlation for DL distinguishers in a closed form under the sole assumption that the differential part and the linear part are independent.

However, the exact expression is computationally infeasible because it requires exhausting all intermediate masks Γ_m.

Another method to consider the dependence between the two parts of a DL distinguisher is to divide the block cipher E into three parts, that is $E = E_2 \circ E_m \circ E_1$. The middle part E_m, which connects E_1 and E_2, is used to take the dependency between E_1 and E_2 into account. Generally, the correlation of E_m is evaluated by experiments using a sufficiently large number of random inputs. Alternatively, Bar-On et al. introduced the Differential-Linear Connectivity Table (DLCT) technique to formally derive the correlation of E_m when it covers only one S-box layer [1]. However, it is infeasible to derive the correlation of E_m based on DLCT technique when E_m involves multiple rounds. In addition, the methods mentioned above share the commonality that they require manual and extensive computing resources to search for DL distinguishers. In 2023, Bellini et al. proposed a fully automatic search tool to search for DL distinguishers of ARX ciphers based on Mixed-Integer Linear Programming (MILP) and Mixed-Integer Quadratic Constraint Programming (MIQCP) techniques [3]. In Bellini et al.'s model, the differential part E_1 and the linear part E_2 are modeling by the techniques presented in [13]. To calculate the correlation of the middle part E_m, Bellini et al. introduced a continuous difference propagation framework, inspired by Coutinho et al.'s Continuous Diffusion Analysis [11], and modeled the continuous difference propagations of each operation. As a result, [3] improved the latest 14-round key-recovery attack against SPECK32/64 with time complexity and data complexity 2^{58} and 2^{31}, respectively. Another automated tool for searching DL distinguishers of ARX ciphers was proposed by Lv et al. in 2023 [21]. One of the foundations of their automated search tool is transforming an arbitrary matrix multiplication chain into MIQCP. As a result, [21] presented the lowest time complexity attacks against 12–14 rounds of SPECK32 to date. Recently, inspired by Bellini et al.'s method, Zhou et al. proposed continuous difference propagation of the AND operation and constructed an MILP/MIQCP-based fully automated model for searching for DL distinguishers of SIMON-like ciphers [26]. An important factorto consider is that the automated model may not be solvable when the size of the model is too large. In [26], Zhou et al. first obtain the optimal differential characteristic for a certain number of rounds, and then extend this optimal characteristic into a complete DL distinguisher. However, using one of the optimal differential characteristics to derive a DL distinguisher is only one of the feasible ways. A better distinguisher may be obtained by considering more differential characteristics. In addition, the automated search tools mentioned above utilize the correlation of a single DL trail (under some explicit conditions [21]) to provide a good estimate of the correlation of a DL distinguisher. In fact, the exact bias of a DL distinguisher needs to exhaust all output differences of E_1 and input masks of E_2. Therefore, it is necessary to develop an automated tool that can search for long-round DL distinguishers and improve the accuracy of estimated correlations simultaneously.

Our Contributions. In this paper, we introduce a new framework based on MILP and MIQCP to automatically search for DL distinguishers of ARX based ciphers. Our framework is capable of searching for long-round DL distinguishers and can more accurately calculate the correlation of distinguishers. Our main contributions include the following three aspects:

Propose an Automated Model Based on a `divide-and-conquer` Strategy. Compared with differential cryptanalysis and linear cryptanalysis, one of the primary advantages of DL cryptanalysis is that attackers can independently construct high-probability differentials and high-correlation linear approximations. Therefore, we propose an automated tool to search for DL distinguishers based on the `divide-and-conquer` strategy. Specifically, we first independently search for all high-probability differential characteristics and high-correlation linear trails. Then, the middle part, serving as a link, is used to connect the differential part and the linear part mentioned above to form a complete DL trail, and the DL trails with competitive correlations are selected.

Consider DL Clustering to Evaluate the Correlation of the Distinguishers More Accurately. In fact, the exact correlation of a DL distinguisher is the sum of the correlations of all DL trails. Therefore, we exhaust all/part of the output differences of the differential part and the input masks of the linear part, and sum the correlations of multiple DL trails as the correlations of the DL distinguishers.

Find the Best Distinguishers and Construct a 45-Round DL Attack for CHAM-64/128. To verify the effectiveness of our automated tools, we apply it to search for DL distinguishers of CHAM-64/128. As a result, we obtain DL distinguishers for CHAM-64/128 covering from 9 to 41 rounds. In addition, the validity of the distinguishers, whose absolute value of theoretical correlations is higher than 2^{17}, is verified by experiments. Finally, we propose a 45-round DL attack whose data and time complexities are $2^{60.2}$ and $2^{117.71}$, respectively. Our results and comparisons with the published works are summarized in Table 1.

Organization of the Paper. The rest of this paper is organized as follows. In Sect. 2, we introduce some notations and briefly review some basic background that will be used later. In Sect. 3, two strategies for searching for DL distinguishers are introduced in detail. Then, our automated models are applied to CHAM-64/128 in Sect. 4. We conclude the paper in Sect. 5.

2   Notations and Preliminaries

2.1   Notations

Notations used in this paper are summarised in Table 2.

Assuming that the probability of a differential $\Delta_{in} \rightarrow \Delta_m$ is p and the correlation of a linear approximation $\Gamma_m \rightarrow \Gamma_{out}$ is q, we refer to the probability weight and the correlation weight of $\Delta_{in} \rightarrow \Delta_m$ and $\Gamma_m \rightarrow \Gamma_{out}$ as $|\log p|$ and

Table 1. Our results and comparisons with the published works on CHAM-64/128.

Method	Attack type	Round	Reference
Differential	Distinguisher	39	[24]
Linear	Distinguisher	34	[24]
Boomerang	Distinguisher	35	[24]
Impossible differential	Distinguisher	18	[24]
Zero-correlation linear	Distinguisher	21	[24]
Differential-linear	Distinguisher	35	[24]
Integral	Distinguisher	16	[24]
Rotational-XOR	Distinguisher	16	[24]
Differential	Distinguisher	39	[16]
Linear	Distinguisher	34	[17]
Differential	Distinguisher	40	[8]
Differential	Key-recovery attack	52	[8]
Differential-linear	Distinguisher	**41**	This paper
Differential-linear	Key-recovery attack †	45	This paper

† The data and time complexities of our 45-round DL attack are $2^{60.2}$ and $2^{117.71}$, respectively

Table 2. Notations.

Symbol	Description
$\mathbb{F}_2$	finite field with only two elements 0 and 1
$\mathbb{F}_2^n$	n-dimensional vector space over $\mathbb{F}_2$
$\mathbb{R}$	the real number domain
$\mathbb{N}$	the set of natural numbers
$\mathcal{B}$	the set of real numbers between 1 and -1
x_i	the i-th bit of $x \in \mathbb{F}_2^n$, where $0 \leq i \leq n - 1$
$\|x\|$	the absolute value of x
$x + y$	the addition of x and y in the real domain
$x \times y$	the multiplication of x and y in the real domain
$x \cdot y$	the inner product of x and y, $x \cdot y = \bigoplus_{i=0}^{n-1} x_i y_i$
$x \oplus y$	bitwise exclusive OR of x and y
$x \boxplus y$	addition of x and y modulo 2^n
$x \lll r$	left rotation of x by r bits
$x \ggg r$	right rotation of x by r bits

$|(\log|q|)|$, respectively. In order to simplify the notations, we will use p_w and q_w to represent the probability weight and the correlation weight of $\Delta_{in} \to \Delta_m$ and $\Gamma_m \to \Gamma_{out}$, respectively. In addition, the absolute value of the correlation is referred to as correlation without explicit specification.

2.2 Differential-Linear Cryptanalysis

Differential-linear cryptanalysis was introduced by Langford and Hellman in [20]. As shown in Fig. 1, a cipher E is divided into two subciphers E_1 and E_2, such that $E = E_2 \circ E_1$. Then, one needs to construct a differential distinguisher and a linear distinguisher of E_1 and E_2, respectively.

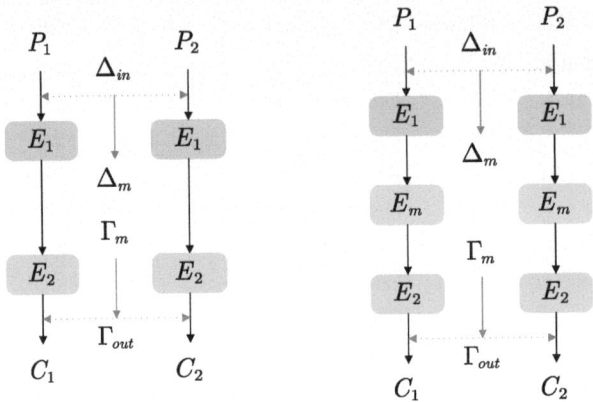

Fig. 1. A DL distinguisher with two parts (left) and three parts (right).

Assume that the probability of the differential $\Delta_{in} \xrightarrow{E_1} \Delta_m$ is $\mathrm{Pr}_{x \in \mathbb{F}_2^n}[E_1(x) \oplus E_1(x \oplus \Delta_{in}) = \Delta_m] = p$, and the correlation of the linear approximation $\Gamma_m \xrightarrow{E_2} \Gamma_{out}$ is $\mathbf{Cor}_{x \in \mathbb{F}_2^n}[\Gamma_m \cdot x \oplus \Gamma_{out} \cdot E_2(x)] = q$. Then, the overall correlation of the DL distinguisher $\Delta_{in} \xrightarrow{E} \Gamma_{out}$ is

$$\mathbf{Cor}_{x \in \mathbb{F}_2^n}[\Gamma_{out} \cdot E(x) \oplus \Gamma_{out} \cdot E(x \oplus \Delta_{in})] = pq^2$$

under the following two assumptions:

Assumption 1. The cases where the differential $\Delta_{in} \xrightarrow{E_1} \Delta_m$ is not satisfied, $\mathrm{Pr}_{x \in \mathbb{F}_2^n}[\Gamma_m \cdot (E_1(x) \oplus E_1(x \oplus \Delta_{in})) = 0 \mid E_1(x) \oplus E_1(x \oplus \Delta_{in}) \neq \Delta_m] = 1/2$.
Assumption 2. There is independence between E_1 and E_2.

As for the first assumption, subsequent researches have shown that it may fail in practice. For example, Biham et al. emphasized that this assumption is not necessarily accurate, and the overall bias should be computed more accurately or verified experimentally. Then, Blondeau et al. [9] provided an exact expression (as shown in Eq. 1) of the correlation for DL distinguisher in a closed form under the sole assumption that the two parts are independent.

$$\mathbf{Cor}_{x \in \mathbb{F}_2^n}(\Gamma_{out} \cdot (E(x) \oplus E(x \oplus \Delta_{in}))) =$$
$$\sum_{\Gamma_m} \mathbf{Cor}_{x \in \mathbb{F}_2^n}(\Gamma_m \cdot (E_1(x) \oplus E_1(x \oplus \Delta_{in}))) \mathbf{Cor}_{y \in \mathbb{F}_2^n}^2(\Gamma_m \cdot y \oplus \Gamma_{out} \cdot E_2(y)). \tag{1}$$

However, the exact expression above is computationally infeasible due to the need of exhausting all intermediate masks Γ_m.

As for the second assumption, a common strategy is to divide the cipher into three subciphers E_1, E_m, and E_2, such that $E = E_2 \circ E_m \circ E_1$ and the correlation of the middle part E_m

$$\mathbf{Cor}_{x \in \mathcal{S}}[\Gamma_m \cdot E_m(x) \oplus \Gamma_m \cdot E_m(x \oplus \Delta_m)] = r$$

is typically determined through experiments, where $\mathcal{S}$ represents the set of samples over which the correlation is computed. In particular, one can also utilize the DLCT introduced by Bar-On et al. to formalize the correlation r when E_m only consists of a few operations [1]. The total correlation of E with form $E = E_2 \circ E_m \circ E_1$ is prq^2 and the data complexity that distinguishes the cipher E from a Pseudo Random Permutation is $\epsilon p^2 r^2 q^4$, where $\epsilon \in \mathbb{N}$ is a small constant.

In fact, Bar-On et al. also pointed out that the exact correlation of E is

$$\sum_{\Delta_m, \Gamma_m} \Pr[\Delta_{in} \xrightarrow{E_1} \Delta_m] \mathbf{Cor}(\Delta_m \xrightarrow{E_m} \Gamma_m) \mathbf{Cor}^2(\Gamma_m \xrightarrow{E_2} \Gamma_{out}), \qquad (2)$$

and it relies on round independence within E_1 and E_2 [1].

2.3 Continuous Analysis of Difference Propagation

In [11], Coutinho et al. proposed a new technique called Continuous Diffusion Analysis (CDA). The main idea of CDA is to generalize cryptographic primitives into a continuous mathematical function and create continuous operators from Boolean operators. This allows for expressing bits of cryptographic primitives as probabilities or correlations. For example, consider two independent random input variables, $a, b \in \mathbb{F}_2$, and an output variable, $c \in \mathbb{F}_2$, of the XOR operation, then c equals 1 if one of the following two conditions is met. That is, $a = 0, b = 1$ and $a = 1, b = 0$. Let $\Pr[a = 1] = p_1$ and $\Pr[b = 1] = p_2$, then $\Pr[c = 1] = p_3 = (1 - p_1)p_2 + p_1(1 - p_2)$. Expressing p_1, p_2, and p_3 as functions of their correlations $\epsilon_{p_i} \in \mathcal{B}$ $(1 \leq i \leq 3)$, we have $p_i = 1/2 + \epsilon_{\epsilon_{p_i}}/2$ and $\epsilon_{p_1} \oplus \epsilon_{p_2} = \epsilon_{p_3} = -\epsilon_{p_1}\epsilon_{p_2}$. Furthermore, one can create continuous versions of entire cryptographic primitives by assuming similar independence properties among the input variables of various cryptographic operations.

Inspired by Coutinho's framework, Bellini et al. [3] defined a more formal continuous difference propagation and constructed continuous functions for the difference propagation of ARX operators (the XOR, majority (MAJ) function, rotation, and modular addition operations).

Proposition 1 (Continuous difference propagation of XOR [3]). *Let $x, y \in \mathcal{B}^n$, then the continuous difference propagation of XOR is given by*

$$x \oplus_{\mathcal{C},\Delta} y = -xy.$$

Proposition 2 (Continuous difference propagation of Left and Right Rotation [3]). *Let $x = (x_{n-1}, x_{n-2}, \cdots, x_0) \in \mathcal{B}^n$ ($r \in \mathbb{N}$ and $0 \leq r \leq n - 1$), then the continuous difference propagation of the rotation to the left, and to the right, by r, respectively, is given by*

$$(x_{n-1}, x_{n-2}, \cdots, x_0) \lll_{\mathcal{C},\Delta} = (x_{n-r-1}, x_{n-r-2}, \cdots, x_0, x_{n-1}, x_{n-2}, \cdots, x_{n-r}),$$

$$(x_{n-1}, x_{n-2}, \cdots, x_0) \ggg_{\mathcal{C},\Delta} = (x_{r-1}, x_{r-2}, \cdots, x_0, x_{n-1}, x_{n-2}, \cdots, x_r).$$

Proposition 3 (Continuous difference propagation of MAJ [3]). *The MAJ function is defined as $MAJ(a, b, c) = ab + bc + ca$, where $a, b, c \in \mathbb{F}_2$. Let $x, y, z \in \mathcal{B}^n$, the continuous difference propagation of the MAJ function is given by*

$$MAJ_{\mathcal{C},\Delta}(x, y, z) = 1/4(x + y + z + xyz).$$

Proposition 4 (Continuous difference propagation of Modular Addition Operation [3]). *Let $x, y, z \in \mathcal{B}^n$, then the continuous difference propagation of the addition modulo 2^n function is given by*

$$x \boxplus_{\mathcal{C},\Delta} y = (x_{n-1} \oplus_{\mathcal{C},\Delta} y_{n-1} \oplus_{\mathcal{C},\Delta} c_{n-1}, \cdots, x_0 \oplus_{\mathcal{C},\Delta} y_0 \oplus_{\mathcal{C},\Delta} c_0),$$

where c_i is calculated recursively as follow:

$$c_i = \begin{cases} -1.0 & i = 0, \\ MAJ_{\mathcal{C},\Delta}(x_{i-1}, y_{i-1}, c_{i-1}) & 1 \leq i \leq n - 1. \end{cases}$$

2.4   Modeling the Differential Part, Linear Parts, and Middle Part

In 2019, Fu et al. proposed MILP models to automatic search for differential characteristics and linear trials of ARX ciphers [13]. In addition, [3] introduced modeling rules for the middle part. For a more detailed explanation of the modeling rules, please refer to [13] and [3].

3   Finding Differential-Linear Distinguishers with MILP/MIQCP

In this section, we will introduce two strategies to search for DL distinguishers. The first strategy involves integrating the models of the three parts into a complete model. Due to limited computing resources, the first strategy cannot be used to search for DL distinguishers that involve a large number of rounds. As a comparison, our second strategy involves searching for differential characteristics and linear trails independently, utilizing the `divide-and-conquer` idea. Subsequently, we merge the differential characteristics and linear trails into complete DL trails by the middle part. There are two advantages for the second modeling strategy. First, instead of searching for r-round complete DL trails, we focus on searching for r_1-round differential characteristics and r_2-round linear trails independently ($r_1 + r_2 < r$). The reduction of the search space enables the derivation of long-round DL distinguishers. In addition, the second modeling strategy is able to exhaust all/part of intermediate differences Δ_m and masks Γ_m, which allows us to derive a more accurate overall correlation according to Eq. 2.

3.1   The First Modeling Strategy

In the first modeling strategy, we initially characterize the differential part, the middle part, and the linear part separately, and then merge them to form a complete MILP model $\mathcal{M}_0$. Next, we will introduce the objective function of $\mathcal{M}_0$ in detail.

Let the number of rounds of the differential part, the middle part, and the linear part be r_d, r_m, and r_l, respectively. Let the r_1-th round probability weight variables and the r_2-th round correlation weight variables in the MILP model be $p_w^{r_1}[i]$ and $q_w^{r_2}[j]$ respectively, where $0 \leq i \leq n-2, 1 \leq j \leq n-1, 0 \leq r_1 \leq r_d - 1, r_d + r_m \leq r_2 \leq r_d + r_m + r_l - 1$. Then, the objective function of $\mathcal{M}_0$ is

$$\min \left\{ \sum_{r_1=0}^{r_d-1} \sum_{i=0}^{n-2} p_w^{r_1}[i] + |\log(|\mathbf{Cor}(\Delta_m \xrightarrow{E_m} \Gamma_m)|)| + 2 \times \sum_{r_2=r_d+r_m}^{r_d+r_m+r_l-1} \sum_{j=1}^{n-1} q_w^{r_2}[j] \right\},$$

where $\log(|\mathbf{Cor}(\Delta_m \xrightarrow{E_m} \Gamma_m)|) = \log|\sum_{0 \leq i \leq n-1}(C_i \times \Gamma_m^i)|$ represents the correlation weight of the middle part, and $\vec{C} = (C_{n-1}, C_{n-2}, \cdots, C_0) \in \mathcal{B}^n$ and $\Gamma_m = (\Gamma_m^{n-1}, \Gamma_m^{n-2}, \cdots, \Gamma_m^0) \in \mathbb{F}_2^n$ represent the output variables of the middle part of $\mathcal{M}_0$ and the input mask of the linear part, respectively.

In this paper, our MILP models are solved by the solver `Gurobi`[1]. When $r_d + r_m + r_l$ is sufficiently large, the model $\mathcal{M}_0$ cannot be solved with limited computing resources. An important reason is that $\mathcal{M}_0$ includes numerous binary variables, continuous variables, multiplication operations, and involves some ready-made functions in `Gurobi`, such as `LOG_2` and `ABS`.

3.2   The Second Modeling Strategy

Our second strategy mainly consists of five steps. First, we build an MILP model to search for the minimum probability weight of r_d-round differential characteristics (resp. the minimum correlation weight of r_l-round linear trails). Then, a new MILP model is built to search for all r_d-round input-output difference pairs (Δ_{in}, Δ_m), where the probabilities weight fall within a specific range. The lower bound of the above range is the minimum probability weight obtained in the first

---

[1] https://www.gurobi.com/.

step, while the upper bound is determined by available computing resources. Similarly, we search all r_l-round input-output linear mask pairs (Γ_m, Γ_{out}) with a specific range of correlation weight in the same manner. In the third step, we use an r_m-round middle part to connect r_d-round difference pairs (Δ_{in}, Δ_m) and r_l-round linear mask pairs (Γ_m, Γ_{out}) to form $(r_d + r_m + r_l)$-round DL trails. Then, all $(R = r_d + r_m + r_l)$-round DL trails $\boldsymbol{\Delta_{in}^R} \xrightarrow{E_1} \boldsymbol{\Delta_m^R} \xrightarrow{E_m} \boldsymbol{\Gamma_m^R} \xrightarrow{E_2} \boldsymbol{\Gamma_{out}^R}$ with competitive correlation weights will be preserved. Subsequently, for each $\boldsymbol{\Delta_{in}^R}$ and $\boldsymbol{\Gamma_{out}^R}$, we search for all/part of r_d-round differential characteristics with the input difference $\boldsymbol{\Delta_{in}^R}$ and all/part of r_l-round linear trails with the output mask $\boldsymbol{\Gamma_{out}^R}$ according to the available computing resources. Finally, after calculating the correlation weights of the DL distinguishers $\boldsymbol{\Delta_{in}^R} \xrightarrow{E} \boldsymbol{\Gamma_{out}^R}$ according to Eq. 2, we select the R-round DL distinguisher $\boldsymbol{\Delta_{in,min}^R} \xrightarrow{E} \boldsymbol{\Gamma_{out,min}^R}$ with the minimum correlation weight. Next, we will introduce the second strategy in detail.

The First Step. The first step is to search for the minimum probability weight and the minimum correlation weight of r_1-round differential characteristics and r_2-round linear trails, respectively. This goal can be achieved by constructing two MILP models $\mathcal{M}_1$ and $\mathcal{M}_2$. The objective functions of these two models are $\min\{\sum_{0 \le r \le r_1-1} \sum_{0 \le i \le n-2} p_w^r[i]\}$ and $\min\{\sum_{0 \le r \le r_2-1} \sum_{1 \le i \le n-1} q_w^r[i]\}$ respectively, where $p_w^r[i]$ and $q_w^r[i]$ represent the r-th round probability weight variable and correlation weight variable in the MILP models, respectively.

The Second Step. The second step involves searching for all r_3-round input-output difference pairs (Δ_{in}, Δ_m) of E_1, where the probability weight p_w^{r3} fall in the range of $p_{w,min}^{r3} \le p_w^{r3} \le p_{w,max}^{r3}$. The lower bound $p_{w,min}^{r3}$ is the minimum probability weight of r_3-round differential characteristics, while the upper bound $p_{w,max}^{r3}$ is selected by the adversary according to actual computing resources. Correspondingly, we also search for all r_4-round input-output linear mask pairs (Γ_m, Γ_{out}). The correlation weight q_w^{r4} fall in the range of $q_{w,min}^{r4} \le q_w^{r4} \le q_{w,max}^{r4}$, where $q_{w,min}^{r4}$ is the minimum correlation weight of r_4-round linear trails, $q_{w,max}^{r4}$ is selected by the adversary according to actual computing resources.

We also construct two MILP models $\mathcal{M}_3$ and $\mathcal{M}_4$ in the second step. Compared with $\mathcal{M}_1$ (resp. $\mathcal{M}_2$), model $\mathcal{M}_3$ (resp. $\mathcal{M}_4$) adds the following constraint:

$$p_{w,min}^{r3} \le \sum_{r=0}^{r_3-1} \sum_{i=0}^{n-2} p_w^r[i] \le p_{w,max}^{r3} \text{ (resp. } q_{w,min}^{r4} \le \sum_{r=0}^{r_4-1} \sum_{i=1}^{n-1} q_w^r[i] \le q_{w,max}^{r4}).$$

Remark 1. In the second step, our main goal is to generate a significant number of distinct input-output difference pairs (Δ_{in}, Δ_m) (resp. input-output linear mask pairs (Γ_m, Γ_{out})) for the third step. We approximate the probabilities (resp. correlations) of the differentials (resp. linear approximations) using the probabilities (resp. correlations) of the best differential characteristics (resp. linear trails). Calculating the exact probability of all differentials $\Delta_{in} \xrightarrow{E_1} \Delta_m$ (resp. the exact correlation of all linear approximations $\Gamma_m \xrightarrow{E_2} \Gamma_{out}$) intended for the third step with limited computing resources is impractical. Therefore, we need to collect a sufficient number of distinct input-output difference pairs (Δ_{in}, Δ_m) (resp. input-output linear mask pairs (Γ_m, Γ_{out})) and estimate the probability (resp. correlations) of the corresponding best differential characteristics (resp. linear trails). Simultaneously, we disregard the differential characteristics (resp. linear trails) with lower probabilities.

The Third Step. In the third step, we will search for R-round DL trails with competitive correlation weights. This goal can be achieved by obtaining multiple different solutions of the MILP model. Assume that the maximum number of rounds of differential characteristics (resp. linear trails) is r_d^{max} (resp. r_l^{max}) in the second step. We consider all possible combinations of r_d, r_m, and r_l such that $r_d + r_m + r_l = R$, where $1 \le r_d \le r_d^{max}$, $1 \le r_l \le r_l^{max}$, and $1 \le r_m$.

Then, for each combination of r_d, r_m, and r_l, we exhaust all r_d-round input-output difference pairs (Δ_{in}, Δ_m) and all r_l-round input-output linear mask pairs (Γ_m, Γ_{out}) obtained in the second step. Since each entry (Δ_{in}, Δ_m) (resp. (Γ_m, Γ_{out})) is accompanied by the corresponding probability weights $p_{w,(\Delta_{in}, \Delta_m)}^{r_d}$ (resp. correlation weight $q_{w,(\Gamma_m, \Gamma_{out})}^{r_l}$), we can calculate the correlation weights

$$p_{w,(\Delta_{in}, \Delta_m)}^{r_d} + |\log(|\mathbf{Cor}(\Delta_m \xrightarrow{E_m} \Gamma_m)|)| + 2 \times q_{w,(\Gamma_m, \Gamma_{out})}^{r_l},$$

of all possible DL trails mentioned above, where $\log(|\mathbf{Cor}(\Delta_m \xrightarrow{E_m} \Gamma_m)|)$ represents the correlation weight of the middle part, as described in the first modeling strategy. Subsequently, the DL trails are sorted in ascending order based on their correlation weights, and several $(R = \mathbf{r_d} + \mathbf{r_m} + \mathbf{r_l})$-round DL trails $\Delta_{in}^{\mathbf{R}} \xrightarrow{E_1} \Delta_m^{R} \xrightarrow{E_m} \Gamma_m^{R} \xrightarrow{E_2} \Gamma_{out}^{\mathbf{R}}$ with lower correlation weights are selected.

The Fourth Step. For each input difference $\Delta_{in}^{\mathbf{R}}$ and output mask $\Gamma_{out}^{\mathbf{R}}$ of the R-round DL trails obtained in the third step, we will search for all/part of $\mathbf{r_d}$-round differential characteristics (resp. $\mathbf{r_l}$-round linear trails) with the input difference $\Delta_{in}^{\mathbf{R}}$ (resp. the output mask $\Gamma_{out}^{\mathbf{R}}$) based on the available computing resources.

Correspondingly, we construct two MILP model $\mathcal{M}_5$ and $\mathcal{M}_6$. Compared with $\mathcal{M}_1$ (resp. $\mathcal{M}_2$), model $\mathcal{M}_5$ (resp. $\mathcal{M}_6$) makes the following modifications:

1. Add a constraint $\Delta_{in} = \Delta_{in}^{\mathbf{R}}$ (resp. $\Gamma_{out} = \Gamma_{out}^{\mathbf{R}}$).
2. Add a constraint $\sum_{r=0}^{\mathbf{r_d}-1} \sum_{i=0}^{n-2} p_w^r[i] \le p_{w,max}^{\mathbf{r_d}}$ (resp. $\sum_{r=0}^{\mathbf{r_l}-1} \sum_{i=1}^{n-1} q_w^r[i] \le q_{w,max}^{\mathbf{r_l}}$). Also, $p_{w,max}^{\mathbf{r_d}}$ (resp. $q_{w,max}^{\mathbf{r_l}}$) is a positive integer chosen by the adversary based on the state size of the primitives.
3. Delete the objective function.

For each $\Delta_{in}^{\mathbf{R}}$ and $\Gamma_{out}^{\mathbf{R}}$ obtained in the third step, we store all $\mathbf{r_d}$-round input-output difference pairs $(\Delta_{in}^{\mathbf{R}}, \Delta_m^*)$ and the corresponding probability weight $p_{w,(\Delta_{in}^{\mathbf{R}}, \Delta_m^*)}^{\mathbf{r_d}}$ and all $\mathbf{r_l}$-round input-output mask pairs $(\Gamma_m^*, \Gamma_{out}^{\mathbf{R}})$ and the corresponding correlation weight $q_{w,(\Gamma_m^*, \Gamma_{out}^{\mathbf{R}})}^{\mathbf{r_l}}$.

The Fifth Step. For each $\boldsymbol{\Delta}_{\mathbf{in}}^{\mathbf{R}}$ and $\boldsymbol{\Gamma}_{\mathbf{out}}^{\mathbf{R}}$ obtained in the third step, we select the R-round DL distinguisher $\boldsymbol{\Delta}_{\mathbf{in,min}}^{\mathbf{R}} \xrightarrow{E} \boldsymbol{\Gamma}_{\mathbf{out,min}}^{\mathbf{R}}$ with the maximum absolute value of the correlation $|\mathbb{C}|$ by exhausting $(\boldsymbol{\Delta}_{\mathbf{in}}^{\mathbf{R}}, \Delta_m^*)$ and $(\Gamma_m^*, \boldsymbol{\Gamma}_{\mathbf{out}}^{\mathbf{R}})$ obtained in the fourth step, where $\mathbb{C}$ is equal to

$$\sum_{(\boldsymbol{\Delta}_{\mathbf{in}}^{\mathbf{R}}, \Delta_m^*),(\Gamma_m^*, \boldsymbol{\Gamma}_{\mathbf{out}}^{\mathbf{R}})} 2^{p_{w,(\boldsymbol{\Delta}_{\mathbf{in}}^{\mathbf{R}}, \Delta_m^*)}^{\mathrm{rd}}} \times \mathbf{Cor}(\Delta_m^* \xrightarrow{E_m} \Gamma_m^*) \times 2^{2 \times q_{w,(\Gamma_m^*, \boldsymbol{\Gamma}_{\mathbf{out}}^{\mathbf{R}})}^{\mathrm{rl}}}.$$

4   Application to CHAM-64/128

4.1   Description of CHAM

CHAM [24] is a family of lightweight block ciphers that proposed by Koo et al. at ICISC'17. In 2019, a revised version of CHAM with an increased number of rounds was proposed to ensure sufficient security redundancy. There are three versions of CHAM, CHAM-64/128, CHAM-128/128, and CHAM-128/256.

CHAM-64/128 adopts the generalized 4-branch Feistel structure, and encrypts a plaintext (X_0, Y_0, Z_0, W_0) of four 16-bit words to a ciphertext (X_r, Y_r, Z_r, W_r) of four 16-bit words under a 128-bit key by applying 88 iterations of the key-dependent round function. The round function of CHAM-64/128 is depicted in Fig. 2, and the i-th round function of CHAM-64/128 can be formed as

$$(X_{i+1}, Y_{i+1}, Z_{i+1}, W_{i+1}) \leftarrow (Y_i, Z_i, W_i, ((X_i \oplus i) \boxplus ((Y_i \lll \alpha_i) \oplus k_i)) \lll \beta_i),$$

where $0 \le i \le r - 1$, $\alpha_i = 1$ and $\beta_i = 8$ when i is even and $\alpha_i = 8$ and $\beta_i = 1$ when i is odd, k_i is the i-th round key.

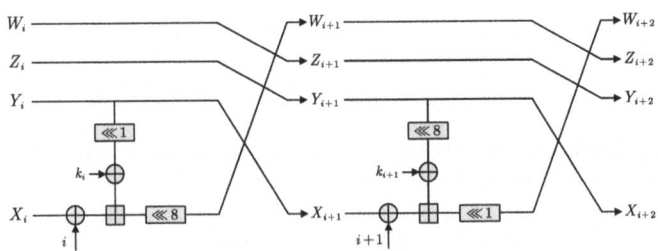

Fig. 2. Two consecutive round functions of CHAM begin with the even i-th round.

4.2   Differential-Linear Distinguisher of CHAM-64/128

According to the search framework described in Subsect. 3.2, we first prepare two MILP models and evaluate the minimum probability weight p_w and the minimum correlation weight q_w of CHAM-64/128. Since the linear part may

Table 3. The minimum probability weight p_w and the minimum correlation weight q_w of CHAM-64/128.

Round	1	2	3	4	5	6	7	8	9	10	11	12	13	14	15
p_w	0	0	0	0	1	1	2	3	4	5	6	7	8	9	11
q_w †	0	0	0	0	0	0	0	1	1	2	3	4	4	5	7
q_w ‡	0	0	0	0	0	0	1	1	2	2	3	4	5	5	7
Round	16	17	18	19	20	21	22	23	24	25	26	27	28	29	30
p_w	14	15	16	19	21	23	25	28	30	32	34	38	39	–	–
q_w †	8	9	10	11	12	13	14	16	17	18	20	21	22	23	25
q_w ‡	8	9	10	11	12	13	14	16	17	18	19	21	22	23	24

Table 4. The number of input-output difference pairs (#DP) and input-output mask pairs (#MP).

Round	4	5	6	7	8	9	10	11
Pr	$1/2^{-5}$ †	$2^{-1}/2^{-6}$	$2^{-1}/2^{-6}$	$2^{-2}/2^{-7}$	$2^{-3}/2^{-8}$	$2^{-4}/2^{-9}$	$2^{-5}/2^{-10}$	$2^{-6}/2^{-11}$
#DP	133523	59758	8746	5105	5026	5186	5663	5327
|**Cor**| ‡	$1/2^{-2}$	$1/2^{-2}$	$1/2^{-2}$	$1/2^{-3}$	$2^{-1}/2^{-4}$	$2^{-1}/2^{-4}$	$2^{-2}/2^{-5}$	$2^{-3}/2^{-6}$
#MP	456847	65879	9675	10245	22814	6888	18156	42380
|**Cor**| §	$1/2^{-2}$	$1/2^{-2}$	$1/2^{-2}$	$2^{-1}/2^{-3}$	$2^{-1}/2^{-4}$	$2^{-2}/2^{-4}$	$2^{-2}/2^{-5}$	$2^{-3}/2^{-6}$
#MP	190650	40083	6553	9416	19138	6372	18450	41608
Round	12	13	14	15	16	17	18	19
Pr	$2^{-7}/2^{-12}$	$2^{-8}/2^{-13}$	$2^{-9}/2^{-14}$	$2^{-11}/2^{-16}$	$2^{-14}/2^{-19}$	$2^{-15}/2^{-20}$	$2^{-16}/2^{-21}$	$2^{-19}/2^{-24}$
#DP	5080	43916	3208	5260	30971	15996	7024	26284
|**Cor**| ‡	$2^{-4}/2^{-7}$	$2^{-4}/2^{-7}$	$2^{-5}/2^{-8}$	$2^{-7}/2^{-9}$	$2^{-8}/2^{-9}$	$2^{-9}/2^{-10}$	$2^{-10}/2^{-10}$	–
#MP	97146	27392	51968	72952	10216	20260	673	–
|**Cor**| §	$2^{-4}/2^{-7}$	$2^{-5}/2^{-7}$	$2^{-5}/2^{-8}$	$2^{-7}/2^{-9}$	$2^{-8}/2^{-9}$	$2^{-9}/2^{-9}$	–	–
#MP	97334	27984	49776	69612	9760	776	–	–

† a/b represents the probability Pr (resp. the absolute value of the correlation |**Cor**|) fall in the range of $a \geq \text{Pr} \geq b$ (resp. $a \geq |\textbf{Cor}| \geq b$).
‡ The linear part begins with an even round.
§ The linear part begins with an odd round.

begin with an odd or even round, we independently searched for the minimum correlation weights in these two cases. The results are shown in Table 3.

Then, we build MILP models to search for input-output difference pairs (Δ_{in}, Δ_m) and input-output mask pairs (Γ_m, Γ_{out}). According to computing resource constraints, we limit the differential probability and correlation to a reasonable range in our models. The results are shown in Table 4.

Exhausting the input-output difference pairs and input-output mask pairs obtained in the second step, we utilize the middle part to connect the differential part and the linear part to derive R-round DL trails $\mathbf{\Delta}_{in}^{R} \xrightarrow{E_1} \Delta_m^R \xrightarrow{E_m} \Gamma_m^R \xrightarrow{E_2} \Gamma_{out}^{R}$ with the maximum correlation $|\mathbf{Cor}_1|$. In addition, we also store R-round DL trails with a correlation $|\mathbf{Cor}_2|$, where $|\mathbf{Cor}_1/\mathbf{Cor}_2| \leq 2^1$. That is, multiple R-round DL trails are stored for a certain R. Part of the results are shown in Table 5.

Table 5. Part of the DL trails for 30 to 41 rounds of CHAM-64/128.

Round	r_d	r_m	r_l	p	r	q	Cor
$0x8020400000400020 \xrightarrow{E_1} 0x2000000000808040 \xrightarrow{E_m} 0x0000000000010100 \xrightarrow{E_2} 0x0200000000000004$							
30	12	11	7	2^{-9}	$2^{-1.503209}$	2^{-1}	$2^{-12.503209}$
$0x0020001010000800 \xrightarrow{E_1} 0x4000204040000080 \xrightarrow{E_m} 0x0001800000000001 \xrightarrow{E_2} 0x0002000000000000$							
31	13	11	7	2^{-10}	$2^{-4.416966}$	2^{0}	$2^{-14.416966}$
$0x8020400000400020 \xrightarrow{E_1} 0x8040002000010100 \xrightarrow{E_m} 0x0001010000000004 \xrightarrow{E_2} 0x0600000000000000$							
32	15	10	7	2^{-12}	$-2^{-2.173490}$	2^{-1}	$-2^{-16.173490}$
$0x8020400000400020 \xrightarrow{E_1} 0x2000000000808040 \xrightarrow{E_m} 0x0000000000010100 \xrightarrow{E_2} 0x8004000202000100$							
33	12	11	10	2^{-9}	$2^{-1.503209}$	2^{-3}	$2^{-16.503209}$
$0x0040002020000000 \xrightarrow{E_1} 0x8040002000010100 \xrightarrow{E_m} 0x0001010000000004 \xrightarrow{E_2} 0x0104040002000002$							
34	13	10	11	2^{-10}	$-2^{-2.173490}$	2^{-4}	$-2^{-20.173490}$
$0x0020001010000800 \xrightarrow{E_1} 0x4000204040000080 \xrightarrow{E_m} 0x0001800000000001 \xrightarrow{E_2} 0x8004000302000100$							
35	13	11	11	2^{-10}	$2^{-4.416966}$	2^{-3}	$2^{-20.416966}$
$0x8020400000400020 \xrightarrow{E_1} 0x8040002000010100 \xrightarrow{E_m} 0x0001010000000004 \xrightarrow{E_2} 0x0104040002000002$							
36	15	10	11	2^{-12}	$-2^{-2.173490}$	2^{-4}	$-2^{-22.173490}$
$0x9020480000400020 \xrightarrow{E_1} 0x4080800001000080 \xrightarrow{E_m} 0x0001800000000001 \xrightarrow{E_2} 0x8004000302000100$							
37	16	10	11	2^{-15}	$-2^{-4.937414}$	2^{-3}	$-2^{-25.937414}$
$0x0082000101000080 \xrightarrow{E_1} 0x0400020588000000 \xrightarrow{E_m} 0x0001010000000004 \xrightarrow{E_2} 0x0104040002000002$							
38	18	9	11	2^{-17}	$-2^{-4.120247}$	2^{-4}	$-2^{-29.120247}$
$0x0200410020419000 \xrightarrow{E_1} 0x0001020001000281 \xrightarrow{E_m} 0x0001800000000001 \xrightarrow{E_2} 0x8004000302000100$							
39	19	9	11	2^{-20}	$-2^{-3.626414}$	2^{-3}	$-2^{-29.626414}$
$0x0200410020419000 \xrightarrow{E_1} 0x0001020001000281 \xrightarrow{E_m} 0x0001800000000001 \xrightarrow{E_2} 0x06c203000100000d$							
40	19	9	12	2^{-20}	$-2^{-3.626414}$	2^{-5}	$-2^{-33.626414}$
$0x8020400000400020 \xrightarrow{E_1} 0x4081220000000280 \xrightarrow{E_m} 0x8180008000608000 \xrightarrow{E_2} 0x8004000303000100$							
41	19	7	15	2^{-19}	$-2^{-3.285529}$	2^{-7}	$-2^{-36.285529}$

Next, for each fixed input difference $\mathbf{\Delta}_{in}^{R}$ (resp. fixed output mask Γ_{out}^{R}) and the corresponding number of rounds $\mathbf{r_d}$ (resp. $\mathbf{r_l}$) obtained in the third step, we build new MILP models to derive all $\mathbf{r_d}$-round input-output difference pairs $(\mathbf{\Delta}_{in}^{R}, \Delta_m^*)$ (resp. all $\mathbf{r_l}$-round input-output mask pairs $(\Gamma_m^*, \Gamma_{out}^{R})$). The range of differential probability (resp. the correlation) is limited to a reasonable level in our models, considering the available computing resources. Partial results of the fourth step are shown in Table 6. It is worth noting that the fixed input differences and output masks in Table 6 correspond to those in Table 5. For example, in the second row of Table 6 (the number of rounds is 30), Δ_{in}^{R} and Γ_{out}^{R} are $0x8020400000400020$ and $0x0200000000000004$, respectively.

Table 6. The number of input-output difference pairs (#DP) with the input difference Δ_{in}^{R} and the number of input-output mask pairs (#MP) with the output mask Γ_{out}^{R}.

Round	r_d	r_m	r_l	Pr	$|Cor|$	#DP	#MP
30	12	11	7	$2^{-7}/2^{-17}$	$2^{-1}/2^{-11}$	1658	20481
31	13	11	7	$2^{-8}/2^{-18}$	$2^{-0}/2^{-11}$	4853	1
32	15	10	7	$2^{-11}/2^{-21}$	$2^{-1}/2^{-11}$	10230	8181
33	12	11	10	$2^{-7}/2^{-17}$	$2^{-2}/2^{-10}$	1658	9896
34	13	10	11	$2^{-8}/2^{-18}$	$2^{-3}/2^{-10}$	4221	25688
35	13	11	11	$2^{-8}/2^{-18}$	$2^{-3}/2^{-10}$	4853	26973
36	15	10	11	$2^{-11}/2^{-21}$	$2^{-3}/2^{-11}$	10230	25688
37	16	10	11	$2^{-14}/2^{-24}$	$2^{-3}/2^{-10}$	16890	26973
38	18	9	11	$2^{-16}/2^{-28}$	$2^{-3}/2^{-10}$	37961	25688
39	19	9	11	$2^{-21}/2^{-29}$	$2^{-3}/2^{-10}$	22302	26973
40	19	9	12	$2^{-21}/2^{-29}$	$2^{-4}/2^{-11}$	22302	6991
41	19	7	15	$2^{-17}/2^{-26}$	$2^{-7}/2^{-12}$	37961	56248

Finally, for each Δ_{in}^{R} and Γ_{out}^{R} obtained in the third step, we calculate the correlation of the DL distinguishers $\Delta_{in}^{R} \xrightarrow{E} \Gamma_{out}^{R}$ of CHAM-64/128 covering from 9 to 41 rounds by exhausting all/part of $(\Delta_{in}^{R}, \Delta_m^{*})$ and $(\Gamma_m^{*}, \Gamma_{out}^{R})$ obtained in the fourth step, according to the available computing resources. Then, the R-round DL distinguishers with the minimum correlation weight are selected. The results are shown in Table 7. We verified the correlation of the 9- to 33-round DL distinguishers mentioned above. Each experiment on the 9- to 29-round DL distinguishers randomly selects one key and 2^{20} plaintext pairs that match the input difference. Each experiment on the 30- to 33-round DL distinguishers randomly selects one key and 2^{28} plaintext pairs that match the input difference. Each of the above experiments is repeated 100 times. The experimental results are shown in Table 7.

Table 7. Correlations of R-round DL distinguishers.

R	r_d	r_m	r_l	Theory	Exper.	DL distinguisher
9	4	1	4	2^0	2^0	0x8000000000000000 $\xrightarrow{E}$ 0x0000010000000000
10	4	2	4	2^0	2^0	0x8000000000000000 $\xrightarrow{E}$ 0x0000000200000000
11	4	2	5	2^0	2^0	0x8000000000000000 $\xrightarrow{E}$ 0x0002000000000000
12	4	4	4	2^0	2^0	0x8000000000000000 $\xrightarrow{E}$ 0x0000000200000000
13	4	4	5	2^0	2^0	0x8000000000000000 $\xrightarrow{E}$ 0x0002000000000000
14	5	3	6	$2^{-0.000044}$	$2^{-0.000044}$	0x0000000000004000 $\xrightarrow{E}$ 0x0000000200000000
15	5	5	5	$2^{-0.000044}$	$2^{-0.000042}$	0x0000000000004000 $\xrightarrow{E}$ 0x0002000000000000
16	5	7	4	$2^{-0.003366}$	$2^{-0.001485}$	0x0000000000004000 $\xrightarrow{E}$ 0x0100000000000002
17	5	7	5	$2^{-0.118191}$	$2^{-0.115145}$	0x8000000000000000 $\xrightarrow{E}$ 0x0002000000000000
18	6	6	6	$2^{-0.171430}$	$2^{-0.111548}$	0x0000000000004000 $\xrightarrow{E}$ 0x0100000000000000
19	5	7	7	$2^{-0.178222}$	$2^{-0.118215}$	0x0000000000004000 $\xrightarrow{E}$ 0x0002000000000000
20	7	7	6	$2^{-0.767947}$	$2^{-0.437351}$	0x8000400000000000 $\xrightarrow{E}$ 0x0100000000000000
21	7	9	5	$2^{-1.153692}$	$2^{-0.646930}$	0x8000400000000000 $\xrightarrow{E}$ 0x0002000000000000
22	7	10	5	$2^{-2.049319}$	$2^{-0.625822}$	0x2000000000000000 $\xrightarrow{E}$ 0x0100000000000000
23	8	10	5	$2^{-2.897291}$	$2^{-1.521606}$	0xc000200000000000 $\xrightarrow{E}$ 0x0002000000000000
24	9	10	5	$2^{-4.046592}$	$2^{-2.565614}$	0x0040002020000000 $\xrightarrow{E}$ 0x0100000000000000
25	10	10	5	$2^{-4.894415}$	$2^{-3.501904}$	0x0080004040002000 $\xrightarrow{E}$ 0x0002000000000000
26	10	12	4	$2^{-5.811487}$	$2^{-4.094048}$	0x8020400000400020 $\xrightarrow{E}$ 0x0100000000000000
27	10	12	5	$2^{-6.083107}$	$2^{-3.209424}$	0x0040002020000000 $\xrightarrow{E}$ 0x0002000000000000
28	13	9	6	$2^{-7.691440}$	$2^{-4.769114}$	0x8200010000018000 $\xrightarrow{E}$ 0x1800000000000000
29	12	12	5	$2^{-8.000000}$	$2^{-4.774067}$	0x8020400000400020 $\xrightarrow{E}$ 0x0002000000000000
30	12	11	7	$2^{-10.005469}$	$2^{-6.145092}$	0x8020400000400020 $\xrightarrow{E}$ 0x0200000000000004
31	13	11	7	$2^{-11.987090}$	$2^{-5.212926}$	0x0020001010000800 $\xrightarrow{E}$ 0x0002000000000000
32	15	10	7	$2^{-13.467578}$	$2^{-6.494287}$	0x8020400000400020 $\xrightarrow{E}$ 0x0600000000000000
33	12	11	10	$2^{-13.917806}$	$2^{-10.030818}$	0x8020400000400020 $\xrightarrow{E}$ 0x8004000202000100
34	13	10	11	$2^{-17.270648}$	–	0x0040002020000000 $\xrightarrow{E}$ 0x0104040002000002
35	13	11	11	$2^{-17.894912}$	–	0x0020001010000800 $\xrightarrow{E}$ 0x8004000302000100
36	15	10	11	$2^{-19.233251}$	–	0x8020400000400020 $\xrightarrow{E}$ 0x0104040002000002
37	16	10	11	$2^{-22.730538}$	–	0x9020480000400020 $\xrightarrow{E}$ 0x8040000302000100
38	18	9	11	$2^{-26.301733}$	–	0x0082000101000080 $\xrightarrow{E}$ 0x0104040002000021
39	19	9	11	$2^{-27.111276}$	–	0x0200410020419000 $\xrightarrow{E}$ 0x8004000302000100
40	19	9	12	$2^{-30.790308}$	–	0x0200410020419000 $\xrightarrow{E}$ 0x06c203000100000d
41	19	7	15	$2^{-31.020688}$	–	0x8020400000400020 $\xrightarrow{E}$ 0x8004000203000100

4.3   Differential-Linear Attack on **CHAM-64/128**

In this subsection, we will propose a 45-round DL attack on CHAM-64/128 based on 41-round distinguishers. In fact, we found eight distinguishers with the same input difference and a correlation higher than 2^{-32}, as shown in Table 8. We use the aforementioned eight distinguishers to construct a 45-round DL attack. As shown in Fig. 3, the details of the attack are as follows.

Table 8. Correlations of 41-round DL distinguishers.

Round	r_d	r_m	r_l	Correlation	DL distinguisher
41	19	7	15	$2^{-31.073540}$	$0x8020400000400020 \xrightarrow{E} 0x8006000203000100$
41	19	7	15	$2^{-31.020688}$	$0x8020400000400020 \xrightarrow{E} 0x8004000203000100$
41	19	7	15	$2^{-31.052990}$	$0x8020400000400020 \xrightarrow{E} 0x8006000202000100$
41	19	7	15	$2^{-31.065394}$	$0x8020400000400020 \xrightarrow{E} 0x8004000202000100$
41	19	7	15	$2^{-31.063001}$	$0x8020400000400020 \xrightarrow{E} 0x8006000303000100$
41	19	7	15	$2^{-31.021054}$	$0x8020400000400020 \xrightarrow{E} 0x8004000303000100$
41	19	7	15	$2^{-31.091326}$	$0x8020400000400020 \xrightarrow{E} 0x8006000302000100$
41	19	7	15	$2^{-31.043496}$	$0x8020400000400020 \xrightarrow{E} 0x8004000302000100$

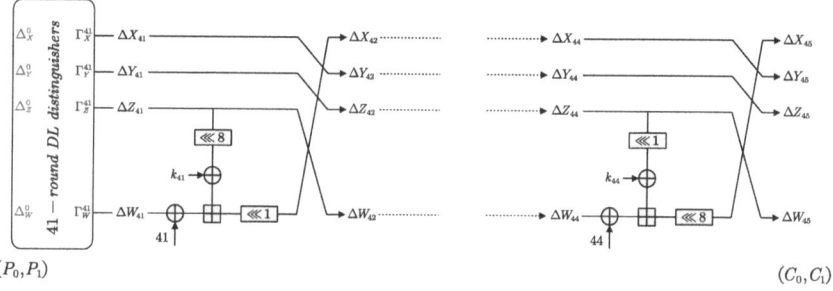

Fig. 3. The structure of 45-round DL attack of CHAM-64/128.

1. Select $2^{2 \times 31.1}/8 = 2^{59.2}$ plaintext pairs (P_0, P_1) with the difference $0x802040$ 0000400020. Encrypt the plaintext pairs by 45 round and obtain the ciphertext pairs (C_0, C_1).
2. Guess the 48-bit keys k_{44}, k_{43}, k_{42}. For each of 2^{48} values, decrypt the ciphertext pairs by three rounds to get the intermediate state pairs $(X_{42}^0, X_{42}^1), (Y_{42}^0, Y_{42}^1), (Z_{42}^0, Z_{42}^1)$, and (W_{42}^0, W_{42}^1).

3. For each of the 2^{48} values, guess the least significant 15 bits of k_{41}. For each of the 2^{63} guessed keys, initialize a counter counter and decrypt the intermediate state pairs $(X_{42}^0, X_{42}^1), (Y_{42}^0, Y_{42}^1), (Z_{42}^0, Z_{42}^1)$, and (W_{42}^0, W_{42}^1) by one round to obtain the intermediate state differences $\Delta X_{41}, \Delta Y_{41}, \Delta Z_{41}$, and ΔW_{41}. If any of the following eight equations are satisfied, the counter counter increases by one.

$$\Delta X_{41}[15] \oplus \Delta X_{41}[2] \oplus \Delta X_{41}[1] \oplus \Delta Y_{41}[1] \oplus \Delta Z_{41}[9] \oplus \Delta Z_{41}[8] \oplus \Delta W_{41}[8] = 0,$$
$$\Delta X_{41}[15] \oplus \Delta X_{41}[1] \oplus \Delta Y_{41}[1] \oplus \Delta Z_{41}[9] \oplus \Delta Z_{41}[8] \oplus \Delta W_{41}[8] = 0,$$
$$\Delta X_{41}[15] \oplus \Delta X_{41}[2] \oplus \Delta X_{41}[1] \oplus \Delta Y_{41}[1] \oplus \Delta Z_{41}[9] \oplus \Delta W_{41}[8] = 0,$$
$$\Delta X_{41}[15] \oplus \Delta X_{41}[2] \oplus \Delta Y_{41}[1] \oplus \Delta Z_{41}[9] \oplus \Delta W_{41}[8] = 0,$$
$$\Delta X_{41}[15] \oplus \Delta X_{41}[2] \oplus \Delta X_{41}[1] \oplus \Delta Y_{41}[1] \oplus \Delta Y_{41}[0] \oplus \Delta Z_{41}[9] \oplus \Delta Z_{41}[8] \oplus \Delta W_{41}[8] = 0,$$
$$\Delta X_{41}[15] \oplus \Delta X_{41}[1] \oplus \Delta Y_{41}[1] \oplus \Delta Y_{41}[0] \oplus \Delta Z_{41}[9] \oplus \Delta Z_{41}[8] \oplus \Delta W_{41}[8] = 0,$$
$$\Delta X_{41}[15] \oplus \Delta X_{41}[2] \oplus \Delta X_{41}[1] \oplus \Delta Y_{41}[1] \oplus \Delta Y_{41}[0] \oplus \Delta Z_{41}[9] \oplus \Delta W_{41}[8] = 0,$$
$$\Delta X_{41}[15] \oplus \Delta X_{41}[2] \oplus \Delta Y_{41}[1] \oplus \Delta Y_{41}[0] \oplus \Delta Z_{41}[9] \oplus \Delta W_{41}[8] = 0,$$

where $\Delta X_{41}[i], \Delta Y_{41}[i], \Delta Z_{41}[i]$, and $\Delta W_{41}[i]$ ($0 \le i \le 15$) represent the i-th bit of $\Delta X_{41}, \Delta Y_{41}, \Delta Z_{41}$, and ΔW_{41}, respectively.
4. If $|counter/2^{59.2}|$ is much greater than $1/2$, the currently guessed key is a candidate key. Finally, exhaust the remaining 65-bit keys and the candidate keys to obtain the correct key.

In fact, we can determine the values of (X_{42}^0, X_{42}^1) and (W_{42}^0, W_{42}^1) after guessing the 48-bit round keys k_{44}, k_{43}, and k_{42}. Thus, if we guess the least significant 15 bits of k_{41}, the values of $(X_{41}^0[i], X_{41}^1[i])$ and $\Delta X_{41}[15]$ can be determined, where $0 \le i \le 14$, $\Delta X_{42}[i] = X_{42}^0[i] \oplus X_{42}^1[i]$, $\Delta W_{42}[i] = W_{42}^0[i] \oplus W_{42}^1[i]$, and $\Delta X_{41}[i] = X_{41}^0[i] \oplus X_{41}^1[i]$. The data and time complexities of our 45-round DL attack are $2 \times 2^{59.2} = 2^{60.2}$ and $2^{60.2} + 2^{48} \times 2^{60.2} \times 4/45 + 2^{63} \times 2^{60.2} \times 1/45 + 2 \times 2^{65} \approx 2^{117.71}$ 45-round encryption, respectively.

5 Conclusion

In this paper, we proposed an automated tool that is able to search for long-round DL distinguishers and more accurately calculate the correlation of DL distinguishers. The scale of existing MILP models that search for complete DL distinguishers increases rapidly as the number of rounds increases. However, it is infeasible to solve large-scale models with limited computing resources. Therefore, we proposed a divide-and-conquer strategy and built MILP models for the differential part and the linear part separately. Subsequently, we combine the differential characteristics and linear trails by the middle part to form a complete DL trails. On the other hand, the accurate correlation of a DL distinguisher is the sum of the correlations of multiple DL trails. Thus, our automated tool considered all/part of DL trails involving the same input differences and output masks under constrained computing resources, aiming to obtain more accurate correlations as much as possible. As an application, we found DL distinguishers that cover from 9- to 41-round of CHAM-64/128, and verified the effectiveness of the DL distinguishers whose absolute value of theoretical correlations is higher than 2^{-17} by experiments. To the best of our knowledge, our 41-round distinguisher is the longest distinguisher for CHAM-64/128 in the single-key scenario. Finally, we proposed a 45-round DL attack based on eight 41-round distinguishers. It should be emphasized that our main focus is on proposing an efficient automated tool for searching long-round distinguishers. In future work, we will attempt to propose an improved key-recovery attack framework for ARX ciphers.

Acknowledgement. We would like to thank the anonymous reviewers for their helpful comments. This work was supported by the Science and Technology on Communication Security Laboratory Foundation (Grant No. 6142103012207), the National Natural Science Foundation of China (Grant No. 62272147), the Natural Science Foundation of Hubei Province of China (Grant No. 2024AFB573).

References

1. Bar-On, A., Dunkelman, O., Keller, N., Weizman, A.: DLCT: a new tool for differential-linear cryptanalysis. In: Ishai, Y., Rijmen, V. (eds.) EUROCRYPT 2019. LNCS, vol. 11476, pp. 313–342. Springer, Cham (2019). https://doi.org/10.1007/978-3-030-17653-2_11

2. Beaulieu, R., Shors, D., Smith, J., Treatman-Clark, S., Weeks, B., Wingers, L.: The SIMON and SPECK lightweight block ciphers. In: ACM 2015, pp. 175:1–175:6. ACM (2015). https://doi.org/10.1145/2744769.2747946

3. Bellini, E., Gerault, D., Grados, J., Makarim, R.H., Peyrin, T.: Fully automated differential-linear attacks against ARX ciphers. In: Rosulek, M. (eds.) CT-RSA 2023. LNCS, vol. 13871, pp. 252–276. Springer, Cham (2023). https://doi.org/10.1007/978-3-031-30872-7_10

4. Biham, E., Biryukov, A., Shamir, A.: Cryptanalysis of skipjack reduced to 31 rounds using impossible differentials. In: Stern, J. (ed.) EUROCRYPT 1999. LNCS, vol. 1592, pp. 12–23. Springer, Heidelberg (1999). https://doi.org/10.1007/3-540-48910-X_2

5. Biham, E., Dunkelman, O., Keller, N.: Enhancing differential-linear cryptanalysis. In: Zheng, Y. (ed.) ASIACRYPT 2002. LNCS, vol. 2501, pp. 254–266. Springer, Heidelberg (2002). https://doi.org/10.1007/3-540-36178-2_16

6. Biham, E., Shamir, A.: Differential cryptanalysis of DES-like cryptosystems. J. Cryptol. **4**, 3–72 (1991). https://doi.org/10.1007/BF00630563

7. Biryukov, A., De Cannière, C., Quisquater, M.: On multiple linear approximations. In: Franklin, M. (ed.) CRYPTO 2004. LNCS, vol. 3152, pp. 1–22. Springer, Heidelberg (2004). https://doi.org/10.1007/978-3-540-28628-8_1

8. Biryukov, A., Teh, J.S., Udovenko, A.: Advancing the meet-in-the-filter technique: applications to CHAM and KATAN. In: Smith, B., Wu, H. (eds.) SAC 2022. LNCS, vol. 13742, pp. 355–375. Springer, Cham (2024). https://doi.org/10.1007/978-3-031-58411-4_16

9. Blondeau, C., Leander, G., Nyberg, K.: Differential-linear cryptanalysis revisited. J. Cryptol. **30**, 859–888 (2017). https://doi.org/10.1007/s00145-016-9237-5

10. Bogdanov, A., Rijmen, V.: Linear hulls with correlation zero and linear cryptanalysis of block ciphers. Des. Codes Cryptogr. **2014**(70), 369–383 (2014). https://doi.org/10.1007/s10623-012-9697-z

11. Coutinho, M., De Sousa, R.T., Borges, F.: Continuous diffusion analysis. IEEE Access **2020**(8), 123735–123745 (2020). https://doi.org/10.1109/ACCESS.2020.3005504

12. Dinu, D., Perrin, L., Udovenko, A., Velichkov, V., Großschädl, J., Biryukov, A.: Design strategies for ARX with provable bounds: SPARX and LAX. In: Cheon, J.H., Takagi, T. (eds.) ASIACRYPT 2016. LNCS, vol. 10031, pp. 484–513. Springer, Heidelberg (2016). https://doi.org/10.1007/978-3-662-53887-6_18

13. Fu, K., Wang, M., Guo, Y., Sun, S., Hu, L.: MILP-based automatic search algorithms for differential and linear trails for speck. In: Peyrin, T. (ed.) FSE 2016. LNCS, vol. 9783, pp. 268–288. Springer, Heidelberg (2016). https://doi.org/10.1007/978-3-662-52993-5_14

14. Hong, D., Lee, J.-K., Kim, D.-C., Kwon, D., Ryu, K.H., Lee, D.-G.: LEA: a 128-bit block cipher for fast encryption on common processors. In: Kim, Y., Lee, H., Perrig, A. (eds.) WISA 2013. LNCS, vol. 8267, pp. 3–27. Springer, Cham (2014). https://doi.org/10.1007/978-3-319-05149-9_1

15. Hong, D., et al.: HIGHT: a new block cipher suitable for low-resource device. In: Goubin, L., Matsui, M. (eds.) CHES 2006. LNCS, vol. 4249, pp. 46–59. Springer, Heidelberg (2006). https://doi.org/10.1007/11894063_4

16. Huang, M., Wang, L.: Automatic tool for searching for differential characteristics in ARX ciphers and applications. In: Hao, F., Ruj, S., Sen Gupta, S. (eds.) INDOCRYPT 2019. LNCS, vol. 11898, pp. 115–138. Springer, Cham (2019). https://doi.org/10.1007/978-3-030-35423-7_6

17. Huang, M., Wang, L.: Automatic search for the linear (hull) characteristics of ARX ciphers: applied to speck, sparx, chaskey, and CHAM-64. Secur. Commun. Netw. **2020**, 4898612:1–4898612:14 (2020). https://doi.org/10.1155/2020/4898612

18. Khovratovich, D., Nikolić, I.: Rotational cryptanalysis of ARX. In: Hong, S., Iwata, T. (eds.) FSE 2010. LNCS, vol. 6147, pp. 333–346. Springer, Heidelberg (2010). https://doi.org/10.1007/978-3-642-13858-4_19

19. Knudsen, L.R.: Deal-a 128-bit block cipher. Complexity **258**(2), 216 (1998). https://api.semanticscholar.org/CorpusID:9745358

20. Langford, S.K., Hellman, M.E.: Differential-linear cryptanalysis. In: Desmedt, Y.G. (ed.) CRYPTO 1994. LNCS, vol. 839, pp. 17–25. Springer, Heidelberg (1994). https://doi.org/10.1007/3-540-48658-5_3

21. Lv, G., Jin, C., Cui, T.: A MIQCP-based automatic search algorithm for differential-linear trails of ARX ciphers (long paper). Cryptology ePrint Archive, Report 2023/259 (2023). https://eprint.iacr.org/2023/259

22. Matsui, M.: Linear cryptanalysis method for DES cipher. In: Helleseth, T. (ed.) EUROCRYPT 1993. LNCS, vol. 765, pp. 386–397. Springer, Heidelberg (1994). https://doi.org/10.1007/3-540-48285-7_33

23. US National Bureau of Standards. Data Encryption Standard, Federal Information Processing Standards publications no. 46 (1977)

24. Roh, D., et al.: Revised version of block cipher CHAM. In: Seo, J.H. (ed.) ICISC 2019. LNCS, vol. 11975, pp. 1–19. Springer, Cham (2020). https://doi.org/10.1007/978-3-030-40921-0_1

25. Wagner, D.: The boomerang attack. In: Knudsen, L. (ed.) FSE 1999. LNCS, vol. 1636, pp. 156–170. Springer, Heidelberg (1999). https://doi.org/10.1007/3-540-48519-8_12

26. Zhou, Y., Wang, S., Hu. B.: MILP/MIQCP-based fully automatic method of searching for differential-linear distinguishers for simon-like ciphers. IET Inf. Secur. **2024**(01), 1–39 (2024). https://doi.org/10.1049/2024/8315115

Security Analysis of **CMAC** in the Multi-user Model

Xiangyang Zhang[1] , Yaobin Shen[2] , and Lei Wang[1(✉)]

[1] Shanghai Jiao Tong University, Shanghai 200240, China
{xiangyang.zhang,wanglei_hb}@sjtu.edu.cn
[2] Xiamen University, Xiamen 361005, China
yaobin.shen@xmu.edu.cn

Abstract. CMAC, also known as OMAC1, is an efficient message authentication code (MAC) and has been standardized by NIST and other organizations. It has been widely applied in IPSec, IKE and many wireless networks. Multi-user security captures a practical scenario where an adversary targets a particular service related to multiple users. Lots of MAC constructions have been rigorously analyzed in the multi-user model. However, the concrete analysis for CMAC in the multi-user model is still a blank in the literature. To fill the gap, we provide a concrete multi-user security bound for CMAC in this paper. Our bound is better than that from generic reduction and we observe that the online security of CMAC in the multi-user model does not degrade from the single-user model.

Keywords: CMAC · OMAC1 · Multi-User Security · MAC · Message Authentication Code

1 Introduction

Message Authentication Code (MAC) is one of the most widely used symmetric-key cryptographic protocols. It provides the integrity of messages and authenticates their origin. Given a message M, it allows a sender in possession of a secret key K to compute an authentication tag T, which can then be verified by the receiver provided that it has also possession of the key. The tag should be hard to forge, i.e., without knowledge of the key, it should be computationally infeasible to compute the tag corresponding to any new message.

A MAC scheme is typically built from a blockcipher. The well-known CBC MAC [19] is the simplest one of such kind. However, the raw CBC MAC is secure just for messages with the same fixed length of multiple of the block size n [3]. Different variants of CBC MAC have been proposed to handle varying-length messages, including EMAC [10], XCBC [8], TMAC [24], OMAC [20]. EMAC (Encrypted MAC), first suggested in [10], is obtained by encrypting $\mathrm{CBC}_{K_1}(M)$ by E again with a new key K_2. Thus, two key schedule operations for the underlying blockcipher E are needed for EMAC. What's more, an entire extra padding block

10^{n-1} must be appended if the bit length of the message is already a multiple of n, which is a "wasting" of one blockcipher invocation. In 2000, Black and Rogaway [7,8] proposed the XCBC construction to get rid of extra padding in EMAC, in particular when the message length is a multiple of block size. In XCBC, only one key scheduling is required and three different keys are used. Later, Kurosawa and Iwata [24,25] proposed TMAC (Two-key CBC MAC) and reduced the number of keys to two. Further, in a year, they [20] proposed OMAC (One-key CBC MAC) and managed to reduce the number of keys to one by deriving the last two keys from the first one.

Among all these constructions, OMAC is one of the best choices. OMAC is a generic name for OMAC1 and OMAC2. In 2005, the NIST standardized OMAC1 in SP 800-38B [15] under the name CMAC. Also the IETF specified AES-CMAC in RFC 4493 [35]. CMAC has been widely used in the IPSec protocol [33] and the Internet Key Exchange (IKE) protocol [23]. Moreover, it has been broadly applied within various wireless networks, such as LoRaWAN, controller area network (CAN), IEEE 802.15.4 et al. In these networks, CMAC can guarantee that only authenticated devices are granted access, thereby mitigating the risk of unauthorized access and ensuring the protection of transmitted data from tampering.

Let n, k be, respectively, the block size and the key size of the underlying blockcipher. Assume that the adversary makes at most q queries of total block length of σ and that ℓ is the maximum block length of all the queries. The designers of CMAC [20] originally proved that, under the assumption that the underlying blockcipher is a pseudorandom permutation (PRP), CMAC is secure up to $O(\frac{\ell^2 q^2}{2^n})$. Later they improved the security bound [21] by $O(\frac{\sigma^2}{2^n})$. In 2009, Nandi [31] presented an improved PRF bound of $O(\frac{q\sigma}{2^n})$ if $\ell \leq 2^{n/3}$, that is the best bound up to now.

The exploration of multi-user security originated with the development of public-key encryption by Bellare et al. [2] and the notion of multi-user security was subsequently adapted to the context of symmetric encryption by Biham [6]. In the multi-user setting, an adversary is granted access to a particular service which relates to multiple users, and has the ability to distribute its queries adaptively across these users to facilitate its efforts. As pointed by Bellare and Tackmann [5], multi-user security and conventional single-user security are qualitatively not distinct but quantitatively they are. Multi-user security can be implied by single-user security through a generic reduction. Assuming u is the number of users, the adversary's multi-user advantage is upper bounded by u times the corresponding single-user advantage. However, the multi-user advantage could degrade much more slowly as demonstrated in a sequence of recent publications [1,9,17,18,26,28]. Most proofs of multi-user security are given in the ideal-cipher model that captures how offline computations affect security. In the ideal-cipher model, a blockcipher is chosen uniformly at random from the set of all blockciphers. An adversary is permitted to make primitive queries to the ideal cipher as well as construction ones. Security related to construction queries is called "online security" while that related to primitive queries is called "offline security."

The study of the multi-user security of MACs are relatively limited in the literature. Notable works include the results of Chatterjee et al. [11], Morgan et al. [27] and Bellare et al. [1]. The first two consider a generic reduction for MACs where the multi-user security is derived by multiplying the number of users u with the single-user security. The last one considers the multi-user security of a hash-based MAC with a dedicated approach. In addition, Shen et al. [34] have shown the multi-user security bounds of double-block-hash-then-sum (DbHtS) MAC [13] which includes SUM-ECB [36], LightMAC_Plus [29] and PMAC_Plus [37]. However, several flaws in their proof were identified by Guo and Wang [16] and Datta et al. [14]. Moreover, Datta et al. [14] also demonstrated a tight multi-user beyond-birthday-bound bound for DbHtS MAC. Very recently, Naito [30] investigated the multi-user security of blockcipher-based hash-then-encrypt-type MACs and showed the multi-user security bound of some MACs of this type, including EMAC, XCBC and TMAC. However, CMAC is not one of this type for its single key property and thus Naito's results cannot be applied to it. The multi-user security of CMAC has not been addressed in the literature until now. Therefore, the following question arises naturally.

"to what extent will the number of users affect the security bound of CMAC?"

Our Contribution. Our work is motivated by the standardization and the wide application of CMAC mode. As mentioned before, Nandi [31] has proved that, in the single-user setting, CMAC is secure up to $O(\frac{q\sigma}{2^n})$ if $\ell \leq 2^{n/3}$ (ℓ is maximum block length of all the queries) in the sense of pseudorandom function (PRF) security. Thus by generic reduction, the multi-user security bound for CMAC is

$$O(\frac{uq\sigma}{2^n}) \text{ with } \ell \leq 2^{n/3}$$

where u is assumed to be the number of users and can be adaptively chosen by the adversary. If u is large enough (e.g. as large as q), the bound will degrade greatly.

In this paper, we further provide a concrete multi-user security bound for CMAC and claim that the online security of CMAC does not degrade from the single-user model. We focus on the multi-user PRF security of CMAC in the ideal-cipher model and get the bound mainly by the H-coefficient technique. We show the advantage of the adversary in the multi-user setting is of the order[1]

$$\frac{q\sigma}{2^n} + \frac{up}{2^k} \text{ with } \ell \leq 2^{n/4}$$

where the attacker $\mathcal{D}$ makes, at most, p ideal-cipher queries, q evaluation queries of total block length of σ. The result shows that the multi-security bound of CMAC reaches the birthday-bound security, and although the offline security degrades (from k bits) to $k - \log_2 u$ bits, the online security stays the same as the single-user security.

---

[1] We omit lower-order terms and constant factors.

Organization. In Sect. 2, we introduce the foundational notations employed throughout this paper. A concise overview is provided for related multi-user PRF security model, followed by a brief description of the H-coefficient technique used in our proof. Furthermore, Sect. 3 introduces the specifications of the CMAC construction. Proceeding to Sect. 4, we present the multi-user security result for CMAC mode, followed by an overview of the proof. Section 5 is dedicated to a thorough and rigorous proof of our main theorem, utilizing the H-coefficient technique. Lastly, we conclude the paper in Sect. 6.

2 Preliminaries

Notations. For a positive integer b, $[b]$ represents the set $\{1, \cdots, b\}$. Let A be a set, then the operation of picking x from set A uniformly at random denoted by $x \xleftarrow{\$} A$. For two sets A and B, $A \cup B = \{x | x \in A \text{ or } x \in B\}$ and $A \cap B = \{x | x \in A \text{ and } x \in B\}$. Further, if $B \subset A$, $A \backslash B = \{x | x \in A \text{ and } x \notin B\}$. $\{0,1\}^*$ denotes the set of bit strings of arbitrary length and $\{0,1\}^n$ denotes the set of all n-bit strings. An n-bit string consisting of zeroes only will be denoted with 0^n. $|X|$ denotes the bit length of string $X \in \{0,1\}^*$. For any two strings $X, Y \in \{0,1\}^*$, XY or $X\|Y$ denotes their concatenation. If $|X| = |Y|$, $X \oplus Y$ denotes their bitwise exclusive-or (XOR). $\mathbb{GF}(2^n)$ is the finite field defined on the set $\{0,1\}^n$. Moreover, $+$ and $\cdot$ represent the field addition and multiplication over $\mathbb{GF}(2^n)$ respectively. For a two-dimensional set $\mathsf{P} = \{(x_1, y_1), \cdots, (x_p, y_p)\}$, $\mathsf{dom}(\mathsf{P}) = \{x | (x, y) \in \mathsf{P}\}$, $\mathsf{rng}(\mathsf{P}) = \{y | (x, y) \in \mathsf{P}\}$ and if $x \in \mathsf{dom}(\mathsf{P})$, then $\mathsf{P}(x) = y$ such that $(x, y) \in \mathsf{P}$.

For an input string M, $M_1 \| \cdots \| M_m \xleftarrow{n} M$ denotes parsing M into blocks $M_1, \cdots, M_m$ where $|M_1| = |M_2| = \cdots = |M_{m-1}| = n$ and $1 \leq |M_m| \leq n$. Then two padding methods, pad and pad_1, are defined for the last block M_m. For M_m with $|M_m| < n$, $\mathsf{pad}(M_m)$ is the string of length n obtained by appending to the right a "1" bit followed by $n - |M_m| - 1$ "0" bits, namely, $\mathsf{pad}(M_m) = M_m \| 10^{n-|M_m|-1}$. For M_m with $|M_m| \leq n$, $\mathsf{pad}_1(M_m)$ is defined as

$$\mathsf{pad}_1(M_m) = \begin{cases} M_m \| 10^{n-|M_m|-1} & \text{if } |M_m| < n \\ M_m & \text{if } |M_m| = n. \end{cases}$$

2.1 Multi-user PRF Security

It is well known that pseudorandom functions (PRFs) are secure MACs. For example, refer to [3]. Therefore, we will capture the multi-user security of CMAC as a multi-user PRF. As a prerequisite, we provide an overview of multi-user PRF security.

Let $F : \mathcal{K} \times \mathcal{X} \to \mathcal{Y}$ be a keyed function with a key space $\mathcal{K}$, an input space $\mathcal{X}$ and an output space $\mathcal{Y}$. Let $\mathcal{F}(\mathcal{X}, \mathcal{Y})$ denote the set of all functions from $\mathcal{X}$ to $\mathcal{Y}$ and a random element f of $\mathcal{F}(\mathcal{X}, \mathcal{Y})$ is a random function that associates to each $X \in \mathcal{X}$ a random value $f(X) \in \mathcal{Y}$. In the multi-user setting, consider u users and each executes the function F with their respective key K_i for $i \in [u]$. Each K_i is sampled independently and uniformly at random from $\mathcal{K}$. The distinguisher $\mathcal{D}$ has access to all users as oracles. $\mathcal{D}$ is allowed to make queries to user i's oracle in the form of (i, M), and gets $T \leftarrow F_{K_i}(M)$. These queries are referred to as *evaluation* queries (also construction queries). The advantage of the distinguisher $\mathcal{D}$ to distinguish the oracles $F_{K_1}, \cdots, F_{K_u}$ from random functions $f_1, \cdots, f_u$ is formally defined as

$$\mathsf{Adv}_F^{\mathrm{muprf}}(\mathcal{D}) = \Big| \Pr[K_1, \cdots, K_u \xleftarrow{\$} \mathcal{K} : \mathcal{D}^{F_{K_1}, \cdots, F_{K_u}} \Rightarrow 1]$$
$$- \Pr[f_1, \cdots, f_u \xleftarrow{\$} \mathcal{F}(\mathcal{X}, \mathcal{Y}) : \mathcal{D}^{f_1, \cdots, f_u} \Rightarrow 1] \Big|.$$

procedure Initialize	procedure Eval(i, M)
1: $K_1, K_2, \cdots, K_u \xleftarrow{\$} \mathcal{K}$	1: $Y_1 \leftarrow F_{K_i}(M)$
2: $f_1, f_2, \cdots, f_u \xleftarrow{\$} \mathcal{F}(\mathcal{X}, \mathcal{Y})$	2: $Y_0 \leftarrow f_i(M)$
3: $b \xleftarrow{\$} \{0, 1\}$	3: **return** Y_b
procedure Prim(J, X)	procedure Finalize(b')
1: **if** $X = (+, x)$ **then return** $E_J(x)$	1: **return** $(b' = b)$
2: **if** $X = (-, y)$ **then return** $E_J^{-1}(y)$	

Fig. 1. Game $\mathbf{G}_F^{\mathrm{muprf\text{-}IC}}$ defining multi-user PRF security of a function F.

Further, if the keyed function F is based on a blockcipher and particular emphasis is given to the impact of offline computations on security, $\mathcal{D}$ can be granted additional access to the underlying blockcipher, denoted by E. In this case the underlying blockcipher E is considered as an ideal cipher. $\mathcal{D}$ can make forward or inverse queries to E under the key J he chooses. This is the ideal-cipher model mentioned before and these queries are *primitive* queries. As depicted in Fig. 1, in the ideal-cipher model the advantage of the distinguisher $\mathcal{D}$ to distinguish the oracles $F_{K_1}, \cdots, F_{K_u}$ from random functions $f_1, \cdots, f_u$ is formally defined as

$$\mathsf{Adv}_F^{\mathrm{muprf\text{-}IC}}(\mathcal{D}) = \Big| \Pr[K_1, \cdots, K_u \xleftarrow{\$} \mathcal{K} : \mathcal{D}^{F_{K_1}, \cdots, F_{K_u}, E^{\pm}} \Rightarrow 1]$$
$$- \Pr[f_1, \cdots, f_u \xleftarrow{\$} \mathcal{F}(\mathcal{X}, \mathcal{Y}) : \mathcal{D}^{f_1, \cdots, f_u, E^{\pm}} \Rightarrow 1] \Big|.$$

2.2 The H-Coefficient Technique

The main proof in this paper adopts the H-coefficient technique [12,32]. Here we provide a brief description, which presents all necessary information to follow and verify our proof, and refer interested readers to [12,32] for the complete definition. We focus on information-theoretic distinguisher $\mathcal{D}$ that is not computationally bounded. Hence, without loss of generality we assume $\mathcal{D}$ is deterministic. Suppose $\mathcal{D}$ interacts with one of two oracles, the "real world" oracle

O or the "ideal world" oracle Q. Let X (resp. Y) be the probability distribution of the transcript when $\mathcal{D}$ interacts with O (resp. Q). A transcript τ is the query-response tuples that $\mathcal{D}$ receives. We say a transcript τ is *attainable* if $\Pr[Y = \tau] > 0$.

Theorem 1 ([12,32]). *Let $\mathcal{T}$ be the set of all attainable transcripts that is $\mathcal{T} = \{\tau \mid \Pr[Y = \tau] > 0\}$. Partition $\mathcal{T}$ into disjoint subsets $\mathcal{T}_{good}$ and $\mathcal{T}_{bad}$ such that $\mathcal{T} = \mathcal{T}_{good} \bigcup \mathcal{T}_{bad}$. If there are two real values $0 \leq \epsilon_1, \epsilon_2 \leq 1$ such that*

- *for each $\tau \in \mathcal{T}_{good}$, it holds that*

$$\frac{\Pr[X = \tau]}{\Pr[Y = \tau]} \geq 1 - \epsilon_1$$

- *for a transcript τ sampled from $\mathcal{T}$ uniformly at random, it holds that*

$$\Pr[\tau \in \mathcal{T}_{bad}] \leq \epsilon_2$$

then the advantage of $\mathcal{D}$ is upper bounded as

$$\mathbf{Adv}(\mathcal{D}) \leq \epsilon_1 + \epsilon_2.$$

3   Specification of CMAC

A blockcipher E is a function $E : \mathcal{K} \times \{0,1\}^n \to \{0,1\}^n$ where $\mathcal{K}$ is the key space. $E(K, \cdot) = E_K(\cdot)$ is a permutation on $\{0,1\}^n$. The block size is n and the key length is denoted as k.

CMAC is a blockcipher-based construction and requires only one key K of the underlying blockcipher E. In order to reach the single-key security, two masks, $L \cdot u$ and $L \cdot u^2$, are introduced to CMAC where $L = E_K(0^n)$. Here u^2, u are polynomials, representing n-bit strings $0^{n-3}100$ and $0^{n-2}10$ respectively and $L \cdot u$, $L \cdot u^2$ are field multiplications over $\mathbb{GF}(2^n)$. We call L "a mask". For an input string $M = M_1 \cdots M_m$ with $|M_1| = |M_2| = \cdots = |M_{m-1}| = n$ and $1 \leq |M_m| \leq n$,

- If $|M_m| = n$, then CMAC computes exactly the same as the CBC MAC, except for XORing a mask $L \cdot u$ before encrypting the last block.
- Otherwise, 10^i padding ($i = n - |M_m| - 1$) is appended to M and CMAC computes exactly the same as the CBC MAC for the padded message, except for XORing another mask $L \cdot u^2$ before encrypting the last block.

The pseudocode of CMAC and an illustration for 3-block messages are given in Fig. 2. To streamline the notations employed in our subsequent security analysis we rephrase line $7 - 9$ in Fig. 2(a) as follows

$$X_m \leftarrow Y_{m-1} \oplus \mathsf{pad}_1(M_m) \oplus L \cdot \delta$$

where $\mathsf{pad}_1(X)$ previously defined in Sect. 2 and δ is defined as

$$\delta = \begin{cases} u^2 & \text{if } |M_m| \leq n \\ u & \text{if } |M_m| = n. \end{cases}$$

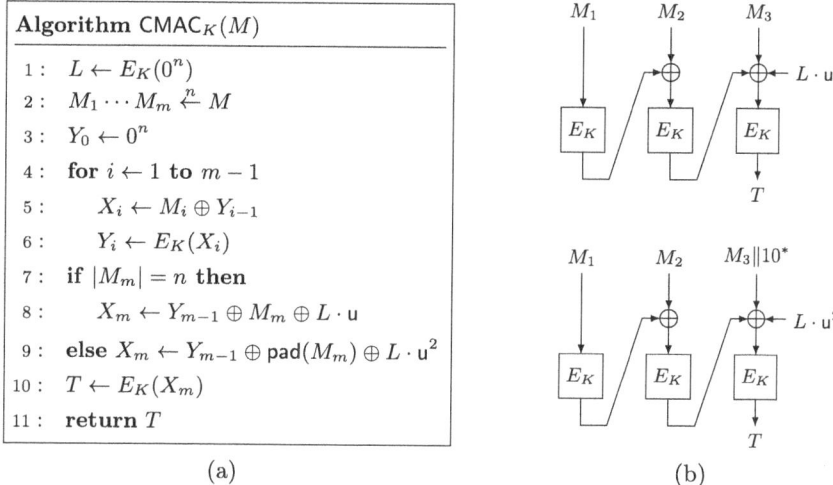

Algorithm CMAC$_K(M)$

1: $L \leftarrow E_K(0^n)$
2: $M_1 \cdots M_m \overset{n}{\leftarrow} M$
3: $Y_0 \leftarrow 0^n$
4: **for** $i \leftarrow 1$ **to** $m-1$
5:     $X_i \leftarrow M_i \oplus Y_{i-1}$
6:     $Y_i \leftarrow E_K(X_i)$
7: **if** $|M_m| = n$ **then**
8:     $X_m \leftarrow Y_{m-1} \oplus M_m \oplus L \cdot \mathsf{u}$
9: **else** $X_m \leftarrow Y_{m-1} \oplus \mathsf{pad}(M_m) \oplus L \cdot \mathsf{u}^2$
10: $T \leftarrow E_K(X_m)$
11: **return** T

(a)   (b)

Fig. 2. Definition of CMAC. The left figure (a) is CMAC's pseudocode and the right figure (b) is an illustration of CMAC for 3-block messages. In figure (b), the top is for the case where the last block of the message is a full block while the bottom is for the case where the last block of the message is a partial block. Note that $L = E_K(0^n)$.

4 Multi-user Security of CMAC

The following Theorem 2 establishes an upper bound on the multi-user PRF advantage of CMAC against all information-theoretic adversaries.

Theorem 2. *Let* $E : \{0,1\}^k \times \{0,1\}^n \to \{0,1\}^n$ *be a blockcipher that we model as an ideal blockcipher. Then for any computationally unbounded adversary* $\mathcal{D}$ *that makes at most* p *ideal-cipher queries and* q *evaluation queries of total block length of* σ *across* u *users, he can distinguish* CMAC *from random functions with an advantage*

$$\mathrm{Adv}^{\text{muprf-IC}}_{\text{CMAC}}(\mathcal{D}) \leq \frac{14q\sigma + q^2}{2^n} + \frac{q^2 + up}{2^k} + \frac{pq + 2pq\sqrt{\ell}}{2^{n+k}} + \frac{16pq\ell^4}{2^{2n+k}}$$

where ℓ *is the maximum block length of messages for all evaluation queries and* $\ell \leq 2^{n/4}$.

Note that there is a limitation of $\ell \leq 2^{n/4}$ in the bound[2]. However, this may not matter, as most applications use messages with a block length less than $2^{n/4}$.

4.1 Proof Overview

Before delving into the detailed analysis of Theorem 2, we provide a proof sketch in this section.

---

[2] In the single-user model, the assumption is $\ell \leq 2^{n/3}$..

We concentrate on the multi-user PRF security of CMAC in the ideal-cipher mode. Our proof is mainly based on the H-coefficient technique. The novelty of this research lies in the identification of specific bad events, and the approach to bounding the probability of these events within our specified target range. These two aspects are also at the core of the H-coefficient technique.

Bounding the occurrence of these events proves challenging in contrast to standard model. Our security analysis is built in the ideal-cipher model, where the adversary can evaluate the underlying blockcipher. Consequently, we must consider the likelihood that the adversary possesses comprehensive knowledge of all input-output pairs resulting from blockcipher evaluations. Therefore, it is reasonable to give the adversary more information, capturing an even stronger notion of security, but which nevertheless facilitates our proof. Specifically, after finishing his query and before his final output, the distinguisher $\mathcal{D}$ is given all the internal input-output values together with all the user keys and corresponding masks. $\mathcal{D}$ is given true values in the real world while in the ideal world, all these values given to $\mathcal{D}$ is (randomly) simulated. Thus there may be something wrong with the compatibility of input-output pairs in the ideal world. Among all the transcripts from the ideal world oracle, some transcripts may lead to inconsistency for the permutation or possible attacks. We defined these undesirable events as "bad". It is the most crucial step to recognize these bad events and upper bound the probabilities of them.

1. To ease the analysis, we would like to ensure that the user keys of any two distinct users are different. It will help us avoid some insignificant but intricate bad events. See bad_1 in Sect. 5.1.
2. For CMAC, a mask L_i is computed by encrypting 0^n. If the distinguisher $\mathcal{D}$ tries to catch a mask by guessing a key and then making a forward primitive query of 0^n, he may get some inconsistency in the ideal world. We set a bad event if he guesses a user key correctly. See bad_2 in Sect. 5.1.
3. To ease the analysis, when simulating the input-output pairs in the ideal world, the oracle maintains the compatibility of the internal input-output pairs for each user both among themselves and with the primitive entries under the same key. Thus we mainly concentrate on the compatibility of the final input-output pairs for each user. In Sect. 5.1, bad_3 and bad_4 are set for the compatibility between the final input-output pairs and the primitive entries under the same key, bad_5 and bad_6 are set for the inner compatibility of the final input-output pairs, bad_7 and bad_8 are set for the compatibility between the final input-output pairs and the internal input-output pairs.

After upper bounding the probability of each bad event, we demonstrate that the ratio of the interpolation probability in the real world to that in the ideal world is lower bounded by 1. Details of the proof can be found in Sect. 5.

5   Proof Details of Theorem 2

We present a full proof in this section.

5.1   Oracle Setting and Bad Events

Our proof is based on the H-coefficient technique. The general setting involves a computationally unbounded distinguisher $\mathcal{D}$ interacting with one of two oracles, namely the "real world" oracle or the "ideal world" oracle. Before the distinguisher $\mathcal{D}$ begins his query, an initialization procedure Initialize is performed, where user keys K_i (in the real world) or random functions f_i (in the real world) are sampled. $\mathcal{D}$ can make two types of queries, primitive queries to the ideal cipher and evaluation queries to one of the oracles. Note that these two types of queries can be made in an interleaved manner. Without loss of generality, we assume that $\mathcal{D}$ is deterministic and never repeats a prior query. The distinguishing game is elaborated in Fig. 3. $\mathcal{D}$ makes its final decision as a deterministic function of the transcript obtained. The "real world" oracle corresponds to game $\mathbf{G}_{\mathsf{CMAC}}^{\mathrm{Real\text{-}muprf}}$ with challenge bit $b = 1$ while the "ideal world" oracle corresponds to game $\mathbf{G}_{\mathsf{CMAC}}^{\mathrm{Ideal\text{-}muprf}}$ with challenge bit $b = 0$. Compared with the multi-user PRF definition in Fig. 1, we depict the two world separately in Fig. 3 and perform a slightly modified distinguishing game. Specifically, after the distinguisher $\mathcal{D}$ finishes his query and before he makes his final decision, the oracle reveals more additional information (in the KeyReveal and IOReveal procedures) to $\mathcal{D}$. This can only help the distinguisher.

In order of precedence, there are roughly two distinct phases for each oracle: first the interaction phase, and then the revealing phase. In the interaction phase, the oracle handles the queries (including evaluation queries and primitive queries) made by the distinguisher $\mathcal{D}$. In the subsequent revealing phase, the oracle grants the distinguisher $\mathcal{D}$ more information. The revealing phase is further divided into two sequential stages that will be detailed later. A bad event can occur at any point for any stage. To apply the H-coefficient technique, our objective is to establish an upper bound on the probability of all such bad events. Therefore, it is reasonable to make an assumption that no preceding bad events have occurred. In particular, we analyze the i-th bad event under the condition that none of the preceding $i - 1$ bad events has occurred.

For any *attainable* transcript (achievable in the ideal world), we say that it is bad if any of the defined 8 bad events occurs. If an *attainable* transcript is not classified as *bad*, we term it as *good*. Denote $\mathcal{T}_{\mathrm{re}}$ and $\mathcal{T}_{\mathrm{id}}$ be the probability distributions of the transcript when $\mathcal{D}$ interacts with the real world and the ideal world respectively.

To simplify notations, we utilize the same notations for the transcripts in both the real world and the ideal world. Assume the number of users is u. Assume further that q evaluation queries of total block length of σ are made by $\mathcal{D}$ and among them q_i evaluation queries of total block length of σ_i are made to user i. Hence $\sum_{i=1}^{u} q_i = q$ and $\sum_{i=1}^{u} \sigma_i = \sigma$. We also suppose that $\mathcal{D}$ makes at most p primitive queries to the ideal cipher.

Interaction Phase. Firstly, we focus on the interaction phase. When the interaction begins in the real world, the oracle samples $K_1, K_2 \cdots, K_u \xleftarrow{\$} \mathcal{K}$ for different users and then answers all queries honestly.

- **Evaluation queries:** For each query $\mathsf{Eval}(i, M^{i,j})$ with $i \in [u], j \in q_i$ and $M^{i,j} \in \mathcal{M}$, the real world oracle responds honestly with:

$$T^{i,j} \leftarrow \mathsf{CMAC}_{K_i}(M^{i,j}), \text{ return } T^{i,j}.$$

We associate each evaluation query with an entry $(\mathsf{Eval}, i, M^{i,j}, T^{i,j})$.
- **Primitive queries:** For each primitive query, the ideal-cipher oracle responds truthfully. Specifically, answer with $E_J(x)$ for the forward query $\mathsf{Prim}(J, (x, +))$ and answer with $E_J^{-1}(y)$ for the inverse query $\mathsf{Prim}(J, (y, -))$. For all the primitive queries, we maintain a set P for primitive queries and associate each primitive query with an entry of the form $(x, y)_J$ in P where $y = E_J(x)$ for the forward query $\mathsf{Prim}(J, (x, +))$ and $x = E_J^{-1}(y)$ for the inverse query $\mathsf{Prim}(J, (y, -))$. Totally there are p elements at most in P for the reason that $\mathcal{D}$ makes no redundant local query. To facilitate the subsequent analysis, we gather all the primitive queries associated with a common key K and compile them into a designated set denoted as P^K. In a formal sense, $\mathsf{P}^K = \{(x, y) | (x, y)_J \in \mathsf{P}, J = K\}$. In the absence of any primitive queries associated with the key K, P^K is defined as empty.

Now turn to the ideal world. Let $\mathcal{F}(\mathcal{M}, \{0, 1\}^n)$ denote the set of all functions from the message space $\mathcal{M}$ to $\{0, 1\}^n$ and a random element f of $\mathcal{F}(\mathcal{M}, \{0, 1\}^n)$ associates to each string $M \in \mathcal{M}$ a random string $f(M) \in \{0, 1\}^n$. In the interaction phase, the ideal world oracle samples $f_1, f_2, \cdots, f_u \xleftarrow{\$} \mathcal{F}(\mathcal{M}, \{0, 1\}^n)$ to simulate the CMAC construction and then answers all queries as follows.

- **Evaluation queries:** For each query $\mathsf{Eval}(i, M^{i,j})$ with $i \in [u], j \in q_i$ and $M^{i,j} \in \mathcal{M}$, the ideal world oracle responds randomly with:

$$T^{i,j} \leftarrow f_i(M^{i,j}), \text{ return } T^{i,j}.$$

Also we associate each evaluation query with an entry $(\mathsf{Eval}, i, M^{i,j}, T^{i,j})$.
- **Primitive queries:** For each primitive query, the ideal-cipher oracle responds truthfully as the way in the real world. Notations associated with primitive queries adhere to those employed in the real world.

After the distinguisher $\mathcal{D}$ has finished his queries in the interaction phase, we arrange the visible information to the distinguisher $\mathcal{D}$ as the following transcript:

$$\tau = \{(\mathsf{Eval}, i, M^{i,j}, T^{i,j})_{i \in [u], j \in [q_i]}, \mathsf{P}\}.$$

We define no bad events for the ideal world in the interaction phase.

Revealing Phase. After the distinguisher $\mathcal{D}$ finishes his querying and before he makes his final decision, more information is revealed to the distinguisher in the revealing phase. Specifically, $\mathcal{D}$ is granted both the underlying blockcipher keys and masks of all users. In the real world, $\mathcal{D}$ is given the true values. While in the ideal world, $\mathcal{D}$ is instead given dummy values $K_i \xleftarrow{\$} \{0, 1\}^n$ and $L_i \xleftarrow{\$} \{0, 1\}^n$ for $i \in [u]$, which are chosen uniformly at random and independent of the transcript.

$G_{CMAC}^{Real\text{-}muprf}$	$G_{CMAC}^{Ideal\text{-}muprf}$
procedure Initialize	**procedure** Initialize
1: $K_1, K_2, \cdots, K_u \xleftarrow{\$} \mathcal{K}$	1: $f_1, f_2, \cdots, f_u \xleftarrow{\$} \mathcal{F}(\mathcal{M}, \{0,1\}^n)$
2: $q \leftarrow 0$	2: $q \leftarrow 0$
procedure Eval(i, M)	**procedure** Eval(i, M)
1: $T \leftarrow \mathsf{CMAC}_{K_i}(M)$	1: $T \leftarrow f_i(M)$
2: $q \leftarrow q + 1$	2: $q \leftarrow q + 1$
3: $Z[q] \leftarrow (i, M, T)$	3: $Z[q] \leftarrow (i, M, T)$
4: **return** T	4: **return** T
procedure Prim(J, X)	**procedure** Prim(J, X)
1: **if** $X = (+, x)$ **then return** $E_J(x)$	1: **if** $X = (+, x)$ **then return** $E_J(x)$
2: **if** $X = (-, y)$ **then return** $E_J^{-1}(y)$	2: **if** $X = (-, y)$ **then return** $E_J^{-1}(y)$
procedure KeyReveal	**procedure** KeyReveal
	1: $K_1, K_2, \cdots, K_u \xleftarrow{\$} \mathcal{K}$
1: **for** $i = 1$ **to** u	2: **for** $i = 1$ **to** u
2: $L_i \leftarrow E_{K_i}(0^n)$	3: $L_i \xleftarrow{\$} \{0,1\}^n$
3: **return** $K_1, \cdots, K_u, L_i, \cdots, L_u$	4: **return** $K_1, \cdots, K_u, L_i, \cdots, L_u$
procedure IOReveal	**procedure** IOReveal
1: **for** $i = 1$ **to** u	1: **for** $i = 1$ **to** u
2: $\mathsf{P}_i \leftarrow \{(0, L_i)\}, \mathsf{P}'_i \leftarrow \emptyset$	2: $\mathsf{P}_i \leftarrow \{(0, L_i)\}, \mathsf{P}'_i \leftarrow \emptyset$
3: **for** $t = 1$ **to** q	3: **for** $t = 1$ **to** q
4: $(i, M, T) \leftarrow Z[t]$	4: $(i, M, T) \leftarrow Z[t]$
5: **if** $|M| \leq n$	5: **if** $|M| \leq n$
6: $x \leftarrow \mathsf{pad}_1(M) \oplus L_i \cdot \delta, y = T$	6: $x \leftarrow \mathsf{pad}_1(M) \oplus L_i \cdot \delta, y = T$
7: $\mathsf{P}'_i \leftarrow \mathsf{P}'_i \cup \{(x, y)\}$	7: $\mathsf{P}'_i \leftarrow \mathsf{P}'_i \cup \{(x, y)\}$
8: **else if** $|M| > n$	8: **else if** $|M| > n$
9: $M_1 \cdots M_m \xleftarrow{n} M$	9: $M_1 \cdots M_m \xleftarrow{n} M$
10: $0^n \leftarrow y_0$	10: $0^n \leftarrow y_0$
11: **for** $s = 1$ **to** $m - 1$	11: **for** $s = 1$ **to** $m - 1$
12: $x_s \leftarrow M_s \oplus y_{s-1}$	12: $x_s \leftarrow M_s \oplus y_{s-1}$
13: **if** $x_s \in \mathsf{dom}(\mathsf{P}^{K_i}), y_s \leftarrow \mathsf{P}^{K_i}(x_s)$	13: **if** $x_s \in \mathsf{dom}(\mathsf{P}^{K_i}), y_s \leftarrow \mathsf{P}^{K_i}(x_s)$
14: **else if** $x_s \in \mathsf{dom}(\mathsf{P}_i), y_s \leftarrow \mathsf{P}_i(x_s)$	14: **else if** $x_s \in \mathsf{dom}(\mathsf{P}_i), y_s \leftarrow \mathsf{P}_i(x_s)$
15: **else** $y_s \leftarrow E_{K_i}(x_s)$	15: **else** $y_s \leftarrow \{0,1\}^n \setminus \mathsf{dom}(\mathsf{P}_i \cup \mathsf{P}^{K_i})$
16: $\mathsf{P}_i \leftarrow \mathsf{P}_i \cup \{(x_s, y_s)\}$	16: $\mathsf{P}_i \leftarrow \mathsf{P}_i \cup \{(x_s, y_s)\}$
17: $x_m \leftarrow y_{m-1} \oplus \mathsf{pad}_1(M_m) \oplus L_i \cdot \delta$	17: $x_m \leftarrow y_{m-1} \oplus \mathsf{pad}_1(M_m) \oplus L_i \cdot \delta$
18: $y_m \leftarrow T$	18: $y_m \leftarrow T$
19: $\mathsf{P}'_i \leftarrow \mathsf{P}'_i \cup \{(x_m, y_m)\}$	19: $\mathsf{P}'_i \leftarrow \mathsf{P}'_i \cup \{(x_m, y_m)\}$
20: **return** $\mathsf{P}_1, \cdots, \mathsf{P}_u, \mathsf{P}'_1, \cdots, \mathsf{P}'_u$	20: **return** $\mathsf{P}_1, \cdots, \mathsf{P}_u, \mathsf{P}'_1, \cdots, \mathsf{P}'_u$
procedure Finalize(b)	**procedure** Finalize(b)
1: **return** b	1: **return** b

Fig. 3. Distingushing game for multi-user CMAC. The left part is the oracle in the real world while the right one is that in the ideal world.

These steps are presented in the procedure KeyReveal of Fig. 3. The revealed values are collected and stored in multi-sets K and L where elements are allowed to repeat, namely, $K = \{K_1, \cdots, K_u\}$ and $L = \{L_1, \cdots, L_u\}$.

At this juncture, the first stage of the revealing phase has been concluded. Now, the transcript is updated to

$$\tau = \{\mathsf{K}, \mathsf{L}, (\mathsf{Eval}, i, M^{i,j}, T^{i,j})_{i \in [u], j \in [q_i]}, \mathsf{P}\}.$$

Now we define the first bad event bad_1 in the ideal world. As the dummy keys provided to the distinguisher are sampled independently and uniformly at random, the occurrence of key collisions is possible. If such collisions take place, the compatibility analysis between the corresponding users becomes quite intricate. To simplify the analysis and avoid further complexity, we categorize the event of two keys colliding as a bad event.

bad_1 We say an *attainable* transcript τ is *bad* if there exist $i, j \in [u]$ such that $i \neq j$ but $K_i = K_j$.

Then we define the second bad event as bad_2 in the ideal world. $\mathcal{D}$ can guess a user key J and then make a primitive query $\mathsf{Prim}(J, (0^n, +))$ to get the corresponding mask. Note that in the ideal world, all the masks are sampled uniformly at random. If it turns out that J collides with any user key, inconsistencies will arise. So to remove this kind of inconsistencies, we define the following simplified bad event:

bad_2 We say an *attainable* transcript τ is *bad* if there exists an entry $(x, y)_J \in \mathsf{P}$ such that $x = 0^n$ and $J = K_i$ with $i \in [u]$.

Now the second stage of the revealing phase begins. In this stage, the distinguisher $\mathcal{D}$ is granted all the input-output (hereafter shortened as IO) pairs, including the intermediate IO pairs and the final IO pair, for each evaluation query. Two sets, P_i and P'_i, are maintained for each user $i \in [u]$. P_i is used to collect all the intermediate IO pairs for user i and is initialized as $\{(0, L_i)\}$. In contrast, P'_i is used to collect all the final IO pairs for user i and is initialized as empty. Refer to procedure IOReveal in Fig. 3 for more details of the revealing. Indeed, the distinguisher $\mathcal{D}$ can be provided with outputs only both in the real world and in the ideal world because it enables the computation of all corresponding inputs based on the information received. However, to enhance the clarity of both the definition and the computation of bad events, the distinguisher is furnished with all inputs simultaneously, which can only help him and has no impact on the bounds to be established.

After the disclosure process of IO pairs, the information available to the distinguisher $\mathcal{D}$ consists of the revealed keys and masks, the evaluation queries together with their intermediate IO pairs and final IO pairs, and the primitive queries. Note that the values in L are separated into P_i's. Thus the final transcript can be represented as

$$\tau = \{\mathsf{K}, (\mathsf{Eval}, i, M^{i,j}, T^{i,j})_{i \in [u], j \in [q_i]}, \mathsf{P}, \mathsf{P}_1, \cdots, \mathsf{P}_u, \mathsf{P}'_1, \cdots, \mathsf{P}'_u\}.$$

Now we define bad events that occur in the disclosure process of IO pairs. The key point is to find out the inconsistencies among P_i, P'_i and P_L. According the revealing procedure in the ideal world, IO pairs in P_i and P^{K_i} are consistent naturally. Therefore, in the subsequent discussion, we define three different types of bad events in the ideal world: 1) the collisions between P'_i and P^{K_i} for each user; 2) the inner collisions in P'_i for each user; 3) the collisions between P'_i and P_i for each user. Specifically, we define another six bad events. Among them, the following bad_3 and bad_4 are defined to remove input collisions and output collisions respectively occurring between P^{K_i} and P'_i for each user.

bad_3 We say an *attainable* transcript τ is *bad* if there exist $(x, y) \in P^{K_i}$ and $(x', y') \in P'_i$ such that $x = x'$.

bad_4 We say an *attainable* transcript τ is *bad* if there exist $(x, y) \in P^{K_i}$ and $(x', y') \in P'_i$ such that $y = y'$.

Then the following bad_5 and bad_6 are defined to remove output collisions and input collisions respectively occurring in P'_i for each user.

bad_5 We say an *attainable* transcript τ is *bad* if there exist $(x, y) \in P'_i$ and $(x', y') \in P'_i$ such that $y = y'$.

bad_6 We say an *attainable* transcript τ is *bad* if there exist $(x, y) \in P'_i$ and $(x', y') \in P'_i$ such that $x = x'$.

At last, the following bad_7 and bad_8 are defined to remove input collisions and output collisions respectively occurring between P_i and P'_i for each user.

bad_7 We say an *attainable* transcript τ is *bad* if there exist $(x, y) \in P_i$ and $(x', y') \in P'_i$ such that $x = x'$.

bad_8 We say an *attainable* transcript τ is *bad* if there exist $(x, y) \in P_i$ and $(x', y') \in P'_i$ such that $y = y'$.

The subsequent lemma provides an upper bound on the probability of each bad event. Its detailed proof is presented in Appendix A.

Lemma 1.

$$\Pr[\tau \in bad_1] \leq \frac{q^2}{2^k}.$$

$$\Pr[\tau \in bad_2] \leq \frac{up}{2^k}.$$

$$\Pr[\tau \in bad_3] \leq \frac{2qp\sqrt{\ell}}{2^{n+k}} + \frac{16qp\ell^4}{2^{2n+k}}.$$

$$\Pr[\tau \in bad_4] \leq \frac{qp}{2^{n+k}}.$$

$$\Pr[\tau \in bad_5] \leq \frac{q^2}{2^n}.$$

$$\Pr[\tau \in bad_6 \cup bad_7] \leq \frac{12q\sigma}{2^n}.$$

$$\Pr[\tau \in bad_8] \leq \frac{2q\sigma}{2^n}.$$

Hence by Lemma 1, we have

$$\Pr[\mathcal{T}_{\mathrm{id}} \in \mathsf{bad}] \leq \sum_{i=1}^{5} \Pr[\tau \in \mathsf{bad}_i] + \Pr[\tau \in \mathsf{bad}_6 \cup \mathsf{bad}_7] + \Pr[\tau \in \mathsf{bad}_8] \qquad (1)$$

$$\leq \frac{14q\sigma + q^2}{2^n} + \frac{q^2 + up}{2^k} + \frac{pq + 2pq\sqrt{\ell}}{2^{n+k}} + \frac{16pq\ell^4}{2^{2n+k}}.$$

5.2   Transcript Ratio

Recall that the ultimate transcript takes the form

$$\tau = \{\mathsf{K}, (\mathrm{Eval}, i, M^{i,j}, T^{i,j})_{i \in [u], j \in [q_i]}, \mathsf{P}, \mathsf{P}_1, \cdots, \mathsf{P}_u, \mathsf{P}_1', \cdots, \mathsf{P}_u'\}$$

and that we have defined $\mathsf{P}^K = \{(x, y)|(x, y)_J \in \mathsf{P}, J = K\}$.

Suppose that a transcript τ is *good*. We define the set Q^K with a superscript K to represent the union set of all IO pairs in P_i. Formally, we have

$$\mathsf{Q}^K = \begin{cases} \mathsf{P}_i, & \text{if } K \in \mathsf{K} \text{ where } \mathsf{K} = \{K_1, \cdots, K_u\}; \\ \emptyset, & \text{otherwise.} \end{cases}$$

and in a similar way we denote the set S^K as

$$\mathsf{S}^K = \begin{cases} \mathsf{P}_i', & \text{if } K \in \mathsf{K} \text{ where } \mathsf{K} = \{K_1, \cdots, K_u\}; \\ \emptyset, & \text{otherwise.} \end{cases}$$

Let

$$s = \sum_{K \in \{0,1\}^k} |\mathsf{S}^K|.$$

Then we have $s \leq q$.

In the ideal world, for a good transcript τ, we have $\mathsf{P}^K \cap \mathsf{Q}^K = \emptyset$ for each $K \in \{0,1\}^n$. Let $\mathsf{V}^K = \mathsf{P}^K \cup \mathsf{Q}^K$, then we can get

$$\Pr[\mathcal{T}_{\mathrm{id}} = \tau] = 2^{-ku} \cdot 2^{-qn} \prod_{K \in \{0,1\}^k} \prod_{i=0}^{|\mathsf{V}^K|-1} \frac{1}{2^n - i}.$$

On the other hand, in the real world, $\mathsf{P}^K, \mathsf{Q}^K$ and S^K indicate pairs (x, y) such that $E_K(x)$ must be y and hence there exist no conflicting information among $\mathsf{P}^K, \mathsf{Q}^K$ and S^K for each $K \in \{0,1\}^n$. Specifically, $\mathsf{P}^K \cap \mathsf{Q}^K \cap \mathsf{S}^K = \emptyset$. Let $\mathsf{W}^K = \mathsf{P}^K \cup \mathsf{Q}^K \cup \mathsf{S}^K$ and $|\mathsf{W}^K| \leq p + \sigma$. Then

$$\Pr[\mathcal{T}_{\mathrm{re}} = \tau] = 2^{-ku} \prod_{K \in \{0,1\}^k} \prod_{i=0}^{|\mathsf{W}^K|-1} \frac{1}{2^n - i}.$$

Therefore

$$\frac{\Pr[\mathcal{T}_{re} = \tau]}{\Pr[\mathcal{T}_{id} = \tau]} = 2^{qn} \prod_{K \in \{0,1\}^k} \prod_{i=0}^{|\mathsf{S}^K|-1} \left(\frac{1}{2^n - |V(K)| - i}\right)$$

$$\geq \prod_{K \in \{0,1\}^k} \prod_{i=0}^{|\mathsf{S}^K|-1} \left(\frac{2^n}{2^n - |\mathsf{V}^K| - i}\right)$$

$$\geq 1. \tag{2}$$

5.3   Wrapping Up

With Eq. (1) and Eq. (2), by Theorem 1, we have

$$\mathrm{Adv}_{\mathsf{CMAC}}^{\mathrm{muprf\text{-}IC}}(\mathcal{D}) \leq \frac{14q\sigma + q^2}{2^n} + \frac{q^2 + up}{2^k} + \frac{pq + 2pq\sqrt{\ell}}{2^{n+k}} + \frac{16pq\ell^4}{2^{2n+k}}.$$

6   Conclusions and Future Work

In this paper, we have provided a concrete multi-user security bound for CMAC that has been standardized and widely applied. Our result shows that in the multi-user model CMAC maintains the same online security bound as in the single-user model. In the future, we may continue elaborating on concrete multi-user security analysis of other constructions, including other MAC schemes. Furthermore, we may also try to consider the generic properties in the multi-user model for some constructions that share the same paradigm.

Acknowledgments. This study was funded by the National Key Research and Development Program of China (2019YFB2101601) and the National Natural Science Foundation of China (62372294).

A   A Proof Details of Lemma 1

Firstly we establish an upper bound on $\Pr[\tau \in \mathsf{bad}_1]$. Recall that the event bad_1 occurs when there exist two distinct users i and j such that $K_i = K_j$. As the keys of each user are sampled independently and uniformly at random in the ideal world, for any two fixed i and j, the probability that $K_i = K_j$ holds is exactly 2^{-k}. Therefore, considering all the pairs of the users, we can conclude that

$$\Pr[\tau \in \mathsf{bad}_1] \leq \frac{u^2}{2^k} \leq \frac{q^2}{2^k}.$$

Then we establish an upper bound on $\Pr[\tau \in \mathsf{bad}_2]$. Recall that the event bad_2 occurs when there exists an entry $(x, y)_J \in \mathsf{P}$ such that $x = 0^n$ and $J = K_i$ with $i \in [u]$. $\mathcal{D}$ can make p primitive queries at most and thus he can guess p

different keys at most. For a particular user $i \in [u]$, the chance that there exists a primitive query such that $J = K_i$ holds is bounded by $p/2^k$. Considering all the users, we have

$$\Pr[\tau \in \mathsf{bad}_2] \leq \frac{up}{2^k}.$$

Next we establish an upper bound on $\Pr[\tau \in \mathsf{bad}_3]$. Observe that CMAC processes the first $m - 1$ blocks of a message M in a CBC MAC manner, where m represents the total block length of M. For any two distinct messages M_1 and M_2 with block length $m \leq 2^{n/4}$, Bellare et al. [4,22] show that

$$\Pr[\mathsf{CBC}_K(M_1) = \mathsf{CBC}_K(M_2)] \leq \frac{2\sqrt{m}}{2^n} + \frac{16m^4}{2^{2n}}.$$

Building on this, we can derive the following lemma.

Lemma 2. *For any $M \in \{0,1\}^{mn}$ with $m \leq 2^{n/4}$ and any $Y \in \{0,1\}^n$ it follows that*

$$\Pr[\mathsf{CBC}_K(M) = Y] \leq \frac{2\sqrt{m}}{2^n} + \frac{16m^4}{2^{2n}}.$$

Proof. Let $M_1 = X\|Y$ and $M_2 = 0^n$. Then the event $\mathsf{CBC}_K(M) = Y$ is the same as $\mathsf{CBC}_K(M_1) = \mathsf{CBC}_K(M_2)$. Hence we can obtain

$$\Pr[\mathsf{CBC}_K(M) = Y] = \Pr[\mathsf{CBC}_K(M_1) = \mathsf{CBC}_K(M_2)]$$
$$\leq \frac{2\sqrt{m}}{2^n} + \frac{16\,m^4}{2^{2n}}.$$

Now we consider domain collisions between P'_i and a primitive entry $(x,y)_J$. For a fixed primitive entry $(x,y)_J$ and a specific user, the probability that $K_i = J$ holds is $1/2^k$. Assume that ℓ is the maximum block length of messages for all evaluation queries. By Lemma 2, for fixed $(x,y) \in \mathsf{P}^{K_i}$ and $(x',y') \in \mathsf{P}'_i$, the probability that $x' = x$ holds is bounded by $\frac{2\sqrt{\ell}}{2^n} + \frac{16\ell^4}{2^{2n}}$. With $|\mathsf{P}'_i| \leq q_i$ and $|\mathsf{P}^{K_i}| \leq p$, such a bad event happens for a user is bounded $\frac{2q_i p\sqrt{\ell}}{2^{n+k}} + \frac{16q_i p\ell^4}{2^{2n+k}}$. Therefore, taking into account all the users, we can get

$$\Pr\left[\tau \in \mathsf{bad}_3\right] \leq \sum_{i=1}^{u} \left(\frac{2q_i p\sqrt{\ell}}{2^{n+k}} + \frac{16q_i p\ell^4}{2^{2n+k}}\right)$$
$$\leq \frac{2qp\sqrt{\ell}}{2^{n+k}} + \frac{16qp\ell^4}{2^{2n+k}}.$$

Now we establish an upper bound on $\Pr[\tau \in \mathsf{bad}_4]$. In this case, we consider range collisions between P'_i and a primitive entry $(x,y)_J$. For a fixed primitive entry $(x,y)_J$ and a specific user i, the probability that $K_i = J$ holds is $1/2^k$. Further, for a primitive entry $(x,y)_J$ and a fixed $(x',y') \in \mathsf{P}'_i$ the probability that $y = y'$ satisfies is $1/2^{n+k}$. For a specific user i, considering all the primitive entries and $|P'_i| \leq q_i$ the probability that such a bad event happens is bounded by $q_i p / 2^{n+k}$. Therefore, by varying over all possible choices of users, we have

$$\Pr[\tau \in \mathsf{bad_4}] \leq \sum_{i=1}^{u} \frac{q_i p}{2^{n+k}} \leq \frac{qp}{2^{n+k}}.$$

Next we establish an upper bound on $\Pr[\tau \in \mathsf{bad_5}]$. All the elements in $\mathsf{rng}(P'_i)$, that are the set of the responded tags for evaluation queries, are sampled uniformly at random. Then for any fixed $(x, y), (x', y') \in P'_i$, the probability of $y = y'$ is $1/2^n$. with $|P'_i| \leq q_i$, it follows that, for each user i, the probability of $y = y'$ is bounded by $q_i^2 / 2^n$. Therefore, considering all the users, we can obtain:

$$\Pr[\tau \in \mathsf{bad_3}] \leq \sum_{i=1}^{u} \frac{q_i^2}{2^n} \leq \frac{q^2}{2^n}.$$

Next we jointly constrain the probabilities of $\mathsf{bad_6}$ and $\mathsf{bad_7}$. Prior to this, we introduce the following lemma extracted from the referenced paper [31] For additional details, please refer to the paper.

Lemma 3 ([31]). *For CMAC in the single-user setting, if the distinguisher makes q evaluation queries of total block length of σ with block length of each message is m_i for $1 \leq i \leq q$, the probability that there exist collisions between final inputs and intermediate inputs is upper bounded by*

$$\frac{4(q-1)\sigma}{2^n} + \sum_{1 \leq s < t \leq q} \frac{(m_s + m_t)^4}{2^{2n}}.$$

Note that in Lemma 3, "collisions between final inputs and intermediate inputs" encompass both the collisions between two final inputs and the collisions between a final input and an intermediate input. That is the reason that we bound the probabilities of $\mathsf{bad_6}$ and $\mathsf{bad_7}$ together. As Lemma 3 specifically pertains to a single user, expanding our consideration to include all users, we have

$$\Pr[\tau \in \mathsf{bad_6} \cup \mathsf{bad_7}] \leq \sum_{i=1}^{u} \left(\frac{4(q_i - 1)\sigma_i}{N} + \sum_{1 \leq s < t \leq q_i} \frac{\left(m^{i,s} + m^{i,t}\right)^4}{N^2} \right)$$

$$\leq \sum_{i=1}^{u} \frac{12 q_i \sigma_i}{2^n} \leq \frac{12 q \sigma}{2^n}.$$

Now we establish an upper bound on $\Pr[\tau \in \mathsf{bad_8}]$. For each user i, the set P_i contains, at most, $\sigma_i - q_i$ pairwise distinct elements When $|P_i| = \sigma_i - q_i$ it indicates that there exist no collisions among intermediate inputs (excluding final inputs) and among intermediate outputs, and in such circumstances $\mathsf{bad_8}$ is most likely to occur. To streamline the analysis, we systematically index the elements in P_i based on their order of occurrence. Specifically, $P_i = \{(x_1^i, y_1^i), \cdots, (x_{\sigma_i - q_i}^i, y_{\sigma_i - q_i}^i)\}$. We set an event E_j^i as true if $y_j^i \notin \mathsf{rng}(P'_i)$

with $1 \leq i \leq u, 1 \leq j \leq \sigma_i - q_i$. Additionally, we define another event $\mathsf{E}^i_{\leq j}$ as $\bigcup^j_{t=1} \mathsf{E}^i_t$. It is observed that

$$\Pr\left[\mathsf{E}^i_{j+1} = 1 \mid \mathsf{E}^i_{\leq j} = 1\right] \geq \frac{2^n - q_i - j}{2^n - j},$$

and hence

$$\Pr\left[\mathsf{E}^i_{\leq \sigma_i - q_i} = 1\right] \geq \prod^{\sigma_i - q_i}_{j=1} \frac{2^n - q_i - j}{2^n - j} = \prod^{\sigma_i - q_i}_{j=1} \left(1 - \frac{q_i}{2^n - j}\right).$$

The consideration of all users leads us to conclude that

$$\Pr\left[\bigcap^u_{i=1} \mathsf{E}^i_{\leq \sigma_i - q_i} = 1\right] \geq \prod^u_{i=0} \prod^{\sigma_i - q_i}_{j=0} \left(1 - \frac{q_i}{2^n - j}\right).$$

$$\geq \prod^u_{i=0}\left(1 - \frac{q_i(\sigma_i - q_i)}{2^n - (\sigma_i - q_i)}\right)$$

$$\geq 1 - \sum^u_{i=0} \frac{q_i(\sigma_i - q_i)}{2^n - (\sigma_i - q_i)}.$$

Assuming that $\sigma \leq 2^{n-1}$, we can get

$$\Pr\left[\tau \in \mathsf{bad_8}\right] = 1 - \Pr\left[\bigcap^u_{i=1} \mathsf{E}^i_{\leq \sigma_i - q_i} = 1\right]$$

$$\leq \sum^u_{i=0} \frac{q_i(\sigma_i - q_i)}{2^n - (\sigma_i - q_i)} \leq \frac{q\sigma}{2^n - \sigma} \leq \frac{2q\sigma}{2^n}.$$

References

1. Bellare, M., Bernstein, D.J., Tessaro, S.: Hash-function based PRFs: AMAC and its multi-user security. In: Fischlin, M., Coron, J.-S. (eds.) EUROCRYPT 2016. LNCS, vol. 9665, pp. 566–595. Springer, Heidelberg (2016). https://doi.org/10.1007/978-3-662-49890-3_22
2. Bellare, M., Boldyreva, A., Micali, S.: Public-key encryption in a multi-user setting: security proofs and improvements. In: Preneel, B. (ed.) EUROCRYPT 2000. LNCS, vol. 1807, pp. 259–274. Springer, Heidelberg (2000). https://doi.org/10.1007/3-540-45539-6_18
3. Bellare, M., Kilian, J., Rogaway, P.: The security of the cipher block chaining message authentication code. J. Comput. Syst. Sci. **61**(3), 362–399 (2000)
4. Bellare, M., Pietrzak, K., Rogaway, P.: Improved security analyses for CBC MACs. In: Shoup, V. (ed.) CRYPTO 2005. LNCS, vol. 3621, pp. 527–545. Springer, Heidelberg (2005). https://doi.org/10.1007/11535218_32
5. Bellare, M., Tackmann, B.: The multi-user security of authenticated encryption: AES-GCM in TLS 1.3. In: Robshaw, M., Katz, J. (eds.) CRYPTO 2016. LNCS, vol. 9814, pp. 247–276. Springer, Heidelberg (2016). https://doi.org/10.1007/978-3-662-53018-4_10

6. Biham, E.: How to decrypt or even substitute des-encrypted messages in 228 steps. Inf. Process. Lett. **84**(3), 117–124 (2002)
7. Black, J., Rogaway, P.: CBC MACs for arbitrary-length messages: the three-key constructions. In: Bellare, M. (ed.) CRYPTO 2000. LNCS, vol. 1880, pp. 197–215. Springer, Heidelberg (2000). https://doi.org/10.1007/3-540-44598-6_12
8. Black, J., Rogaway, P.: CBC macs for arbitrary-length messages: the three-key constructions. J. Cryptol. **18**(2), 111–131 (2005)
9. Bose, P., Hoang, V.T., Tessaro, S.: Revisiting AES-GCM-SIV: multi-user security, faster key derivation, and better bounds. In: Nielsen, J.B., Rijmen, V. (eds.) EUROCRYPT 2018. LNCS, vol. 10820, pp. 468–499. Springer, Cham (2018). https://doi.org/10.1007/978-3-319-78381-9_18
10. Bosselaers, A., Preneel, B.: Integrity Primitives for Secure Information Systems: Final Ripe Report of Race Integrity Primitives Evaluation, vol. 1007. Springer, Heidelberg (1995)
11. Chatterjee, S., Menezes, A., Sarkar, P.: Another look at tightness. In: Miri, A., Vaudenay, S. (eds.) SAC 2011. LNCS, vol. 7118, pp. 293–319. Springer, Heidelberg (2012). https://doi.org/10.1007/978-3-642-28496-0_18
12. Chen, S., Steinberger, J.: Tight security bounds for key-alternating ciphers. In: Nguyen, P.Q., Oswald, E. (eds.) EUROCRYPT 2014. LNCS, vol. 8441, pp. 327–350. Springer, Heidelberg (2014). https://doi.org/10.1007/978-3-642-55220-5_19
13. Datta, N., Dutta, A., Nandi, M., Paul, G.: Double-block hash-then-sum: a paradigm for constructing BBB secure PRF. IACR Trans. Symmetric Cryptol. **2018**(3), 36–92 (2018)
14. Datta, N., Dutta, A., Nandi, M., Talnikar, S.: Tight multi-user security bound of dbhts. IACR Trans. Symmetric Cryptol. 192–223 (2023)
15. Dworkin, M.J.: Recommendation for block cipher modes of operation: the CMAC mode for authentication. NIST SP 800-38B (2005)
16. Guo, T., Wang, P.: A note on the security framework of two-key DbHtS MACs. In: Alcaraz, C., Chen, L., Li, S., Samarati, P. (eds.) ICICS 2022. LNCS, vol. 13407, pp. 55–68. Springer, Cham (2022). https://doi.org/10.1007/978-3-031-15777-6_4
17. Hoang, V.T., Tessaro, S.: Key-alternating ciphers and key-length extension: exact bounds and multi-user security. In: Robshaw, M., Katz, J. (eds.) CRYPTO 2016. LNCS, vol. 9814, pp. 3–32. Springer, Heidelberg (2016). https://doi.org/10.1007/978-3-662-53018-4_1
18. Hoang, V.T., Tessaro, S.: The multi-user security of double encryption. In: Coron, J.-S., Nielsen, J.B. (eds.) EUROCRYPT 2017. LNCS, vol. 10211, pp. 381–411. Springer, Cham (2017). https://doi.org/10.1007/978-3-319-56614-6_13
19. ISO/IEC: Information Technology – Security Techniques – Message Authentication Codes (MACs) – Part 1: Mechanisms Using a Block Cipher. ISO/IEC 9797-1:2011 (2011)
20. Iwata, T., Kurosawa, K.: OMAC: one-key CBC MAC. In: Johansson, T. (ed.) FSE 2003. LNCS, vol. 2887, pp. 129–153. Springer, Heidelberg (2003). https://doi.org/10.1007/978-3-540-39887-5_11
21. Iwata, T., Kurosawa, K.: Stronger security bounds for OMAC, TMAC, and XCBC. In: Johansson, T., Maitra, S. (eds.) INDOCRYPT 2003. LNCS, vol. 2904, pp. 402–415. Springer, Heidelberg (2003). https://doi.org/10.1007/978-3-540-24582-7_30
22. Jha, A., Nandi, M.: Revisiting structure graph and its applications to CBC-MAC and EMAC. IACR Cryptol. ePrint Arch. 161 (2016). http://eprint.iacr.org/2016/161

23. Kaufman, C., Hoffman, P.E., Nir, Y., Eronen, P., Kivinen, T.: Internet Key Exchange Protocol Version 2 (IKEv2). RFC 7296 (2014). https://www.rfc-editor.org/info/rfc7296

24. Kurosawa, K., Iwata, T.: TMAC: two-key CBC MAC. In: Joye, M. (ed.) CT-RSA 2003. LNCS, vol. 2612, pp. 33–49. Springer, Heidelberg (2003). https://doi.org/10.1007/3-540-36563-X_3

25. Kurosawa, K., Iwata, T.: TMAC: two-key CBC MAC. IEICE Trans. Fundam. Electron. Commun. Comput. Sci. **87-A**(1), 46–52 (2004)

26. Luykx, A., Mennink, B., Paterson, K.G.: Analyzing multi-key security degradation. In: Takagi, T., Peyrin, T. (eds.) ASIACRYPT 2017. LNCS, vol. 10625, pp. 575–605. Springer, Cham (2017). https://doi.org/10.1007/978-3-319-70697-9_20

27. Morgan, A., Pass, R., Shi, E.: On the adaptive security of MACs and PRFs. In: Moriai, S., Wang, H. (eds.) ASIACRYPT 2020. LNCS, vol. 12491, pp. 724–753. Springer, Cham (2020). https://doi.org/10.1007/978-3-030-64837-4_24

28. Mouha, N., Luykx, A.: Multi-key security: the even-mansour construction revisited. In: Gennaro, R., Robshaw, M. (eds.) CRYPTO 2015. LNCS, vol. 9215, pp. 209–223. Springer, Heidelberg (2015). https://doi.org/10.1007/978-3-662-47989-6_10

29. Naito, Y.: Blockcipher-based MACs: beyond the birthday bound without message length. In: Takagi, T., Peyrin, T. (eds.) ASIACRYPT 2017. LNCS, vol. 10626, pp. 446–470. Springer, Cham (2017). https://doi.org/10.1007/978-3-319-70700-6_16

30. Naito, Y.: The multi-user security of macs via universal hashing in the ideal cipher model. In: Oswald, E. (ed.) CT-RSA 2024. LNCS, vol. 14643, pp. 51–77. Springer, Cham (2024). https://doi.org/10.1007/978-3-031-58868-6_3

31. Nandi, M.: Improved security analysis for OMAC as a pseudorandom function. J. Math. Cryptol. **3**(2), 133–148 (2009)

32. Patarin, J.: The "coefficients H" technique. In: Avanzi, R.M., Keliher, L., Sica, F. (eds.) SAC 2008. LNCS, vol. 5381, pp. 328–345. Springer, Heidelberg (2009). https://doi.org/10.1007/978-3-642-04159-4_21

33. Poovendran, R., Song, J., Lee, J.: The AES-CMAC-96 Algorithm and Its Use with IPsec. RFC 4494 (2006). https://doi.org/10.17487/RFC4494. https://www.rfc-editor.org/info/rfc4494

34. Shen, Y., Wang, L., Gu, D., Weng, J.: Revisiting the security of DbHtS MACs: beyond-birthday-bound in the multi-user setting. In: Malkin, T., Peikert, C. (eds.) CRYPTO 2021. LNCS, vol. 12827, pp. 309–336. Springer, Cham (2021). https://doi.org/10.1007/978-3-030-84252-9_11

35. Song, J., Poovendran, R., Lee, J., Iwata, T.: The AES-CMAC algorithm. Technical report, RFC 4493 (2006)

36. Yasuda, K.: The sum of CBC MACs is a secure PRF. In: Pieprzyk, J. (ed.) CT-RSA 2010. LNCS, vol. 5985, pp. 366–381. Springer, Heidelberg (2010). https://doi.org/10.1007/978-3-642-11925-5_25

37. Yasuda, K.: A new variant of PMAC: beyond the birthday bound. In: Rogaway, P. (ed.) CRYPTO 2011. LNCS, vol. 6841, pp. 596–609. Springer, Heidelberg (2011). https://doi.org/10.1007/978-3-642-22792-9_34

Quantum Key Recovery Attacks on 4-Round Iterated Even-Mansour with Two Keys

Ravi Anand[1], Shibam Ghosh[2], Takanori Isobe[3], and Rentaro Shiba[4,5(✉)]

[1] Indrapastha Institute of Information Technology Delhi, Delhi, India
`ravi.anand@iiit.ac.in`
[2] Computer Science Department, University of Haifa, Haifa, Israel
`sghosh03@campus.haifa.ac.il`
[3] University of Hyogo, Kobe, Japan
`takanori.isobe@ai.u-hyogo.ac.jp`
[4] Mitsubishi Electric Corporation, Kamakura, Japan
[5] Nagoya University, Nagoya, Japan
`shiba.rentaro.k7@s.mail.nagoya-u.ac.jp`

Abstract. In this paper, we propose quantum key recovery attacks on 4-round iterated Even-Mansour (IEM) with a key schedule that applies two keys alternately. We first show that a conditional periodic function such that one of the secret keys appears as a period conditionally can be constructed using the encryption function and internal permutations. By applying the offline Simon's algorithm to this function, we construct a key recovery attack with a complexity of $O(\sqrt{N} \log N)$ for $N = 2^n$, where n is the block size and one secret key size. Using quantum queries, this attack outperforms the generic quantum attack, *i.e.*, Grover's search which takes the time complexity of $O(N)$. Moreover, we propose the quantum version of the multibridge attack proposed by Dinur *et al.* in ASIACRYPT 2014 to analyze the 4-round IEM. As a result, we show that the quantum multibridge attack can achieve the optimal complexity of $O(N)$ even if we have only $O(1)$ data without quantum queries, while the classical attack requires $O(N)$ data to achieve the same time complexity. Furthermore, we show that the quantum multibridge attack slightly outperforms Grover's search when considering the quantum circuit depth for these attacks.

Keywords: Cryptanalysis · quantum attack · multibridge attack · iterated Even-Mansour

1 Introduction

The Even-Mansour (EM) scheme [11] is a well-known approach for constructing a block cipher E from a public pseudo-random permutation $P : \{0,1\}^n \mapsto \{0,1\}^n$ and two n-bit keys $\mathsf{K}_0, \mathsf{K}_1$. The Even-Mansour (EM) cipher $E : \{0,1\}^{2n} \times \{0,1\}^n \mapsto \{0,1\}^n$ is defined as:

$$E_{\mathsf{K}_0,\mathsf{K}_1}(x) = P(x \oplus \mathsf{K}_0) \oplus \mathsf{K}_1$$

N. Mouha and N. Nikiforakis (Eds.): ISC 2024, LNCS 15257, pp. 87–103, 2025.
https://doi.org/10.1007/978-3-031-75757-0_5

The EM cipher has been studied intensively due to its simplicity and security has been discussed in both classical and quantum settings.

The structure obtained by iterating an EM scheme is called an Iterated Even-Mansour (IEM) scheme, which is also referred to as an abstraction of many concrete block ciphers. Given r permutations $P_1, \ldots, P_r : \{0,1\}^n \mapsto \{0,1\}^n$, and the secret key $\mathsf{K} = \mathsf{K}_0 \| \mathsf{K}_1 \| \cdots \| \mathsf{K}_r \in \{0,1\}^{(r+1)n}$, the r-round IEM cipher is defined as follows:

$$E_{\mathsf{K}}(x) = P_r(P_{r-1}(\cdots P_1(x \oplus \mathsf{K}_0) \cdots)) \oplus \mathsf{K}_r. \tag{1}$$

Analyzing the security of the IEM ciphers is useful for deriving lower bounds on the number of queries and the computational cost required for the attacks since its internal permutations correspond to the round functions of concrete block ciphers and are assumed to be random. Moreover, the security of IEM ciphers varies depending on the number of permutations used and the key schedule, making it very useful for determining the foundational constructions of block ciphers.

To date, various security analyses have been proposed for several variants of EM and IEM ciphers. In [8], Chen and Steinberger analyzed the tight security bound of Eq. (1) and proved that it is $2^{\frac{r}{r+1}n}$. In [10], Dinur et al. proposed the *multibridge attack* for recovering the secret key of the 4-round variants of the IEM ciphers with two independent n-bit keys. They showed that the secret key of 4-round 2-key IEM ciphers can be recovered with the optimal complexity of $N = 2^n$, and the trade-off curve of $DT = N^2$ can be obtained by applying the multibridge attack.

In the case of quantum security, Kuwakado and Morii [19] was the first to show that a 1-round 2-key EM cipher can be attacked using Simon's algorithm with the time complexity of $O(\log N)$ in the Q2 model. The same paper also shows that the keys of this scheme can be recovered with time complexity of $O(N^{1/3})$ and a qRAM of size $O(N^{1/3})$ by applying a quantum collision search algorithm [6] in the Q1 model. Leander and May [20] described a method to combine the quantum algorithms of Simon and ch1Grover, termed Grover-meets-Simon (GMS), and it can be applied to the analysis of FX constructions. In [2], the offline Simon's algorithm was proposed. The offline Simon's algorithm is a variant of GMS where the quantum state the attacker wants to evaluate is prepared at the beginning of the algorithm. The authors showed that the offline Simon's algorithm can recover the keys of 1-round 2-key EM with $O(N^{1/3} \log N)$ time complexity and $O(\log N)$ quantum memory.

1.1   Motivation

As mentioned above, the quantum security of EM has been intensively studied. On the other hand, for IEM schemes, although several studies on the quantum security are conducted [3,7,16,24], it is insufficient because of the large number of variants. Specifically, for the 4-round IEM with two keys (i.e., $2n$-bit secret key), which was analyzed classically by Dinur et al. [10], the efficient key recovery attacks using quantum algorithms have not been proposed, despite the fact that the similar construction is used as the basis of several block ciphers such as LED-128 [15] PRINCE v2 [4] and QARMA v2 [1]. Thus, in this paper, we analyze the quantum key recovery security of this construction. For simplicity, we refer to this IEM cipher as 4-IEM in the rest of the paper. We will briefly describe the construction of 4-IEM in Sect. 2.1.

1.2   Our Contribution

Our aim in this paper is to analyze the security of 4-IEM, which uses four permutations P_1, P_2, P_3, P_4 and the $2n$-bit master key $K = K_0 \| K_1$ with the alternating key schedule. In the rest of the paper, we denote the classical and quantum data complexities and the classical and quantum time complexities as D_C, D_Q, T_C, and T_Q, respectively. Here, the quantum data complexity D_Q indicates the number of quantum queries.

In this paper, we propose efficient quantum attacks on 4-IEM. One of our attacks is based on the offline Simon's algorithm [2], a quantum search algorithm that employs Simon's algorithm as a subroutine. We show that the conditional periodic function can be constructed by exploiting the construction of 4-IEM. Since this function has a period that becomes the true value of one of the secret keys under the condition that the guess of another key value is correct, we can search two keys by using the offline Simon's algorithm [2] with quantum queries. As a result, we show that two keys of 4-IEM can be identified with the complexity of $T_Q = \sqrt{N} \log N$ and $D_Q = \log N$. Moreover, we show that this attack can be converted to the quantum attack in the Q1 model under the assumption that the attacker can make a superposition of all possible plaintext and ciphertext pairs by only classical queries, *i.e.*, the attacker can have the full codebook. Although this requires $D_C = N$ classical queries and matches the quantum time complexity of Grover's search, some advantages might be gained in some settings since the number of quantum computations can be reduced. We also show the application of the offline Simon's algorithm based attack to LED-128 [15].

Furthermore, we also propose a quantum adaptation of the multibridge attack presented in [10] dubbed the quantum multibridge attack to 4-IEM in the Q1 model. We show how to incorporate quantum computations to enhance the efficiency of the classical multibridge attack. As a result, we show that the quantum multibridge attack can achieve the complexity of $T_Q = N$ even if $D_C = 1$, and the time complexity is independent of the data complexity, while the classical one requires $D_C = N$ data to achieve $T_C = N$. This complexity matches Grover's search. However, considering the depth of quantum circuits, the time complexity of the quantum multibridge attack becomes $T_Q = N/2$ when we consider the complexity of Grover's search as $T_Q = N$, since the quantum multibridge attack requires only $O(1)$ evaluations for full-round encryptions. Table 1 summarizes the results of our study.

Paper Organization. The rest of the paper is structured as follows: Sect. 2 briefly describes 4-IEM, basis of quantum computation and algorithms, and the previous

Table 1. Comparison of the optimal complexities. (The time quantum complexity of the quantum multibridge attack is relative to Grover's algorithm when considering the depth of the quantum circuit.)

Method	Setting	Classical Data (D_C)	Classical Time (T_C)	Quantum Data (D_Q)	Quantum Time (T_Q)	Trade-off	Reference
Multibridge	Classical	N	N	-	-	$DT = N^2$	[10]
Grover (Generic)	Q1/Q2	1	-	-	N	-	[14]
Offline Simon's	Q2	-	-	$\log N$	$\sqrt{N}\log N$	-	Sect. 3
Offline Simon's with full codebook	Q1	N	N	-	$\sqrt{N}\log N$	-	Sect. 3
Quantum Multibridge	Q1	1	-	-	$N/2$	-	Sect. 4

attack against 4-IEM. In Sect. 3, we show a quantum attack on 4-IEM using the offline Simon's algorithm. In Sect. 4, we propose the quantum multibridge attack. After that, we conclude the paper in Sect. 5.

2   Preliminaries

2.1   Iterated Even-Mansour Schemes with Two Keys

In this paper, we focus on the 4-IEM cipher that uses two independent n-bit keys K_0 and K_1, i.e., a $2n$-bit master key $\mathsf{K} = \mathsf{K}_0||\mathsf{K}_1$. The two keys K_0 and K_1 are XOR-ed alternately as shown in Fig. 1.

$$E_\mathsf{K}(x) = P_4(P_3(P_2(P_1(x \oplus \mathsf{K}_0) \oplus \mathsf{K}_1) \oplus \mathsf{K}_0) \oplus \mathsf{K}_1) \oplus \mathsf{K}_0.$$

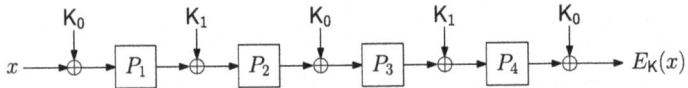

Fig. 1. 4-round IEM with alternating two keys (4-IEM)

This type of key schedule is used for some block cipher instances, such as LED-128, PRINCE v2 and QARMA v2.

2.2   Basis of Quantum Computation

We assume that the readers have some basic knowledge of quantum computation. For more details, see [21]. In the following, we will give brief explanations about quantum adversary models, some quantum algorithms, and qRAM.

Quantum Adversary Models. Quantum attacks are performed by an attacker who possesses a quantum computer and utilizes quantum computation. In [23], Zhandry shows that there are two quantum adversary models, depending on the capabilities of the adversary.

Q1 model The adversary can perform offline quantum computation and online classical queries.

Q2 model The adversary can perform offline quantum computation and quantum superposition queries.

The Q1 model is considered more realistic than the Q2 model. Despite their lack of apparent practicality, attacks obtained in the Q2 model are of particular interest as they are powerful attacks, often with very low cost.

Quantum Amplitude Amplification (QAA). Quantum amplitude amplification (QAA) was introduced by Brassard, Høyer and Tapp [5], which will be used in the attacks described in this paper. QAA is a quantum search algorithm, and it can be viewed as a generalized version of Grover's algorithm [14].

Theorem 1 ([5]). *Let* $\chi : \{0,1\}^n \to \{0,1\}$ *be a boolean function, and* $G = \{x|\chi(x) = 1\}$ *be a set of good elements and* $B = \{x|\chi(x) = 0\}$ *be a set of bad elements. Assume* $\mathcal{A}$ *is a quantum algorithm on* n *qubits, without measurement, that applied to an initial zero state produces the superposition:* $\mathcal{A}|0\rangle = \sum_{x \in G} \alpha_x |x\rangle + \sum_{y \in B} \alpha_y |y\rangle$. *Let* $a = \sum_{x \in G} |\alpha_x|^2 > 0$ *be the probability of obtaining a good element* x *if we measure* $\mathcal{A}|0\rangle$. *Furthermore, let the unitary operators* $\mathcal{S}_\chi$ *and* $\mathcal{S}_0$ *be defined as follows:*

$$\mathcal{S}_\chi : |x\rangle \mapsto \begin{cases} -|x\rangle & \text{if } x \in G \\ |x\rangle & \text{if } x \in B \end{cases}, \mathcal{S}_0 : |x\rangle \mapsto \begin{cases} -|x\rangle & \text{if } x = 0 \\ |x\rangle & \text{otherwise} \end{cases}$$

Define $\mathbf{Q} = -\mathcal{A}\mathcal{S}_0\mathcal{A}^{-1}\mathcal{S}_\chi$ *and set* $m = \lfloor \frac{\pi}{4\theta_a} \rfloor$, *where* $\theta_a \in [0, \pi/2]$ *is the constant defined by* $\sin^2 \theta_a = a$. *Then, if we compute* $\mathbf{Q}^m \mathcal{A}|0\rangle$ *and measure the system, the result is a good element with probability at least* $\max(1 - a, a)$.

We represent the operation $\mathbf{Q} = -\mathcal{A}\mathcal{S}_0\mathcal{A}^{-1}\mathcal{S}_\chi$ in two phases. The algorithm $\mathcal{A}$ is called the SETUP phase, and $\mathcal{S}_\chi$ is called the FLIP phase. Thus, the whole procedure is denoted as

$$\text{QAA(SETUP, FLIP)} = \text{QAA}(\mathcal{A}, \mathcal{S}_\chi),$$

which is equivalent to $\mathbf{Q}^m \mathcal{A}$. Grover's algorithm is the special case when $H^{\otimes n}$ is used as $\mathcal{A}$. In this paper, whenever we use QAA, we give a proper description of the SETUP and FLIP phases. Besides, we set the iteration number m to $1/\sqrt{a}$ where a good element can be measured with an overwhelming probability.

Simon's Algorithm. Simon's algorithm [22] is a quantum algorithm for finding hidden Boolean period in a function. Simon's algorithm aims to solve the following problem.

Problem 1. Given a function $f : \{0,1\}^n \mapsto \{0,1\}^n$, find $S \in \{0,1\}^n \setminus \{0\}^n$ such that $f(x) = f(x \oplus S)$.

Simon's algorithm finds S in $O(\log N)$, where solving this problem with classical oracle access to f requires $N^{1/2}$ queries to f.

For several cryptographic constructions, Simon's algorithm may obtain the secret key directly as the period S or obtain effective secret information for attacks.

The subroutine for Simon's algorithm is as follows:

1. Prepare $n+1$ qubits. Consider the first n qubits as the first register and the last 1 qubit as the second register: $|0\rangle^{\otimes n}|0\rangle$
2. Apply $H^{\otimes n}$ to the first register: $\sum_{x \in \{0,1\}^n} |x\rangle|0\rangle$
3. Make a quantum query to f: $\sum_{x \in \{0,1\}^n} |x\rangle|f(x)\rangle$
4. Measure the second register and the state of the second register is collapsed to a constant a: $\sum_{x \in \{0,1\}^n | f(x) = a} |x\rangle|a\rangle$
5. Apply H to the first register: $\sum_{y \in \{0,1\}^n} \sum_{x \in \{0,1\}^n | f(x) = a} (-1)^{x \cdot y}|y\rangle|a\rangle$
6. Measure the first register to get a value of y.

We omitted the normalized values of superpositions for simplicity. We repeat the subroutine above $O(\log N)$ times to get a set of values $Y = \{y : y \cdot S = 0\}$. By using the set, we can find S from this Y if the system Y is not full rank.

Grover-Meets-Simon. Grover-Meets-Simon (GMS) algorithm [20], was proposed as a combination of Grover algorithm and Simon algorithm. The core idea of GMS is to check periodic property as a condition inside Grover algorithm. This was proposed to analyze FX schemes in the Q2 model. FX schemes [17,18] are defined as $\mathsf{FX}_{\mathsf{K},\mathsf{K}_{in},\mathsf{K}_{out}}(x) = E_{\mathsf{K}}(x \oplus \mathsf{K}_{in}) \oplus \mathsf{K}_{out}$ where E_{K} is a secure block cipher. GMS consists of an outer loop of Grover's algorithm and an inner subroutine of Simon's algorithm. We describe the core algorithm with the following function:

$$f(\mathsf{K}, x) = \mathsf{FX}_{\mathsf{K},\mathsf{K}_{in},\mathsf{K}_{out}(x)} \oplus E_{\mathsf{K}}(x) = E_{\mathsf{K}}(x \oplus \mathsf{K}_{in}) \oplus \mathsf{K}_{out} \oplus E_{\mathsf{K}}(x)$$

Note that, only if K is the correct key, $f(\mathsf{K}, \cdot)$ is periodic as $f(\mathsf{K}, x) = f(\mathsf{K}, x \oplus \mathsf{K}_{in})$ with period K_{in}. Thus, one can use Grover search over K with the periodicity of $f(\mathsf{K}, \cdot)$ as a testing condition inside Grover iteration.

The Offline Simon's Algorithm. The offline Simon's algorithm [2] is a variant of the GMS. Unlike GMS, we first make a superposition as a database by making queries of the target constructions. In the superposition, all the possible inputs and corresponding outputs of the target algorithm are included. The superposition can also be created from offline queries, and it allows for the elimination of superposition queries. Thus, the offline Simon's algorithm can be used also in the $Q1$ model.

qRAM. The quantum random access memory (qRAM) is a quantum operator that represents the behavior of classical RAM. Assume that there is a data array $\{x_1, x_2 \cdots x_M\}$, where M is the number of elements. Then, the qRAM is an efficient implementation achieving the following unitary:

$$|i\rangle|y\rangle \rightarrow |i\rangle|y \oplus x_i\rangle$$

where x_i is an element stored in the position of address i in qRAM. We define this operation as qRAM Read. This operation can be performed with a superposition of all addresses.

2.3 Multibridge Attack

Dinur *et al.* [10] proposed the multibridge attack on 4-IEM cipher and showed that the master key of this cipher can be recovered with the complexity of $D_C = T_C = N$. Similar to the dissection technique, this method dissects the cipher into four parts that are processed separately. However, unlike dissection, the parts are not sequential but instead nested. After that, like the splice-and-cut technique, it connects or bridges two outer parts and two inner parts based on the intermediate encryption values of the cipher. Finally, the attack exploits a self-similarity property of the cipher to connect another pair of intermediate encryption values using another bridge. In the multibridge attack, the attacker assumed that the relation shown in Fig. 2 holds for a fixed constant Δ. The attack works as follows:

1. At first, query D_C plaintexts x to the encryption oracle E_{K} and compute $d(x) = x \oplus E_{\mathsf{K}}(x)$. For each x, store $(d(x), x)$ in a table L_1.
2. For each of the N/D_C arbitrary values of Δ:
   (a) Let the value after P_1 be α. For each of the N possible values of α:
      i. Assume that the value before P_4 is $\alpha \oplus \Delta$. Compute $P_1^{-1}(\alpha) \oplus P_4(\alpha \oplus \Delta)$ and search for matches with this values of $d(x)$ in L_1 (This is the first *bridge*, denoted in red in Fig. 2 that connects intermediate values, after P_1 and before P_4, respectively).
      ii. For each match, obtain x_j and compute $\hat{\mathsf{K}}_0 = x_j \oplus P_1^{-1}(\alpha)$ as a possible value of K_0 and store $\hat{\mathsf{K}}_0$ in L_2, next to α.
   (b) Let the value before P_2 be β. For each of the N possible values of β:
      i. From the self-similarity of the cipher, the value after P_3 is $\beta \oplus \Delta$. Compute $\hat{\mathsf{K}}_0 = P_2(\beta) \oplus P_3^{-1}(\beta \oplus \Delta)$ and search for matches in L_2 (This is the second *bridge*, denoted in blue in Fig. 2 that connects intermediate values, before P_2 and after P_3, respectively).
      ii. For each match, obtain α and calculate $\hat{\mathsf{K}}_1 = \alpha \oplus \beta$ as a possible value of K_1.
      iii. Test the suggested key pair $(\hat{\mathsf{K}}_0, \hat{\mathsf{K}}_1)$ by trial encryptions, and if it succeeds, return it.

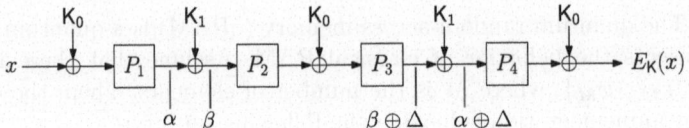

Fig. 2. Multibridge attack on 4-IEM

In this attack, the attacker tries to independently guess K_0 and K_1 for N/D_C constants Δ. Each key is guessed from an intermediate value which takes N possible values. Thus, the data complexity of the attack is D_C and the time complexity of attack is $T_C = (N/D_C)(N + N) \approx N^2/D_C$. The complexity is optimal when $D_C = T_C = N$.

3   Quantum Key Recovery Attack on 4-IEM

In this section, we introduce a quantum key recovery attack on 4-IEM that leverages the offline Simon's algorithm. This algorithm can be utilized within the Q1 model for certain cryptographic constructions, as it enables the elimination of quantum queries in Grover-Meets-Simon (GMS) algorithm by utilizing a superposition created through offline queries. However, for our initial attack on 4-IEM, we are unable to reduce the number of queries below N. Consequently, we primarily focus on the scenario where the attacker generates the initial superposition via quantum queries, referred to as the Q2 model. We employ the offline Simon's algorithm in our attack, ensuring its applicability within the Q1 model, as will be demonstrated later in this section.

For our first attack, consider the following two functions F and G constructed from 4-IEM encryption and internal permutations and their inverses as

$$F : \{0,1\}^n \times \{0,1\}^n \to \{0,1\}^n, F(\kappa, x) = P_3(P_2(x) \oplus \kappa),$$
$$G : \{0,1\}^n \times \{0,1\}^n \to \{0,1\}^n, G(\kappa, x) = P_4^{-1}(E_K(P_1^{-1}(x) \oplus \kappa) \oplus \kappa).$$

G includes an offline computation of E_K. Furthermore, for simplicity we write $F(\kappa, \cdot) = f_\kappa(\cdot)$ and $G(\kappa, \cdot) = g_\kappa(\cdot)$ in the parametrized form with respect to the parameter $\kappa \in \{0,1\}^n$. Note that, when $\kappa = K_0$, $i.e.$, κ is a right value, we can rewrite g_{K_0} as

$$\begin{aligned} g_{K_0}(x) &= P_4^{-1}(E_K(P_1^{-1}(x) \oplus K_0) \oplus K_0) \\ &= P_4^{-1}(P_4(P_3(P_2(P_1(P_1^{-1}(x) \oplus K_0 \oplus K_0) \oplus K_1) \oplus K_0) \oplus K_1) \oplus K_0 \oplus K_0) \\ &= P_3(P_2(x \oplus K_1) \oplus K_0) \oplus K_1 \end{aligned}$$

Thus, if we set $\kappa = K_0$, we get

$$f_{K_0}(x) \oplus g_{K_0}(x) = P_3(P_2(x) \oplus K_0) \oplus P_3(P_2(x \oplus K_1) \oplus K_0) \oplus K_1.$$

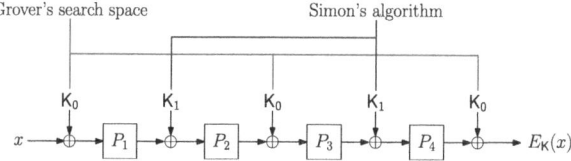

Fig. 3. Application of GMS to 4-IEM

This implies that, for the correct value of $\kappa = \mathsf{K}_0$, $(F \oplus G)(\mathsf{K}_0, x) = f_{\mathsf{K}_0} \oplus g_{\mathsf{K}_0}(x)$ is a periodic function with period K_1. Thus, we can apply Grover-meets-Simon(GMS) [20] or the offline Simon's algorithm [2] as shown in Fig. 3.

In our algorithm, the attacker is required to query both of the plaintexts and K_0 because the starting point of this algorithm is the value after P_1. In the Q2 model, the attacker is assumed to perform quantum queries. Therefore, the attacker can query to the plaintexts space and K_0 space. The attack procedure is as follows:

1. For a small constant $c\,(\geq 1)$, we start from the following superposition:

$$\overset{cn}{\bigotimes}\left(\sum_{x\in\{0,1\}^n}|x\rangle|g_\kappa(x)\rangle\right)\otimes\sum_{\kappa\in\{0,1\}^n}|\kappa\rangle$$

2. Using cn superposition queries to f, the following superposition state can be obtained:

$$\overset{cn}{\bigotimes}\left(\sum_{x\in\{0,1\}^n}|x\rangle|f_\kappa \oplus g_\kappa(x)\rangle\right)\otimes\sum_{\kappa\in\{0,1\}^n}|\kappa\rangle$$

3. After applying $(H^{\otimes n}\otimes I_n)^{cn}$, we have:

$$\left(\sum_{x_1,u_1}(-1)^{u_1\cdot x_1}|u_1\rangle|(f_\kappa \oplus g_\kappa)(x_1)\rangle\right)\otimes\cdots\otimes\left(\sum_{x_{cn},u_{cn}}(-1)^{u_{cn}\cdot x_{cn}}|u_{cn}\rangle|(f_\kappa \oplus g_\kappa)(x_{cn})\rangle\right)$$

$$\otimes\sum_{\kappa\in\{0,1\}^n}|\kappa\rangle.$$

4. Define the following Boolean function H_{GMS} and a FLIP operator $\mathcal{S}_{H_{GMS}}$ over the domain of κ:

$$H_{GMS}(\kappa)=\begin{cases}1, & \text{if } f_\kappa \oplus g_\kappa \text{ is periodic}\\0, & \text{otherwise}\end{cases}\quad,\mathcal{S}_{H_{GMS}}:|\kappa\rangle=\begin{cases}-|\kappa\rangle, & \text{if } H_{GMS}(\kappa)=1\\|\kappa\rangle, & \text{if } H_{GMS}(\kappa)=0.\end{cases}$$

The quantum subroutine of H_{GMS} performs Simon's algorithm to check if $(f_\kappa \oplus g_\kappa)$ is periodic or not. In H_{GMS}, the dimension d of the vector space spanned by $u_1,\ldots,u_{cn}$ is computed.
If $d < n$, $f_\kappa \oplus g_\kappa$ is periodic for the input κ and H_{GMS} returns 1, otherwise $f_\kappa \oplus g_\kappa$ is not periodic for the input and $H_{GMS}(\kappa)$ returns 0. The FLIP operator $\mathcal{S}_{H_{GMS}}$ flips the phase if $H_{GMS} = 1$. After constructing this function, amplify the amplitude of $|\kappa\rangle$ such that $f_\kappa \oplus g_\kappa$ is periodic.

5. After identifying the K_0, fix $\kappa = K_0$ and apply single Simon's algorithm to $f_{K_0} \oplus g_{K_0}$. As K_0 is assumed to be known in this step, the simple application of Simon's algorithm can identify K_1.

Complexity Analysis. This quantum attack starts with making a superposition cn of all possible plaintext and ciphertext pairs. Here, we assume that the superposition is created by quantum queries. Therefore, the (quantum) data complexity is $D_Q = \log N$. The time complexity corresponds to the cost for quantum computation of the offline Simon's algorithm. Thus, the offline quantum computation for identifying K_0 and K_1 takes the time complexity of $T_Q = \sqrt{N} \log N$.

The Q1 Attack with Full Codebook

Now we discuss an attack on 4-IEM in the Q1 model. As we use the offline Simon's algorithm, we start the algorithm by creating a superposition of all possible plaintexts and ciphertexts. If the attacker can collect all possible plaintexts and ciphertexts by classical queries, the quantum attack without quantum queries is also possible. In this setting, the attacker first creates a superposition over N plaintext and ciphertexts pairs by only classical queries. We use the method proposed in [2] to create the superposition. The procedure is as follows:

1. Start with two n qubit registers: $|0\rangle^{\otimes n}|0\rangle^{\otimes n}$.
2. Apply $H^{\otimes}$ to the first register: $\sum_{x \in \{0,1\}^n} |x\rangle|0\rangle$.
3. For each $y \in \{0,1\}^n$, query y to E_K classically. Write $E_K(y)$ in the second register if the first contains the value y: $\sum_{x \in \{0,1\}^n} |x\rangle|E_K(x)\rangle$.

The output superposition can be viewed as a quantum keyed oracle, but it exists offline. Therefore, if the attacker can construct this superposition, s.he executes the quantum attack based on the offline Simon's algorithm without superposition queries. In this setting, N classical queries are required in the online phase. On the other hand, the time complexity is the same as the Q2 model, *i.e.*, $T_Q = \sqrt{N} \log N$.

In [12], the authors assumed that quantum computers require a lot of execution of error corrections, which degrades the performance. Under the assumption of [12], modern classical computers are faster per operation than quantum computers. Therefore, we can say that N times classical queries are faster than N times Grover's iterations following the assumption. Thus, in this setting, our quantum attack based on the offline Simon's algorithm may outperform Grover's search.

Application to LED-128

LED-128 is a variant of a lightweight block cipher family LED [15], which takes a 64-bit plaintext and a 128-bit secret key as the input. LED-128 employs the IEM with two alternating keys as the underlying construction. LED-128 iterates the *step*, which consists of XORing half of the secret key and application of the public permutation consisting of the 4-round AES-like round function. The full LED-128 has total 12 steps.

The best know attack in classical setting against the LED-128 is the application of the attack against the 3-round IEM proposed in [9], which can attack up to 8-step LED-128. However, for the 4-step LED-128, Dinur et al. show that direct application of the multibridge attack is the most efficient attack in the classical setting with the complexity $D_C = T_C = 2^{64}$.

Our quantum attack can be applied to attack on 4-step LED-128 directly. Our attack in the Q2 model requires $T_Q = \sqrt{N} \log N$ with $D_Q = \log N$ quantum data. Thus, applying this attack to 4-round LED-128 requires $T_Q = 2^{32} \cdot 2^6 = 2^{38}$ with $D_Q = 64 = 2^6$ quantum data. In the Q1 model, considering that the attacker has a full codebook, the data complexity becomes $D_C = 2^{64}$ and time complexity remain the same, i.e., $T_Q = 2^{32} \cdot 2^6 = 2^{38}$.

4   The Quantum Multibridge Attack

In this section, we propose the quantum multibridge attack, which can be applied to recover two keys of 4-IEM without quantum queries. In this attack, we first make D_C classical queries to get QAA to find two intermediate values and a constant, which forms a bridge between them. The procedure of our attack is as follows:

1. Make offline queries of D_C plaintexts and create a list of queried data and the values calculated from the response and store the list in a qRAM.
2. Amplify N/D_C possible values of Δ
   (a) Create a superposition over D_C candidates for K_0 based on the list created in the first step.
   (b) Create a superposition over D_C candidates of key pair (K_0, K_1) based on the list of candidates for K_0.
   (c) Run a quantum search algorithm to identify a right key pair (K_0, K_1).
   (d) Test (K_0, K_1) by a trial encryption.

The first step is in the online phase, and the other steps are offline. In the following, we explain the detailed procedure of our attack.

The Attack Procedure. Similarly to the original multibridge attack, our attack begins by initializing variables, as depicted in Fig. 2. The *online* phase involves querying plaintexts x and obtaining their corresponding ciphertexts $E_K(x)$. By calculating $d(x) = x \oplus E_K(x)$ for each plaintext, we prepare a list L such that $L(d(x)) = (d(x), x)$ and store it in the qRAM, where x is a plaintext indexed by $d(x)$. In the offline phase, we search Δ from N/D_C possible values by using QAA in the actual algorithm. However, for simplicity, we describe the procedure of the offline phase for a fixed Δ. The procedure of the offline phase of the quantum multibridge attack under a fixed Δ is as follows:

1. Iterate the following procedure D_C times:
    (a) we apply the first QAA, namely $\mathcal{F}_1 = \mathsf{QAA}(\mathcal{A}_1, \mathcal{S}_1)$.
        i. The SETUP phase $\mathcal{A}_1 = H^{\otimes n}$. In other words, this is Grover's algorithm.
        ii. To define the FLIP phase $\mathcal{S}_1$, we consider the function f, defined over all possible values of $\alpha \in \{0,1\}^n$ as $f_\Delta(\alpha) = P_1^{-1}(\alpha) \oplus P_4(\alpha \oplus \Delta)$. Furthermore, we define the following Boolean function based on f:

$$F_\Delta(\alpha) = \begin{cases} 1 & \text{if } f_\Delta(\alpha) \text{ has a match in } L \\ 0 & \text{otherwise.} \end{cases}$$

In other words, F_Δ validates if there is a x such that $f_\Delta(\alpha) = d(x)$ and $(d(x), x) \in L$, as shown in Fig. 4.

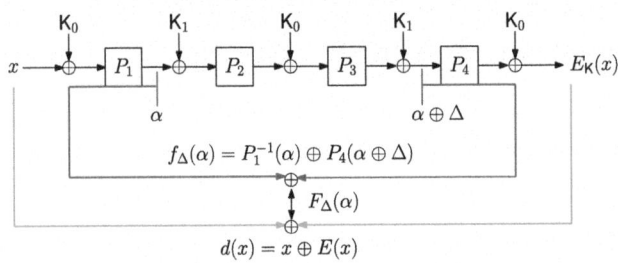

Fig. 4. Validation of **STEP 1**

The FLIP phase consists of the unitary $\mathcal{S}_1 = \mathcal{S}_{F_\Delta}$ which flips the phase of $|\alpha\rangle$ if $F_\Delta(\alpha) = 1$. Note that, $\mathcal{S}_{F_\Delta}$ can be implemented with two calls to O_{F_Δ}, which is a quantum offline circuit for computing F_Δ. We start with a superposition of

$$|\psi_0\rangle = \sum_{\alpha \in \{0,1\}^n} |\alpha\rangle.$$

Run QAA where $\mathcal{Q} = -\mathcal{A}_1 \mathcal{S}_0 \mathcal{A}_1^{-1} \mathcal{S}_1$ Then, we have

$$|\psi_0\rangle \xrightarrow{\mathsf{QAA}} |\psi_1\rangle = \sum_{\alpha \in \{0,1\}^n | F_\Delta(\alpha)=1} |\alpha\rangle.$$

    (b) In this step, apply qRAM Read to $|\psi_1\rangle$ to create a superposition of all possible K_0. We read values of x indexed by $d(x) = f_\Delta(\alpha)$ from L. The operation is as follows:

$$|\psi_1\rangle \xrightarrow{\text{Compute } f_\Delta(\alpha) \text{ and } P_1^{-1}(\alpha)} \sum_{\alpha \in \{0,1\}^n | F_\Delta(\alpha)=1} |\alpha\rangle |f_\Delta(\alpha)\rangle |P_1^{-1}(\alpha)\rangle$$

$$\xrightarrow{\text{qRAM Read}} \sum_{\alpha \in \{0,1\}^n | F_\Delta(\alpha)=1} |\alpha\rangle |f_\Delta(\alpha) = d(x)\rangle |P_1^{-1}(\alpha) \oplus x\rangle$$

Measure α and $P_1^{-1}(\alpha) \oplus x$ and store them next to the corresponding $d(x)$ in L.
2. Now we apply another QAA, namely $\mathcal{F}_2 = \mathsf{QAA}(\mathcal{A}_2, \mathcal{S}_2)$.
   (a) We start with the description of $\mathcal{A}_2$. The algorithm $\mathcal{A}_2$ is $\mathcal{A}_2 = \mathsf{QAA}(\mathcal{A}_3, \mathcal{S}_3)$ where $\mathcal{A}_3$ is $H^{\otimes n}$. To define $\mathcal{S}_3$, consider the function $g_\Delta(\beta) = P_2(\beta) \oplus P_3^{-1}(\beta \oplus \Delta)$ defined over all possible values of $\beta \in \{0,1\}^n$ and corresponding Boolean function:

$$G_\Delta(\beta) = \begin{cases} 1, & \text{if there is } P_1^{-1}(\alpha) \oplus x \in L \text{ s.t. } g_\Delta(\beta) = P_1^{-1}(\alpha) \oplus x \\ 0, & \text{otherwise .} \end{cases}$$

Thus, $G_\Delta(\beta) = 1$ if and only if there is $P_1^{-1}(\alpha) \oplus x$ such that $P_1^{-1}(\alpha) \oplus x = g_\Delta(\beta)$, as shown in Fig. 5, which is exactly the multibridge property we need.

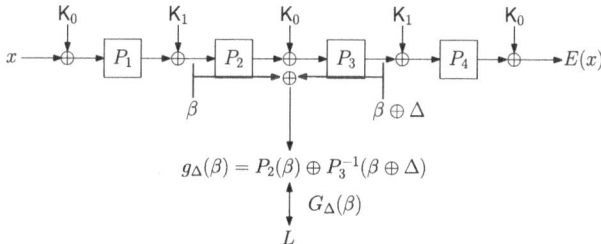

Fig. 5. Validation of **STEP 2**

Thus, the FLIP phase consists of the unitary $\mathcal{S}_3 = \mathcal{S}_{G_\Delta}$ which flips the phase of $|\beta\rangle$ if $G_\Delta(\beta) = 1$. Note that, $\mathcal{S}_{G_\Delta}$ can be implemented with two calls to O_{G_Δ}, which is a quantum offline circuit for computing G_Δ. We start with the following initial state:

$$|\psi_2\rangle = \sum_{\beta \in \{0,1\}^n} |\beta\rangle.$$

We run QAA with $\mathbf{Q} = -\mathcal{A}_3 \mathcal{S}_0 \mathcal{A}_3^{-1} \mathcal{S}_3$ and we have:

$$|\psi_2\rangle \xrightarrow{\mathsf{QAA}} \sum_{\beta \in \{0,1\}^n | G_\Delta(\beta)=1} |\beta\rangle$$

By computing $|g_\Delta(\beta)\rangle$ and reading the values of α such that stored with $P_1^{-1}(\alpha) \oplus x$ where $|g_\Delta(\beta)\rangle = P_1^{-1}(\alpha) \oplus x$, from L, we can obtain the following superposition.

$$|\psi_3\rangle = \sum_{\{\alpha \in \{0,1\}^n | F_\Delta(\alpha)=1\}} \sum_{\{\beta \in \{0,1\}^n | G_\Delta(\beta)=1\}} |g_\Delta(\beta)\rangle |\alpha \oplus \beta\rangle.$$

Let $\mathcal{K}$ be a set that contains all key pairs generated from a pair of (α, β) for a Δ. Then, $|\psi_3\rangle$ can be expressed as

$$|\psi_3\rangle = \sum_{\hat{K}_0||\hat{K}_1 \in \mathcal{K}} |\hat{K}_0\rangle|\hat{K}_1\rangle = \sum_{\hat{K}=\hat{K}_0||\hat{K}_1 \in \mathcal{K}} |\hat{K}\rangle$$

where $\hat{K}_0$ and $\hat{K}_1$ are the candidates for K_0 and K_1, respectively.

(b) Finally, we define $\mathcal{S}_2$. This operator simply flips the phase of $|\hat{K}\rangle$ if $\hat{K}$ is a valid key and we check this by trial encryptions over a small set of plaintext-ciphertext pairs $\mathcal{M} = \{(m_i, c_i)|0 \leq i < s\}$, where s is a small constant[1]. Define the following Boolean function:

$$H_\Delta(\hat{K}) = \begin{cases} 1 & \text{if } E_K(m_i) = c_i, \forall(m_i, c_i) \in \mathcal{M} \\ 0 & \text{otherwise.} \end{cases}$$

E_K is the quantum circuit of 4-IEM which uses $K = \hat{K}_0||\hat{K}_1$ as the secret key. Note that, with a guessed key pair, it is possible to prepare such a circuit offline. Now define a unitary operator $\mathcal{S}_3 = \mathcal{S}_H$ which flips the sign if $H_\Delta(\hat{K}) = 1$.

Thus, we run QAA with $\mathbf{Q} = -\mathcal{A}_2 \mathcal{S}_0 \mathcal{A}_2^{-1} \mathcal{S}_3$ with initial state $|\psi_3\rangle$ and perform a final measuring of the whole state.

Complexity Analysis

The online phase requires D_C online classical queries and D_C simple computations to compute $d(x)$. In the following, we analyze the complexity of each offline steps.

STEP 1. This is an offline phase. In this step we apply $\mathcal{F}_1 = \text{QAA}(\mathcal{A}_1, \mathcal{S}_1)$ which is a simple Grover's algorithm for creating a superposition state of D_C solutions from a uniform superposition state. Since, there are D_C numbers of α such that $x_{f_\Delta(\alpha)} \in L$, the superposition after applying $\mathcal{S}_1 = \mathcal{S}_{F_\Delta}$ is as follows:

$$\mathcal{S}_1|\psi_0\rangle = \sqrt{(N - D_C)/N} \sum_{\substack{\alpha \in \{0,1\}^n \\ |F_\Delta(\alpha)=0}} |\alpha\rangle - \sqrt{D_C/N} \sum_{\substack{\alpha \in \{0,1\}^n \\ |F_\Delta(\alpha)=1}} |\alpha\rangle$$

Therefore, the number of iterations is $\sqrt{N/D_C}$. We iterate this QAA operation D_C times to store all D_C solutions to L. Thus, the complexity of this step is $\sqrt{N/D_C} \times D_C = \sqrt{ND_C}$.

---

[1] In [13], this number is sufficient if it satisfies $s > \lceil 2k/n \rceil$, where k is the secret key size. Thus, it is small enough that it does not affect the time complexity.

STEP 2. Similar to the **STEP 1**, the SETUP phase of $\mathcal{F}_2 = \mathsf{QAA}(\mathcal{A}_2, \mathcal{S}_2)$, namely $\mathcal{A}_2$ is a simple Grover's algorithm for creating a superposition state of D_C solutions from a uniform superposition state. Since, there are D_C numbers of β such that $G_\Delta(\beta) = 1$, application of $\mathcal{S}_3 = \mathcal{S}_{G_\Delta}$ is as follows:

$$S_3|\psi_2\rangle = \sqrt{(N - D_C)/N} \sum_{\substack{\beta \in \{0,1\}^n \\ |G_\Delta(\beta)=0}} |\beta\rangle - \sqrt{D_C/N} \sum_{\substack{\beta \in \{0,1\}^n \\ |G_\Delta(\beta)=1}} |\beta\rangle$$

Thus, the number of iterations is $\sqrt{N/D_C}$, which is the complexity of the SETUP phase of $\mathcal{F}_2$. Finally, in the FLIP phase, if we apply $\mathcal{S}_2 = \mathcal{S}_H$ to $|\psi_3\rangle$, then the superposition state is as follows:

$$S_2|\psi_3\rangle = \sum_{\hat{\mathsf{K}} \in \mathcal{K}} |\hat{\mathsf{K}}\rangle = \sqrt{(D_C - 1)/D_C} \sum_{\hat{\mathsf{K}}|H(\hat{\mathsf{K}})=0} |\hat{\mathsf{K}}\rangle - \sqrt{1/D_C} \sum_{\hat{\mathsf{K}}|H(\hat{\mathsf{K}})=1} |\hat{\mathsf{K}}\rangle$$

As the number of possible key pairs is D, $\mathcal{F}_2$ requires $\sqrt{D}$ iterations. The operations from creating $|\psi_3\rangle$ to identifying a right key pair is a sequential execution of $\mathcal{A}_2$ and $\mathcal{S}_2$. Thus, the cost of this sequence requires $\sqrt{N/D_C} \times \sqrt{D_C} = \sqrt{N}$.

Overall Complexity. We also search for the right value of Δ by QAA. Since the search space of Δ is N/D_C, the search cost is $\sqrt{N/D_C}$. In summary, the overall complexity is as follows:

$$T_Q = D_C + \sqrt{N/D_C}(\sqrt{ND_C} + \sqrt{N}) = D_C + N \approx N$$

The optimal complexity is $T_Q = N$, and the time complexity of the quantum version of the multibridge attack is independent of the amount of data. Therefore, $D_C = 1$ is sufficient and no qRAM is required to achieve the optimal time complexity.

Comparison with Grover's Search. Although this attack does not outperform Grover's search, the quantum multibridge attack does not need exponential times evaluations for full round encryption of 4-IEM. In the quantum multibridge attack, the quantum search operations are executed for quantum oracles consisting of XOR of two permutations. We can assume each execution of these functions takes about $1/4$ of a full round encryption time. Therefore, when we consider the complexity of Grover's search as N, the time complexity of the quantum multibridge attack when $D_C = 1$ becomes:

$$T_Q = 1 + \sqrt{N}(\sqrt{N}/4 + \sqrt{N}/4) \approx N/2.$$

Thus, the multibridge attack slightly outperforms Grover's search when considering the depth of the quantum circuit.

5 Conclusion

In this paper, we propose quantum key recovery attacks against 4-IEM, which was analyzed classically by Dinur *et al.* [10] We show that our attack based on the offline Simon's algorithm is highly efficient when the attacker can make superposition queries, *i.e.*, in the Q2 model. Besides, we show that this attack can be used in the Q1 model, under the assumption that the attacker can create the full codebook using classical queries. Moreover, we propose a quantum version of the multibridge attack [10]. The result shows that the quantum version can achieve $T_Q = N$ even if $D_C = 1$, while the classical one requires $D_C = N$ to achieve the time complexity of $T_C = N$. Furthermore, we show that the quantum multibridge attack slightly more efficient than Grover's search, when considering the depth of the quantum circuit. Specifically, the result shows that the time complexity of the quantum multibridge attack becomes $T_Q = N/2$, when we consider the time complexity of Grover's search as $T_Q = N$.

References

1. Avanzi, R., et al.: The tweakable block cipher family qarmav2. IACR Cryptol. ePrint Arch. 929 (2023)
2. Bonnetain, X., Hosoyamada, A., Naya-Plasencia, M., Sasaki, Yu., Schrottenloher, A.: Quantum attacks without superposition queries: the offline Simon's algorithm. In: Galbraith, S.D., Moriai, S. (eds.) ASIACRYPT 2019. LNCS, vol. 11921, pp. 552–583. Springer, Cham (2019). https://doi.org/10.1007/978-3-030-34578-5_20
3. Bonnetain, X., Schrottenloher, A., Sibleyras, F.: Beyond quadratic speedups in quantum attacks on symmetric schemes. In: Dunkelman, O., Dziembowski, S. (eds.) EUROCRYPT 2022. LNCS, vol. 13277, pp. 315–344. Springer, Cham (2022). https://doi.org/10.1007/978-3-031-07082-2_12
4. Božilov, D., et al.: PRINCEv2. In: Dunkelman, O., Jacobson, Jr., M.J., O'Flynn, C. (eds.) SAC 2020. LNCS, vol. 12804, pp. 483–511. Springer, Cham (2021). https://doi.org/10.1007/978-3-030-81652-0_19
5. Brassard, G., Hoyer, P., Mosca, M., Tapp, A.: Quantum amplitude amplification and estimation. Contemp. Math. **305**, 53–74 (2002)
6. Brassard, G., Hoyer, P., Tapp, A.: Quantum algorithm for the collision problem. arXiv preprint quant-ph/9705002 (1997)
7. Cai, B., Gao, F., Leander, G.: Quantum attacks on two-round even-mansour. Front. Phys. **10**, 1028014 (2022)
8. Chen, S., Steinberger, J.: Tight security bounds for key-alternating ciphers. In: Nguyen, P.Q., Oswald, E. (eds.) EUROCRYPT 2014. LNCS, vol. 8441, pp. 327–350. Springer, Heidelberg (2014). https://doi.org/10.1007/978-3-642-55220-5_19
9. Dinur, I., Dunkelman, O., Keller, N., Shamir, A.: Key recovery attacks on 3-round even-mansour, 8-step LED-128, and full AES². In: Sako, K., Sarkar, P. (eds.) ASIACRYPT 2013. LNCS, vol. 8269, pp. 337–356. Springer, Heidelberg (2013). https://doi.org/10.1007/978-3-642-42033-7_18
10. Dinur, I., Dunkelman, O., Keller, N., Shamir, A.: Cryptanalysis of iterated even-mansour schemes with two keys. In: Sarkar, P., Iwata, T. (eds.) ASIACRYPT 2014. LNCS, vol. 8873, pp. 439–457. Springer, Heidelberg (2014). https://doi.org/10.1007/978-3-662-45611-8_23

11. Even, S., Mansour, Y.: A construction of a cipher from a single pseudorandom permutation. J. Cryptol. **10**(3), 151–162 (1997)
12. Gidney, C., Ekerå, M.: How to factor 2048 bit RSA integers in 8 hours using 20 million noisy qubits. Quantum **5**, 433 (2021)
13. Grassl, M., Langenberg, B., Roetteler, M., Steinwandt, R.: Applying Grover's algorithm to AES: quantum resource estimates. In: Takagi, T. (ed.) PQCrypto 2016. LNCS, vol. 9606, pp. 29–43. Springer, Cham (2016). https://doi.org/10.1007/978-3-319-29360-8_3
14. Grover, L.K.: A fast quantum mechanical algorithm for database search. In: STOC, pp. 212–219. ACM (1996)
15. Guo, J., Peyrin, T., Poschmann, A., Robshaw, M.: The LED block cipher. In: Preneel, B., Takagi, T. (eds.) CHES 2011. LNCS, vol. 6917, pp. 326–341. Springer, Heidelberg (2011). https://doi.org/10.1007/978-3-642-23951-9_22
16. Hosoyamada, A., Aoki, K.: On quantum related-key attacks on iterated even-mansour ciphers. In: Obana, S., Chida, K. (eds.) IWSEC 2017. LNCS, vol. 10418, pp. 3–18. Springer, Cham (2017). https://doi.org/10.1007/978-3-319-64200-0_1
17. Kilian, J., Rogaway, P.: How to protect DES against exhaustive key search. In: Koblitz, N. (ed.) CRYPTO 1996. LNCS, vol. 1109, pp. 252–267. Springer, Heidelberg (1996). https://doi.org/10.1007/3-540-68697-5_20
18. Kilian, J., Rogaway, P.: How to protect des against exhaustive key search (an analysis of DESX). J. Cryptol. **14**, 17–35 (2001)
19. Kuwakado, H., Morii, M.: Security on the quantum-type even-mansour cipher. In: ISITA, pp. 312–316. IEEE (2012)
20. Leander, G., May, A.: Grover meets simon – quantumly attacking the FX-construction. In: Takagi, T., Peyrin, T. (eds.) ASIACRYPT 2017. LNCS, vol. 10625, pp. 161–178. Springer, Cham (2017). https://doi.org/10.1007/978-3-319-70697-9_6
21. Nielsen, M.A., Chuang, I.L.: Quantum Computation and Quantum Information, vol. 2. Cambridge University Press, Cambridge (2001)
22. ch1Simon, D.R.: On the power of quantum computation. In: FOCS, pp. 116–123. IEEE Computer Society (1994)
23. Zhandry, M.: How to construct quantum random functions. In: FOCS, pp. 679–687. IEEE Computer Society (2012)
24. Zhang, P., Luo, Y.: Quantum key recovery attacks on tweakable even-mansour ciphers. Quantum Inf. Process. **22**(9), 336 (2023)

Machine Learning

Optimizing Label-Only Membership Inference Attacks by Global Relative Decision Boundary Distances

Jiacheng Xu[ID], Jianpeng Hu, Chunqing Yu, and Chengxiang Tan[✉]

School of Electronic and Information Engineering, Tongji University, Shanghai, China
{2011263,hujianpeng,chunqingyu,jerrytan}@tongji.edu.cn

Abstract. A sample's distance from the decision boundary is a crucial indicator for predicting whether a given sample is a member of the training set in label-only membership inference attacks. Traditional attacks search for the minimum adversarial point for each sample to obtain the decision boundary distance and use a fixed threshold to determine if it is a member sample. However, during the search process, the randomness of the initial adversarial samples may lead to local optimal traps and, ultimately, to incorrect decision boundary distances. Similarly, a fixed threshold may lead to membership misclassification because there is some overlap in the distribution of decision boundary distances for members and nonmembers. To assess the problem of inaccurate decision boundary distances and misclassification, we propose a novel attack method under the label-only setting called the global adaptive membership inference attack. We propose a new low-dimensional rotational search algorithm to find the globally optimal initial point in the broader decision boundary, thus reducing the instability caused by random initial points. We also propose and employ the relative boundary distance instead of a single decision boundary distance to find an adaptive threshold for each sample. Extensive experiments show that our global adaptive MIA outperforms current label-only membership inference attacks in the CIFAR10 and CIFAR100 datasets, especially for the true positive rate at low false positive rates metric.

Keywords: membership inference · machine learning · decision-based attack

1 Introduction

Machine learning algorithms have been trained on increasingly sensitive or private information such as medical history [12,40], political orientation [2,3], and criminal records [27,36]. However, recent research has shown that trained models can unexpectedly reveal personal information [1,21,29]. As one of the simplest forms of these information leaks, membership inference attacks (MIA) have attracted much attention. For a given sample and a trained target model, MIA

© The Author(s), under exclusive license to Springer Nature Switzerland AG 2025
N. Mouha and N. Nikiforakis (Eds.): ISC 2024, LNCS 15257, pp. 107–126, 2025.
https://doi.org/10.1007/978-3-031-75757-0_6

aims to infer whether it is a member sample involved in model training or a nonmember sample outside the training set. While most MIAs [4,28,38] require the model to output confidence values as a precondition for an attack, more and more research is now focusing on the label-only label MIA [7,9,19], a more realistic MIA that only requires the model predicted labels. The classification robustness to perturbations of each sample has been taken as a new proxy for the confidence value, and the intuition behind this attack is that member samples are more challenging to perturb than nonmember samples [14,30,31]. Unfortunately, while current label-only MIAs perform successfully in highly overfitted models, they fail to work well in more generalized models. The effectiveness of these attacks raises concerns because there are far more well-generalized models than overfitted models in reality.

In this paper, we re-examine the problem of current label-only MIAs, provide a fine-grained analysis of traditional attacks under different overfitting degree models, and explain their successes and failures, respectively. The main reason for the high performance of these attacks under the overfitted model is that they perform much better on misclassified samples than on correctly classified samples. Since the balanced set used for evaluation consists of half members and half nonmembers, many nonmember samples are misclassified under the overfitted model, dramatically increasing the attack performance. The main reason for the low performance of these attacks under the well-generalized model is that they do not accurately measure the sample's robustness and miss the sample's complexity. These attacks utilize decision boundary distances computed by the untargeted HopSkipJump Algorithm (HSJA) to represent the robustness of the samples. However, Vo et al. [33] demonstrated that different initial adversarial images could critically impact the decision boundary distances even given the same source image. Apart from the inaccuracy introduced by the initial image, the diversity of the samples also reduces the attack performance because some nonmembers may also have large decision boundary distances, and it is not easy to distinguish members from nonmembers well with a fixed threshold.

To address the above problems, we propose a novel label-only MIA called global adaptive membership inference attack and introduce a more rational evaluation method. First, we propose the cbalanced set, a balanced set with all samples correctly classified, as the new evaluation set. Second, we present a low-dimensional rotational search algorithm called Ldrsa, which traverses the entire decision boundary to obtain the global optimum decision boundary distance. Under the same evaluation dataset and query costs, our method produces more diminutive and more stable decision boundary distances. Finally, we define and propose the relative decision boundary distance to replace the single decision boundary distance as the new membership score. The membership score represents the likelihood that the sample is a member, and the relative decision boundary distance represents the difference in decision boundary distance before and after the sample participates in model training, equivalent to implementing an adaptive decision boundary distance threshold for each sample.

Abstractly, our contribution can be summarized as follows: (1)We propose a low-dimensional rotational search algorithm called Ldrsa to obtain the global optimum decision boundary distance. (2)We propose an adaptive attack method employing the relative decision boundary distance as the new membership score, accurately distinguishing between members and nonmembers. Extensive experiments demonstrate that our attack method outperforms traditional attacks across different datasets and models.

2   Background: Membership Inference Attack

The essence of MIA is not concerned with the leakage of the specific value of a sample but with the leakage of the membership of a sample, i.e., whether a sample increases the probability of being identified as a member by participating in the model training, similar to differential privacy [11]. Hence, MIA can also be seen as one of the smallest and simplest forms of privacy leakage.

Definition. Given a sample x, a trained machine learning model M, a training dataset D_{train} and some auxiliary information denoted as I, we follow a common definition of membership inference attack [20]: $A(x, M, I) \rightarrow \{0, 1\}$, where A means the membership inference attack, 1 means $x \in D_{train}$ and 0 means $x \notin D_{train}$.

Evaluation. Since the output of MIA is binary, the evaluation of MIA can be summarized as a classical inference game [39], and MIA's performance has been measured with balanced set and average-case metrics in most studies. However, Carlini et al. [4] have argued that average-cases metrics such as the area under curve(AUC) are nonsense at a high error rate and suggested a new metirc called true positive rate(TPR) at a low false positive rate(FPR) instead. Similarly, Jayaraman et al. [15] have noticed that a balanced set consisting of members and nonmembers of the same size is impractical and suggested an imbalanced dataset. In this paper, we take TPR at low FPR and AUC as our evaluation metrics, and we define and propose a cbalanced set for the new evaluation dataset. The cbalanced dataset details are in Sect. 3.1.

Principle. Although the implementations of MIAs vary, they share the same principle of finding a suitable 'proxy' for each sample that can distinguish between members and nonmembers as much as possible. In most cases, such a proxy is closely related to the confidence values of the samples, and the rationale behind this is that member samples generally have lower confidence values than nonmember samples in overfitting models, which is why these methods are also known as score-based MIA. However, confidence values are not as easy to obtain, and defenders can easily mislead score-based attacks by modifying the confidence values [16,22]. Therefore, several researchers proposed the label-only MIA [7,19], whose adversary only has the query access to the model and only requires the predicted label. Similar to the intuition behind score-based MIAs, the intuition behind these label-only MIAs is that members are less susceptible to perturbation than nonmembers. In other words, members have more considerable decision boundary distances than nonmembers. The details of the intuition can be seen in Sect. 3.2.

3   Method

This section introduces a global adaptive MIA that mixes Ldrsa and HSJA to obtain the global optimum decision boundary distance and sets an adaptive membership score threshold for each sample. We start by outlining the threat model and estimation mechanism. Then, we describe the rationale behind our attack and explain its effectiveness. Finally, we go on to the specifics of our attack pipeline and show how it is organized.

3.1   Threat Model And Estimation Mechanism

In this paper, we concentrate on a practical, black-box MIA scenario in which the target model solely outputs the hard label results without providing any confidence score. Furthermore, we suppose that the query cost limits the number of requests an adversary can send. The threat above model complies with the requirements for most label-only MIAs [7,19], while our evaluation procedures differ from the traditional methodology.

Evaluation Dataset. Most label-only MIAs use a balanced dataset as the evaluation dataset, which consists of an equal number of records randomly selected from the training and test sets. However, we believe that this evaluation dataset overestimates the potential membership leakage problem of previous label-only MIAs for two main reasons. On the one hand, traditional attacks perform much better on misclassified samples than on correctly classified samples. On the other hand, the increase in the number of misclassified samples due to model overfitting reinforces the impact of the misclassified sample assessment results on the overall assessment results. Therefore, we propose a new evaluation dataset called the cbalanced dataset that retains the characteristics of the balanced dataset while requiring the same prediction labels for each sample point as the ground truth.

Evaluation Metric. Most label-only MIAs measured the effectiveness of their attacks using average-case metrics like AUC and accuracy. However, Rezaei et al. [26] pointed out that the true positive rate at a false positive rate (TPR at low FPR) metric better indicates actual privacy threats than these metrics because it represents identifying a larger sample of members at a low error rate. Carlini et al. [4] also mentioned that building solutions with low false positive rates was common practice in many computer security domains. Therefore, we used the TPR at low FPR and the ROC curve on a logarithmic scale as new evaluation metrics and retained the AUC metric for completeness of comparison.

3.2   Attack Intuition

We propose our global adaptive MIA based on the following intuitions.

Intuition I. It is well-known that most member samples become correctly labeled and progressively move away from the decision boundary during training. Therefore, our first intuition is that members' average decision boundary distance is usually larger than that of nonmembers. Although this intuition is the same as in previous attacks, our approach to obtaining decision boundary distances is quite different. Compared with the traditional untargeted HSJA algorithm, our proposed Ldrsa algorithm rotates each adversarial point so that it traverses the adversary space, and finally obtains accurate and stable decision boundary distances, as detailed in Sect. 3.3.

Intuition II. Assuming the right to exclude any sample from the training set and then retrain the target model, our second intuition is that the value of the change in the decision boundary distance before and after a member is excluded from the training set is significantly larger than that of a nonmember. For instance, given a sample (x, y), training algorithm Υ, training dataset D_{train}, we first define the trained model $M = \Upsilon(D_{train})$ and the exclusion model $M_{exc} = \Upsilon(D_{train} \setminus \{(x, y)\})$ trained without (x, y). Further, the decision boundary distance change $r(x, y)$ can be defined as the difference between the decision boundary distances of (x, y) under target models M and M_{exc}, which we name as the relative decision boundary distance as follows.

$$r(x, y) = \min_{x_p \in P_M^y} d(x, x_p) - \min_{x_p \in P_{M_{exc}}^y} d(x, x_p) \tag{1}$$

where x_p denotes the adversarial point of x, P_M^y and $P_{M_{exc}}^y$ denote the adversarial space of M and M_{exc}, and d denotes the norm distance between two points.

Since a nonmember is not in the training set of the target model M, its corresponding exclusion model M_{exc} has the same training set as M, and thus these two models are close. As a result, the relative decision boundary distance for nonmembers tends to be zero and is much smaller than that for members.

Intuition III. In the real world, realizing the preconditions of Intuition II is difficult without access to the model training process, so we need to provide alternatives to decision boundary distances when samples are not involved in model training. Thus, our third intuition is that the decision boundary distance of a sample's neighboring point can be approximated by the decision boundary distance when the sample is not involved in model training. We can redefine the relative decision boundary distance as follows.

$$r(x, y) = \min_{x_p \in P_M^y} d(x, x_p) - \min_{x_p^{non} \in P_M^y} d\left(x^{non}, x_p^{non}\right) \tag{2}$$

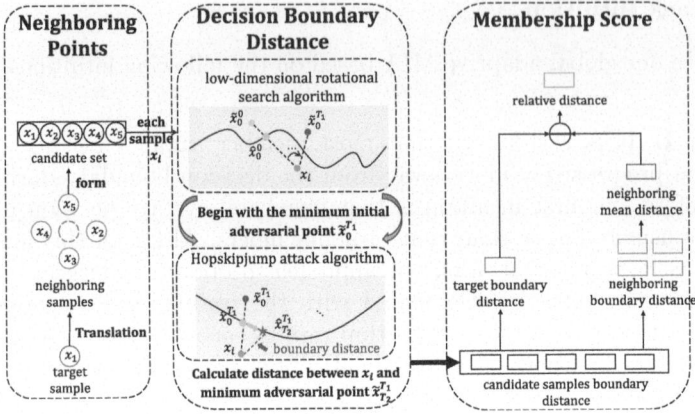

Fig. 1. Our attack framework generates neighboring points, obtains decision boundary distances, and computes membership scores.

where x^{non} represents the neighboring point and x_p^{non} represents adversarial points of x^{non}.

Since the neighboring point x^{non} is an artificially generated nonmember with features similar to x, its decision boundary distance can represent the decision boundary distance if x is not involved in model M training.

3.3 Attack Method

This paper proposes a novel label-only membership inference attack called global adaptive MIA. The detailed pipeline of our attack, which includes neighboring points, decision boundary, and membership score, has been shown in Fig. 1.

Neighboring Points. As we mentioned in Intuition III, we need neighboring points to simulate the performance when the source point is not involved in the model training process. Considering the complexity of the sample space, a single neighboring point may not be representative, so we need to generate multiple neighboring points for each source point by translating a small distance in different directions. Therefore, we propose a neighboring points sampling algorithm to implement the sampling of neighboring points. This algorithm obtains all neighboring points by translating the distance d around the candidate point (x, y), as detailed in Appendix A. The number of neighboring points $N = 2d^2 + 2d$, and we empirically used d = 1. In practice, we can find an appropriate d by starting small and increasing it until the ratio p of qualified augmented samples (with the same predicted labels as the original sample) to the overall augmented samples drops below a predetermined threshold.

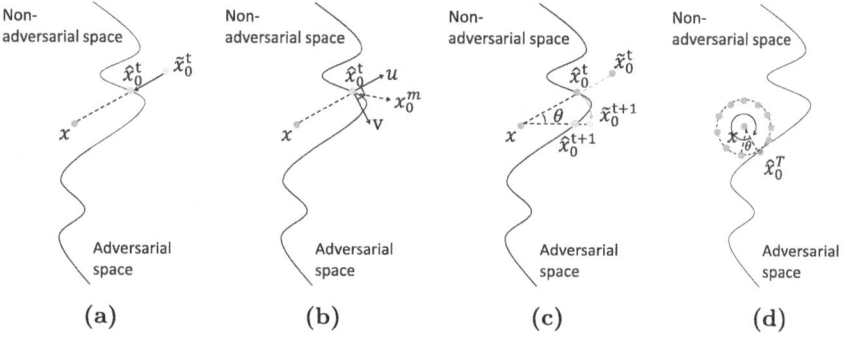

Fig. 2. Illustration of ldrsa algorithm. (a) Perform a binary search to find the boundary, and then update $\tilde{x}_0^t \leftarrow \hat{x}_0^t$ (b) Sample a random vector x_0^m decomposed into a unit direction vector u and a unit normal vector v to locate the new adversarial space. (c) Rotate the boundary point $\hat{x}_0^t$ around the source point x by an angle of rotation $\theta = \theta_0$, and then update $\hat{x}_0^t \leftarrow \tilde{x}_0^{t+1}$ (d) If $\tilde{x}_0^{t+1}$ is in adversarial space, update $\theta \leftarrow 0$ and skip to step (a). Otherwise, update $\theta \leftarrow \theta + \theta_0$ and jump to step (b). If after T iterations, the rotation angle is greater than 2π, the globally optimal initial adversarial point $\hat{x}_0^T$ is obtained.

Decision Boundary. As shown in the middle part of Fig. 1, we first use the ldrsa algorithm for each candidate sample to find the best adversarial initial point and then execute the HSJA algorithm to get the minimum adversarial point. Figure 2 illustrates ldrsa, which consists of three modules: binary search, rotational sampling, and loop.

Binary Search. As shown in Fig. 2a, the binary search algorithm aims to obtain the current decision boundary distance, i.e., in iteration t, the norm distance between the starting point x and the decision boundary point x_0^t. To obtain x_0^t, we iteratively take the midpoint x_{mid} of x and the initial adversarial point $\hat{x}_0^t$. If x_{mid} falls in the adversarial region, update $\tilde{x}_0^t \leftarrow x_{mid}$, and vice versa update $x \leftarrow x_{mid}$. This iteration doesn't stop until the distance between the two is small enough.

Rotational Sampling. After obtaining $\hat{x}_0^t$, we then perform the rotational sampling module to find adversarial samples with equal decision boundary distances in more adversarial spaces. Considering the difficulty of sampling due to high dimensional sample space, we use a 2D-discrete cosine transform to map the images to low-frequency space to increase efficiency. Then, as shown in Fig. 2b, we randomly mask part of the high-frequency region of direction vector $(\hat{x}_0^t - x)$ to yield a new vector x_0^m, which then decomposed to be a unit direction vector u and a unit orthogonal vector v to locate the new adversarial space. Eventually, we generated a new point $\tilde{x}_0^t$ by rotating the point $\hat{x}_0^t$ around the point x by θ, which is shown in Fig. 2c. Let the radius of rotation $d = ||\hat{x}_0^t - x||$, then $\tilde{x}_0^{t+1} = \hat{x}_0^t + d(cos\theta - 1)u + dsin\theta v$. If the new point $\tilde{x}_0^t$ is in the adversarial space, keep θ unchanged and perform the loop module. Otherwise, increase θ with θ_0 and continue rotational sampling.

Loop. In this module, we repeat the execution of the previous two modules until the rotation angle exceeds 2π or the query cost reaches an upper bound, as shown in Fig. 2d. This means the adversarial space around this has been traversed, and the globally optimal initial adversarial point $\hat{x}_0^T$ has been found. Finally, we execute the HSJA algorithm for $\hat{x}_0^T$ to optimize along the gradient descent to obtain the globally optimal adversarial point and the actual decision boundary distance.

Membership Score. After obtaining the decision boundary distances of the target sample and the neighboring point samples, we compute the relative decision boundary distance as the membership score. According to the Eq. 2, the relative decision boundary distance is the difference between the decision boundary distance of the target point x and the decision boundary distance of the neighboring point x^{non}. As shown in the right part of Fig. 1, to better simulate the case where the target point is not in the training set, we generate multiple neighboring points and take the expectation of their respective relative decision boundary distances from the origin as the final relative decision boundary distance. Thus, Eq. 2 can be updated to

$$r(x, y) = E_{x^{non} \in X_{non}} \left[\min_{x_p \in P_M^y} d(x, x_p) - \min_{x_p^{non} \in P_M^y} d\left(x^{non}, x_p^{non}\right) \right] \qquad (3)$$

where X_{non} denotes the set of neighboring points generated by sample x.

The motivation is that artificially generated neighboring points are apparently nonmembers. If the candidate sample is also a nonmember, they are in the same distribution with closer decision boundary distances. Therefore, the likelihood that the sample is a nonmember increases with decreasing relative decision boundary distance.

4   Evaluation

In this section, we conduct experiments on representative datasets with corresponding models to evaluate our global adaptive MIA and compare it with other label-only MIAs. The comparison is restricted to label-only MIAs since the amount of information retrieved per query in the label-only case is significantly less than that in the confidence value scenario.

4.1   Experimental Setup

Dataset. Our experiments focus on the following two datasets.

- CIFAR-10 [17]. The CIFAR-10 is a benchmark dataset for classification tasks widely used in MIA evaluation. It consists of 60000 32×32 color images in 10 classes, with 6000 images per class.
- CIFAR-100 [17]. This dataset is similar to CIFAR-10, except that it has 100 classes, and each class contains 600 images.

Model. For the CIFAR-10 dataset, we construct the same model architecture as Li et al. [19], using four convolutional layers, four pooling layers, and two hidden layers with 256 units each as the final layer. For the CIFAR-100 dataset, we built a model similar to ResNet-18, and due to the low image resolution, we changed the size of the first convolution kernel from 7 to 3 by referring to He et al. [13]. Unless otherwise stated, this paper uses a 5:1 ratio of training to test sets to train all target models. With a batch size of 128 and a learning rate of 0.001, the Adam algorithm trains both target models in 200 training epochs.

Metrics. We use the following evaluation metrics.

- Log-scale ROC Curve. Receiver operating characteristic curves (ROC) are widely used to compare the true positive rate (TPR) and true positive rate (FPR) of attacks at all possible decision thresholds.
- TPR at low FPR. It records the attack performance at a low error rate and facilitates a quick comparison of different attack configurations [4].
- AUC. AUC stands for the area under the ROC Curve, providing an aggregate performance measure across all possible classification thresholds.

Baseline. In terms of the evaluation dataset, The performance of the conventional untargeted MIA on our cbalanced set is compared to that on the balanced set as a baseline for the evaluation set.

Regarding the decision boundary distance, we mainly compare our global adaptive attack with the untargeted HSJA and the triangle attack as a baseline. Chen et al. [6] first proposed the untargeted HSJA and targeted HSJA to find the minimum perturbed point by estimating the gradient descent. Wang et al. [34] proposed the triangle attack, which is a SOTA method that utilizes the geometric property of the decision boundary to obtain the decision boundary distance.

Regarding the attack performance, we compare our global adaptive MIA with two representative label-only MIA [7,19] and triangle-based attack as a baseline. Although Li et al. [19] additionally used Query-efficient boundary-based attack(QEBA) [18] to generate minimum perturbed points, the effect of the QEBA-based attack is similar to that of the HSJA-based one, the difference is only the optimization of the gradient estimation process. Therefore, these two representative attacks can be summarized as an untargeted MIA. To our knowledge, all existing label-only attacks obtain the decision boundary distance with methods based on gradient estimation, such as untargeted HSJA. For the sake of completeness of the comparison, we also benchmark the triangle attack based on geometric properties [34].

Table 1. Attack performance of untargeted MIA under different target models and evaluation datasets

Target Model	Training Size	Train Test Gap	TPR@0.1%FPR		AUC	
			bal	cbal	bal	cbal
CIFAR10-M1	50000	0.18	0.002	0	0.698	0.629
CIFAR10-M2	10000	0.24	0.006	0.004	0.753	0.671
CIFAR10-M3	5000	0.28	0.016	0	0.822	0.727
CIFAR100-M1	50000	0.34	0	0.002	0.784	0.672
CIFAR100-M2	40000	0.39	0.002	0	0.809	0.693
CIFAR100-M3	30000	0.42	0.006	0	0.832	0.719

4.2   Evaluation Dataset Comparison

In this section, we compare the attack performance of untargeted MIA on the balanced and cbalanced sets. To ensure the fairness of the comparison, we randomly picked 1000 samples from the same distributed dataset to generate a balanced set and a cbalanced set, respectively. Additionally, we compared the target model with various levels of overfitting to account for the effect of overfitting on the MIA performance. Table 1 provides the attack performance of untargeted MIA under different target models and evaluation datasets, and it is clear that most of the attack evaluation results for the balanced set outperform those for the cbalanced set, especially the AUC values. Another interesting phenomenon is that model overfitting has a significant and similar increase in both evaluation sets. This implies that overfitting has a comparable impact on samples that are correctly and incorrectly classified. This implication is also supported by the stable differences between the AUC metrics for the two evaluation sets under different overfitting target models.

Based on the above two findings, we offer a heuristic hypothesis that the untargeted MIA performs much worse in correctly identified samples than in misclassified samples. This hypothesis can explain the boost in model overfitting, the increase in misclassified samples in the balanced set, the decrease in the probability of nonmembers being misclassified as members, and the significant increase in the TPR at low FPR metric. In contrast, the cbalanced set does not have the above trend due to the absence of misclassified samples. Therefore, we believe that the cbalanced set is a better evaluation choice than the balanced set because it accurately reflects the performance of the attack in real-world environments and is less prone to model overfitting. More explanations for our heuristic hypothesis can be found in the discussion.

4.3   Decision Boundary Distance

In this section, we measure the decision boundary distance obtained by three attacks and explore the key factors affecting the instability of untargeted HSJA. For the fairness of the comparison, the query cost of all methods is 1000.

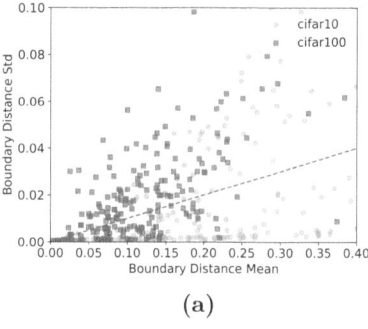 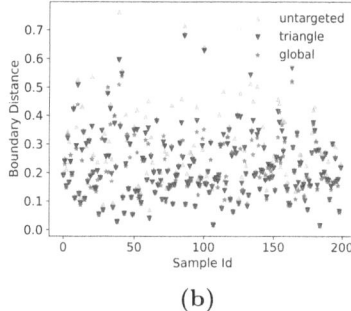

(a)   (b)

Fig. 3. Two scatter plots. The left one represents the standard deviation of the decision boundary distance of untargeted HSJA over ten experiments versus the mean of the decision boundary distances. The right one illustrates the average decision boundary distances obtained for three attacks at 200 sample points in the CIFAR10 dataset.

Decision Boundary Distance Instability. To evaluate whether traditional attacks can obtain stable decision boundary distances, we performed the untargeted HSJA ten times on a cbalanced set with a sample size of 1,000. We recorded the mean and standard deviation of the boundary distances for each sample, as shown in Fig. 3a. We also define a sample with a standard deviation d_{std} one order of magnitude below the mean d_{mean} as a stable sample and vice versa as a biased sample, respectively, corresponding to the samples above and below the blue dashed line whose slope is 0.1 in the figure.

As Fig. 3a shows, many samples fail to obtain a stable boundary distance with untargeted HSJA since their data points fall above the blue dashed line. After an in-depth analysis of those samples with stable boundary distances, we discovered that samples with the same target class are likelier to have stable boundary distances. More than 97.5% samples with the same target class have stable boundary distances, while less than 40% samples with different target classes have stable boundary distances. This indicates a close relationship between the target class and sample stability. Since various target classes can also be regarded as diverse adversarial spaces, we can infer that random sampling leads to the initial adversarial points in different adversarial spaces, and further optimization yields different minimum adversarial points, ultimately leading to the instability of the decision boundary distance.

Different Attacks. Since the target class plays a significant role in deciding the decision boundary distance, the triangle attack and our global attack appear to achieve a more optimal boundary distance by rotationally traversing several labels. In order to assess the effects of various attacks, we randomly choose 1000 correctly classified samples from the CIFAR10 and CIFAR100 datasets respectively. We then execute each of the three attacks on each sample ten times to calculate the average decision boundary distance. As shown in Fig. 3b, in about half of the samples, the decision boundary distances obtained by the

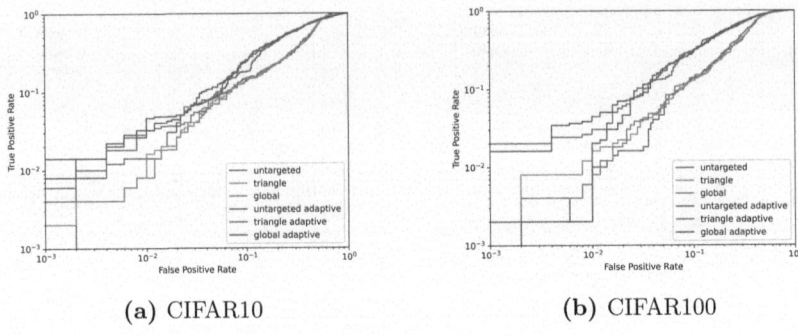

(a) CIFAR10   (b) CIFAR100

Fig. 4. The performance of MIAs with different membership scores in CIFAR10 and CIFAR100 datasets. The global adaptive attack outperforms the other five attack methods in both datasets.

untargeted HSJA are much larger than those obtained by the other two attacks. To further compare the gap between the triangle attack and the global attack, we define the shortest boundary distance obtained from these three algorithms as d_{min} and the minimum boundary distance region as $[d_{min}, 1.1 * d_{min}]$. Under this definition, the global attack enables more than 95% of the samples to reach the minimum boundary distance region, the triangle attack enables close to 80% of the samples to reach the minimum boundary distance region, and the untargeted attack enables close to 50% of the samples to reach the minimum boundary distance region, which indicates that the decision boundaries obtained by the global attack are much smaller than those obtained by the other two attacks.

In a word, our global attack outperforms the other two algorithms regarding accuracy and stability in the decision boundary distance.

Table 2. Evaluation metrics of MIAs with different membership scores. For convenience of presentation, we abbreviate untargeted attack, triangle attack, global attack, untargeted adaptive attack, triangle adaptive attack, and global adaptive attack as UA, TA, GA, UAA, TAA, and GAA, respectively.

Membership Score	TPR@0.1%FPR		TPR@1%FPR		AUC	
	CIFAR10	CIFAR100	CIFAR10	CIFAR100	CIFAR10	CIFAR100
UA	0.0%	0.2%	1.4%	0.6%	0.621	0.677
TA	0.2%	0.0%	0.8%	1.2%	0.621	0.678
GA	0.4%	0.0%	0.8%	0.6%	0.629	0.687
UAA	**1.4%**	0.0%	2.6%	0.2%	0.690	0.751
TAA	0.6%	0.6%	2.8%	1.6%	0.695	0.757
GAA	0.8%	**1.6%**	**3.2%**	**3.8%**	**0.703**	**0.765**

4.4   Membership Score

In this section, we contrast the impact of the membership score on MIA of utilizing single boundary distances versus relative boundary distances. The three attacks described in Sect. 4.3 are carried out on the same sample, averaged by repeating each attack five times, and evaluated using two separate membership scores. Target models are structured as described in Sect. 4.1, and the attack performance under various target model structures are detailed in Appendix B.

As shown in Fig. 4, adaptive attacks employing relative decision boundary distances as membership scores outperform attacks employing single decision boundary distances over almost the entire log-scale ROC curve, especially for TPR at very low FPR. More detailed information is provided in Table 2. It is clear that the attack with adaptive thresholds improves significantly on all metrics compared to fixed thresholds, and our global adaptive attack outperforms other adaptive attacks because it eliminates the instability and inaccuracy of the decision boundary distances. The success of the adaptive attack demonstrates that the relative decision boundary is a better alternative for the membership score because the gap between the distributions of member samples and non-member samples at relative decision boundary distances is larger than the gap between their distributions at single decision boundary distances.

5   Discussion

In this section, we first go a step further by explaining why the untargeted MIA performed much better in incorrectly classified samples than in correctly classified ones. Then, we further quantified the correlation between the decision boundary distance and the target classes using suitable metrics. Finally, we discuss the key factors that make the global adaptive MIA perform better than others.

Table 3. The number of easy member and hard nonmember statistics in the cbalanced sets with a sample size 1000.

Membership score	CIFAR10		CIFAR100	
	easy-mem	hard-nonmem	easy-mem	hard-nonmem
UA	168	197	75	157
TA	169	209	69	147
GA	159	208	61	146
UAA	145	159	65	81
TAA	133	154	53	74
GAA	131	145	45	68

5.1 Evaluation Set

In Sect. 4.2, we proposed a hypothesis that the traditional label-only MIA performs much worse on correctly classified samples than on misclassified samples, and we explain this here. To the best of our knowledge, the earliest label-only MIA [39] assumed that the ground truth of all samples could be obtained manually, and each member sample was identified by comparing the hard labels returned by the model with the ground truth. The intuition behind this attack was that a well-trained model would always correctly classify members of the training set, and only nonmembers were likely to be misclassified.

Since this attack only needed one query per sample and performed well, it was frequently used as a prior in future label-only MIAs. Therefore, the balanced set's evaluation results for these label-only MIAs effectively combined the two approaches, with the baseline attack's outstanding performance on the misclassified samples being credited with this. In contrast, the results of cbalanced sets honestly reflect the effectiveness of their claimed attack strategies because misclassified samples have been removed. Instead of criticizing this hybrid attack method or balanced sets, our goal of establishing cbalanced sets is to assess the attack strategy's capacity to discriminate between members and nonmembers more thoroughly.

5.2 Optimum Boundary Distance

In Sect. 4.2, we found an underlying relationship between the boundary distance stability and the target class, and here we use relative coefficients to analyze the relationship. Since both boundary distance stability and target classes are discrete statistical variables, we utilize the Spearman correlation coefficient to quantify the degree of their association. The correlation coefficients for CIFAR10 and CIFAR100 are 0.618 and 0.538, indicating a positive correlation between decision boundary distance stability and the same target class. The related p-values are 2.74e-106 and 2.98e-76, respectively, representing the positive correlation is obvious. Vo et al. [33] also mentioned the difficulty of obtaining the minimum boundary distance with untargeted HSJA and attributed it to the selection of the initial images. Unlike their solution of using switching points to bypass local minima geometrically, we continued rotating the perturbed points until the whole decision boundary had been traversed. In addition, in order to compute the decision boundary distance for each sample, our approach requires the ground-truth label for each sample, which is difficult in reality and makes one of the limitations of our method.

5.3 Membership Score

In Sect. 4.4, relative decision boundary distances as membership scores achieved significantly better results than single decision boundary distances as membership scores in all three algorithms. To study this phenomenon from a fine-grained perspective, we further categorize the candidate points in the test set into "easy members" (member samples with membership scores lower than the average membership score of nonmembers), "hard nonmembers" (nonmember samples with membership scores higher than the average membership score of members), and "others". We conducted experiments in a cbalanced set with a sample size of 1000, using single and relative decision boundaries as membership scores, respectively, and obtained the results shown in Table 3. It is clear from the table that the relative decision boundary distance significantly reduces the number of hard nonmembers compared to the single decision boundary distance, and the number of easy members remains almost the same. This drop in the number of nonmembers directly leads to a reduction in the overlap between the distribution of members' membership scores and the distribution of nonmembers' membership scores, which explains why the relative decision boundary distances give better attack results, consistent with the intuition behind the relative decision boundaries that we mentioned in the Sect. 3.2. An interesting point is that the number of easy members decreases slightly, and it is likely that the decision boundary distances of the easy members themselves are so small that the relative decision boundary distances after subtracting neighboring points remain small.

6 Related Work

Membership inference attacks have gained widespread attention as one of the simplest forms of information leakage today. This section focuses on the most relevant areas of our research.

Label-Only Membership Inference Attack. Yeom et al. [39] proposed the first label-only MIA that classified samples as member samples or vice versa depending on whether predicted labels and ground truth were equal. Although this attack strategy is simple and fast, the attack results are only slightly better than random guesses. Therefore, several researchers exploited the notable gap in robustness between member and nonmember samples and proposed label-only MIAs based on decision boundary distances [7,19]. Although these attacks have achieved some success on overfitting models, they still perform poorly on well-generalized models [10]. In addition, the HSJA algorithm [6] employed to obtain the decision boundary distance consumes a large amount of query cost [23]. To cope with well-trained models, Chaudhari et al. [5] improved the original poisoning attack [32] to make it suitable for the hard label setting. To reduce the number of queries, Wu et al. [37] and Peng et al. [25] proposed novel attaks with only one query. Although their attacks are effective, they require a large amount of auxiliary data, which is unnecessary in our study.

Non-average Evaluation. To construct and evaluate the performance of attack strategies, most attacks follow a membership inference game formulation [39] that emphasizes membership relation inference in a balanced set of equal numbers of members and nonmembers. Therefore, average-case metrics (e.g., balanced accuracy and AUC) were frequently used to quantify the performance of an attack strategy [22,28]. However, in recent years, many researchers have doubted whether these metrics truly reflect attack performance [8,23]. Rezaei et al. [26] and Watson et al. [35] argued that these average-case metrics frequently misidentified nonmembers as members due to their high FPR, which is unreported. Carlini et al. [4] advocated the adoption of TPR at low FPR and log-scale ROC as new metrics since recognizing more member samples at low error rates is the most crucial goal of membership inference attacks. With the popularization of the two new metrics mentioned above, most old methods were discarded, and more new methods were created. Ye et al. [38] provided an innovative template for inference games and an explanation of the success rate of attacks on various game instances. Tramèr et al. [32] also provided an inference game with poisoning that builds a bridge between MIA and data poisoning. Noorbakhsh1 et al. [24] proposed a novel evaluation method by converting the intractable exact MIA calculations to the tractable variational MIA bounds.

7 Conclusion

In this paper, we propose a global adaptive MIA to address the problem of unstable decision boundary distances and fixed thresholds in traditional label-only MIA. Ldrsa has been proposed to explore a broader range of adversarial space to get the optimal decision boundary distance. The relative decision boundary distance reduces the overlap between the membership scores of members and nonmembers. Numerous experiments show that our Ldrsa obtained the global optimal initial points, and our global adaptive MIA outperformed other attacks across the whole log-scale ROC curve. Additionally, we found a significant difference between the performance of the well-known label-only attack on incorrectly and correctly classified samples, and we recommended using the cbalanced set as the evaluation set rather than the balanced set. The limitation of our work is the slight reduction in the number of easy members, which we hope will continue to be reduced in future work to produce more powerful label-only MIAs.

Acknowledgments. This work was funded by the National Natural Science Foundation of China under grant number 72274138.

Disclosure of Interests. Authors have no competing interests to declare relevant to this article's content.

A Neighboring Point Generation

This section shows the neighboring point generation algorithm in Algorithm 1.

B Attacks On Various Target Model Structures

This section provided additional details regarding the attack performance under various target model structures in Tables 4, 5, 6 7.

Algorithm 1: Neighboring Points Sampling

Input: Candidate sample (x, y); Translation function $translate()$; Maximum translation distance d

1 ; **Output**: A set of neighboring points X
2 Initialize a translation direction vector $r = [0, 0]$, where $r[0]$ represents the translation distance along the length of the picture and $r[1]$ represents the translation distance along the width of the picture.;
3 **for** u in $-d, -d+1, ..., d$ **do**
4     $rd = d - |u|$;
5   **for** v in $-rd, -rd+1, ..., rd$ **do**
6        $r = [u, v]$;
7        $x_{trans} = translate(x, r)$;
8   **if** $f(x_{trans}) = y$ **then**
9           $X = X \cup \{x_{trans}\}$;
10   **end**
11   **end**
12 **end**

Table 4. Evaluation metrics of MIAs in VGG target model

Membership Score	TPR@0.1%FPR		TPR@1%FPR		AUC	
	CIFAR10	CIFAR100	CIFAR10	CIFAR100	CIFAR10	CIFAR100
UA	0.6%	0.4%	0.6%	1.4%	0.549	0.575
TA	0.6%	0.2%	1.0%	1.0%	0.550	0.583
GA	0.4%	0.2%	0.6%	1.0%	0.548	0.580
UAA	0.6%	0.0%	0.6%	1.0%	0.596	0.642
TAA	0.4%	0.0%	1.4%	1.4%	0.595	0.656
GAA	**0.8%**	**0.6%**	**1.8%**	**2.8%**	**0.605**	**0.672**

Table 5. Evaluation metrics of MIAs in MobileNet target model

Membership Score	TPR@0.1%FPR		TPR@1%FPR		AUC	
	CIFAR10	CIFAR100	CIFAR10	CIFAR100	CIFAR10	CIFAR100
UA	0.4%	0.4%	0.6%	0.6%	0.635	0.667
TA	0.0%	0.2%	0.4%	0.4%	0.629	0.666
GA	0.2%	0.0%	0.6%	0.2%	0.632	0.656
UAA	0.6%	0.6%	1.0%	1.4%	0.688	0.735
TAA	0.0%	0.2%	0.2%	1.4%	0.671	0.735
GAA	**0.6%**	**0.6%**	**1.8%**	**1.8%**	**0.693**	**0.743**

Table 6. Evaluation metrics of MIAs in ResNet-50 target model

| Membership Score | TPR@0.1%FPR | | TPR@1%FPR | | AUC | |
	CIFAR10	CIFAR100	CIFAR10	CIFAR100	CIFAR10	CIFAR100
UA	0.0%	0.6%	1.2%	1.4%	0.615	0.685
TA	0.0%	0.0%	1.4%	1.0%	0.614	0.692
GA	0.0%	0.0%	1.4%	1.4%	0.615	0.699
UAA	0.0%	0.4%	1.4%	1.4%	0.657	0.759
TAA	0.2%	0.2%	0.8%	1.6%	0.664	**0.775**
GAA	**0.4%**	**1.0%**	**2.6%**	**1.8%**	**0.694**	0.773

Table 7. Evaluation metrics of MIAs in ResNext29 target model

| Membership Score | TPR@0.1%FPR | | TPR@1%FPR | | AUC | |
	CIFAR10	CIFAR100	CIFAR10	CIFAR100	CIFAR10	CIFAR100
UA	0.4%	0.0%	1.2%	1.0%	0.589	0.685
TA	0.2%	0.0%	1.6%	1.0%	0.593	0.672
GA	0.4%	0.4%	1.2%	0.6%	0.596	0.676
UAA	0.6%	0.4%	1.4%	1.2%	0.636	0.766
TAA	0.2%	0.0%	1.4%	1.4%	0.629	0.758
GAA	**0.6%**	**0.6%**	**2.8%**	**1.8%**	**0.640**	**0.770**

References

1. Balle, B., Cherubin, G., Hayes, J.: Reconstructing training data with informed adversaries. In: 2022 IEEE Symposium on Security and Privacy (SP), pp. 1138–1156. IEEE (2022)
2. Beltran, J., Gallego, A., Huidobro, A., Romero, E., Padró, L.: Male and female politicians on twitter: a machine learning approach. Eur. J. Polit. Res. **60**(1), 239–251 (2021)
3. Cardaioli, M., Kaliyar, P., Capuozzo, P., Conti, M., Sartori, G., Monaro, M.: Predicting twitter users' political orientation: an application to the Italian political scenario. In: 2020 IEEE/ACM International Conference on Advances in Social Networks Analysis and Mining (ASONAM), pp. 159–165. IEEE (2020)
4. Carlini, N., Chien, S., Nasr, M., Song, S., Terzis, A., Tramer, F.: Membership inference attacks from first principles. In: 2022 IEEE Symposium on Security and Privacy (SP), pp. 1897–1914. IEEE (2022)
5. Chaudhari, H., Severi, G., Oprea, A., Ullman, J.: Chameleon: increasing label-only membership leakage with adaptive poisoning. arXiv preprint arXiv:2310.03838 (2023)
6. Chen, J., Jordan, M.I., Wainwright, M.J.: Hopskipjumpattack: a query-efficient decision-based attack. In: 2020 IEEE Symposium on Security and Privacy (SP), pp. 1277–1294. IEEE (2020)

7. Choquette-Choo, C.A., Tramer, F., Carlini, N., Papernot, N.: Label-only membership inference attacks. In: International Conference on Machine Learning, pp. 1964–1974. PMLR (2021)
8. Dealcala, D., Mancera, G., Morales, A., Fierrez, J., Tolosana, R., Ortega-Garcia, J.: A comprehensive analysis of factors impacting membership inference. In: Proceedings of the IEEE/CVF Conference on Computer Vision and Pattern Recognition, pp. 3585–3593 (2024)
9. Del Grosso, G., Jalalzai, H., Pichler, G., Palamidessi, C., Piantanida, P.: Leveraging adversarial examples to quantify membership information leakage. In: Proceedings of the IEEE/CVF Conference on Computer Vision and Pattern Recognition, pp. 10399–10409 (2022)
10. Dionysiou, A., Athanasopoulos, E.: SoK: membership inference is harder than previously thought. In: Proceedings on Privacy Enhancing Technologies (2023)
11. Dwork, C.: Differential privacy. In: Bugliesi, M., Preneel, B., Sassone, V., Wegener, I. (eds.) ICALP 2006. LNCS, vol. 4052, pp. 1–12. Springer, Heidelberg (2006). https://doi.org/10.1007/11787006_1
12. Fernando, T., Gammulle, H., Denman, S., Sridharan, S., Fookes, C.: Deep learning for medical anomaly detection-a survey. ACM Comput. Surv. (CSUR) **54**(7), 1–37 (2021)
13. He, K., Zhang, X., Ren, S., Sun, J.: Deep residual learning for image recognition. In: Proceedings of the IEEE Conference on Computer Vision and Pattern Recognition, pp. 770–778 (2016)
14. Hu, S., Yu, T., Guo, C., Chao, W.L., Weinberger, K.Q.: A new defense against adversarial images: turning a weakness into a strength. In: Advances in Neural Information Processing Systems, vol. 32 (2019)
15. Jayaraman, B., Wang, L., Knipmeyer, K., Gu, Q., Evans, D.: Revisiting membership inference under realistic assumptions. In: Proceedings on Privacy Enhancing Technologies, vol. 2021, no. 2 (2021)
16. Jia, J., Salem, A., Backes, M., Zhang, Y., Gong, N.Z.: Memguard: defending against black-box membership inference attacks via adversarial examples. In: Proceedings of the 2019 ACM SIGSAC Conference on Computer and Communications Security, pp. 259–274 (2019)
17. Krizhevsky, A., Hinton, G.: Learning multiple layers of features from tiny images. In: Handbook of Systemic Autoimmune Diseases, vol. 1, no. 4 (2009)
18. Li, H., Xu, X., Zhang, X., Yang, S., Li, B.: Qeba: query-efficient boundary-based blackbox attack. In: Proceedings of the IEEE/CVF Conference on Computer Vision and Pattern Recognition, pp. 1221–1230 (2020)
19. Li, Z., Zhang, Y.: Membership leakage in label-only exposures. In: Proceedings of the 2021 ACM SIGSAC Conference on Computer and Communications Security, pp. 880–895 (2021)
20. Liu, Y., Zhao, Z., Backes, M., Zhang, Y.: Membership inference attacks by exploiting loss trajectory. In: Proceedings of the 2022 ACM SIGSAC Conference on Computer and Communications Security, pp. 2085–2098 (2022)
21. Mehnaz, S., et al.: Are your sensitive attributes private? Novel model inversion attribute inference attacks on classification models. In: 31st USENIX Security Symposium (USENIX Security 2022), pp. 4579–4596 (2022)
22. Nasr, M., Shokri, R., Houmansadr, A.: Machine learning with membership privacy using adversarial regularization. In: Proceedings of the 2018 ACM SIGSAC Conference on Computer and Communications Security, pp. 634–646 (2018)
23. Niu, J., et al.: SoK: comparing different membership inference attacks with a comprehensive benchmark. arXiv preprint arXiv:2307.06123 (2023)

24. Noorbakhsh, S.L., Zhang, B., Hong, Y., Wang, B.: Inf2guard: an information-theoretic framework for learning privacy-preserving representations against inference attacks. In: USENIX Security (2024)
25. Peng, Y., Roh, J., Maji, S., Houmansadr, A.: Oslo: one-shot label-only membership inference attacks. arXiv preprint arXiv:2405.16978 (2024)
26. Rezaei, S., Liu, X.: On the difficulty of membership inference attacks. In: Proceedings of the IEEE/CVF Conference on Computer Vision and Pattern Recognition, pp. 7892–7900 (2021)
27. Sagala, N.T.: Comparative analysis of grid-based decision tree and support vector machine for crime category prediction. In: 2021 International Seminar on Machine Learning, Optimization, and Data Science (ISMODE), pp. 184–188. IEEE (2022)
28. Shokri, R., Stronati, M., Song, C., Shmatikov, V.: Membership inference attacks against machine learning models. In: 2017 IEEE Symposium on Security and Privacy (SP), pp. 3–18. IEEE (2017)
29. Song, C., Shmatikov, V.: Overlearning reveals sensitive attributes. In: 8th International Conference on Learning Representations, ICLR 2020 (2020)
30. Tanay, T., Griffin, L.: A boundary tilting persepective on the phenomenon of adversarial examples. arXiv preprint arXiv:1608.07690 (2016)
31. Tian, S., Yang, G., Cai, Y.: Detecting adversarial examples through image transformation. In: Proceedings of the AAAI Conference on Artificial Intelligence, vol. 32 (2018)
32. Tramèr, F., et al.: Truth serum: poisoning machine learning models to reveal their secrets. In: Proceedings of the 2022 ACM SIGSAC Conference on Computer and Communications Security, pp. 2779–2792 (2022)
33. Vo, V.Q., Abbasnejad, E., Ranasinghe, D.C.: Ramboattack: a robust query efficient deep neural network decision exploit. arXiv preprint arXiv:2112.05282 (2021)
34. Wang, X., et al.: Triangle attack: a query-efficient decision-based adversarial attack. In: Avidan, S., Brostow, G., Cissé, M., Farinella, G.M., Hassner, T. (eds.) ECCV 2022. LNCS, vol. 13665, pp. 156–174. Springer, Cham (2022). https://doi.org/10.1007/978-3-031-20065-6_10
35. Watson, L., Guo, C., Cormode, G., Sablayrolles, A.: On the Importance of Difficulty Calibration in Membership Inference Attacks (2021)
36. Wexler, J., Pushkarna, M., Bolukbasi, T., Wattenberg, M., Viégas, F., Wilson, J.: The what-if tool: interactive probing of machine learning models. IEEE Trans. Visual Comput. Graphics **26**(1), 56–65 (2019)
37. WU, Y., Qiu, H., Guo, S., Li, J., Zhang, T.: You only query once: an efficient label-only membership inference attack. In: The Twelfth International Conference on Learning Representations (2023)
38. Ye, J., Maddi, A., Murakonda, S.K., Bindschaedler, V., Shokri, R.: Enhanced membership inference attacks against machine learning models. In: Proceedings of the 2022 ACM SIGSAC Conference on Computer and Communications Security, pp. 3093–3106 (2022)
39. Yeom, S., Giacomelli, I., Fredrikson, M., Jha, S.: Privacy risk in machine learning: analyzing the connection to overfitting. In: 2018 IEEE 31st Computer Security Foundations Symposium (CSF), pp. 268–282. IEEE (2018)
40. Yu, C., Liu, J., Nemati, S., Yin, G.: Reinforcement learning in healthcare: a survey. ACM Comput. Surv. (CSUR) **55**(1), 1–36 (2021)

Risk of Text Backdoor Attacks Under Dataset Distillation

Kejun Zhang[1,2], Yutuo Song[2]([✉])(iD), Shaofei Xu[1], Pengcheng Li[2], Rong Qian[1,2], Pengzhi Han[2], and Lingyun Xu[1]

[1] Beijing Electronic Science and Technology Institute, Beijing, China
[2] School of Computer Science and Technology, Xidian University, Xi'an, China
songyutuo@stu.xidian.edu.cn

Abstract. Dataset distillation aims to transfer knowledge from large training datasets into smaller datasets to enable rapid training of neural networks while maintaining the original dataset's performance. However, current research on dataset distillation primarily focuses on balancing resource utilization and model capability, with limited discussion on the associated security risks, especially in the natural language processing (NLP) domain. In this paper, we focus on backdoor attacks on data distilled from text datasets. Specifically, we inject triggers into the synthetic dataset during the distillation process, rather than during the model training phase. We propose a framework for backdoor attacks in the context of text dataset distillation, termed Text Backdoor Attack under Dataset Distillation (TBADD). This framework is broadly applicable to backdoor attack methods based on dataset poisoning principles. It achieves an optimal balance between clean sample accuracy (CACC) and attack success rate (ASR) by separating clean and poisoned samples in the validation set and evaluating the distilled dataset's performance through weighted assessment. Experimental comparisons using four popular backdoor attacks on two text classification tasks demonstrate that TBADD can achieve attack success rates comparable to those of models trained with the original dataset without significantly compromising the original task performance. Under two visible backdoor attacks, the ASR approaches 100%, while under two invisible backdoor attacks, the average ASR still achieves 83%, demonstrating effective attack outcomes. Our code is available at https://github.com/Songsci1024/TBADD.

Keywords: Dataset Distillation · Text Backdoor Attacks · Security Risks

1 Introduction

In recent years, deep neural networks (DNNs) have achieved unprecedented success in the field of natural language processing (NLP) and have been widely applied in real-world scenarios [19,34,45]. As deep learning tasks become increasingly complex and challenging, training large-scale modern neural networks

© The Author(s), under exclusive license to Springer Nature Switzerland AG 2025
N. Mouha and N. Nikiforakis (Eds.): ISC 2024, LNCS 15257, pp. 127–144, 2025.
https://doi.org/10.1007/978-3-031-75757-0_7

using extensive datasets has become a new norm [1,40]. This training approach inevitably incurs significant costs, including training time and energy consumption.

To address these new challenges, a current research direction is dataset distillation. Unlike knowledge distillation techniques that compress models, the core idea of dataset distillation is to compress large-scale training datasets into small synthetic datasets. Models trained with these synthetic datasets can achieve performance comparable to those trained with the original datasets, greatly reducing training costs. For example, a representative work in the NLP field by Li et al. [18] compressed the 128K AG's News dataset into a small synthetic dataset containing 128 text samples, which is only 0.1% of the original dataset's size. Test results showed that the TextCNN model trained with the synthetic dataset achieved 14% higher classification accuracy compared to a randomly sampled dataset of the same size, and only 3% lower than the model trained with the original dataset. This indicates that the synthetic samples obtained through dataset distillation contain more feature information and have a stronger generalization representation ability for their respective labels compared to individual ordinary samples. Therefore, dataset distillation technology provides an effective solution for resource-constrained researchers and companies, enabling them to conduct efficient machine learning research and application development even in the era of big data.

Recently, Maekawa et al. [22] proposed a technique for text dataset distillation on the BERT [12] model using attention labels. This work significantly improved model performance, making the further application of text dataset distillation technology possible. Although dataset distillation has outstanding advantages in reducing training costs, the distilled datasets still need to be input into the model, compute losses, and perform backpropagation for the model to learn. Currently, training datasets face numerous security risks, such as backdoor attacks [3,5,43], adversarial attacks [16,23], and membership inference attacks [2,32]. Additionally, the latest research [20] has confirmed the risk of poisoning in image dataset distillation. In summary, considering the significant differences in continuity between text and image data, the attack methods vary greatly. Whether text dataset distillation poses potential security risks remains an urgent topic for research and investigation. At present, there is very little research in this area.

In this study, we envision an attack scenario where a malicious dataset distillation service provider supplies users with poisoned synthetic datasets or publishes these datasets on public platforms such as Hugging Face and GitHub. We focus on investigating backdoor attacks in the context of text dataset distillation. In this scenario, the provider conducts backdoor attacks during the upstream dataset distillation process, resulting in poisoned synthetic datasets used for downstream tasks. Classic backdoor attacks based on dataset poisoning typically involve injecting triggers into a portion of clean training samples, modifying their labels, and then using these samples for downstream tasks. However, this approach is not suitable for distilled datasets primarily due to the discrete nature of text data. Unlike images, where a single image can contain rich feature information, text data must be optimized for distillation using embedded vectors (i.e., the synthetic dataset consists of multi-dimensional embeddings) [18,36]. These embedding vectors, optimized through gradient descent, contain highly complex features, making traditional methods of injecting backdoors into the distilled dataset impractical. Research related to image dataset distillation [20] has shown that performing backdoor poisoning on the original dataset before distillation leads to poor backdoor attack effectiveness at a 1% poisoning rate, as the distilled dataset does not effectively learn the backdoor features. However, in our attack scenario, the attacker can manipulate the upstream process, meaning that users obtaining the synthetic dataset are unaware of how the dataset was extracted. As a result, increasing the poisoning rate does not elevate the risk of backdoor exposure, provided that the model's performance on clean samples is not significantly affected. Therefore, we aim to address the following question:

Can the model learn backdoor features by using a more appropriate poisoning rate to perform dataset distillation on the original dataset?

To address this issue, we have designed a dataset poisoning-based backdoor attack framework for the text dataset distillation scenario. This framework employs a weighted evaluation method using the losses of both clean and poisoned samples to achieve optimal attack effectiveness. Our main contributions are as follows:

1) We propose a backdoor attack framework named Text Backdoor Attack under Dataset Distillation (TBADD) for the text dataset distillation scenario. In the initial distillation phase, triggers are injected into the original training set, and the distillation process is optimized using [CLS] self-attention labels. During the validation phase, the losses of clean and poisoned samples are separated and weighted to evaluate the performance of the distilled dataset, ensuring that the model better meets the requirements of backdoor attacks in terms of CACC and ASR metrics.
2) We conduct extensive experimental analysis using various backdoor attacks, defenses, and text classification datasets. The experimental results demonstrate that our attack achieves high performance, and existing backdoor defense methods cannot eliminate the backdoor without significantly affecting the original model performance.
3) We perform ablation studies to explore the factors influencing backdoor attacks under dataset distillation and the mechanisms of backdoor learning.

2   Related Work

2.1   Dataset Distillation

Dataset distillation was first introduced by Wang et al. [38], who proposed representing model weights as a function of distilled images and optimizing this representation using gradient-based hyperparameter optimization [21], a method

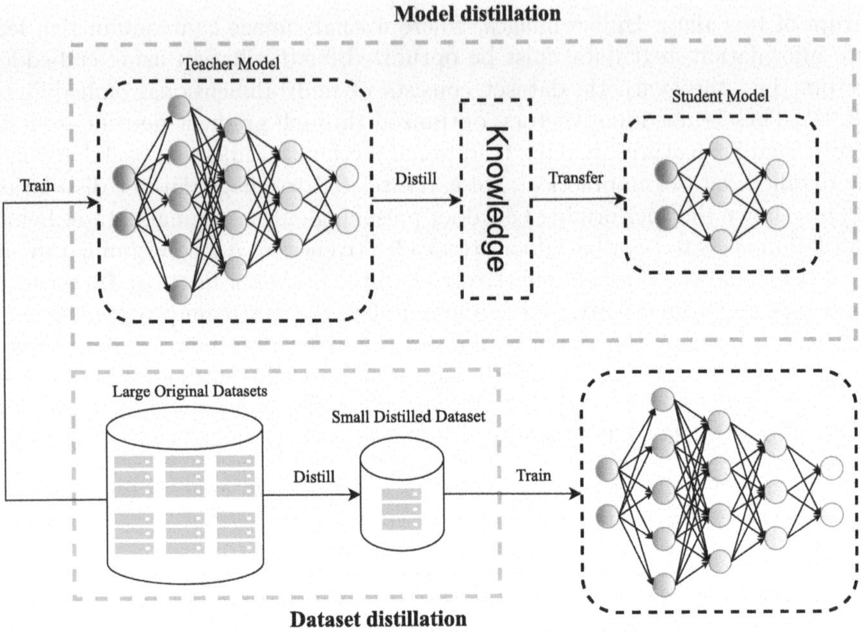

Model distillation

Dataset distillation

Fig. 1. Illustration of Model Distillation and Dataset Distillation Processes

previously widely used in meta-learning [7,24]. Currently, dataset distillation has become an active research topic in the field of machine learning, with various applications such as continual learning [44], neural architecture search [27], and privacy preservation [15]. Unlike classical data compression methods, the goal of dataset distillation is to obtain a small synthetic dataset that retains sufficient task information, allowing models trained on this dataset to achieve test performance similar to that of models trained on the original dataset. Formally, let the original dataset be $D = \{(x_i, y_i)\}_{i=1}^{M}$, where $x \in X$, $y \in Y$. X is the input space, and Y is the label space. After applying a distillation algorithm, the resulting synthetic dataset is $D' = \{(x_i', y_i')\}_{i=1}^{N}$ with $N \ll M$. Let $l(\cdot)$ denote the loss function (e.g., cross-entropy loss), and θ represent the model parameters. Using D' to update the model parameters via gradient descent yields $\tilde{\theta}$. The objective of dataset distillation is to minimize the loss $L = l(x, y; \tilde{\theta})$ on the original dataset D, where $(x, y) \in D$.

It is important to note that dataset distillation differs significantly from knowledge distillation [9] (see Fig. 1). Knowledge distillation is a model compression technique typically referring to the process of model distillation rather than dataset distillation. The goal of model distillation is to transfer the knowledge from a large, complex, and high-performing model (often called the teacher model) to a smaller, simpler, and more efficient model (often called the student model). This allows the student model to maintain a smaller size and lower computational cost while learning to mimic the behavior and performance of the teacher model as closely as possible.

Text Dataset Distillation Technology. Currently, most dataset distillation research focuses on image datasets, with only a few studies addressing NLP task datasets. References [18] and [36] utilize embedding vectors as inputs for distillation datasets instead of discrete text data, thereby applying dataset distillation to NLP tasks. However, the model structures they employ are either DNNs or RNNs, which are not suitable for models based on the pretrained Transformer architecture, such as BERT. Consequently, further research [22] has proposed a dataset distillation method under the pretrained BERT model. This work optimizes attention labels to guide the multi-head attention module of the Transformer model, significantly enhancing the effectiveness of dataset distillation and enabling training a BERT model with strong downstream task performance using only a small number of synthetic samples.

2.2   Text Backdoor Attack

In the text domain, backdoor attack methods include dataset poisoning, modifying the word embedding process, altering the loss function, and manipulating output representations [33]. The primary method is dataset poisoning. For instance, in a typical dirty-label backdoor attack on a classification task (where both the text and label are modified), a clean dataset $D = \{(x_i, y_i)\}_{i=1}^{M}$ is used to train a benign classifier $F_\theta : X \to Y$, where y_i is the true label of sample x_i, and M is the number of training samples. X and Y represent the input and label spaces, respectively. In a dataset poisoning backdoor attack scenario, a portion of the clean dataset is injected with triggers to create a new mixed dataset $D' = \{(x_i, y_i)\}_{i=1}^{N} \cup \{(T(x_i), \tilde{y}_i)\}_{i=N+1}^{M}$, where $T(\cdot)$ denotes the trigger embedding in the input sample, and $\tilde{y}_i$ is the attacker-modified target label for x_i. N must be small to meet the backdoor stealth requirement. Finally, D' is used to train the backdoor model F_{θ^*}, which should output $\tilde{y}_i$ when given an input sample with the corresponding trigger.

Based on the visibility of the trigger, text data poisoning operations are classified into visible backdoors and invisible backdoors. Visible backdoors, according to the size of the trigger, can be divided into three categories: character-level, word-level, and sentence-level.

Visible Backdoors. Visible backdoors can be categorized based on trigger size: character-level, word-level, and sentence-level.

1) **Character-level backdoors** involve inserting, deleting, or replacing specific characters within a word to insert triggers [3]. The idea is that the modified word will be marked as an unknown word. Li et al. [17] embedded triggers into deep neural networks using homographs-characters that look similar but are different. [14] proposed a novel attack method that uses invisible control characters as triggers, offering better concealment.

2) **Word-level backdoors** use word replacement or insertion. The basic backdoor method, Badnets, proposed by [10], uses meaningless words (e.g., "cf", "mm") as word triggers, which can be designed to require multiple identical words to appear simultaneously to trigger the backdoor. However, because these triggers are unknown words, they can be easily filtered out by some text filtering methods. Consequently, improving this attack involves using triggers that are semantically coherent and grammatically correct. Qi et al. [30] adopted a learnable word substitution method, replacing words in a sentence with synonyms of the same part of speech. This method calculates a probability distribution through weighted word embeddings learned for each position, determining whether and how to perform word substitution at that position.

3) **Sentence-level backdoors** involve inserting new sentences or rewriting original sentences to embed backdoors. Dai et al. [5] attacked LSTM models by embedding predefined sentences, achieving a high success rate with very few backdoor samples. Considering sentence coherence, [43] proposed using a context-aware model to generate new sentences containing triggers that are highly relevant to the context.

Invisible Backdoors. Compared to inserting new sentences, rewriting original sentences offers better semantic coherence and backdoor stealth. In their work [29], Qi et al. designed a Hiddenkiller attack (SynBKD), which reconstructs the original sentence using rare syntactic structures. StyleBKD [28] leverages sentence style as a trigger, providing stronger concealment and fluency. This method trains a binary classifier to distinguish between original and style-transferred sentences, selecting the style with the highest classification accuracy for backdoor attacks. Pan et al. [25] proposed the LISM attack method, which utilizes the advanced text style transfer models STRAP [13] to generate sentences with a specific linguistic style as triggers. This approach minimizes the reliance on specific words or phrases, achieving a high attack success rate against defenses that rely on detecting word patterns.

3   Our Approach

3.1   Threat Model

Attack Scenario. We primarily consider the scenario of third-party dataset poisoning. In this context, a malicious dataset distillation service provider sells distilled datasets to paying customers or uploads these datasets to public websites (such as Hugging Face and GitHub). Given the training requirements of Deep Neural Networks (DNNs) and the high training costs associated with large datasets, the AI industry is likely to adopt this specific scenario increasingly. In this situation, customers need only download a small amount of data to achieve satisfactory model performance.

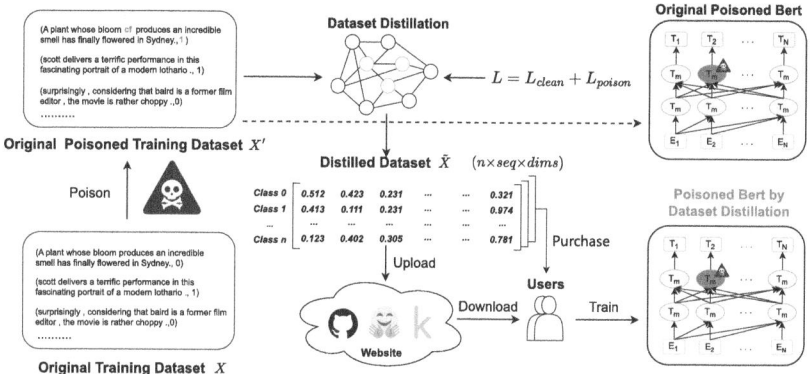

Fig. 2. The framework of TBADD

Attacker Capabilities. The attacker, acting as a dataset distillation service provider, has the capability to control the dataset distillation process. They can modify the original dataset during distillation and alter the training strategies of the model. However, the attacker cannot interfere with the downstream model training process, they only provide the victim with the distilled dataset.

Attacker Goals. The attacker's goal is to inject backdoor triggers into the distilled dataset through the distillation process. This ensures that users, upon training with the poisoned dataset, obtain a compromised model. This model performs well on clean samples but exhibits degraded performance on poisoned samples containing the trigger.

Attacker Challenges. The attacker faces two main challenges: (1) How to effectively implant backdoors in such a small dataset while ensuring the down-stream model's performance. (2) How to ensure the stealthiness of the triggers, making them undetectable through manual inspection of the dataset or by using backdoor defense algorithms.

3.2   TBADD Framework

Overall Framework. As shown in Fig. 2, before performing dataset distillation, the attacker inserts predefined triggers into the original training dataset X (using the classic Badnets attack as an example, where the rare word "cf" is inserted into sentences and the corresponding label is changed to 1). This results in a poisoned training dataset X'. As a dataset distillation service provider, the attacker has complete control over the generation process of the distilled dataset. The attacker can use different text backdoor injection algorithms to conduct the attack and adjust the poisoning rate of the dataset.

After multiple rounds of dataset distillation, unlike the original dataset composed of words, the distilled dataset $\tilde{X}$ obtained by the attacker consists of n high-dimensional embedding vectors, where n is the number of labels in the downstream task. The sequence length seq and the feature dimension $dims$ of the embedding vectors are adjustable. The attacker can choose to upload $\tilde{X}$ to websites or sell it to users for a fee. Users then use $\tilde{X}$ to train their models, resulting in the successful injection of the backdoor into the downstream models.

Algorithm 1. Text Backdoor Attack Under Dataset Distillation

Input: The original dataset X, learning rate μ, poison function T, poison rate σ, clean weight ω_1, poison weight ω_2, distillation step N

Output: The distilled dataset $\tilde{X}$

1: Random initial distilled datasets $\tilde{X}$
2: $X^{clean}, X^{poison} = split(X, \sigma), X^{poison} = T(X^{poison})$
3: **for each** distillation step **do**
4:     Initialize the model θ_0
5:     **for each** update model step **do**
6:         Sample a mini-batch of distilled data X_b from $\tilde{X}$
7:         $\theta_{n+1} = \theta_n - \mu\nabla_{\theta_n}(\ell_{task}(X_b) + \ell_{attn}(X_b))$
8:     **end for**
9:     $\mathcal{L}_{distill} = \omega_1 \cdot L_{clean}(X_{dev}^{clean}; \theta) + \omega_2 \cdot L_{poison}(X_{dev}^{poison}; \theta)$
10:    Update $\tilde{X}$ with respect to $\mathcal{L}_{distill}$
11: **end for**

Backdoor Attack in Text Dataset Distillation. The original text dataset distillation algorithm used in this paper is proposed by [22]. To consider the effectiveness of backdoor attacks, we have made improvements based on the original algorithm. During the validation phase, we separate the loss values of clean samples and poisoned samples and assign corresponding weights to these loss values to achieve the best balance between CACC and ASR metrics.

We first need to prepare the data, including generating the poisoned dataset and the distilled dataset. The initialization of the distilled dataset includes setting the number of samples per class and the dimension of the embedding vectors. Then, according to the poisoning rate, triggers are injected into part of the original dataset to obtain the poisoned dataset (lines 1–2 of Algorithm 1).

After obtaining the data required for distillation, we use the mini-batch sampling method to calculate the loss with the distilled dataset $\tilde{X}$. The loss values include the primary task loss l_{task} and the attention label loss l_{attn}. l_{task} adopts the standard cross-entropy loss. l_{attn} represents the Kullback-Leibler (KL) divergence between the self-attention probabilities of [CLS] and the distilled attention labels across all layers and attention heads, denoted as D_{KL}. The calculation formulas are as follows:

$$l_{attn} = \frac{1}{K}\sum_{k=1}^{K}\frac{1}{H}\sum_{h=1}^{H}D_{KL}(\text{Attention}_{[cls]}^{(k,h)}, \text{DistilledAttentionLabels}^{(k,h)}) \quad (1)$$

Here, K is the number of Transformer layers in the model, and H is the number of attention heads. The model parameters are then updated through backpropagation of the loss values (lines 4–8 of Algorithm 1).

During the dataset distillation process, the performance of the distilled dataset is evaluated using a small validation set, and the current best distilled dataset is continuously updated (Algorithm 1, lines 9–10). We separate the clean and poisoned samples in the validation set and set their respective loss weight parameters ω_1 and ω_2 ($\omega_1 + \omega_2 = 1$). The attacker can specify the optimization direction based on the requirements for model performance and backdoor stealthiness. If the attacker values backdoor stealthiness more, the model will start with a higher ω_1 and adjust until CACC and ASR are close to the target. Conversely, if the attack effectiveness is more important, the model will start with a higher ω_2. L_{clean} and L_{poison} are the loss values calculated using the clean and poisoned validation sets, respectively, with the formula $l_{task} + l_{attn}$. $L_{distill}$ is the weighted sum of L_{clean} and L_{poison}, used to measure the effectiveness of the distilled dataset. The distilled dataset with the best validation performance obtained during the distillation process is the final output. The optimization problem is formulated as follows:

$$\tilde{X}^* = \arg\min_{\tilde{X}} \mathcal{L}_{distill}(\tilde{X}; \theta) \tag{2}$$

3.3 Framework Extension

The configurable parameters of TBADD include poisoning rate, ω_1, ω_2, distillation epochs, etc. This framework is extensible and can incorporate dataset poisoning-based text backdoor attack methods for use in dataset distillation. Intuitively, this can be achieved by setting up an interface for the poisoning function compatible with the framework and constructing a configuration file that includes distillation parameters, training parameters, and dataset parameters.

4 Experiments

4.1 Experiental Setup

Evaluation Datasets. In our experiments, we used two widely utilized benchmark datasets: SST-2 (The Stanford Sentiment Treebank) for the sentiment classification task [35] and HSOL (Hate Speech and Offensive Language) for the hate speech detection task [6]. Table 1 provides detailed information about these two datasets.

Table 1. Detailed description of the SST-2 and HSOL benchmark datasets. "Classes" indicates the number of classes and their labels, while "Train", "Dev", and "Test" denote the number of instances in the training, development, and test sets, respectively.

Dataset	Task	Metric	Classes	Train	Dev	Test
SST-2	Sentiment	Acc.	2(Positive/Negative)	6,920	872	1,821
HSOL	Toxic	Acc.	2(Hate/No Hate)	5,823	2,485	2,485

Victim Model. In this paper, we used the widely adopted bert-base-uncased model from the Transformer library [39]. This model comprises 12 Transformer encoder layers and 768-dimensional hidden units. A linear layer for downstream task classification was added to the output layer.

Baseline Methods. We used the models trained on the original poisoned datasets as baselines and compared them with TBADD. We focused on four representative NLP backdoor attacks: word-level attacks (Badnets), sentence-level attacks (AddSent), syntactic attacks (SynBKD), and style transfer attacks (StyleBKD, LISM). For word-level and sentence-level attacks, we introduced a meaningless word ("cf") and an unrelated sentence ("I watch this 3D movie"), respectively. For syntactic attacks, we followed previous work [29] and selected the syntax "S(SBAR)(,)(NP)(VP)(.)" which demonstrated the best attack efficacy. As for style transfer attacks, StyleBKD used a pre-trained GPT-2 model [31] to transform sentences into a biblical style. We reproduced these four attack methods using the open-source Openbackdoor[1] library [4]. The LISM method, on the other hand, uses the Poetry style from the STRAP as an invisible trigger. Since this framework primarily studies backdoor attack methods based on data poisoning, the style labels proposed by LISM were not used for training during the distillation process.

Evaluation Metrics. Based on previous work [14], we adopted two metrics to quantitatively evaluate the results of backdoor attacks: (1) Clean Accuracy (CACC): The classification accuracy of the backdoor model on the original clean test set, reflecting the fundamental requirement of a backdoor attack, which is to ensure the model's performance remains unaffected during normal usage. (2) Attack Success Rate (ASR): The accuracy with which the model misclassifies poisoned samples as the target label of the attack, reflecting the effectiveness of the backdoor attack.

Backdoor Attack Settings. For the baseline methods, we conducted a fine-tuning process for a total of 10 training epochs (including 3 initial warm-up epochs), with a learning rate set to 2e-5. We used the dirty-label poisoning method, where only samples with non-target labels were poisoned. The poisoning

---

[1] https://github.com/thunlp/OpenBackdoor/.

rate of the datasets for both TBADD and baseline experiments was uniformly set to 10%.

Dataset Distillation Settings. The distillation algorithm[2] employed in this study adopts the state-of-the-art text dataset distillation algorithm proposed by [22], referred to as DD. We reused the majority of the parameters from the original paper's experiments, with some adjustments made to certain hyperparameters. We conducted DD for 100 epochs, with a fixed initial learning rate (lr_inputs_embeds) of 1e-2 during dataset distillation. For training the target model during validation, the initial learning rate of model parameters (lr_init) was also fixed at 1e-2. The attention label ($attention\_label\_type$) was set to correspond to the word "[cls]". Labels in the distilled dataset were represented using hard labels. The batch size for the distilled dataset ($train\_batch\_size$) was fixed at 128. The ratio of ω_1 to ω_2 was set to 1:1. The validation of the victim model was conducted 50 times.

4.2 Attack Results

Table 2. TBADD overall attack performance. "No Attack" and "No Attack DD" denote training on the clean original dataset and training on the clean distilled dataset.

Datasets	SST-2		HSOL	
Attack	CACC	ASR	CACC	ASR
No Attack	0.914	-	0.950	-
No Attack DD	0.889	-	0.949	-
Badnets	0.908	1.000	0.953	0.999
Badnets_TBADD	0.877	1.000	0.950	1.000
AddSent	0.906	1.000	0.953	1.000
AddSent_TBADD	0.878	0.997	0.943	1.000
SynBKD	0.885	0.940	0.943	0.991
SynBKD_TBADD	0.853	0.896	0.922	0.980
StyleBKD	0.861	0.910	0.923	0.801
StyleBKD_TBADD	0.842	0.862	0.905	0.721
LISM	0.892	0.763	0.935	0.767
LISM_TBADD	0.832	0.807	0.889	0.710

The results in Table 2 demonstrate that the four types of backdoor attacks under the TBADD framework are capable of effectively injecting backdoors into the distilled dataset. Our main observations are as follows:

---

[2] https://github.com/arumaekawa/dataset-distillation-with-attention-labels/.

TBADD has only a slight impact on the accuracy of the original task. The average decrease in CACC is 3.32% and 1.96% for the two datasets. This is because some features are inevitably lost after the compression of the original dataset through distillation. For example, the accuracy of No Attack DD under SST-2 decreases by 2.5% compared to No Attack. However, considering the small decrease in CACC performance, especially the 0.3% decrease for Badnets_TBADD under HSOL, it can ensure the performance of downstream models (attacker challenge 1).

TBADD performs best in terms of attack effectiveness on Badnets and AddSent methods, achieving nearly 100% attack success rate. The other two invisible backdoor attacks also exhibit good performance, especially the SynBKD_TBADD method under HSOL, with an ASR of 98%, which is only 1.1% lower than the baseline. Meanwhile, we observed that LISM_TBADD improved the ASR by 4.4% over the baseline in the SST-2 dataset but did not show any improvement in the HSOL dataset. This discrepancy can be attributed to the nature of the SST-2 dataset, which is an emotion annotation task dataset. The distilled models trained on SST-2 are more sensitive to language style. In contrast, the distilled models on HSOL tend to focus more on semantic and logical features.

4.3 Defense Results

Non-inference Stage Backdoor Defense. Non-inference stage backdoor defense mainly relies on detecting and filtering suspicious samples by leveraging the anomalous behaviors of poisoned samples compared to clean ones. The non-inference stage refers to the period before the model is deployed, during which there are two critical phases of defense: before and during model training.

1) **Before model training.** Defenders can resist backdoors by screening the text dataset. However, distilled datasets are represented by multidimensional embedding vectors, unlike discrete symbolic information, making it difficult for humans to intuitively understand or visualize data in high-dimensional space. This characteristic is brought about by the distillation algorithm. Furthermore, current methods for reverse-engineering tokens from embeddings [11] have low precision and recall in long sentence recovery tasks. Therefore, the method of manually screening the dataset is difficult to detect backdoors. Additionally, existing defense methods based on training datasets are essentially premised on input information being text [26,42], so backdoor defense during this period cannot resist TBADD.

2) **During model training.** Considering that using distilled datasets for training only requires a few simple parameter updates, unlike traditional model training methods that require multiple rounds of iteration, it is difficult to capture poisoned features during this process [37].

Inference Stage Backdoor Defense. Inference stage backdoor defense is conducted after model training, involving anomaly detection or fine-tuning of samples input into the model. In this experiment, two inference-stage deployment defense algorithms, STRIP [8] and RAP [41], were selected for experimentation. We reused the defense algorithm hyperparameters provided by Openbackdoor to conduct relevant tests on the SST-2 dataset. The results are shown in Table 3. It can be observed that STRIP cannot effectively resist TBADD, with a high success rate of attacks. Conversely, RAP demonstrates effective defense against Badnets_TBADD, but the CACC drops by 16%. For the other three types of attacks, although the decline in CACC is less pronounced, RAP fails to accurately detect backdoor samples. Therefore, backdoor defense methods cannot eliminate TBADD backdoors without significantly impacting the original performance of the model.

Table 3. The Performance of TBADD Under Different Backdoor Defenses

Defend	No defense		STRIP		RAP	
Attack	CACC	ASR	CACC	ASR	CACC	ASR
Badnets_TBADD	0.877	1.000	0.854	0.930	0.710	0.143
AddSent_TBADD	0.878	0.997	0.810	0.975	0.817	0.430
SynBKD_TBADD	0.853	0.896	0.831	0.843	0.816	0.764
StyleBKD_TBADD	0.842	0.862	0.831	0.830	0.800	0.512
LISM_TBADD	0.832	0.807	0.841	0.727	0.775	0.680

4.4   Ablation Study

In this section, we propose an ablation study to evaluate the impact of various hyperparameter choices in our experiments. Our analysis primarily focuses on the following aspects:

Impact of Loss Weights ω_1 and ω_2. $\omega_1 : \omega_2$ reflects the importance of clean sample accuracy and backdoor attack success rate when evaluating the performance of the target model. We conduct additional experiments using Syn-BKD_TBADD on the SST-2 dataset to explore the influence of $\omega_1 : \omega_2$ on backdoor attacks. The results, as shown in Fig. 3, indicate that as the proportion of ω_1 decreases, the accuracy of clean samples under the same poisoning rate also decreases, while the success rate of backdoor attacks increases. Loss weights have a significant impact on the results when the poisoning rate is 10% and 20%. Choosing a larger ω_1 may result in poor performance of the backdoor attack, but too small a value will also negatively affect the performance of the original task. However, the impact is smaller at poisoning rates of 5% and 30%, indicating that adjusting weights under various poisoning rates is a reasonable approach. The experiment demonstrates that the loss weights affect the final performance of the model. By specifying an optimization strategy and adjusting these two parameters, the attacker can find a relatively satisfactory balance between the ASR and CACC metrics.

Impact of Poisoning Rate. In Fig. 3, the left plot shows a steady downward trend in CACC, with a nearly 5% decrease as the poisoning rate increases from 1% to 30%. Due to the stronger correlation in the poisoned data, the right plot of Fig. 3 shows that when the poisoning rate is between 1% and 10%, the ASR exhibits an overall increasing trend with a substantial rate of increase. As the poisoning rate continues to rise, the ASR begins to increase more slowly and eventually fluctuates between 90% and 94%. Therefore, attackers need to consider that when ASR reaches a certain level, further increasing the poisoning rate will not yield higher attack gains but will instead lead to a decline in CACC and an increased risk of backdoor exposure.

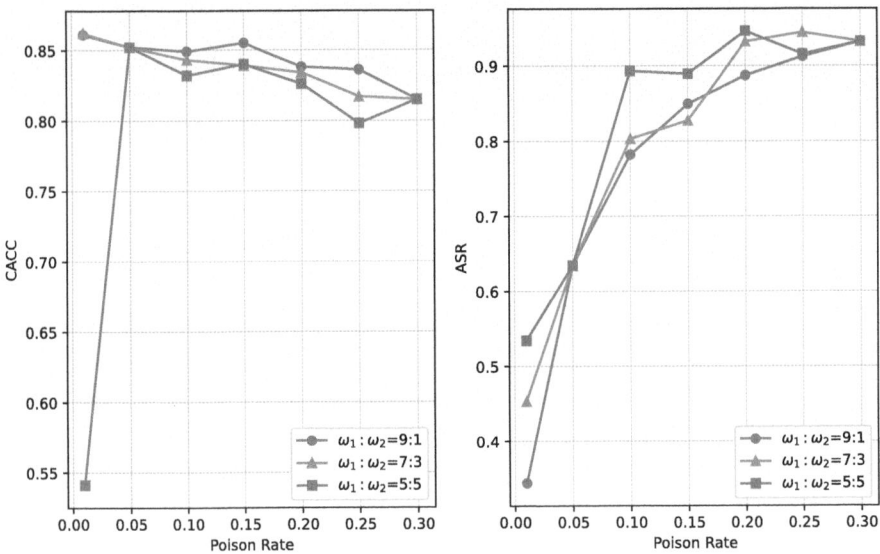

Fig. 3. The Impact of $\omega_1 : \omega_2$ and Poison Ratio

Impact of Distillation Epochs. Figure 4 illustrate the effect of dataset distillation epochs (ranging from 10 to 400) on backdoor attacks using the SST-2 datasets. The following observations can be made:

1) **Initial Epochs.** When the model is trained for only 10 epochs, CACC is below 60%, indicating that the distilled dataset cannot capture the generalization features of the original dataset. Despite the low accuracy for clean samples, ASR reaches a high level. For instance, in AddSent_TBADD and StyleBKD_TBADD, the results are only about 10% lower than the optimal ASR. This suggests that in the early stages of distillation, the dataset tends to extract simpler backdoor features, effectively learning "shortcuts." which is consistent with the observation in [37] that backdoor models are inclined to learn backdoor features during the initial training phase.

2) **Intermediate Epochs.** At 50 epochs, both CACC and ASR show significant improvement. The model starts to balance between learning the generalization features of clean samples and the specific backdoor features.

3) **Later Epochs.** Beyond 200 epochs, the CACC and ASR become relatively stable with minimal changes. This indicates that the model has reached a point where additional training epochs do not substantially impact the performance, maintaining a balance between CACC and ASR.

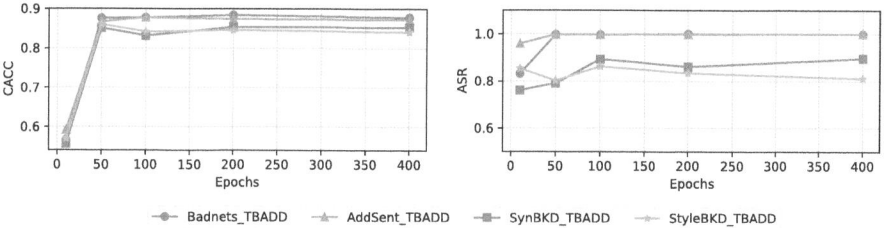

Fig. 4. The Impact of Distillation Epochs

5   Conclusion

In this study, we propose a backdoor attack framework under text dataset distillation (TBADD), which poisons distilled datasets and impacts model security. Our experiments demonstrate that TBADD exhibits strong attack capabilities, effectively countering inference-stage backdoor defenses. Additionally, we observe a tendency for dataset distillation to learn "shortcuts", which provides insights for defending against backdoor attacks during the distillation process. We hope this work will promote further research in backdoor defense and raise awareness among practitioners to ensure the reliability of training data and models.

Acknowledgments. We would like to thank the anonymous ISC2024 reviewers for their valuable comments and suggestions. This work was supported by the Fundamental Research Funds for the Central Universities (Grant Nos. 3282023012, 3282023033), Cybersecurity Team Development 2024 (Grant No. 3282024056) and the Open Fund Project of the Key Laboratory of Cybersecurity, MOE.

References

1. Brown, T., et al.: Language models are few-shot learners. In: Advances in Neural Information Processing Systems, vol. 33, pp. 1877–1901 (2020)
2. Carlini, N., Chien, S., Nasr, M., Song, S., Terzis, A., Tramer, F.: Membership inference attacks from first principles. In: 2022 IEEE Symposium on Security and Privacy (SP), pp. 1897–1914. IEEE (2022)

3. Chen, X., et al.: BadNL: backdoor attacks against NLP models with semantic-preserving improvements. In: Proceedings of the 37th Annual Computer Security Applications Conference, pp. 554–569 (2021)

4. Cui, G., Yuan, L., He, B., Chen, Y., Liu, Z., Sun, M.: A unified evaluation of textual backdoor learning: frameworks and benchmarks. In: Advances in Neural Information Processing Systems, vol. 35, pp. 5009–5023 (2022)

5. Dai, J., Chen, C., Li, Y.: A backdoor attack against LSTM-based text classification systems. IEEE Access **7**, 138872–138878 (2019)

6. Davidson, T., Warmsley, D., Macy, M., Weber, I.: Automated hate speech detection and the problem of offensive language. In: Proceedings of the International AAAI Conference on Web and Social Media, vol. 11, pp. 512–515 (2017)

7. Finn, C., Abbeel, P., Levine, S.: Model-agnostic meta-learning for fast adaptation of deep networks. In: International Conference on Machine Learning, pp. 1126–1135. PMLR (2017)

8. Gao, Y.: Design and evaluation of a multi-domain trojan detection method on deep neural networks. IEEE Trans. Dependable Secure Comput. **19**(4), 2349–2364 (2021)

9. Gou, J., Yu, B., Maybank, S.J., Tao, D.: Knowledge distillation: a survey. Int. J. Comput. Vision **129**(6), 1789–1819 (2021)

10. Gu, T., Dolan-Gavitt, B., Garg, S.: Badnets: identifying vulnerabilities in the machine learning model supply chain. arXiv preprint arXiv:1708.06733 (2017)

11. Gupta, S., Huang, Y., Zhong, Z., Gao, T., Li, K., Chen, D.: Recovering private text in federated learning of language models. In: Advances in Neural Information Processing Systems, vol. 35, pp. 8130–8143 (2022)

12. Kenton, J.D.M.W.C., Toutanova, L.K.: Bert: pre-training of deep bidirectional transformers for language understanding. In: Proceedings of NAACL-HLT, pp. 4171–4186 (2019)

13. Krishna, K., Wieting, J., Iyyer, M.: Reformulating unsupervised style transfer as paraphrase generation. In: Proceedings of the 2020 Conference on Empirical Methods in Natural Language Processing (EMNLP), pp. 737–762 (2020)

14. Kurita, K., Michel, P., Neubig, G.: Weight poisoning attacks on pretrained models. In: Proceedings of the 58th Annual Meeting of the Association for Computational Linguistics, pp. 2793–2806 (2020)

15. Li, G., Togo, R., Ogawa, T., Haseyama, M.: Dataset distillation for medical dataset sharing. arXiv preprint arXiv:2209.14603 (2022)

16. Li, L., Ma, R., Guo, Q., Xue, X., Qiu, X.: Bert-attack: adversarial attack against BERT using BERT. In: Proceedings of the 2020 Conference on Empirical Methods in Natural Language Processing (EMNLP), pp. 6193–6202 (2020)

17. Li, S., et al.: Hidden backdoors in human-centric language models. In: Proceedings of the 2021 ACM SIGSAC Conference on Computer and Communications Security, pp. 3123–3140 (2021)

18. Li, Y., Li, W.: Data distillation for text classification. arXiv preprint arXiv:2104.08448 (2021)

19. Liu, S., Zhang, X., Zhang, S., Wang, H., Zhang, W.: Neural machine reading comprehension: methods and trends. Appl. Sci. **9**(18), 3698 (2019)

20. Liu, Y., Li, Z., Backes, M., Shen, Y., Zhang, Y.: Backdoor attacks against dataset distillation. arXiv preprint arXiv:2301.01197 (2023)

21. Maclaurin, D., Duvenaud, D., Adams, R.: Gradient-based hyperparameter optimization through reversible learning. In: International Conference on Machine Learning, pp. 2113–2122. PMLR (2015)

22. Maekawa, A., Kobayashi, N., Funakoshi, K., Okumura, M.: Dataset distillation with attention labels for fine-tuning BERT. In: Proceedings of the 61st Annual Meeting of the Association for Computational Linguistics (Volume 2: Short Papers), pp. 119–127 (2023)

23. Morris, J., Lifland, E., Yoo, J.Y., Grigsby, J., Jin, D., Qi, Y.: Textattack: a framework for adversarial attacks, data augmentation, and adversarial training in NLP. In: Proceedings of the 2020 Conference on Empirical Methods in Natural Language Processing: System Demonstrations, pp. 119–126 (2020)

24. Nichol, A., Achiam, J., Schulman, J.: On first-order meta-learning algorithms. arXiv preprint arXiv:1803.02999 (2018)

25. Pan, X., Zhang, M., Sheng, B., Zhu, J., Yang, M.: Hidden trigger backdoor attack on {NLP} models via linguistic style manipulation. In: 31st USENIX Security Symposium (USENIX Security 2022), pp. 3611–3628 (2022)

26. Pei, H., Jia, J., Guo, W., Li, B., Song, D.: Textguard: provable defense against backdoor attacks on text classification. arXiv preprint arXiv:2311.11225 (2023)

27. Prabhakar, S.N., Deshwal, A., Mishra, R., Kim, H.: Distilnas: neural architecture search with distilled data. IEEE Access **10**, 124990–124998 (2022)

28. Qi, F., Chen, Y., Zhang, X., Li, M., Liu, Z., Sun, M.: Mind the style of text! adversarial and backdoor attacks based on text style transfer. In: Proceedings of the 2021 Conference on Empirical Methods in Natural Language Processing, pp. 4569–4580 (2021)

29. Qi, F., et al.: Hidden killer: invisible textual backdoor attacks with syntactic trigger. In: Proceedings of the 59th Annual Meeting of the Association for Computational Linguistics and the 11th International Joint Conference on Natural Language Processing (Volume 1: Long Papers), pp. 443–453 (2021)

30. Qi, F., Yao, Y., Xu, S., Liu, Z., Sun, M.: Turn the combination lock: learnable textual backdoor attacks via word substitution. In: Proceedings of the 59th Annual Meeting of the Association for Computational Linguistics and the 11th International Joint Conference on Natural Language Processing (Volume 1: Long Papers), pp. 4873–4883 (2021)

31. Radford, A., et al.: Language models are unsupervised multitask learners. In: OSDI 2004: Sixth Symposium on Operating System Design and Implementation, pp. 137–150 (2004)

32. Salem, A., Zhang, Y., Humbert, M., Fritz, M., Backes, M.: ML-leaks: model and data independent membership inference attacks and defenses on machine learning models. In: Network and Distributed Systems Security Symposium 2019. Internet Society (2019)

33. Sheng, X., Han, Z., Li, P., Chang, X.: A survey on backdoor attack and defense in natural language processing. In: 2022 IEEE 22nd International Conference on Software Quality, Reliability and Security (QRS), pp. 809–820. IEEE (2022)

34. Singh, S.P., Kumar, A., Darbari, H., Singh, L., Rastogi, A., Jain, S.: Machine translation using deep learning: an overview. In: 2017 International Conference on Computer, Communications and Electronics (Comptelix), pp. 162–167. IEEE (2017)

35. Socher, R., et al.: Recursive deep models for semantic compositionality over a sentiment treebank. In: Proceedings of the 2013 Conference on Empirical Methods in Natural Language Processing, pp. 1631–1642 (2013)

36. Sucholutsky, I., Schonlau, M.: Soft-label dataset distillation and text dataset distillation. In: 2021 International Joint Conference on Neural Networks (IJCNN), pp. 1–8. IEEE (2021)

37. Tang, R.R., Yuan, J., Li, Y., Liu, Z., Chen, R., Hu, X.: Setting the trap: capturing and defeating backdoors in pretrained language models through honeypots. In: Advances in Neural Information Processing Systems, vol. 36, pp. 73191–73210 (2023)
38. Wang, T., Zhu, J.Y., Torralba, A., Efros, A.A.: Dataset distillation. arXiv preprint arXiv:1811.10959 (2018)
39. Wolf, T., et al.: Transformers: state-of-the-art natural language processing. In: Proceedings of the 2020 Conference on Empirical Methods in Natural Language Processing: System Demonstrations, pp. 38–45 (2020)
40. Yang, A., et al.: Baichuan 2: open large-scale language models. arXiv preprint arXiv:2309.10305 (2023)
41. Yang, W., Lin, Y., Li, P., Zhou, J., Sun, X.: Rap: robustness-aware perturbations for defending against backdoor attacks on NLP models. In: Proceedings of the 2021 Conference on Empirical Methods in Natural Language Processing, pp. 8365–8381 (2021)
42. Zhai, S., et al.: NCL: textual backdoor defense using noise-augmented contrastive learning. In: ICASSP 2023-2023 IEEE International Conference on Acoustics, Speech and Signal Processing (ICASSP), pp. 1–5. IEEE (2023)
43. Zhang, X., Zhang, Z., Ji, S., Wang, T.: Trojaning language models for fun and profit. In: 2021 IEEE European Symposium on Security and Privacy (EuroS&P), pp. 179–197. IEEE (2021)
44. Zhou, Y., Nezhadarya, E., Ba, J.: Dataset distillation using neural feature regression. In: Advances in Neural Information Processing Systems, vol. 35, pp. 9813–9827 (2022)
45. Zulqarnain, M., Ghazali, R., Hassim, Y.M.M., Rehan, M.: A comparative review on deep learning models for text classification. Indonesian J. Electr. Eng. Comput. Sci. **19**(1), 325–335 (2020)

Mobile Security and Trusted Execution

Emulating Android Device Drivers via Borrowed Execution Context

Alex Le Blanc[1]([⊠]) and Ivan Pustogarov[2]

[1] University of Waterloo, Waterloo, ON, Canada
a6leblan@uwaterloo.ca
[2] Concordia University, Montreal, QC, Canada
ivan.pustogarov@concordia.ca

Abstract. The ability to emulate isolated code parts in binary low-level system code such as an operating system's kernel is often both necessary and beneficial from the security analysis point of view, as it significantly reduces the search space to more interesting parts, and also because complete kernel images are very difficult or often impossible to emulate as a whole using existing emulators. In this paper, we consider this problem of emulating isolated code compartments for Android binary kernel images.

To this end, we present a framework that allows emulation of device drivers directly from binary Android kernel images by "borrowing" emulated execution context from a running stock Linux kernel. It works by injecting the Android kernel under test into the same memory space as the stock Linux kernel, logically unlinking specific isolated parts from its original kernel, and reattaching them to the stock Linux kernel.

We evaluate the correctness of our approach on a set of 56 drivers from 10 different kernels, for which it was successful in borrowing the execution context in all cases. By further extending it with coverage-based fuzzing, we fuzzed a set of 23 IOCTL drivers and discovered 4 zero-day vulnerabilities (some high-severity) which were confirmed by Google's security team.

Keywords: Emulation · Android kernel · fuzzing · device drivers

1 Introduction

Dynamic analysis is one of the proven and effective methods for finding security bugs. Moreover, it achieves its full potential in an emulated environment: emulation allows for a fine-grained control of the execution through internal state introspection, which, in turn, enables a number of useful types of instrumentation without the need to purchase physical copies of the device.

When it comes to dynamic analysis of binary low-level system code, such as an operating system's kernel (or firmware), one of the common tasks is to emulate and analyze only specific isolated parts rather the whole system. There are two reasons for this. First, it is more effective from a security analysis point of view

© The Author(s), under exclusive license to Springer Nature Switzerland AG 2025
N. Mouha and N. Nikiforakis (Eds.): ISC 2024, LNCS 15257, pp. 147–167, 2025.
https://doi.org/10.1007/978-3-031-75757-0_8

to focus on specific bug-prone parts, e.g., network packet parsing code in a network driver, or a system call handler, as it significantly reduces the search space in otherwise large system. Second, emulating a complete operating system kernel can be problematic or impossible due to the absence of a large number of emulated versions of the hardware that the low-level system code would require to boot and operate. In fact, one of the more popular emulators, Qemu [1], can properly boot kernels compiled for only a handful of hardware boards[1]. This makes, in many cases, focusing on isolated code compartments the only possible solution in terms of the amount of the hardware whose emulated versions need to be added.

Unfortunately, isolating and emulating code starting from an arbitrary location without booting the kernel first is far from obvious. This is usually hindered by missing execution context, i.e., various kernel structures and subsystems that would otherwise be initialized during the normal boot process. Without a valid execution context, the portion of the code that we try to emulate will most likely result in undefined behavior. This usually manifests as memory access violation errors when it tries to interact with uninitialized kernel memory. In this paper, we approach this problem of emulating isolated code parts for binary Android kernels images and we focus on device drivers added by the manufacturers, which usually are much less audited compared to the core kernel subsystems and historically have been a source of many vulnerabilities.

More specifically, when the execution moves to a logically separate code compartment (i.e., a driver), which is a part of a larger system (i.e., the kernel), it is expected that registers and memory at specific address ranges are initialized (i.e., are set to particular values). It is also expected that specific kernel functions, which are not part of the driver itself, are present at specific memory addresses. If such expected/valid execution context is present, the emulation will correspond to an execution run on a real device, and it becomes possible to reason about the device's security properties. If, on the other hand, the execution context is set arbitrarily, then with overwhelming probability, the emulation will not correspond to an actual device behavior. Without being able to emulate the original Android kernel, getting a precise and valid execution context is non-trivial, and the space of all possible values is too large for exhaustive search.

Our key observation is that the execution context of the stock Linux kernel configuration (that can be emulated) might be close enough to the execution context expected by individual parts of Android kernels (e.g., device drivers). Our main idea is to load the Android kernel alongside the already booted (in an emulator) stock Linux kernel, and then redirect the execution to the driver for the analysis. More precisely, we run the stock Linux kernel and then inject the Android kernel's binary into the same memory space. In this way, the two kernels "live" alongside each other, but only the stock kernel is in charge of running the system, i.e., interacting with emulated peripherals and maintaining all the kernel structures required for proper operation. We connect the injected Android kernel to the running stock kernel by redirecting calls to standard kernel functions

---

[1] While some of the peripherals, such as camera, or IR sensor, might indeed not be needed, in general, there is always a number of hardware components that are critical and are required during the boot process.

(such as `printk`) and control data structures to the corresponding versions in the stock kernel. Once the kernels are connected, we finally identify the initialization functions of the driver and move the execution there.

A different approach for a related problem was proposed in [11] in which the authors suggested a way to insert drivers originally developed for custom Android kernels into the stock Linux kernel, thus enabling emulation of these drivers. While similar in spirit, that approach has two fundamental limitations which we also try to solve in the current work. First, the approach in [11] is limited to device drivers only, while we consider an approach that, in principle, can be used to direct execution to any part/subsystem of an Android kernel. Second, and most importantly, the system presented in [11] requires drivers to be recompiled from the source code. At the same time, kernel images are shipped to end users in binary form (including initial release and system updates). Because of this, there is no guarantee that, in general, the OEM's published source code[2] exactly matches the binary running on the devices; moreover, some bugfixes can be included only into the distributed kernel binaries. In addition, the source code for some drivers might simply not be available. Working on binary kernel images (e.g., extracted from system updates) does not have the aforementioned limitations.

We implemented our approach as the LiLi framework (as in Linux in Linux). To evaluate LiLi, we used drivers from ten different Android kernels, from four vendors (Lineage[3], Huawei, HTC, and Samsung). We used 56 unique drivers to test LiLi's correctness in transferring Linux execution context. LiLi was successful in all cases. We then further extended our framework with coverage-based fuzzing and tested it on a set of 23 drivers. We ultimately discovered four zeroday vulnerabilities in Google smart TV kernels while obtaining only a handful of false positives. All discovered vulnerabilities were confirmed by Google's Android Security Team, and two of them were assigned a severity rating of "High", while another received a "Moderate" rating. Moreover, one of the high-severity vulnerabilities was discovered in one of the core Android subsystems, ION, which potentially affects a much broader set of Android devices. We received a total of 6,000 USD as bounties for reporting the vulnerabilities.

Our Contributions. In summary, we make three main contributions:

1. **LiLi (Linux in Linux).** We present LiLi, a framework that enables emulation and fuzzing of selected parts of custom Android kernels such as device drivers.
2. **Fuzzing emulated drivers.** We emulate and fuzz drivers from 10 different custom Android kernels.
3. **Discovery of zero-day vulnerabilities.** We discover 4 zero-day vulnerabilities, all of which were confirmed by Google's Android security team.

---

[2] Linux kernel is developed under GPL which in theory requires OEMs to publish their source code. In practice it remains a grey area especially when it comes to kernel modules and device drivers, many of which, in fact, come in binary form only.

[3] Lineage operating systems are custom modifications of existing kernels from other vendors. In this project, we look at four Lineage kernels based on Google, Huawei, Fairphone, and BQ kernels.

2   Background

Executable and Linkable Format (ELF). The executable and linkable format (ELF) is the standard file format for executable and relocatable object
files for a number of Unix-based systems including Linux and Android. Linux
kernel binaries themselves (e.g., vmlinux), as well as any drivers inserted at runtime, i.e., loadable kernel modules, follow this format. There are two main types
of metadata that are of particular interest to us, namely symbols and relocations. We also refer to a third type, sections, which are contiguous parts of the
binary that serve some common purpose (e.g., there is a ".text" section for
code, a ".rodata" section for read-only data, etc.).

An ELF symbol provides a reference to some part of a binary. It can be thought
of as a structure that holds information about a function or data object (e.g., a
variable). These symbols are stored in the .symtab section. Examples of the information stored in these structures are: (1) *Section index*: the ELF section that
this symbol belongs to; (2) *Value*: typically the offset of the symbol relative to
its section, but can also be a CRC checksum; (3) *Binding*: the visibility of the
symbol, typically denoted as either "local" if the scope of the symbol is limited to
a single file, or "global" if it can be made available to other files during linking;
(4) *Symbol name:* points to the symbol name in the string table section. A symbol
may belong to undefined category (in which case the section index and offset are
undefined). These are symbols that have been referenced in a compilation unit,
but which have not been defined by this compilation unit. They are resolved once
the value of a symbol is known (e.g., during linking process).

ELF relocation entries are added to a compilation unit by the compiler to
keep track of instructions that reference symbols whose location is either yet
unknown (i.e., undefined symbols) or might change. For instance, a loadable
kernel module might have a branch instruction (call or bl) to kernel-defined
printk. But during compilation, the actual address of printk is not yet known
to the module (and might even be different for different target kernels). For
this, ELF binaries include a *relocation entry* in a dedicated ELF section that
signals to the kernel module loading subsystem that this instruction's target
address should be patched/replaced by the actual address. Each relocation entry
contains information such as: (1) *Offset*: the location where a relocation needs to
be performed; (2) *Info*: contains both the index of the symbol referred to (such as
for our object in the example above), and the type of relocation; (3) *Addend*: the
offset from the relevant symbol that we are interested in (e.g., we might need the
address of a field of a structure, rather than of the structure itself). The kernel (or
program loader) then uses relocation and symbol entries to dynamically patch
each instruction to point to the correct destination.

We use relocations to connect the injected and the emulated kernels together
by adding new relocation entries.

Loadable Kernel Modules (LKMs). A device driver can either be compiled
as a constituent part of the kernel and is therefore automatically initialized at
boot-time; or be compiled as an LKM, i.e., a separate ELF binary (usually having

.ko filename extension) that can be loaded and removed from the kernel at run-time. LKMs designate their initialization routine via a pointer stored in the .gnu.linkonce.this_module section. LiLi makes use of LKM kernel subsystem to inject one Android kernel into another kernel. To specify the precise location in the injected kernel that we wish to redirect execution to, we take advantage of the initialization pointer.

The Evasion Kernel. The evasion kernel is a part of the EASIER framework [11], an ex-vivo dynamic analysis framework for Android device drivers. It is a modified version of a stock Vanilla Linux kernel that allows one to insert LKMs that were compiled for arbitrary Android host kernels. The EASIER framework provides a way to generate simplistic models for missing peripherals from the code itself with sufficiently good success rate. In this work, we use EASIER to generate hardware models for a small number of missing peripherals that are expected by the code compartments that we test. We note however that the Evasion kernel can be replaced by developing simplified hardware models of the required peripherals either manually or using another similar tool.

vmlinux. When compiling a kernel, the compiler starts by individually compiling the various source files it contains into separate object files. These object files are then linked together into a single object file, namely vmlinux.o. Then, vmlinux.o is statically linked to produce vmlinux, which is then compressed and combined with decompressing code to produce a bootable kernel image: zImage (or bzImage). Therefore, vmlinux is effectively an uncompressed version of the bootable kernel image (minus the booting metadata).

3 Overview

If it was possible to emulate Android kernels as a whole with off-the-self emulators, running driver code would not be an issue either. Unfortunately, the vast majority of Android kernels will not boot in an emulator. This motivates the high-level goal of LiLi: if we cannot boot a complete kernel in an emulator, is it still possible to emulate its isolated parts, e.g., built-in device drivers? One of the first (and naïve) alternative approaches would be to simply copy the Android kernel binary under test into an emulated memory space, set the program counter to the first instruction of the function that we want to emulate (e.g., driver's entry function), and start to execute instruction by instruction, until we reach the end of the function. Such an approach might be valid, but only for very simple and, most importantly, self-contained code, which is not the case for the majority of drivers.

To better understand the problem, consider the code snippet in Listing 1.1. This code illustrates four different categories of problems with the naïve approach above. The code consists of two functions: a) module_init(), which is supposed to be called by the kernel when the driver is loaded, and b) driver_probe(), which is supposed to be called by the kernel once the driver is registered and the device is detected. Assume we set the instruction pointer at the first instruction of module_init() and start emulated execution.

Uninitialized Pointers. When the execution reaches line 7, it tries to access global pointer `current`[4]. This pointer is defined/initialized outside of the `module_init()` function (and outside of the driver code), and, thus, will remain uninitialized for our naïve emulation. As a result, when `module_init()` tries to dereference it, a segmentation fault will occur. Moreover, the structure pointed by `current` contains a number of other pointers. With a large number of kernel-defined pointers, identifying all of them and manually setting them to correct values is not feasible.

Uninitialized Global Variables in Standard Kernel API. A related problem happens when the driver code tries to use standard kernel API functions in line 9, for example the `vmalloc()` memory allocation routine. Internally, this routine uses the `totalram_pages`[5] global variable to find where to allocate new memory. This global variable is supposed to be initialized during kernel boot; otherwise the behavior of `vmalloc()` would be undefined.

Unmapped Memory. Another problem arises when the code tries to map physical pages (line 13). Usually the kernel maps all physical memory at a specific (virtual memory) offset (conventionally called *linear mapping*) early in the boot process. On many architectures, a call to `kmap()` will return the corresponding address from this mapping. If physical memory was not mapped (which is the case for the code snippet in Listing 1.1), the pointer dereference in line 14 will result in an unmapped memory exception.

```
1  static struct platform_driver ex_plaform_driver = {
2      .probe      = driver_probe,
3  ...
4  }
5  int module_init() {
6  ...
7      struct files_struct *files = current->files; /* problem 1 */
8  ...
9      data = vmalloc(PAGE_SIZE); /* problem 2 */
10 ...
11     struct page *p;
12 ...
13     v = kmap(p); /* problem 3 */
14     *(int *)v = 42;
15 ...
16     platform_driver_register(&ex_plaform_driver); /* problem 4 */
17 ...
18 }
19
20 int driver_probe() { ... }
```

Listing 1.1. Difficulties with naïve approach to emulation.

Asynchronous Function Calls. Properly initializing all required memory might be difficult even within the scope of one driver. This is because some functions are intended to be called by the kernel asynchronously. In line 16, the code calls `platform_driver_register`, which registers callback function

---

[4] The `current` pointer refers to the user process currently executing. During the execution, for example (but not limited to) of a system call, the current process is the one that invoked the call. Kernel code can get process-specific information by using it [13]. On arm64 architecture, it is stored in the `sp_el0` machine-specific register.

[5] Defined in `mm/page_alloc.c`.

`driver_probe` with the kernel. It is then up to the kernel to call this callback at an appropriate time. The driver itself never calls this function. This usually will leave a subset of driver-defined variables uninitialized, causing problems similar to those in the previous cases.

In this paper, we use the term *execution context* to denote all variables/structures that the driver (or isolated code portion) under test might need/use during the execution. The execution context must be initialized to proper values so that the emulated execution is identical to the execution on the physical device. Only in this case can we reason about code's security proprieties. We also note that these types of problems are not specific to kernel emulation, but applicable, to varying extent, to other types of code too (e.g., userspace programs).

The goal of LiLi is, thus, to reconstruct and provide a valid execution context for an isolated part of Android kernel code (in this paper, to a built-in Android device driver). Our key observation is that custom Android kernels and the stock Linux kernel share most of the core subsystems, and, thus, the execution context maintained by the stock Linux kernel (which can be booted and emulated) might be close enough to the execution context expected by Android kernel drivers. We refer to the stock Linux kernel that will provide the execution context as the *donor kernel*, the code/driver that we would like to test and that does not initially have an execution context as *orphan code*, and the kernel to which the *orphan code* originally belongs as the *original kernel*.

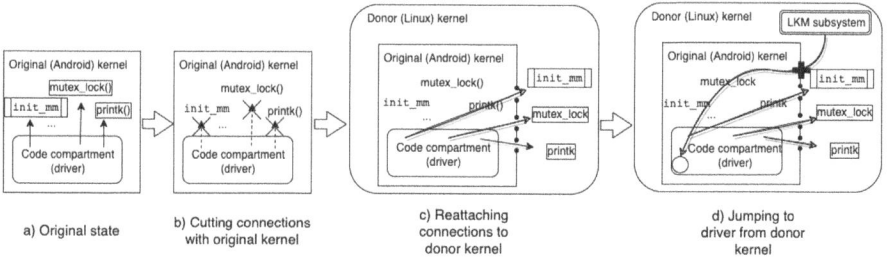

Fig. 1. Overview of LiLi: attaching orphan code to donor's execution context

LiLi's task is, through a series of transformations, to make the orphan code assimilate the execution context provided by the donor kernel. The overview of this process is shown in Fig. 1. At the beginning (Step a), the orphan code is attached to the original kernel through a series of links; they connect it to the original kernel's (uninitialized) data structures and functions that operate on these structures. Thus, at Step b, LiLi cuts these original connections by replacing all references to these structures and functions with undefined symbols.

LiLi then reattaches (re-links) the orphan code to the donor Linux kernel at Step c. This is done in two sub-stages: first by adding new relocation entries that are specifically crafted to point to the donor's kernel code, and, during the second sub-stage, transforming the original kernel binary (that includes the orphan code) to a loadable kernel module. When this *surrogate module* is loaded into the donor kernel during the next steps, the donor kernel's module loading subsystem is forced, by the new relocations, to reattach the orphan code to itself. During this step, it might happen that the orphan code depends on a small number of functions/subsystems for which there are no alternatives in the donor kernel. In this case, we can redirect such calls to stub functions that return immediately (effectively skipping such calls). For references to data objects that have no alternatives in the donor kernel, LiLi refers to the objects from the original kernel, because either the object does not need to be initialized and everything works as intended, or it does need to be initialized, in which case the issues that arise are no different than if we had stubbed the object. Here, these objects are also recursively detached from the original kernel and reattached to the donor kernel, similar to the orphan code (e.g., if this objects stores a pointer to `printk`).

During Step c, we also need to make the donor kernel compatible with the orphan code as much as possible. For this, we align the donor's kernel-driver API to match the original kernel through its configuration. Once this is done, as the last step (Step d), LiLi instructs the donor kernel to pivot the execution to the code under test by adding a function pointer to a specific section in the surrogate module.

We finally proceed by booting the Linux donor kernel in Qemu, which creates the proper execution context. We then insert the original kernel transformed into a surrogate module (with includes the orphan code) into the donor kernel. We can then proceed to fuzzing the driver. More specifically, we focus on IOCTL system calls. For this step we chose to use syzkaller, but any other kernel fuzzer would work too.

4   Implementation

LiLi's goal is to make the orphan (driver) code run within the donor kernel's execution context. For this it first needs to be disconnected from the original kernel. The orphan code is functionally connected to its original kernel through the use of API calls[6] (e.g., `printk` or `vmalloc`) and global data structures (e.g., `init_mm`). To cut these connections we need to: (a) precisely *locate the code and data* that belongs to the driver (which will effectively define the border between the driver and the original kernel); (b) *find all instructions and data* within the driver code that reference functions/data outside of the driver code. In practical terms, cutting connections and reattaching them to the donor kernel means patching these instructions/data (in our specific implementation, the patching happens dynamically, i.e., when the donor kernel runs in the emulator).

4.1   Locating Driver's Code and Data in the Original Kernel Binary

The original kernel's `vmlinux` contains a symbol table[7], and some of the symbol entries will naturally belong to the driver code. These entries, in turn, will contain

---

[6] More precisely, ones exported by the original kernel functions and variables.

[7] For stripped kernel binaries which don't have the corresponding ELF section, we can still extract the symbol table: the kernel stores it internally as it needs it at run-time.

the offsets and sizes of `vmlinux` parts that store the driver's code and data. Our goal for this subsection is, thus, to identify these symbols.

In order to find the driver's symbols, we consider two main types: local and non-local. Each type of symbol will require a different approach.

Local Symbols. For local symbols, we refer to symbols that have a binding of "LOCAL". These symbols represent functions and variables that are limited only to the scope of the file that defines them (e.g., static functions). When compiling a C file, the GCC compiler will normally place all these local symbols together in the symbol table right after a debugging symbol of type "FILE" whose name is the name of the compiled source file. When linking multiple `.o` files together, the GNU linker will place these groups of local symbols sequentially in the new symbol table, each group still preceded by the corresponding "FILE" symbol. Thus, we can search the symbol table for everything between the FILE symbol with a source file's name and the next FILE symbol. More specifically, we take all such symbol table entries for symbols that have non-zero size (to remove debugging symbols).

Non-local Symbols. As for non-local symbols (i.e., symbols with "GLOBAL" and "WEAK" bindings), the challenge is that they are necessarily listed after all the LOCAL symbols in the symbol table, without a nearby symbol that identifies the source file that defines them (like the aforementioned FILE symbols). We must instead directly scan the source file itself to recover the names of these global symbols (via `ctags`). For each of these symbols, we then scan the `vmlinux` symbol table for the GLOBAL symbol with the same name (or WEAK symbol if the function has the "`__weak`" descriptor). We use the driver source code for the sole purpose of identifying function names and names of `.c` files. We never need to compile the driver, nor analyze its functions' bodies, and the code that we test during fuzzing comes directly from the kernel binary image. We discuss an alternative approach in Sect. 6.

Variable Declarations Behind Preprocessing Macros. Some variable declarations can be hidden behind macros which makes it more difficult to identify them without using a C preprocessor. To get around this, if we have a GLOBAL object symbol that is not a part of the list of driver symbols, we search the donor kernel's `System.map` file to find if that symbol exists there, and if it does not, we assume that this symbol should have been declared by the driver.

4.2 Instructions of Interest

At this point, we have categorized all the symbols in the original kernel's `vmlinux` into those that belong to the driver, and those that do not. Moreover, from these symbols we also have located `vmlinux` segments[8] that contain the driver's code Our next task is to scan these segments for instructions that reference code and data outside of the driver. These will be the very connections that we cut later.

---

[8] We mean contiguous parts of the binary here, not ELF program segments.

There are two types of instructions which are of interest to us: (a) branch instructions that call a function outside of the driver; (b) sequences of instructions that access data outside of the driver. Recovering the destination of a branch (e.g., bl) is relatively straightforward by looking at its argument[9]. We check if this destination address points to outside of the driver code, and if this is the case, we save the location of this instruction for future use. We also resolve its destination address to a symbol (e.g., printk) and save it too (saving the symbol name is important as it will be used to reattach the driver to the donor kernel).

Finding places where the driver accesses data objects external to the driver is more complicated. Unlike function calls where a single bl instruction immediately gives us the destination, access to data objects involves more than one instruction. By using the reference manual for ARMv8 we narrowed down two pairs of instructions that can cross page boundaries[10] for data access: (adrp; add), and (adrp; ldr) (note that these instructions are always paired). The argument to adrp instruction gives us the page for the object, and the argument to either add or ldr gives us the offset of the object in this page. We, thus, find the relative (to PC) destination address of data object as

(adrp_dest << 12 + add_dest) or

(adrp_dest << 12 + ldr_offset)

depending on which pair of instructions was used[11]. For example, the code might contain the following instructions: (adrp x0, n_pages; add x0, offset) or, alternatively, (adrp x0, n_pages; ldr x1, [x0, offset]); the object address will be computed as (pc + n_pages << 12 + offset).

One of the difficulties that required a bit more sophisticated analysis is that these pairs of instructions are non-atomic, i.e., the two instructions in a pair can be interspersed by another unrelated instruction. Moreover, different pairs can even overlap. To tackle this problem, we use a list to keep track of unpaired adrp instructions, to then compare the registers used by subsequent add and ldr instruction with those of the adrp's in the list. If the registers match, then the two destinations are added to obtain the precise destination of that pair (and the adrp can be removed from the list). We then resolve these destinations to specific symbols using the symbol table.

Finally, similarly to branch instructions, we save for future use the locations of (adrp;add)/(adrp;ldr) pairs together with the symbol names they reference.

4.3   Data of Interest

While the original kernel's vmlinux is statically linked, it still contains relocations that patch data objects if the CONFIG_RELOCATABLE configuration option

---

[9] There is the case of indirect calls, such as bl x0, but these are usually used to reference the code in the driver itself. This was also the case in all our experiments.

[10] Accesses within page boundaries will point back to the driver. No re-linking is required in this case.

[11] The destination address computed in this way may fall in the middle of a data object. While it was never the case in our experiments, one can use symbol start address and symbol size to find if an address falls within the boundaries of a data object.

is enabled (e.g., for KASLR to shift objects in memory), which was always the case for all the kernels under test.

LiLi therefore recreates these relocations in the surrogate module. Each such original relocation in `vmlinux` references an absolute address. We thus first search for the symbol corresponding to this address in `vmlinux`'s symbol table. LiLi then creates a relocation with the object's address and the found symbol. If `CONFIG_RELOCATABLE` is disabled (which should not be the case for production kernels), we can scan the driver's `data` section and create new relocations for each address that points to a symbol.

4.4   Re-linking

At this point, we should have a table that contains information about all connections (links) from the driver to the original kernel: for both functions and data objects. This table has the following format (*link_type, [from]:instr_address, [to]:destination_symbol*), where *link type* is either `func` or `data_object`, *instr_address* is the address of an instruction in the driver that references the original kernel, and *destination_symbol* is the name of the specific symbol that this instruction references. This table, in fact, can be seen as a *restored* simplistic and abbreviated version of the relocation table that was used (and discarded) when `vmlinux` itself was compiled and linked.

Now, equipped with this recovered relocation table, we can correctly disconnect the driver from the original kernel and reattach (re-link) it to the donor kernel. There are two ways to achieve this: we can either re-link the driver statically by rewriting the donor kernel binary, or we can do it dynamically (i.e., during donor kernel's runtime). In our implementation, we use a dynamic approach: ideally we would want to avoid any modifications to the donor kernel so that our approach is as generic as possible regarding kernel versions. But more importantly, the Linux kernel, at its very core, already has a way to accommodate additional code dynamically via the loadable kernel module subsystem; we are going to hijack this functionality.

From a high level, we transform the original kernel (together with the driver) into a loadable kernel module compatible with the donor kernel. We call the resulting module *surrogate module*. During this transformation, we incorporate the recovered relocation table into this new module. We then let the donor kernel do the rest: when we load the surrogate module, the donor kernel is forced by the added relocation entries to patch all necessary instructions, effectively reattaching the driver to itself. In the rest of this section, we will provide more technical details regarding our implementation.

Initializing Surrogate Module. We start by generating a simple C file that contains basic, minimally required ELF sections needed in a kernel module (e.g., `.modinfo`) and compiling it into a `.ko` file. LiLi then extracts the entirety of the original kernel's `vmlinux` image, debugging sections aside, and copies it into this file's `.text` section.

The reason we copy parts that may not be necessary for our particular driver is that all the code in `vmlinux` is statically linked and is position-independent (i.e., PC-relative), meaning that we will need to maintain the same offsets between instructions and their destinations. Moreover, it is important that the whole binary goes into one section, because otherwise upon module insertion, separate ELF sections may be loaded into different memory regions in the kernel, potentially causing the relative offsets used by the instructions to point to unintended destinations. Note that copying the entire `vmlinux` image like this, while formally preserving existing symbol and relocation tables in the output file, effectively disables them for kernel loading subsystems (as they are now residing in one single section together with everything else).

Adding Symbols and Relocations. Once we have the skeleton ELF file for the surrogate module, we can start adding symbols and relocations from our recovered simplistic relocation table. This procedure consists of two sub-steps. First, LiLi adds a new empty symbol section, and for each entry in the table, creates a new symbol entry with the same name but `UNDEF` as the value in case this name is present in the donor kernel. This will instruct the donor kernel that these symbols should be resolved, and it will resolve them to the donor kernel's version of these symbols. During the second sub-step, LiLi recreates the actual relocation table from our simplistic table, using the same values for the instruction address and symbol name. Once added, this should instruct the donor kernel to patch the corresponding instructions and point them to its own symbols.

This procedure with adding symbols and relocations effectively prepares the driver to be unlinked from the original kernel and linked to the donor kernel. In our experiments, this address resolution technique always worked correctly.

Driver Entry Points. As the last step, we need to: (a) identify the driver's entry/initialization functions, and (b) make the donor kernel jump to these functions. We first note that all initialization functions are prefixed by "`__initcall_`" in `vmlinux`'s symbol table at compile time. Moreover, depending on the intended call order, a different suffix is appended to the function's name by the compiler (suffix of 1 means it's called before ones with 1 s, which are before 2, which are before 2 s, etc.). Thus, by looking for the `__initcall_` prefix among the driver's LOCAL symbols, we can recover the names of the driver's initialization functions. Then, by looking at the suffixes of these symbol names, we can recover the order in which these functions should be called.

In order to solve (b), we note that when loading a module, the kernel LKM subsystem looks at the module's `.gnu.linkonce.this_module` section at a particular offset, where it expects to find a pointer to the initialization function; we use this feature to finally redirect execution to the driver. In order to accommodate multiple initialization functions using a single available slot in `.gnu.linkonce.this_module`, we create a trampoline code that calls each of the built-in driver's initialization functions in the correct order. We inject this trampoline at the beginning of the surrogate module's `.text` section (since there is only irrelevant system code there anyways). We then add a relocation entry in `.rela.gnu.linkonce.this_module` that refers to the trampoline. This ensures that all the initialization functions are called at load-time.

5   Evaluation

In this section, we evaluate two aspects of LiLi. First, we check if LiLi can correctly unlink a built-in driver from its original kernel and then re-link it to the donor kernel. Second, we test if the re-linked drivers can: (a) run in the context of the donor kernel, and (b) be fuzzed. More importantly, we test if LiLi can be used to find new bugs, with our primary focus on IOCTL handlers.

For emulation and fuzzing, we use three components external to LiLi: Qemu as the emulator; the evasion kernel from the EASIER framework as the donor kernel; and syzkaller as the fuzzer. The reason for choosing the evasion kernel as the donor kernel is that Android drivers often require a specific peripheral. Without an emulated version of these peripherals (usually not implemented by Qemu), achieving acceptable code coverage is difficult. The EASIER framework can be used to substitute the missing peripherals with simplistic models derived from the driver code itself. This allows us to test LiLi without implementing emulated versions of the hardware. We also extended the evasion framework to accommodate more types of drivers. More specifically, we added support for I2C drivers in addition to platform drivers provided by EASIER. Finally, we extended EASIER's evasion kernel by porting several Android subsystems, thus, extending the set of drivers that EASIER can handle even further.

5.1   Experimental Dataset

In order to test LiLi's re-linking capabilities, we use 56 different IOCTL drivers from 10 different Android kernels: Samsung (Galaxy S9, Galaxy Note 9), Huawei (P20 Pro, Mate 10 Pro), HTC (Exodus, U12+) and Lineage (Fairphone_sdm632, Xiaomi_msm8937, Bq_msm8953, Amlogic). As in this paper we focus on Android, we also verified that these drivers were not simultaneously a part of the vanilla Linux kernel.

For emulation and fuzzing experiments, we use 23 drivers from the same kernels. This is due to limitations of the EASIER framework to create emulated versions of the peripherals in all cases (indeed, this not a limitation of LiLi itself). See Appendix C for the list of drivers, and whether we were able to obtain a device models for each of them.

5.2   LiLi's Correctness

In order to test LiLi's correctness in unlinking and re-linking built-in device drivers, we need to first verify that it fully recovers and restores all the relocations, and second, that it can be loaded to the donor kernel. To do that, we first notice that during normal driver compilation, the kernel build system,

160   A. Le Blanc and I. Pustogarov

before creating the final `vmlinux` file, compiles each driver/subsystem separately, producing a `built-in.o` file. This intermediate file contains all the relocations that would be further used (and discarded) by the building system to link it to `vmlinux`. As we had access to the source code of the original kernels, we could use `builtin.o` files for each of the drivers to get their relocation and symbol tables[12]. We then check if they match the relocations and symbols reconstructed and extracted from `vmlinux` by LiLi.

Following this methodology, we verified that the relocation and symbol tables were correctly recovered by LiLi and were similar between the surrogate module and the corresponding built-in.o for all 56 drivers. In all these cases, the generated surrogate modules were accepted by the donor (evasion) kernel.

5.3   Fuzzing Results and Analysis

All our fuzzing tests were performed on arm64 `c7g.metal` AWS EC2 instances running Ubuntu 20.04 with 128 GiB of RAM. For instrumentation and address sanitizing, we use `KCOV` and `KASAN`, respectively. Table 1 summarizes these experiments. For each driver, the table shows its size, the amount of time it was fuzzed, code coverage, and the number of unique crashes. Each driver was fuzzed for the duration of 3 to 4.5 h with the average of 1,134 covered blocks per driver (as reported by syzkaller). Based on the code coverage, and the fact that these drivers extensively use the kernel API, we conclude that all the drivers under test were able to successfully use the donor kernel's execution context. We further categorize the drivers into three groups based on type and number of crashes.

Group 1. This group includes drivers 1 through 11 in Table 1 (i.e., 48% of drivers). Fuzzing them resulted in discovering 4 zero day vulnerabilities. All these drivers produced sufficient code coverage without any false positives, i.e., they could be analyzed precisely. This also indicates that LiLi can be used to find new bugs.

Group 2. Drivers from the second group (12 to 17) resulted in a small number of unique crashes. However, we were not able to identify the exact cause of these crashes through additional manual analysis, and we thus classified them as false positives[13].

Group 3. The third group includes drivers from 18 to 23 which produced several false positive crashes. Drivers from this group internally use the `msm` Android subsystem which LiLi also re-linked to the evasion kernel. Upon manual analysis, we found that `msm` subsystem recursively depended on yet another subsystem not present in the donor kernel. In this case, our prototype of LiLi redirected all calls to that subsystem with function stubs. This means that the drivers from

---

[12] We note that these object files were used only to obtain the ground truth about correct relocations; LiLi does not require these object files.

[13] We believe however that some of these crashes were caused by actual vulnerabilities.

group 3 were operating under only partially recovered execution context. We note however that even in this case, we had only a handful of false positives, and moreover, the drivers from this group achieved reasonable code coverage. One solution to this problem would be to recursively re-link all Android kernel subsystems used by the driver instead of using a fixed depth level (2 in our case).

Table 1. Fuzzing Results.

#	Driver	Kernel	LOC	Fuzzing Statistics		
				CPU-hours	Cov	Crashes
1	meson_ion_delay_alloc	Lineage Amlogic	500	219	1425	1
2	ionvideo	Lineage Amlogic	1566	194	2453	2
3	amaudio2	Lineage Amlogic	1465	197	1261	1
4	anc_hs	Huawei P20 Pro	1080	293	802	0
5	hicam_buf	Huawei Mate 10	630	194	1158	0
6	efuse64	Lineage Amlogic	879	196	1205	0
7	meson_uvm_allocator	Lineage Amlogic	395	196	1127	0
8	vout2_mod	Lineage Amlogic	1721	196	1148	0
9	vout_mod	Lineage Amlogic	1744	193	1144	0
10	cvbs_out	Lineage Amlogic	1881	198	1272	0
11	hbtp_input	Lineage BQ	1387	213	1809	0
12	dolby_fw	Lineage Amlogic	540	253	1124	3
13	audio_data	Lineage Amlogic	224	203	814	2
14	video_composer	Lineage Amlogic	2544	199	1222	1
15	sensors_ssc	Lineage Xiaomi	356	205	1417	1
16	anc_hs_default	Huawei P20 Pro	156	264	1426	1
17	maxim	Huawei P20 Pro	879	198	1182	2
18	msm_ispif	Lineage Xiaomi	1832	194	593	4
19	msm_ispif_32	Lineage Xiaomi	1326	193	859	3
20	msm_csiphy	Lineage Xiaomi	2355	292	598	3
21	msm_csid	Lineage Xiaomi	1153	195	594	3
22	msm_flash	Lineage Xiaomi	1207	267	593	3
23	msm_ir_led	Lineage BQ	360	213	861	4

CPU-hours = fuzzing time * 64 (the number of cores used)
Cov = total number of basic blocks of kernel code reached

5.4 Discovered Vulnerabilities

The four previously unreported bugs were found in the Lineage Amlogic kernel[14].
Given that the Lineage Amlogic kernel is based on Android TV kernels, we
have reported these bugs to Google's Android Security Team, and they were all
confirmed. In Table 2, we provide the type of vulnerabilities and Google's severity
assignment. We provide more technical details about each of the vulnerabilities
in Appendix A.

Table 2. Newly Discovered Vulnerabilities

Driver	Vulnerability Type	Severity
meson_ion_delay_alloc	Double free	High
meson_ion_delay_alloc	Memory leak	High
ionvideo	Arbitrary write	Moderate
amaudio2	Null ptr dereference	N/A

6 Limitations

In our implementation, in order for LiLi to identify the driver's symbols, it needs
to find the names of its functions and data objects. Currently, this is done by
scanning the orphan code's source files, but we only need function declarations,
and there is no requirement to parse function bodies, nor compile the files. An
alternative approach that we can use is to recover function names directly from
the vmlinux binary. To do this, we start with a single function name, e.g., the
ioctl handler that we want to analyze. As a local function symbol, it should fall
between two FILE symbols in the symbol table. Taking all entries between these
two FILE symbols allows us to obtain the remaining local symbols that belong
to the driver. In order to find all of the driver's global symbols, we analyze all
call sites in vmlinux that either belong to this initial set or jump to this set. We
then update our initial list of symbols (and filter out standard kernel API) by
recursively repeating the same procedure on this updated set.

7 Conclusion

In this paper, we approached the problem of emulating arbitrary Android kernel
images, the majority of which are not supported by existing emulators. We proposed LiLi, a tool that can be used to disconnect isolated parts of an Android

---

[14] Three of these were found directly through the fuzzing experiments, and one was
found upon manual code inspection of a driver that contained one of the other three
bugs.

kernel image, such as built-in drivers, and to re-link them to a version of the Linux kernel that can be emulated. We applied LiLi to a collection of Android kernel drivers from various vendors, which allowed us to fuzz test them. Following an analysis of the results of these experiments, we discovered 4 zero-day vulnerabilities, all of which were confirmed by the manufacturer (Google).

We believe the approach implemented by LiLi can be used to simplify dynamic analysis of various parts of custom Android kernels which can otherwise be difficult to test, making the dynamic analysis of the Android kernel more accessible. To this end, we make LiLi available as open-source on Github[15], where we also provide extended experimental results.

A   Discovered Vulnerabilities: Technical Details

In this appendix, we elaborate on each discovered vulnerability from Sect. 5.

Double Free. Driver `meson_ion_delay_alloc` defines IOCTL `UVM_IOC_ALLOC`. Here, it calls `uvm_alloc_buffer`, which allocates a `uvm_buffer` based on data passed through the IOCTL's `arg` parameter, and stores a pointer to the buffer in a `dma_buf`. This same function then tries to give the `dma_buf` a file descriptor `fd`, and if this fails, it then `kfree`'s the `uvm_buffer`. However, the `dma_buf`'s reference count will also be dropped, causing the release function `meson_uvm_release` to be called, where the `dma_buf`'s `uvm_buffer` is once again `kfree`'d. Hence, we have a pointer that is double freed, which produces undefined behaviour. One way to reliably cause the `fd` registration to fail is to repeatedly call `UVM_IOC_ALLOC`. This will register `dma_buf`'s over and over, until the maximum number of given `fd`'s has been reached.

Memory Leak. Command `UVM_IOC_ALLOC` from driver `meson_ion_delay_alloc` allocates a `uvm_buffer` based on data passed through the IOCTL's `arg` parameter. If another driver has the file descriptor for this buffer (e.g., if a user-space program is interacting with both drivers), then it can call `dma_buf_map_attachment` on this buffer, which will eventually call `meson_uvm_alloc_buffer`. This uses `ion_alloc`, which allocates a buffer inside memory pools belonging to the `ion` subsystem, based on data in the `uvm_buffer`. This includes the buffer's size, which it takes from a field in the `uvm_buffer` allocated as a result of the `UVM_IOC_ALLOC` IOCTL. Since the `meson` driver does not contain any checks for this buffer size provided by the user-space, this means that an application interacting with these two drivers could create buffers of arbitrary size in the `ion` memory pools, potentially draining them and denying other processes from using these pools. Note that this would not normally be found by fuzzing, as its exploitation requires a fair amount of set-up (e.g., there needs to be a custom driver on top of the `meson` driver).

---

[15] https://github.com/AlexLB99/LiLi.

Arbitrary Write. The `ionvideo` driver defines IOCTL `vidioc_qbuf`, which takes as input a pointer p to a `v4l2_buffer`. Then, the `vidioc_qbuf` function writes to an array at index `p->index`, but without first validating the value of `p->index`. Since the contents of the `v4l2_buffer` that p points to are user-provided, a user could control the write address of this particular operation.

Null Ptr Deref. The `amaudio` driver creates multiple `dev` files at insertion time (`amaudio2_out`, `amaudio2_in`, etc.). Several of these files use the same IOCTL handler, wherein some commands call `mutex_lock` on `amaudio->sw.lock` and `amaudio->hw.lock`. However, these locks are only initialized via `mutex_init` in the `open` function if the file being opened is `amaudio2_out`. Thus, invoking IOCTLs that lock these locks with other `dev` files that use the same IOCTL handler (e.g., `amaudio2_in`) will result in an attempt to lock an uninitialized lock, ultimately causing a null pointer dereference.

B   Related Works

Given the variety of challenges surrounding dynamic analysis techniques, in many cases, researchers limit the scope of their work to a single type of driver. vUSBf [14], which provides a framework that increases the performance of USB device driver fuzzing, by using the USB redirection protocol to communicate with these devices in virtual environments (with virtualization enabled). Similarly, POTUS [9] also enables the fuzzing of USB drivers in virtual machines, but allows for emulation of arbitrary USB devices as well, improving ease of use. Peng and Payer [10] would later propose a similar tool, but this time with a lesser reliance on symbolic execution, mitigating the associated overhead and scalability issues. Another popular area of focus is the kernel's WiFi drivers and devices. Some approaches will emulate certain WiFi devices in order to fuzz drivers that use these devices (e.g., Keil and Kolbitsch [6], with IEEE 802.11 devices), typically with the goal of finding vulnerabilities in the syscall interface. In contrast, PeriScope [15] explores the hardware-OS boundary by monitoring the two primary types of read accesses (MMIO and DMA) issued by drivers to their devices, and injecting fuzzed values whenever such a read is encountered. Overall, these techniques perform well in their niche, however, they naturally lack the breadth that we aim for.

There are also more generalized tools that allow for the automated analysis of the Linux kernel and its drivers. For instance, Charm [17] runs the device driver in a virtual machine, and provides a way for that driver to communicate with physical devices. It achieves this by redirecting I/O calls issued by the driver through a customized USB channel. SURROGATES [7] and AVATAR [18] offer similar functionality, but for embedded systems. These techniques opt to redirect I/O accesses to physical devices using FPGA bridges and the JTAG debugger backend, respectively. All of these approaches take an additional step toward complete driver emulation, but they still rely on the presence of physical hardware, which can be expensive and difficult to acquire. Moreover, even with the problem of hardware being resolved, there are still some challenges on the software side. This is especially evident in the case of Charm, which deals with kernel drivers. In order to resolve all the associated software dependencies, the authors mention that an experienced security analyst would normally take several days to port a driver to a custom kernel that can be emulated.

One prevalent solution to the problem of missing peripherals is the use of symbolic execution. For instance, SymDrive [12] allows for the creation of symbolic devices that specialized instrumented x86 Linux kernel drivers can interact with. This is done with the help of the S2E [4] platform, which can be used to symbolically execute an entire operating system's stack. Another example is FIE [5], which can be used to detect vulnerabilities in MSP430 microcontroller firmware. It uses the KLEE [3] symbolic execution engine, and intercepts a driver's accesses to memory-mapped registers (used for hardware interaction), returning custom symbolic values provided by FIE. In a similar way to PeriScope (sans the symbolic execution), FIE is therefore able to execute a driver without the presence of its corresponding devices. This technique only targets simple firmware programs relevant to MSP430 microcontrollers, meaning there is no guarantee that a similar technique could be used for the analysis of more complex drivers. More generally, symbolic execution techniques tend to suffer from slowness caused by the constraint solving problem, as well as path explosion issues. Moreover, in order to find bugs, custom checkers need to be used to solve the constraints produced as output of symbolic execution. Different kinds of bugs will require different checkers, and writing these takes time and experience.

Other techniques (e.g., [2,8,16]) opt for a static approach to vulnerability detection. The advantage of static approaches is that they allow to entirely bypass the challenge of code execution. However, getting false positives is a flaw that is universal across static analysis techniques. The more false positives there are, the more time and expertise is needed to identify real bugs.

Finally, the EASIER framework [11] mitigates some of the challenges of dynamic analysis (e.g., needing hardware or complex emulation) by resolving certain hardware and software dependencies, and by taking advantage of its dynamicity to allow for easy verification of false positives. However, it, like similar dynamic techniques, still depends on the insertion of a separately compiled stand-alone module into an emulator, rather than the insertion of a portion of a kernel binary. In other words, using it requires access to the source code of the entire kernel, as well as the ability to compile LKMs against that kernel. Not only is this not always possible, but it also limits itself to only the emulation of drivers, as opposed to any other selected part of the kernel.

C   Experimental Dataset

In Table 3, we include the 56 drivers from our initial testing set. We also indicate in the DM (Device Model) column those for which the Evasion framework was able to reconstruct a correct device model. For all these drivers, LiLi was able to reconstruct the correct relocation table.

Table 3. Experimental dataset

Driver	DM	Driver	DM	Driver	DM	Driver	DM
audio							
maxim	✓	tfa98xx	X	anc_hs	✓	anc_hs_default	✓
dolby_fw	✓	amaudio2	✓	audio_info	✓	efuse64	✓
camera							
hicam_buf	✓	hwcam_cfgdev	X	laser_module	X	msm	X
msm_csiphy	✓	msm_actuator	X	msm_ispif	✓	msm_ispif_32	✓
msm_isp	X	msm_sensor_driver	X	msm_flash	✓	msm_csid	✓
msm_eeprom	X	msm_cpp	X	cam_cci_dev	X	msm_ir_led	✓
msm_ir_cut	X	cam_eeprom_dev	X	cam_flash_dev	X	cam_actuator_dev	X
vm	X						
video							
msm_vidc_4l2	X	amlvideo2	X	picdec	X	ionvideo	✓
video_composer	✓	videotunnel	X	vout_serve	✓	vout2_serve	✓
vbs_out	✓	wifi_dt	X				
other							
hismart_ar	X	msm_rng	X	sde_rotator_dev	X	msm_vidc_4l2	X
msm_glink_pkt	X	qseecom	X	qcedev	X	sensors_ssc	✓
radio-iris	X	mdss_rotator	X	hbtp_input	✓	nq-nci	X
pn547	X	smartcard	X	aml_aucpu	X	meson_ion_delay_alloc	✓
meson_uvm_allocator	✓	msm_smd_pkt	X				

References

1. Bellard, F.: Qemu, a fast and portable dynamic translator. In: USENIX Annual Technical Conference, FREENIX Track, California, USA, vol. 41, p. 46 (2005)
2. Bessey, A.: A few billion lines of code later: using static analysis to find bugs in the real world. Commun. ACM **53**(2), 66–75 (2010)
3. Cadar, C., Dunbar, D., Engler, D.R., et al.: Klee: unassisted and automatic generation of high-coverage tests for complex systems programs. In: OSDI, vol. 8, pp. 209–224 (2008)
4. Chipounov, V., Kuznetsov, V., Candea, G.: S2e: a platform for in-vivo multi-path analysis of software systems. ACM Sigplan Notices **46**(3), 265–278 (2011)
5. Davidson, D., Moench, B., Ristenpart, T., Jha, S.: FIE on firmware: finding vulnerabilities in embedded systems using symbolic execution. In: 22nd USENIX Security Symposium (USENIX Security 2013), pp. 463–478 (2013)
6. Keil, S., Kolbitsch, C.: Stateful fuzzing of wireless device drivers in an emulated environment. Black Hat Japan (2007)
7. Koscher, K., Kohno, T., Molnar, D.: SURROGATES: enabling near-real-time dynamic analyses of embedded systems. In: 9th USENIX Workshop on Offensive Technologies (WOOT 15) (2015)
8. Machiry, A., Spensky, C., Corina, J., Stephens, N., Kruegel, C., Vigna, G.: DR.CHECKER: a soundy analysis for linux kernel drivers. In: 26th USENIX Security Symposium (USENIX Security 2017), pp. 1007–1024 (2017)

9. Patrick-Evans, J., Cavallaro, L., Kinder, J.: POTUS: probing off-the-shelf USB drivers with symbolic fault injection. In: 11th USENIX Workshop on Offensive Technologies (WOOT 17). USENIX Association, Vancouver (2017). https://www. usenix.org/conference/woot17/workshop-program/presentation/patrick-evans
10. Peng, H., Payer, M.: USBFuzz: A framework for fuzzing USB drivers by device emulation. In: 29th USENIX Security Symposium (USENIX Security 2020), pp. 2559–2575 (2020)
11. Pustogarov, I., Wu, Q., Lie, D.: Ex-vivo dynamic analysis framework for android device drivers. In: 2020 IEEE Symposium on Security and Privacy (SP), pp. 1088–1105. IEEE (2020)
12. Renzelmann, M.J., Kadav, A., Swift, M.M.: SymDrive: testing drivers without devices. In: 10th USENIX Symposium on Operating Systems Design and Implementation (OSDI 2012), pp. 279–292 (2012)
13. Rubini, A., Corbet, J.: Linux Device Drivers. Nutshell handbooks, O'Reilly & Associates (2001). https://books.google.ca/books?id=97eyKSX0oCYC
14. Schumilo, S., Spenneberg, R., Schwartke, H.: Don't trust your usb! how to find bugs in usb device drivers. Blackhat Europe (2014)
15. Song, D., et al.: Periscope: an effective probing and fuzzing framework for the hardware-os boundary. In: 2019 Network and Distributed Systems Security Symposium (NDSS), pp. 1–15. Internet Society (2019)
16. Stuart, H.: Hunting bugs with coccinelle. Master's Thesis (2008)
17. Talebi, S.M.S., Tavakoli, H., Zhang, H., Zhang, Z., Sani, A.A., Qian, Z.: Charm: facilitating dynamic analysis of device drivers of mobile systems. In: 27th USENIX Security Symposium (USENIX Security 2018), pp. 291–307 (2018)
18. Zaddach, J., Bruno, L., Francillon, A., Balzarotti, D., et al.: Avatar: a framework to support dynamic security analysis of embedded systems' firmwares. In: NDSS, vol. 14, pp. 1–16 (2014)

Software Security

SyzLego: Enhancing Kernel Directed Greybox Fuzzing via Dependency Inference and Scheduling

Chengxiang Liao, Ruipeng Wang, Yuwei Li, Juxing Chen, Yang Li,
and Zulie Pan$^{(\boxtimes)}$

National University of Defense Technology, Changsha, China
{lcx,wangruipeng,liyuwei,chenjuxing,liyanghf,panzulie17}@nudt.edu.cn

Abstract. The security of the kernel is crucial for the operating system (OS) and all user applications. Directed greybox fuzzing (DGF) is an efficient method for testing specific target sites in programs. Unlike conventional user-space application fuzzing, kernel directed fuzzing requires generating the correct sequence of syscalls and fulfilling their arguments appropriately in order to test the target site. However, the current neglect of implicit dependencies between syscalls makes fuzzing inefficient. In addition, the task scheduling, not suitable for DGF in the kernel, hinders the speed of reaching the target site.

To address these challenges, we present *SyzLego*, a general DGF solution for Linux kernel. *SyzLego* leverages a novel static analysis to enhance syscall dependency inference and adjust task scheduling for DGF. *SyzLego* first extracts nested function pointers and applies a type-matching instruction filter to infer implicit dependencies between functions. It then combines these implicit dependencies to enhance syscall dependency inference and adjusts task scheduling to suit DGF. We implement *SyzLego* and evaluate it against the state-of-the-art SyzDirect using a dataset of known bugs. The results demonstrate that *SyzLego* outperforms SyzDirect, achieving an average speedup of 2.94 and a maximum speedup of 22.46 across all reached target sites.

Keywords: Directed greybox fuzzing · Linux kernel fuzzing · Static analysis · OS security

1 Introduction

The security of the kernel is crucial for the whole operating system (OS) and all user applications. Recently, OS fuzzing becomes a popular technique for automatically discovering vulnerabilities and discovers a large number of bugs and vulnerabilities (e.g. Syzbot [5]). Reviewing bugs and vulnerabilities of this magnitude is a labor-intensive task. In this context, directed greybox fuzzing (DGF) becomes an efficient way to generate test cases that can trigger the special target sites in the tested program to stress-test the specific code area [1,2,4,10,13,14,24,31]. However, existing works mainly focus on user-space applications.

© The Author(s), under exclusive license to Springer Nature Switzerland AG 2025
N. Mouha and N. Nikiforakis (Eds.): ISC 2024, LNCS 15257, pp. 171–189, 2025.
https://doi.org/10.1007/978-3-031-75757-0_9

Unlike user-space applications, which have a fixed entry point, OS kernels implement hundreds of syscalls as the primary interface for interacting with the kernel. For example, the Linux kernel defines over 300 syscalls and Syzkaller describes nearly 4000 syscall variants [7]. For a specific target site in OS kernels, only a few syscalls are relevant. ① To effectively generate the correct sequence of syscalls to test the target site, DGF needs to understand the dependencies between syscalls and identify those relevant to the target site. Otherwise, DGF could not generate correct test sequences to trigger the target site effectively across the prohibitively large search space. However, existing works [14,24] neglect implicit dependencies, leading to generating many invalid syscall sequences for triggering the target site. Meanwhile, it is challenging to extract implicit dependencies due to the complexity of OS kernels, including indirect calls, shared variables, and nested structures. ② Additionally, during fuzzing, existing works use a similar task scheduling mode designed for coverage-guided fuzzing, which prioritizes Triage tasks to validate the coverage of test cases over Smash tasks to test the kernel. However, coverage in DGF is not as critical as it is in coverage-guided fuzzing. Consequently, a better task scheduling suitable for DGF is demanded.

To address the aforementioned problems, we present *SyzLego*, a general directed greybox fuzzing solution for Linux kernel based on SyzDirect. Similar to SyzDirect, *SyzLego* targets specific sites within the Linux kernel for testing. *SyzLego* introduces a novel static analysis method to infer implicit dependencies between syscalls, leveraging the design of the Linux kernel. Additionally, *SyzLego* optimizes task scheduling to be more suitable for DGF. Specifically, *SyzLego* first extracts function pointers nested in virtual tables and marks them as anchor functions. Second, it filters the function pointers using a type-matching instruction filter algorithm. Third, it infers relevant syscalls based on the modeling data [24]. During fuzzing, *SyzLego* uses a customized generation and mutation algorithm to synthesize test cases according to the inferred information. Furthermore, *SyzLego* employs a distance-based task scheduling approach to prioritize the most promising tasks.

We implemented the prototype of *SyzLego* based on SyzDirect and LLVM [12]. We evaluated *SyzLego* against SyzDirect using a dataset containing 39 known bugs. Among these, 18 target sites could be reached by at least one fuzzer within 12 h. The results demonstrate that *SyzLego* achieves an average speedup of 6.75 and 2.94 over SyzDirect in 6 cases and across all reached target sites, respectively

In summary, we make the following contributions:

- We propose a novel static analysis method to infer implicit dependencies between syscalls in Linux kernel and an optimized task scheduling for DGF.
- We present the design and implementation of *SyzLego*, a directed greybox fuzzing prototype for Linux kernel, which leverages the identified information and feedback to guide fuzzing.
- We conduct a comprehensive evaluation of *SyzLego* against the state-of-the-art DGF solution. The results demonstrate that *SyzLego* can reach the target faster than SyzDirect.

2   Motivation

2.1   Motivation Example

As shown in Fig. 1, a buggy target is in `rds_rdma_extra_size` (line 25 in (d)), which can lead to an excessive allocation size for `kcalloc` and a kernel warning, if `args` → `nr_local` is too large. When performing a backward control flow analysis from the buggy target, it can only be reached from `rds_sendmsg` via syscall `sendmsg` and `sendmmsg` (i.e. the orange part of (a), `sendmsg$rds` is a variant of `sendmsg`).

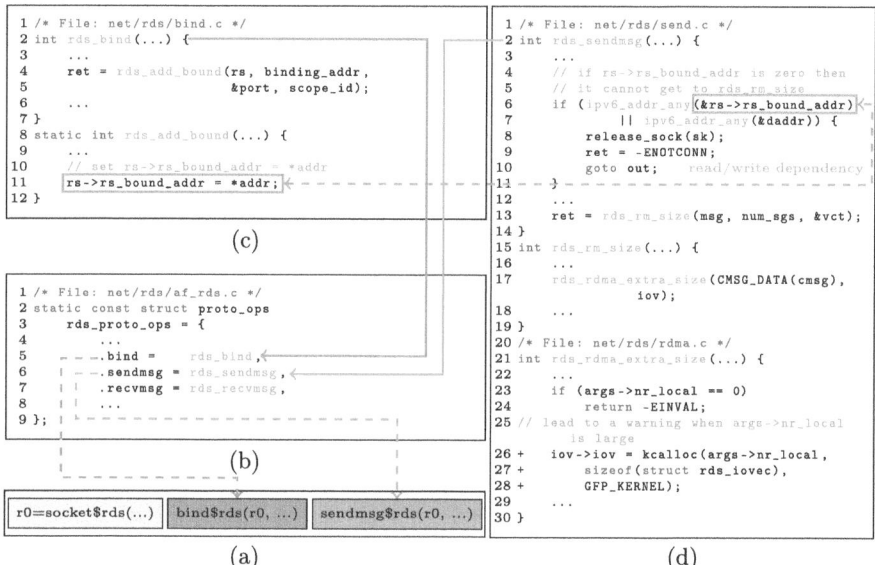

Fig. 1. An example of a buggy target [19], control-flow and corresponding syscalls in Linux kernel. (a) shows the corresponding syscalls in the PoC of this buggy target. (b) shows the virtual table of the structure (`rds_proto_ops`) that is control-flow reachable to the buggy target. (c) shows a partial implementation of the function `rds_bind`, which can write the value of `rs_bound_addr`. (d) shows the buggy target in `rds_rdma_extra_size`, which can lead to an excessive allocation size for `kcalloc` and a kernel warning (line 25 in (d)). And `rds_rdma_extra_size` can be reached through the call chain of `rds_sendmsg` → `rds_rm_size` → `rds_rdma_extra_size`, where the control-flow can be affected by a read/write dependency corresponding to line 6 in (d) and line 11 in (a), respectively.

SyzDirect [24] solved this problem by modeling Linux kernel code and Syzlang description [7] to get entry syscalls, i.e., `sendmsg$rds`. However, they overlook a critical syscall, which is `bind$rds` (i.e. the green part of (a)). Although `bind$rds` seems irrelevant to the target site, the control-flow from `rds_sendmsg` to `rds_rm_size` (the blue rectangle covered part of line 6 in (d)) is affected by `rds_add_bound` (the blue rectangle covered part of line 11 in (c)), and the write operation can be reached from `rds_bind` via syscall `bind$rds`. Therefore, test cases without syscall `bind$rds` (even if with syscall `sendmsg$rds`) can not trigger the buggy target.

2.2 Implicit Dependency

For DGF in OS kernels, the goal is to generate a specific sequence of syscalls and appropriately fill their arguments to synthesize the test cases. Typically, Syzkaller generates test cases by combining syscalls, which results in a vast search space due to the multitude of potential combinations. Many of these combinations are invalid or ineffective for triggering the target site because of the large number of syscalls. Although SyzDirect [24] reduces the search space by inferring entry syscalls, it remains challenging to generate the correct sequence of syscalls due to the lack of consideration for dependencies between syscalls.

There are two different types of dependencies between syscalls: explicit dependency and implicit dependency [17]. **Explicit Dependency:** if a syscall A generates a resource that another syscall B will use as an argument, we call that syscall B explicitly dependent on syscall A. In Fig. 1 (a), `bind$rds` and `sendmsg$rds` are explicitly dependent on `socket$rds`. **Implicit Dependency:** if the execution of a syscall B is affected by another syscall A through some shared variables, we call that syscall B implicitly dependent on syscall A. In Fig. 1 (a), `sendmsg$rds` is implicitly dependent on `bind$rds`. However, the current solution [24] only notices the explicit dependency between syscalls and applies the static-learning algorithm [23] to infer it. Yet the implicit dependency that plays an important role in getting the relevant syscalls are ignored. For instance, as mentioned above, the faulty patch in Fig. 1 shows that there is a read/write dependency between `rds_sendmsg` and `rds_add_bound` (i.e. syscall `sendmsg$rds` depends on `bind$rds` implicitly).

Challenge I: Implicit Dependency Extraction. Analyzing implicit dependencies between syscalls in Linux kernel is challenging due to the extensive use of shared variables, such as global variables, shared memory, and arguments. Furthermore, tracking these shared variables is difficult because of the complexity of the Linux kernel. For instance, the implicit dependency in the faulty patch shown in Fig. 1 is influenced by the argument. Both `rds_sendmsg` and `rds_bind` take the same argument (`struct socket *`) and then read (line 6 in (d)) and write (line 11 in (c)) the value of `rs → rs_bound_addr` (i.e. part of the argument `struct socket *`), respectively. The read and write operations are independent (i.e., without any control flow dependencies). Therefore, it is challenging to track the data flow via arguments in the Linux kernel, as it is easy to get lost in indirect calls or become confused by multi-level pointers nested within structures.

2.3   Intuition1: Modular Virtual Table Functions

Thanks to Linux kernel employs modular programming, where functions serve merely as interfaces, so many related functions will be polymerized together and nested in a structure or an array (i.e., the virtual tables).

Insight: If we extract the functions from a virtual table (neighbor functions), it is more likely that these functions have dependencies among each other compared to other functions. Therefore, combined with the backward control flow analysis on call graph (CG), we can match each function on the function paths with their neighbor functions. Then, we can get a subset of functions that may have dependencies with current target site.

2.4   Task Schedule

Currently, most OS kernel fuzzing techniques are based on Syzkaller [6], which explores the OS kernel by executing a series of test cases (i.e., a sequence of syscalls). The state-of-the-art DGF used for Linux kernel is SyzDirect [24], which is also based on Syzkaller and thus inherits a similar task scheduling mode. The primary difference is that SyzDirect replaces the Triage-Queue and Smash-Queue with a priority queue, where tasks with shorter distances have higher priority. Syzkaller-like fuzzers use a task queue with three types of tasks: **Candidate**, **Triage**, and **Smash**. ① When a Candidate task is obtained, Syzkaller adopts test case in the task and executes it. ② When a Triage task is obtained, Syzkaller tries to validate the new coverage found by the test case, performs minimization, and updates the global coverage map. ③ When a Smash task is obtained, Syzkaller mutates the test case in the task multiple times (default is 100) to generate many new test cases and executes them one by one to test the Linux kernel. In summary, the Triage task is for coverage validation and the Smash task is for testing.

The default task scheduling in Syzkaller prioritizes Triage tasks over Smash tasks indefinitely. This approach is effective when using Syzkaller to fuzz Linux kernel with coverage guidance, as any new coverage is considered interesting. Each instance of ''new coverage'' must be validated to significantly reduce the work queue, preventing many false positives from contaminating the task queue. However, in DGF, some "new coverage" is not pertinent to triggering the target site.

Additionally, due to the high startup overhead of OS kernels, Syzkaller-like fuzzers use a persistent mode to fuzz OS kernels, whereas AFL-like fuzzers typically use a fork-server to maintain a clean state. To mitigate the cumulative impact of continuous fuzzing on the kernel, Syzkaller restarts the Virtual Machine (VM) periodically (default is 1 h). When the VM is restarted, all unfinished tasks in the task queue, including seeds in unfinished Smash tasks, are discarded. SyzVegas [25] has demonstrated the importance of task scheduling for coverage-guided fuzzers, modeling it as a Multi-Armed Bandit Problem and achieving promising results in coverage guidance.

Challenge II: Task Effectiveness Identification. It is challenging to determine the effectiveness of a task before executing it, as it is difficult to measure the potential benefits and costs of each task. To identify the task scheduling pattern in DGF, we conducted a simple experiment on SyzDirect to measure the proportion of times Triage and Smash tasks were selected and discarded during the first two hours. The results, shown in Fig. 2, indicate that Triage tasks are picked more than 95% of the time on average, while Smash tasks have a discard rate of up to 80% on average. Although these seeds may hold significant potential, they lose the opportunity to be smashed and are simply added to the corpus where seeds have already been smashed. Thus, it seems unfair for fuzzer to treat them the same as seeds that have undergone the Smash process.

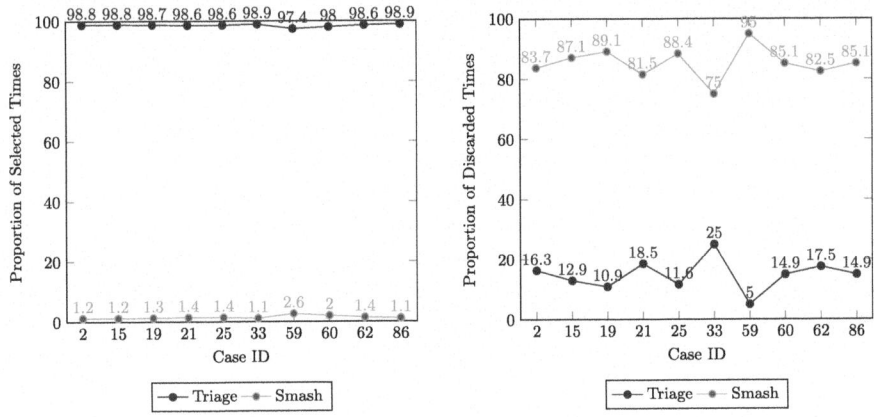

Fig. 2. The proportion of times Triage and Smash tasks were selected and discarded for 10 different target sites during the first two hours.

2.5   Intuition2: Making Fully Use of Feedback

As mentioned above, the Triage task is used for coverage validation. Consequently, this implies that the potential seed in a Triage task may exhibit some coverage that cannot be consistently reproduced. In other words, the benefits (e.g., coverage, distance, etc.) derived from this test case are likely to be significantly less than the initially observed benefits. However, in DGF, there are two different types of feedback information: coverage and distance. In this context, distance information is more important than coverage.

Insight: If a Triage task with a test case has a greater distance than a Smash task, prioritizing such a Triage task may waste time in triggering the target. Because such validation is likely to yield fewer benefits for DGF compared to executing the closer Smash task.

3 Design

3.1 Overview

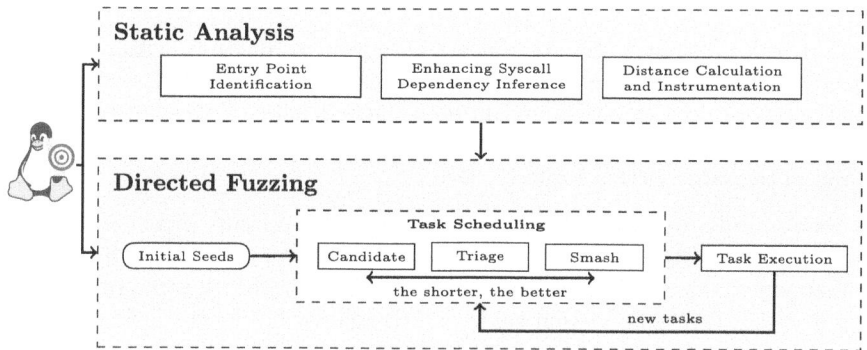

Fig. 3. Overview of *SyzLego*.

In this paper, we propose *SyzLego*, a general DGF solution for Linux kernel. Similar to other DGF for Linux kernel, *SyzLego* takes a designated target code location in Linux kernel source code as input and follows the workflow presented in Fig. 3 to synthesize test cases to trigger the target site in Linux kernel. *SyzLego* consists of two components: Static Analysis and Directed Fuzzing. During static analysis, first, *SyzLego* applies Entry Point Identification [24] to identify the entry syscalls. Then *SyzLego* applies Enhancing Syscall Dependency Inference to get the relevant syscalls. Last, *SyzLego* calculates the distance and instruments Linux kernel. After getting the static guides *SyzLego* will start the Directed Fuzzing. During the task schedule stage of the fuzzing loop, we adjust the priority of tasks in task queue based on the distance to the target site.

We have developed *SyzLego* based on SyzDirect, retaining its entry point identification. Additionally, *SyzLego* employs the same distance calculation and energy scheduling methods as SyzDirect, which are also used in AFLGo. Finally, we enhanced syscall dependency inference and task scheduling by implementing approximately 1,000 lines of C++ for an LLVM [12] pass, and 200 lines of Golang based on SyzDirect.

3.2 Enhancing Syscall Dependency Inference

As mentioned before, it is very hard to analyze implicit dependencies between syscalls, due to the extensive use of shared variables. Take Fig. 1 as an example, the execution of `rds_sendmsg` is affected by `rs`→`rs_bound_addr` (line 6 in (d)), and this variable is written in function `rds_add_bound` (line 11 in (c)). However, this read/write dependency is connected by the shareable variable `rs`, which even comes from the argument of two different syscalls (`sendmsg$rds` and `bind$rds`, respectively). Therefore, it is challenging to catch these dependencies between syscalls by using generic control flow analysis and data flow analysis.

To overcome this challenge, instead of using generic control flow analysis or data flow analysis, we exploit the design of Linux kernel to extract potential impact between modules. In essence, Linux kernel employs modular programming, where many functions serve merely as interfaces, with their implementations provided within specific modules. Consequently, functions within a module are highly likely to operate on the same resource of that module. Therefore, these functions typically exhibit significant inter-dependencies. This brings us the following key insight: we can infer the implicit dependencies between functions stored in the same virtual table.

Functional Group. There are many virtual tables in Linux kernel and a single virtual table usually polymerizes some functions and resources as a whole object. In this paper, the term **neighbor functions** refers to a collection of functions stored within the same virtual table, which collectively form a cohesive **functional group**. Also, take the patch in Fig. 1 as an example, we can find that `rds_sendmsg` and `rds_bind` are neighbor functions, stored at `rds_proto_ops` as shown in Fig. 1 (b) from lines 3–7, as function pointers in such a virtual table correspond to socket→ops.sendmsg and socket→ops.bind, respectively. We can see that they correspond to syscall sendmsg$rds and bind$rds by further referring to syzlang descriptions. Therefore, `rds_sendmsg` and `rds_bind` (there are many other functions like `rds_recvmsg`, etc.) belong to a same functional group. And we name this functional group as `rds_proto_ops`, respectively.

Identifying all functional groups by searching through all virtual tables in Linux kernel is a straightforward task. However, after identifying these functional groups, we cannot assume that all neighbor functions will influence the control flow from the entry syscall to the specific target site, due to the substantial dependencies and code complexity within a single module. For example, in Fig. 1, the functional group `rds_proto_ops` includes many functions, such as `rds_sendmsg`, `rds_bind`, `rds_recvmsg`, etc. However, the execution from `rds_sendmsg` to the target site (line 25 in (d)) is not affected by `rds_recvmsg`. Therefore, even neighbor functions belonging to the same functional group may not impact the specific target site. Consequently, it is necessary to adopt strategies to filter out irrelevant neighbor functions.

As previously mentioned, accurately identifying read-write operations on the same variable by analyzing the data flow, including arguments and shared variables, throughout the entire Linux kernel is challenging. Nevertheless, a coarse analysis can be employed to filter out functions that do not affect the control flow to the specific target site. Typically, read-write operations on the same variable involve the same variable type. Thus, a type-matching instruction filter method can be used to filter out functions that do not potentially perform read-write operations influencing the control flow to the specific target site.

Given a target site, we first extract the nested structure types for each field within all nested structures. We then perform a backward control flow analysis from the target site using type-based indirect call analysis [16] to construct the call graph (CG) and control flow graph (CFG) and identify all conditional variable types. Then, for each function in Linux, we trace its control flow to identify all write operations, extract the nested type of the written destination and match these nested written types with the conditional variable types previously identified. Finally, for each neighbor function, if it can reach any function in $KeyCmpWritingFuncs$ on the CG, the neighbor function will be retained. Following this, we can exclude neighbor functions that can not affect the control flow to the target.

Algorithm 1: Type-Matching Instruction Filter Algorithm

Input: Linux kernel: L and Target site: T.
Output: potential functions may write variables in $KeyCmpSet$: $KeyCmpWritingFuncs$.
   // Initialize a type maps in nested structures
1 $TypeInfo \leftarrow InitialStructure(L)$;
   // Initialize a set of condition-variables on the paths to T
2 $CmpTypeSet \leftarrow GetKeyCmpType(L, T, TypeInfo)$;
3 $KeyCmpWritingFuncs \leftarrow \emptyset$;
4 **foreach** $F \in L$ **do**
5   **foreach** $WriteInst \in F$ **do**
6        $destAddrType \leftarrow TypeInfo[WriteInst.destination]$;
7   **if** $destAddrType \in CmpTypeSet$ **then**
8           $KeyCmpWritingFuncs \leftarrow$
           $KeyCmpWritingFuncs \cup \{destAddrType\}$;

9 **return** $KeyCmpWritingFuncs$;

Algorithm 2: GetKeyCmpType

Input: Linux kernel: L, Target site: T and type maps: $TypeInfo$.
Output: a set of condition-variables type on the path to T: $CmpTypeSet$.
1 $CmpTypeSet \leftarrow \emptyset$;
2 **for** *each path to T* **do**
3   **foreach** *condition c on path* **do**
4        $CmpTypeSet \leftarrow CmpTypeSet \cup \{TypeInfo[c]\}$;

5 **return** $CmpTypeSet$;

By doing Algorithm 1, we can filter out functions in functional groups but may not be useful to trigger the target site.

Enhancing Syscall Dependency Inference. After getting the functional groups filtered, we can identify the potential implicit dependencies within each functional group. Leveraging these functional groups allows us to infer the implicit dependencies between syscalls and enhance the selection of relevant syscalls.

SyzDirect [24] denotes the first functions executed after the dispatch process as **anchor functions** and maps the anchor functions to syscall entries by modeling the Linux kernel. In short, for the anchor functions, they first match the anchor functions to corresponding syscalls, and for other functions, they perform a backward control flow searching to get the reachable anchor functions and then map them to syscall entries by anchor functions. Therefore, we can map any functions to the corresponding syscalls by reusing the modeling data, and then, we can get all syscalls corresponding to a functional group.

Given a target site within Linux kernel, we first identify the function containing the target site and designate it as the **target kernel function**. We then perform a backward control flow analysis from the target kernel function and record all execution paths. For each path, we scan each function along the path and locate it within the stored functional group. For each located functional group, we extract all neighbor functions that belong to it and apply the type-matching instruction filter algorithm to filter out irrelevant functions, forming a set of **candidate functions**. Next, for each candidate function, we map it to derive relevant syscalls by utilizing the modeling data and static-learning algorithm. Finally, the combination of all the relevant syscalls is taken as the definitive result for enhancing syscall dependency inference for the target site.

For example, in Fig. 1, the target site is line 25 in (d). We first identify the target kernel function as `rds_rdma_extra_size`, and then perform a backward control flow analysis, getting in the control flow path: `rds_sendmsg` → ⋯ → `rds_rdma_extra_size`. Next, we scan each function along this control flow path and determine that `rds_sendmsg` belongs to the functional group `rds_proto_ops`, including neighbor functions like `rds_bind`, `rds_recvmsg`, etc. We then apply the filter algorithm to exclude irrelevant functions, forming a set of candidate functions, like `rds_bind`. By using the modeling data, we can map `rds_sendmsg` and `rds_bind` to `sendmsg$rds` and `bind$rds`, respectively. By further using the static-learning algorithm we can find both `sendmsg$rds` and `bind$rds` explicitly dependent on `socket$rds`. Finally, we obtain the definitive result for enhancing syscall dependency inference for the target site.

3.3   Task Scheduling Policy

The objective of directed fuzzing differs from that of coverage-guided fuzzing in terms of task scheduling. As previously mentioned, the purposes of the Triage task and the Smash task are coverage validation and testing, respectively. On one hand, prioritizing a Smash task may result in false positives due to delayed execution of the Triage task. On the other hand, focusing solely on Triage tasks, as done by SyzDirect, may reduce the opportunities to synthesize test cases for the specific target site. Therefore, an optimal task scheduling policy should balance these two tasks to enhance the efficiency of directed fuzzing.

The general task scheduling process in SyzDirect is illustrated in Fig. 4 (a). Compared to coverage-guided fuzzers, DGF typically uses the distance to the target site as a new feedback metric to determine the interest level of a test case. Consequently, SyzDirect has modified the Triage and Smash task queues to priority queues, favoring tasks with closer distances to the target site.

Task distance refers to the distance of the test case within that task. Consider two tasks: a Triage task and a Smash task. The distance from the Smash

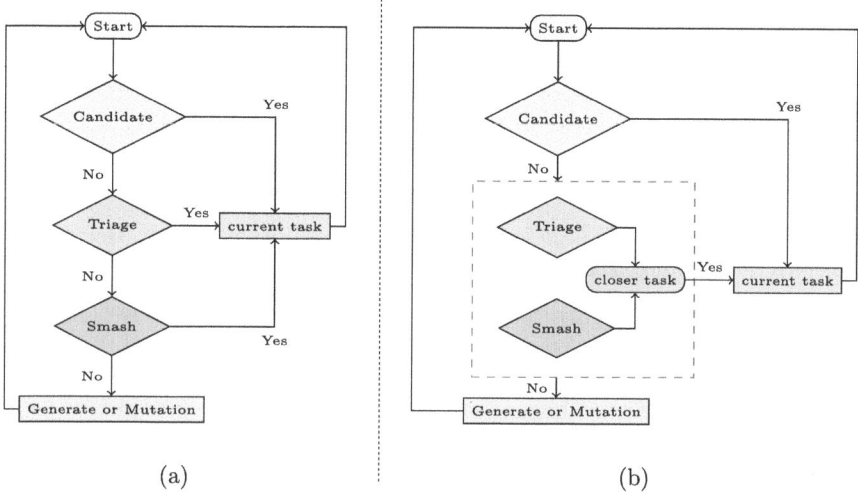

(a)   (b)

Fig. 4. Overview of task scheduling in SyzDirect (a) and *SyzLego* (b).

task to the target site is shorter than that of the Triage task. It is evident that the closer task is more likely to generate new test cases that successfully trigger the target site. However, when the distances of two tasks are equal, it becomes challenging to determine which one is preferable. In such cases, it is advisable to maintain the scheduling policy used in Syzkaller and SyzDirect.

To address this, we modified the task selection policy in SyzDirect by incorporating a distance comparison mechanism into the original task selection process, as shown in Fig. 4 (b):

1. Prioritize the Candidate task as the highest priority, given that it represents the most promising seeds from the syz-manager with substantial potential.
2. Group the Triage and Smash tasks together, selecting the one with the closest distance to the target site as the current task.
3. If the closest distances of the Triage and Smash tasks are equal, prioritize the Triage task.

4   Evaluation

In this section, we evaluate the performance of *SyzLego* in DGF within the Linux kernel. We primarily compare *SyzLego* with SyzDirect, the state-of-the-art DGF tool for the Linux kernel. To assess the contribution of each component of *SyzLego*, we conduct an ablation study.

In summary, we aim to answer the following research questions and study:

– RQ1: How does the *SyzLego* perform in reaching the target site?
– RQ2: How does each component individually contribute to the performance of *SyzLego*?
– A case study highlighting some noteworthy observations.

4.1   Evaluation Setup

Evaluation Dataset. We adopt a subset of known bugs tested in SyzDirect [20]. Due to the limitations of computational resources, we select these target sites based on their time cost in the evaluation results of SyzDirect. The final dataset consists of 39 bugs, and we evaluate *SyzLego* on its ability to reach the target sites.

Baseline Fuzzer. As *SyzLego* is implemented based on SyzDirect, the state-of-the-art DGF for Linux kernel, we primarily compare *SyzLego* with SyzDirect.

Basic Settings. As there is randomness in fuzzing experiments, we follow the setup used in SyzDirect. For each case, we run 10 iterations and use the hitting-round (Runs) and Time-to-Exposure (TTE) as evaluation metrics, which are widely adopted in directed fuzzing studies [1,2]. Specifically, the hitting-round represents the number of times a fuzzer triggers the target bug or reaches the target site in repeated experiments. TTE is the first time a fuzzer triggers the target bug or reaches the target site. We calculate the arithmetic average of TTE across multiple repeated experiments as μTTE. If a fuzzer does not trigger the target within the fuzzing timeout (e.g., 12 h), the TTE for that case is considered as the timeout. We adapt the configuration provided by the default setting of SyzDirect. All experiments are conducted on a server machine with 104 Intel(R) Xeon(R) Gold 6230R CPUs (2.10GHz) and 219GB RAM, running a 64-bit Ubuntu 20.04 LTS system.

4.2   RQ1: How Does the *SyzLego* Perform in Reaching the Target Site?

In this experiment, we apply *SyzLego* to the dataset and compare its performance with SyzDirect. Out of the 39 target sites, 18 can be reached by at least one fuzzer within 12 h. Table 1 presents the exact time (μTTE) and hitting-rounds when the fuzzer reaches each target site. Specifically, *SyzLego* achieves significantly faster target reaching in cases 1, 2, 5, 33, 60, and 82 compared to SyzDirect, achieving an average speedup of 6.75 and 2.94 over SyzDirect in these 6 cases and across all reached target sites, respectively.

4.3   RQ2: How Does Each Component Individually Contribute to the Performance of *SyzLego*?

As mentioned above, *SyzLego* consists of two components: enhancing syscall dependency inference and task scheduling. To evaluate the contribution of each component, we designed and implemented $SyzLego_{task}$, a variant of *SyzLego*, which modifies only the task scheduling of SyzDirect without enhancing syscall dependency inference, whereas *SyzLego* is the full version of our solution. We then reran the experiment on the dataset using *SyzLego* and $SyzLego_{task}$ with a 12-hour limit and compared them with SyzDirect. Additionally, we repeated each experiment 10 times for each case.

Table 1. The performance of *SyzLego*, *SyzLego$_{task}$* and SyzDirect in reaching target sites.

Case ID	Fuzzer	Runs	μTTE(s)	Speedup	Case ID	Fuzzer	Runs	μTTE(s)	Speedup
1	*SyzLego*	8/10	29800	1.32		*SyzLego*	10/10	4993	3.97
	SyzLego$_{task}$	7/10	36295	1.08	33	*SyzLego$_{task}$*	9/10	9056	2.19
	SyzDirect	8/10	39210	/		SyzDirect	10/10	19821	/
2	*SyzLego*	10/10	159	22.46		*SyzLego*	2/10	31041	0.99
	SyzLego$_{task}$	10/10	2812	1.27	49	*SyzLego$_{task}$*	3/10	30616	1.01
	SyzDirect	9/10	3578	/		SyzDirect	4/10	30864	/
4	*SyzLego*	10/10	10	1.00		*SyzLego*	4/10	36167	1.19
	SyzLego$_{task}$	10/10	9	1.11	50	*SyzLego$_{task}$*	3/10	37371	1.16
	SyzDirect	10/10	10	/		SyzDirect	0/10	43200	/
5	*SyzLego*	10/10	9435	3.24		*SyzLego*	10/10	500	6.70
	SyzLego$_{task}$	10/10	11747	2.61	60	*SyzLego$_{task}$*	10/10	492	6.80
	SyzDirect	8/10	30603	/		SyzDirect	10/10	3347	/
9	*SyzLego*	10/10	10	1.10		*SyzLego*	1/10	41954	1.03
	SyzLego$_{task}$	10/10	10	1.10	61	*SyzLego$_{task}$*	0/10	43200	1.00
	SyzDirect	10/10	11	/		SyzDirect	0/10	43200	/
13	*SyzLego*	10/10	11	0.90		*SyzLego*	10/10	14	0.78
	SyzLego$_{task}$	10/10	10	1.01	74	*SyzLego$_{task}$*	10/10	11	1.00
	SyzDirect	10/10	10	/		SyzDirect	10/10	11	/
23	*SyzLego*	8/10	22831	1.18		*SyzLego*	10/10	446	2.79
	SyzLego$_{task}$	7/10	24393	1.10	82	*SyzLego$_{task}$*	10/10	789	1.58
	SyzDirect	6/10	26951	/		SyzDirect	10/10	1244	/
24	*SyzLego*	8/10	11705	0.91		*SyzLego*	9/10	7595	0.93
	SyzLego$_{task}$	8/10	12873	0.83	95	*SyzLego$_{task}$*	8/10	7545	0.94
	SyzDirect	8/10	10696	/		SyzDirect	9/10	7077	/
25	*SyzLego*	10/10	9	1.11		*SyzLego*	10/10	14222	1.25
	SyzLego$_{task}$	10/10	10	1.00	99	*SyzLego$_{task}$*	8/10	17834	1.00
	SyzDirect	10/10	10	/		SyzDirect	9/10	17829	/

The experimental results, also presented in Table 1, indicate that the two components exhibit different effects on various test target sites. The syscall dependency inference enhancement component demonstrates significant performance improvements in cases 2, 5, and 33, while the task scheduling component shows significant performance improvements in cases 5, 33, 60, and 82.

Table 2. The detailed case analysis. Great is *SyzLego* shows good performance; R1 is easily reachable target sites; R2 is lack of deep analysis for related syscalls; and R3 is the impact of other shallow bugs.

Reason	Cases
Great	1, 2, 5, 33, 60, 82
R1	4, 9, 13, 25, 74
R2	49, 50, 95, 99
R3	23, 61

4.4   A Case Study Highlighting Some Noteworthy Observations

We manually analyzed the reasons why *SyzLego* was slower than SyzDirect in RQ1 and RQ2 by examining the PoCs from Syzbot [5], the source code of the target site, and fuzzing logs. This investigation aimed to identify the factors contributing to the slower performance of *SyzLego* compared to SyzDirect.

For case 24, the significant number of virtual table functions associated with the control flow, coupled with the wide range of variable types affecting the control flow, resulted in a substantial number of false positives in *SyzLego*. For others, in summary, we identified three primary reasons for the slower performance in other cases:

Easily Reachable Target Sites (R1). Some cases (4, 9, 13, 25, and 74) are relatively easy to reach, allowing the fuzzer to quickly synthesize the correct PoC while *SyzLego* remains in its initial state and requires time to assist the fuzzer. Additionally, some cases are quite simple, consisting of one entry syscall and an explicit dependency syscall. Thus, *SyzLego* cannot improve performance in such cases and may even hinder it.

Lack of Deep Analysis for Relevant Syscalls (R2). Triggering the target site requires specific context and arguments for the relevant syscalls. *SyzLego* enhances syscall dependency inference by using specially designed virtual tables in Linux kernel. However, it does not perform a deep analysis of the shared variables in relevant syscalls. Consequently, this analysis may overestimate or underestimate the number of implicit dependencies for the specific syscalls.

The Impact of Other Shallow Bugs (R3). When fuzzing the target kernel, shallow vulnerabilities or bugs will lead to frequent kernel crashes and reboots. Test cases mutated from such seeds are more likely to trigger these crashes. The substantial overhead of the kernel reboot process significantly impairs the efficiency of DGF.

Table 2 presents a detailed case analysis: in cases 1, 2, 5, 33, 60, and 82, *SyzLego* shows good performance; in cases 4, 9, 13, 25, and 74, the performance is average due to *R1*; in cases 49, 50, 95, and 99, the performance is poor due to *R2*; in cases 23 and 61, the performance is poor due to *R3*; in case 24, the performance is poor due to false positives in *SyzLego*.

In this paper, our main technical contributions are enhancing syscall dependency inference by analyzing implicit dependencies and task scheduling. We leave the deep analysis of relevant syscalls as future work and discuss how to improve *SyzLego* later.

5   Limitation and Further Work

5.1   Inaccuracy of Static Analysis

SyzLego exploits the design of Linux kernel and uses a type-matching filter algorithm to filter out neighbor functions that cannot affect the control flow to reach the target. Though *SyzLego* tries to mitigate false positives, the static analysis still has false positives and false negatives. Since we will dynamically adjust the use of this information during fuzzing, fuzzing can help correct some of the errors. As we all know the accuracy of static analysis completely is very challenging. Due to the complexity of Linux kernel, on the one hand, it requires more effective methods and tools to perform perfect control and data flow analysis, on the other hand, it requires a full understanding of Linux kernel and matching each function to Syzlang descriptions.

5.2   Future Analysis of Argument Mutation

Despite the entry syscalls and dependencies, the arguments of each syscall are important to reach the target site. However, the arguments make a huge search space, and most of the combination of the arguments is invalid for triggering the target site. In this paper, we only promote a method to address the implicit dependency between syscalls, thus it is still difficult to get correct arguments of the syscall sequence. We plan to explore how the identify dependent syscalls more accurately and how to perform directed mutations on the arguments in the future.

5.3   Limitation of Distance

Like the state-of-the-art work SyzDirect [24], this paper also focuses on using distance feedback information to guide the fuzzer. However, the distance information is not enough to select seeds and tasks, because, during the fuzzing process, the distance of test cases is usually stuck in a rut, meaning that all the seeds and tasks with the same distance in a period of time, and the fuzzer will perform the same actions as the coverage-guided fuzzer. We plan to instrument Linux kernel to get more feedback information to guide the fuzzer, when there is not any new coverage or distance feedback in the future.

6   Related Work

6.1   Directed Greybox Fuzzing on User-Space Applications

There has been substantial research on DGF, primarily focusing on user-space applications [1,2,4,10,13,31]. AFLGo [1], the first DGF solution for user-space applications, introduces a novel distance metric for fuzzing specific target sites. Subsequent DGF techniques have employed two major strategies to quickly approach the target site: `distance-guided exploration` [1,2,4,13] and `invalid input pruning` [10,31]. The first strategy collects runtime feedback to calculate the distance to the target location, prioritizing test cases with shorter distances. The second strategy filters out test cases that cannot reach the target location or follow infeasible execution paths, thereby improving exploration efficiency. Unlike user-space applications, which typically have a fixed entry point, OS kernels usually provide many API functions (i.e., syscalls) and take a sequence of syscalls as input. Therefore, existing DGF solutions have limitations in dealing with OS kernels.

6.2   Kernel Fuzzing

Linux kernel, as a critical part of the OS, is a popular target for fuzzing. Since the syscall interface is the main communication interface, many efforts have focused on testing the kernel through the syscall interface [3,8,9,11,17,18,21–23,25,27,28,30]. In addition to using code coverage as feedback, many studies have utilized other techniques to improve testing efficiency, such as enhanced coverage [26,30], static analysis [17], symbolic execution [11], dynamic analysis [23], deep learning [27] and reinforcement learning [25]. Many works try to mitigate the shortcomings of manually written specifications by human experts [8,22,28]. Given that the input to the Linux kernel consists of a sequence of syscalls, many studies have focused on capturing the dependencies between syscalls. Moonshine [17] defines two types of dependencies between syscalls: explicit and implicit dependencies, and applies a combination of static analysis and trace extraction to distill the seeds of Syzkaller [6]. Healer [23] utilizes resource descriptions to identify the resources generated and used by syscalls to capture explicit dependencies and determines implicit dependencies through dynamic execution using coverage feedback. MOCK [27] designs a neural network language model to efficiently capture dependencies within calling contexts and help generate high-quality test cases. To fully test the subsystems of the Linux kernel, many studies have focused on USB interfaces [18], driver interrupts [3,9], and direct memory access (DMA) [21]. However, these works are all coverage-guided, aiming to cover more kernel code and bugs, while *SyzLego* aims to fuzz specific target sites.

6.3   Directed Greybox Fuzzing on OS Kernels

Currently, there are only a few DGF works for OS kernels [14,15,24,29]. GREBE [15] takes a directed fuzzing approach to explore more error behaviors of a kernel bug and DDrace [29] only uses existing DGF techniques to find concurrency UAF in Linux drivers. As the first directed fuzzing framework for OS kernels, G-Fuzz [14] primarily targets gVisor and also implements a variant called G-Fuzz-Linux for directed fuzzing of the Linux kernel. G-Fuzz proposes an automatic method based on static analysis and expert knowledge to infer which syscalls are related to the given target before fuzzing. Unlike AFLGo [1], G-Fuzz does not instrument the kernel to obtain distance information. Instead, it records the distance of each basic block into a file and calculates the distance information based on coverage feedback during the fuzzing process. SyzDirect [24], the state-of-the-art DGF solution for the Linux kernel, employs novel static analysis to identify the entry syscalls as well as the conditions on their arguments, achieving promising experimental results. However, it only uses the static-learning algorithm proposed by Healer [23] to deal with explicit dependencies, whereas *SyzLego* aims to capture implicit dependencies between syscalls.

7   Conclusion

In this paper, we present *SyzLego*, a DGF solution for Linux kernel. To address the implicit dependency between syscalls, *SyzLego* employs novel static analysis to identify the relevant syscalls to enhance the syscall dependency inference for DGF in Linux kernel, which greatly narrows down the exploration space of the target site in Linux kernel. With the distance-based task scheduling, *SyzLego* can allocate more power to tasks closer to the target site. Our extensive evaluation on upstream Linux kernels demonstrates that *SyzLego* outperforms the state-of-the-art solution, achieving an average speedup of 2.94 and a maximum speedup of 22.46 across all reached target sites.

Acknowledgment. We would like to thank the anonymous reviewers for their insightful comments that helped improve the quality of the paper. This work is supported by the NSFC under No. 62202484.

References

1. Böhme, M., Pham, V.T., Nguyen, M.D., Roychoudhury, A.: Directed greybox fuzzing. In: Proceedings of the 2017 ACM SIGSAC Conference on Computer and Communications Security, pp. 2329–2344 (2017)
2. Chen, H., Xue, Y., Li, Y., Chen, B., Xie, X., Wu, X., Liu, Y.: Hawkeye: towards a desired directed grey-box fuzzer. In: Proceedings of the 2018 ACM SIGSAC conference on Computer and Communications Security, pp. 2095–2108 (2018)
3. Corina, J., et al.: Difuze: interface aware fuzzing for kernel drivers. In: Proceedings of the 2017 ACM SIGSAC Conference on Computer and Communications Security, pp. 2123–2138 (2017)
4. Du, Z., Li, Y., Liu, Y., Mao, B.: Windranger: a directed greybox fuzzer driven by deviation basic blocks. In: Proceedings of the 44th International Conference on Software Engineering, pp. 2440–2451 (2022)
5. Google: syzbot. https://syzkaller.appspot.com/upstream
6. Google: Syzkaller. https://github.com/google/syzkaller (2022)
7. Google: syzlang. https://github.com/google/syzkaller/blob/master/docs/syscall_descriptions_syntax.md (2022)
8. Hao, Y., et al.: Syzdescribe: principled, automated, static generation of syscall descriptions for kernel drivers. In: 2023 IEEE Symposium on Security and Privacy (SP), pp. 3262–3278. IEEE (2023)
9. Hetzelt, F., Radev, M., Buhren, R., Morbitzer, M., Seifert, J.P.: Via: analyzing device interfaces of protected virtual machines. In: Proceedings of the 37th Annual Computer Security Applications Conference, pp. 273–284 (2021)
10. Huang, H., Guo, Y., Shi, Q., Yao, P., Wu, R., Zhang, C.: Beacon: directed grey-box fuzzing with provable path pruning. In: 2022 IEEE Symposium on Security and Privacy (SP), pp. 36–50. IEEE (2022)
11. Kim, K., Jeong, D.R., Kim, C.H., Jang, Y., Shin, I., Lee, B.: Hfl: hybrid fuzzing on the linux kernel. In: NDSS (2020)

12. Lattner, C., Adve, V.: Llvm: a compilation framework for lifelong program analysis & transformation. In: International Symposium on Code Generation and Optimization, 2004. CGO 2004, pp. 75–86. IEEE (2004)
13. Lee, G., Shim, W., Lee, B.: Constraint-guided directed greybox fuzzing. In: 30th USENIX Security Symposium (USENIX Security 21), pp. 3559–3576 (2021)
14. Li, Y., et al.: G-fuzz: a directed fuzzing framework for gVisor. IEEE Trans. Dependable Secure Comput. **21**(1), 168–185 (2023)
15. Lin, Z., et al.: Grebe: unveiling exploitation potential for linux kernel bugs. In: 2022 IEEE Symposium on Security and Privacy (SP), pp. 2078–2095. IEEE (2022)
16. Lu, K., Hu, H.: Where does it go? refining indirect-call targets with multi-layer type analysis. In: Proceedings of the 2019 ACM SIGSAC Conference on Computer and Communications Security, pp. 1867–1881 (2019)
17. Pailoor, S., Aday, A., Jana, S.: {MoonShine}: optimizing {OS} fuzzer seed selection with trace distillation. In: 27th USENIX Security Symposium (USENIX Security 18), pp. 729–743 (2018)
18. Peng, H., Payer, M.: {USBFuzz}: a framework for fuzzing {USB} drivers by device emulation. In: 29th USENIX Security Symposium (USENIX Security 20), pp. 2559–2575 (2020)
19. shamir rabinovitch: net/rds: fix warn in rds_message_alloc_sgs. https://git.kernel.org/pub/scm/linux/kernel/git/torvalds/linux.git/commit/?id=ea010070d0a74 97253d5a6f919f6dd107450b31a (2018)
20. Robin-Pwner: Syzdirect dataset. https://github.com/seclab-fudan/SyzDirect/blob/main/dataset/dataset.pdf (2024), Accessed 18 Jan 2024
21. Song, D., et al.: Periscope: an effective probing and fuzzing framework for the hardware-os boundary. In: 2019 Network and Distributed Systems Security Symposium (NDSS), pp. 1–15. Internet Society (2019)
22. Sun, H., Shen, Y., Liu, J., Xu, Y., Jiang, Y.: {KSG}: augmenting kernel fuzzing with system call specification generation. In: 2022 USENIX Annual Technical Conference (USENIX ATC 22), pp. 351–366 (2022)
23. Sun, H., et al.: Healer: relation learning guided kernel fuzzing. In: Proceedings of the ACM SIGOPS 28th Symposium on Operating Systems Principles, pp. 344–358 (2021)
24. Tan, X., Zhang, Y., Lu, J., Xiong, X., Liu, Z., Yang, M.: Syzdirect: directed greybox fuzzing for linux kernel. In: Proceedings of the 2023 ACM SIGSAC Conference on Computer and Communications Security, pp. 1630–1644 (2023)
25. Wang, D., Zhang, Z., Zhang, H., Qian, Z., Krishnamurthy, S.V., Abu-Ghazaleh, N.: {SyzVegas}: beating kernel fuzzing odds with reinforcement learning. In: 30th USENIX Security Symposium (USENIX Security 21), pp. 2741–2758 (2021)
26. Wang, Y., et al.: Not all coverage measurements are equal: Fuzzing by coverage accounting for input prioritization. In: NDSS (2020)
27. Xu, J., et al.: Mock: optimizing kernel fuzzing mutation with context-aware dependency. In: Proceedings of the Network and Distributed System Security Symposium (NDSS) (2024)
28. Yang, C., Zhao, Z., Zhang, L.: Kernelgpt: enhanced kernel fuzzing via large language models. arXiv preprint arXiv:2401.00563 (2023)
29. Yuan, M., Zhao, B., Li, P., Liang, J., Han, X., Luo, X., Zhang, C.: Ddrace: finding concurrency uaf vulnerabilities in linux drivers with directed fuzzing. In: 32nd USENIX Security Symposium, USENIX Security 2023, Anaheim, CA, USA, August 9-11 (2023)

30. Zhao, B., et al.: {StateFuzz}: System {Call-Based}{State-Aware} linux driver fuzzing. In: 31st USENIX Security Symposium (USENIX Security 22), pp. 3273–3289 (2022)
31. Zong, P., Lv, T., Wang, D., Deng, Z., Liang, R., Chen, K.: {FuzzGuard}: filtering out unreachable inputs in directed grey-box fuzzing through deep learning. In: 29th USENIX security symposium (USENIX security 20), pp. 2255–2269 (2020)

A Lightweight Defense Scheme Against Usermode Helper Privilege Escalation Using Linux Capability

Jingzi Meng[1,2], Yuewu Wang[3], Lingguang Lei[1,2(✉)], Chunjing Kou[3], and Peng Wang[3]

[1] Key Laboratory of Cyberspace Security Defense, Institute of Information Engineering, Chinese Academy of Sciences, Beijing, China
{mengjingzi,leilingguang}@iie.ac.cn
[2] School of Cyber Security, University of Chinese Academy of Sciences, Beijing, China
[3] School of Cryptology, University of Chinese Academy of Sciences, Beijing, China
{wangyuewu,kouchunjing,p-wang}@ucas.ac.cn

Abstract. A new attack path is discovered in Linux privilege escalation attacks. Among the 50 exploits we have collected over the past 3 years, 19 leverage usermode helper to execute arbitrary code with root privileges, making it the most prevalent attack method. Existing research focuses on protecting permission mechanisms but falls short, as the attackers don't attempt to modify their permissions. Instead, they exploit the regular routine of usermode helper by tampering with the path of usermode helper file which the kernel is about to execute. To address this, we propose a lightweight defense mechanism based on the fine-grained access control provided by Linux capability. The novelty of our approach lies in the fact that we didn't use capability as a process property. Instead, we attach capabilities to valid usermode helper files and verify these files before execution. We identify the optimal point for insertion capability checks by statically analyzing kernel source code through LLVM. Our prototype implementation on Linux v6.6.3 demonstrates that our scheme effectively blocks these privilege escalation attacks with negligible performance overhead.

Keywords: Usermode helper · Capability · Linux privilege escalation attacks · Defense

1 Introduction

Among the attacks faced by the Linux kernel, privilege escalation attacks are particularly severe as they can allow attackers to gain high privileges and complete control over the entire system. Famous vulnerabilities like Dirty COW [8] and Dirty Pipe [6] and their exploitations have demonstrated the severe consequence of privilege escalation attacks. Given the diverse nature of kernel vulnerabilities, comprehensive solutions are challenging. Consequently, current

N. Mouha and N. Nikiforakis (Eds.): ISC 2024, LNCS 15257, pp. 190–208, 2025.
https://doi.org/10.1007/978-3-031-75757-0_10

research focuses on protecting permission mechanisms in Linux kernel, such as restricting the invocation of the kernel function `commit_creds()` to protect a process's credentials (i.e., `cred`) [15], directly protecting the critical data related to process permissions using data integrity protection [4,19,20,24] or measuring data structures in an isolated security domain [31].

However, attack and defense continually evolve. Previous defenses may be ineffective with current attacks. We collect privilege escalation exploits over the past three years and reveal a shift in attack methods, with the most prevalent now exploiting usermode helper functionality to execute malicious code with root privileges. The usermode helper is a normal function of the kernel used to call user space helper programs. Specifically, the kernel spawns a new process to execute the usermode helper represented by a *path* with root privileges. For instance, the `modprobe` program is a usermode helper used to load kernel modules and is invoked via its path `/sbin/modprobe`. While writable paths facilitate custom helper programs, they also present a security risk. Once attackers gain kernel control, they can overwrite these paths to execute arbitrary code. Of the 50 collected exploits, 19 utilize this method, making it the largest proportion.

This new attack vector does not alter the permission data but relies on the normal routine of usermode helper invocation, where the kernel unconditionally executes the helper program pointed to by the *path*. Consequently, previous defenses are no longer effective. To defeat this new attack method, we propose a lightweight defense based on Linux capability. Capability is a privilege mechanism that breaks down root privileges into 41 distinct units, allowing fine-grained control. While capabilities are traditionally granted to processes and checked before accessing sensitive resources, they also support being granted to object files. Thus, we propose a novel usage of capabilities: attaching them to valid files and checking the file's capability before executing it with root privileges.

Particularly, we introduce `CAP_OBJ_UMH` to prevent usermode helper based attacks. To determine the appropriate points to insert capability checks and avoid being bypassed, we need to locate where usermode helpers are actually executed. Since the invocations of the usermode helper are embedded in the extensive kernel code, it's challenging to find them all. To address this, we performed a static analysis of the kernel code with LLVM [18], identifying all usermode helper call locations and constructing callgraphs for each call point. It turns out that all usermode helper calls converge into a single function where we can add the capability check. In addition, we adapted the user space programs. Existing usermode helpers will be placed on the whitelist and will not be subject to the capability check. The kernel will only check permissions when calling helper programs of unknown origin. If a new usermode helper is introduced, it needs to be granted `CAP_OBJ_UMH` before use. A usermode helper replaced by an attacker does not have the capability and, therefore, will not be executed by the kernel.

We implemented a prototype system based on Linux v6.6.3. Experiments demonstrate that our approach effectively blocks all existing usermode helper privilege escalation attacks with negligible performance overhead.

The main contributions of this paper are as follows:

- We perform a comprehensive analysis of a new type of Linux privilege escalation attacks, elucidating the mechanisms employed to gain privileges. Our investigation includes an examination of 50 kernel exploits collected over the past three years, revealing that 19 of these exploits have utilized the standard routine of usermode helpers to execute arbitrary code with root privileges.
- We propose a defense scheme based on Linux capability to defeat this novel attack vector. By leveraging intrinsic properties of capability, we extend its protection to bidirectional, safeguarding the subject before it executes an object. Additionally, we perform static code analysis on the Linux kernel to identify the optimal point for inserting capability checks.
- We develop a prototype of the defense system and demonstrate its effectiveness against usermode helper based attacks. Experimental results indicate that our defense system successfully mitigates the 19 identified exploits with negligible performance overhead.

2   Background

2.1   Linux Usermode Helper

The Linux kernel uses usermode helpers (UMH) as a shared framework for calling user space programs and returning their status to the kernel. Usermode helpers are crucial for offloading complex tasks from the kernel to user space programs. These tasks include complex configuration procedures, dynamic module loading, and device event handling, which are better suited for execution outside the kernel space. The Linux kernel uses root privileges to execute usermode helpers to ensure that these processes have the necessary permissions to perform their intended tasks. This paradigmatic approach not only streamlines the kernel's functionality but also bolsters its flexibility and extensibility.

A common example of usermode helpers is the `modprobe` program, which is used to load kernel modules dynamically. When the kernel encounters a request for a module that is not currently loaded, it can call `modprobe` to load the necessary module from user space. Another example of a usermode helper is `hotplug`. When a USB device is inserted, the usermode helper manages device initialization and configuration.

2.2   Linux Capability

Linux capabilities are designed to mitigate the security risks associated with overprivileged processes. Traditionally, processes with a UID of 0 are known as root processes and have unrestricted access to all system resources. This all-or-nothing privilege model poses a great risk to the system. To address this, Linux capability (introduced in Linux kernel v2.2) divides root privileges into distinct units called capabilities. Each capability corresponds to a specific privileged operation or set of operations. For example, `CAP_SYS_TIME` permits setting the system clock, while CAP_NET_ADMIN enables various network-related operations. Currently, 41 capabilities are defined in the Linux kernel. Figure 1 illustrates the operating mode of capability.

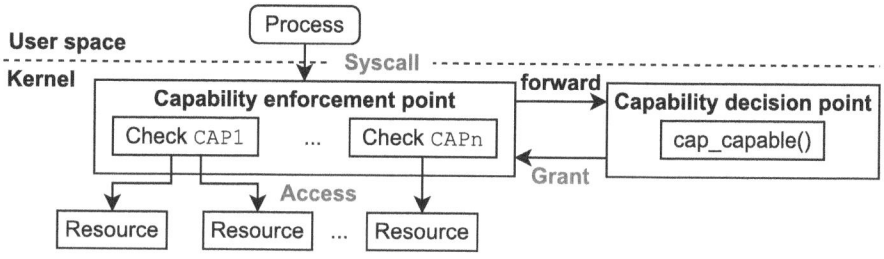

Fig. 1. The operating mode of Linux capability.

Capability is typically used as a property of processes and is checked before accessing sensitive resources. Scattered capability checkpoints forward the access request to a unified capability decision point, which grants or denies access based on the process's capabilities and the required capabilities of sensitive resources. Capability can also be granted to files stored in the file's extended attributes. If an executable file has capabilities, it gains these capabilities when executed.

When developers add new sensitive resources, they can call the capability check function before the access operation, and the capability mechanism will ensure that the sensitive resource is not subject to unauthorized access.

Despite these advantages, capability is not widely used in third-party applications. Developers often prioritize functionality over security, leading them to request root privileges for sensitive operations instead of using capabilities. However, there is a growing trend toward fine-grained access control. For instance, the system management service systemd uses capabilities to manage system services, reducing security risks by configuring services with only necessary capabilities instead of root access.

3 Threat Model of Privilege Escalation Attacks

We assume that the system starts in a trusted state without any pre-existing compromises, meaning the system image has not been tampered with and that the kernel boot process is secure. An attacker does not have any privileges but can exploit kernel vulnerabilities to hijack the control flow and attempt to elevate their privileges. We focus on the general privilege escalation methods instead of mitigating all kernel vulnerabilities. Attacks requiring abnormal operations, such as rebooting the system or replacing the kernel, are outside the scope of this model, as they are likely to alert the user. Additionally, we do not consider side-channel attacks.

4   Analysis of Usermode Helper Attacks

To analyze the current privilege escalation attack landscape, we first collect and categorize the latest exploits that can cause local privilege escalation. Then, we conduct an in-depth analysis of the principles underlying the most prevalent privilege escalation attack.

4.1   Attack Dataset Preparation

For vulnerability collection, we mainly refer to cvedetails.com, exploitdb, and an open-source project on GitHub. CVEdetails.com [17] provides detailed information about Common Vulnerabilities and Exposures (CVEs), with extensive filtering options, allowing us to identify Linux kernel CVEs with privilege escalation impacts over the past three years. We then search for corresponding exploits on ExploitDB [9], a public database with comprehensive exploits for various platforms, including Linux. Additionally, a GitHub project [16] offered links related to Linux kernel security and exploitation, from which we extracted local privilege escalation (LPE) exploits as complementary. In total, we gathered 50 exploits across 37 CVEs, with some CVEs having multiple exploits. The distribution of privilege escalation vectors used in exploits is listed in Table 1.

Table 1. Distribution of privilege escalation vectors.

Category	Escalation vectors	Nums
Use existing kernel components	call malicious usermode helpers	19
	call commit_creds() with root credentials	17
	replace current credentials with root process's credentials	5
Overwrite of permission data	modify read-only file	8
	wrong UID map in overlayfs	1

Our analysis reveals that current privilege escalation attack vectors fall into two categories. The first category is the most dominant. It leverages existing kernel components, such as kernel functions or high-privileged process credentials. The second category directly overwrites permission data to escalate privileges. Vulnerabilities in this category are generally more concealed and more difficult to exploit.

Due to their covert and scattered nature, it's challenging to defend all kernel vulnerabilities. Therefore, most existing research focuses on the first type of privilege escalation attacks. As shown in the Table 1, two primary vectors of privilege escalation in this category are utilizing usermode helpers and invoking commit_creds(). The commit_creds() function is a traditional vector that attackers use to commit fake root credentials once they gain control of the kernel code. Normally, the process credentials, such as UID, undergo permission checks before any changes are made. For example, modifying the UID of the current process involves the system call `setuid`, which enters the kernel and leads to `__sys_setuid()`, where permission checks are performed. Only if these checks are passed can the UID be modified. However, once an attacker hijacks the control flow, he can directly call the `commit_creds()` function to submit root credentials, bypassing the permission checks in `__sys_setuid()`. Lin et al. [15] have introduced a defense method towards attacks based on `commit_creds()`.

While the traditional use of `commit_creds()` remains relatively common, as shown in Table 1, usermode helpers have emerged as the most widely used vector for escalating privileges.

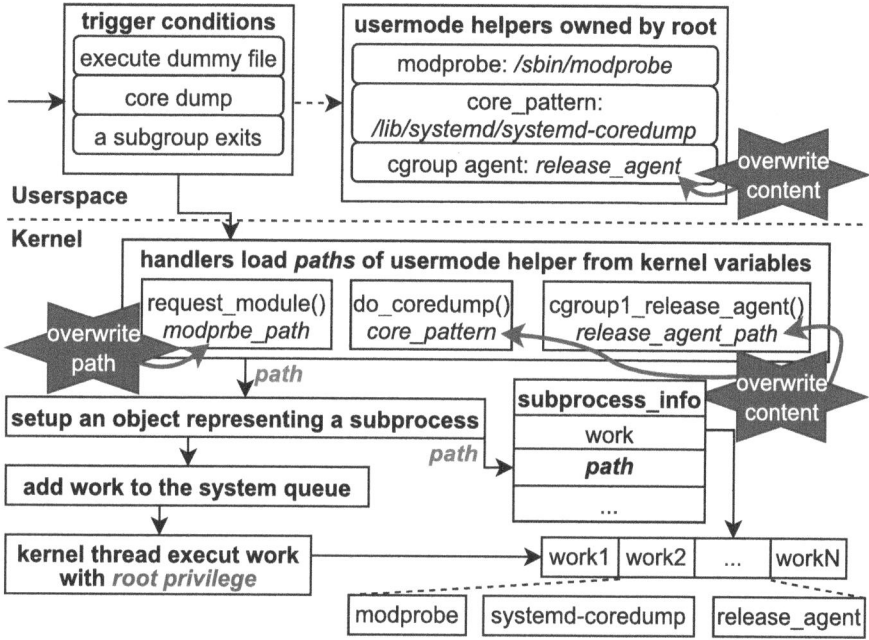

Fig. 2. The principle of usermode helper privilege escalation attacks.

4.2 Attack Vector Leveraging Usermode Helpers

The new approach in privilege escalation attacks exploits the fact that usermode helpers will be executed with root privileges. The normal workflow of usermode helpers is illustrated in Fig. 2. In user space, various usermode helper programs are equipped to handle various conditions. The kernel processes different events through different handler functions, which load the paths of usermode helpers from kernel variables. The kernel then initializes a `subprocess_info` struct with the path and other parameters, then adds `subprocess_info->work` to a system queue. A kernel thread, `kworker`, is responsible for executing tasks in the queue with root privilege, including the newly added subprocess.

This process flow highlights a critical security concern: if an attacker can modify the path or the content of a usermode helper, he can execute arbitrary code with root privileges. In the collected attack code, attackers managed to tamper with real usermode helpers in the following two ways.

(1) Overwrite the path of the usermode helper: The attacker modifies the path related kernel variable so that `subprocess_info->path` point to a malicious program instead of the intended usermode helper.

(2) Tamper with the content of the usermode helper file: The attacker alters the actual usermode helper file with malicious scripts or file path.

Both methods ensure that when the kernel spawns the helper, it executes the attacker's code with root privileges.

Overwrite the Path. Fifteen of the 50 exploits achieve privilege escalation by tampering with the path of the usermode helper to be executed. Fourteen of them overwrite `modprobe_path` kernel variable, while one forges a `subprocess_info` object with a fake path. We begin by describing the mechanism of modifying `modprobe_path` to gain privileges.

The `modprobe_path` variable holds the location of `modprobe` program, which is `/sbin/modprobe` by default. The `modprobe` program is used to load kernel modules and handle unrecognized file types for the kernel, requiring `CAP_SYS_MODULE` to run. To allow customization, the value of `modprobe_path` is not hard-coded but resides on a writable page. Its address can be read from the kernel symbol table, presenting an opportunity for exploitation. If a kernel vulnerability exposes an arbitrary write primitive, such as an out-of-bounds write vulnerability, an attacker can overwrite the value of `modprobe_path` to point to a malicious program. For example, in CVE-2023-0179 [7], a stack buffer overflow exisits due to an integer underflow vulnerability, attackers can overwrite the jumpstack with arbitrary values. If the Kernel Address Space Layout Randomization (KASLR) is bypassed and the address of `modprobe_path` is leaked, an attacker can manage to overwrite its value with a malicious path.

Attackers can trigger a fake usermode helper by executing a file with an unrecognized type in user space, which doesn't require any capability. This process ultimately reaches the kernel via the `execve()` system call. The kernel must determine the type of the program before execution, which involves calling `search_binary_handler()`. This function iterates through a list of binary format handlers, testing each handler's `load_binary()` implementation to recognize and load the program. If all handlers fail, the kernel inspects the first four bytes of the file. If one or more bytes are not ASCII printable characters, the kernel attempts to find the appropriate binary format handler by trying to load a module named `binfmt-WXYZ`, where `WXYZ` represents the hex values of the first four bytes of the executable.

For example, on a dummy file with the first four bytes as 0xFFFFFFFF, the kernel thread handling the `execve()` system call will ultimately try to call `request_module("binfmt-FFFFFFFF")`. The `request_module()` calls `call_modprobe()`, passing on `modprobe_path`. Then, the kernel prepares an `subprocess_info` object representing a process. This object's `work` field defines its job, which is to create a user mode process and execute the program pointed to by its `path`. The `subprocess_info->path` is initialized with the previously passed `modprobe_path`, and the `subprocess_info` is added to the system queue through its `work` field.

Thus, when an unprivileged user executes the dummy file, it triggers the kernel to run `/sbin/modprobe` with root privileges. This mechanism can be exploited if `modprobe_path` has been maliciously modified, allowing attackers to escalate their privileges to root. Another exploit method involves an attacker directly forging a `subprocess_info` object with a path to malicious code. In both scenarios, the attacker controls the path of the usermode helper, enabling privilege escalation.

Overwrite the Content. The second type of attack accomplishes privilege escalation by modifying the content of the usermode helper. Unlike traditional binaries, these usermode helpers are special files linked to kernel variables. The content of these files reflects the values of the associated kernel variables, making them susceptible to two types of exploitation: direct modification through file access interfaces and indirect modification by rewriting the kernel variables. Attackers typically inject the path of their malicious executable into the usermode helper, so when the kernel executes the helper, it effectively runs the attacker's code with root privileges. Recent exploits have predominantly targeted two files: `core_pattern` and `release_agent`.

One exploit directly writes the malicious path to `release_agent` file due to insufficient protection of its file access interface. Located under the root cgroupfs, this file allows users to perform customized cleanup tasks when a subgroup exits. If a subgroup is configured with `notify_on_release` (i.e., the value of the `notify_on_release` file in its own directory is set to 1), then `release_agent` will be called as a usermode helper with root privileges on the subgroup's exits. By default, `release_agent` is empty.

Moreover, the `release_agent` is related to a special struct, `struct cftype`, with a write pointer directing to the file's write function. The function pointed to by `cftype->write` is called when the file is written. Since the kernel lacks permission checks in this function, an attacker can write malicious commands to `release_agent` and trigger a privilege escalation when a subgroup exits. The vulnerability [5] caused widespread concern and can result in container escapes, affecting many local and online container platforms. The kernel has patched this vulnerability by adding a capability check in the files's write function, requiring the capability `CAP_SYS_ADMIN` to modify `release_agent`.

Three exploits modify `/proc/sys/kernel/core_pattern` file through the corresponding kernel variable `core_pattern`. This file specifies the pattern for core dump filenames, which by default is set to `core`, meaning that when a core dump occurs, the generated file is named `core`. If the pattern starts with a '|', the kernel treats the rest of the pattern as an absolute path and executes the file with root privileges. In this case, the core dump is written to the standard input of the specified program instead of to a file. For example, the pattern `|/lib/systemd/systemd-coredump` means that `systemd-coredump` will be called when core dump happens.

`/proc/sys/kernel/core_pattern` is protected by a strict UGO policy, allowing only the root user to modify it. However, it is actually a virtual file that exports the value of the kernel variable `core_pattern`, which is of `ctl_table`. If attackers manage to overwrite the value of this kernel variable, the content of the `core_pattern` file changes accordingly. Similarly, once attackers bypass KASLR, they can read the address of this variable from the kernel symbol table. They can then use the `copy_from_user()` function to write a malicious path starting with '|' to `core_pattern`. This allows the execution of arbitrary programs with root privileges.

5   Design of the Defense System

Our analysis in Sect. 4.2 reveals that privilege escalation via usermode helpers hinges on modifying the usermode helper program the kernel calls. Usermode helpers usually access system resources or change the system state. Although located in the user space, they generally are owned by root and can only be modified by root user. Under normal circumstances, the kernel calls a program with root privileges that can only be written by root, posing no inherent risk of privilege escalation. However, during an attack, an attacker gaining control of kernel code still possesses ordinary privileges, and so does the fake usermode helper. The kernel does not check permissions before executing the usermode helper, resulting in the unconditional execution of fake helper files and successful privilege escalation. Therefore, the fundamental approach to intercepting this type of attack is to introduce permission checks within the normal routine of usermode helper. Three key issues must be considered:

(1) **Location of the check:** Identifying the appropriate place to insert checks to avoid being bypassed.

(2) **Type of permission to check:** Deciding what specific permissions need to be verified.

(3) **System usability:** Ensuring that the introduction of checks does not compromise system functionality.

5.1   Identifing the Location of the Check

Identifying where to introduce permission checks before executing usermode helpers is challenging due to the kernel's complexity. The actual execution of usermode helpers may still be some steps away from the call points. To address this, we first identify the caller functions of usermode helper and then locate the execution points.

Despite their varied origins, the caller functions share the requirement of a path parameter to the usermode helper program. For instance, the attack code targeting `modprobe` will call `call_modprobe()` with a path parameter, which is then passed to `call_usermodehelper_setup()`. Both functions are considered usermode helper caller functions. To identify all relevant call points, we conduct a comprehensive analysis of the kernel source code using LLVM. We perform forward analysis to discover more generalized call points by traversing instructions within known usermode helper calling functions and identifying callees that receive a path-type argument. Similarly, we use backward analysis to find callers of known usermode helper call functions, extracting functions that contain a path-type argument. This approach allows us to identify four key function call points: `call_modprobe()`, `call_usermodehelper()`, `call_usermodehelper_setup()`, and `call_usermodehelper_keys()`.

Inserting permission checks at these caller functions risks being bypassed, as attackers can directly call the execution function. To pinpoint the execution point, we construct call graphs from the caller functions.

Since the kernel frequently uses function pointers for diverse functionalities, known as indirect calls, which are not easily resolved by LLVM, we employ PeX [30], an LLVM-based tool, to find the functions that function pointers actually call. We modify PeX to output the function call chains starting from the identified caller functions. Our analysis reveals that all the identified functions eventually call `call_usermodehelper_setup()`, indicating that the call chain converges at this point. Figure 3 illustrates the relevant functions and their call relationships within the kernel.

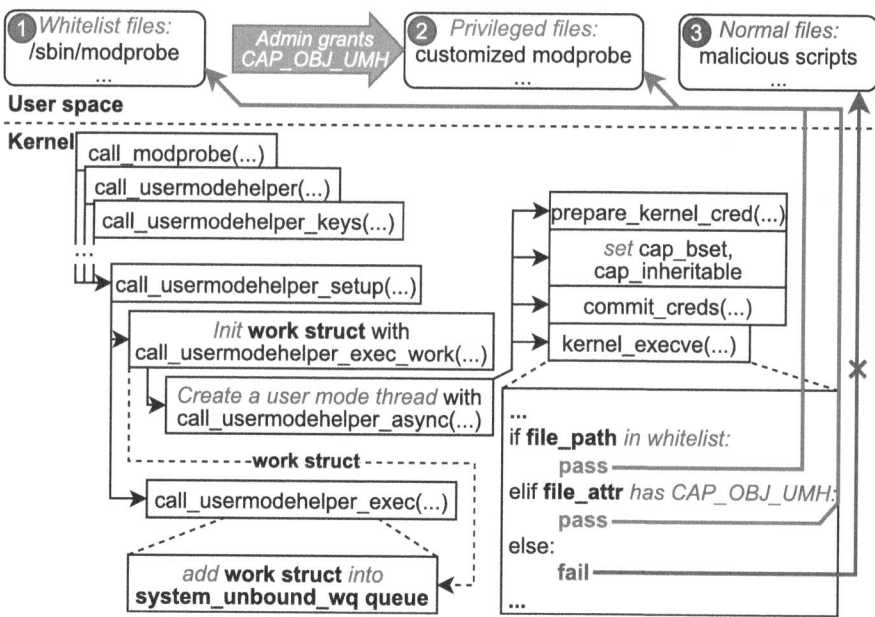

Fig. 3. Function call graph and defense mechanism for usermode helper invocations.

The `call_usermodehelper_setup()` function prepares for usermode helper execution by initializing a `subprocess_info` object. This includes setting the `subprocess_info->path` to the path of the usermode helper to be executed and initializing the `subprocess_info->work` with the kernel function `call_usermodehelper_exec_work()`. This function creates a usermode thread, with the task specified by `call_usermodehelper_exec_async()`. The async function inherits permission data from the parent process, computes credentials for the child process using the `cred` structure, and eventually calls `kernel_execve()` to execute the usermode helper. The `kernel_execve()` is crucial as it generates a structure from the usermode helper's path and executes the binary file. Notably, `call_usermodehelper_exec()`, which is called after `call_usermodehelper_setup()`, adds the `subprocess_info->work` to the system queue. The kernel thread `kworker` handles the work in the queue, creating a new process and executing the usermode helper program.

The function `kernel_execve()` is the final point where the helper path can be modified, but since the path is now a local variable, the attack window is significantly reduced, making it harder for attackers compared to modifying global kernel variables like `modprobe_path`.

5.2   Deciding Permissions to Check

To prevent privilege leakage and ensure the security of usermode helper execution, the kernel must verify that a usermode helper is privileged before executing it. In Linux systems, two primary types of privilege identifiers are used for subject processes: UID (User ID) and capabilities. UID is used for identity-based access control. By default, processes with a UID of 0 (root) have all capabilities, while processes with a non-zero UID have none. Linux capabilities allow for more granular control by enabling specific privileges to be assigned independently to processes. Currently, usermode helpers are owned and modifiable only by root, meaning a UID check could ensure the usermode helper file is root-owned and not subject to unauthorized modification.

However, UID-based checks are coarse-grained. Requiring only root to set usermode helpers increases the frequency of root usage, thus elevating security risks. Capability checks can reduce the necessity for root involvement, thereby minimizing the risk associated with root usage. Modern Linux kernels favor capability checks for sensitive operations, as capabilities provide more precise and limited permission assignments. Given that usermode helpers can be targets for tampering by attackers, invoking these helpers should be treated as a sensitive operation protected by capabilities.

Typically, capabilities protect objects from unauthorized access by checking the capability set of the subject process. However, for usermode helpers, it is crucial to ensure that the program executed by the root process is trustworthy and has special permissions. To address this, we define a new capability, `CAP_OBJ_UMH`, specifically designed to prevent this kind of privilege escalation attacks. The new capability indicates that it is assigned to guest objects (i.e., the usermode helper programs). By requiring usermode helpers to possess a specific capability, we can ensure that only trusted and privileged programs are executed by the kernel with root privileges.

5.3   Maintaining System Usability

To ensure that the newly added permission checks do not impact system usability and user experience, we add current usermode helpers to a whitelist. This eliminates the need for users to authorize the capability to the existing usermode helpers as the capability checks will only apply to usermode helpers that are not on the whitelist. The system administrator is responsible for granting CAP_OBJ_UMH to any custom usermode helpers before they are used. This involves setting capabilities on the usermode helper files. If a file is modified after authorization, its configured capability will be revoked automatically. For new functionalities, kernel developers need to invoke the new usermode helper in the kernel and either add it to the whitelist or ensure it has CAP_OBJ_UMH on the system. This design ensures that even if attackers overwrite the path of the usermode helper, the fake helper lacking CAP_OBJ_UMH will not be executed, thus preventing privilege escalation.

6   Implementation

We used Linux kernel v6.6.3 source code (the latest version at the time of writing) as the target, leveraging LLVM/Clang 12.0 for analysis and modified 159 lines of code.

6.1   Collecting Usermode Helpers

Current usermode helpers on the system are owned by root and need to be found and whitelisted. Since all calls of usermode helpers converge at the function call_usermodehelper_setup(), with its first argument pointing to the path of usermode helper. We can traverse the kernel's bitcode using LLVM to extract the locations where this function is called and the values of its first argument, systematically identifying all usermode helper paths. Specifically, we add a pass to identify the call points of call_usermodehelper_setup() by iterating through the instructions with LLVM object CallInst, and obtain the value of its first argument by CallInst->getArgOperand(0).

We identified 20 usermode helpers in total. Ten of these use hard-coded paths with constant strings, which pose no risk of being tampered with. These usermode helpers perform relatively fixed functions that do not require reconfigurability. For example, /linuxrc is called at boot time to create the root filesystem and start the kernel, which does not need user customization, so its path is fixed. Two paths can be modified by altering kernel startup parameters, which require root privileges and a reboot to take effect. Based on our threat model, the attacker does not have such capabilities. Table 2 lists the remaining 8

Table 2. Paths and trigger conditions of different usermode helpers.

Usermode Helper Path	Kernel Source Location	Trigger Condition
`/sbin/modprobe`	`kernel/module/kmod.c`	Execute a dummy file
`/lib/systemd/systemd-coredump`	`fs/coredump.c`	Core dump
`/sbin/hotplug`	`lib/kobject_uevent.c`	Hotplug event
`release_agent under root cgroup directory`	`kernel/cgroup/cgroup-v1.c`	A child cgroup sets notify_on_release and exits
`/sbin/poweroff`	`kernel/reboot.c`	Emergency system poweroff
`/sbin/ocfs2_hb_ctl`	`fs/ocfs2/stackglue.c`	Unmount an ocfs2 filesystem
`/sbin/nfsdcltrack`	`fs/nfsd/nfs4recover.c`	Manipulate a database storing NFSclient clock info
`/sbin/drbdadm`	`drivers/block/drbd/drbd_nl.c`	Invoke DRBD program suite

usermode helpers, with the kernel source code locations and the paths that may be vulnerable to tampering by an attacker.

Different usermode helpers have different trigger conditions. For example, the trigger for `modprobe` is executing a dummy file. The Table 2 lists the scenarios for each usermode helper. Some scenarios are hard to exploit. For example, the trigger condition for `poweroff` is an error in the system power supply unit or an excessively high temperature. It is much more challenging than executing an unrecognized file in user space. The ease of triggering may explain why `modprobe` is popular in privilege escalation attacks. However, as long as the path can be modified, there exists the possibility of exploitation. Therefore, we consider all these writable paths as objects to be protected.

6.2   Introducing a New Capability

To secure the usermode helpers' execution, we introduce a new capability, `CAP_OBJ_UMH`, defined in `include/linux/capability.h`. This capability ensures that only trusted, privileged programs are executed by the kernel. As illustrated in Sect. 5.1, we identified that all usermode helper calls eventually invoke `kernel_execve()` by passing in a file path of the helper. However, this function is also used in running the init process. To preserve its original functionality, we reimplemented it as `kernel_execve_from_umh()`, especially for UMHs. In this new function, we added a whitelist check and a capability check. File paths not in the whitelist are subject to capability checks.

Capabilities are stored in the file's extended attributes as key-value pairs. We use kernel function `__vfs_getxattr()` to obtain a file's extend attributes, specifying `XATTR_NAME_CAPS` as the attribute key. The inode and dentry information needed by `__vfs_getxattr()` are derived from the file path passed into the `kernel_execve()` function. By checking for `CAP_OBJ_UMH` in the file's capability set, we authenticate the usermode helper file.

6.3   Configuring in User Space

New usermode helpers not included in the initial whitelist require capability configured before use. This configuration should be performed by system administrators who have high privileges. The administrator can configure capability for usermode helpers with the `setcap` command. For example, the command `setcap CAP_OBJ_UMH+p` <*filename*> grants the `CAP_OBJ_UMH` capability to the file specified by *filename*. It is essential that the usermode helper file is protected with UGO (User, Group, Others) mechanism, allowing only the owner to modify it. Therefore, attackers can not tamper with usermode helper files on the whitelist. We add seven usermode helpers to the whitelist, as shown in Table 2, with the exception of `release_agent`, which does not have an absolute path.

Among the eight usermode helpers listed in the table, six points to executables and are safeguarded by UGO, while `core_pattern` and `release_agent` correspond to kernel variables that are susceptible to an additional risk of modification. Although the default value of `core_pattern` in the kernel is `core`, it is reset by the system service manager `systemd` to `|/lib/systemd/systemd-coredump`. So we add `/lib/systemd/systemd-coredump` to the whitelist. Even if an attacker can overwrite the `core_pattern` using kernel vulnerabilities, the malicious path that passes to `kernel_execve()` will be checked with capability.

The `release_agent` is dynamically generated at runtime, depending on where the cgroup is mounted. Its execution is triggered when a subgroup exits. By default, this file is empty, meaning no action is taken. If a user needs to use `release_agent` to execute customized code, he must configure the `CAP_OBJ_UMH` for it after writing to this file.

7 Evaluation

In this section, we conduct a security evaluation of our defense system and then evaluate the prototype's performance. The experimental platform is a laptop with an Intel Core i7-8550U CPU @ 1.8 GHz and 8 GB memory (DDR4-2400). The operating system is Ubuntu 24.04. We evaluate the performance of the original Linux kernel v6.6.3 and the modified kernel on the laptop natively.

Table 3. Protection results of different types of usermode helper-based attacks.

CVE-ID	Trigger	Mitigated	CVE-ID	Trigger	Mitigated
2023-2598	hijack function pointer	✓	2022-2586	modprobe	✓
			2022-32250	modprobe	✓
2023-3609	core_pattern	✓	2022-32250	modprobe	✓
2023-3776	core_pattern	✓	2022-2586	modprobe	✓
2023-4622	core_pattern	✓	2022-0185	modprobe	✓
2022-0492	release_agent	✓	2022-0185	modprobe	✓
2023-0179	modprobe	✓	2022-34918	modprobe	✓
2023-1829	modprobe	✓	2022-27666	modprobe	✓
2023-5178	modprobe	✓	2024-1086	modprobe	✓
2023-31248	modprobe	✓	2024-0582	modprobe	✓

7.1 Security

To verify the effectiveness of our defense system, we reproduced 19 exploits of privilege escalation attacks by leveraging usermode helper in our experimental VMs. Among them, we reverted the patches to expose the vulnerabilities that had been fixed in the experiment kernel version. We found that all 19 exploits (shown in Table 3) failed to achieve privilege escalation under our modification. Among the 19 exploits, 14 overwrite the path of `modprobe` helper program, 3 overwrite the content of `core_pattern`, one leverages the helper file `release_agent`, and one directly calls `call_usermodehelper_setup()` with a fake `subprocess_info` structure. The results prove that our defense system can effectively block different types of usermode helper-based privilege escalation attacks.

7.2 Performance

First, we used the ftrace tool [21] to perform a breakdown analysis of the modified `kernel_execve()` function to count the overhead from the extra checking operations we introduced. Specifically, we prepared a script file as a newly introduced usermode helper with `CAP_OBJ_UMH` set and wrote its path into `core_pattern` file, which will be executed when core dump happens. Then, we triggered a core dump by sending signal `SIGABRT`. It reported that these extra operations cost 41.917us while the whole `kernel_execve` cost 1709.456us. For usermode helpers on the whitelist, the additional check overhead was less than 1us.

Table 4. Performance of the defense system.

Benchmarks	1 Parallel Copy			8 Parallel Copies		
	Original	Modified	Overhead	Original	Modified	Overhead
Dhrystone 2 using register variables	4584.3	4558.8	0.56%	15419.8	15457.5	−0.24%
Double-Precision Whetstone	1578.3	1577.3	0.06%	7401.3	7418.5	−0.23%
Execl Throughput	556.5	548.1	1.51%	2400.2	2396	0.17%
File Copy 1024 bufsize 2000 maxblocks	1482	1469.5	0.84%	4457.6	4491.6	−0.76%
File Copy 256 bufsize 500 maxblocks	897.2	891.6	0.62%	2841	2868.7	−0.98%
File Copy 4096 bufsize 8000 maxblocks	2546.6	2435.9	4.35%	9096.8	9124.1	−0.30%
Pipe Throughput	580.8	582.1	−0.22%	1948.9	1954.2	−0.27%
Pipe-based Context Switching	366.5	363	0.95%	1160.5	1185.4	−2.15%
Process Creation	259.6	250.5	3.51%	2131.9	2142.3	−0.49%
Shell Scripts (1 concurrent)	1114.4	1072.2	3.79%	5707.1	5712.4	−0.09%
Shell Scripts (8 concurrent)	5210.8	5208.9	0.04%	5336.5	5342.6	−0.11%
System Call Overhead	264.6	264.5	0.04%	861.7	860.1	0.19%
System Benchmarks Index Score	1012.3	998.6	1.35%	3549	3564.5	−0.44%

We then also used the UnixBench [22] to evaluate the impact of our modifications on the overall performance of the system. The results are illustrated in Table 4, which shows that our modification introduces negligible overhead to the system.

8   Related Work

Kernel developers and security researchers have made a number of efforts to defend privilege escalation attacks.

Defense Through Kernel Configuration. To prevent attacks utilizing usermode helpers, the kernel introduced a pair of configurations. Enabling `CONFIG_STATIC_USERMODEHELPER` routes all usermode helper calls to a single executable defined by `CONFIG_STATIC_USERMODEHELPER_PATH`, which then delegates to the appropriate helper based on its first argument. [10, 26] provide simple examples of the single usermode helper implementation in user space. Setting `CONFIG_STATIC_USERMODEHELPER_PATH` to an empty string disables all usermode helpers. However, disabling usermode helpers or enforcing static paths can impact system functionality and availability. Consequently, these options have not been widely adopted in mainstream Linux distributions.

Use of Capability. Some efforts are aimed at facilitating the use of capability to implement the principle of least privilege. Work such as Decap [11] and LiCA [25] establishes the relationship between system calls and capability through static analysis, while others like TCLP [14] and MiniCon [12] try to restrict the capability of the container through triggered system calls.

Other Defense Methods. Security researchers focus on preventing privilege escalation attacks by restricting the attacker's abilities and protecting privileged data. PET [27] can prevent certain types of kernel errors from being exploited, making it harder to tamper with the paths of usermode helpers. Lin et al. [15] introduce a defense method that checks if the newly committed process credentials exceed the actual privileges of the process during `commit_creds()`. This method only counters `commit_creds()`-type attacks. Traditional data flow integrity approaches use data flow graphs to verify legitimate object access and, therefore, protect the privilege credentials, but they often impose significant performance overhead [2, 3, 23]. Alternative data protection schemes have been proposed. DOPE [19] restricts access to sensitive data during kernel space exploitation, but usermode helpers are running in the user space. AKO [29] adds observation points in system call handlers, comparing the permission information recorded before and after the call to identify privilege escalation attacks. Similarly, PriviGuard [1] monitors sensitive data at system call entry points and uses stack canaries for protection. KDRM [13] relocates kernel privilege data to a new page during system calls to protect it. Some methods focus on specific data protection. Sentry [24] only safeguards structure data, and PrivWatcher [4] moves process credentials to a read-only region. xMP [20] can also protect process credentials via intercepting LSM hooks. Wei et al. [28] protect the SELinux context data of processes to limit the damage that can be inflicted on the system even after an attacker gains root privileges. Furthermore, CPEED [31] measures process state in a secure environment and intervenes immediately if permission data changes.

While these studies are effective in mitigating attacks based on modifying the permissions of the attacker's process, they do not apply to attacks that utilize usermode helpers' root privileges to execute malicious codes.

9   Conclusion

Privilege escalation attacks can have serious consequences, and previous defenses may not be effective against current attacks. In this paper, we collect a dataset containing 50 Linux kernel privilege escalation exploits from the last three years and classify them by their vectors of gaining privileges. We discover that an increasing number of exploits leverage usermode helpers. After performing an in-depth analysis of this new attack vector, we propose a lightweight defense based on Linux capabilities. Using LLVM to analyze kernel source code statically, we insert capability checks right before the kernel executes usermode helpers. Our defense mechanism effectively defeats existing attacks while maintaining negligible performance overhead.

Acknowledgments. We would like to thank the anonymous reviewers for their valuable comments and suggestions. This work is supported by the National Key R&D Program of China under Award No. 2023YFB3105804.

References

1. PrivGuard: Protecting Sensitive Kernel Data From Privilege Escalation Attacks — IEEE Journals & Magazine — IEEE Xplore (2018)
2. Akritidis, P., Cadar, C., Raiciu, C., Costa, M., Castro, M.: Preventing memory error exploits with WIT. In: 2008 IEEE Symposium on Security and Privacy (sp 2008), pp. 263–277 (2008). https://doi.org/10.1109/SP.2008.30. iSSN: 2375-1207
3. Castro, M., Costa, M., Harris, T.: Securing software by enforcing data-flow integrity (2006)
4. Chen, Q., Azab, A.M., Ganesh, G., Ning, P.: Privwatcher: non-bypassable monitoring and protection of process credentials from memory corruption attacks. In: Proceedings of the 2017 ACM on Asia Conference on Computer and Communications Security, ASIA CCS 2017, pp. 167-178. Association for Computing Machinery, New York (2017). https://doi.org/10.1145/3052973.3053029
5. CVE-2022-0492 (2022). https://cve.mitre.org/cgi-bin/cvename.cgi?name=CVE-2022-0492
6. CVE-2022-0847 (2022). https://cve.mitre.org/cgi-bin/cvename.cgi?name=CVE-2022-0847
7. CVE-2023-0179 (2023). https://cve.mitre.org/cgi-bin/cvename.cgi?name=CVE-2023-0179
8. Dirty COW Vulnerability (2016). https://en.wikipedia.org/wiki/Dirty_COW
9. Exploit database (2024). https://www.exploit-db.com/

10. First public implementation of usermode helper in LinuxKit (2017). https://github.com/linuxkit/linuxkit/blob/master/pkg/init/usermode-helper.c

11. Hasan, M.M., Ghavamnia, S., Polychronakis, M.: Decap: depriviliging programs by reducing their capabilities. In: Proceedings of the 25th International Symposium on Research in Attacks, Intrusions and Defenses, RAID 2022, pp. 395–408. Association for Computing Machinery, New York (2022). https://doi.org/10.1145/3545948.3545978

12. Kang, H., Kim, J., Shin, S.: MiniCon: automatic enforcement of a minimal capability set for security-enhanced containers. In: 2021 IEEE International IOT, Electronics and Mechatronics Conference (IEMTRONICS), pp. 1–5 (2021). https://doi.org/10.1109/IEMTRONICS52119.2021.9422529

13. Kuzuno, H., Yamauchi, T.: KDRM: kernel data relocation mechanism to mitigate privilege escalation attack. In: Li, S., Manulis, M., Miyaji, A. (eds.) Network and System Security, pp. 61–76. Springer, Cham (2023). https://doi.org/10.1007/978-3-031-39828-5_4

14. Lee, S., Seo, J., Nam, J., Shin, S.: Poster: TCLP: enforcing least privileges to prevent containers from kernel vulnerabilities. In: Proceedings of the 2019 ACM SIGSAC Conference on Computer and Communications Security, CCS 2019, pp. 2665–2667. Association for Computing Machinery, New York (2019). https://doi.org/10.1145/3319535.3363282

15. Lin, X., Lei, L., Wang, Y., Jing, J., Sun, K., Zhou, Q.: A measurement study on linux container security: attacks and countermeasures. In: Proceedings of the 34th Annual Computer Security Applications Conference, ACSAC 2018, pp. 418–429. Association for Computing Machinery, New York (2018). https://doi.org/10.1145/3274694.3274720

16. Linux kernel exploitation (2024). https://github.com/xairy/linux-kernel-exploitation?tab=readme-ov-file#lpe

17. Linux kernel (operating system) : Product details, threats and statistics (2024). https://www.cvedetails.com/product/47/Linux-Linux-Kernel.html?vendor_id=33

18. LLVM Project (2023). https://llvm.org/

19. Maar, L., Schwarzl, M., Rauscher, F., Gruss, D., Mangard, S.: Dope: domain protection enforcement with pks. In: Proceedings of the 39th Annual Computer Security Applications Conference, ACSAC 2023, pp. 662–676. Association for Computing Machinery, New York (2023). https://doi.org/10.1145/3627106.3627113

20. Proskurin, S., Momeu, M., Ghavamnia, S., Kemerlis, V.P., Polychronakis, M.: xMP: selective memory protection for kernel and user space. In: 2020 IEEE Symposium on Security and Privacy (SP), pp. 563–577 (2020). https://doi.org/10.1109/SP40000.2020.00041. iSSN: 2375-1207

21. Rostedt, S., Oltmanns, E., Dunlap, R., Morton, A., Kacur, J., Teigland, D.: ftrace - function tracer (2017). https://www.kernel.org/doc/html/v4.17/trace/ftrace.html

22. Smith, B., Grehan, R., Yager, T., Niemi, D.C., Voellm, A.F.: Byte-unixbench: a unix benchmark suite. Technical report (2011)

23. Song, C., Lee, B., Lu, K., Harris, W.R., Kim, T., Lee, W.: Enforcing kernel security invariants with data flow integrity. In: Proceedings of the 2016 Annual Network and Distributed System Security Symposium (NDSS), San Diego, CA (2016)

24. Srivastava, A., Giffin, J.: Efficient protection of kernel data structures via object partitioning. In: Proceedings of the 28th Annual Computer Security Applications Conference, ACSAC 2012, pp. 429–438. Association for Computing Machinery, New York (2012)

25. Sun, M., Song, Z., Ren, X., Wu, D., Zhang, K.: LiCA: a fine-grained and path-sensitive linux capability analysis framework. In: Proceedings of the 25th International Symposium on Research in Attacks, Intrusions and Defenses, RAID 2022, pp. 364–379. Association for Computing Machinery, New York (2022). https://doi.org/10.1145/3545948.3545966
26. The userspace side of Linux' CONFIG_STATIC_USERMODEHELPER (2019). https://github.com/tych0/huldufolk/tree/master
27. Wang, Z., Chen, Y., Zeng, Q.: PET: prevent discovered errors from being triggered in the linux kernel. In: 32nd USENIX Security Symposium (USENIX Security 2023), pp. 4193–4210. USENIX Association, Anaheim (2023). https://www.usenix.org/conference/usenixsecurity23/presentation/wang-zicheng
28. Wei, L., Zuo, Y., Ding, Y., Dong, P., Huang, C., Gao, Y.: Security identifier randomization: a method to prevent kernel privilege-escalation attacks. In: 2016 30th International Conference on Advanced Information Networking and Applications Workshops (WAINA), pp. 838–842 (2016). https://doi.org/10.1109/WAINA.2016.19
29. Yamauchi, T., Akao, Y., Yoshitani, R., Nakamura, Y., Hashimoto, M.: Additional kernel observer: privilege escalation attack prevention mechanism focusing on system call privilege changes. Int. J. Inf. Secur. **20**(4), 461–473 (2021). https://doi.org/10.1007/s10207-020-00514-7
30. Zhang, T., Shen, W., Lee, D., Jung, C., Azab, A.M., Wang, R.: PeX: a permission check analysis framework for linux kernel. In: Proceedings of the 28th USENIX Security Symposium, pp. 1205–1220 (2019). https://www.usenix.org/conference/usenixsecurity19/presentation/zhang-tong
31. Zhou, M., et al.: Container privilege escalation and escape detection method based on security-first architecture. In: 2023 IEEE International Conference on High Performance Computing & Communications, Data Science & Systems, Smart City & Dependability in Sensor, Cloud & Big Data Systems & Application (HPCC/DSS/SmartCity/DependSys), pp. 490–498 (2023). https://doi.org/10.1109/HPCC-DSS-SmartCity-DependSys60770.2023.00073

Multi-Party Computation

Balance-Based ZKP Protocols for Pencil-and-Paper Puzzles

Shohei Kaneko[1]([✉]) [ID], Pascal Lafourcade[2] [ID], Lola-Baie Mallordy[3] [ID], Daiki Miyahara[1,4]([✉]) [ID], Maxime Puys[2] [ID], and Kazuo Sakiyama[1] [ID]

[1] The University of Electro-Communications, Tokyo, Japan
{shohei.kaneko,miyahara}@uec.ac.jp
[2] Université Clermont Auvergne, CNRS, Clermont Auvergne INP, Mines Saint-Etienne, LIMOS, 63000 Clermont-Ferrand, France
[3] University Clermont Auvergne, LIMOS, CNRS UMR (6158), Aubière, France
[4] National Institute of Advanced Industrial Science and Technology, Tokyo, Japan

Abstract. In this paper, we propose zero-knowledge proof (ZKP) protocols using physical objects for four pencil-and-paper puzzles: the well-known Sudoku as well as Makaro, Futoshiki, and Kakuro. That is, our protocols allow a prover to convince a verifier that the prover knows a solution to a puzzle without relying on the use of computers. While previous physical ZKP protocols for puzzles have mainly relied on decks of cards, our research introduces a novel approach utilizing a balance scale and coins to design balance-based ZKP protocols; moreover we show its flexibility by adapting it to the four different puzzles. We compare the number of coins and operations in our protocols with the existing card-based protocols and show that, for certain puzzles, our balance-based protocol outperforms the card-based method. Finally, we prove that our protocols achieve perfect completeness, perfect soundness and are perfectly zero-knowledge.

Keywords: Card-based cryptography · Zero-knowledge proof · Balance scale · Pencil-and-paper puzzle · Sudoku

1 Introduction

Alice, a hungry girl, goes to a fish market in the East Coast of the US with no money as depicted in Fig. 1. She spots a stand selling fish, with a big sign claiming *"Free fish for anyone who can solve my four puzzles"*. She comes closer and sees that the puzzles are four pencil games: Sudoku, Makaro, Futoshiki, and Kakuro. She cannot miss such a golden opportunity, and starts searching for the solutions. After several hours racking her brain without finding any solution, she screams at the merchant: *"Grifter, your puzzles are impossible!"*. The merchant calmly tells her *"I can prove I know all of the solutions"*. The merchant cannot give away its solutions, or people would come flocking to its stand asking for free

© The Author(s), under exclusive license to Springer Nature Switzerland AG 2025
N. Mouha and N. Nikiforakis (Eds.): ISC 2024, LNCS 15257, pp. 211–231, 2025.
https://doi.org/10.1007/978-3-031-75757-0_11

fish. What he needs to do is a *zero-knowledge proof* (ZKP) to Alice, allowing to convince her that he knows a solution without revealing it. He remembers that Murata et al. [31] proposed similar protocols using a PEZ dispenser. However, there are no PEZ dispensers at the fish market; the merchant only has a *balance* and *coins* on his stand, to weigh the fishes he sells. In this research, we propose a method to assist merchants, designing ZKP protocols using a balance and coins.

1.1   Zero-Knowledge Proof

Zero-knowledge proofs (ZKPs), introduced in 1985 by Goldwasser et al. [11], allow a prover P to convince a verifier V that a given statement is true without revealing any further information. ZKPs give a model that is not limited to computer use, but may also be applied in real life using everyday objects. In 1990, Quisquater et al. [32] published the well-known story of the Ali Baba cave to illustrate this concept, which made the first instance of a physical ZKP.

A ZKP protocol for a solution to a pencil-and-paper puzzle should satisfy three properties as follows:

Completeness: If P knows a solution of a given grid, it can convince V.
Soundness: If P does not provide a correct solution of a given grid, V rejects P with a sufficiently high probability.
Zero-knowledge: The verifier V is not given any information other than that the prover P can solve the puzzle.

These properties can come in three different flavours: perfect, statistical and computational. Perfect completeness means that an honest prover will always convince an honest verifier on a true statement, perfect soundness means that it is impossible to prove a false statement, and perfect zero-knowledge means that transcripts can be perfectly simulated and leak no information whatsoever. Perfect soundness can be relaxed to statistical soundness, where a prover must have a negligible probability of falsely convincing the verifier. It can be relaxed further to computational soundness, where any way to cheat must be computationally infeasible. Completeness and zero-knowledge can be relaxed in the same way. Our proposed protocols achieve the stronger versions of these properties: perfect completeness, perfect soundness, and perfect zero-knowledge based on some physical assumptions.

It was shown that for any NP-complete problem, there exists an interactive ZKP [10]. An extension by Ben-Or et al. [3] showed that every provable statement can be proven in zero-knowledge. The puzzles introduced in this paper have all been proven to be NP-complete: Sudoku and Kakuro in 2003 [50], Makaro in 2018 [17], and Futoshiki in 2021 [22]. Thus, there should exist ZKP protocols for such puzzles; however, a concrete procedure using a balance has not been addressed.

Fig. 1. Alice visits the fish market.

Table 1. Comparison of the complexity of our balance-based protocols with the existing card-based ones. We consider $n \times n$ grids except for the standard 9×9 Sudoku grid. In Sudoku, n_e is the number of empty cells. In Futoshiki, i is the number of inequality symbols. In Makaro, n_s represents the number of rooms with size s, $2 \leq s \leq s_0$ for some s_0, c is the number of arrow cells, d is the number of cells adjacent to arrow cells, and e is the number of bold lines between two adjacent cells in different rooms. In Kakuro, t represents the number of triangular cells, n_h is the number of uninterrupted rows and columns of length h, $2 \leq h \leq h_0 < n$ for some h_0, and w is the number of white cells.

	Balance-Based			Card-Based	
	Coins	Shuffles	Comparisons	Cards	Shuffles
Sudoku	243	27	$686 + 2n_c$	90 [45]	45 [45]
Futoshiki	n^2	$2n$	$2(n-1)(\sum_{k=1}^n k) + 2\binom{n}{2} + n_e + i$	–	–
Makaro	$\sum_{s=2}^{s_0} s n_s + 2e + s_0$	$\sum_{s=2}^{s_0} n_s + e$	$\sum_{s=2}^{s_0}(n_s \times \sum_{k=1}^s k) + d - c + 3e$	$2s_0 - 1 + s_0 \sum_{s=2}^{s_0} n_s) + (s_0 - 1)s_0$ [5]	$2(\sum_{s=2}^{s_0} n_s + c + e)$ [5]
Kakuro	$t + 2w$	t	$t + \sum_{\ell=2}^{\ell_0}(n_\ell \binom{\ell}{2}) + w$	$81(t + 81)$ [28]	$3t + 1$ [28]

1.2 Contributions

We propose a new perspective on ZKPs for pencil puzzles, replacing decks of cards with a balance and coins. To prove our method's adaptability, we show it can be applied to four different puzzles. We develop ZKP protocols for Sudoku, Makaro, Futoshiki, and Kakuro, which all provide perfect completeness, perfect soundness, and perfect zero-knowledge.

Table 1 indicates the number of coins, shuffles, and comparisons used in our balance-based protocol, as well as the number of cards and shuffles used in the existing card-based protocols. In Kakuro, it can be observed that the number of coins used in the balance-based protocol is less than the number of cards used in the card-based protocol [28]. In Futoshiki, our balance-based protocol directly verifies an inequality using the property of a balance, although there is no card-based protocol yet. From these observations, it can be inferred that in certain puzzles, balance-based protocols may reduce the number of physical entities and rounds of operation, making them easier to execute compared to card-based protocols. We note that a type of shuffle used in card-based ZKP protocols is costly to implement, while our balance-based protocol uses a common and easy-to-implement shuffle.

1.3   Related Work

In 2009, the first physical ZKP applied to Sudoku was proposed [12], using a deck of cards. This leads to several improvement results [36,45,48]. In addition to Sudoku, there are many card-based ZKP protocols, such as Nurimisaki [34], Kurodoko [34], Juosan [26], Usowan [27], Herugolf [27], Five cells [27,44], Nurikabe [33], Hitori [33], Heyawake [33], Makaro [5,36], Nonogram [6,37], Numberlink [40], Bridges [42], Cryptarithmetic [16], Akari [4], Takuzu [4,26], Kakuro [4,28], KenKen [4], Shikaku [43], Slitherlink [21], Sumplete [14], Suguru [35], Topswops [20], Pancake Sorting [19], ABC End View [8,39], Ball Sort [38], Goishi Hiroi [39], Ripple Effect [41], 15 puzzle [47], graph problems [24], and Moon-or-Sun [13]. However, few solutions try to incorporate other everyday objects other than cards. Such examples include: PEZ dispenser [1,2,31], coins (where their weights are not considered, but rather the toss of coins with result either head or tail) [18,23], polarizing plates [46], dial lock [29], tamper-evident seals [30], balls in bags [25], and marbles in an auction protocol [7]. These protocols are not for ZKPs, but for secure multiparty computations, which enable us to compute a given function over private inputs without revealing anything. Our study proposes a ZKP protocol using a balance and coins, which to our knowledge is the first of its kind. That is, our study explores computations performed by comparisons. It should be noted that a ZKP protocol for Sudoku can be constructed by comparisons. As for Futoshiki, we are the first ones to propose a physical ZKP protocol. Our ZKP protocols using everyday objects could inspire further research. This study, along with research on card-based cryptography, aims to answer the question: "What is the easiest way to perform cryptographic tasks, such as secure computation and zero-knowledge proof systems, without using computers?"

The computational complexity of pencil-and-paper puzzles has been widely studied [15], and a large number of puzzles are proved to be NP-complete as shown in a recent survey [49]. To the best of our knowledge, no research has employed an NP-hardness proof to construct a physical ZKP protocol because such an NP-hardness proof is shown by a reduction (mostly from the SAT problem), while a physical ZKP protocol is constructed directly to eliminate overhead.

2   Model

To describe our ZKP protocols visually, we introduce our use of coins and balances. We use balances similar to the Roberval balance, which is depicted in Fig. 2. We assume an ideal balance that tilts at a constant angle toward the heavier side regardless of the weight difference. That is, from seeing how the balance tilts, we cannot obtain information on the weights of coins placed on its plates other than which is heavier.

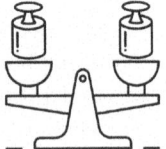

Fig. 2. The Roberval balance.

2.1 Actions

Our protocols use a coin represented as $\bigcirc$ of various weights (their weights are indistinguishable by just looking at them). We sometimes denote a stack of several coins by $\textcircled{)\!)\!)}$ for simplicity. In addition to moving coins, our protocols make use of two specific operations on coins: *Compare* and *Shuffle*.

Compare: We represent a comparison of two stacks of coins using a balance as follows: $\textcircled{)\!)\!)} \mid \textcircled{)\!)\!)}$. This operation returns three results: *Left*, *Right*, and *Even*, referring to the heavier stack between the two stacks, and no more information.

Shuffle: Shuffling several coins is represented as follows: $[\bigcirc_1 \bigcirc_2 \cdots \bigcirc_m] \rightarrow [\bigcirc_{r(1)} \bigcirc_{r(2)} \cdots \bigcirc_{r(m)}]$, where r is a uniformly distributed random permutation chosen from the symmetric group of degree m. This operation returns the coins rearranged completely random: after shuffling, the order of m coins is rearranged according to r (the underscripts number are given to identify the new positions; however, the coins are indistinguishable in practice).

2.2 Protocol

In our balance-based ZKP protocol for a puzzle, a prover P first places a coin on a cell of the given grid, such that the weight of the coin represents the number filled in the cell in a solution P has. This means that P needs to know a specific weight of a coin beforehand without a verifier V knowing it. This is possible if P uses a balance without V observing it, and we omit this in a protocol description. Additionally, only P should handle coins (whose weights directly represent a solution) throughout protocols, so as not to give V any information on the weights of the coins.

3 Sudoku

Sudoku is a famous puzzle, which gained popularity in 1986 when it was published by the Japanese puzzle company, Nikoli[1]. In this game, any number from 1 to 9 is placed in an empty cell. A typical Sudoku grid is a 9×9 grid, divided into 3×3 blocks. Initially, some cells are filled with numbers. In Fig. 3, we give a simple example of a Sudoku grid and its solution. The goal is to fill the cells so that each row (there are 9 rows), each column (there are 9 columns), and each block (there are 9 blocks) contains distinct numbers from 1 to 9.

3.1 ZKP Protocol

We present a ZKP protocol for Sudoku using a balance and coins. That is, this protocol enables a prover P (*i.e.*, the merchant) to convince a verifier V (*i.e.*, the hungry girl) that P knows a solution of a given Sudoku puzzle (in the fish market introduced in Sect. 1). Its security proof is given in Sect. 3.2.

---

[1] https://www.nikoli.co.jp/en/.

8				5	1			
		1			8			
	4		2				9	
			3					2
1	2	3	4		6	7	8	9
6					1			1
	8				9	5		
		2				4		
		7	6					

8	3	9	7	6	5	1	2	4
2	6	1	3	9	4	8	7	5
7	4	5	2	8	1	3	9	6
5	9	4	8	3	7	6	1	2
1	2	3	4	5	6	7	8	9
6	7	8	9	1	2	5	4	3
3	8	6	1	4	9	2	5	7
9	1	2	5	7	3	4	6	8
4	5	7	6	2	8	9	3	1

Fig. 3. An example of a Sudoku puzzle and its solution introduced in the Nikoli's website: https://www.nikoli.co.jp/en/puzzles/sudoku/.

Setup Phase: According to P's solution, the prover P places three ◯s on each cell so that the weight of each coin placed on a cell is equal to the number filling the cell. More precisely, the coins are placed in two phases:

1. For each initially filled cell, V places three ◯s, each with the corresponding weight.
2. For each empty cell, P places three ◯s according to its solution.
3. V checks that P executed the setup honestly, *i.e.*, all the three coins placed on each empty cell have the same weight. For this, P performs two comparisons for each empty cell and confirms that they result in even, as follows:

$$\bigcirc_1\bigcirc_2\bigcirc_3 \;\rightarrow\; \bigcirc_1 \mid \bigcirc_2 \;\&\; \bigcirc_1 \mid \bigcirc_3,$$

where the three coins are specified by the subscripts.

Verification Phase: The prover and the verifier execute the following steps to confirm that the nine coins placed in the first row (resp. column or block) match those in each of the other rows (resp. columns or blocks), *i.e.*, the numbers 1 through 9 each appear only once in each row (resp. column or block).

1. P picks a ◯ on each cell of the first row and shuffle them: [⬭] → ⬭. Let us denote these nine coins by $R_1 = \{\bigcirc_1^1, \bigcirc_2^1, \dots, \bigcirc_9^1\}$.
2. V confirms that R_1 has all different weights, as follows:
   - For each of all possible pairs in R_1, *i.e.*, $\bigcirc_i^1$ and $\bigcirc_j^1$, $1 \le i < j \le 9$, the prover P compares them as follows:

$$\bigcirc_i^1 \mid \bigcirc_j^1 \quad \text{for all } i \text{ and } j \text{ such that } 1 \le i < j \le 9.$$

   - If the comparison results in even, then V rejects P's solution.
3. P picks a ◯ on each cell of another row, say the k-th row, $2 \le k \le 9$, and shuffle them: [⬭] → ⬭. Let us denote these coins by $R_k = \{\bigcirc_1^k, \bigcirc_2^k, \dots, \bigcirc_9^k\}$.
4. V confirms that only a single coin among R_1 has the same weight as a coin among R_k. For this, it proceeds as follows, for each coin $\bigcirc_i^1$, $1 \le i \le 9$, among R_1.

(a) P compares $\bigcirc_i^1$ with each coin $\bigcirc_j^k$ among R_k, as follows:

$$\bigcirc_i^1 \mid \bigcirc_j^k \quad \text{for all } \bigcirc_j^k \in R_k.$$

- If the comparison results in even, then P returns $\bigcirc_i^1$ to R_1 but removes $\bigcirc_j^k$ from R_k.
- Otherwise, P returns the two coins.

(a) If none of the above comparisons result in even, V rejects P's solution.

5. Repeat the above steps from step 3 for another k. Note that there is no need to shuffle R_1.
6. Repeat the above steps for columns and blocks.

In this way, the verifier V is convinced that each row (resp. column or block) contains distinct numbers from 1 to 9, because for any two rows (resp. columns or blocks), there exists exactly one cell that contains the same number as the one in the other row (resp. column or block). Note that P is the only one manipulating the coins associated with the solution, otherwise V could learn information on their weights when manipulating them.

Efficiency: The numbers of coins, shuffles, and comparisons are summarized in Table 1. Let n_e denote the number of empty cells in a given Sudoku grid. This protocol uses $243\,(=3\times 81)$ coins, $27\,(=9\times 3)$ shuffles, and $1188 + 2n_e$ comparisons (but will be improved in Sect. 3.3). Let us count the number of comparisons. First, in the setup phase, two comparisons are performed for each empty cell, *i.e.*, $2n_e$ comparisons. In the verification phase, we first compare nine coins in R_1 one by one, *i.e.*, $36\,(=\binom{9}{2})$ comparisons. Then we compare nine coins in R_1 with nine coins in R_2 one by one, but the number of coins in R_2 decreases by one after comparing a coin in R_1 with all coins in R_2. Thus, in the worst case, we need $45\,(=\sum_{k=1}^{9} k)$ comparisons. Because there are eight rows (resp. columns or blocks) excluding the first row, the number of comparisons becomes $1188\,(=36\times 3+45\times 8\times 3)$. Therefore, the total number of comparisons becomes $1188 + 2n_e$. For an $n\times n$ Sudoku grid, this protocol uses $3n^2$ coins and requires $3n$ shuffles and $3(n-1)\sum_{k=1}^{n} k+3\binom{n}{2}+2n_e$ comparisons. Table 1 shows the case for $n=9$.

3.2   Security

We prove the three properties of ZKP for our proposed protocol.

Lemma 1 (Perfect Completeness – Sudoku). *If P provides a correct solution of a given Sudoku grid, V is always convinced.*

Proof. If P provides a correct solution, it is clear that both R_1 and R_k can be regarded as $\{1, 2, \ldots, 9\}$. Therefore, comparing every pair of numbers in R_1 cannot result in even, and comparing a number in R_1 with each number in R_k should result in even when the same numbers are compared.   □

Lemma 2 (Perfect Soundness – Sudoku). *If P does not provide a correct solution of a given Sudoku grid, V always rejects P's solution.*

Proof. Without loss of generality, assume that P gives an incorrect solution for a row, *i.e.*, there are two or more coins of the same weight $\ell \in \{1, \ldots, 9\}$ among nine coins in the same row. If such coins are included in R_1, then they are detected when comparing them because every possible pair of coins in R_1 is compared in step 2. Otherwise, *i.e.*, they are included in any R_k, $2 \leq k \leq 9$, they can be detected in step 4 as follows. The first time that P compares such a coin of weight ℓ in R_k with a coin of weight ℓ in R_1, the coin of weight ℓ is removed from R_k. Then, since R_1 no longer contains a coin of weight ℓ, there should exist a coin in R_1 such that no comparison with it and any coin in R_k results in even. Therefore, V can always rejects an incorrect solution.   □

Lemma 3 (Perfect Zero-Knowledge – Sudoku). *The verifier V is not given any information other than that the prover P can solve a given Sudoku grid.*

Proof. Note that V must not know the weight of even one coin placed on an empty cell; otherwise, V knows a number filled with the corresponding cell in the solution. Since the weight of a coin is indistinguishable from its appearance, once P places a coin on a cell, its weight cannot be known unless V picks it. Note that our protocol lets P handle the coins when they need to be moved or touched as noted in Sect. 2.2.

Informally, our protocol is zero-knowledge because it shuffles nine coins in R_1 and R_k in steps 1 and 3, respectively, to hide information about positions of cells where the nine coins are originally placed. This means that comparisons in steps 2 and 4 leak no information about the solution, except whether the placement of coins is valid or not.   □

Formally, we construct a simulator not in possession of a solution of a given puzzle to prove the zero-knowledge property. For this, we refer to [12], where a simulation-based proof for a card-based ZKP protocol for Sudoku is provided. Their proof replaces the standard rewind ability for a simulator with the ability to arbitrarily swap sequences of cards with another at any time. We apply this technique to construct a simulator for our protocol, ensuring indistinguishability from an honest prover, *i.e.*, it has the ability to arbitrarily swap coins with another one. The simulator acts as follows.

- In the setup phase, the simulator places three identical coins of any weight on each empty cell.
- In step 1 of the verification phase, when R_1 is shuffled, the simulator swaps R_1 with nine coins of weights 1 through 9.
- In step 3, when R_k is shuffled, the simulator swaps R_k with nine coins of weights 1 through 9.

Since a shuffling action provides a randomized order of coins, the comparison results performed in steps 2 and 4 are completely indistinguishable from those provided by an honest prover.   □

3.3   Discussion

Number of Comparisons: We can further reduce the number of comparisons by employing a method similar to the binary search when comparing R_1 with R_2. This is because after executing step 2, the weight of every coin in R_1 is determined from the 36 comparison results performed in step 2. If we compare a coin of weight five with every coin in R_2, then we can classify R_2 into four coins of weights less than five, four coins of weights greater than five, and the coin of weight five. This reduces the number of comparisons required, because the four coins of weights less (greater) than five do not need to be compared with the one of weight greater (less) than five. Recursively applying this method, the number of comparisons required for comparing R_1 and R_2 is 25, which is less than the one derived in the efficiency paragraph, *i.e.*, 45. The total number of comparisons is $686 \, (= 36 + 25 \times (8 + 9 + 9))$, where R_1 used for the verification of rows is also used for columns and blocks (excluding comparisons performed in the setup phase). Moreover, another improvement can be considered, such as rearranging the order of comparisons, *e.g.*, comparing R_3 and R_4 after comparing R_1 and R_2 and then comparing R_3 and R_1 might reduce the number of comparisons.

Card-Based Protocol: Placing three identical coins on each cell is the same as in the existing card-based ZKP protocol proposed by Gradwohl *et al.*. [12], in which three cards each having the same number are placed on each cell. Note that this protocol is different from the protocol in Table. 1. Their protocol does not confirm that each of three cards has the same number, and hence, it does not achieve perfect soundness. In our protocol, since we encode a number with the weight of a coin, we can confirm that each of three coins has the same weight using a balance, achieving perfect soundness.

4   Futoshiki

Futoshiki is a puzzle developed by Tamaki Seto in 2001, played on an $n \times n$ square grid. A Futoshiki grid includes white cells and inequality signs. In Fig. 4, we give an example of a 4×4 Futoshiki grid and its solution. The goal is to place one number in every white cells on the board according to the following constraints:

1. Each row and each column contains all the numbers 1 through n.
2. The numbers must satisfy the inequality signs.

4.1   ZKP Protocol

The main difference from Sudoku is that the numbers must also satisfy the inequality rule. We detail our protocol for an $n \times n$ grid. Our protocol achieves perfect completeness, perfect soundness and is perfectly zero-knowledge. The proofs are given in Sect. 4.2.

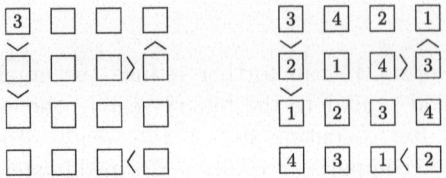

Fig. 4. An example of a Futoshiki puzzle and its solution generated in Futoshiki.com: https://www.futoshiki.com.

Setup: The setup phase is almost the same as in our proposed protocol for Sudoku (Sect. 3). That is, according to P's solution, the prover P places two $\bigcirc$s on every cell, and P compares the two $\bigcirc$s to show V that they have the same weight.

Verification: P and V execute the following steps:

1. To verify that the numbers on both sides of each inequality sign satisfy the rule, P compares two $\bigcirc$s placed on both sides of the sign: $\bigcirc \mid \bigcirc$. V observes that the balance gives the expected result; if not, V rejects P's solution. After performing each comparison, P moves the $\bigcirc$s to their original positions.
2. To verify that each row and column contains all the numbers from 1 to n, P and V use the same method as for Sudoku (Sect. 3).

Efficiency: Let i denote the number of inequality sings in a given $n \times n$ grid. This protocol uses n^2 coins and performs $2n$ shuffles and $2(n-1)(\sum_{k=1}^{n} k) + 2\binom{n}{2} + n_e + i$ comparisons. Compared to Sudoku, the number of comparisons is reduced by $(n-1)\sum_{k=1}^{n} k + \binom{n}{2}$ due to the absence of blocks, but it increases by i for the inequality verification. The shuffles are also reduced by n compared to Sudoku due to the absence of blocks. In the inequality verification, because no shuffling is performed, it does not impact the total number of shuffle operations.

4.2   Security

We prove the security of the Futoshiki protocol. A proof for completeness is omitted because it is clear from the protocol description.

Lemma 4 (Perfect Completeness – Futoshiki). *If P knows a solution of a given Futoshiki grid, he can always convince V.*

Lemma 5 (Perfect Soundness – Futoshiki). *If P does not provide a correct solution of a given Futoshiki grid, V always rejects P.*

Proof. When P gives an incorrect solution, the following two situations are possible:

– A row (resp. column) contains the same number at least twice. In this case, V will reject P's solution in the same way as in Sudoku (see Lemma 2).

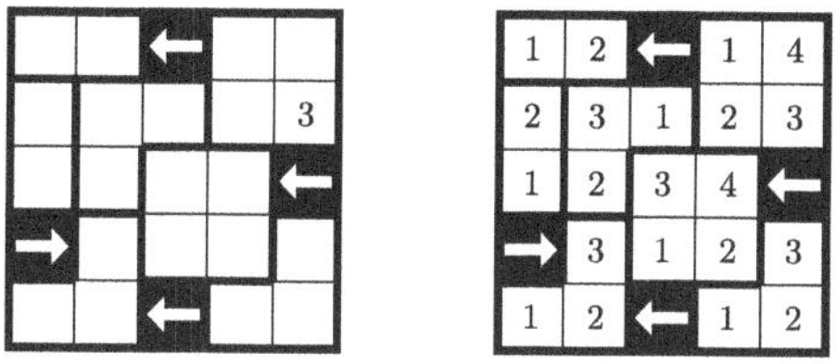

Fig. 5. An example of a Makaro puzzle and its solution introduced in the Nikoli's website: https://www.nikoli.co.jp/en/puzzles/makaro/.

– A pair of numbers does not verify the inequality sign between them. In this case, when V observes the result of the comparison, it will notice that the inequality is not satisfied and V will reject P's solution.

Therefore, V will always reject an invalid solution. □

Lemma 6 (Perfect Zero-Knowledge – Futoshiki). *The verifier V is not given any information other than that the prover P can solve the Futoshiki grid.*

Proof. We show that no information has been leaked other than that the prover P can solve the Futoshiki grid in both of the verification phases:

– In step 1, when V checks whether the numbers satisfy the inequality rule, as V does not touch the coins but only observes the result of the balance, V can only learn which coin is heavier (the coins are visually indistinguishable). Hence V still does not learn anything on P's solution except that it is correct.
– In step 2, V cannot learn anything on the numbers P placed on each cell for the same reason as in the Sudoku ZKP protocol (Lemma 3).

Therefore, V cannot learn anything throughout the whole process, except whether the solution is valid or not.

Formally, a simulator acts as follows.

– In the setup phase, the simulator arbitrarily places two identical coins on each empty cell.
– In step 1, before comparing two coins, it swaps the two coins so that the comparison result matches the inequality sign.
– In step 2 of the verification phase, it acts in the same way as in the proof for Lemma 2.

Since the simulator places coins to respect the inequality signs, the comparison results performed in step 1 are indistinguishable from those provided by an honest prover. □

5   Makaro

Makaro is another grid game proposed by Nikoli. A Makaro grid is made of white cells, and black cells filled with an arrow. In Fig. 5, we give an example of a 5×5 Makaro grid. The goal is to place one number in every white cells on the grid according to the following constraints:

1. The areas separated by bold lines are called rooms, and each room is filled with one number from 1 to the number of cells in that room.
2. In the case of a black cell with an arrow, the cell to which the arrow points must be the cell with the highest number out of the vertically and horizontally adjacent cells to that black cell.
3. Adjacent cells cannot have the same number.

5.1   ZKP Protocol

The main difference from Sudoku is that the cells must be filled according to the arrow rule, *i.e.*, the number pointed by the arrow must be the highest among the adjacent cells. This property is easy to verify using a balance. Our protocol achieves perfect completeness, perfect soundness and is perfectly zero-knowledge. The proofs are given in Sect. 5.2.

Setup: As in the protocol for Sudoku (Sect. 3), according to P's solution, the prover P places several $\bigcirc$s each of the corresponding weight on every cell, and P compares them to show V that they have the same weight. In the following, we assume that the number of coins placed is sufficient for clarity. The correct number of coins is computed later.

Verification: The prover P and the verifier V execute the following steps:

1. To verify that a $\bigcirc$ on each cell pointed by an arrow is the heaviest, P compares it with each other adjacent $\bigcirc$ around the arrow: $\bigcirc \,|\, \bigcirc$. If the coin pointed by the arrow is ever found lighter than another, V rejects P's solution. The coins are moved to their original positions after each comparison.
2. Let $s_0 \, (\geq 2)$ denotes the size of the largest room in the given grid. To verify that each room contains different coins with weight from 1 to the size of the room, it proceeds as follows.
   (a) V prepares additional s_0 coins with weight from 1 to s_0.
   (b) For a room of size s, $1 \leq s \leq s_0$, the prover P picks a $\bigcirc$ from each cell and shuffle the s coins: $[\,\bigcirc\!\!\!\gg\,]$. Let R denote these s coins.
   (c) Let R_0 denote the s coins with weight from 1 to s among the s_0 coins prepared. Using R_0 and R, the verifier V confirms that they are identical in the same way as for Sudoku (Sect. 3) as follows.
      i. P compares a coin in R_0 with each coin in R.
         – If the comparison results in even, then P returns $\bigcirc$ to R_0 but removes $\bigcirc$ from R.
         – Otherwise, P returns the two coins.

Table 2. The numbers required for each verification in our Makaro protocol

	Coins	Shuffles	Comparisons
Setup	–	–	$2e$
Arrow	–	–	$d - c$
Room	$\sum_{s=2}^{s_0} sn_s + s_0$	$\sum_{s=2}^{s_0} n_s$	$\sum_{s=2}^{s_0}(n_s \sum_{k=1}^{s} k)$
Adjacency	$2e$		e
Total	$\sum_{s=2}^{s_0} sn_s + s_0 + 2e$	$\sum_{s=2}^{s_0} n_s + e$	$\sum_{s=2}^{s_0}(n_s \sum_{k=1}^{s} k) + d - c + 3e$

     ii. If none of the above comparisons result in even, V rejects P's solution.

    iii. Repeat step 2(c)i for another coin in R_0 until all the coins in R_0 are compared.

  (d) Repeat step 2(b) for another room until all the rooms are confirmed.

3. To verify that no identical coins are next to each other, for each of such a pair of coins, P shuffles the two $\bigcirc$s: $[\bigcirc\bigcirc]$, and compares them: $\bigcirc | \bigcirc$. If the balance shows even, V rejects P's solution. The two coins are no longer used and are removed.

Efficiency: Let n_s denote the number of rooms with size s, $2 \leq s \leq s_0$ for some s_0, c the number of arrows, d the number of cells adjacent to arrow cells, and e the number of bold lines between two adjacent cells in different rooms. This protocol uses $\sum_{s=2}^{s_0} sn_s + s_0 + 2e$ coins and performs $\sum_{s=2}^{s_0} n_s + e$ shuffles and $\sum_{s=2}^{s_0}(n_s \sum_{k=1}^{s} k) + d - c + 3e$ comparisons. Table 2 summarizes those numbers required for each verification in the protocol. We first note that the number of rooms is represented as $\sum_{s=2}^{s_0} n_s$ and the number of cells is $\sum_{s=2}^{s_0} sn_s$. Therefore, in the room verification, the protocol uses a coin placed on every cell as well as the additional s_0 coins, *i.e.*, $\sum_{s=2}^{s_0} sn_s + s_0$ coins, and shuffles coins placed on each room, *i.e.*, $\sum_{s=2}^{s_0} n_s$ shuffles. The number of comparisons follows the same approach as for Sudoku: for a room of size s, the number of comparisons is $\sum_{k=1}^{s} k$ in the worst case, and since there are n_s rooms of size s for $2 \leq s \leq s_0$, the total number of comparisons is $\sum_{s=2}^{s_0}(n_s \sum_{k=1}^{s} k)$. In the arrow verification, the number of comparisons is $d - c$ because the cells indicated by the arrows are compared with other cells, *i.e.*, $d - c$ equals to the number of such other cells. In the adjacency verification, the protocol uses a coin placed on each of two cells separated by a bold line, shuffles the two coins, and compares them. Thus, the numbers of coins, shuffles, and comparisons are $2e$, e, and e, respectively. Finally, in the setup, the protocol compares coins placed on the same cell each other if there are multiple coins placed on the same cell. Since the room verification needs a coin placed on every cell, the number of comparisons is equal to the number of coins placed on cells for the other verifications. The adjacency verification needs such $2e$ coins placed on cells, and hence, the setup should perform $2e$ comparisons.

5.2   Security

We prove the security of the Makaro protocol. A proof for completeness is omitted because it is clear from the protocol description.

Lemma 7 (Perfect Completeness – Makaro). *If P knows a solution of a given Makaro grid, he can always convince V.*

Lemma 8 (Perfect Soundness – Makaro). *If P does not provide a collect solution of a given Makaro grid, V always rejects P.*

Proof. When P gives an incorrect solution, the following three situations are possible.

- A room of size s contains twice the same number, or a number not in $\{1, \ldots, s\}$. In this case, V will reject P's solution as in Sudoku (see Lemma 2).
- The number in the cell pointed by the arrow is not the highest. In this case, a comparison using the balance reveals that the coin in that cell is not the heaviest, and V rejects P's solution.
- Adjacent cells contains the same number. In this case, the balance will result in even when comparing the coins in these cells, and V will reject P's solution.

Therefore, when P does not give the correct answer, V will always reject.   □

Lemma 9 (Perfect Zero-Knowledge – Makaro). *The verifier V is not given any information other than that the prover P can solve the Makaro grid.*

Proof. We show that no information has been leaked other than that the prover P can solve the Makaro grid through the following three checks in the verification phase:

- In step 1, when comparing the coins around the arrow cell, V does not learn anything except for which is the heaviest because the coins are visually indistinguishable and V never touches them and only observes the balance results.
- In step 2, V does not learn anything except that each room of size s contains one and only one number i for all $i \in \{1, \ldots, s\}$ for the exact same reason as for Sudoku (see Lemma 3).
- In step 3, when V checks that no adjacent cells contain the same number, as the coins are shuffled before the comparison and never reused after, V cannot learn anything except whether they are of different weight.

Therefore, V cannot learn anything throughout the whole process, except whether the solution is valid or not.

Formally, a simulator acts as follows.

- In the setup phase, the simulator places coins such that two identical coins are placed on the same cell if two coins should be placed on the same cell.
- In step 1, before comparing two coins, it swaps the coin placed on the cell pointed by an arrow with a coin of weight 2 and swaps the other coin with a coin of weight 1.

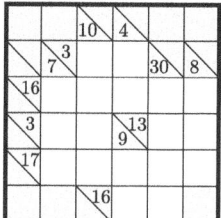

Fig. 6. An example of a Kakuro puzzle and its solution introduced in the Nikoli's website: https://www.nikoli.co.jp/en/puzzles/kakuro/.

- In step 2(b), when s coins are shuffled, it swaps them with s coins weighted from 1 to s.
- In step 3, when two coins are shuffled, it swaps them with two coins of different weights.

This should make the comparison results performed in the protocol indistinguishable from those provided by an honest prover. □

6 Kakuro

Kakuro (or *Kakkuro*) was the most popular logic puzzle in Japanese printed press until 1992, when Sudoku took the top spot. The Kakuro grid has white cells and gray cells separated by diagonal lines into two triangular rooms. In Fig. 6, we give an example of a 6×6 Kakuro grid and its solution. The goal is to place one number in every white cells on the grid according to the following constraints:

1. The number in the upper right corner of the oblique line represents the sum of the numbers entering the consecutive white cells to its right.
2. The number in the lower left corner of the oblique line represents the sum of the numbers entering the consecutive white cells below it.
3. Each connected (*i.e.*, uninterrupted by a gray cell) row or column cannot contain twice the same number.

6.1 ZKP Protocol

By using a balance, it is easy to compare the numbers in the cells separated by diagonal lines with the sum of the numbers in the continuously connected cells. We detail our ZKP protocol. It achieves perfect completeness, perfect soundness and is perfectly zero-knowledge. The proofs are given in Sect. 6.2.

Setup: P and V fill the grid in two steps:

1. For each triangular cell, V places a coin ◯ of the indicated weight.
2. According to its solution, P places two coins ◯s on each white cell.

Verification: P and V execute the following steps:

1. For each triangular cell with a number, to verify if the weight of the coin on the cell is equal to the sum of the weights of the coins on consecutive white cells from the triangle cell, P and V follow these steps:
   - P compares the $\bigcirc$ representing the number on the triangular cell with the $\bigcirc$s on the consecutive white cells: $\bigodot\, |\, \bigcirc$.
   - If the comparison does not result in even, then V rejects P's solution.
   - P moves the $\bigcirc$s to their original positions.[2]
2. For each uninterrupted row (or column), V verifies that the coin placed on each cell is of a different weight than those placed on the other cells in the same way as steps 1 and 2 for Sudoku (Sect. 3).

Efficiency: Let t denote the number of triangular cells, n_ℓ the number of uninterrupted rows and columns of length ℓ, $2 \leq \ell \leq \ell_0$ for some ℓ_0, and w the number of white cells. This protocol uses a total of $t + 2w$ coins and performs t shuffles because in step 2, it applies a shuffle for each of uninterrupted rows and columns. The number of comparisons is $t + \sum_{\ell=2}^{\ell_0}\left(n_\ell\binom{\ell}{2}\right) + w$ because in step 2, it performs comparisons for all possible pairs of cells within each of uninterrupted rows and columns (and in step 1, a comparison is needed for each of triangular cells).

6.2 Security

We prove the security of the Kakuro protocol. A proof for completeness is omitted because it is clear from the protocol description.

Lemma 10 (Perfect Completeness – Kakuro). *If P knows a solution of a given Kakuro grid, he can always convince V.*

Lemma 11 (Perfect Soundness – Kakuro). *If P does not provide a correct solution of a given Kakuro grid, V always rejects P's solution.*

Proof. When P gives an incorrect solution, the following two situations are possible.

- A number in a triangular cell and the sum of the subsequent numbers from that triangle cell are not equal. In this case, the weight of the coin $\bigcirc$ representing the triangular cell number and the sum of the weights of the coins $\bigcirc$ in the consecutive white cells from that triangle cell are not equal, causing the balance to be unbalanced. Hence, V will reject P's solution.
- The same number is included twice in a block formed by consecutive white cells either vertically or horizontally. In this case, during the comparison of the coins $\bigcirc$ in the white cells of the block, the weights of two coins are equal, resulting in the balance being even. Hence, V will reject P's solution.

---

[2] For this, P and V should memorize the order of $\bigcirc$s when they are placed on the balance.

Therefore, when P does not give the correct answer, V will always reject its solution.   □

Lemma 12 (Perfect Zero-Knowledge – Kakuro). *The verifier V cannot learn any information other than that the prover P can solve the Kakuro grid.*

Proof. We show that no information has been leaked other than that the prover P can solve the Kakuro grid through each step of the verification phase:

- In step 1, V checks that the number in the triangular cell is equal to the sum of the subsequent numbers. The coins ◯s from consecutive white cells are stacked before placing them on the scale. Hence V does not learn anything on their individual weight (they are visually indistinguishable), except that the sum of their weight is the same as the weight of the corresponding coin ◯.
- In step 2, V ensures that uninterrupted rows and columns do not contain twice the same number. The coins ◯s are shuffled, and each pair of coins is compared. Since the initial positions of each coin cannot be identified, V cannot determine the numbers on the white cells.

Hence, V cannot learn anything on P's solution throughout the whole protocol. Formally, a simulator acts as follows.

- In the setup phase, the simulator arbitrarily places two identical coins on each white cell.
- In step 1 of the verification phase, before comparing, it swaps the coins placed on the consecutive white cells with the same number of coins such that the total weight of them is equal to the number on the triangular cell.
- In step 2, it acts in the same way as in the proof for Lemma 2.

This should make the comparison results performed in the protocol indistinguishable from those provided by an honest prover.   □

7   Concluding Remarks

In this paper, we constructed ZKP protocols using a balance scale for four pencil-and-paper puzzles. We demonstrated the security of our proposed solutions, showing that they are perfectly complete, sound, and zero-knowledge. As a future work, we aim to explore other similar games. Additionally, we would like to investigate improvements that allow for the execution of the protocol with fewer coins and steps for the puzzles presented in this paper.

An analogous verification was considered in [9], where one confirms whether two cups contain the same number of marbles, say $X = Y$ or not. Because our model employs a balance to confirm which is heavier, say $X \geq Y$ or not, we considered an entirely different mechanism to construct a ZKP protocol. As can be observed from our ZKP protocols, Sudoku ZKP can be conducted only based on verifying $X = Y$ because it involves repeating the verification of whether a coin in a set is equal to each one in the other set.

Acknowledgements. We thank the anonymous referees, whose comments have helped us to improve the presentation of the paper. This work was supported in part by JSPS KAKENHI Grant Number JP23H00479, the ANR project MobiS5 (ANR-18-CE39-0019), the ANR project SEVERITAS (ANR-20-CE39-0009) and the ANR Project PRIVA-SIQ (ANR-23-CE39-0008).

References

1. Abe, Y., Iwamoto, M., Ohta, K.: Efficient private PEZ protocols for symmetric functions. In: Hofheinz, D., Rosen, A. (eds.) TCC 2019. LNCS, vol. 11891, pp. 372–392. Springer, Cham (2019). https://doi.org/10.1007/978-3-030-36030-6_15

2. Balogh, J., Csirik, J.A., Ishai, Y., Kushilevitz, E.: Private computation using a PEZ dispenser. Theor. Comput. Sci. **306**(1), 69–84 (2003)

3. Ben-Or, M., et al.: Everything provable is provable in zero-knowledge. In: Goldwasser, S. (ed.) CRYPTO 1988. LNCS, vol. 403, pp. 37–56. Springer, New York (1990). https://doi.org/10.1007/0-387-34799-2_4

4. Bultel, X., Dreier, J., Dumas, J., Lafourcade, P.: Physical zero-knowledge proofs for Akari, Takuzu, Kakuro and KenKen. In: Demaine, E.D., Grandoni, F. (eds.) Fun with Algorithms. LIPIcs, vol. 49, pp. 8:1–8:20. Schloss Dagstuhl (2016)

5. Bultel, X., et al.: Physical zero-knowledge proof for Makaro. In: Izumi, T., Kuznetsov, P. (eds.) SSS 2018. LNCS, vol. 11201, pp. 111–125. Springer, Cham (2018). https://doi.org/10.1007/978-3-030-03232-6_8

6. Chien, Y.-F., Hon, W.-K.: Cryptographic and physical zero-knowledge proof: from sudoku to nonogram. In: Boldi, P., Gargano, L. (eds.) FUN 2010. LNCS, vol. 6099, pp. 102–112. Springer, Heidelberg (2010). https://doi.org/10.1007/978-3-642-13122-6_12

7. Dreier, J., Jonker, H., Lafourcade, P.: Secure auctions without cryptography. In: Ferro, A., Luccio, F., Widmayer, P. (eds.) Fun with Algorithms. LNCS, vol. 8496, pp. 158–170. Springer, Cham (2014). https://doi.org/10.1007/978-3-319-07890-8_14

8. Fukasawa, T., Manabe, Y.: Card-based zero-knowledge proof for the nearest neighbor property: zero-knowledge proof of ABC end view. In: Batina, L., Picek, S., Mondal, M. (eds.) Security, Privacy, and Applied Cryptography Engineering. LNCS, vol. 13783, pp. 147–161. Springer, Cham (2022). https://doi.org/10.1007/978-3-031-22829-2_9

9. Glaser, A., Barak, B., Goldston, R.J.: A zero-knowledge protocol for nuclear warhead verification. Nature **510**, 497–502 (2014)

10. Goldreich, O., Kahan, A.: How to construct constant-round zero-knowledge proof systems for NP. J. Cryptol. **9**(3), 167–189 (1991)

11. Goldwasser, S., Micali, S., Rackoff, C.: The knowledge complexity of interactive proof-systems (extended abstract). In: Sedgewick, R. (ed.) STOC 1985, pp. 291–304. ACM (1985)

12. Gradwohl, R., Naor, M., Pinkas, B., Rothblum, G.N.: Cryptographic and physical zero-knowledge proof systems for solutions of Sudoku puzzles. Theor. Comput. Syst. **44**(2), 245–268 (2009)

13. Hand, S., Koch, A., Lafourcade, P., Miyahara, D., Robert, L.: Check alternating patterns: a physical zero-knowledge proof for Moon-or-Sun. In: Shikata, J., Kuzuno, H. (eds.) IWSEC 2023. LNCS, vol. 14128, pp. 255–272. Springer, Cham (2023). https://doi.org/10.1007/978-3-031-41326-1_14

14. Hatsugai, K., Ruangwises, S., Asano, K., et al.: NP-completeness and physical zero-knowledge proofs for sumplete, a puzzle generated by ChatGPT. New Gener. Comput. **42**, 429–448 (2024). https://doi.org/10.1007/s00354-024-00267-0

15. Hearn, R.A., Demaine, E.D.: Games, Puzzles, and Computation. CRC Press, Boca Raton (2009)

16. Isuzugawa, R., Miyahara, D., Mizuki, T.: Zero-knowledge proof protocol for cryptarithmetic using dihedral cards. In: Kostitsyna, I., Orponen, P. (eds.) UCNC 2021. LNCS, vol. 12984, pp. 51–67. Springer, Cham (2021). https://doi.org/10.1007/978-3-030-87993-8_4

17. Iwamoto, C., Haruishi, M., Ibusuki, T.: Herugolf and Makaro are NP-complete. In: Ito, H., Leonardi, S., Pagli, L., Prencipe, G. (eds.) Fun with Algorithms. LIPIcs, vol. 100, pp. 24:1–24:11. Schloss Dagstuhl, Dagstuhl (2018)

18. Komano, Y., Mizuki, T.: Coin-based secure computations. Int. J. Inf. Secur. **21**, 833–846 (2022)

19. Komano, Y., Mizuki, T.: Card-based zero-knowledge proof protocol for pancake sorting. In: Bella, G., Doinea, M., Janicke, H. (eds.) Innovative Security Solutions for Information Technology and Communications. LNCS, vol. 13809, pp. 222–239. Springer, Cham (2023). https://doi.org/10.1007/978-3-031-32636-3_13

20. Komano, Y., Mizuki, T.: Physical zero-knowledge proof protocol for Topswops. In: Su, C., Gritzalis, D., Piuri, V. (eds.) Information Security Practice and Experience, ISPEC 2022, LNCS, vol. 13620, pp. 537–553. Springer, Cham (2022). https://doi.org/10.1007/978-3-031-21280-2_30

21. Lafourcade, P., Miyahara, D., Mizuki, T., Robert, L., Sasaki, T., Sone, H.: How to construct physical zero-knowledge proofs for puzzles with a "single loop" condition. Theor. Comput. Sci. **888**, 41–55 (2021)

22. Lloyd, H., Crossley, M., Sinclair, M., Amos, M.: J-pop: Japanese puzzles as optimization problems. IEEE Trans. Games **14**(3), 391–402 (2021)

23. Minamikawa, Y., Shinagawa, K.: Coin-based cryptographic protocols without hand operations. IEICE Trans. Fundamentals **E107.A**(8), 1178–1185 (2024)

24. Miyahara, D., Haneda, H., Mizuki, T.: Card-based zero-knowledge proof protocols for graph problems and their computational model. In: Huang, Q., Yu, Y. (eds.) Provable and Practical Security. LNCS, vol. 13059, pp. 136–152. Springer, Cham (2021). https://doi.org/10.1007/978-3-030-90402-9_8

25. Miyahara, D., Komano, Y., Mizuki, T., Sone, H.: Cooking cryptographers: secure multiparty computation based on balls and bags. In: IEEE Computer Security Foundations Symposium, pp. 1–16. IEEE, NY (2021)

26. Miyahara, D., et al.: Card-based ZKP protocols for Takuzu and Juosan. In: Farach-Colton, M., Prencipe, G., Uehara, R. (eds.) Fun with Algorithms. LIPIcs, vol. 157, pp. 20:1–20:21. Schloss Dagstuhl (2021)

27. Miyahara, D., Robert, L., Lafourcade, P., Mizuki, T.: ZKP protocols for Usowan, Herugolf, and Five Cells. Tsinghua Sci. Technol. **29**(6), 1651–1666 (2024)

28. Miyahara, D., Sasaki, T., Mizuki, T., Sone, H.: Card-based physical zero-knowledge proof for Kakuro. IEICE Trans. Fundamentals **102**(9), 1072–1078 (2019)

29. Mizuki, T., Kugimoto, Y., Sone, H.: Secure multiparty computations using a dial lock. In: Cai, J.-Y., Cooper, S.B., Zhu, H. (eds.) TAMC 2007. LNCS, vol. 4484, pp. 499–510. Springer, Heidelberg (2007). https://doi.org/10.1007/978-3-540-72504-6_45

30. Moran, T., Naor, M.: Basing cryptographic protocols on tamper-evident seals. Theor. Comput. Sci. **411**(10), 1283–1310 (2010)

31. Murata, S., Miyahara, D., Mizuki, T., Sone, H.: Public-PEZ cryptography. In: Susilo, W., Deng, R.H., Guo, F., Li, Y., Intan, R. (eds.) ISC 2020. LNCS, vol. 12472, pp. 59–74. Springer, Cham (2020). https://doi.org/10.1007/978-3-030-62974-8_4

32. Quisquater, J.-J., et al.: How to explain zero-knowledge protocols to your children. In: Brassard, G. (ed.) CRYPTO 1989. LNCS, vol. 435, pp. 628–631. Springer, New York (1990). https://doi.org/10.1007/0-387-34805-0_60

33. Robert, L., Miyahara, D., Lafourcade, P., Mizuki, T.: Card-based ZKP for connectivity: applications to Nurikabe, Hitori, and Heyawake. New Gener. Comput. **40**(1), 149–171 (2022)

34. Robert, L., Miyahara, D., Lafourcade, P., Mizuki, T.: Physical ZKP protocols for Nurimisaki and Kurodoko. Theor. Comput. Sci. **972**, 114071 (2023)

35. Robert, L., Miyahara, D., Lafourcade, P., Libralesso, L., Mizuki, T.: Physical zero-knowledge proof and NP-completeness proof of Suguru puzzle. Inf. Comput. **285**, 104858 (2022)

36. Ruangwises, S.: Two standard decks of playing cards are sufficient for a ZKP for Sudoku. New Gener. Comput. **40**(1), 49–65 (2022)

37. Ruangwises, S.: An improved physical ZKP for Nonogram and Nonogram color. J. Comb. Optim. **45**, 122 (2023)

38. Ruangwises, S.: Physical zero-knowledge proof for ball sort puzzle. In: Della Vedova, G., Dundua, B., Lempp, S., Manea, F. (eds.) Unity of Logic and Computation, CiE 2023, LNCS, vol. 13967, pp. 246–257. Springer, Cham (2023). https://doi.org/10.1007/978-3-031-36978-0_20

39. Ruangwises, S.: Physically verifying the first nonzero term in a sequence: Physical ZKPs for ABC end view and Goishi Hiroi. In: Li, M., Sun, X., Wu, X. (eds.) Frontiers of Algorithmics. LNCS, vol. 13933, pp. 171–183. Springer, Cham (2023). https://doi.org/10.1007/978-3-031-39344-0_13

40. Ruangwises, S., Itoh, T.: Physical zero-knowledge proof for Numberlink puzzle and k vertex-disjoint paths problem. New Gener. Comput. **39**(1), 3–17 (2021)

41. Ruangwises, S., Itoh, T.: Physical zero-knowledge proof for ripple effect. Theor. Comput. Sci. **895**, 115–123 (2021)

42. Ruangwises, S., Itoh, T.: Physical ZKP for connected spanning subgraph: applications to bridges puzzle and other problems. In: Kostitsyna, I., Orponen, P. (eds.) UCNC 2021. LNCS, vol. 12984, pp. 149–163. Springer, Cham (2021). https://doi.org/10.1007/978-3-030-87993-8_10

43. Ruangwises, S., Itoh, T.: How to physically verify a rectangle in a grid: a physical ZKP for Shikaku. In: Fraigniaud, P., Uno, Y. (eds.) Fun with Algorithms. LIPIcs, vol. 226, pp. 24:1–24:12. Schloss Dagstuhl, Dagstuhl (2022)

44. Ruangwises, S., Iwamoto, M.: Printing protocol: Physical ZKPs for decomposition puzzles. New Gener. Comput. **42**, 331–343 (2024). https://doi.org/10.1007/s00354-024-00266-1

45. Sasaki, T., Miyahara, D., Mizuki, T., Sone, H.: Efficient card-based zero-knowledge proof for Sudoku. Theor. Comput. Sci. **839**, 135–142 (2020)

46. Shinagawa, K., et al.: Secure computation protocols using polarizing cards. IEICE Trans. Fund. **99-A**, 1122–1131 (2016)

47. Tamura, Y., Suzuki, A., Mizuki, T.: Card-based zero-knowledge proof protocols for the 15-puzzle and the token swapping problem. In: ACM ASIA Public-Key Cryptography Workshop, pp. 11–22. ACM, New York (2024)

48. Tanaka, K., Mizuki, T.: Two UNO decks efficiently perform zero-knowledge proof for Sudoku. In: Fernau, H., Jansen, K. (eds.) Fundamentals of Computation Theory. LNCS, vol. 14292, pp. 406–420. Springer, Cham (2023). https://doi.org/10.1007/978-3-031-43587-4_29
49. Uehara, R.: Computational complexity of puzzles and related topics. Interdiscip. Inf. Sci. **29**(2), 119–140 (2023)
50. Yato, T., Seta, T.: Complexity and completeness of finding another solution and its application to puzzles. IEICE Trans. Fundamentals **86**(5), 1052–1060 (2003)

ChronoCloak: An Integrated Solution for Mitigating Premature Disclosure in Oblivious Digital Dissemination

Ahmed Zawia[(✉)] and M. Anwar Hasan

University of Waterloo, Waterloo, ON, Canada
{azawia,ahasan}@uwaterloo.ca

Abstract. With the increasing use of online digital content delivery, such as games, videos, and magazine articles, there are scenarios where it is crucial to prevent premature revelation of the distributed content and, at the same time, allow a recipient to choose any specific item of the content bundle in a privacy-preserving manner. In this work, we propose an integrated solution, namely ChronoCloak, which aims to address both the premature exposure of the sender data and the privacy preservation of the receiver interaction. ChronoCloak allows a sender to transmit a set of secrets through a puzzle, which can be solved via a lengthy computation. Upon solving the puzzle, the receiver recovers only a subset of the secrets that is oblivious to the sender. It also allows the receiver to securely outsource the computation (with public verifiability), yet only the intended receiver can retrieve a subset of secrets using the puzzle solution. We also propose an ideal functionality for ChronoCloak and provide a generic construction implementing this functionality in the random oracle model, using an ideal oblivious transfer functionality and a time lock-like function.

Keywords: Delay-based cryptography · Oblivious transfer · Trapdoor verifiable delay functions · Time-lock puzzles

1 Introduction

In certain cases of digital content distribution, it is crucial for the distributor to be able to send a selection of time-locked items (e.g., games, videos, or magazine articles) to a recipient who can then choose and unlock one of those items after a predetermined time in a privacy preserving manner so that the distributor is unaware of the recipient's choice. For example, the publisher of a weekly magazine may send digital copies of encrypted articles of an upcoming issue to its reader base in advance. Then, a *pay-per-article* subscriber, on or after the publication date, can decrypt one of the articles of their choice that is oblivious to the publisher. The core issues, namely time-locking of contents and their oblivious transfer, in the aforementioned applications can potentially be addressed by carefully deploying relevant cryptographic primitives and other necessary

N. Mouha and N. Nikiforakis (Eds.): ISC 2024, LNCS 15257, pp. 232–251, 2025.
https://doi.org/10.1007/978-3-031-75757-0_12

functional blocks. For example, one existing solution is a time-release oblivious transfer employing a verifiable ID-based encrypted blind signature [45], where a trusted third party (time server) is used to ensure the release of the message at a predetermined time in the future. Time tokens can be broadcast periodically only if the server is online. In the work of [36], privacy is guaranteed only for a limited period of time. As in [36,45] uses a time server to release a private key that enables the sender to learn the receiver's choice after a specified amount of time has passed. A second solution can be constructed using [8]'s framework, which is an inefficient method of constructing similar functionality using multiple primitives. However, no concrete construction has been proposed. As trusted setup can be difficult to perform securely, using multiple primitives as a solution may require multiple calls to a trusted setup. This significantly complicates the system setup process thereby increasing potential security risks. We then ask: if both issues occur simultaneously in a system, how can we address them in a single solution?

Contributions. In this work, we consider an integrated approach to address time-delayed decryption and oblivious transfer and propose a solution called *ChronoCloak*. Through ChronoCloak, the sender and receiver interact via secret trapdoors and construct a joint puzzle. After solving the puzzle via a lengthy computation (i.e., a sequential computation of length $T \in \mathbb{N}$), a subset of the sender's secrets can be obliviously retrieved by the receiver. More importantly, our ChronoCloak allows the recipient to outsource the lengthy computation to an external solver without worrying that the latter can decrypt the sender's secret. This is because the puzzle is jointly generated by both the sender's and the intended recipient's secret trapdoors and, therefore, recovering the transmitted secret requires more than just the solution to the puzzle - it also requires the recipient's secret trapdoor. In this article, we introduce an ideal functionality for ChronoCloak and present a generic construction that implements this functionality in the random oracle model, integrating an ideal oblivious transfer functionality along with a time lock-like function.

Related Work. As discussed previously, in the literature there are proposals for constructing Oblivious Transfer (OT) protocols with time-release delays, among which [21,36,45] are the most pertinent. The problem of sending messages into the future with conditional oblivious transfer was considered by Crescenzo et al. [21]. In the case of delayed release, the authors of [45] incorporate a trusted third party as a time server to ensure the scheduled release of the message. In the work of [36], however, the receiver's choice privacy is maintained within a constrained time frame. Similar to [45], the work in [36] uses a time server to release a private key that allows the sender to learn the receiver's choice after a specified time. As the time server generally requires output some secrets at every time interval, the reliability and security requirement for the protocol's trusted-party extends beyond the one-time setup of initializing the protocol parameters.

Delay-Based Primitives. Aside from time servers, several cryptographic primitives have been proposed to guarantee time delay, such as time-lock puzzles (TLP) [41], proof of sequential work [1,20,33,37], and verifiable delay functions (VDF) [17,25,35,39,44] (and its relative trapdoor VDF [44,46]). Furthermore, the security treatment of these primitives lacks composability guarantees, and thus, integrating them securely into more complex protocols is not intuitive. This shortfall can be addressed by modeling them in the universal composability framework [12]. There are also several studies that discuss maintaining composability in delay-based primitives, including [3,8,9,24,26,30], some with and some without public verifiability.

Oblivious Transfer. The concept of oblivious transfer was initially introduced by [40]. Since then, it has been a crucial building block in many secure multiparty computations [18,29]. Over time, different constructions of OT protocols have been developed based on different assumptions. One notable example is the Chou-Orlandi OT scheme [19], which is a three-round OT based on Diffie-Hellman (DH) key exchange. Although the Chou-Orlandi scheme did not achieve UC security [7,27,34], their core idea inspired the design of secure and more efficient OT protocols such as [4,14,31,42]. Also, there are a number of isogeny-based oblivious transfer constructions, including [2,5,6,32,42,43]. In [2], the authors propose a framework for developing cryptographic primitives which is amenable to group-actions such as CSIDH [16] and CSI-FiSh [10]. Using their framework, the authors describe the construction of a variety of cryptographic primitives, including an (inefficient) statistically sender-private OT protocol. A notable work by Lai et al. [31] introduced efficient OT construction based on the *reciprocal* CSIDH assumption, using a *quadratic twist map* to reduce a 3-round Chou-Orlandi OT scheme to 2 rounds. They incorporated a "proof of decryption" (PoD) mechanism, achieving UC security. Their PoD assumption, however, had a security flaw, which was rectified in the revised version [32], resulting in a four-round OT scheme. An optimized OT extension introduced in [5] reduces isogeny computations, resulting in a weaker notion of OT security, i.e., OT with selective failure attack. Additionally, they proposed two optimal OTs with 4 and 2 rounds for different models. On the other hand, we note that some of the isogeny-based schemes such as [6,42,43] have been affected by recent attack [15] on SIDH, but there is no known way to extend such attacks to the general isogeny problem. There are several other assumptions that can be used to construct oblivious transfer such as lattice-based [38], and code-based [11,22,23].

2   Background

Notations. We use $A \parallel B$ to denote the concatenation of a string representation of A and B. We use the calligraphic font to denote a finite set (e.g., $\mathcal{B}$). The size of a set $\mathcal{B}$ is represented by $|\mathcal{B}|$. We denote the process of uniformly sampling a random element e from $\mathcal{B}$ by $e \leftarrow_\$ \mathcal{B}$, whereas the deterministic choice of an element e from $\mathcal{B}$ is referred to by $e \leftarrow \mathcal{B}$. The process of executing an algorithm Alg on a uniformly random distribution is denoted by $a \leftarrow_\$ \mathsf{Alg}$, where a is the output. On the other hand, the deterministic process of executing an algorithm Alg is denoted by $a \leftarrow \mathsf{Alg}$. A function's composition is denoted by $\circ$ such that $\mathsf{f}_1 \circ \mathsf{f}_2(x) = \mathsf{f}_1(\mathsf{f}_2(x))$ for a valid input x. The set $\{1, \ldots, n\}$ is denoted by $[n]$ for a positive integer n. The process of sampling the vector $(z_i)_{i \in [n]}$ of size n

for a uniform distribution on $\mathcal{B}^n$ is denoted by $z \leftarrow_\$ \mathcal{B}^n$ such that $z_i \leftarrow_\$ \mathcal{B}$ for all $i \in [n]$. $\Pr[\mathsf{Ev} : \mathsf{Ev}_1, \mathsf{Ev}_2, \ldots, \mathsf{Ev}_n]$ refers to the probability of the event Ev arising after orderly events $\mathsf{Ev}_1, \mathsf{Ev}_2, \ldots, \mathsf{Ev}_n$. Finally, a scheme's security level is represented by $\lambda \in \mathbb{N}$.

2.1   Overview of the Security Model

The following is a brief overview of the security model used in our protocol, based on universally composable (UC) security [12]. We then present related definitions, including those for oblivious transfer and the random oracle.

Functionality. In the UC framework, the ideal functionality F acts as a trusted third party, e.g., two party computations involve F that maps inputs to outputs, is defined as $\mathsf{F} = (\mathsf{F}_1, \mathsf{F}_2) : \{0,1\}^* \times \{0,1\}^* \rightarrow \{0,1\}^* \times \{0,1\}^*$. The first party, whose input is x_1, wants the output $\mathsf{F}_1(x_1, x_2)$, and the second party, whose input is x_2, wants the output $\mathsf{F}_2(x_1, x_2)$. The security of the model relies on the fact that each party can only compute the output for their own input, without knowing the other party's input. **Static corruption:** In static corruption, corrupted parties remain corrupted during protocol execution, while honest parties remain honest. **Distinguisher** Suppose Env is the environment entity that decides parties' inputs (including the adversary's auxiliary input) and receives all parties' outputs, Env serves as an interactive distinguisher between two distributions.

Malicious Adversarial Model. A malicious adversary A has no restrictions on their actions-it can deviate from the construction specification, changes its input, and alters its strategy. **Real Execution** Parties interact directly to carry out construction execution. **Ideal execution** Parties interact through the construction's intended ideal functionality, F. **Hybrid Execution** It involves parties interacting not only with each other, as in real execution, but also with a trusted entity computing functionalities (e.g., F_{RO}) over which a simulator ($\tilde{\mathsf{A}}$) has some control. Briefly, in the UC framework, after parties have obtained their inputs, the honest party sends its private input to F, and a simulation sends the adversary's input to F. The simulation interacts with the adversary (corrupting a party P_i) as a blackbox; hence, it needs to extract the input from the adversary through normal construction's rounds of interaction, and passes it to F. In the following steps, F provides the adversary's output to the simulator, which in turn passes it on to the adversary to complete the construction rounds (for more information, see [28, Section 2.3.1]). Upon notification by the simulator, it is then F's responsibility to release the honest party's output. In this work, we assume that the simulator $\tilde{\mathsf{A}}$ is probabilistic polynomial-time. Generally speaking, as an interactive distinguisher, Env interacts with the adversary during the execution to ultimately distinguish between the real execution and the ideal execution. Furthermore, the constructions in this article will be presented in a hybrid model due to the limitations of the UC framework outlined by Canetti et al. [13].

Definition 1. *Against malicious adversaries, a construction Γ securely implements a deterministic functionality F if*

$$\exists \text{ a simulator } \tilde{\mathsf{A}} \text{ s.t. } \mathsf{Hybrid}^{\hat{\mathsf{F}}}_{\Gamma, A, Env} \overset{c}{=} \mathsf{Ideal}_{F, \tilde{\mathsf{A}}, Env},$$

for any probabilistic polynomial-time adversary A *and distinguisher* Env, *where* $\mathsf{Ideal}_{F,\tilde{A},Env}$ *represents all parties' output distribution ensemble from the ideal execution of* F *(in which one of the parties is corrupted by* $\tilde{A}$*), and* $\mathsf{Hybrid}_{\Gamma,A,Env}^{\hat{F}}$ *represents all parties' output ensemble from the real execution in which parties (one of whom is corrupted by* A*) have access to a functionality* $\hat{F}$ *(e.g.,* F_{RO}*).*

Related Definitions

Oblivious Transfer Protocol, F_{OT}. A 1-out-of-2 oblivious transfer protocol allows for the transmission of one of two messages obliviously. This protocol involves a trusted setup party, a sender (P_S), and a receiver (P_R), typically requiring n rounds of interaction. The sender holds two secret messages, m_0 and m_1, while the receiver has a choice bit i. Through n rounds of interaction, the sender and receiver transfer a secret message, allowing the receiver to reconstruct the selected message, m_i. In Fig. 1, we present the ideal functionality of 1-out-of-2 oblivious transfer protocol, namely F_{OT}.

<u>Commit</u>: Upon receiving (Commit, *sid*, P_S, $i \in \{0,1\}$) from P_R, check if a (P_R, P_S, *sid*, $i \in \{0,1\}$) was previously stored. If yes, ignore; otherwise, store (P_R, P_S, *sid*, $i \in \{0,1\}$) and output (Commit, *sid*, P_R) to P_S.

<u>Challenge</u>: Upon receiving (Challenge, *sid*, P_R, m_0, m_1) from P_S, check if a (P_R, P_S, *sid*, i) was previously stored. If not, ignore; otherwise, send (Challenge, *sid*, P_S, m_i) to P_R and (Challenge, *sid*, P_R) to P_S.

Fig. 1. Oblivious transfer ideal functionality (F_{OT}).

Random Oracle Functionality, F_{RO}. Below we present F_{RO}, which initiates with an empty record.

<u>Initiate</u>: Upon receiving (Initiate, *sid*) from $\tilde{A}$, setup an empty record **H**, representing the state of $F_{RO} : \{0,1\}^* \to \mathcal{H}$; and no further messages of this type is accepted.

<u>Query</u>: Upon receiving (Query, *sid*, inString $\in \{0,1\}^*$) from participant P, return (Query, *sid*, *str* $\in \mathcal{H}$) as follows: (i) If (-, inString) $\notin$ **H** (i.e., previously, there is no record containing an entry inString in **H**), sample *str* $\leftarrow_\$ \mathcal{H}$ and then add the tuple (*str*, inString) to **H**. (ii) If there is a record containing inString in **H**, retrieve *str* from **H** (i.e., retrieve (*str*, inString) $\leftarrow$ **H**).

Fig. 2. The random oracle ideal functionality (F_{RO}).

3   Underlined UC Framework and Operation Unit

In this section, we present an overview of the underlined UC framework. We first present an informal definition related to a generic sequential function. Following this, we highlight the concept of capturing the abstract progression of computations through a series of ticks from a global ticker F_{clk}. To capture computation costs (expressed in ticks from F_{clk}), we then introduce an *operation unit* (OU) and its ideal functionality (F_{OU}), which each party accesses to execute a protocol's algorithms.

Long Sequential Functions. We use T to characterize a function's difficulty, representing the amount of sequential work required to compute its output for any random input with a polynomially large number of parallel computations. A short function has a small T, while a function with a large T is considered a long function. Throughout this work, we refer to the long sequential function as SeqEval. SeqEval is defined with parameters for its domain and range. A shorter version of SeqEval, referred to as a shortcut or trapdoor, is denoted by tr.

UC Framework and a Global Ticker. As depicted in Fig. 3, our framework relies on the ideal functionality of a global ticker (F_{clk}) from [9], providing "ticks" (representing a unit of time) on a one-at-a-time basis. F_{clk} is designed to capture the units of passing time and starts with an empty record of enrolled functionalities and parties. Our work implicitly assumes that all relevant functionalities and parties of a protocol are enrolled with F_{clk}.

Enrollment: Upon receiving Enroll from a party P (resp. from functionality F), add P to **P** (resp. add F to **F**); then send back Enrolled.
Ticked request: Upon receiving IsTicked from $F \in \mathbf{F}$ and $F \notin L_F$, add F to L_F, and send ticked to F; otherwise, send NotTicked to F.
Ready: Upon receiving Ready from $P \in \mathbf{P}$, add P to L_P, and send Success to P.
Tick: Upon receiving tick from Env, if $\mathbf{P} = L_p$, set both $L_p = \varnothing$ and $L_F = \varnothing$, and send ticked to the adversary $\tilde{\mathcal{A}}$. Otherwise, send NotTicked to Env.

Fig. 3. The functionality of F_{clk}-global ticker from [9].

F_{clk}'s ticks are initiated by the environment Env's query Tick, but F_{clk} will only tick if all parties have sent (in an arbitrary order) a Ready query. Moreover, to emulate a delay based on computation, parties do not (directly) receive notification of ticks (excluding simulator $\tilde{\mathcal{A}}$). They rather discretely query the relevant functionalities, which in turn respond appropriately to each query based on its internal state. Upon query such as Elicitate, functionalities first check (via IsTicked) with F_{clk} to determine if a tick has occurred. In such a case, the functionality Tick interface will be triggered internally. Then the functionality will return an appropriate message (on request) to the relevant party(ies). As soon as all relevant functionalities have responded, the party will submit a Ready query to F_{clk}, requesting an advance to the next tick. For clarity, we assume that the query messages to/from F_{clk} are handled implicitly in our protocol due to their repetitiveness.

Generally, the environment is capable of conducting computations instantaneously relative to other parties, e.g., it can perform computation before activating honest parties. To effectively simulate time delay and to align with a more realistic model, we propose a global operation unit OU, mandating that all parties utilize this OU for conducting any form of arbitrary computation. This OU operates under tick-based functionality, governed by F_{clk}, ensuring no party, including the environment, can advance computationally ahead of others; thereby constraining the environment's advantage.

Modeling Operation Unit. Here we introduce an operation unit OU with a finite instruction set (INST). OU is formally defined as follows: OU : INST × STR → STR, where STR is the input/output space. Each party P has *private access* to OU, through which P executes algorithm steps. To execute an algorithm, P translates the steps into a sequence of instructions (i.e., a sequence of instructions executing a step S is referred to as $\mathbf{Inst}_S = \{\mathsf{Inst}_j\}_{j \in [k]}$ s.t. $k \in \mathbb{N}$ and all $\mathsf{Inst} \in \mathsf{INST}$) and parses the input in STR's format. P has the flexibility to construct $\mathbf{Inst}_S$ arbitrarily (of polynomial size), reflecting the strategy used to achieve the desired output.

OU's execution model: Let τ_F be a *global* function that takes $\mathbf{Inst}_S$ as input and outputs an integer $\tau \in \mathbb{N}$, representing the number of ticks required for $\mathbf{Inst}_S$'s execution. To emulate computation costs (in ticks), we introduce the ideal functionality F_{OU}, which captures the process of executing OU described earlier. To mimic OU's execution cost, F_{OU} computes the instruction sequence $\mathbf{Inst}_S$ instantly on a given input in but withholds the output until $\tau = \tau_F(\mathbf{Inst}_S, in)$ ticks have elapsed. As depicted in Fig. 4, to initiate a session with F_{OU}, P sends (Initiate, sid) to F_{OU}, which creates two empty lists, namely $\mathbf{L}_{in}$ and $\mathbf{L}_{out}$. To perform an execution, P submits (Evaluate, sid, $\mathbf{Inst}_S$, in) to F_{OU}. Promptly, F_{OU} evaluates the instruction sequence, storing the query and the execution output in $\mathbf{L}_{in}$, then it informs P with τ. At every tick, for every query in $\mathbf{L}_{in}$, if $\tau = 0$, move the query from $\mathbf{L}_{in}$ to $\mathbf{L}_{out}$, otherwise it decreases τ by one. After τ ticks have passed, P sends Elicitate query to F_{OU}, which returns all queries of P, containing the execution outputs. To simplify the notations, for evaluating Solve.SeqEval, P simply sends (Evaluate, sid, SeqEval, $\hat{in} := \mathbf{c} \parallel \mathsf{RandSeed}$) to F_{OU}, instead of submitting a set of explicit instructions as (Evaluate, sid, $\mathbf{Inst}_{\mathsf{SeqEval}} \leftarrow \mathsf{P}(\mathsf{SeqEval})$, $in \leftarrow \mathsf{P}(\hat{in})$) to F_{OU}. In light of the above discussion, we can define T to be $\tau_F(\mathsf{SeqEval}, \mathbf{c})$.

Initiate: Upon receiving (Initiate, sid) from P_j, store sid and initiate two empty lists, namely $\mathbf{L}_{in}^j$ and $\mathbf{L}_{out}^j$. Output (Success, sid) to P_j.

Evaluate: Upon receiving (Evaluate, sid, $\mathbf{Inst}_S$, $in \in \mathsf{STR}$) from P_j, compute $out \leftarrow \mathsf{OU}(\mathbf{Inst}_S, in)$ and $\tau = \tau_F(\mathbf{Inst}_S, in)$. Add $(P_j, \mathbf{Inst}_S, sid, \tau, out)$ to $\mathbf{L}_{in}^j$, and Send (Success, sid, $\mathbf{Inst}_S$, τ) to P_j.

Tick: In every tick, and for every query in $\mathbf{L}_{in}^j$, if $\tau > 0$, then decrease τ by one and update the query. If $\tau = 0$, then move it from $\mathbf{L}_{in}^j$ and add it to $\mathbf{L}_{out}^j$.

Elicitate: Upon receiving (Elicitate, sid) from P_j, pop all entries in $\mathbf{L}_{out}^j$ with $(P_j, \cdots)$ and send (Elicitate, sid, $\mathbf{resp}$) to P_j, where $\mathbf{resp}$ denotes the popped entries.

Fig. 4. The ideal functionality of the operation unit, F_{OU}.

4   ChronoCloak

Here, we present a formal definition of ChronoCloak and its desired properties.

Definition 2 (ChronoCloak). *ChronoCloak is a tuple of algorithms (Setup, Commit, Challenge, Solve, Verify, Open) defined as follows, where $\mathcal{M}$, $\mathcal{S}$, $\mathcal{C}$, $\mathcal{Y}$, and Π refer to the message, secret, challenge, answer, and proof spaces, respectively.*

- *Setup: a randomized algorithm that takes a security parameter λ and a difficulty T. It runs in time $\mathsf{Poly}(\lambda)$ and outputs a public parameter pp.*
- *Commit: a randomized algorithm that takes pp and $i \in \{0,1\}$; it selects a random secret $sk_r \leftarrow_\$ \mathcal{S}$, and generates and outputs, in time $\mathsf{Poly}(\lambda)$, a commitment c' of i, and sk_r.*
- *Challenge: a randomized algorithm with input pp, $(m_0, m_1) \in \mathcal{M}^2$, and $c' \in \mathcal{C}$. It selects $sk_c \leftarrow_\$ \mathcal{S}$, and computes and returns, in time $\mathsf{Poly}(\lambda)$, a challenge $c \in \mathcal{C}$ of c'.*
- *Solve: an algorithm that runs in time T with $\mathsf{Poly}(\lambda)$ parallel processors. It takes as an input pp and a challenge $c \in \mathcal{C}$; it returns an answer $a \in \mathcal{Y}$ and a proof $\pi \in \Pi$.*
- *Verify: a deterministic algorithm that receives pp and $c \in \mathcal{C}$ with its proposed answer $a \in \mathcal{Y}$ and proof $\pi \in \Pi$. In time polynomial in $\log T$ and λ, it returns* ACCEPT *if a is the correct unique answer to c with respect to π, otherwise it returns* REJECT.
- *Open: a deterministic algorithm that runs in time $\mathsf{Poly}(\log T, \lambda)$. It takes as an input pp, sk_r, and a challenge $c \in \mathcal{C}$ with its answer $a \in \mathcal{Y}$ and proof $\pi \in \Pi$; with the knowledge of $sk_r \in \mathcal{S}$, it returns $m_i \in \{m_0, m_1\}$ if a is the unique answer to c regarding π, otherwise it returns $\perp$.*

ChronoCloak Properties. Let $\mathcal{A}$ be adversary represented by a set of polynomially bounded algorithms (or/and strategies, which are both referred to by A), e.g., $\mathcal{A} := (A_1, A_2)$. Let A_1 be an offline algorithm, running on time $Poly(T, \lambda)$ that outputs pc a pre-computation of pp. Furthermore, it is the internal coin tosses of ChronoCloak's algorithms that yield all the probabilities. The outputs generated by an algorithm and enclosed within brackets [-] are secret, e.g., sk_r is the secret output of $(\mathbf{c}', [sk_r]) \leftarrow_\$ \mathsf{Commit}(pp, i)$. The following assumes that all statements are true for any λ, T and $pp \leftarrow_\$ \mathsf{Setup}(1^\lambda, T)$. ChronoCloak's properties are:

- *Correctness.* For every $\{m_0, m_1\} \leftarrow_\$ \mathcal{M}^2$, and $i \in \{0, 1\}$ and for every honest challenge $\mathbf{c} \leftarrow_\$ \mathsf{Challenge}(pp, \mathbf{c}')$ of an honest $(\mathbf{c}', [sk_r]) \leftarrow_\$ \mathsf{Commit}(pp, i)$, $\mathsf{Open}(pp, [sk_r], \mathbf{c}, \mathbf{a}, \pi)$ always returns the intended m_i from an honest answer $(\mathbf{a}, \pi) \leftarrow \mathsf{Solve}(pp, \mathbf{c})$ that Verify accepts with probability one.
- *Uniqueness.* ChronoCloak is unique only if, for every challenge $\mathbf{c} \in \mathcal{C}$ of $\mathbf{c}'$, there exists exactly one valid answer (i.e., $\mathbf{a}, \pi \leftarrow \mathsf{Solve}(pp, \mathbf{c})$), that Verify accepts, and this is the only answer through which Open returns $m \in \{m_0, m_1\}$, satisfying:

$$\Pr\left[\begin{array}{c} \mathbf{a}' \neq \mathbf{a} \\ \text{and} \\ \left(\begin{array}{c} \mathsf{Verify}(pp, \mathbf{a}', \pi') = \mathrm{ACCEPT} \\ \text{or} \\ \mathsf{Open}(pp, sk_r', \mathbf{c}, \mathbf{a}', \pi') \neq \bot \end{array}\right) \end{array} : \begin{array}{l} pp \leftarrow_\$ \mathsf{Setup}(1^\lambda, T), (\mathrm{pc}) \leftarrow \mathsf{A}_1(pp), \\ (\mathbf{c}', [sk_r]) \leftarrow \mathsf{A}_2(\mathsf{Commit}, pp, [i]), \\ \mathbf{c} \leftarrow_\$ \mathsf{Challenge}(pp, \mathbf{c}', [m_0, m_1] \in \mathcal{M}^2), \\ (\mathbf{a}, -) \leftarrow \mathsf{Solve}(pp, \mathbf{c}), \\ (\mathbf{a}', \pi', sk_r') \leftarrow \mathsf{A}_3(pp, \mathrm{pc}, [sk_r], \mathbf{c}). \end{array}\right]$$

is a negligible function of λ, for any adversary $\mathcal{A} := (\mathsf{A}_1, \mathsf{A}_2, \mathsf{A}_3)$. Although the answer $\mathbf{a}$ must be unique, the proof π does not.
- *Sequentiality.* ChronoCloak is sequential only if no adversary $\mathcal{A}$ can obtain the correct answer before an honest solver. Let $\mathsf{A}_{\mathrm{short}}$ be an online algorithm that proposes $\mathbf{a}'$ in a shorter time than executing $\mathsf{Solve}(pp, \mathbf{c})$ (i.e., in less time than T). For any adversary $\mathcal{A} := (\mathsf{A}_1, \mathsf{A}_2, \mathsf{A}_{\mathrm{short}})$, we have

$$\Pr\left[\mathbf{a}' = \mathbf{a} : \begin{array}{l} pp \leftarrow_\$ \mathsf{Setup}(1^\lambda, T), \mathrm{pc} \leftarrow \mathsf{A}_1(pp), \\ (\mathbf{c}', [sk_r]) \leftarrow \mathsf{A}_2(\mathsf{Commit}, pp, [i]), \\ \mathbf{c} \leftarrow_\$ \mathsf{Challenge}(pp, \mathbf{c}', [m_0, m_1] \in \mathcal{M}^2), \\ \mathbf{a}' \leftarrow \mathsf{A}_{\mathrm{short}}(pp, \mathrm{pc}, \mathbf{c}), \\ (\mathbf{a}, \pi) \leftarrow \mathsf{Solve}(pp, \mathbf{c}). \end{array}\right]$$

is a negligible function of λ. This must also hold for both $\mathcal{A}_2 \in \mathcal{A}$ and $\mathcal{A}_2 \notin \mathcal{A}$.
- *Hiding.* ChronoCloak is hiding only if, for every challenge $\mathbf{c} \in \mathcal{C}$ of $\mathbf{c}'$, and answer $\mathbf{a} \leftarrow \mathsf{Solve}(pp, \mathbf{c})$, it holds that:

$$\left| \Pr\left[b' = b : \begin{array}{l} pp \leftarrow_\$ \mathsf{Setup}(1^\lambda, T), (\mathrm{pc}, [m_0, m_1]) \leftarrow \mathsf{A}_1(pp), \\ (\mathbf{c}', [sk_r]) \leftarrow \mathsf{Commit}(pp, [i]), [b] \leftarrow_\$ \{0, 1\}, \\ \mathbf{c} \leftarrow_\$ \mathsf{Challenge}(pp, \mathbf{c}', \left[\begin{array}{ll} [m_0, m_1] & \text{for } b = 0 \\ [m_0', m_1'] \leftarrow_\$ \mathcal{M}^2 & \text{for } b = 1 \end{array}\right]), \\ (\mathbf{a}, \pi) \leftarrow \mathsf{Solve}(pp, \mathbf{c}), b' \leftarrow \mathsf{A}_4(pp, \mathrm{pc}, \mathbf{c}', \mathbf{c}, \mathbf{a}). \end{array}\right] - \frac{1}{2} \right|$$

is a negligible function of λ, for any adversary $\mathcal{A} := (\mathsf{A}_1, \mathsf{A}_4)$.
- *Secrecy.* ChronoCloak is secretive only if there is no adversary, corrupting the receiver, inferring any extra information than inferred by an honest receiver. Hence, for any adversary $\mathcal{A} := (\mathsf{A}_1, \mathsf{A}_2, \mathsf{A}_3, \mathsf{A}_5, \mathsf{A}_6)$, we have

$$\Pr\left[\begin{array}{l} \hat{m}_{1-i} = m_{1-i}, \\ \text{and } \hat{m}_i = m_i \end{array} : \begin{array}{l} pp \leftarrow_\$ \mathsf{Setup}(1^\lambda, T), \mathrm{pc} \leftarrow \mathsf{A}_1(pp), \\ (\mathbf{c}', [sk_r]) \leftarrow \mathsf{A}_2(\mathsf{Commit}, pp, [i]), \\ \mathbf{c} \leftarrow_\$ \mathsf{Challenge}(pp, \mathbf{c}', [m_0, m_1] \in \mathcal{M}^2), \\ (\mathbf{a}', -, sk_r') \leftarrow \mathsf{A}_3(pp, \mathrm{pc}, [sk_r], \mathbf{c}), \hat{m}_i \leftarrow \mathsf{A}_5(pp, \mathrm{pc}, [sk_r'], \mathbf{c}, \mathbf{a}') \\ \hat{m}_{1-i} \leftarrow \mathsf{A}_6(pp, \mathrm{pc}, [sk_r'], \mathbf{c}, \mathbf{a}', \hat{m}_i). \end{array}\right]$$

is a negligible function of λ.

– *Privacy.* ChronoCloak is private only if the $\mathbf{c}'_i$ of i is indistinguishable from $\mathbf{c}'_{i'}$ of i'. For any adversary $\mathcal{A}$, we have

$$\left| \Pr \left[\mathcal{A}(pp, \mathbf{c}') = i : \begin{array}{l} pp \leftarrow_\$ \mathsf{Setup}(1^\lambda, T), \\ [i] \leftarrow_\$ \{0,1\}, \\ \mathbf{c}' \leftarrow_\$ \mathsf{Commit}(pp, [i]) \end{array} \right] - 1/2 \right|$$

is a negligible function of λ.

The Ideal Functionality of ChronoCloak. Now, we present the ideal functionality $\mathsf{F_{CC}}$ that captures ChronoCloak features, shown in Fig. 5, which involves a series of interactions among participants. By submitting an Enrollment message

---

<u>Enrollment</u>: Upon receiving (Enroll, sid) from a party P_j, add P_j to $\mathcal{P}$; then send back (Enrolled, sid).

<u>Commit</u>: Upon receiving (Commit, sid, P_S, i) from P_R, add the tuple (P_R, P_S, sid, $m_0 = \varnothing$, $m_1 = \varnothing$, i, $T = \varnothing$, $\chi_0 = \varnothing$, $\chi_T = \varnothing$) to **InState**, where χ_j is the chronicle progress; and no further messages of this type is accepted. Output (Commit, sid, P_R) to P_S.

<u>Challenge</u>: Upon receiving (Challenge, sid, P_R, T, m_0, m_1) from P_S, if Commit is received, sample $(\mathbf{c}_j)_{j \in [T+1]} \leftarrow_\$ \mathcal{C}^T$ s.t. $\nexists \mathbf{c}_j = \mathbf{c}_k \; \forall j \neq k$. Assign **ChronoSteps**[$\mathbf{c}_j$] $= \mathbf{c}_{j+1} \; \forall j \in [T+1]$ and updates (P_S, P_R, sid, m_0, m_1, T, $\chi_0 = \mathbf{c}_1$, $\chi_T = \mathbf{c}_{T+1}$, $\pi_{\textbf{list}} = [\varnothing]$) in **InState**. Lastly, broadcast (Challenge, sid, χ_0) to $\mathcal{P}$ and no further messages of this type is accepted.

<u>Advance</u>: Upon receiving (Step, sid, χ) from P_j, perform the following: (i) If **ChronoSteps**[χ] is defined, add (P_j, Step, sid, χ, $\chi' :=$ **ChronoSteps**[χ]) to $\mathbf{L}_{in}$ and skip the next step. (ii) If **ChronoSteps**[χ] is not defined, sample $\chi' \leftarrow_\$ \mathcal{C}$, set **ChronoSteps**[$\chi$] $= \chi'$ and add (P_j, Step, sid, χ, χ') to $\mathbf{L}_{in}$.

<u>Prove</u>: Upon receiving (Prove, sid, χ, χ') from P_j, add (P_j, Prove, sid, REJECT) to $\mathbf{L}_{in}$ if $(\chi, \chi') \neq (\chi_0, \chi_T)$, and skip next. A non-corrupt P_S: If there is no $(\mathsf{P}_j, \pi) \in \pi_{\textbf{list}}$, append $(\mathsf{P}_j, \pi \leftarrow_\$ \Pi)$ to $\pi_{\textbf{list}}$, then add (P_j, Prove, sid, π) to $\mathbf{L}_{in}$. A corrupt P_S: Forward the query to $\tilde{\mathcal{A}}$ and wait to receive π'. If $\pi' \notin \Pi$, halt; otherwise add (P_j, Prove, sid, π') to $\mathbf{L}_{in}$.

<u>Verify</u>: Upon receiving (Verify, sid, χ, χ', π') from P_j, add (P_j, Verify, sid, REJECT) to $\mathbf{L}_{in}$ if $(\chi, \chi') \neq (\chi_0, \chi_T)$ or $(-, \pi') \notin \pi_{\textbf{list}}$; otherwise add ($\mathsf{P}_j$, Verify, sid, ACCEPT) to $\mathbf{L}_{in}$.

<u>Open</u>: Upon receiving (Open, sid, χ, χ', π') from P_R, send P_R the response (Open, sid, REJECT) if $(\chi, \chi') \neq (\chi_0, \chi_T)$ or $(-, \pi') \notin \pi_{\textbf{list}}$; if not, add ($\mathsf{P}_R$, Open, sid, m_i) to $\mathbf{L}_{in}$.

<u>Tick</u>: At every tick, set $\mathbf{L}_{out} \leftarrow \mathbf{L}_{in}$ and $\mathbf{L}_{in} \leftarrow \varnothing$.

<u>Elicitate</u>: Upon receiving (Elicitate, sid) from P_j, pop all entries in $\mathbf{L}_{out}$ with (P_j, $\cdots$) and send (Elicitate, sid, **resp**) to P_j, where **resp** denotes the popped entries. If (P_j, Prove, sid, π') $\in$ **resp**, send (P_j, (χ_T, π')) to P_R.

Fig. 5. The ideal functionality of ChronoCloak, $\mathsf{F_{CC}}$.

to F_{CC}, participants are added to the Participant List ($\mathcal{P}$). A receiver P_R initiates interactions by submitting Commit to F_{CC} with a choice i. Upon receiving notice of P_R's query from F_{CC}, the sender P_S responds by sending (m_0, m_1) via Challenge to F_{CC}. F_{CC} broadcasts a challenge (χ_0) to all parties in $\mathcal{P}$. $P_j \in \mathcal{P}$ prompts sequential Advance queries to F_{CC}, obtaining $\{\chi_k\}_{k \in [T]}$ after all T-ticks, where to obtain χ_k at a tick, P_j must have χ_{k-1} from the previous tick. Note that, following each tick, all parties receive their respective responses from F_{CC} by calling Elicitate. Once T ticks have elapsed, P_j can obtain a proof π from F_{CC} by sending Prove with (χ_0, χ_T). Upon obtaining/receiving (χ_T, π') from F_{CC}, P_R retrieves m_i by invoking Open on F_{CC}, completing the ChronoCloak process.

5   Generic ChronoCloak

In this section, we present a generic ChronoCloak based on the functionalities F_{RO}, F_{OT}, and F_{OU}. We then prove that our protocol securely realizes F_{CC}, thereby proving that Definition 2 of ChronoCloak is simulatable implying the ideal functionality for F_{CC}. In particular, we instantiate our protocol using Definition 2 of (Setup, Commit, Challenge, Solve, Verify, Open), and then we show that if our ChronoCloak is Commit-Challenge simulatable[1], then it is a UC-securely realizing F_{CC} in the random oracle mode. In light of this, we will use F_{OT}, shown in Fig. 1, as a building block for Commit-Challenge. Additionally, our protocol achieves a time T delay through a long sequential function SeqEval with difficulty T. As discussed in Sect. 3, parties exclusively use F_{OU} to execute all functions, including the evaluation of SeqEval. Let Hash be a hash function, modeled by the random oracle F_{RO}, defined as $\{0,1\}^* \to \{0,1\}^{2\lambda}$, where Hash takes arbitrary input and serializes it as a string of bits.

5.1   The Protocol

In Fig. 6, we present a ChronoCloak protocol $\Gamma_{F_{CC}}$ based on Definition 2, which is defined by the parameters $(\mathcal{M}, \mathcal{S}, \mathcal{C}, \mathcal{Y} := \mathcal{C}, \Pi)$.

Discussion.

Correctness. For $\Gamma_{F_{CC}}$ to be correct, we assume that SeqEval and $tr_{sk} \in \mathcal{F}$ are commutative actions on $\mathcal{C}$'s elements for any $sk \in \mathcal{S}$ (i.e., for any element in the set $\mathcal{C}$, both sequences of actions—$tr_{sk} \circ$ SeqEval and SeqEval $\circ tr_{sk}$—are equivalent). Specifically, if $\hat{y} = tr_{sk}(\text{SeqEval}(x))$ and $\hat{y}' = \text{SeqEval}(tr_{sk}(x))$, then $\hat{y} = \hat{y}'$, $\forall x \in \mathcal{C}$ and $\forall sk \in \mathcal{S}$. The correctness requirement is feasible, as most efficient delay-based primitives with public verifiability rely on some algebraic structure satisfying the commutativity property. An example is the sequential function SeqEval introduced by Rivest et al. [41], which involves (T-times) repeated squaring in a group with an unknown order, G. In this context, $tr_{sk}(\cdot)$ is then defined

---

[1] This means that a simulator can extract the receiver's (and the sender's) input during or after the Commit-Challenge phase, but before the solving process begins.

Initialization [Setup]. A trusted party P_{TTP} generates a set of public parameters $pp \leftarrow_\$ \mathsf{Setup}(\lambda, T)$ which includes (i) a description of $\mathsf{Solve.SeqEval} : \mathcal{C} \to \mathcal{C}^a$ to be the T-long function with a public challenge and answer (i.e., $x, y \in \mathcal{C}$ such that $y \leftarrow \mathsf{SeqEval}(x)$), and (ii) a description of a large ensemble of short trapdoors $\mathcal{F}$ given a secret space $\mathcal{S}$ (i.e., $\mathsf{tr}_{sk} \leftarrow \mathcal{F}$ given $sk \leftarrow_\$ \mathcal{S}$). P_{TTP} sends (Setup, P_{TTP}, pp) to all parties.

Preparation [Enrollment]. Initially, P_S and P_R share a common input pp and $sid \in \{0,1\}^*$. Using a private input $i \in \{0,1\}$, the receiver (P_R) decides which message to obtain. In response to a receiver's request, the sender (P_S) prepares the relevant message set $(m_0, m_1) \in \mathcal{M}^2$.

Message 1 [Commit]. Instantiated by F_{OT}, P_R sends (Commit, sid, P_S, i) to F_{OT}.

Message 2 [Challenge]. Upon receiving (Commit, sid, P_R) from F_{OT}, P_S performs the following

- computes $\hat{x} \leftarrow \mathsf{tr}_{sk_c}(x)$ and $\hat{y} \leftarrow \mathsf{tr}_{sk_c}(y)$, where $\mathsf{tr}_{sk_c} \leftarrow \mathcal{F}$ for $sk_c \leftarrow_\$ \mathcal{S}$.
- sends (Query, sid, $\hat{x} \parallel \hat{y}$) to F_{RO}, and waits to receive (Query, sid, k). Then it sets $k^{\text{MSB}} \parallel k^{\text{LSB}} = k$, where k^{MSB} and $k^{\text{LSB}} \in \{0,1\}^\lambda$.
- computes $\hat{m}_0 = m_0 \oplus k^{\text{MSB}}$, $\hat{m}_1 = m_1 \oplus k^{\text{MSB}}$, and $\mathsf{sig} := sk_c \oplus k^{\text{LSB}}$.
- sends (Query, sid, $\mathsf{sig} \parallel sk_c \parallel k^{\text{LSB}}$) to F_{RO}, and waits to receive (Query, sid, cm_{sig}).

P_S sends (Challenge, sid, P_R, $\hat{m}_0, \hat{m}_1$) to F_{OT}. If (Challenge, sid, P_R) is received, P_S sends (Challenge, sid, P_S, $\mathbf{c} := (\hat{x}, \mathsf{sig}, cm_{\text{sig}})$) to P_R.

Message 3 [Solve]. Upon receiving (Challenge, sid, P_S, $\hat{m}_i$) from F_{OT} and (Challenge, sid, P_S, $\mathbf{c}$) from P_S, P_R sends (Evaluate, sid, Solve, $\hat{in} := (pp, \mathbf{c}.\hat{x})$) to F_{OU} and awaits to receive (Evaluate, sid, $\mathbf{Inst}_{\text{Solve}}$, T). To obtain $(\mathbf{a}' := \hat{y}', \pi \in \Pi)$, P_R sends T consecutive (Elicitate, sid) queries to the F_{OU}, stopping upon receiving the Tth response (Elicitate, sid, $\mathbf{resp}$) with a non-empty $\mathbf{resp} \neq \varnothing$.

Output [Open]. Upon obtaining $(\hat{y}', \pi)$, P_R performs the following

- checks that $\mathsf{Verify}(pp, \mathbf{c}.\hat{x}, (\hat{y}', \pi)) = \text{ACCEPT}$; if no, it outputs $\bot$.
- sends (Query, sid, $\hat{x} \parallel \hat{y}'$) to F_{RO}, and waits to receive (Query, sid, k). Then it sets $k^{\text{MSB}} \parallel k^{\text{LSB}} = k$.
- computes $sk_c := \mathbf{c}.\mathsf{sig} \oplus k^{\text{LSB}}$; then it sends (Query, sid, $\mathbf{c}.\mathsf{sig} \parallel sk_c \parallel k^{\text{LSB}}$) to F_{RO}, and waits to receive (Query, sid, cm'_{sig}).
- checks that $cm'_{\text{sig}} = \mathbf{c}.cm_{\text{sig}}$, $\hat{x} = \mathsf{tr}_{sk_c}(x)$, and $\hat{y} = \mathsf{tr}_{sk_c}(y)$; if no, it outputs $\bot$; otherwise, it continues next.

Finally, P_R computes $m_i = \hat{m}_i \oplus k^{\text{MSB}}$

---

^{a} We use this notation (i.e., $\mathsf{Solve.SeqEval}$) to indicate the function $\mathsf{SeqEval}$ being a part of Solve algorithm.

Fig. 6. Proposed ChronoCloak protocol $\Gamma_{\mathsf{F}_{\text{CC}}}$ implementing F_{CC}.

as $\mathrm{tr}_{sk}(x) = x^{sk}$. For all $x \in G$, the functions SeqEval and tr_{sk} commute as follows: $\mathsf{SeqEval} \circ \mathrm{tr}_{sk}(x) = (x^{sk})^{2^T} = \mathrm{tr}_{sk}(x^{2^T}) = \mathrm{tr}_{sk} \circ \mathsf{SeqEval}(x)$, which satisfies $\hat{y} = \mathrm{tr}_{sk}(y)$. Another example can be found in the work of [46].

Alternative Approach. When designing a ChronoCloak protocol, it may seem intuitive to time-lock each secret message with a challenge and then use $\mathsf{F_{OT}}$ to transmit either of these challenges. This approach, however, may leak the receiver's choice in two instances: the first instance is in the public-solving model, in which the receiver reveals the transmitted challenge to the public solver. One could argue that the receiver may obfuscate the transmitted challenge to conceal their choice before sending it to the solver; however, this obfuscation method has several problems, such as the difficulty of disputing an improperly constructed challenge (or commitment) without the receiver revealing their concealed secret and thus their choice. The second instance results from a selective fault attack (by the sender) in which one of the messages contains a maliciously corrupted challenge.

Furthermore, our construction is more efficient. Compared to the alternative approach, which requires the creation of two challenges, their commitments (i.e., two commitments), one OT operation, and one concealing operation (for a public solver), while our construction only requires the creation of one challenge, its commitment, and one OT operation.

Real-World Example. The constructed protocol of ChronoCloak must maintain being a "function" (i.e., being unique), where each challenge has only one solution that allows message extraction, and which the verifier accepts (i.e., it is infeasible to find another answer that Verify outputs accepts or that Open outputs anything but $\bot$). Consider a real-world example: If a sender transmits a valid challenge $\mathbf{c}$ (that has an answer $\mathbf{a}$), and the receiver finds an alternative answer $\mathbf{a}'$ (with its proof) that also passes verification, the receiver can then show that $\mathbf{c}$ is not properly constructed given $\mathbf{a}'$. This can affect applications where the receiver has to compensate for received content.

Scalability. Our ChronoCloak protocol scales well for multiple receivers, allowing a sender to transmit content to many receivers with a single challenge, though requiring one OT operation for each receiver. The protocol scales well because the solution to the challenge ensures that all receivers obtain their chosen content *obliviously*. However, this work does not extend effectively to the scenario of multiple senders and receivers, where each sender needs to generate its own challenge and a corresponding solution, thereby affecting scalability. The solution to this limitation was left for future work.

5.2   Security

We will now provide a proof that $\Gamma_{\mathsf{F_{CC}}}$ securely implements $\mathsf{F_{CC}}$.

Theorem 1. *The protocol $\Gamma_{\mathsf{F_{CC}}}$ is securely UC-implementing $\mathsf{F_{CC}}$ in $(\mathsf{F_{RO}}, \mathsf{F_{OT}}, \mathsf{F_{OU}})$-hybrid model under a malicious adversary (A) with static corruption, and for any PPT environment Env.*

Proof. To prove the theorem, we construct the simulators $\tilde{\mathcal{A}}'_S$ and $\tilde{\mathcal{A}}'_R$ (see Figs. 7 and 8). Env produces inputs sent to the appropriate parties (i.e., $\mathsf{P}_S \xleftarrow{send}$ (m_0, m_1), $\mathsf{P}_R \xleftarrow{send} i$, $\mathsf{A} \xleftarrow{send}$ aux). The simulator provides *the malicious adversary* with the matching inputs. $\tilde{\mathcal{A}}'_S$ (resp. $\tilde{\mathcal{A}}'_R$) simulates $\Gamma_{\mathsf{F_{CC}}}$ in the presence of a copy of A_S (resp. A_R), corrupting the sender (resp. receiver, and solver). The simulations emulate the random oracle $\mathsf{F_{RO}}$ with empty state. Hence, it responds to any query from/to $\mathsf{F_{RO}}$ and keeps track of all queries and responses.

Security with Corrupted Sender and Honest Receiver. We present $\tilde{\mathcal{A}}'_S$ who passes the inputs $([m_0, m_1], \mathsf{aux})$ from Env to A_S.

---

1. *Initialization and Preparation*: On Env's inputs (λ, T), $\tilde{\mathcal{A}}'_S$ simulates Setup honestly. Then, A_S is invoked with inputs (m_0, m_1, aux) from Env.
2. *Message 1 [Commit]*: As an honest receiver, $\tilde{\mathcal{A}}'_S$ sends (Commit, *sid*, P_R, $i' = 0$) to $\mathsf{F_{OT}}$ with a dummy input (e.g., $i' = 0$).
3. *Message 2 [Challenge]*: Upon receiving (Challenge, *sid*, A_S, $\hat{m}_i$) from $\mathsf{F_{OT}}$ and (Challenge, *sid*, A_S, $\mathbf{c} = (\hat{x}, \mathsf{sig}, cm_{\mathsf{sig}})$) from A_S, $\tilde{\mathcal{A}}'_S$ observes all queries (i.e., inString $\in \mathsf{F_{RO}.H}$) to $\mathsf{F_{RO}}$. Accordingly, $\tilde{\mathcal{A}}'_S$ identifies a record in $\mathsf{F_{RO}.H}$ with a prefix $(str_1, \hat{\mathbf{c}}.\hat{x} \,\|\, str_2) \in \mathsf{F_{RO}.H}$, which allows it to obtain $k^{\mathsf{MSB}} \,\|\, k^{\mathsf{LSB}} = k \leftarrow str_1$, the answer $\hat{y} \leftarrow str_2$, and the secret $sk_c := \mathbf{c}.\mathsf{sig} \oplus k^{\mathsf{LSB}}$ (Note that there might be multiple records with the same prefix, i.e., $\hat{\mathbf{c}}.\hat{x} \,\|\, str_2$). $\tilde{\mathcal{A}}'_S$ also identifies a record of form $(str_1, \mathbf{c}.\mathsf{sig} \,\|\, sk_c \,\|\, k^{\mathsf{LSB}}) \in \mathsf{F_{RO}.H}$, which allows it to obtain $cm'_{\mathsf{sig}} \leftarrow str_1$, if there is no record of such, it sets $cm'_{\mathsf{sig}} = \bot$. Following that, it checks for $\hat{y}$ as follows: $cm'_{\mathsf{sig}} \overset{?}{=} \mathbf{c}.cm_{\mathsf{sig}}$, $\hat{x} \overset{?}{=} \mathsf{tr}_{sk_c}(x)$, and $\hat{y} \overset{?}{=} \mathsf{tr}_{sk_c}(y)$. If the validation passes, $\tilde{\mathcal{A}}'_S$ computes $m_0 = \mathbf{c}.\hat{m}_0 \oplus k^{\mathsf{MSB}}$, $m_1 = \mathbf{c}.\hat{m}_1 \oplus k^{\mathsf{MSB}}$; otherwise, $\tilde{\mathcal{A}}'_S$ sets $(m_0, m_1) \leftarrow_\$ \mathcal{M}^2$.
4. *Message 3 [Solve]*: After above, $\tilde{\mathcal{A}}'_S$ sends (Challenge, *sid*, P_R, T, m_0, m_1) to $\mathsf{F_{CC}}$, and waits for (Challenge, *sid*, χ_0). Then, $\tilde{\mathcal{A}}'_S$ sends (Evaluate, *sid*, $\mathsf{Inst_{Solve}} \leftarrow \tilde{\mathcal{A}}'_R(\mathsf{Solve})$, $in \leftarrow \tilde{\mathcal{A}}'_R(pp, \mathbf{c}.\hat{x})$) to $\mathsf{F_{OU}}$, and receives (Evaluate, *sid*, $\mathsf{Inst_{Solve}}$, τ). In the event that A_S did not query either or both of (Query, *sid*, $\hat{x} \,\|\, str_1$) and (Query, *sid*, $\mathsf{sig} \,\|\, sk_c \,\|\, k^{\mathsf{LSB}}$), $\tilde{\mathcal{A}}'_S$ tracks all queries to $\mathsf{F_{RO}}$, and if a query for an answer passes the validation in Step 3, it responses in accordance to the messages submitted to $\mathsf{F_{CC}}$ (i.e., m_0, m_1).
5. *Output [Open]*: After τ ticks, $\tilde{\mathcal{A}}'_S$ responds to all Prove query from $\mathsf{F_{CC}}$ with $\bot$
   - if $\mathbf{a} = \hat{y}$ obtained from Step 3 is not equal to $\hat{y}'$ obtained from $\mathsf{F_{OU}}$ (and skip next);
   - and if the challenge $\mathbf{c}$ is not well formed, i.e., $cm'_{\mathsf{sig}} \neq \mathbf{c}.cm_{\mathsf{sig}}$, $\hat{x} \neq \mathsf{tr}_{sk_c}(x)$, or $\hat{y} \neq \mathsf{tr}_{sk_c}(y)$ for sk_c obtained using $\hat{y}$ (and skip next);
   - otherwise it responds with $\pi \in \Pi$.
   Lastly, once P_R, in the ideal execution, receives m_i, $\tilde{\mathcal{A}}'_S$ returns A_S's output to Env.

Fig. 7. A simulation $\tilde{\mathcal{A}}'_S$ for $\Gamma_{\mathsf{F_{CC}}}$.

Below, we show that $\tilde{\mathcal{A}}'_S$'s output is indistinguishable from the real execution and aligns with the ideal execution. $\tilde{\mathcal{A}}'_S$ operates honestly within the simulation by generating pp and acting as a trusted receiver, rendering it indistinguishable from a real execution. Furthermore, in Step 2, $\tilde{\mathcal{A}}'_S$ does not know P_R's input (in the ideal case), so it uses fixed choice, i.e., $i' = 0$. Despite this, Env cannot distinguish whether i' matches P_R's input or not. This is due to ChronoCloak's 'privacy' assumption, which holds given the ideal functionality $\mathsf{F_{OT}}$. As such, the two executions remain identical.

Additionally, to participate in the ideal execution, $\tilde{\mathcal{A}}'_S$ must send m_0 and m_1 to the $\mathsf{F_{CC}}$ at an early stage (i.e., before obtaining $\hat{y}$). However, since $\tilde{\mathcal{A}}'_S$ does not possess both secret messages, m_0 and m_1, it cannot consistently participate in the ideal execution as a real execution would. Fortunately, in Step 3, $\tilde{\mathcal{A}}'_S$ can extract and forward both secret messages m_0 and m_1 using sig, cm_{sig} and through $\mathsf{F_{RO}}$. If it cannot extract both messages, $\tilde{\mathcal{A}}'_S$ will select a random message(s) of the same length (i.e., representing the case in which the adversary did not inquire $\mathsf{F_{RO}}$). This indicates that A_S sends a random string(s) (i.e., $\hat{m}_0$, and $\hat{m}_1$), which implies sending a message(s) that are unknown to A_S (since A_S did not acquire the corresponding key, k^{MSB}). Later on, if A_S makes additional query(s) for the missing key, $\tilde{\mathcal{A}}'_S$ returns a suitable key that corresponds to the message sent to $\mathsf{F_{CC}}$ (in Step 4). However, the probability of A_S forming a valid challenge that passes in Step 5 is negligible since it has to predict the output of the query to $\mathsf{F_{RO}}$ in such a way that $k^{\mathrm{MSB}} = \mathsf{sig} \oplus sk_c$ (same for cm_{sig}). In this case, the simulator sends a null proof message. Accordingly, the $\tilde{\mathcal{A}}'_S$ can participate in ideal execution with interaction consistent with input from Env and the adversary's strategy. As a result, both executions are indistinguishable.

Security with Honest Sender and Corrupted Receiver. We present $\tilde{\mathcal{A}}'_R$ who passes the inputs $([i], \mathsf{aux})$ from Env to A_R.

Below, we show that the view generated by $\tilde{\mathcal{A}}'_R$ cannot be distinguished from the real execution and is consistent with the ideal execution. While in the simulation, $\tilde{\mathcal{A}}'_R$ behaves primarily as an honest sender, it deviates from honest execution in Step 3 (as it does not have P_S's inputs m_0 and m_1, in the ideal case). In more detail, $\tilde{\mathcal{A}}'_R$ sends to $\mathsf{F_{OT}}$ bogus challenge (i.e., $(\hat{m}_0, \hat{m}_1) \leftarrow_\$ \mathcal{M}^2$, $\mathsf{sig} \leftarrow_\$ \{0,1\}^\lambda$, and $cm_{\mathsf{sig}} \leftarrow_\$ \mathsf{F_{RO}}.\mathcal{H}$) hoping to receive $m_{i'}$ from $\mathsf{F_{CC}}$ later on (i.e., after τ ticks). For this reason, $\tilde{\mathcal{A}}'_R$ must first extract A_R's choice, i.e., i', which it can with the help of $\mathsf{F_{OT}}$ (see Step 2). So far, $\tilde{\mathcal{A}}'_R$ has sent (to $\mathsf{F_{OT}}$) two random messages, which is equivalent to sending true messages with an unknown key (i.e., $\hat{m}_{i'} = m_{i'} \oplus k^{\mathrm{MSB}}$ for $k^{\mathrm{MSB}} \leftarrow_\$ \{0,1\}^\lambda$). Env hence distinguishes between both executions if it can determine whether $\hat{m}_{i'}$ generated at random or through $(k^{\mathrm{MSB}} \| \cdots) \leftarrow \mathsf{Hash}(\hat{x} \| \hat{y})$. This event is negligible since Hash is assumed to be modeled as a random oracle; thus, the probability of distinguishing between executions is negligible without the knowledge of $\hat{y}$.

Further, $\tilde{\mathcal{A}}'_R$ in Step 4 advances step by step at each tick to retrieve χ_T, enabling it to obtain $m_{i'}$ from $\mathsf{F_{CC}}$. However, $\tilde{\mathcal{A}}'_R$ differs from the real execution in that it aborts when A_R sends a query of form (Query, sid, $\hat{x} \| \hat{y}$) (to $\mathsf{F_{RO}}$) before $\tilde{\mathcal{A}}'_R$. The probability of this abort is equal to the probability of A_R breaking the ChronoCloak's 'sequentiality' assumption of Solve (i.e., obtaining the answer $\mathbf{a}$ before time T). After τ ticks, $\tilde{\mathcal{A}}'_R$ can only know one of the two

1. *Initialization and Preparation*: The simulator obtains (λ, T) from the environment as a common public input. Then, A_R is invoked with inputs (i, aux) from Env.
2. *Message 1 [Commit]*: Upon receiving (Commit, A_R, sid) from F_{OT}, $\tilde{\mathcal{A}}'_R$ receives A_R's choice i' (which may differ from i) from A_R's messages to F_{OT}.
3. *Message 2 [Challenge]*: After above, $\tilde{\mathcal{A}}'_S$ samples two bogus messages $(\hat{m}_0, \hat{m}_1)$ $\leftarrow_\$ \mathcal{M}^2$. Then, it computes $\mathbf{c} := (\hat{x} \leftarrow \mathsf{tr}_{sk_c}(x), \mathsf{sig} \leftarrow_\$ \{0,1\}^\lambda, cm_{\mathsf{sig}} \leftarrow_\$ F_{RO}.\mathcal{H})$ and $\hat{y} \leftarrow \mathsf{tr}_{sk_c}(y)$, where $\mathsf{tr}_{sk_c} \leftarrow \mathcal{F}$ for $sk_c \leftarrow_\$ \mathcal{S}$. Finally, it sends (Challenge, sid, A_R, $\hat{m}_0, \hat{m}_1$) to F_{OT}. If (Challenge, sid, A_R) is received, $\tilde{\mathcal{A}}'_S$ sends (Challenge, sid, P_S, $\mathbf{c} := (\hat{x}, \mathsf{sig}, cm_{\mathsf{sig}})$) to A_R.
   Simultaneously, $\tilde{\mathcal{A}}'_R$ sends (Commit, sid, P_S, i') to F_{CC}. After that, it awaits the F_{CC}'s (Challenge, sid, χ_0) messages. Lastly, $\tilde{\mathcal{A}}'_R$ sends (Evaluate, sid, $\mathbf{Inst}_{\mathsf{SeqEval}} \leftarrow \tilde{\mathcal{A}}'_R(\mathsf{Solve.SeqEval})$, $in \leftarrow \tilde{\mathcal{A}}'_R(\mathbf{c}.\hat{x})$) to F_{OU}, and receives (Evaluate, sid, $\mathbf{Inst}_{\mathsf{SeqEval}}$, τ).
4. *Message 3 [Solve]*: At every tick, $\tilde{\mathcal{A}}'_R$ obtains the current sequential step χ' by sending (Elicitate, sid) to F_{CC}. Then, $\tilde{\mathcal{A}}'_R$ updates $\tau \leftarrow \tau - 1$ and sends (Step, sid, χ') to F_{CC}. $\tilde{\mathcal{A}}'_R$ outputs ABORT, if $\tau > 0$ and $\tilde{\mathcal{A}}'_R$ observes a query sent to F_{RO} by A_R of form (Query, sid, $\hat{x} \| \hat{y}$).
5. *Output [Open]*: When $\tau = 0$, $\tilde{\mathcal{A}}'_R$ obtains $m_{i'}$ from F_{CC} by sending Prove and Open calls. Upon receiving (Query, sid, $\hat{x} \| \hat{y}$) from A_R, $\tilde{\mathcal{A}}'_R$ computes $k^{\mathsf{MSB}} = m_{i'} \oplus \hat{m}_{i'}$ and $k^{\mathsf{LSB}} = sk_c \oplus \mathsf{sig}$, and sends (Query, sid, $k^{\mathsf{MSB}} \| k^{\mathsf{LSB}}$) to A_R. Also, for any query of form (Query, sid, $\mathsf{sig} \| sk_c \| k^{\mathsf{LSB}}$), $\tilde{\mathcal{A}}'_R$ responds by (Query, sid, cm_{sig}).

Fig. 8. A simulation $\tilde{\mathcal{A}}'_R$ for $\Gamma_{F_{CC}}$.

messages (i.e., only $m_{i'}$), whereas Env knows both (i.e., $m_{i'}$ and $m_{1-i'}$). Env would, however, require to obtain the other message $\hat{m}_{1-i'}$ sent through F_{OT} (by $\tilde{\mathcal{A}}'_R$) to distinguish $m_{1-i'}$ from $\overline{m}_{1-i'} := \hat{m}_{1-i'} \oplus k^{MSB}$. Therefore, this is infeasible due to ChronoCloak's 'secrecy' assumption, which preserved through the functionality of F_{OT}. In Step 5, $\tilde{\mathcal{A}}'_R$ can answer A_R's query to F_{RO} with the appropriate key $k^{\mathsf{MSB}} \| k^{\mathsf{LSB}} = k$ in accordance with $m_{i'}$. Yet, both executions will become distinguishable in case A_R obtains an alternative valid answer $\hat{y}'$ ($\neq \hat{y}$) accepted by Verify, in which $\tilde{\mathcal{A}}'_R$'s challenge $\mathbf{c}$ is quite unlikely to be well-formed given $\hat{y}'$ under the Hash assumption. This contradicts ChronoCloak's 'uniqueness' assumption and is therefore infeasible. As a result, $\tilde{\mathcal{A}}'_R$ can simulate the protocol with interactions that are consistent with inputs from the environment and the strategy of the adversary, whereby the two executions are indistinguishable.

6   Conclusion

In this article, we have presented a new construct called ChronoCloak, intended to address the issue of premature exposure of sender's data and privacy-preserving of receiver's interaction. In the context of oblivious digital dissemination, ChronoCloak has the potential to be a viable integrated solution to mitigate premature disclosure. As opposed to its existing counterparts, the proposed ChronoCloak is based on an integrated model and does not require a time server. Essentially, ChronoCloak enables a sender to transmit secrets through a puzzle that must be solved via lengthy computation. By solving the puzzle, only a subset of the secrets is revealed to the receiver, which is oblivious to the sender. Moreover, the receiver may outsource the computation (with public verification), but only the intended recipient is able to retrieve a subset of secrets using the solution to the puzzle. In this work, we define an ideal functionality for ChronoCloak and present a protocol to implement this functionality in the random oracle model by integrating an ideal OT functionality with a time lock-like function.

Acknowledgments. We sincerely thank the anonymous reviewers for their valuable comments and thoughtful suggestions.

References

1. Abusalah, H., Kamath, C., Klein, K., Pietrzak, K., Walter, M.: Reversible proofs of sequential work. In: Ishai, Y., Rijmen, V. (eds.) EUROCRYPT 2019. LNCS, vol. 11477, pp. 277–291. Springer, Cham (2019). https://doi.org/10.1007/978-3-030-17656-3_10
2. Alamati, N., De Feo, L., Montgomery, H., Patranabis, S.: Cryptographic group actions and applications. In: Moriai, S., Wang, H. (eds.) ASIACRYPT 2020. LNCS, vol. 12492, pp. 411–439. Springer, Cham (2020). https://doi.org/10.1007/978-3-030-64834-3_14
3. Arapinis, M., Lamprou, N., Zacharias, T.: Astrolabous: a universally composable time-lock encryption scheme. In: Tibouchi, M., Wang, H. (eds.) ASIACRYPT 2021. LNCS, vol. 13091, pp. 398–426. Springer, Cham (2021). https://doi.org/10.1007/978-3-030-92075-3_14
4. Badrinarayanan, S., Masny, D., Mukherjee, P.: Efficient and tight oblivious transfer from PKE with tight multi-user security. In: Applied Cryptography and Network Security - 20th International Conference, ACNS 2022, LNCS, vol. 13269, pp. 626–642. Springer, Cham (2022). https://doi.org/10.1007/978-3-031-09234-3_31
5. Badrinarayanan, S., Masny, D., Mukherjee, P., Patranabis, S., Raghuraman, S., Sarkar, P.: Round-optimal oblivious transfer and MPC from computational CSIDH. In: Boldyreva, A., Kolesnikov, V. (eds.) Public-Key Cryptography - PKC 2023. LNCS, vol. 13940, pp. 376–405. Springer, Cham (2023). https://doi.org/10.1007/978-3-031-31368-4_14
6. Barreto, P., Oliveira, G., Benits, W.: Supersingular isogeny oblivious transfer. IACR Cryptol. ePrint Arch. p. 459 (2018), https://eprint.iacr.org/2018/459
7. Barreto, P.S.L.M., David, B., Dowsley, R., Morozov, K., Nascimento, A.C.A.: A framework for efficient adaptively secure composable oblivious transfer in the ROM. CoRR **abs/1710.08256** (2017). http://arxiv.org/abs/1710.08256
8. Baum, C., David, B., Dowsley, R., Kishore, R., Nielsen, J.B., Oechsner, S.: CRAFT: composable randomness beacons and output-independent abort MPC from time. In: Boldyreva, A., Kolesnikov, V. (eds.) Public-Key Cryptography - PKC 2023. LNCS, vol. 13940, pp. 439–470. Springer, Cham (2023). https://doi.org/10.1007/978-3-031-31368-4_16

9. Baum, C., David, B., Dowsley, R., Nielsen, J.B., Oechsner, S.: TARDIS: a foundation of time-lock puzzles in UC. In: Canteaut, A., Standaert, F.-X. (eds.) EUROCRYPT 2021. LNCS, vol. 12698, pp. 429–459. Springer, Cham (2021). https://doi.org/10.1007/978-3-030-77883-5_15

10. Beullens, W., Kleinjung, T., Vercauteren, F.: CSI-FiSh: efficient isogeny based signatures through class group computations. In: Galbraith, S.D., Moriai, S. (eds.) ASIACRYPT 2019. LNCS, vol. 11921, pp. 227–247. Springer, Cham (2019). https://doi.org/10.1007/978-3-030-34578-5_9

11. Branco, P., Döttling, N., Srinivasan, A.: A framework for statistically sender private OT with optimal rate. In: Handschuh, H., Lysyanskaya, A. (eds.) Advances in Cryptology – CRYPTO 2023. Lecture Notes in Computer Science, vol. 14081, pp. 548–576. Springer, Cham (2023). https://doi.org/10.1007/978-3-031-38557-5_18

12. Canetti, R.: Universally composable security: a new paradigm for cryptographic protocols. In: Proceedings 42nd IEEE Symposium on Foundations of Computer Science, pp. 136–145 (2001). https://doi.org/10.1109/SFCS.2001.959888

13. Canetti, R., Kushilevitz, E., Lindell, Y.: On the limitations of universally composable two-party computation without set-up assumptions. J. Cryptol. **19**(2), 135–167 (2006). https://doi.org/10.1007/s00145-005-0419-9

14. Canetti, R., Sarkar, P., Wang, X.: Efficient and round-optimal oblivious transfer and commitment with adaptive security. In: Moriai, S., Wang, H. (eds.) ASIACRYPT 2020. LNCS, vol. 12493, pp. 277–308. Springer, Cham (2020). https://doi.org/10.1007/978-3-030-64840-4_10

15. Castryck, W., Decru, T.: An efficient key recovery attack on SIDH. In: Hazay, C., Stam, M. (eds.) Advances in Cryptology - EUROCRYPT 2023. LNCS, vol. 14008, pp. 423–447. Springer, Cham (2023). https://doi.org/10.1007/978-3-031-30589-4_15

16. Castryck, W., Lange, T., Martindale, C., Panny, L., Renes, J.: CSIDH: an efficient post-quantum commutative group action. In: Peyrin, T., Galbraith, S. (eds.) Advances in Cryptology - ASIACRYPT 2018. LNCS, vol. 11274, pp. 395–427. Springer, Cham (2018). https://doi.org/10.1007/978-3-030-03332-3_15

17. Chávez-Saab, J., Rodríguez-Henríquez, F., Tibouchi, M.: Verifiable isogeny walks: Towards an isogeny-based postquantum VDF. In: Selected Areas in Cryptography - 28th International Conference, SAC 2021. LNCS, vol. 13203, pp. 441–460. Springer (2021). https://doi.org/10.1007/978-3-030-99277-4_21

18. Chor, B., Goldreich, O., Kushilevitz, E., Sudan, M.: Private information retrieval. In: 36th Annual Symposium on Foundations of Computer Science, Milwaukee, Wisconsin, USA, 23–25 October 1995, pp. 41–50. IEEE Computer Society (1995). https://doi.org/10.1109/SFCS.1995.492461

19. Chou, T., Orlandi, C.: The simplest protocol for oblivious transfer. In: Lauter, K., Rodríguez-Henríquez, F. (eds.) LATINCRYPT 2015. LNCS, vol. 9230, pp. 40–58. Springer, Cham (2015). https://doi.org/10.1007/978-3-319-22174-8_3

20. Cohen, B., Pietrzak, K.: Simple proofs of sequential work. In: Nielsen, J.B., Rijmen, V. (eds.) EUROCRYPT 2018. LNCS, vol. 10821, pp. 451–467. Springer, Cham (2018). https://doi.org/10.1007/978-3-319-78375-8_15

21. Di Crescenzo, G., Ostrovsky, R., Rajagopalan, S.: Conditional oblivious transfer and timed-release encryption. In: Stern, J. (ed.) EUROCRYPT 1999. LNCS, vol. 1592, pp. 74–89. Springer, Heidelberg (1999). https://doi.org/10.1007/3-540-48910-X_6

22. David, B., Dowsley, R., Nascimento, A.C.A.: Universally composable oblivious transfer based on a variant of LPN. In: Gritzalis, D., Kiayias, A., Askoxylakis, I.

(eds.) CANS 2014. LNCS, vol. 8813, pp. 143–158. Springer, Cham (2014). https://doi.org/10.1007/978-3-319-12280-9_10

23. Döttling, N., Garg, S., Hajiabadi, M., Masny, D., Wichs, D.: Two-round oblivious transfer from CDH or LPN. In: Canteaut, A., Ishai, Y. (eds.) EUROCRYPT 2020. LNCS, vol. 12106, pp. 768–797. Springer, Cham (2020). https://doi.org/10.1007/978-3-030-45724-2_26

24. Eldefrawy, K., Jakkamsetti, S., Terner, B., Yung, M.: Standard model time-lock puzzles: defining security and constructing via composition. IACR Cryptol. ePrint Arch, p. 439 (2023). https://eprint.iacr.org/2023/439

25. Ephraim, N., Freitag, C., Komargodski, I., Pass, R.: Continuous verifiable delay functions. In: Canteaut, A., Ishai, Y. (eds.) EUROCRYPT 2020. LNCS, vol. 12107, pp. 125–154. Springer, Cham (2020). https://doi.org/10.1007/978-3-030-45727-3_5

26. Freitag, C., Komargodski, I., Pass, R., Sirkin, N.: Non-malleable time-lock puzzles and applications. In: Nissim, K., Waters, B. (eds.) TCC 2021. LNCS, vol. 13044, pp. 447–479. Springer, Cham (2021). https://doi.org/10.1007/978-3-030-90456-2_15

27. Genç, Z.A., Iovino, V., Rial, A.: The simplest protocol for oblivious transfer revisited. Inf. Process. Lett. **161**, 105975 (2020). https://doi.org/10.1016/J.IPL.2020.105975

28. Hazay, C., Lindell, Y.: Efficient Secure Two-Party Protocols: Techniques and Constructions, 1st edn. Springer-Verlag, Berlin, Heidelberg (2010)

29. Ishai, Y., Prabhakaran, M., Sahai, A.: Founding cryptography on oblivious transfer – efficiently. In: Wagner, D. (ed.) CRYPTO 2008. LNCS, vol. 5157, pp. 572–591. Springer, Heidelberg (2008). https://doi.org/10.1007/978-3-540-85174-5_32

30. Katz, J., Loss, J., Xu, J.: On the security of time-lock puzzles and timed commitments. In: Pass, R., Pietrzak, K. (eds.) TCC 2020. LNCS, vol. 12552, pp. 390–413. Springer, Cham (2020). https://doi.org/10.1007/978-3-030-64381-2_14

31. Lai, Y.-F., Galbraith, S.D., Delpech de Saint Guilhem, C.: Compact, efficient and UC-secure isogeny-based oblivious transfer. In: Canteaut, A., Standaert, F.-X. (eds.) EUROCRYPT 2021. LNCS, vol. 12696, pp. 213–241. Springer, Cham (2021). https://doi.org/10.1007/978-3-030-77870-5_8

32. Lai, Y.F., Galbraith, S.D., de Saint Guilhem, C.D.: Compact, efficient and uc-secure isogeny-based oblivious transfer. Cryptology ePrint Archive, Paper 2020/1012 (2020). https://eprint.iacr.org/2020/1012

33. Lenstra, A.K., Wesolowski, B.: Trustworthy public randomness with sloth, unicorn, and TRX. Int. J. Appl. Cryptogr. **3**(4), 330–343 (2017). https://doi.org/10.1504/IJACT.2017.10010315

34. Li, B., Micciancio, D.: Equational security proofs of oblivious transfer protocols. In: Abdalla, M., Dahab, R. (eds.) PKC 2018. LNCS, vol. 10769, pp. 527–553. Springer, Cham (2018). https://doi.org/10.1007/978-3-319-76578-5_18

35. Loe, A.F., Medley, L., O'Connell, C., Quaglia, E.A.: A practical verifiable delay function and delay encryption scheme. IACR Cryptol. ePrint Arch. p. 1293 (2021). https://eprint.iacr.org/2021/1293

36. Ma, X., Xu, L., Zhang, F.: Oblivious transfer with timed-release receiver privacy. J. Syst. Softw. **84**(3), 460–464 (2011). https://doi.org/10.1016/j.jss.2010.11.886

37. Mahmoody, M., Moran, T., Vadhan, S.P.: Publicly verifiable proofs of sequential work. In: Kleinberg, R.D. (ed.) Innovations in Theoretical Computer Science, ITCS 2013, Berkeley, CA, USA, 9-12 January 2013, pp. 373–388. ACM (2013). https://doi.org/10.1145/2422436.2422479

38. Micciancio, D., Sorrell, J.: Simpler statistically sender private oblivious transfer from ideals of cyclotomic integers. In: Moriai, S., Wang, H. (eds.) ASIACRYPT 2020. LNCS, vol. 12492, pp. 381–407. Springer, Cham (2020). https://doi.org/10.1007/978-3-030-64834-3_13

39. Pietrzak, K.: Simple verifiable delay functions. In: Blum, A. (ed.) 10th Innovations in Theoretical Computer Science Conference, ITCS 2019, 10–12 January 2019, San Diego, California, USA. LIPIcs, vol. 124, pp. 60:1–60:15. Schloss Dagstuhl - Leibniz-Zentrum für Informatik (2019). https://doi.org/10.4230/LIPIcs.ITCS.2019.60

40. Rabin, M.O.: How to exchange secrets with oblivious transfer. Tech. Report. TR-81; Aiken Computation Lab, Harvard University: Cambridge, MA, USA (1981)

41. Rivest, R.L., Shamir, A., Wagner, D.A.: Time-lock puzzles and timed-release crypto. Technical Report, Massachusetts Institute of Technology, USA (1996)

42. de Saint Guilhem, C.D., Orsini, E., Petit, C., Smart, N.P.: Semi-commutative masking: a framework for isogeny-based protocols, with an application to fully secure two-round isogeny-based OT. In: Krenn, S., Shulman, H., Vaudenay, S. (eds.) CANS 2020. LNCS, vol. 12579, pp. 235–258. Springer, Cham (2020). https://doi.org/10.1007/978-3-030-65411-5_12

43. Vitse, V.: Simple oblivious transfer protocols compatible with supersingular isogenies. In: Buchmann, J., Nitaj, A., Rachidi, T. (eds.) AFRICACRYPT 2019. LNCS, vol. 11627, pp. 56–78. Springer, Cham (2019). https://doi.org/10.1007/978-3-030-23696-0_4

44. Wesolowski, B.: Efficient verifiable delay functions. In: Ishai, Y., Rijmen, V. (eds.) EUROCRYPT 2019. LNCS, vol. 11478, pp. 379–407. Springer, Cham (2019). https://doi.org/10.1007/978-3-030-17659-4_13

45. Xu, L., Zhang, F., Tang, S.: Timed-release oblivious transfer. Secur. Commun. Netw. **7**(7), 1138–1149 (2014). https://doi.org/10.1002/sec.845

46. Zawia, A., Hasan, M.A.: A new class of trapdoor verifiable delay functions. In: Jourdan, G.V., Mounier, L., Adams, C., Sèdes, F., Garcia-Alfaro, J. (eds.) Foundations and Practice of Security, pp. 71–87. Springer Nature Switzerland, Cham (2023). https://doi.org/10.1007/978-3-031-30122-3_5

Large-Plaintext Functional Bootstrapping with Small Parameters for BGV Encoding

Yan Xu[1,2], Guizhen Zhu[3], Huaxiong Wang[4], and Li-Ping Wang[1,2](✉)

[1] Key Laboratory of Cyberspace Security Defense, Institute of Information Engineering, CAS, Beijing, China
`wangliping@iie.ac.cn`
[2] School of Cyber Security, University of Chinese Academy of Sciences, Beijing, China
[3] Data Communication and Science Technology Research Institute, Beijing, China
[4] School of Physical and Mathematical Sciences, Nanyang Technological University, Singapore, Singapore

Abstract. Functional bootstrapping refreshes the noise of a ciphertext and computes a function homomorphically. It is commonly used to calculate activation functions in privacy-preserving machine learning. However, existing functional bootstrapping requires enormous parameters to evaluate any function for a BGV ciphertext of a large plaintext. In this paper, we first introduce a basic functional bootstrapping algorithm for small plaintexts, which requires only one run of FHEW-like bootstrapping, while other similar methods require extra costs. Then, we provide a homomorphic digit decomposition algorithm that reduces the number of involved FHEW-like bootstrapping procedures by half compared with the work of Micciancio and Polyakov (ASIACRYPT 2022). Finally, based on our above algorithms, we propose a functional bootstrapping algorithm for BGV ciphertexts of large plaintexts that supports 64-bit plaintexts when $N = 4096$, where N is the largest dimension used. Compared with the latest BGV/BFV-based functional bootstrapping, for a 12-bit plaintext, the bit size of the largest ciphertext modulus is reduced by 867 bits, N is reduced by a factor of 16, and the computational cost is reduced by a factor of 80.

Keywords: Fully homomorphic encryption · Functional bootstrapping · BGV · FHEW

1 Introduction

Fully homomorphic encryption (FHE) is one of the most popular choices for secure cloud computing, due to its ability to perform arbitrary computations on encrypted data without knowing the secret decryption key. FHE schemes resort to noisy ciphertexts for security reasons, but the noise increases with each homomorphic operation, eventually destroying the underlying message. Gentry introduced the bootstrapping technique to reduce the noise and hence constructed

N. Mouha and N. Nikiforakis (Eds.): ISC 2024, LNCS 15257, pp. 252–272, 2025.
https://doi.org/10.1007/978-3-031-75757-0_13

the first plausible FHE scheme [17]. Since the breakthrough work, significant progress has been made in promoting FHE toward practicality [5,6,9,11,16,18].

Ducas and Micciancio further proposed functional bootstrapping, which refreshes the noise of a ciphertext and homomorphically calculates a function at the same time [15]. The bootstrapping of the FHEW scheme [15] and its improvement [11] compute an NAND gate. Currently, most functional bootstrapping algorithms are constructed using the FHEW scheme. In [4,12], an antiperiodic function was evaluated using the FHEW-like bootstrapping. In [7,13,14,20,24,25,29], the algorithms were improved to support larger plaintexts and any functions by combining multiple FHEW-like bootstrapping procedures. Functional bootstrapping is commonly applied to compute non-polynomial functions such as the activation functions of machine learning. Although the BGV, BFV, and CKKS schemes also support evaluating non-polynomial functions homomorphically via polynomial approximation [10,22], the cost grows exponentially with the desired precision [28]. Higher precision with less overhead is achievable through functional bootstrapping.

Privacy-preserving machine learning sometimes needs to compute polynomial functions, and the BGV scheme has many advantages over other popular FHE schemes for homomorphic calculations of polynomials. The above FHEW-like functional bootstrapping algorithms do not support efficient batching, and the CKKS scheme has noisy decryption results. Both BFV and BGV support exact homomorphic calculations and batching over finite fields. However, previous studies have shown that BGV slightly outperforms BFV in the homomorphic computation of deep circuits and large plaintexts [23], and this advantage is pronounced in the homomorphic computation of deep neural networks [27].

Therefore, combining functional bootstrapping and the BGV scheme is highly valuable. In this regard, we mainly consider how to evaluate non-polynomial functions for BGV ciphertexts using functional bootstrapping. In a BGV ciphertext, the message is encoded into the least significant bits (LSBs), and the plaintext modulus and the ciphertext modulus are often coprime. The BGV ciphertext can be transformed into a ciphertext where the message is encoded in the most significant bits (MSBs), using the transformation between LSB and MSB encodings of [3]. Then functional bootstrapping algorithms, such as [24,25], can be used to compute any non-polynomial function on this ciphertext.

However, we recommend using a BGV-based functional bootstrapping algorithm directly on the BGV ciphertext to compute non-polynomial functions. Because when the error and the plaintext are small enough, this method requires only one run of the FHEW-like bootstrapping whereas previous similar methods required extra costs, such as more runs of the FHEW-like bootstrapping [14,24,25,29], extra BGV/BFV homomorphic multiplications [13], or losing a single-bit precision of the plaintext [4,12]. Additionally, this advantage becomes more apparent when using the BGV-based functional bootstrapping to decompose large plaintexts homomorphically. Furthermore, some useful cryptosystems heavily rely on running bootstrapping directly on the BGV ciphertexts, such as the deniable homomorphic encryption scheme [1]. So, we propose new BGV-based functional bootstrapping algorithms that directly refresh BGV ciphertexts and meanwhile homomorphically compute any functions. A BGV/BFV-based functional bootstrapping is also proposed in [26], but our method is better when processing a small number of plaintexts due to our smaller parameters.

Our Contributions. Firstly, we introduce a basic functional bootstrapping algorithm for BGV ciphertexts of small plaintext modulus. The algorithm is based on the structure of the BGV ciphertexts and follows the FHEW bootstrapping framework. It can directly process a BGV ciphertext to reduce its noise and compute any function on its plaintext. Unlike previous functional bootstrapping algorithms for any functions, this algorithm runs the FHEW-like bootstrapping only once without extra costs.

Then, we provide a homomorphic digit decomposition algorithm for BGV. This algorithm employs our basic functional bootstrapping to decompose the plaintext of a BGV ciphertext into some smaller integers homomorphically. In addition, this algorithm reduces the number of FHEW-like bootstrapping operations by about half compared with the homomorphic digit decomposition of [25]. It also enables its outputs to support more homomorphic operations compared with the HomDecomp-Reduce of [29]. Besides, this algorithm can support 32-bit and 64-bit plaintexts when the dimension of bootstrapping keys, N, is 2^{11} and 2^{12} respectively, whereas [25,29] cannot.

Next, we propose a functional bootstrapping algorithm for BGV ciphertexts of large plaintexts. This algorithm combines our homomorphic digit decomposition and the tree-based method of [20]. In this algorithm, parameters and costs are much smaller than those in [26]. For instance, the bit size of the largest ciphertext modulus is reduced by 867 bits and the computational cost is reduced by a factor of 80 when processing an LWE ciphertext of a 12-bit plaintext. Besides, this algorithm allows the bit size of the plaintext to be 64 bits, whereas [26] cannot. As for the packing procedure in this algorithm, we leverage the structural properties of the test polynomials used in this algorithm as well as the optimization principle of [20] to improve the method of [11]. Let $t = B_t^{\ell_t}$ be the plaintext modulus where $B_t, \ell_t \in \mathbb{Z}^+$. Then, although we expand the size of the packing key by B_t times, the computational cost of packing is reduced by a factor of $O(\frac{\log N}{B_t})$, and the noise caused by packing is reduced by a factor of $\frac{N}{B_t}$.

Organization. This paper is organized as follows. In Sect. 2, we describe some preliminaries on the BGV scheme and the GSW scheme. In Sect. 3, we introduce a new homomorphic digit decomposition algorithm, a new packing method, and new functional bootstrapping algorithms for the BGV scheme. In Sect. 4, we offer some parameter sets for our algorithms and compare them with previous works. We conclude the paper in Sect. 5.

2 Preliminaries

Notations. We denote the set of integers by $\mathbb{Z}$, and its quotient ring by $\mathbb{Z}_q = \mathbb{Z}/q\mathbb{Z}$ with $\left[-\frac{q}{2}, \frac{q}{2}\right)$ as the representative interval. We set $\mathcal{R} = \mathbb{Z}[X]/(X^N+1)$ and $\mathcal{R}_q = \mathcal{R}/q\mathcal{R}$ where $N \in \mathbb{Z}^+$ is a power of two. For $a \in \mathcal{R}$, define $[a]_q = a \mod q$ with coefficients reduced into the range $\left[-\frac{q}{2}, \frac{q}{2}\right)$. We denote column vectors by bold lowercase letters, e.g. $\boldsymbol{a}$, and denote matrices by bold capital letters, e.g. $\boldsymbol{A}$. We define $[n] = \{0, 1, \ldots, n-1\}$ and use $\langle .,. \rangle$ to denote the inner product operation. We also use $(a_0, \ldots, a_{n-1})$ or $(a_i)_{i \in [n]}$ to denote a column vector. For an n-dimensional vector $\boldsymbol{a} \in \mathcal{R}_q^n$, the i-th component of $\boldsymbol{a}$ is written as $a_i = \sum_{j=0}^{N-1} a_{i,j} X^j \in \mathcal{R}_q$, where $a_{i,j} \in \mathbb{Z}_q$. If D is a set, then $a \overset{\$}{\leftarrow} D$ denotes sampling a uniformly from D. If χ is a probability distribution, then $a \overset{\$}{\leftarrow} \chi$ denotes sampling a according to χ. The variance of a random variable x is represented by $\mathsf{Var}(x)$. $\lfloor . \rceil$, $\lfloor . \rfloor$, and $\lceil . \rceil$ denote the rounding, floor, and ceiling functions, respectively. For $a = \sum_{i=0}^{N-1} a_i X^i \in \mathcal{R}$, we define its norm as $\|a\| = \max_{i \in [N]} |a_i|$ and define its variance as $\mathsf{Var}(a) = \max_{i \in [N]} \mathsf{Var}(a_i)$. For $\boldsymbol{a} = (a_i)_{i \in [n]} \in \mathcal{R}^n$, define $\mathsf{Var}(\boldsymbol{a}) = \max_{i \in [n]} \mathsf{Var}(a_i)$. The definition of a gadget matrix is as follows.

Definition 1 (Gadget Matrix). *The gadget vector is defined as* $\boldsymbol{g} = (1, B, \ldots, B^{\ell-1}) \in \mathbb{Z}^\ell$, *where* $B \in \mathbb{Z}^+$ *is its base,* $\ell \in \mathbb{Z}^+$. *The gadget matrix is defined as* $\boldsymbol{G} = \boldsymbol{I}_2 \otimes \boldsymbol{g} \in \mathbb{Z}^{2\ell \times 2}$, *where* $\otimes$ *denotes the Kronecker product. For any* $k, q \in \mathbb{Z}^+$ *and* $\boldsymbol{x} \in \mathcal{R}_q^k$, *define* $\mathsf{G}^{-1}(\boldsymbol{x}) = \boldsymbol{y} \in \mathcal{R}_B^{k\ell}$ *such that* $x_i = \sum_{j=0}^{\ell-1} B^j \cdot y_{i \cdot \ell + j}$ *for* $i \in [k]$ *where* $\ell = \lceil \log_B q \rceil$, *and use* σ_B^2 *to denote the upper bound of* $\mathsf{Var}(\boldsymbol{y})$.

Throughout the paper, we set a plaintext modulus $t = B_t^{\ell_t}$ where $B_t, \ell_t \in \mathbb{Z}^+$, and we let t and N coprime. Let $B \in \mathbb{Z}^+$ denote the gadget base. Let λ denote the computational security parameter, implying a λ-bit security level. All logarithms are base 2, and all calculations are carried out over $\mathcal{R}$ unless otherwise noted.

2.1 The BGV Scheme

The following is the BGV scheme [6] and related algorithms written in a style suitable for our algorithms. Let χ be a zero-centered discrete Gaussian distribution over $\mathcal{R}$. Let $q \in \mathbb{Z}^+$ be a ciphertext modulus. We sample a secret key $\boldsymbol{s}' \overset{\$}{\leftarrow} \mathcal{R}_q^n$ and set $\boldsymbol{s} = (-\boldsymbol{s}', 1)$. For a plaintext $\mu \in \mathcal{R}_t$, the BGV encryption (see Algorithm 1) yields a BGV ciphertext $\boldsymbol{c} \in \mathcal{R}_q^{n+1}$ of μ under the key $\boldsymbol{s}'$ with an error e. Note that $\boldsymbol{c}$ is in $\mathcal{R}_q^2$ when $n = 1$, and $\boldsymbol{c}$ is in $\mathbb{Z}_q^{n+1}$ when $N = 1$. In addition, we can decrypt $\boldsymbol{c}$ by computing $[[\langle \boldsymbol{c}, \boldsymbol{s} \rangle]_q]_t$. For simplicity, we only consider the symmetric version, while the public key version can be found in [6]. Lemma 1 shows the correctness of Algorithm 1, and its proof is given in Appendix A.1.

Lemma 1 (BGV Encryption). *For a plaintext* $\mu \in \mathcal{R}_t$, *a secret key* $\boldsymbol{s}' \overset{\$}{\leftarrow} \mathcal{R}_q^n$ *and* $n, q, t \in \mathbb{Z}^+$, $\mathsf{BGV.Enc}(\mu, \boldsymbol{s}', n, q, t)$ *outputs a BGV ciphertext* $\boldsymbol{c} \in \mathcal{R}_q^{n+1}$ *such that* $\langle \boldsymbol{c}, \boldsymbol{s} \rangle = \mu + t \cdot e \pmod{q}$ *where* $e \in \mathcal{R}$ *is the error.*

For the secret keys used in this paper, set $z = (-z', 1)$ and $\tilde{z} = (-\tilde{z}', 1)$ where $z' = \sum_{i=0}^{N-1} z_i' X^i \in \mathcal{R}$, $\tilde{z}' = (z_i')_{i\in[N]}$ and z_i' is chosen from a zero-centered discrete Gaussian distribution over $\mathbb{Z}$ with variance σ_z^2 for $i \in [N]$, and set $s = (-s', 1)$ where $s' = (s_i')_{i\in[n]} \in \{0, 1, -1\}^n$ and the Hamming weight of s' is $h_s \in \mathbb{Z}^+$.

As for homomorphic operations, homomorphic addition is the addition of BGV ciphertexts, and homomorphic multiplication of two BGV ciphertexts includes tensor product and relinearization [6]. Moreover, we can get a ciphertext of $d \cdot \mu$ by $[d \cdot c]_q = ([d \cdot c_0]_q, \ldots, [d \cdot c_n]_q)$ for $d \in \mathcal{R}$.

Modulus switching [6,19] (see Algorithm 2) is capable of changing the modulus of a ciphertext and is usually used after each homomorphic multiplication to reduce noise in the BGV scheme. Lemma 2 shows the correctness of Algorithm 2, and its proof is given in Appendix A.2.

Lemma 2 (Modulus Switching). *Adapt the notations of Algorithm 2. Let $q' \mid q$ and $q = q' = 1 \pmod{t}$. Let c be a BGV ciphertext such that $\langle c, s \rangle = \mu + t \cdot e \pmod{q}$. Assume $|[\langle c, s \rangle]_q| < \frac{q}{2} - \frac{qt(h_s+1)}{2q'}$. If $c_{\mathsf{ms}} \leftarrow \mathsf{MS}(c, q, q', t)$, then $c_{\mathsf{ms}} \in \mathbb{Z}_{q'}^{n+1}$ satisfies $\langle c_{\mathsf{ms}}, s \rangle = \mu + t \cdot e_{\mathsf{ms}} \pmod{q'}$ and $\mathsf{Var}([\langle c_{\mathsf{ms}}, s \rangle]_{q'}) \le (\frac{q'}{q})^2 \cdot \mathsf{Var}([\langle c, s \rangle]_q) + (\frac{q'}{q})^2 \cdot \mathsf{Var}(\langle \delta, s \rangle)$. We set $\mathsf{Var}(\delta) \le \frac{t^2 q^2}{12q'^2}$. Then $\mathsf{Var}([\langle c_{\mathsf{ms}}, s \rangle]_{q'}) \le (\frac{q'}{q})^2 \cdot \mathsf{Var}([\langle c, s \rangle]_q) + \frac{t^2(h_s+1)}{12}$.*

We use SampleExtract of [11] to extract a BGV ciphertext of μ_0 from a BGV ciphertext of $\mu = \sum_{i=0}^{N-1} \mu_i X^i$ (see Algorithm 3). Lemma 3 shows the correctness, and its proof is given in Appendix A.3.

Lemma 3 (Extraction). *Adapt the notations of Algorithm 3. Let c be a BGV ciphertext satisfying $\langle c, z \rangle = \mu + t \cdot e \pmod{q}$ where $\mu = \sum_{i=0}^{N-1} \mu_i X^i$ and $e = \sum_{i=0}^{N-1} e_i X^i$. Then, $\mathsf{Extract}(c, q)$ outputs a BGV ciphertext $c' \in \mathbb{Z}_q^{N+1}$ satisfying $\langle c', \tilde{z} \rangle = \mu_0 + t \cdot e_0 \pmod{q}$.*

Key switching [6] (see Algorithm 5) changes the secret key of a ciphertext while keeping the plaintext of the ciphertext unchanged. Lemma 4 shows the correctness, and its proof is given in Appendix A.4.

Lemma 4 (Key Switching). *Adapt the notations of Algorithm 5. Let c satisfy $\langle c, \tilde{z} \rangle = \mu + t \cdot e \pmod{q}$. Let $KSK \leftarrow \mathsf{KSKeyGen}(\tilde{z}', s', \ell, q, t)$ satisfy $\langle ksk_{i\ell+j}, s \rangle = B^j z_i' + t \cdot e_{i\ell+j} \pmod{q}$ for $i \in [N]$ and $j \in [\ell]$ where $\ell = \lceil \log_B q \rceil$. If $c_{\mathsf{ks}} \leftarrow \mathsf{KS}(c, KSK, q)$, then $\langle c_{\mathsf{ks}}, s \rangle = \mu + t \cdot (e + e_{\mathsf{ks}}) \pmod{q}$ where $e_{\mathsf{ks}} = -\sum_{i=0}^{N-1} \sum_{j=0}^{\ell-1} \bar{c}_{i\ell+j} \cdot e_{i\ell+j}$. Set $\mathsf{Var}(e_i) \le \sigma_{\mathsf{ks}}^2$ for $i \in [N\ell]$. Then $\mathsf{Var}(e_{\mathsf{ks}}) \le \ell N \sigma_B^2 \sigma_{\mathsf{ks}}^2$.*

Algorithm 1. BGV Encryption

1: **procedure** BGV.Enc($\mu \in \mathcal{R}_t, s', n, q, t$)
2:     $a \xleftarrow{\$} \mathcal{R}_q^n, e \xleftarrow{\$} \chi$
3:     $c \leftarrow ([a]_q, [\langle a, s' \rangle + t \cdot e + \mu]_q)$
4:     **return** $c \in \mathcal{R}_q^{n+1}$

Algorithm 2. Modulus Switching

1: **procedure** MS($c \in \mathbb{Z}_q^{n+1}, q, q', t$)
2:     $x \leftarrow \frac{q}{q'}$
3:     $\delta \leftarrow t \cdot [-t^{-1} \cdot c]_x$
4:     $c_{\mathsf{ms}} \leftarrow [\frac{1}{x} \cdot (c + \delta)]_{q'}$
5:     **return** $c_{\mathsf{ms}} \in \mathbb{Z}_{q'}^{n+1}$

Algorithm 3. Extraction

1: **procedure** Extract($c = (\sum_{i=0}^{N-1} c_{0,i} X^i, \sum_{i=0}^{N-1} c_{1,i} X^i) \in \mathcal{R}_q^2, q$)
2:     $c_0' \leftarrow c_{0,0}$
3:     **for** $i = 1$ to $N - 1$ **do**
4:         $c_i' \leftarrow [-c_{0,N-i}]_q$
5:     $c_N' \leftarrow c_{1,0}$
6:     **return** $c' = (c_0', \ldots, c_N') \in \mathbb{Z}_q^{N+1}$

2.2 The GSW Scheme

The following is the (Ring-)GSW scheme used in our bootstrapping. The description is written in BGV style. Algorithm 6 presents the GSW encryption, and Algorithm 7 describes the external product of a BGV ciphertext and a GSW ciphertext. For variance estimation, similar to [11], we assume that all the coefficients of the errors of BGV or GSW ciphertexts that occur in all the linear combinations we consider are independent. Lemma 5 and Lemma 6 show the correctness of Algorithm 6 and Algorithm 7, and their proofs are given in Appendix A.5 and Appendix A.6, respectively.

Lemma 5 (GSW Encryption). *For a plaintext $\mu \in \{0,1\}$, a ciphertext modulus $Q \in \mathbb{Z}^+$, a secret key $z' \in \mathcal{R}$, $t \in \mathbb{Z}^+$ and $\ell = \lceil \log_B Q \rceil$, GSW.Enc($\mu, z', \ell, Q, t$) outputs a GSW ciphertext $C \in \mathcal{R}_Q^{2\ell \times 2}$ satisfying $Cz = te + \mu Gz$ (mod Q) where $z = (-z', 1)$, e is the error of C.*

Lemma 6 (External Product). *Adapt the notations of Algorithm 7. Let c be a BGV ciphertext satisfying $c^\top z = \mu' + te'$ (mod Q). Let $\ell = \lceil \log_B Q \rceil$. Let C be a GSW ciphertext satisfying $Cz = te + \mu Gz$ (mod Q) where $\mu \in \{0,1\}$. Then ExtMul(c, C, Q) outputs a BGV ciphertext $c_{\mathsf{mult}} \in \mathcal{R}_Q^2$ satisfying $c_{\mathsf{mult}}^\top z = \mu' \cdot \mu + t \cdot e_{\mathsf{mult}}$ (mod Q) where $e_{\mathsf{mult}} = \mu e' + x^\top e$. Furthermore, let $\mathsf{Var}(x) \leq \sigma_B^2$ and $\mathsf{Var}(e) \leq \sigma^2$. Then $\mathsf{Var}(e_{\mathsf{mult}}) \leq \mathsf{Var}(e') + 2\ell N \sigma_B^2 \sigma^2$.*

3 Functional Bootstrapping for BGV

In this section, given a BGV ciphertext of a message $\mu \in \mathbb{Z}_t$, we attempt to calculate a BGV ciphertext of $f(\mu)$ for any function $f : \mathbb{Z}_t \to \mathbb{Z}_t$. For small plaintexts, following the FHEW bootstrapping framework, we present a basic

Algorithm 4. Key-Switching Key Generation
1: **procedure** KSKeyGen($\tilde{z}' = (z'_i)_{i \in [N]}, s', \ell, q, t$)
2:     **for** $i = 0$ to $N - 1$ **do**
3:         **for** $j = 0$ to $\ell - 1$ **do**
4:             $ksk_{i\ell+j} \leftarrow \text{BGV.Enc}(B^j z'_i, s', n, q, t)$
5:     **return** $\boldsymbol{KSK} = (\boldsymbol{ksk}_i)_{i \in [N\ell]}$

Algorithm 5. Key Switching
1: **procedure** KS($\boldsymbol{c} = (c_i)_{i \in [N+1]} \in \mathbb{Z}_q^{N+1}, \boldsymbol{KSK} = (\boldsymbol{ksk}_i)_{i \in [N\ell]}, , q$)
2:     $\bar{\boldsymbol{c}} = (\bar{c}_i)_{i \in [N\ell]} \leftarrow \mathsf{G}^{-1}((c_0, \ldots, c_{N-1}))$
3:     $c_{\mathsf{ks}} \leftarrow [(\boldsymbol{0}, c_N) - \sum_{i=0}^{N-1} \sum_{j=0}^{\ell-1} \bar{c}_{i\ell+j} \cdot \boldsymbol{ksk}_{i\ell+j}]_q$
4:     **return** $c_{\mathsf{ks}} \in \mathbb{Z}_q^{n+1}$

functional bootstrapping algorithm to achieve this task. For larger plaintexts, we first introduce a new homomorphic digit decomposition algorithm to decompose μ into smaller integers $\{\mu_0, \ldots, \mu_{\ell_t - 1}\}$ such that $\mu = \sum_{i=0}^{\ell_t - 1} B_t^i \cdot \mu_i$ where $t = B_t^{\ell_t}$ and $\mu_i \in \mathbb{Z}_{B_t}$ for $i \in [\ell_t]$. Next, we propose a new packing algorithm to homomorphically construct the test polynomials required in our functional bootstrapping, utilizing the ciphertexts of the coefficients of the test polynomials. Then, combining the above algorithms, we introduce a new functional bootstrapping algorithm for larger plaintexts and analyze its noise growth and its success probability.

3.1 Basic Functional Bootstrapping

Given a BGV ciphertext $\boldsymbol{c} \in \mathbb{Z}_{2N}^{n+1}$ of a small message $\mu \in \mathbb{Z}_t$ such that $[\langle \boldsymbol{c}, \boldsymbol{s} \rangle]_{2N} = \mu + te$, we construct a basic BGV-based functional bootstrapping algorithm to compute a BGV ciphertext of $f(\mu)$ for any function $f : \mathbb{Z}_t \to \mathbb{Z}_t$, following the FHEW bootstrapping framework.

As stated in [20], for an input ciphertext whose plaintext is encoded in the MSBs, only an antiperiodic function can be computed by directly performing one run of FHEW-like bootstrapping, and thus extra costs are needed to compute an arbitrary function [13,14,24,25,29]. However, we consider inputting a BGV ciphertext whose plaintext is encoded in the LSBs. If the error of the input

Algorithm 6. GSW Encryption
1: **procedure** GSW.Enc($\mu \in \{0, 1\}, z', \ell, Q, t$)
2:     **for** $i = 0$ to $2\ell - 1$ **do**
3:         $\boldsymbol{y}_i \leftarrow \text{BGV.Enc}(0, z', 1, Q, t)$
4:     $\boldsymbol{Y} \leftarrow (\boldsymbol{y}_0^\top, \ldots, \boldsymbol{y}_{2\ell-1}^\top)$
5:     $\boldsymbol{C} \leftarrow [\boldsymbol{Y} + \mu \cdot \boldsymbol{G}]_Q$ where $\boldsymbol{G} = \boldsymbol{I}_2 \otimes (1, B, \ldots, B^{\ell-1})$
6:     **return** $\boldsymbol{C} \in \mathcal{R}_Q^{2\ell \times 2}$

Algorithm 7. External Product

1: **procedure** ExtMul($c \in \mathcal{R}_Q^2, C \in \mathcal{R}_Q^{2\ell \times 2}, Q$)
2:     $x \leftarrow \mathsf{G}^{-1}(c)$
3:     $c_{\mathsf{mult}}^\top \leftarrow [x^\top C]_Q$
4:     **return** $c_{\mathsf{mult}} \in \mathcal{R}_Q^2$

Algorithm 8. Bootstrapping Key Generation

1: **procedure** BootKeyGen($s' = (s_i')_{i \in [n]}, z', \ell, Q, t$)
2:     **for** $i = 0$ to $n - 1$ **do**
3:         **if** $s_i' = 1$ **then**
4:             $s_{i,0}' \leftarrow 1, s_{i,1}' \leftarrow 0$
5:         **else if** $s_i' = -1$ **then**
6:             $s_{i,0}' \leftarrow 0, s_{i,1}' \leftarrow 1$
7:         **else if** $s_i' = 0$ **then**
8:             $s_{i,0}' \leftarrow 0, s_{i,1}' \leftarrow 0$
9:         $\boldsymbol{BK}_{2i} \leftarrow \mathsf{GSW.Enc}(s_{i,0}', z', \ell, Q, t)$
10:       $\boldsymbol{BK}_{2i+1} \leftarrow \mathsf{GSW.Enc}(s_{i,1}', z', \ell, Q, t)$
11:     **return** $\boldsymbol{BK} = (\boldsymbol{BK}_i)_{i \in [2n]}$

---

ciphertext is small enough, then we need only one run of FHEW-like bootstrapping without extra costs to compute any function.

As shown in Algorithm 9, our basic BGV-based functional bootstrapping algorithm includes computing $\sum_{i=0}^{N-1} u_i X^i = tv X^{-\frac{N}{2} - [\langle c, s \rangle]_{2N}}$, where the test polynomial tv is designed as $\sum_{i=0}^{N-1} f([i - \frac{N}{2}]_t) X^i$ to make $u_0 = f(\mu)$, and then extracting u_0 homomorphically. The bootstrapping key is constructed by BGV-based GSW ciphertexts, as shown in Algorithm 8, and we use σ_{bk}^2 to denote the upper bound of the error variance of the key. Let bootstrapping key $\boldsymbol{BK} \leftarrow$ BootKeyGen(s', z', ℓ, Q, t) where $\ell = \lceil \log_B Q \rceil$. Theorem 1 shows the correctness of Algorithm 9, and its proof is given in Appendix A.7.

Theorem 1. *Let $c \in \mathbb{Z}_{2N}^{n+1}$ be a BGV ciphertext such that $[\langle c, s \rangle]_{2N} = \mu + t \cdot e$ and $|[\langle c, s \rangle]_{2N}| < \frac{N}{2}$. Let $v \in \mathcal{R}_Q^2$ be a BGV ciphertext of $tv = \sum_{i=0}^{N-1} f([i - \frac{N}{2}]_t) X^i \in \mathcal{R}$ satisfying $\langle v, z \rangle = tv + t \cdot e_{\mathsf{tv}} \pmod{Q}$. Then, $\mathsf{BasicFB}(c, \boldsymbol{BK}, v, Q)$*

Algorithm 9. Basic Functional Bootstrapping

1: **procedure** BasicFB($c = (c_i)_{i \in [n+1]} \in \mathbb{Z}_{2N}^{n+1}, (\boldsymbol{BK}_i)_{i \in [2n]}, v \in \mathcal{R}^2, Q$)
2:     $c_{\mathsf{br}} \leftarrow [X^{-c_n - \frac{N}{2}} \cdot v]_Q$
3:     **for** $i = 0$ to $n - 1$ **do**
4:         $C \leftarrow [G + (X^{c_i} - 1) \cdot \boldsymbol{BK}_{2i} + (X^{-c_i} - 1) \cdot \boldsymbol{BK}_{2i+1}]_Q$
5:         $c_{\mathsf{br}} \leftarrow \mathsf{ExtMul}(c_{\mathsf{br}}, C, Q)$
6:     $c_{\mathsf{out}} \leftarrow \mathsf{Extract}(c_{\mathsf{br}}, Q)$
7:     **return** $c_{\mathsf{out}} \in \mathbb{Z}_Q^{N+1}$

---

outputs a BGV ciphertext $c_{\text{out}} \in \mathbb{Z}_Q^{N+1}$ that satisfies $\langle c_{\text{out}}, \tilde{z} \rangle = f(\mu) + t \cdot e_{\text{out}} \pmod{Q}$, where $\text{Var}(e_{\text{out}}) \leq \text{Var}(e_{\text{tv}}) + 8n\ell N \sigma_B^2 \sigma_{\text{bk}}^2$.

If the modulus of the input BGV ciphertext c is q satisfying $q = 2N = 1 \pmod{t}$ and $2N \mid q$, then we use MS to change the modulus to $2N$. But when t is very large, we need a very large N by this method, as $N > \frac{t}{2}$ is required. In addition, the asymptotic cost of Algorithm 9 is $O(\ell n N \log N)$ which is greatly affected by N, when employing Fast Fourier Transformations (FFTs). To reduce the complexity, we will introduce another method in Sect. 3.4 that only requires $N > \frac{B_t}{2}$ where $B_t < t$.

3.2   Homomorphic Digit Decomposition

For a BGV ciphertext $c \in \mathbb{Z}_q^{n+1}$ of a large message $\mu \in \mathbb{Z}_t$ with a large ciphertext modulus q, we construct a new homomorphic digit decomposition algorithm to get BGV ciphertexts of smaller integers $\{\mu_0, \ldots, \mu_{\ell_t-1}\}$ such that $\mu = \sum_{i=0}^{\ell_t-1} B_t^i \cdot \mu_i$ where $t = B_t^{\ell_t}$ and $\mu_i \in \mathbb{Z}_{B_t}$ for $i \in [\ell_t]$.

The idea behind our homomorphic digit decomposition algorithm is as follows: For ease of description, define the phase of a BGV ciphertext $c \in \mathbb{Z}_q^{n+1}$ under the secret key s as $\varphi = [\langle c, s \rangle]_q$, and consider the decomposition from the perspective of phases. For a phase $\varphi_0 = \mu + t e_0 = \sum_{i=0}^{\ell_t-1} B_t^i \mu_i + B_t^{\ell_t} e_0 \pmod{q}$ with an error e_0, view $\sum_{i=1}^{\ell_t-1} B_t^{i-1} \mu_i + B_t^{\ell_t-1} e_0$ as an error e'. Thus, $\varphi_0 = \mu_0 + B_t e' \pmod{q}$. Then, use MS to change the ciphertext modulus of φ_0 from q to $2N$, obtaining a phase $\varphi_0' = \mu_0 + B_t e_0' \pmod{2N}$ with an error e_0'. Next, employ BasicFB to compute a function $f(x) = [x]_{B_t}$ on φ_0' with bootstrapping keys whose plaintext moduli are B_t^2, obtaining a phase $u_0 = \mu_0 + B_t^2 e_{\text{out},0} \pmod{q}$ with an error $e_{\text{out},0}$. After that, compute $\varphi_1 = [(\varphi_0 - u_0)B_t^{-1}]_q$. So, $\varphi_1 = e' - B_t e_{\text{out},0} = \sum_{i=1}^{\ell_t-1} B_t^{i-1} \mu_i + B_t^{\ell_t-1} e_1 \pmod{q}$, where $e_1 = e_0 - B_t^{2-\ell_t} e_{\text{out},0}$. Perform the above MS and BasicFB on φ_1 again to obtain a phase $u_1 = \mu_1 + B_t^2 e_{\text{out},1} \pmod{q}$ with an error $e_{\text{out},1}$. By analogy, we get phases $\{u_j\}_{j \in [\ell_t]}$ where $u_j = \mu_j + B_t^2 e_{\text{out},j} \pmod{q}$ with an error $e_{\text{out},j}$ for $j \in [\ell_t]$.

Based on this idea, we propose a new homomorphic digit decomposition algorithm for BGV ciphertexts, as shown in Algorithm 10. Theorem 2 shows the correctness and the noise growth of Algorithm 10.

Theorem 2. *Adapt the notations of Algorithm 10. Let $c \in \mathbb{Z}_q^{n+1}$ be a BGV ciphertext such that $[\langle c, s \rangle]_q = \mu + te$ where $\mu = \sum_{j=0}^{\ell_t-1} B_t^j \mu_j \in \mathbb{Z}_t$ and $\text{Var}(e) \leq E_{\text{in}}$. Let $BK \leftarrow \text{BootKeyGen}(s', z', \ell, q, B_t^2)$ and $KSK \leftarrow \text{KSKeyGen}(\tilde{z}', s', \ell, q, B_t^2)$ where $\ell = \lceil \log_B q \rceil$. If $\{c_{\text{out},j}\}_{j \in [\ell_t]} \leftarrow \text{Decomp}(c, BK, KSK, q)$, $2N \mid q$, $q = 1 \pmod{t}$, $2N = 1 \pmod{B_t}$,*

$$|[\langle c_j', s \rangle]_q| < \frac{q}{2} \cdot \left(1 - \frac{B_t(h_s + 1)}{2N}\right) \text{ for } j \in [\ell_t], \tag{1}$$

$$|[\langle c_{\text{ms},j}, s \rangle]_{2N}| < \frac{N}{2} \text{ for } j \in [\ell_t], \tag{2}$$

Algorithm 10. Homomorphic Digit Decomposition

1: **procedure** Decomp($c \in \mathbb{Z}_q^{n+1}, \boldsymbol{BK}, \boldsymbol{KSK}, q$)
2:      $c_0' \leftarrow c, \; v \leftarrow (0, \sum_{i=0}^{N-1} [i - \frac{N}{2}]_{B_t} X^i)$
3:      **for** $j = 0$ to $\ell_t - 2$ **do**
4:          $c_{\mathsf{ms},j} \leftarrow \mathsf{MS}(c_j', q, 2N, B_t)$
5:          $c_{\mathsf{boot},j} \leftarrow \mathsf{BasicFB}(c_{\mathsf{ms},j}, \boldsymbol{BK}, v, q)$
6:          $c_{\mathsf{out},j} \leftarrow \mathsf{KS}(c_{\mathsf{boot},j}, \boldsymbol{KSK}, q)$
7:          $c_{j+1}' \leftarrow (c_j' - c_{\mathsf{out},j}) \cdot B_t^{-1} \bmod q$
8:      $c_{\mathsf{ms},\ell_t-1} \leftarrow \mathsf{MS}(c_{\ell_t-1}', q, 2N, B_t)$
9:      $c_{\mathsf{boot},\ell_t-1} \leftarrow \mathsf{BasicFB}(c_{\mathsf{ms},\ell_t-1}, \boldsymbol{BK}, v, q)$
10:     $c_{\mathsf{out},\ell_t-1} \leftarrow \mathsf{KS}(c_{\mathsf{boot},\ell_t-1}, \boldsymbol{KSK}, q)$
11:     **return** $\{c_{\mathsf{out},j} \in \mathbb{Z}_q^{n+1}\}_{j \in [\ell_t]}$

$$|[\langle c_{\mathsf{out},j}, s \rangle]_q| < \frac{q}{2} \; for \; j \in [\ell_t]. \tag{3}$$

Then $c_{\mathsf{out},j} \in \mathbb{Z}_q^{n+1}$ *satisfies* $\langle c_{\mathsf{out},j}, s \rangle = \mu_j + B_t^2 \cdot e_{\mathsf{out},j} \pmod{q}$ *where* $\mathsf{Var}(e_{\mathsf{out},j}) \le E_{\mathsf{boot}} + E_{\mathsf{ks}}$ *for* $j \in [\ell_t]$, $E_{\mathsf{boot}} = 8n\ell N\sigma_B^2\sigma_{\mathsf{bk}}^2$ *and* $E_{\mathsf{ks}} = \ell N\sigma_B^2\sigma_{\mathsf{ks}}^2$.

Proof. For step 3 to step 7, consider the j-th iteration ($j \in [\ell_t - 1]$). Assume that we have c_j' such that $\langle c_j', s \rangle = \sum_{k=j}^{\ell_t-1} B_t^{k-j}\mu_k + B_t^{\ell_t-j}e_j' = \mu_j + B_t(\sum_{k=j+1}^{\ell_t-1} B_t^{k-(j+1)}\mu_k + B_t^{\ell_t-(j+1)}e_j') \pmod{q}$ and $\mathsf{Var}(e_j') \le E_j'$. By step 2, $c_0' = c$ and $E_0' = E_{\mathsf{in}}$. By step 4 and step 8, based on Lemma 2, we get $\langle c_{\mathsf{ms},j}, s \rangle = \mu_j + B_t e_{\mathsf{ms},j} \pmod{2N}$ and $\mathsf{Var}([\langle c_{\mathsf{ms},j}, s \rangle]_{2N}) \le (\frac{2N}{q})^2 \mathsf{Var}([\langle c_j', s \rangle]_q) + \frac{B_t^2(h_s+1)}{12} \le (\frac{2N}{q})^2 B_t^{2(\ell_t-j)} E_j' + \frac{B_t^2(h_s+1)}{12}$ for $j \in [\ell_t]$. By step 5, according to Theorem 1, we get $\langle c_{\mathsf{boot},j}, \tilde{z} \rangle = \mu_j + B_t^2 e_{\mathsf{boot},j} \pmod{q}$ where $\mathsf{Var}(e_{\mathsf{boot},j}) \le E_{\mathsf{boot}}$. By step 6 and Lemma 4, we get $\langle c_{\mathsf{out},j}, s \rangle = \mu_j + B_t^2 e_{\mathsf{out},j} \pmod{q}$ where $e_{\mathsf{out},j} = e_{\mathsf{boot},j} + e_{\mathsf{ks},j}$ and $\mathsf{Var}(e_{\mathsf{ks},j}) \le E_{\mathsf{ks}}$. By step 7, we get $\langle c_{j+1}', s \rangle = (\sum_{k=j}^{\ell_t-1} B_t^{k-j}\mu_k + B_t^{\ell_t-j}e_j' - \mu_j - B_t^2 e_{\mathsf{out},j})B_t^{-1} = \sum_{k=j+1}^{\ell_t-1} B_t^{k-(j+1)}\mu_k + B_t^{\ell_t-(j+1)}e_{j+1}' \pmod{q}$, where $e_{j+1}' = e_j' - B_t^{-\ell_t+j+2}e_{\mathsf{out},j}$. Therefore, after $\ell_t - 1$ times of iteration, we get $\langle c_{\ell_t-1}', s \rangle = \mu_{\ell_t-1} + B_t e_{\ell_t-1}' \pmod{q}$ where $e_{\ell_t-1}' = e_{\ell_t-2}' - e_{\mathsf{out},\ell_t-2}$. By step 9 and step 10, based on Theorem 1 and Lemma 4, we get $\langle c_{\mathsf{out},\ell_t-1}, s \rangle = \mu_{\ell_t-1} + B_t^2 e_{\mathsf{out},\ell_t-1} \pmod{q}$ where $\mathsf{Var}(e_{\mathsf{out},\ell_t-1}) \le E_{\mathsf{boot}} + E_{\mathsf{ks}}$. $\quad\square$

Then, we estimate the success probability P_{decomp} of obtaining correct results from Algorithm 10. Adapt the notations of the proof of Theorem 2. The correctness conditions, Eqs. (1), (2) and (3), can also be written as

$$|e_j'| < \frac{q}{2B_t^{\ell_t-j}} \cdot \left(1 - \frac{B_t(h_s+1)}{2N}\right) - \frac{1}{2}, \tag{4}$$

$$|e_{\mathsf{ms},j}| < \frac{N}{2B_t} - \frac{1}{2}, \tag{5}$$

$$|e_{\mathsf{out},j}| < \frac{q}{2B_t^2} - \frac{1}{2B_t}, \tag{6}$$

for $j \in [\ell_t]$. From the proof, we derive that for $j \in [\ell_t]$, $\mathsf{Var}(e'_j) \leq E_{\mathsf{in}} + (\frac{B_t^2}{t})^2 \cdot (\frac{B_t^{j}-1}{B_t-1})^2 \cdot (E_{\mathsf{boot}} + E_{\mathsf{ks}})$, $\mathsf{Var}(e_{\mathsf{ms},j}) \leq (\frac{2NB_t^{\ell_t-j-1}}{q})^2 \cdot \mathsf{Var}(e'_j) + \frac{h_s+1}{12}$, and $\mathsf{Var}(e_{\mathsf{out},j}) \leq E_{\mathsf{boot}} + E_{\mathsf{ks}}$. Let $P_{0,j}$, $P_{1,j}$ and $P_{2,j}$ represent the probabilities that the conditions Eqs. (4), (5), and (6) are satisfied, respectively. Then $P_{\mathsf{decomp}} = \prod_{j=0}^{\ell_t-1}(P_{0,j} \cdot P_{1,j} \cdot P_{2,j})$.

Our homomorphic digit decomposition algorithm has many advantages, although it requires the error of the input ciphertext c to be small enough. Like the HomDecomp-Reduce of [29], Algorithm 10 needs to run the FHEW-like bootstrapping only once to homomorphically compute each μ_j whereas the homomorphic digit decomposition of [25] needs two runs. Besides, [25,29] can only be used when q is a power of two, but Algorithm 10 is also suitable for other values of q. In addition, for an output ciphertext, let η be the ratio of its error size to its modulus. In the HomDecomp-Reduce of [29], we have $\eta \approx \frac{|e_{\mathsf{boot}}+x|}{2B_t N}$ where e_{boot} is the error caused by the FHEW-like bootstrapping and $|x| < \frac{N}{2}$. In Algorithm 10, $\eta \approx \frac{|e_{\mathsf{boot}}|}{q}$ is much smaller, and thus our outputs support more homomorphic operations compared with [29], because $q \gg 2NB_t$ as shown in Sect. 4.

3.3   Homomorphic Packing

Consider a function $y : \mathbb{Z}_{B_t} \to \mathbb{Z}_t$. Let c be a BGV ciphertext satisfying $[\langle c, s\rangle]_{2N} = \mu + B_t e$. As mentioned in Sect. 3.1, to compute a BGV ciphertext of $y(\mu)$ from c by Algorithm 9, we need a test vector $tv = \sum_{i=0}^{N-1} y([i - \frac{N}{2}]_{B_t}) X^i$. Given $\{c_m\}_{m \in [B_t]}$, where the BGV ciphertext $c_m = (c_{m,i})_{i \in [N+1]}$ satisfies $[[\langle c_m, \tilde{z}\rangle]_Q]_t = y([m]_{B_t})$ for $m \in [B_t]$, we describe how to pack them into a BGV ciphertext $c_{\mathsf{pack}} \in \mathcal{R}_Q^2$ of tv.

The idea behind our packing method is as follows: For each value of $m \in [B_t]$, we construct a polynomial $\rho_m = \sum_{i=0}^{N-1} \rho_{m,i} X^i$ by setting $\rho_{m,i} = 1$ if $[i - \frac{N}{2}]_{B_t} = [m]_{B_t}$ and $\rho_{m,i} = 0$ otherwise for $i = 0, \ldots, N-1$. Then, we obtain an equation: $tv = \sum_{m=0}^{B_t-1} y([m]_{B_t})\rho_m = \sum_{m=0}^{B_t-1}(c_{m,N} - \sum_{i=0}^{N-1}\langle \mathsf{G}^{-1}(c_{m,i}), g\rangle \cdot z'_i) \cdot \rho_m \bmod Q \bmod t$. Next, we set the packing key as $\boldsymbol{PaK} = \{\boldsymbol{pak}_k\}_{k \in [B_t N\ell]}$, where $\boldsymbol{pak}_k$ is constructed as a BGV ciphertext of $B^j z'_i \rho_m$ with an error e_k, $k = mN\ell + i\ell + j$, $\ell = \lceil \log_B Q \rceil$, $\mathsf{Var}(e_k) \leq \sigma_{\mathsf{pak}}^2$ for $m \in [B_t], i \in [N], j \in [\ell]$, as shown in Algorithm 11. Our technique relies on a circular security assumption. Hence, by the above equation, we can use the key $\boldsymbol{PaK}$ to pack the BGV ciphertexts $\{c_m\}_{m \in [B_t]}$, as shown in Algorithm 12. The correctness is shown in the following theorem, and its proof is given in Appendix A.8.

Theorem 3. Let $c_m \in \mathbb{Z}_Q^{N+1}$ satisfy $[\langle c_m, \tilde{z}\rangle]_Q = y([m]_{B_t}) + t\varepsilon_m$ and $\mathsf{Var}(\varepsilon_m) \leq E$ for $m \in [B_t]$. Let $(\boldsymbol{PaK}, \boldsymbol{\rho}) \leftarrow \mathsf{PackKeyGen}(z', \ell, t, Q)$ where $\ell = \lceil \log_B Q \rceil$. If $c_{\mathsf{pack}} \leftarrow \mathsf{Pack}(\{c_m\}_{m \in [B_t]}, \boldsymbol{PaK}, \boldsymbol{\rho}, Q)$, then we have $\langle c_{\mathsf{pack}}, z\rangle = t(e + e_{\mathsf{pack}}) + \sum_{i=0}^{N-1} y([i-\frac{N}{2}]_{B_t})X^i \pmod{Q}$ where $\mathsf{Var}(e) \leq E$ and $\mathsf{Var}(e_{\mathsf{pack}}) \leq B_t N\ell\sigma_B^2\sigma_{\mathsf{pak}}^2$.

Then, we compare our packing method with the methods proposed in [8,11]. Using the public functional key switching of [11] and the LWEs-to-RLWE algorithm of [8] to generate c_{pack}, the packing keys include ℓN and $\ell \log N$ RLWE

Algorithm 11. Packing Key Generation

1: **procedure** PackKeyGen($z' = \sum_{i=0}^{N-1} z_i' X^i, \ell, t, Q$)
2:    **for** $m = 0$ to $B_t - 1$ **do**
3:       **for** $i = 0$ to $N - 1$ **do**
4:          **if** $[i - \frac{N}{2}]_{B_t} = [m]_{B_t}$ **then**
5:             $\rho_{m,i} \leftarrow 1$
6:          **else**
7:             $\rho_{m,i} \leftarrow 0$
8:       $\rho_m \leftarrow \sum_{i=0}^{N-1} \rho_{m,i} X^i$
9:       **for** $i = 0$ to $N - 1$ **do**
10:         **for** $j = 0$ to $\ell - 1$ **do**
11:            $\pmb{pak}_{m \cdot N\ell + i \cdot \ell + j} \leftarrow \mathsf{BGV.Enc}(B^j z_i' \rho_m, z', 1, Q, t)$
12:    **return** $\pmb{PaK} = (\pmb{pak}_k)_{k \in [B_t N\ell]}, \pmb{\rho} = (\rho_m)_{m \in [B_t]}$

Algorithm 12. Homomorphic Packing

1: **procedure** Pack($\{\pmb{c}_m \in \mathbb{Z}_Q^{N+1}\}_{m \in [B_t]}, (\pmb{pak}_k)_{k \in [B_t N\ell]}, (\rho_m)_{m \in [B_t]}, Q$)
2:    **for** $m = 0$ to $B_t - 1$ **do**
3:       $\pmb{z}_m = (z_{m,j})_{j \in [N\ell]} \leftarrow \mathsf{G}^{-1}((c_{m,0}, \ldots, c_{m,N-1}))$
4:       $\pmb{c}_{\mathsf{pack}} \leftarrow [\pmb{c}_{\mathsf{pack}} + \sum_{i=0}^{N-1} \sum_{j=0}^{\ell-1} z_{m,i \cdot \ell + j} \cdot \pmb{pak}_{m \cdot N\ell + i \cdot \ell + j}]_Q$
5:    $\pmb{c}_{\mathsf{pack}} \leftarrow (0, [\sum_{m=0}^{B_t-1} c_{m,N} \cdot \rho_m]_Q) - \pmb{c}_{\mathsf{pack}}$
6:    **return** $\pmb{c}_{\mathsf{pack}} \in \mathcal{R}_Q^2$

---

samples, and their variances of e_{pack} are NV_{ks} and $\frac{(N^2-1)V_{ks}}{3}$, respectively, where $V_{ks} \leq N\ell\sigma_B^2\sigma_{\mathsf{pak}}^2$. Besides, their asymptotic costs are $O(\ell N^2 \log N)$ integer multiplications when using FFTs (Fast Fourier Transformations). In our design, the packing key includes $\ell N B_t$ RLWE samples, but the asymptotic cost is $O(\ell N^2 B_t)$ integer multiplications, reduced by a factor of $O(\frac{\log N}{B_t})$. Our variance of e_{pack} is reduced by a factor of $\frac{N}{B_t}$ and $\frac{N^2-1}{3B_t}$ compared with [8,11], respectively.

3.4   Functional Bootstrapping for Large Plaintexts

Given a BGV ciphertext $\pmb{c} \in \mathbb{Z}_q^{n+1}$ of a message $\mu = \sum_{i=0}^{\ell_t-1} B_t^i \mu_i \in \mathbb{Z}_t$ satisfying $[\langle \pmb{c}, \pmb{s} \rangle]_q = \mu + te$ where $t = B_t^{\ell_t}$ is large and $\mu_i \in \mathbb{Z}_{B_t}$ for $i \in [\ell_t]$, we set out to refresh its noise while simultaneously generating a BGV ciphertext encrypting of $f(\mu)$ for any function $f : \mathbb{Z}_t \to \mathbb{Z}_t$.

Inspired by the tree-based method for combining functional bootstraps of [20], we introduce a new functional bootstrapping algorithm for large plaintexts, as shown in Algorithm 13. For clarity, the main steps of the algorithm are described below from the perspective of plaintext. Firstly, apply Decomp to get $\{\mu_i\}_{i \in [\ell_t]}$. Then, for $j \in [k_0]$ where $k_0 = \frac{t}{B_t}$, use μ_0 and a test polynomial $tv_{0,j} = \sum_{i=0}^{N-1} f([i - \frac{N}{2}]_{B_t} + B_t[j]_{k_0}) X^i$ to compute $f(\mu_0 + B_t[j]_{k_0}) = f(\mu_0 + B_t([j]_{B_t} + B_t \cdot \frac{[j]_{k_0} - [j]_{B_t}}{B_t}))$ by BasicFB. Next, for $j \in [k_1]$ where $k_1 = \frac{t}{B_t^2}$, pack $\{f(\mu_0 + B_t([m]_{B_t} + B_t[j]_{k_1}))\}_{m \in [B_t]}$ into a test polynomial

---

Algorithm 13. Functional Bootstrapping for Larger Plaintexts

1: **procedure** LargeFB($c \in \mathbb{Z}_q^{n+1}, f, \boldsymbol{BK}, \overline{\boldsymbol{BK}}, \boldsymbol{KSK}, \boldsymbol{PaK}, \rho, q, Q$)
2:     **for** $j = 0$ to $B_t^{\ell_t-1} - 1$ **do**
3:         $\boldsymbol{v}_{0,j} \leftarrow (0, \sum_{i=0}^{N-1} f([i - \frac{N}{2}]_{B_t} + B_t \cdot [j]_{B_t^{\ell_t-1}}) X^i)$
4:     $\{c_i\}_{i \in [\ell_t]} \leftarrow$ Decomp($c, \boldsymbol{BK}, \boldsymbol{KSK}, q$)
5:     **for** $d = 0$ to $\ell_t - 2$ **do**
6:         $c_{\mathsf{ms},d} \leftarrow$ MS($c_d, q, 2N, B_t$)
7:         **for** $j = 0$ to $B_t^{\ell_t-(d+2)} - 1$ **do**
8:             **for** $m = 0$ to $B_t - 1$ **do**
9:                 set $\alpha \in [B_t^{\ell_t-(d+1)}]$ s.t. $[\alpha]_{B_t^{\ell_t-(d+1)}} = B_t \cdot [j]_{B_t^{\ell_t-(d+2)}} + [m]_{B_t}$
10:                 $\hat{c}_m \leftarrow$ BasicFB($[c_{\mathsf{ms},d}, \overline{\boldsymbol{BK}}, \boldsymbol{v}_{d,\alpha}, Q$)
11:                 $\boldsymbol{v}_{d+1,j} \leftarrow$ Pack($\{\hat{c}_m\}_{m \in [B_t]}, \boldsymbol{PaK}, \rho, Q$)
12:     $c_{\mathsf{ms},\ell_t-1} \leftarrow$ MS($c_{\ell_t-1}, q, 2N, B_t$)
13:     $c_{\mathsf{out}} \leftarrow$ BasicFB($c_{\mathsf{ms},\ell_t-1}, \overline{\boldsymbol{BK}}, \boldsymbol{v}_{\ell_t-1,0}, Q$)
14:     **return** $c_{\mathsf{out}} \in \mathbb{Z}_Q^{N+1}$

$tv_{1,j} = \sum_{i=0}^{N-1} f(\mu_0 + B_t[i - \frac{N}{2}]_{B_t} + B_t^2[j]_{k_1})X^i$ by Pack, and then use μ_1 and $tv_{1,j}$ to compute $f(\sum_{i=0}^{1} B_t^i \mu_i + B_t^2[j]_{k_1})$ by BasicFB. By analogy, we finally obtain $f(\sum_{i=0}^{\ell_t-1} B_t^i \mu_i) = f(\mu)$. The following theorem demonstrates the correctness.

Theorem 4. *Adapt the notations of Algorithm 13. Let $\boldsymbol{c} \in \mathbb{Z}_q^{n+1}$ be a BGV ciphertext of $\mu \in \mathbb{Z}_t$ such that $[\langle \boldsymbol{c}, \boldsymbol{s} \rangle]_q = \mu + te$. Let $\ell = \lceil \log_B q \rceil$, $\ell' = \lceil \log_B Q \rceil$, $\boldsymbol{BK} \leftarrow$ BootKeyGen(s', z', ℓ, q, B_t^2), $\overline{\boldsymbol{BK}} \leftarrow$ BootKeyGen(s', z', ℓ', Q, t), $\boldsymbol{KSK} \leftarrow$ KSKeyGen($\tilde{z}', s', \ell, q, B_t^2$), $(\boldsymbol{PaK}, \rho) \leftarrow$ PackKeyGen(z', ℓ', t, Q). Assume $\boldsymbol{c}_j$ can be decrypted correctly for all $j \in [\ell_t]$. For any function $f : \mathbb{Z}_t \rightarrow \mathbb{Z}_t$, if $2N \mid q$, $q = 1 \pmod{t}$, $c_{\mathsf{out}} \leftarrow$ LargeFB($c, f, \boldsymbol{BK}, \overline{\boldsymbol{BK}}, \boldsymbol{KSK}, \boldsymbol{PaK}, \rho, q, Q$), $2N = 1 \pmod{B_t}$,*

$$|[\langle \boldsymbol{c}_j, \boldsymbol{s} \rangle]_q| < \frac{q}{2} \cdot \left(1 - \frac{B_t(h_s+1)}{2N}\right) \text{ for } j \in [\ell_t], \tag{7}$$

$$|[\langle \boldsymbol{c}_{\mathsf{ms},j}, \boldsymbol{s} \rangle]_{2N}| < \frac{N}{2} \text{ for } j \in [\ell_t], \tag{8}$$

$$|[\langle \boldsymbol{c}_{\mathsf{out}}, \tilde{z} \rangle]_Q| < \frac{Q}{2}, \tag{9}$$

then $\boldsymbol{c}_{\mathsf{out}} \in \mathbb{Z}_Q^{N+1}$ satisfies $\langle \boldsymbol{c}_{\mathsf{out}}, \tilde{z} \rangle = f(\mu) + te_{\mathsf{out}} \pmod{Q}$ where $\mathsf{Var}(e_{\mathsf{out}}) \leq \ell_t E'_{\mathsf{boot}} + (\ell_t - 1)E_{\mathsf{pack}}$, $E'_{\mathsf{boot}} = 8n\ell' N\sigma_B^2 \sigma_{\mathsf{bk}}^2$ and $E_{\mathsf{pack}} = B_t N\ell' \sigma_B^2 \sigma_{\mathsf{pak}}^2$.

Proof. By step 4, based on Theorem 2, we get $c_i \in \mathbb{Z}_q^{n+1}$ such that $[\langle \boldsymbol{c}_i, \boldsymbol{s} \rangle]_q = \mu_i + B_t^2 e_i$ where $\mu = \sum_{i=0}^{\ell_t-1} B_t^i \mu_i$, $\mathsf{Var}(e_i) \leq E_{\mathsf{boot}} + E_{\mathsf{ks}}$ for $i \in [\ell_t]$, $E_{\mathsf{boot}} = 8n\ell N\sigma_B^2 \sigma_{\mathsf{bk}}^2$ and $E_{\mathsf{ks}} = \ell N\sigma_B^2 \sigma_{\mathsf{ks}}^2$. As for step 5 to step 11, consider the d-th iteration ($d = 0, \ldots, \ell_t - 2$), we suppose a ciphertext $\boldsymbol{v}_{d,\alpha} \in \mathcal{R}_Q^2$ is already obtained, satisfying $[\langle \boldsymbol{v}_{d,\alpha}, z \rangle]_Q = \sum_{i=0}^{N-1} f(\sum_{j=0}^{d-1} B_t^j \mu_j + B_t^d[i - \frac{N}{2}]_{B_t} +$

$B_t^{d+1}[\alpha]_{B_t^{\ell_t-(d+1)}})X^i + te_{\mathsf{tv},d,\alpha}$ where $\mathsf{Var}(e_{\mathsf{tv},d,\alpha}) \le E_{\mathsf{tv},d}$ for $\alpha \in [B_t^{\ell_t-(d+1)}]$ and $d = 1,\ldots,\ell_t - 2$. Set $E_{\mathsf{tv},0} = 0$. By step 6, based on Lemma 2, we get $c_{\mathsf{ms},d} \in \mathbb{Z}_{2N}^{n+1}$ such that $\langle c_{\mathsf{ms},d}, s \rangle = \mu_d + B_t e_{\mathsf{ms},d} \pmod{2N}$ where $\mathsf{Var}([\langle c_{\mathsf{ms},d}, s \rangle]_{2N}) \le (\frac{2NB_t^2}{q})^2 \mathsf{Var}(e_d) + \frac{B_t^2(h_s+1)}{12}$. By step 10, based on Theorem 1, we get $\hat{c}_m \in \mathbb{Z}_Q^{N+1}$ such that $\langle \hat{c}_m, \tilde{z} \rangle = f(\sum_{j=0}^{d-1} B_t^j \mu_j + B_t^d \mu_d + B_t^{d+1}[\alpha]_{B_t^{\ell_t-(d+1)}}) + t\hat{e}_m = f(\sum_{j=0}^{d} B_t^j \mu_j + B_t^{d+1} \cdot [m]_{B_t} + B_t^{d+2} \cdot [j]_{B_t^{\ell_t-(d+2)}}) + t\hat{e}_m \pmod{Q}$ where $\mathsf{Var}(\hat{e}_m) \le E_{\mathsf{tv},d} + E'_{\mathsf{boot}}$ for $j \in [B_t^{\ell_t-(d+2)}]$ and $m \in [B_t]$. By step 11, according to Theorem 3, we get $v_{d+1,j} \in \mathcal{R}_Q^2$ such that $[\langle v_{d+1,j}, z \rangle]_Q = \sum_{i=0}^{N-1} f(\sum_{j=0}^{d} B_t^j \mu_j + B_t^{d+1}[i - \frac{N}{2}]_{B_t} + B_t^{d+2}[j]_{B_t^{\ell_t-(d+2)}})X^i + te_{\mathsf{tv},d+1,j}$ where $\mathsf{Var}(e_{\mathsf{tv},d+1,j}) \le E_{\mathsf{tv},d+1} = E_{\mathsf{tv},d} + E'_{\mathsf{boot}} + E_{\mathsf{pack}}$ for $j \in [B_t^{\ell_t-(d+2)}]$.

After $\ell_t - 1$ iterations, we get $v_{\ell_t-1,0} \in \mathcal{R}_Q^2$ such that $[\langle v_{\ell_t-1,0}, z \rangle]_Q = \sum_{i=0}^{N-1} f(\sum_{j=0}^{\ell_t-2} B_t^j \mu_j + B_t^{\ell_t-1}[i - \frac{N}{2}]_{B_t})X^i + te_{\mathsf{tv},\ell_t-1,0}$ where $\mathsf{Var}(e_{\mathsf{tv},\ell_t-1,0}) \le E_{\mathsf{tv},\ell_t-1} = (\ell_t - 1)(E'_{\mathsf{boot}} + E_{\mathsf{pack}})$. By step 12, based on Lemma 2, we get $c_{\mathsf{ms},\ell_t-1} \in \mathbb{Z}_{2N}^{n+1}$ such that $\langle c_{\mathsf{ms},\ell_t-1}, s \rangle = \mu_{\ell_t-1} + B_t e_{\mathsf{ms},\ell_t-1} \pmod{2N}$ where $\mathsf{Var}([\langle c_{\mathsf{ms},\ell_t-1}, s \rangle]_{2N}) \le (\frac{2NB_t^2}{q})^2 \mathsf{Var}(e_{\ell_t-1}) + \frac{B_t^2(h_s+1)}{12}$. Applying Theorem 1 in step 13, our algorithm outputs a BGV ciphertext $c_{\mathsf{out}} \in \mathbb{Z}_Q^{N+1}$ satisfying $\langle c_{\mathsf{out}}, s \rangle = f(\sum_{j=0}^{\ell_t-2} B_t^j \mu_j + B_t^{\ell_t-1} \mu_{\ell_t-1}) + te_{\mathsf{out}} = f(\mu) + te_{\mathsf{out}} \pmod{Q}$, where $\mathsf{Var}(e_{\mathsf{out}}) \le E_{\mathsf{tv},\ell_t-1} + E'_{\mathsf{boot}} = \ell_t E'_{\mathsf{boot}} + (\ell_t - 1)E_{\mathsf{pack}}$.   □

Then, we estimate the success probability P_{fb} of obtaining correct results from Algorithm 13. Adapt the notations of the proof of Theorem 4. The correctness conditions of Algorithm 13, Eqs. (7), (8) and (9), can also be written as

$$|e_j| < \frac{q}{2B_t^2} \cdot \left(1 - \frac{B_t(h_s+1)}{2N}\right) - \frac{1}{2B_t}, \tag{10}$$

$$|e_{\mathsf{ms},j}| < \frac{N}{2B_t} - \frac{1}{2}, \tag{11}$$

$$|e_{\mathsf{out}}| < \frac{Q}{2t} - \frac{1}{2}, \tag{12}$$

for $j \in [\ell_t]$. And from the proof, we derive that $\mathsf{Var}(e_j) \le E_{\mathsf{boot}} + E_{\mathsf{ks}}$, $\mathsf{Var}(e_{\mathsf{ms},j}) \le (\frac{2NB_t}{q})^2 \cdot \mathsf{Var}(e_j) + \frac{h_s+1}{12}$, and $\mathsf{Var}(e_{\mathsf{out}}) \le \ell_t E'_{\mathsf{boot}} + (\ell_t - 1)E'_{\mathsf{pack}}$, for $j \in [\ell_t]$. Let $P_{0,j}$, $P_{1,j}$, $P_{3,j}$, $P_{4,j}$ and P_5 represent the probabilities that the conditions Eqs. (4), (5), (10), (11), and (12) are satisfied respectively. Then $P_{\mathsf{fb}} = \prod_{j=0}^{\ell_t-1}(P_{0,j} \cdot P_{1,j} \cdot P_{3,j} \cdot P_{4,j}) \cdot P_5$. Notably, when the confidentiality of f is required, $v_{0,j}$ must be a BGV ciphertext with non-zero noise $e_{\mathsf{f},j}$ for $j \in [B_t^{\ell_t-1}]$. Let $\mathsf{Var}(e_{\mathsf{f},j}) \le \sigma_{\mathsf{f}}^2$. Then we should add σ_{f}^2 to the upper bound of $\mathsf{Var}(e_{\mathsf{out}})$ in Theorem 4.

As for applications, using the homomorphic encoding and decoding of [21], we can combine our algorithms with existing BGV-based algorithms for complex homomorphic operations, such as calculating non-polynomial functions like tanh and sigmoid, evaluating multilayer perceptrons and deep neural networks, and searching in a lookup table.

4   Parameters and Comparison

In this section, we provide our recommended parameter sets and compare our algorithm with related works. We use the central limit theorem and the error function erf to calculate the success probability of our algorithms. In addition, we utilize the fact that if a random variable X follows a Gaussian distribution with mean 0 and variance σ^2, then $\Pr(|X| < x) = \mathsf{erf}(\frac{x}{\sqrt{2}\sigma})$ for any $x \in \mathbb{R}$, where $\mathsf{erf}(x) = \frac{2}{\sqrt{\pi}} \int_0^x e^{-\eta^2} \mathrm{d}\eta$. Consequently, given the success probability and the security parameter λ that are expected, we can use Theorem 2 and Theorem 4 to select proper parameter sets.

We provide parameter sets Par 1-3 for Algorithm 10 and Par 4-7 for Algorithm 13 in Table 1. In this table, t is the plaintext modulus, N is the dimension of the bootstrapping keys, Q is the largest modulus used, n and q are the dimension and the modulus of the input ciphertexts, respectively. For other parameters in Theorem 2 and Theorem 4, we choose $\sigma_B^2 = 1/3$, $\sigma_z^2 = \sigma_{\mathsf{bk}}^2 = \sigma_{\mathsf{pak}}^2 = \sigma_{\mathsf{ksk}}^2 = E_{\mathsf{in}} = 3.2$, and $h_s = 64$. And we let parameters guarantee λ-bit security by the LWE estimator of [2].

Table 1. Parameters for digit decomposition and functional bootstrapping

Parameter	[25]	[29]	Par 1	Par 2	Par 3	[26]	Par 4	[26]	Par 5	Par 6	Par 7
$\lceil \log t \rceil$	20	20	20	32	64	9	9	12	12	32	64
n	1305	1340	1305	1305	1305	1024	1024	1024	1024	2048	4096
$\log N$	11	11	10	11	12	15	11	15	11	11	12
$\lceil \log q \rceil$	28	35	27	39	71	16	22	20	22	39	71
$\lceil \log Q \rceil$	28	35	27	39	71	673	30	900	33	55	89

As for homomorphic digit decomposition, we set $B_t = 16$, $P_{\mathsf{decomp}} > 1 - 2^{32}$ and $\lambda \geq 128$. We find that N and Q in Algorithm 10 are smaller than those of [25,29] when $\lceil \log t \rceil = 20$. In addition, when $N = 2^{11}$, Algorithm 10 supports $\lceil \log t \rceil = 32$ whereas [25,29] cannot. Moreover, our algorithm even supports 64-bit plaintexts when $N = 2^{12}$ and thus has a wider range of application prospects.

As for functional bootstrapping, we set $P_{\mathsf{fb}} > 1 - 2^{30}$ and $\lambda \geq 125$. We choose $B_t = 2$ for Par 4-6 and choose $B_t = 16$ for Par 7. Compared with the BGV/BFV-based functional bootstrapping of [26], N and Q in Algorithm 13 are much smaller when $\lceil \log t \rceil = 9$ and 12. Particularly, Q in our algorithm has 867 fewer bits when $\lceil \log t \rceil = 12$. Besides, when $N = 2^{12}$ and $\lceil \log Q \rceil = 89$, Algorithm 13 allows $\lceil \log t \rceil = 64$ while [26] cannot. Moreover, due to the inability of [26] to homomorphically compute functions that include privacy information, it is not possible for [26] to use the digit decomposition to evaluate functions on a large plaintext homomorphically.

Next, compare the complexity of homomorphically computing any function f on a BGV ciphertext of a plaintext $\mu \in \mathbb{Z}_t$. It is known that a polynomial multiplication over $\mathcal{R}$ includes $cN \log N$ integer multiplications when using FFTs where c is some constant number. Then, in Algorithm 13, the number of integer multiplications is $(n+1)(-1+7\ell_t+N\ell_t\ell)+4nd(\ell_t\ell+\ell'(1+b))+2b\ell'N^2$, where $\ell = \lceil \log_B q \rceil$, $\ell' = \lceil \log_B Q \rceil$, $b = B_t^{\ell_t-1}$, $d = cN\log N$. The algorithm of [26] includes homomorphic linear transformation, homomorphic function evaluation by calculating the equivalent polynomial of the evaluated function f, homomorphic decoding, and extraction. So, the number of integer multiplications included in the algorithm of [26] is $N(2q-2\sqrt{q}+nN)+4d\ell'(\sqrt{N}+\sqrt{n}-1)+(2\sqrt{q}+N+n-2)(3N+4d+2d\ell')$. Detailed complexity analysis is given in Appendix B. When $\lceil \log t \rceil = 12$, in Algorithm 13, set the gadget bases for $\mathbb{Z}_q$ and $\mathbb{Z}_Q$ to $2^{1.3}$ and 2^{17}, respectively, then Algorithm 13 includes $3.4788 \times 10^{10} + 3.9697 \times 10^{11}c$ integer multiplications, maintaining $P_{fb} > 1 - 2^{30}$. In the algorithm of [26], if the Residue Number System is used to decompose an operation with a large modulus Q into several operations with 32-bit moduli, the bit size of the gadget base for $\mathbb{Z}_Q$ is set to 32 in general. Then, the computational cost of the algorithm of [26] is $3.3979 \times 10^{13} + 3.2023 \times 10^{13}c$ integer multiplications, which is about 80 times that of Algorithm 13. Therefore, Algorithm 13 is better than the algorithm of [26] to compute any functions on a small number of large plaintexts by FHE.

5   Conclusion

We propose a new homomorphic digit decomposition algorithm and new functional bootstrapping algorithms for BGV. Our decomposition algorithm has better efficiency, less noise, and smaller parameters compared with [25,29]. When processing an LWE ciphertext of a large plaintext, in our functional bootstrapping algorithm, the bit size of the largest modulus is reduced by 867 bits, and the computational cost is reduced by a factor of 80, compared with [26]. Besides, our packing method used in the above algorithms produces less noise and costs less than [8,11]. In future work, we intend to further optimize our algorithm and explore ways to implement it.

Acknowledgments. Li-Ping Wang is supported by the National Natural Science Foundation of China under Grant No. 62372446. The research of Huaxiong Wang is supported by Singapore Ministry of Education Academic Research Fund Tier 2 Grant MOE-000623-00.

A   Proofs

A.1   Proof of Lemma 1

Proof. By Algorithm 1, we obtain $c = ([a]_q, [\langle a, s' \rangle + te + \mu]_q)$ where $a \in \mathcal{R}_q^n$ and $e \in \mathcal{R}$. Then $\langle c, s \rangle = \langle -a, s' \rangle + \langle a, s' \rangle + te + \mu = \mu + te \pmod{q}$.   □

A.2   Proof of Lemma 2

Proof. In Algorithm 2, by step 3, $c + \delta = c + t(-t^{-1}c) = 0 \pmod{x}$ and $c + \delta = c \pmod{t}$. So $x \mid (c + \delta)$. Set $c' = \frac{1}{x} \cdot (c + \delta)$. By step 2, $x = 1 \pmod{t}$. Hence, $c' = x \cdot c' = c + \delta = c \pmod{t}$. By step 4, $[c']_{q'} = [c_{\mathsf{ms}}]_{q'}$. Let $[\langle c, s \rangle]_q = \langle c, s \rangle + \alpha \cdot q$. Set $\gamma = \langle c', s \rangle + \alpha \cdot q'$. Then $\gamma = \langle c, s \rangle + \alpha \cdot q = [\langle c, s \rangle]_q = \mu \pmod{t}$.

Besides, $\gamma = \langle c', s \rangle + \alpha \cdot q' = \langle c', s \rangle + \frac{q'}{q} \cdot \langle c, s \rangle - \frac{q'}{q} \cdot \langle c, s \rangle + \alpha \cdot q' = \frac{q'}{q} \cdot (\langle c, s \rangle + \alpha \cdot q) + \langle c' - \frac{q'}{q} \cdot c, s \rangle = \frac{q'}{q} \cdot [\langle c, s \rangle]_q + \frac{q'}{q} \cdot \langle \delta, s \rangle$. Then $|\gamma| < \frac{q'}{q} \cdot (\frac{q}{2} - \frac{qt(h_s+1)}{2q'}) + \frac{1}{x} \cdot \frac{tx}{2} \cdot (h_s + 1) = \frac{q'}{2}$. So $[\langle c_{\mathsf{ms}}, s \rangle]_{q'} = [\langle c', s \rangle]_{q'} = \gamma$.   □

A.3   Proof of Lemma 3

Proof. From the properties of c, we know that, over $\mathcal{R}$, $\langle c, z \rangle = \sum_{i=0}^{N-1}(c_{1,i} - (\sum_{j=0}^{i} c_{0,i-j} \cdot z'_j - \sum_{j=i+1}^{N-1} c_{0,N-(j-i)} \cdot z'_j))X^i = \sum_{i=0}^{N-1}(\mu_i + t \cdot e_i)X^i \pmod{q}$. Therefore, $\langle c', \tilde{z} \rangle = c_{1,0} - (c_{0,0} \cdot z'_0 - \sum_{j=1}^{N-1} c_{0,N-j} \cdot z'_j) = \mu_0 + t \cdot e_0 \pmod{q}$.   □

A.4   Proof of Lemma 4

Proof. $\langle c_{\mathsf{ks}}, s \rangle = c_N - \sum_{i=0}^{N-1} \sum_{j=0}^{\ell-1} \bar{c}_{i\ell+j} \cdot \langle \mathbf{ksk}_{i\ell+j}, s \rangle = c_N - \sum_{i=0}^{N-1} \sum_{j=0}^{\ell-1} \bar{c}_{i\ell+j} \cdot (B^j z'_i + te_{i\ell+j}) = c_N - \sum_{i=0}^{N-1} c_i z'_i - t \cdot (\sum_{i=0}^{N-1} \sum_{j=0}^{\ell-1} \bar{c}_{i\ell+j} e_{i\ell+j}) = \mu + te + te_{\mathsf{ks}} \pmod{q}$ □

A.5   Proof of Lemma 5

Proof. Adapt the notations of Algorithm 6. According to Lemma 1, we get $\mathbf{y}_i^\top z = t \cdot e_i \pmod{Q}$ for $i \in [2\ell]$, where $e_i \in \mathcal{R}$ is the error of $\mathbf{y}_i$. Therefore, $\mathbf{C} \cdot z = (\mathbf{Y} + \mu \cdot \mathbf{G}) \cdot z = (\mathbf{y}_0^\top, \dots, \mathbf{y}_{2\ell-1}^\top) \cdot z + \mu \mathbf{G}z = (t \cdot e_0, \dots, t \cdot e_{2\ell-1}) + \mu \mathbf{G}z = t \cdot e + \mu \mathbf{G}z \pmod{Q}$, where $e = (e_0, \dots, e_{2\ell-1})$.   □

A.6   Proof of Lemma 6

Proof. $c_{\mathsf{mult}}^\top z = \mathbf{x}^\top \mathbf{C}z = \mathbf{x}^\top (t \cdot e + \mu \mathbf{G}z) = t \cdot \mathbf{x}^\top e + \mu \mathbf{G}^{-1}(c)^\top \mathbf{G}z = t \cdot \mathbf{x}^\top e + \mu c^\top z = t \cdot \mathbf{x}^\top e + \mu(\mu' + t \cdot e') = \mu\mu' + t \cdot (\mu e' + \mathbf{x}^\top e) \pmod{Q}$.   □

A.7   Proof of Theorem 1

Proof. In Algorithm 9, by step 2 to step 5, applying Lemma 6, we obtain $\langle c_{\mathsf{br}}, z \rangle = tv \cdot X^{-\frac{N}{2} - c_n} \cdot X^{c_0 \cdot s'_0} \cdot \dots \cdot X^{c_{n-1} \cdot s'_{n-1}} + t \cdot e_{\mathsf{br}} = tv \cdot X^{-\frac{N}{2} - \langle c, s \rangle} + t \cdot e_{\mathsf{br}} \pmod{Q}$ where $\mathsf{Var}(e_{\mathsf{br}}) \leq \mathsf{Var}(e_{\mathsf{tv}}) + 8n\ell N \sigma_B^2 \sigma_{\mathsf{bk}}^2$. We observe that for $\sum_{i=0}^{N-1} u_i X^i = \sum_{i=0}^{N-1} v_i X^i \cdot X^{-y}$, $u_0 = v_y$ if $y \in [0, N)$ and $u_0 = -v_{y+N}$ if $y \in (-N, 0)$. Let $-\varphi = [-\frac{N}{2} - \langle c, s \rangle]_{2N} = -(\frac{N}{2} + \mu + te)$. Then $\varphi \in (0, N)$. Employing Lemma 3 in step 6, we determine that $\langle c_{\mathsf{out}}, \tilde{z} \rangle = f(\mu) + t \cdot e_{\mathsf{br},0} \pmod{Q}$ where $e_{\mathsf{br}} = \sum_{i=0}^{N-1} e_{\mathsf{br},i} X^i$.   □

A.8   Proof of Theorem 3

Proof. We set $\boldsymbol{z}_m \leftarrow \mathsf{G}^{-1}((c_{m,0}, \ldots, c_{m,N-1}))$ for $m \in [B_t]$. Then, $\sum_{j=0}^{\ell-1} B^j \cdot z_{m,i\ell+j} = c_{m,i}$ for $i \in [N]$ and $m \in [B_t]$. Applying Algorithm 12 yields $\boldsymbol{c}_{\mathsf{pack}} = [(0, \sum_{m=0}^{B_t-1} c_{m,N} \rho_m) - \sum_{m=0}^{B_t-1} \sum_{i=0}^{N-1} \sum_{j=0}^{\ell-1} z_{m,i\cdot\ell+j} \cdot \boldsymbol{pak}_k]_Q$, and Algorithm 11 provides that $\langle \boldsymbol{pak}_k, \boldsymbol{z} \rangle = B^j z_i' \rho_m + t e_k \pmod{Q}$ where $k = mN\ell + i\ell + j$, for $m \in [B_t]$, $i \in [N]$ and $j \in [\ell]$. It is known that $\langle \boldsymbol{c}_m, \tilde{\boldsymbol{z}} \rangle = c_{m,N} - \sum_{i=0}^{N-1} c_{m,i} \cdot z_i' = y([m]_{B_t}) + t \cdot \varepsilon_m \pmod{Q}$ for $m \in [B_t]$. Therefore, $\langle \boldsymbol{c}_{\mathsf{pack}}, \boldsymbol{z} \rangle = \sum_{m=0}^{B_t-1} y([m]_{B_t}) \rho_m + t(e + e_{\mathsf{pack}}) = \sum_{i=0}^{N-1} y([i - \frac{N}{2}]_{B_t}) X^i + t(e + e_{\mathsf{pack}}) \pmod{Q}$, $e = \sum_{m=0}^{B_t-1} \varepsilon_m \rho_m$ and $e_{\mathsf{pack}} = \sum_{m=0}^{B_t-1} \sum_{i=0}^{N-1} \sum_{j=0}^{\ell-1} z_{m,i\cdot\ell+j} \cdot e_k$ where $z_{m,i\cdot\ell+j} \in \mathbb{Z}_B$, $e_k \in \mathcal{R}$ and $k = mN\ell + i\ell + j$ for $m \in [B_t]$, $i \in [N]$ and $j \in [\ell]$. □

B   Complexity Analysis

Here, we analyze the computational cost of the functional bootstrapping algorithm of [26] and Algorithm 13 in detail. We count the computational cost by the number of integer multiplications. So, the computational cost of a polynomial multiplication over $\mathcal{R} = \mathbb{Z}[X]/(X^N+1)$ is $d = cN \log N$ when using FFTs, where c is some constant number. As for the parameters used here, n and q are the dimension and modulus of the input ciphertexts, respectively. N and Q are the dimension and modulus of the output ciphertexts, respectively. t is the plaintext modulus, and B is the gadget base. Set $t = B_t^{\ell_t}$, $\ell = \lceil \log_B q \rceil$, $\ell' = \lceil \log_B Q \rceil$.

The functional bootstrapping algorithm of [26] consists of homomorphic linear transformation, homomorphic function evaluation, homomorphic decoding, and extraction. The homomorphic linear transformation includes $2\sqrt{n}-1$ homomorphic rotations, n homomorphic multiplications of ciphertexts, and an encoding of a matrix in $\mathbb{Z}^{N \times n}$. The computational costs of a homomorphic rotation, a homomorphic multiplication, and an encoding are $2\ell'd$, $(4 + 2\ell')d + 3N$, and nN^2, respectively. In the homomorphic decoding, the steps are similar to the homomorphic linear transformation without the encoding, but n is replaced by N. The homomorphic function evaluation is achieved by calculating the equivalent polynomial of the evaluated function with the Paterson-Stockmeyer method, including $2(\sqrt{q} - 1)$ homomorphic multiplications and $2N\sqrt{q}(\sqrt{q} - 1)$ integer multiplications. Besides, the computational cost of the extraction is 0. Therefore, the computational cost of the algorithm of [26] is $N(2q - 2\sqrt{q} + nN) + 4d\ell'(\sqrt{N} + \sqrt{n} - 1) + (2\sqrt{q} + N + n - 2)(3N + 4d + 2d\ell')$.

Algorithm 13 includes one call to Decomp, ℓ_t calls to MS, $B_t^{\ell_t-2} + B_t^{\ell_t-3} + \cdots + B_t^0 = \frac{1-B_t^{\ell_t-1}}{1-B_t} \approx B_t^{\ell_t-2}$ calls to Pack, and $B_t^{\ell_t-1} + 1$ calls to BasicFB. In addition, Decomp contains $(\ell_t - 1)(n + 1)$ integer multiplications and ℓ_t calls to MS, BasicFB, and KS. Furthermore, the computational costs of MS, KS, and Pack are $3(n + 1)$, $N\ell(n + 1)$, and $2B_t N^2 \ell'$, respectively. Besides, in Algorithm 13, the computational cost of BasicFB is $4n\ell d$ inside Decomp and is $4n\ell'd$ outside Decomp. Consequently, the computational cost of Algorithm 13 is $(n + 1)(-1 + 7\ell_t + N\ell_t\ell) + 4nd(\ell_t\ell + \ell'(1 + b)) + 2b\ell'N^2$, where $b = B_t^{\ell_t-1}$.

References

1. Agrawal, S., Goldwasser, S., Mossel, S.: Deniable fully homomorphic encryption from learning with errors. In: Malkin, T., Peikert, C. (eds.) CRYPTO 2021. LNCS, vol. 12826, pp. 641–670. Springer, Cham (2021). https://doi.org/10.1007/978-3-030-84245-1_22
2. Albrecht, M.R., Player, R., Scott, S.: On the concrete hardness of learning with errors. J. Math. Cryptology **9**(3), 169–203 (2015)
3. Alperin-Sheriff, J., Peikert, C.: Practical bootstrapping in quasilinear time. In: Canetti, R., Garay, J.A. (eds.) CRYPTO 2013. LNCS, vol. 8042, pp. 1–20. Springer, Heidelberg (2013). https://doi.org/10.1007/978-3-642-40041-4_1
4. Boura, C., Gama, N., Georgieva, M., Jetchev, D.: Simulating homomorphic evaluation of deep learning predictions. In: Dolev, S., Hendler, D., Lodha, S., Yung, M. (eds.) CSCML 2019. LNCS, vol. 11527, pp. 212–230. Springer, Cham (2019). https://doi.org/10.1007/978-3-030-20951-3_20
5. Brakerski, Z.: Fully homomorphic encryption without modulus switching from classical GapSVP. In: Safavi-Naini, R., Canetti, R. (eds.) CRYPTO 2012. LNCS, vol. 7417, pp. 868–886. Springer, Heidelberg (2012). https://doi.org/10.1007/978-3-642-32009-5_50
6. Brakerski, Z., Gentry, C., Vaikuntanathan, V.: (leveled) fully homomorphic encryption without bootstrapping. ACM Trans. Comput. Theory **6**(3), 1–36 (2014)
7. Carpov, S., Izabachène, M., Mollimard, V.: New techniques for multi-value input homomorphic evaluation and applications. In: Matsui, M. (ed.) CT-RSA 2019. LNCS, vol. 11405, pp. 106–126. Springer, Cham (2019). https://doi.org/10.1007/978-3-030-12612-4_6
8. Chen, H., Dai, W., Kim, M., Song, Y.: Efficient homomorphic conversion between (ring) LWE ciphertexts. In: Sako, K., Tippenhauer, N.O. (eds.) ACNS 2021. LNCS, vol. 12726, pp. 460–479. Springer, Cham (2021). https://doi.org/10.1007/978-3-030-78372-3_18
9. Cheon, J.H., Kim, A., Kim, M., Song, Y.S.: Homomorphic encryption for arithmetic of approximate numbers. In: Takagi, T., Peyrin, T. (eds.) ASIACRYPT 2017. LNCS, vol. 10624, pp. 409–437. Springer, Cham (2017). https://doi.org/10.1007/978-3-319-70694-8_15
10. Cheon, J.H., Kim, D., Kim, D., Lee, H., Lee, K.: Numerical method for comparison on homomorphically encrypted numbers. In: Galbraith, S.D., Moriai, S. (eds.) ASIACRYPT 2019. LNCS, vol. 11922, pp. 415–445. Springer, Cham (2019). https://doi.org/10.1007/978-3-030-34621-8_15
11. Chillotti, I., Gama, N., Georgieva, M., Izabachène, M.: Faster packed homomorphic operations and efficient circuit bootstrapping for TFHE. In: Takagi, T., Peyrin, T. (eds.) ASIACRYPT 2017. LNCS, vol. 10624, pp. 377–408. Springer, Cham (2017). https://doi.org/10.1007/978-3-319-70694-8_14
12. Chillotti, I., Joye, M., Paillier, P.: Programmable bootstrapping enables efficient homomorphic inference of deep neural networks. In: Dolev, S., Margalit, O., Pinkas, B., Schwarzmann, A.A. (eds.) CSCML 2021. LNCS, vol. 12716, pp. 1–19. Springer, Cham (2021). https://doi.org/10.1007/978-3-030-78086-9_1
13. Chillotti, I., Ligier, D., Orfila, J., Tap, S.: Improved programmable bootstrapping with larger precision and efficient arithmetic circuits for TFHE. In: Tibouchi, M., Wang, H. (eds.) ASIACRYPT 2021. LNCS, vol. 13092, pp. 670–699. Springer, Cham (2021). https://doi.org/10.1007/978-3-030-92078-4_23

14. Clet, P., Boudguiga, A., Sirdey, R., Zuber, M.: Combo: a novel functional bootstrapping method for efficient evaluation of nonlinear functions in the encrypted domain. In: Mrabet, N.E., Feo, L.D., Duquesne, S. (eds.) AFRICACRYPT 2023. LNCS, vol. 14064, pp. 317–343. Springer, Cham (2023). https://doi.org/10.1007/978-3-031-37679-5_14

15. Ducas, L., Micciancio, D.: FHEW: bootstrapping homomorphic encryption in less than a second. In: Oswald, E., Fischlin, M. (eds.) EUROCRYPT 2015. LNCS, vol. 9056, pp. 617–640. Springer, Heidelberg (2015). https://doi.org/10.1007/978-3-662-46800-5_24

16. Fan, J., Vercauteren, F.: Somewhat practical fully homomorphic encryption. IACR Cryptology ePrint Archive, p.144 (2012)

17. Gentry, C.: Fully homomorphic encryption using ideal lattices. In: Proceedings of the 41st Annual ACM Symposium on Theory of Computing, STOC 2009, pp. 169–178. ACM (2009)

18. Gentry, C., Halevi, S.: Implementing gentry's fully-homomorphic encryption scheme. In: Paterson, K.G. (ed.) EUROCRYPT 2011. LNCS, vol. 6632, pp. 129–148. Springer, Heidelberg (2011). https://doi.org/10.1007/978-3-642-20465-4_9

19. Gentry, C., Halevi, S., Smart, N.P.: Homomorphic evaluation of the AES circuit. In: Safavi-Naini, R., Canetti, R. (eds.) CRYPTO 2012. LNCS, vol. 7417, pp. 850–867. Springer, Heidelberg (2012). https://doi.org/10.1007/978-3-642-32009-5_49

20. Guimarães, A., Borin, E., Aranha, D.F.: Revisiting the functional bootstrap in TFHE. IACR Trans. Cryptographic Hardware Embed. Syst. **2021**(2), 229–253 (2021)

21. Halevi, S., Shoup, V.: Bootstrapping for helib. J. Cryptol. **34**(1), 7 (2021)

22. Iliashenko, I., Zucca, V.: Faster homomorphic comparison operations for BGV and BFV. Proc. Priv. Enhancing Technol. **2021**(3), 246–264 (2021)

23. Kim, A., Polyakov, Y., Zucca, V.: Revisiting homomorphic encryption schemes for finite fields. In: Tibouchi, M., Wang, H. (eds.) ASIACRYPT 2021. LNCS, vol. 13092, pp. 608–639. Springer, Cham (2021). https://doi.org/10.1007/978-3-030-92078-4_21

24. Kluczniak, K., Schild, L.: FDFB: full domain functional bootstrapping towards practical fully homomorphic encryption. IACR Trans. Cryptographic Hardware Embed. Syst. **2023**(1), 501–537 (2023)

25. Liu, Z., Micciancio, D., Polyakov, Y.: Large-precision homomorphic sign evaluation using FHEW/TFHE bootstrapping. In: Agrawal, S., Lin, D. (eds.) ASIACRYPT 2022. LNCS, vol. 13792, pp. 130–160. Springer, Cham (2022). https://doi.org/10.1007/978-3-031-22966-4_5

26. Liu, Z., Wang, Y.: Amortized functional bootstrapping in less than 7 ms, with õ(1) polynomial multiplications. In: Guo, J., Steinfeld, R. (eds.) ASIACRYPT 2023. LNCS, vol. 14443, pp. 101–132. Springer, Singapore (2023). https://doi.org/10.1007/978-981-99-8736-8_4

27. Lou, Q., Feng, B., Fox, G.C., Jiang, L.: Glyph: fast and accurately training deep neural networks on encrypted data. In: Advances in Neural Information Processing Systems 33: Annual Conference on Neural Information Processing Systems 2020, NeurIPS 2020, pp. 9193–9202 (2020)

28. Lou, Q., Jiang, L.: SHE: a fast and accurate deep neural network for encrypted data. In: Advances in Neural Information Processing Systems 32: Annual Conference on Neural Information Processing Systems 2019, NeurIPS 2019, pp. 10035–10043 (2019)
29. Ma, S., Huang, T., Wang, A., Zhou, Q., Wang, X.: Fast and accurate: efficient full-domain functional bootstrap and digit decomposition for homomorphic computation. IACR Trans. Cryptographic Hardware Embed. Syst. **2024**(1), 592–616 (2024)

Ripple: Accelerating Programmable Bootstraps for FHE with Wavelet Approximations

Charles Gouert[1]([✉])(iD), Mehmet Ugurbil[2](iD), Dimitris Mouris[2](iD),
Miguel de Vega[2], and Nektarios G. Tsoutsos[1](iD)

[1] University of Delaware, Newark, USA
{cgouert,tsoutsos}@udel.edu
[2] Nillion, Zug, Switzerland
{memo,dimitris,miguelv}@nillion.com

Abstract. Homomorphic encryption can address key privacy challenges in cloud-based outsourcing by enabling potentially untrusted servers to perform meaningful computation directly on encrypted data. While most homomorphic encryption schemes offer addition and multiplication over ciphertexts natively, any non-linear functions must be implemented as costly polynomial approximations due to this restricted computational model. Nevertheless, the CGGI cryptosystem is capable of performing arbitrary univariate functions over ciphertexts in the form of lookup tables through the use of programmable bootstrapping. While promising, this procedure can quickly become costly when high degrees of precision are required. To address this challenge, we propose Ripple: a framework that introduces different approximation methodologies based on discrete wavelet transforms (DWT) to decrease the number of entries in homomorphic lookup tables while maintaining high accuracy. Our empirical evaluations demonstrate significant error reduction compared to plain quantization methods across multiple non-linear functions. Notably, Ripple improves runtime performance for realistic applications, such as logistic regression and Euclidean distance.

Keywords: Cryptography · Homomorphic Encryption · Lookup Tables

1 Introduction

Cloud computing enables corporations to leverage powerful computational resources, while avoiding the cost and upkeep associated with maintaining local computing infrastructure. Along with numerous benefits, this gives rise to privacy concerns over outsourced data as cloud service providers can possibly view

C. Gouert and M. Ugurbil—The first two authors have equal contribution and appear in alphabetical order.

C. Gouert and N.G. Tsoutsos would like to acknowledge the support of the National Science Foundation (Award #2239334).

© The Author(s), under exclusive license to Springer Nature Switzerland AG 2025
N. Mouha and N. Nikiforakis (Eds.): ISC 2024, LNCS 15257, pp. 273–293, 2025.
https://doi.org/10.1007/978-3-031-75757-0_14

data stored on their servers, and malicious actors have increasingly targeted cloud servers as they can be treasure troves of proprietary information from multiple clients [22,31]. While encryption techniques such as AES can be used to protect data confidentiality, the encrypted data must be static and the cloud cannot apply meaningful processing on ciphertexts (aside from storage). Thus, if a client wants to modify their data, they will have to download the ciphertexts, decrypt them, perform a computation to update the plaintext data, re-encrypt them, and re-upload the result to the cloud.

Fully Homomorphic encryption (FHE) is a powerful technique that helps address privacy concerns in cloud computing by allowing computation on encrypted data [13]. With FHE, a client can encrypt sensitive data, upload the corresponding ciphertexts to the cloud, have the cloud apply an arbitrary algorithm such as image classification, and then receive a valid encryption of the results, which can only be decrypted with the client's secret key. In this way, the cloud learns nothing about the contents of the input data, intermediate results, or the output of the encrypted computation.

Nevertheless, for many FHE schemes such as BGV [3] and CKKS [5], evaluating non-linear functions directly remains impossible, as only addition and multiplication operations can be executed over ciphertexts. Conversely, CGGI [7] allows encrypted lookup tables (LUTs), which allow non-linear functions to be computed exactly. Unfortunately, this operation is quite costly and becomes significantly more expensive as the plaintext modulus increases. Likewise, both the time and memory required to generate the lookup tables scale exponentially with the input's precision, with LUT sizes of 32 bits and larger becoming impractical.[1]

One solution to this problem is to simply quantize the LUT inputs (i.e., reduce the bit width) to lower the number of entries in the lookup table, resulting in faster evaluation and LUT generation times. The reduced precision caused by quantization, however, can negatively impact a wide variety of applications that require high precision. For instance, quantization in deep neural networks can result in non-negligible accuracy loss [20] and thus lead to incorrect classifications. Particularly, errors occurring due to quantization in early layers will propagate to subsequent layers, resulting in an avalanche effect, where the errors are compounded in each layer. Indeed, this effect is not limited to privacy-preserving inference and can happen in any application.

In this work, we propose the *Ripple* framework that offers new efficient techniques for encrypted LUT evaluation. Ripple provides all of the same benefits of quantization in terms of latency reduction while minimizing the accuracy loss resulting from reduced precision and bit widths. Our approach leverages the *discrete wavelet transform* (DWT) [28] to approximate non-linear functions and generate significantly smaller lookup tables while maintaining high accuracy. Moreover, Ripple employs multiple DWT families and introduces bespoke FHE-friendly protocols tailored to each family to maximize accuracy and minimize

---

[1] We empirically observed even 32-bit encrypted LUTs with the state-of-the-art TFHE-rs [32] FHE library require approximately 515 GB of RAM and 65 min. For reference, 30-bit LUTs took almost 15 min requiring over 120 GB..

latency. For instance, we find that some DWT families benefit from multiple LUTs while others need only a single LUT evaluation. We apply Ripple to a variety of non-linear functions that are widely used across several domains from machine learning [4,11] to statistics [26], as well as multiple realistic applications for homomorphic encryption [17,29], such as logistic regression inference and edge detection. Our contributions can be summarized as follows:

- We introduce Ripple to construct smaller encrypted LUTs with wavelet techniques without sacrificing accuracy.
- We propose multiple protocols for evaluating wavelet-encoded LUTs in the encrypted domain.
- We implement a suite of commonly adopted non-linear functions and optimize with Ripple, along with a set of benchmarks from various domains.

2 Preliminaries

2.1 Fully Homomorphic Encryption Overview

The key characteristic of all FHE schemes is *malleability*, where ciphertexts can be manipulated to change the underlying plaintext data predictably. All FHE schemes can be roughly divided into two categories depending on the primary computational domain: arithmetic-based schemes and Boolean-based schemes.

We focus on the latter class, where instead of encrypting integers or floating point numbers, Boolean schemes encrypt individual bits (or low-precision integers in certain cases). The addition and multiplication primitives are replaced by encrypted gate operations, such as AND, OR, and NOT gates. In practice, most logic gates are implemented as a series of linear operations between ciphertext polynomials followed by a *functional bootstrap*, which serves to scale the output to the expected value. Because Boolean schemes can support all standard logic gates, they are capable of executing arbitrary algorithms. Contrary to arithmetic-based schemes, this class of cryptosystems is capable of evaluating non-linear functions directly through the use of Boolean circuits.

Additionally, unlike arithmetic-based schemes, Boolean schemes do not need to utilize polynomial approximations. Indeed, non-linear operations can be implemented exactly as a Boolean circuit. As an example, the ReLU activation function is directly mapped to a multi-bit comparator circuit followed by a multiplexer. However, this may require a larger number of Boolean gates and the majority of gate types require at least one bootstrapping operation, resulting in relatively high latency for large circuits. Prior frameworks, such as the Google Transpiler [15], ArctyrEX [19], and HELM [16], exploit the inherent circuit-level parallelism to reduce the latency of circuit evaluation. Still, the performance of these frameworks is limited by the critical path (or greatest depth) of the homomorphic circuit. Additionally, all three approaches rely on logic and/or high-level synthesis methods to convert input programs to optimized Boolean circuits, which results in high pre-processing cost for non-trivial applications.

Alternatively, with proper parameter selection, Boolean schemes can encrypt low-precision integers. In the case of the CGGI cryptosystem [6], this allows for ciphertext addition and multiplication with a public constant, but not multiplication between two ciphertexts. Notably, it still retains the functional bootstrap, which can be utilized to evaluate $N:N$ lookup tables. This approach combines some of the key strengths of both arithmetic-based schemes and the Boolean mode of operation in the form of natively supported multi-bit arithmetic and a mechanism for exactly evaluating non-linear functions.

The primary challenge is the restriction on the size of the plaintext space, but this can be overcome by representing high-precision plaintexts as vectors of ciphertexts, where each encryption encodes a low-precision chunk of the original message. This very methodology is employed in the TFHE-rs library [32] in two different ways: a Chinese remainder theorem (CRT) method and a radix method. The former involves generating multiple residues by reducing an input message by a series of co-prime bases and encrypting each residue as a separate ciphertext. Upon decryption, the residues are combined to form the final higher-precision result. The second method involves decomposing the input data into a series of digits, each of which is decrypted individually. Ripple utilizes the latter approach as it provides a convenient way to truncate ciphertexts, which is an integral operation in the DWT protocols explained in the following section. Truncating the digits of a ciphertext array encoded with the radix decomposition can be done with negligible latency overhead as no FHE operations are required.

Programmable Bootstrapping (PBS). A crucial feature of the DM and CGGI FHE cryptosystems is the *functional bootstrap*, which takes advantage of the programmability of the bootstrapping algorithm employed in these schemes. A polynomial with crafted coefficients that encodes the set of desired output messages is rotated by an encrypted value and the first encrypted coefficient corresponding to the constant term of the polynomial is extracted. These two procedures, *blind rotation* and *extraction*, form the core bootstrapping steps.

By encoding chosen lookup table (LUT) entries in the coefficients of the polynomial to be rotated, one can evaluate a LUT T over a ciphertext. Essentially, this can be done by rotating the LUT polynomial by an encrypted amount (corresponding to the input ciphertext) and extracting the entry corresponding to the constant term. The result is a valid encryption that encodes the mapping from a LUT input to a desired LUT output. Thus, it allows computing arbitrary univariate functions by evaluating a function in the plaintext domain across all possible inputs and encoding them in the polynomial utilized during bootstrapping. This generalized bootstrapping technique is called *programmable bootstrapping (PBS)* [9,24]. Although the LUT needs to be relatively small to maintain efficient cryptographic parameter sets, it has two main advantages. First, it can encode any arbitrary univariate function, and second, it leads to a significant performance boost as it replaces expensive operations that otherwise would require multiple additions and multiplications.

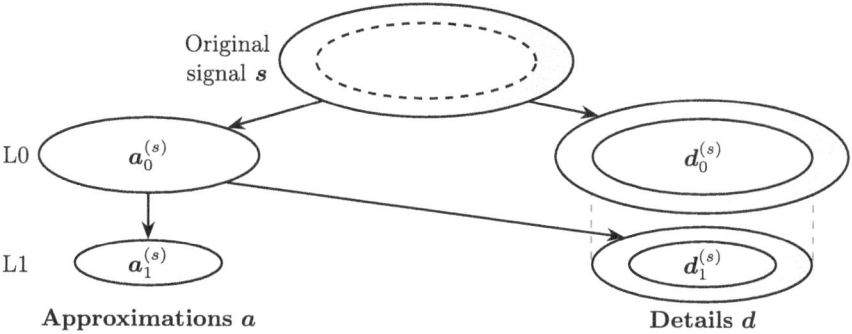

Fig. 1. Two DWT iterations. The signal s can be represented by the approximation $a^{(s)}$ (green) and the details $d^{(s)}$ (gray). (Color figure online)

2.2   The Discrete Wavelet Transform (DWT)

A Discrete Wavelet Transformation (DWT) is a process of splitting a discretely sampled signal into two parts: the approximation and the detail coefficients [28]. The former is half of the size of the original signal but encompasses the most interesting parts of it, while the latter contains information about the error incurred by the approximation coefficients. When combining both the detail coefficients and the approximation, one can reconstruct the original signal. Figure 1 illustrates the original signal on top and two applications of the DWT. In the first level (L0), we deconstruct the signal on top to approximation ($a_0^{(s)}$) and detail coefficients ($d_0^{(s)}$). Then, we can repeat the same process by treating the L0 approximation as a new signal and thus get new approximation ($a_1^{(s)}$) and detail coefficients ($d_1^{(s)}$) at level 1, and so on. In Fig. 1, notice that given the L1 approximation and detail coefficients along with the L0 detail coefficients, it is sufficient for recovering the original signal.

There exist multiple wavelet families such as the Daubechy (Db) and the Biorthogonal wavelets. A special case of Db wavelets is the Db-1 – or *Haar* – wavelet. The core idea in all families is a matrix multiplication with a constant matrix M, where M differs based on the family. Haar uses an orthogonal matrix to obtain the approximation coefficients, which are calculated by averaging every two consecutive points of the original signal. Biorthogonal, on the other hand, relies on two different matrices, where the transpose of one matrix is the inverse of the other. We delve more into the details of both wavelet families in Sect. 3.

Haar DWT. Haar applies a linear transformation to the input and generates the approximation and detail coefficients. Starting with a signal $s = [s_0, \ldots, s_{2N-1}]$ of length $2N$, the Haar DWT generates the approximation coefficients $a = [a_0, \ldots, a_{N-1}]$ and the detail coefficients $d = [d_0, \ldots, d_{N-1}]$, each with N entries. More specifically, the approximations are generated as $a_k = (s_{2k} + s_{2k+1})/2$, while the details are generated by $d_k = (s_{2k} - s_{2k+1})/2$ for $k \in [0, \ldots, N)$.

It is easy to see that when the Haar DWT is applied to a one-hot vector, it results in yet another one-hot vector, albeit scaled. The index of the non-zero value in the new vector is in fact the old index divided by 2, which is akin to removing the last bit of the index. Therefore, we can simply truncate the value to get rid of the least significant bits and end up with the value that we want to do the lookup at. In effect, we have manually applied the Haar DWT transform to the one-hot vector using only truncation.

Biorthogonal DWT. The linear transformation in Haar can be seen as a matrix multiplication with some public orthogonal matrix.[2] The Biorthogonal DWT on the other hand, requires two different matrices, where the transpose of one matrix is the inverse of the other, i.e., $M_1^T = M_2^{-1}$. In this case, M_1 is used for the decomposition of the signal, while M_2 is used for the reconstruction.

In Haar, we observe that the points in the approximation coefficient are averaged from the input signal S and the details are complementary in order to be able to recover S. Conversely, in Biorthogonal wavelets, the approximations and details are computed with weighted averages [28]. Since the Biorthogonal wavelets have more non-zero filters, when the transform is applied to a one-hot vector, the result is not a one-hot vector. Even so, we can manually calculate the resulting vector as it is a weighted average of the two consecutive values starting at the most significant bits of the original index. The weights depend on the least significant bits of the original index; hence, by splitting the original index into the MSBs and LSBs, we can calculate the transformed vector.

3   The Ripple Framework

As mentioned in Sect. 2.1, a key feature of the CGGI cryptosystem is the ability to evaluate a lookup table with the programmable bootstrapping mechanism. Complex non-linear functions can now be encoded as LUTs and evaluated homomorphically, eliminating the need to perform expensive polynomial approximations. Unfortunately, as the size of the LUT grows, this technique becomes prohibitively expensive (recall footnote 1), and thus many non-linearities are impossible to evaluate in applications that require high precision.

We address this challenge by utilizing the DWT to reduce the size of LUTs without sacrificing correctness. Ripple is the first framework to explore wavelet approximations for FHE as a way to accelerate programmable bootstrapping. Our key observation is that if we apply the DWT to signals that represent smooth functions (e.g., logarithm, square root, sigmoid, etc.), then the detail coefficients are relatively small compared to the approximation coefficients. This means that our approximation is sufficient to represent the original signal and we can completely disregard the detail coefficients while maintaining a minimal error relative to the original function. Utilizing this observation, we can zero out the details in Fig. 1, and by just applying the DWT a single time, we can

---

[2] An orthogonal matrix M has the property that $MM^T = I$, where I is the identity matrix. A matrix M is orthogonal if its transpose (M^T) is equal to its inverse (M^{-1}).

halve the size of the LUT. This signal might still be quite big, so we can repeat the same process and half the LUT size even further. Of course, as this is an approximation, the smaller the LUT size, the higher the error we might have. With Ripple, however, these errors are marginal as we show in Sect. 5.

Ripple's Key Observation. The core idea behind Ripple relies on the orthogonality or biorthogonality of the DWT transform applied to the inner product. Consider the fact that the inner product between two vectors $\boldsymbol{v}$ and $\boldsymbol{u}$ is equal to the product between the transpose of the first vector and the second, i.e., $\langle \boldsymbol{v}, \boldsymbol{u} \rangle = \boldsymbol{v}^T \cdot \boldsymbol{u}$. As described in Sect. 2.2, the DWT of both $\boldsymbol{v}$ and $\boldsymbol{u}$ is a multiplication with a matrix M, which we can view as $\mathsf{DWT}(\boldsymbol{v}) = M \cdot \boldsymbol{v}$. This results in a vector $\left[\frac{\boldsymbol{a}^{(v)}}{\boldsymbol{d}^{(v)}}\right]$, where $\boldsymbol{a}^{(v)}$ and $\boldsymbol{d}^{(v)}$ represent the approximation and detail coefficients of $\boldsymbol{v}$, respectively. Similarly for $\mathsf{DWT}(\boldsymbol{u}) = M \cdot \boldsymbol{u}$ we get $\boldsymbol{a}^{(u)}$ and $\boldsymbol{d}^{(u)}$. Observe that using orthogonality,

$$
\begin{aligned}
\langle \mathsf{DWT}(\boldsymbol{v}), \mathsf{DWT}(\boldsymbol{u}) \rangle = \langle M \cdot \boldsymbol{v}, M \cdot \boldsymbol{u} \rangle &= (M \cdot \boldsymbol{v})^T \cdot M \cdot \boldsymbol{u} \\
&= \boldsymbol{v}^T \cdot M^T \cdot M \cdot \boldsymbol{u} = \boldsymbol{v}^T \cdot I \cdot \boldsymbol{u} = \boldsymbol{v}^T \cdot \boldsymbol{u} = \langle \boldsymbol{v}, \boldsymbol{u} \rangle.
\end{aligned}
\tag{1}
$$

We remark that the inner product of two vectors is equal to the sum of the inner product of the approximation coefficients and the inner product of the detail coefficients of the DWT transforms of the vectors, as follows:

$$
(M \cdot \boldsymbol{v})^T \cdot M \cdot \boldsymbol{u} = \left[\frac{\boldsymbol{a}^{(v)}}{\boldsymbol{d}^{(v)}}\right]^T \cdot \left[\frac{\boldsymbol{a}^{(u)}}{\boldsymbol{d}^{(u)}}\right] = \boldsymbol{a}^{(v)T} \cdot \boldsymbol{a}^{(u)} + \boldsymbol{d}^{(v)T} \cdot \boldsymbol{d}^{(u)}.
$$

In Ripple, we represent $\langle \boldsymbol{v}, \boldsymbol{u} \rangle$ as $\langle \boldsymbol{a}^{(v)}, \boldsymbol{a}^{(u)} \rangle + \langle \boldsymbol{d}^{(v)}, \boldsymbol{d}^{(u)} \rangle$ which is approximately equal to the inner product of their respective approximation coefficient vectors $\boldsymbol{a}^{(v)}$ and $\boldsymbol{a}^{(u)}$. By dropping the detail coefficients, we get the approximation of the original inner product via the inner product of the approximation coefficients, which is key to our proposed lookup methodology. Thus, $\langle \boldsymbol{v}, \boldsymbol{u} \rangle = \langle \mathsf{DWT}(\boldsymbol{v}), \mathsf{DWT}(\boldsymbol{u}) \rangle \approx \langle \boldsymbol{a}^{(v)}, \boldsymbol{a}^{(u)} \rangle$.

This works nicely for orthogonal DWTs, but for the Biorthogonal DWT, we need extra considerations. Instead of applying the same transformation to both $\boldsymbol{v}$ and $\boldsymbol{u}$, we have to apply the decomposition matrix to one, while applying the reconstruction matrix to the other. Then, by biorthogonality of these matrices, the same observation holds and $\langle \boldsymbol{v}, \boldsymbol{u} \rangle = \langle M_1 \cdot \boldsymbol{v}, M_2 \cdot \boldsymbol{u} \rangle \approx \langle \boldsymbol{a}^{(v)}, \boldsymbol{a}^{(u)} \rangle$.

Applying Our Observation to the Encrypted Domain. In Eq. (1), we can view $\boldsymbol{v}$ as a one-hot vector where the non-zero value is at the index of the ciphertext and $\boldsymbol{u}$ as a public LUT T' that approximates the full-precision LUT T. Then, the inner product $\langle \boldsymbol{v}, \boldsymbol{u} \rangle$ will yield the lookup value in table T' at the non-zero index of $\boldsymbol{v}$, which is the lookup value at the ciphertext. In particular, $\langle \boldsymbol{a}^{(v)}, \boldsymbol{a}^{(u)} \rangle$ will be an approximation of this lookup. Notably, the approximation of the LUT is easy to calculate since it is in plaintext, while we need a way to efficiently calculate the approximation vector of the one-hot vector that represents the ciphertext. Fortunately, it turns out that this approximation vector can be calculated by a weighted sum of lookups.

Of course, the aforementioned technique is not practical in FHE, but programmable bootstrapping (PBS) can be leveraged for this purpose. Starting with a ciphertext x' (which is a truncated version of the full-precision x) we can evaluate the LUT T' on x' homomorphically and obtain ciphertext $y' = T'(x')$. The novelty of Ripple lies in that x' has fewer bits than x and T' has fewer entries than T, while y' is a close approximation to $y = T(x)$. Ripple focuses on the two most popular DWT families: Haar and Biorthogonal, which are both viable and constitute a tradeoff between accuracy and latency (as discussed in Sect. 5). In the following subsections, we describe how Ripple formulates and evaluates encrypted lookup tables with each of the two DWT families.

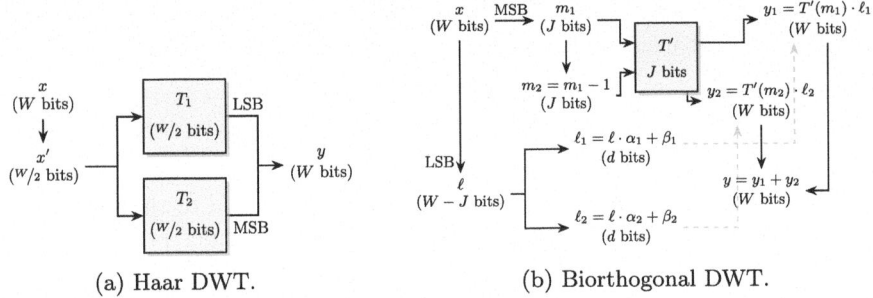

(a) Haar DWT.   (b) Biorthogonal DWT.

Fig. 2. DWT LUT approximating $y = T(x)$. In (a), the approximation computes $y = T_1(x') \parallel T_2(x')$, where $x' = (x \gg W/2)$. In (b), we compute $y = T'(m_1) \cdot \ell_1 + T'(m_2) \cdot \ell_2$, where $m_1 = (x \gg (W - J))$, $m_2 = m_1 - 1$, $\ell = x \mod 2^{W-J}$, $\ell_1 = \ell \cdot \alpha_1 + \beta_1$, and $\ell_2 = \ell \cdot \alpha_2 + \beta_2$ with $\alpha_1, \alpha_2, \beta_1, \beta_2$ being public scalars.

3.1   PBS with Haar DWT

Let W be the bit width of our input radix-decomposed ciphertext vector, where each ciphertext encodes a plaintext digit (as explained in Sect. 2). Naturally, we can represent the function that we want to approximate as a LUT T that maps k-bit inputs to k-bit outputs. For simplicity, we can assume that $k = W$. Creating a LUT of 2^W entries, however, is not always feasible. For instance, $W = 64$ requires generating and storing 2^{64} LUT entries, which is completely impractical. A straightforward option is to truncate our input ciphertexts by J bits and limit T to only have 2^{W-J} entries and operate over $W - J$ bit inputs and outputs. Notably, this truncation simply involves deleting encrypted digits and corresponds exactly to truncation in the plaintext domain. As it turns out, this approximation incurs high errors and is not sufficient for most applications.

Ripple takes a different approach: First, we apply the Haar DWT over the public LUT T iteratively J times by dropping the detail coefficients to end up with an approximation T' of our original function. The new table T' now operates over $W - J$ bits. Observe, however, that our input ciphertext vector is still W-bits long. To index T', Ripple truncates the vector to encode $W - J$ bits so it can be used during PBS to index the LUT. As long as $W - J$ bits is a multiple of the size of our radix digits, the truncation is free. Conveniently, this is the index needed for the approximation vector $\boldsymbol{a}^{(v)}$. This results in an output ciphertext vector also encoding $W - J$ bits.

As we started with an W-bit input ciphertext vector, after approximating the function we need to end up with a W-bit output as well. To do so, we repeat the same process twice by building two LUTs (T_1 and T_2); one for the LSBs and one for the MSBs. In both cases, the truncated $W - J$ bit input ciphertext vector is used to index the LUT. This is illustrated in Fig. 2a, where $J = W/2$. Note that each of T_1 and T_2 has $W/2$ bits and thus takes approximately half the time to be evaluated compared to a W-bit LUT (which is not even possible to practically create for large W). Additionally, both tables can be evaluated in parallel and finally, the two outputs can be concatenated to get the final encrypted result encoding W bits of data.

We remark that, in certain functions, we only need to evaluate the LSB table and we can avoid evaluating T_2 altogether. For instance, any function where the output can fit in less than half the bit width, such as the square root or Sigmoid activation function, only needs a single LUT evaluation.

3.2   PBS with Biorthogonal DWT

The Haar DWT is quite efficient since its approximation vector is again one-hot and hence only has a single approximation that needs to be looked up; however, this benefit also comes at a limitation. Namely, all the points that have the same most significant bits evaluate to the same value. The Biorthogonal DWT overcomes this challenge by making use of the least significant bits of the input ciphertext, as well as the most significant bits. This comes at the cost of doing two lookups followed by two multiplications and an addition, but results in more accurate approximations. In the end, we get significantly better compression, in fact, the same compression used in JPEG2000 [27].

The Biorthogonal DWT follows a similar approach as the Haar DWT, yet incurs more operations as its linear transformation computes weighted averages. Contrary to Haar where we had to evaluate two separate LUTs, in Biorthogonal wavelets we need to evaluate a single LUT (T') across two different indices. We observe that this can also be done using two LUTs, where, as an optimization, the second table T_2 equals the first one (T_1) shifted by an index: $T_2(x) = T_1(x+1 \mod |T_1|)$, where $|T_1|$ refers to the size of T_1.

Figure 2b demonstrates how Ripple approximates an LUT with Biorthogonal wavelets. First, we extract the most significant bits (MSBs) from the input to be used for the lookup, and the least significant bits (LSBs), which will be used to combine the lookups via their weighted average. Starting with a W-bit input x, we split it into two parts of J and $W - J$ bits, which we call m_1 and ℓ, respectively. Here, J is equal to the depth of the DWT applied. The former (m_1) represents the J MSBs of x and it serves two purposes. First, from m_1, we create m_2 as $m_1 - 1$. Then, we use both m_1 and m_2 to index two consecutive entries of the DWT-encoded LUT and end up with ciphertexts $T'(m_1)$ and $T'(m_2)$. The latter (ℓ) represents the $W - J$ LSBs of x and is used to compute two linear expressions with public constant values α_1, α_2, β_1, and β_2 as $\ell_1 = \ell \cdot \alpha_1 + \beta_1$, and $\ell_2 = \ell \cdot \alpha_2 + \beta_2$. These values come from the non-zero entries of the approximation coefficients vector $\boldsymbol{a}^{(v)}$: $\alpha_1 = -1$, $\alpha_2 = 1$, $\beta_1 = 2^J$, and $\beta_2 = 0$. Lastly, we multiply $T'(m_1)$ by ℓ_1 and $T'(m_2)$ by ℓ_2 computing the inner product in the DWT domain, so we go back to W bits and sum the two ciphertexts together to get our final output.

We are usually able to compress the LUT for the Biorthogonal DWT into J bits as these values do not have to cover the entire output range, unlike Haar which requires a W-bit LUT output. However, when this is not possible, we employ a similar method of evaluating multiple LUTs in parallel with the same J-bit inputs and combine the J-bit outputs to form a higher bit-width result.

4   Function-Centric Compression

In this Section, we investigate two optimizations to further reduce the LUT sizes of specific classes of non-linear functions; namely, we propose optimizations for symmetrical functions and functions where the complex non-linearity converges to some value outside a certain interval.

Symmetrical Functions. First, we exploit the symmetry of certain functions to further reduce the LUT size. This class includes common functions in machine learning, such as reciprocal, sigmoid (σ), hyperbolic tangent (tanh), and the error function (erf). More formally, these functions exhibit the following property: $\frac{1}{-x} = -\frac{1}{x}$, $\sigma(-x) = 1 - \sigma(x)$, $\tanh(-x) = -\tanh(x)$ and $\mathsf{erf}(-x) = -\mathsf{erf}(x)$. Therefore, if we know the sign of the input, we can evaluate the function strictly in the positive domain and then use this intermediate result to calculate the actual value by taking into account the sign of the input.

To apply this technique, the function must exhibit symmetry around zero, but we note that any symmetric function can be shifted to exhibit this required symmetry. For example, sigmoid becomes symmetric around zero after it is moved down on the y-axis by 0.5: $\sigma(-x) - 0.5 = -(\sigma(x) - 0.5)$. We stress that this technique easily generalizes to any symmetric function and reduces the size of the LUT by 2× as only half the domain needs to be evaluated.

In general, we call a function $f(x)$ symmetric around the symmetry point $(x_{\mathsf{sym}}, y_{\mathsf{sym}})$ if $f(x_{\mathsf{sym}} - x) - y_{\mathsf{sym}} = c_{\mathsf{sym}} \cdot (f(x_{\mathsf{sym}} + x) - y_{\mathsf{sym}})$, for symmetry constant c_{sym}. The symmetry constant defines the symmetry relationship; for instance if $c_{\mathsf{sym}} = 1$ then the function is reflected along the y-axis (like $f(x) = x^2$) while if $c_{\mathsf{sym}} = -1$ then the function is reflected along both the x and y axes (like $f(x) = \tanh(x)$). It is easy to see that, given $f(x)$ at some value $x_{\mathsf{sym}} + \delta$, we can compute f at $x_{\mathsf{sym}} - \delta$ simply by noting:

$$f(x_{\mathsf{sym}} - \delta) = f(x_{\mathsf{sym}} - \delta) - y_{\mathsf{sym}} + y_{\mathsf{sym}} = c_{\mathsf{sym}} \cdot (f(x_{\mathsf{sym}} + \delta) - y_{\mathsf{sym}}) + y_{\mathsf{sym}}$$
$$= c_{\mathsf{sym}} \cdot f(x_{\mathsf{sym}} + \delta) + (1 - c_{\mathsf{sym}}) \cdot y_{\mathsf{sym}}.$$

Figure 3 demonstrates a function with $x_{\mathsf{sym}}, y_{\mathsf{sym}}$ and $c_{\mathsf{sym}} = -1$. Notice that for sigmoid, we have $x_{\mathsf{sym}} = 0, y_{\mathsf{sym}} = 0.5$ and $c_{\mathsf{sym}} = -1$, hence we get $\sigma(-x) =$

$-\sigma(x) + 1$. Further, if we set $g(x) = f(x_{\mathtt{sym}} + x)$ and use the absolute value $|x - x_{\mathtt{sym}}|$ and the condition $(x - x_{\mathtt{sym}} < 0)$:

$$f(x) = g(x - x_{\mathtt{sym}}) = \begin{cases} g(x - x_{\mathtt{sym}}) & x - x_{\mathtt{sym}} \geq 0, \\ c_{\mathtt{sym}} \cdot g(x_{\mathtt{sym}} - x) + (1 - c_{\mathtt{sym}}) \cdot y_{\mathtt{sym}} & x - x_{\mathtt{sym}} < 0. \end{cases}$$

Note that this equation holds for all positive or negative values x. Thus, we build our LUT based on $g(x)$; we can use this equation to evaluate f at any value x.

Convergent Functions. We also optimize the class of functions that can be approximated by polynomials outside a region. We refer to these functions as piecewise functions and we specifically study the case where we have three intervals: two that we approximate with polynomials and an interval defined by a non-polynomial function that we evaluate with a LUT. Note that this technique can be generalized to any number of intervals.

A special case of this includes functions that are nearly constant outside a certain bounded interval. Coincidentally, sigmoid, tanh, and erf are also prominent examples of this. For instance, sigmoid is nearly 1 above a threshold of 8 and nearly 0 below -8 with less than 0.0003 of maximum difference. For tanh, the maximum difference is 0.0003 outside $[-4, 4]$, while for erf the difference is $1.54 \cdot 10^{-8}$ outside the same interval as tanh.

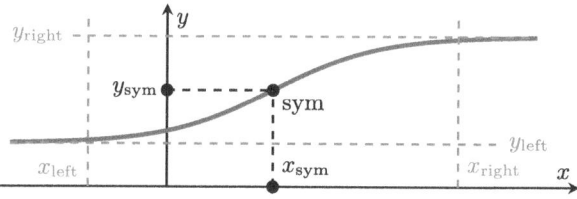

Fig. 3. Sigmoid like function where the symmetry point is $x_{\mathtt{sym}}$ and $y_{\mathtt{sym}}$. $x_{\mathtt{left}}$ and $x_{\mathtt{right}}$ are the convergence bounds for $y_{\mathtt{right}}$ and $y_{\mathtt{left}}$, respectively.

Given a function $f(x)$ and an interval $[x_{\mathtt{left}}, x_{\mathtt{right}}]$, we say this function is convergent if there exists a piecewise polynomial $p(x)$ such that for $x \notin [x_{\mathtt{left}}, x_{\mathtt{right}}]$, $|f(x) - p(x)| < \epsilon$ for a small constant ϵ. To approximate such convergent functions, we can check whether the input is inside the interval and select the lookup value $T(x)$ or the polynomial value accordingly as:

$$f(x) \approx (x \in [x_{\mathtt{left}}, x_{\mathtt{right}}]) \cdot T(x) + p(x).$$

Convergent Symmetrical Functions. Bringing together optimizations for symmetrical and convergent functions, we devise a function evaluation protocol in Algorithm 1 (note that only $f(x) - p(x)$ needs to be symmetric). We start by extracting the most significant bit, which is the sign bit of ct (called ltz for "less than zero" since this bit is 0 for positive values and 1 for negative). Then we

---

Algorithm 1. LUT Evaluation for Symmetric Convergent Functions

---

Public Inputs: func   ▷ Function to be evaluated
   xsym, ysym   ▷ X and Y coordinates of the symmetry point
   csym   ▷ Symmetry coefficient
   threshold   ▷ LUT boundary
Private Input: ct   ▷ Encrypted input value

1: **procedure** EVALUATE(func, xsym, ysym, csym, ct)
2:      ct ← ct - xsym   ▷ Shift to symmetry point
3:      ltz ← EXTRACTSIGN(ct)   ▷ Get the sign bit
4:      sign ← 1 - 2 · ltz   ▷ Calculate the sign as -1 or 1
5:      abs ← sign · ct   ▷ Compute the absolute value
6:      eval ← PBS(abs)   ▷ The LUT evaluation on abs
7:      sym ← $(1 + \text{ltz} \cdot (\text{csym} - 1)) \cdot \text{eval} + \text{ltz} \cdot (1 - \text{csym}) \cdot \text{ysym}$
8:      check ← CMP(abs, threshold)   ▷ Is abs in LUT domain?
9:      poly ← POLY(abs, ltz, check)   ▷ Polynomial evaluation
10:     **return** check · sym + poly

---

calculate the sign as -1 (if ltz is 1) or 1 (if ltz is 0) and the absolute value (abs in line 5 in Algorithm 1) of the ct by multiplying it by the sign. Next, we use the LUT method to look up the function value at abs. Note that this could be the desired DWT LUT and involves truncation and multiplication operations. We bring it all together using the symmetry of the function (in line 7 in Algorithm 1). Next, we check if the abs is in the LUT domain. Notice that since the function is symmetric, we only have to check one end of $[x_{\text{left}}, x_{\text{right}}]$, which we call threshold $= x_{\text{right}} - x_{\text{sym}}$. Then we evaluate the polynomial approximation at abs. Finally, we merge the results using the convergence property.

For example, to evaluate sigmoid, we define PBS(abs) $:= \sigma(\text{abs})$ for abs $\in [0, 8]$, CMP(abs, threshold) $:=$ abs < threshold, and POLY(abs, ltz, check) $:= (1 - \text{check}) \cdot (1 - \text{ltz})$. Then we call EVALUATE with $x_{\text{sym}} = 0, y_{\text{sym}} = 0.5$ and $c_{\text{sym}} = -1$. On the other hand, for a non-convergent symmetrical function like reciprocal $f(x) = \frac{1}{x}$, we set CMP$(\dots) = 1$ and POLY$(\dots) = 0$.

5   Experimental Evaluation

We implemented Ripple using the state-of-the-art TFHE-rs [32] library. In our experiments, we compare Ripple against HELM [16], Romeo [18], and Google Transpiler [15], as well as baseline implementations in TFHE-rs that use LUTs configured for the full bit width of each application. For Ripple, we implemented three variants: (a) a quantized version that is similar to the baseline, but, in this case, we truncate before applying the LUTs in a similar way to preparing inputs for a Haar DWT lookup, (b) a Haar DWT variant, and (c) a Biorthogonal DWT variant. It is expected that the quantized version will outperform both the Haar and Biorthogonal DWT-encoded LUTs in terms of latency, with the last two incurring significantly fewer errors.

Table 1. Overview of runtime improvement (in seconds) and mean absolute error (MAE) over non-linear operations for Ripple using quantization, Haar, and Biorthogonal wavelets. Our baseline uses LUT sizes (T) to be equal to the word size (W), while the Ripple quantized version, as well as the Haar and Biorthogonal DWT variants, use approximations with T bits; k represents the precision.

Op.	W	k	T	Base	Quant.		Haar		Biortho.	
					Time	MAE	Time	MAE	Time	MAE
$\sqrt{x}$				9.5	2.4	2.79e-3	2.3	1.37e-3	3.1	1.92e-5
$1/x$				9.5	2.4	2.45e-4	2.4	1.26e-4	3.1	8.62e-6
$1/\sqrt{x}$				18.1	4.8	2.19e-4	2.4	1.14e-4	3.1	8.24e-6
$\log x$	24	16	12	9.5	2.4	1.73e-3	2.3	8.61e-4	3.1	7.42e-6
$\sigma(x)^*$				19.0	4.8	1.97e-2	2.3	6.37e-5	3.3	6.73e-6
$\mathrm{erf}(x)^*$				9.4	2.4	3.96e-3	2.4	1.28e-4	3.3	8.89e-6
$\tanh(x)^*$				9.5	2.4	3.96e-3	2.4	1.28e-4	3.3	9.41e-6
$\sqrt{x}$				N/A	3.2	6.93e-4	3.2	3.45e-4	4.2	1.35e-6
$1/x$				N/A	3.2	1.57e-5	3.2	8.03e-6	4.2	5.37e-7
$1/\sqrt{x}$				N/A	6.3	1.49e-5	3.2	7.70e-6	4.1	5.07e-7
$\log x$	32	20	16	N/A	3.2	3.99e-4	3.2	1.47e-4	4.1	1.31e-4
$\sigma(x)^*$				N/A	6.3	7.68e-6	3.2	3.97e-6	4.3	4.20e-7
$\mathrm{erf}(x)^*$				N/A	3.1	1.54e-5	3.2	7.95e-6	4.3	5.31e-7
$\tanh(x)^*$				N/A	3.2	1.54e-5	3.2	7.91e-6	4.3	5.19e-7

We perform a series of experiments varying from simple non-linear functions to more elaborate applications (depicted in Appendix A). We utilized a c5.12xlarge AWS EC2 instance with 48 virtual cores running Ubuntu 22.04. For all TFHE-rs modes, we used a parameter set corresponding to approximately 128 bits of security [2]. Specifically, we utilized parameters that allow ciphertexts to hold two data bits and two bits of carry used for intermediate computations. All radix ciphertexts are constructed as vectors of ciphertexts constructed with these parameters. Also, in our experiments, the LUT generations are pre-computed by the server.

Ripple Approximations. In Table 1 we compare the Ripple approximations with both the Haar and Biorthogonal wavelet families against a baseline TFHE-rs implementation (using a non-DWT LUT with the full bit-width) and also a quantized (i.e., approximation) version that truncates half of the bit-width of the inputs. Specifically, we consider non-linear functions including reciprocal, square root, and the sigmoid activation function. Our comparisons emphasize the time to evaluate each non-linear function in seconds as well as the mean absolute error (MAE), which is the sum of absolute errors divided by the number of samples. We perform three blocks of experiments for the same functions with different combinations of word sizes (W), precision values (k), and LUT sizes (T). We experimentally observed that setting T to W/2 yields the fastest runtime while minimizing the MAE. We set the precision k between the T and W because otherwise, quantization misses all the information in the fractional bits.

In Table 1, we observe that the runtime of all quantization, Haar DWT, and Biorthogonal DWT is faster than baseline, and increasingly so as the word size increases. This is intuitive as the LUTs are smaller, and therefore there are fewer PBS operations across the radix ciphertext. In the case of the Biorthogonal DWT, the extra computation associated with the multi-bit additions and multiplications is offset by the parallelism inherent in the algorithm. We observe that, for word size 24, the speedup is around to $3-4\times$, and for word size 32, the baseline is not possible to evaluate on our experimental server, as the RAM required to generate the encrypted LUTs exceeds 500 gigabytes for 32-bit tables. The Haar DWT is usually the same speed as quantization as both involve reducing the bit-width of the input by half and evaluating an LUT, but it is more accurate by halving the error observed. On the other hand, the Biorthogonal DWT is slower than the other two due to the overhead of multiplications, however, it is an order of magnitude more accurate.

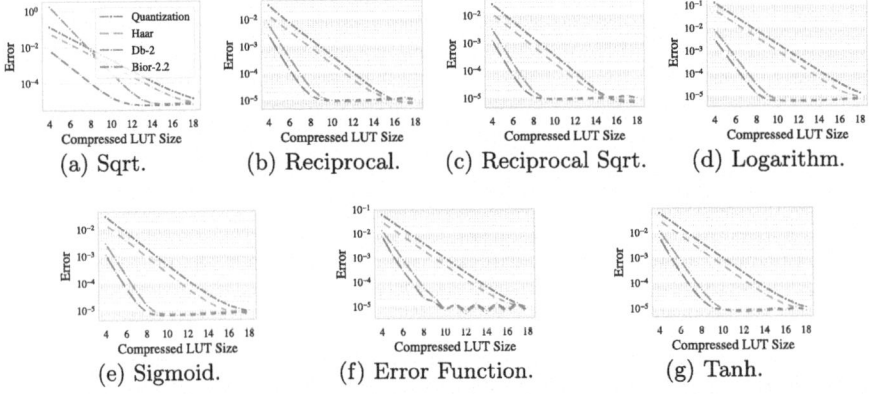

Fig. 4. Approximation errors for multiple non-linear functions for varying compressed LUT sizes with Ripple.

DWT Compression. To better understand the accuracy difference between quantization and various DWT methods (i.e., Haar and Biorthogonal), we plot the average approximation errors for various compressed LUT sizes in Fig. 4. We also evaluate a third DWT variant, Db-2 (which is the second wavelet after Haar in the Debauchies family of wavelets), to illustrate the benefits of Haar and Biorthogonal. We start with a word size of 20 and a precision of 16 and proceed to compress the tables to varying sizes from 4 to 18 bits (the x-axes). Interestingly, the errors vary based on the approximated non-linear function.

From the trend, it is clear that the Haar DWT is twice as accurate as quantization, while Db-2 and Biorthogonal DWTs are (in most cases) orders of magnitude more accurate. The difference in accuracy is most drastic around half the word size, which is 10 in this case. As the LUT size increases, the error of quantization and Haar DWT decreases linearly to the LUT size, while the respective errors of Db-2 and Biorthogonal DWTs decay exponentially to the LUT size until we reach a LUT size of 10–14 bits. The accuracy of the Biorthogonal DWT seems almost equivalent to Db-2 DWT and better by a factor of approximately 2 after some compression threshold. This suggests that Biorthogonal DWT gives better accuracy for the functions under evaluation.

Biorthogonal's superior accuracy, coupled with the fact that Db-2 is more expensive to evaluate due to an increased number of LUT evaluations, leads us to discard it altogether. On the other hand, since Biorthogonal is more expensive than Haar, we can evaluate the trade-off based on our application. If we need higher accuracy, we can go with Biorthogonal DWT, while if speed is of the essence, we can choose Haar DWT.

We observe the trends across the board, however, there are some differences between functions. For square root (Fig. 4a), Db-2 starts performing very poorly as the compressed LUT size decreases past 14. Reciprocal (Fig. 4b) and reciprocal square root (Fig. 4c) follow this trend, except for sizes 15–18 we have that Haar and quantization are more accurate than Biorthogonal and Db-2. Logarithm (Fig. 4d), sigmoid (σ, Fig. 4e), and tanh (Fig. 4g) follow the same trend with slight boundary effects (i.e., divergent behavior around the boundaries) for compressed LUT sizes over 16. Error function (Fig. 4f) experiences boundary effects when DWT is applied an odd number of times, hence we get a zigzag pattern for the error for compressed LUT sizes between 10 and 20 bits. Other functions experience this boundary effect for compressed LUTs with larger bit sizes, resulting in a paradoxically higher error when the compressed LUT size is above 16. The boundary effects can be attributed to DWT filters wrapping around the columns of the DWT matrix.

Table 2. Overview of bounded symmetrical function optimizations. Baseline: we compress a LUT with size equal to the word size (W) to LUT size (T); Optimization: we compress LUT with size (T+3) to LUT size (T). We report the maximum absolute error.

Op.	W	k	T	Haar			Bior.		
				Baseline	Opt.	Diff.	Baseline	Opt.	Diff.
$\sigma(x)$				7.82e-3	2.57e-4	30×	3.60e-5	1.65e-5	2.2×
erf(x)	24	16	12	3.52e-2	1.11e-3	32×	3.34e-4	3.43e-5	9.7×
tanh(x)				3.12e-2	9.82e-4	32×	2.67e-4	3.01e-5	8.9×
$\sigma(x)$				7.81e-3	1.61e-5	485×	3.16e-5	1.04e-6	30×
erf(x)	32	20	16	3.52e-2	6.93e-5	508×	3.16e-4	2.15e-6	147×
tanh(x)				3.12e-2	6.15e-5	507×	2.51e-4	1.90e-6	132×

Function-Centric Compression. In Table 2 we compare Ripple's optimizations for convergent symmetrical functions with both Haar and Biorthogonal wavelet families, against a baseline without the optimizations. We start with a word size equal to 24 bits (or 32 bits) and using the optimizations, we bring this down to 19 bits (or 23 bits), respectively, by reducing the domain of the integer part of the LUT from $[-256, 256]$ to $[0, 8]$ (or from $[-2048, 2048]$ to $[0, 8]$). This means that we now have 19 (or 23 bits) to represent a significantly smaller domain. We compare the maximum absolute error observed using the baseline and optimizations. Specifically, we observe a large decrease in the error for Haar DWT on the order of $30\times$ for 24 bits and $500\times$ for 32 bits, while the decrease for Biorthogonal is about $10\times$ for 24 bits and $100\times$ for 32 bits, respectively. The improvement in Biorthogonal is lower due to its already remarkable compression capabilities. Given the great increase in accuracy, applying these optimizations is beneficial when the computational overhead is acceptable.

6   Related Works

Ducas and Micciancio [12] first proposed the idea of using LUTs to evaluate arbitrary binary gates in FHE, while Chillotti et al. [8] extended this to evaluate arbitrary function evaluation as a tree of leveled multiplexers. Adoption was very limited, however, as it required expressing programs as deterministic automata and needed the control inputs of the multiplexers to be fresh ciphertexts (i.e., could not perform computation with them before to multiplexer). The programmable bootstrapping technique (PBS) introduced in [9] allows for efficient and general-purpose LUT evaluation. HELM [16] built on this technique and introduced a framework for automated conversion from Verilog hardware description language (HDL) to encrypted circuits. HELM employs three modes of operation, one that operates over binary gates, one that operates over integers and utilizes secure LUT evaluations, and a mixed mode that operates over binary circuits and "bridges" to integers to securely evaluate a LUT and then "bridges" back to the binary domain. However, HELM is only compatible with low-precision LUTs as bridging from an integer to bits requires multiple N to 1 LUTs. Conversely, Ripple has high precision and requires smaller LUTs to encode the same amount of information with negligible errors.

Romeo [18] and Google Transpiler [15] follow a similar approach as HELM, in that of relying on an HDL and logic synthesis. The latter, provides two different front-ends, one based on Yosys [30] and another one based on Google XLS [14]. Both works, however, rely on Boolean circuits and neither of them supports LUTs, resulting in costly operations for evaluating non-linear functions.

In a different line of work, Chung et al. [10] evaluate LUTs under FHE with the BGV, BFV, and CKKS cryptosystems. Their idea is to transform LUTs into low-degree multivariate polynomials and utilize the packing (or batching) capabilities of the aforementioned cryptosystems to simultaneously evaluate multiple LUTs. They demonstrate their approach by evaluating AES on an A-100 GPU in over 9.5 min (while batching 2048 ciphertexts). Although the amortized cost per ciphertext is under a second, the latency of this approach is far from practical. On the other hand, Ripple shows a way to accelerate LUT evaluation without sacrificing correctness and is orthogonal to the underlying cryptosystem. As a matter of fact, our techniques introduced in Ripple can be extended for BGV, BFV, and CKKS as well and further accelerate LUT evaluation.

7   Concluding Remarks

In this work, we introduce the Ripple framework that leverages different approximation techniques based on discrete wavelet transform families to reduce the number of homomorphic LUT entries in PBS. Previous works focused either on polynomial approximations or on full-size LUTs; these techniques incur high-performance overheads when high precision is required while the former also introduced non-negligible errors. Ripple, on the other hand, maintains high accuracy while it reduces the LUT sizes. Our empirical evaluations have shown significant error reduction compared to plain quantization methods across various non-linear functions, varying from square root and reciprocal computations to more elaborate sigmoid and hyperbolic tangent functions. A key benefit of Ripple is that it improves performance for several realistic benchmarks without sacrificing accuracy, compared to equivalent applications that utilize the full bit widths and incur slower LUT evaluation runtimes.

A   Evaluation of Applications

Euclidean Distance. This application constitutes a formula for computing the distance between two n-dimensional points $\boldsymbol{u}$ and $\boldsymbol{v}$ in the Euclidean space. It has a plethora of applications from statistics and cluster analysis [4] to facial recognition [25] and has drawn the interest of recent FHE works [17,29]. The Euclidean distance can be computed by $d(\boldsymbol{u}, \boldsymbol{v}) = \sqrt{\sum_{i=1}^{n}(u_i - v_i)^2}$; however, computing non-linearities (e.g., the square root) in the encrypted domain is not a trivial task. Thus, many prior FHE works resort to computing the squared Euclidean distance and return it to the user, who needs to compute the final square root in the clear.

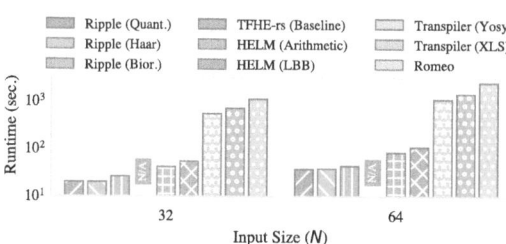

Fig. 5. Runtime comparisons for Euclidean distance between Ripple's three variants (Quantization, Haar DWT, and Biorthogonal DWT), TFHE-rs (baseline), HELM, Google Transpiler, and Romeo for vectors of 32 and 64 elements. Note that HELM, Transpiler, and Romeo only implement the squared Euclidean distance (i.e., without the square root computation). We use a word size W of 32 bits for all frameworks. Lastly, for 32 and 64 bits, TFHE-rs is not applicable (N/A) as the resources required for the LUT are impractical (see footnote 1).

For this benchmark, shown in Fig. 5, we use $W = 32$ bits and use vector lengths 32 and 64 to demonstrate scalability. All Ripple variants perform the full Euclidean distance computation, while the related works compute the squared Euclidean distance and neglect the final square root calculation. We note that the TFHE-rs baseline is unable to evaluate the Euclidean distance with the required wordsize due to the astronomical cost of building 32-bit encrypted LUTs. For the Google Transpiler, we utilize both logic synthesis backends (i.e., Google XLS and Yosys), which optimize the circuit in different ways. For HELM, we utilize both LUT circuit modes (i.e., many-to-many LUTs for the arithmetic mode and a circuit of 2:1 LUTs for "lossless bidirectional bridging" or LBB). Overall, all three Ripple configurations outperform the related works in terms of latency while still taking into account the square root operation. However, as we observed in Table 1 the Haar and Biorthogonal approaches achieve significantly better approximations than the quantization variant. Notably, Haar also exhibits very competitive latencies across all non-linear functions and benchmarks.

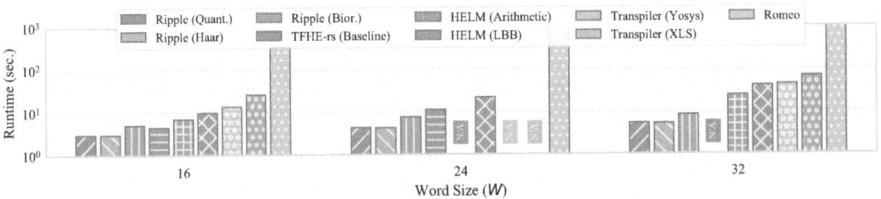

Fig. 6. Runtime comparisons for the logistic regression application for 4 attributes for word sizes of 16, 24, and 32 bits. For 24 bits, the arithmetic mode of HELM as well as both modes of the Google Transpiler are not applicable (N/A) as they rely on native word sizes. Lastly, for 32 bits, the TFHE-rs baseline is also N/A as the resources required for the LUT are impractical (see footnote 1).

Logistic Regression. Logistic Regression (LR) is a widely studied application in FHE from genome-wide association studies [23] to more generic applications [17,29] such as natural language processing [1]. This construction is well-suited to binary classification problems and is akin to a single-layer neural network with a sigmoid activation. In Ripple, we use DWT-encoded LUTs to directly compute the sigmoid activation function. The client decrypts the result, which represents the probability that the encrypted input belongs to the first class.

We utilize the Palmer penguin dataset [21], where each input consists of eight attributes that correspond to the physical characteristics of penguins (e.g., bill length, flipper length, etc.). Since logistic regression is particularly well-suited for binary classification, we remove entries in the dataset corresponding to the Chinstrap species. Figure 6 showcases our LR inference benchmark for four attributes. While our chosen dataset is composed of entries with eight attributes, we truncate it to match the dimensions used in related works. We observe that Ripple is significantly faster than related works and also outperforms the TFHE-rs baseline using the full-bit width. The only exception is W = 16 bits, where the baseline outperforms the Biorthogonal DWT; however, for 24 bits, the Biorthogonal DWT exhibits lower latency than the baseline.

To achieve high accuracy with our chosen dataset we utilize all eight attributes with a wordsize of 24 bits. For this binary classification, all modes achieve 100% accuracy; the baseline latency is 13.3 s per inference, while the Biorthogonal DWT variant classifies in 7.8 s. Lastly, the quantized variant that truncates half of the bits of the LUT input exhibits a latency of 6.2 s, while the Haar DWT slightly outperforms this with a latency of approximately 6 s.

References

1. Alexander Genkin, D.D.L., Madigan, D.: Large-scale Bayesian logistic regression for text categorization. Technometrics **49**(3), 291–304 (2007). https://doi.org/10.1198/004017007000000245

2. Becker, A., Ducas, L., Gama, N., Laarhoven, T.: New directions in nearest neighbor searching with applications to lattice sieving. In: Krauthgamer, R. (ed.) 27th SODA, pp. 10–24. ACM-SIAM (2016). https://doi.org/10.1137/1.9781611974331.ch2

3. Brakerski, Z., Gentry, C., Vaikuntanathan, V.: (Leveled) fully homomorphic encryption without bootstrapping. In: Goldwasser, S. (ed.) ITCS 2012, pp. 309–325. ACM (2012). https://doi.org/10.1145/2090236.2090262

4. Carter, R.L., Morris, R., Blashfield, R.K.: On the partitioning of squared euclidean distance and its applications in cluster analysis. Psychometrika **54**(1), 9–23 (1989)

5. Cheon, J.H., Kim, A., Kim, M., Song, Y.: Homomorphic encryption for arithmetic of approximate numbers. In: Takagi, T., Peyrin, T. (eds.) ASIACRYPT 2017. LNCS, vol. 10624, pp. 409–437. Springer, Cham (2017). https://doi.org/10.1007/978-3-319-70694-8_15

6. Chillotti, I., Gama, N., Georgieva, M., Izabachène, M.: Faster fully homomorphic encryption: bootstrapping in less than 0.1 seconds. In: Cheon, J.H., Takagi, T. (eds.) ASIACRYPT 2016. LNCS, vol. 10031, pp. 3–33. Springer, Heidelberg (2016). https://doi.org/10.1007/978-3-662-53887-6_1

7. Chillotti, I., Gama, N., Georgieva, M., Izabachène, M.: Faster packed homomorphic operations and efficient circuit bootstrapping for TFHE. In: Takagi, T., Peyrin, T. (eds.) ASIACRYPT 2017. LNCS, vol. 10624, pp. 377–408. Springer, Cham (2017). https://doi.org/10.1007/978-3-319-70694-8_14

8. Chillotti, I., Gama, N., Georgieva, M., Izabachène, M.: TFHE: fast fully homomorphic encryption over the torus. J. Cryptol. **33**(1), 34–91 (2020). https://doi.org/10.1007/s00145-019-09319-x

9. Chillotti, I., Joye, M., Paillier, P.: Programmable bootstrapping enables efficient homomorphic inference of deep neural networks. In: Dolev, S., Margalit, O., Pinkas, B., Schwarzmann, A. (eds.) CSCML 2021. LNCS, vol. 12716, pp. 1–19. Springer, Cham (2021). https://doi.org/10.1007/978-3-030-78086-9_1

10. Chung, H., Kim, H., Kim, Y.S., Lee, Y.: Amortized Large Look-up Table Evaluation with Multivariate Polynomials for Homomorphic Encryption. Cryptology ePrint Archive, Paper 2024/274 (2024). https://eprint.iacr.org/2024/274

11. Dubey, S.R., Singh, S.K., Chaudhuri, B.B.: Activation functions in deep learning: a comprehensive survey and benchmark. Neurocomput. **503**(C), 92–108 (2022). https://doi.org/10.1016/j.neucom.2022.06.111
12. Ducas, L., Micciancio, D.: FHEW: bootstrapping homomorphic encryption in less than a second. In: Oswald, E., Fischlin, M. (eds.) EUROCRYPT 2015. LNCS, vol. 9056, pp. 617–640. Springer, Heidelberg (2015). https://doi.org/10.1007/978-3-662-46800-5_24
13. Gentry, C.: A fully homomorphic encryption scheme. Ph.D. thesis, Stanford University (2009)
14. Google Research: Google XLS (2020). https://google.github.io/xls
15. Gorantala, S., et al.: A General Purpose Transpiler for Fully Homomorphic Encryption. Cryptology ePrint Archive, Report 2021/811 (2021). https://eprint.iacr.org/2021/811
16. Gouert, C., Mouris, D., Tsoutsos, N.G.: HELM: Navigating Homomorphic Encryption through Gates and Lookup Tables. Cryptology ePrint Archive, Paper 2023/1382 (2023). https://eprint.iacr.org/2023/1382
17. Gouert, C., Mouris, D., Tsoutsos, N.G.: SoK: new insights into fully homomorphic encryption libraries via standardized benchmarks. PoPETs **2023**(3), 154–172 (2023). https://doi.org/10.56553/popets-2023-0075
18. Gouert, C., Tsoutsos, N.G.: Romeo: conversion and evaluation of HDL designs in the encrypted domain. In: Proceedings of the 57th ACM/EDAC/IEEE Design Automation Conference. DAC 2020, Virtual Event, USA. IEEE Press (2020)
19. Gouert, C., et al.: Accelerated encrypted execution of general-purpose applications. Cryptology ePrint Archive, Report 2023/641 (2023)
20. Hashemi, S., Anthony, N., Tann, H., Bahar, R.I., Reda, S.: Understanding the impact of precision quantization on the accuracy and energy of neural networks. In: Proceedings of the Conference on Design, Automation & Test in Europe, DATE 2017, pp. 1478–1483. European Design and Automation Association, Leuven, BEL (2017)
21. Horst, A., Hill, A., Gorman, K.: Palmer archipelago penguins data in the palmer-penguins R package - an alternative to Anderson's irises. R J. **14**(1) (2022)
22. Juliadotter, N.V., Choo, K.K.R.: Cloud attack and risk assessment taxonomy. IEEE Cloud Comput. **2**(1), 14–20 (2015)
23. Kim, M., Song, Y., Li, B., Micciancio, D.: Semi-parallel logistic regression for GWAS on encrypted data. BMC Med. Genomics **13**(Suppl 7), 99 (2020)
24. Liu, Z., Micciancio, D., Polyakov, Y.: Large-precision homomorphic sign evaluation using FHEW/TFHE bootstrapping. In: Agrawal, S., Lin, D. (eds.) ASIACRYPT 2022, Part II. LNCS, vol. 13792, pp. 130–160. Springer, Heidelberg (2022). https://doi.org/10.1007/978-3-031-22966-4_5
25. Malkauthekar, M.D.: Analysis of euclidean distance and manhattan distance measure in face recognition. In: Third International Conference on Computational Intelligence and Information Technology (CIIT 2013), pp. 503–507. IET, Mumbai (2013). https://doi.org/10.1049/cp.2013.2636
26. Ribeiro, M.I.: Gaussian probability density functions: properties and error characterization. Institute for Systems and Robotics, Lisboa, Portugal (2004)
27. Unser, M., Blu, T.: Mathematical properties of the JPEG2000 wavelet filters. IEEE Trans. Image Process. **12**(9), 1080–1090 (2003)
28. Van Fleet, P.: Discrete Wavelet Transformations: An Elementary Approach with Applications. Wiley, Hoboken (2019). https://books.google.pt/books?id=jGAaxQEACAAJ

29. Viand, A., Jattke, P., Hithnawi, A.: SoK: fully homomorphic encryption compilers. In: 2021 IEEE Symposium on Security and Privacy, pp. 1092–1108. IEEE Computer Society Press (2021). https://doi.org/10.1109/SP40001.2021.00068
30. Wolf, C.: Yosys Open SYnthesis Suite (2016). https://yosyshq.net
31. Yang, P., Xiong, N., Ren, J.: Data security and privacy protection for cloud storage: a survey. IEEE Access **8**, 131723–131740 (2020)
32. Zama: TFHE-rs: A Pure Rust Implementation of the TFHE Scheme for Boolean and Integer Arithmetics Over Encrypted Data (2022). https://github.com/zama-ai/tfhe-rs

Robust Multiparty Computation from Threshold Encryption Based on RLWE

Antoine Urban[1,2(✉)] [iD] and Matthieu Rambaud[1,2] [iD]

[1] Télécom Paris, Paris, France
{antoine.urban,matthieu.rambaud}@telecom-paris.fr
[2] Institut Polytechnique de Paris, Palaiseau, France

Abstract. We consider protocols for secure multi-party computation (MPC) built from FHE under honest majority, i.e., for $n = 2t + 1$ players of which t are corrupt, that are robust. Surprisingly there exists no robust threshold FHE scheme based on BFV to design such MPC protocols. Precisely, all existing methods for generating a common relinearization key can abort as soon as one player deviates. We address this issue, with a new relinearization key (adapted from [CDKS19, CCS'19]) which we show how to securely generate in parallel of the threshold encryption key, in the same broadcast. We thus obtain the first robust threshold BFV scheme, moreover using only one broadcast for the generation of keys instead of two previously.

Of independent interest, as an optional alternative, we propose the first threshold FHE decryption enabling simultaneously: (i) robustness over asynchronous channels with honest majority; (ii) tolerating a power-of-small-prime ciphertext modulus, e.g., 2^e; and (iii) secret shares of sizes quasi-independent of n.

1   Introduction

The generation and use of vast volumes of data to fuel innovative scientific breakthroughs pose a number of challenges in terms of data collection and efficiency. One potential solution lies in the delegation of data processing to public cloud service providers equipped with substantial computing resources. Nonetheless, concerns surrounding the privacy and security of outsourced data and analysis persist. In recent years, there have been notable advancements in cryptographic methods designed to enhance secure computation. Of these techniques, Multiparty Computation (MPC) and Fully Homomorphic Encryption (FHE) have received growing interest due to significant technical breakthroughs.

***Threshold* FHE *(ThFHE)*.** Fully Homomorphic Encryption (FHE) allows for the execution of arbitrary computations on encrypted data without the need

A. Urban—Supported by the Beyond5G project.

M. Rambaud—Supported by the French ANR Project ANR-21-CE39-0009-BARRACUDA.

N. Mouha and N. Nikiforakis (Eds.): ISC 2024, LNCS 15257, pp. 294–314, 2025.
https://doi.org/10.1007/978-3-031-75757-0_15

for decryption. Over the years, several generations of FHE schemes have been proposed, with the latest based on the ring-learning-with-errors (RLWE) assumption gaining traction through implementation, and standardization [2]. Extending these constructions to multiple participants brings up the question of which key to encrypt under. Encrypting inputs under individual keys prevents homomorphic evaluation, while a single key for all players creates a single point of failure for privacy if compromised. To remove this single point of failure and accommodate a broader range of use cases involving multiple players, threshold FHE (ThFHE) schemes have been developed [3], in which a secret key is split into a number of shares, so that only a threshold of players collaborating together can decrypt an encrypted secret.

ThFHE-*Based MPC.* In scenarios involving multiple users, ThFHE-based techniques present a promising set of solutions for secure multiparty computation (MPC), where a set of n players collaborates to compute any function on their inputs, while preserving the confidentiality of the latter, due to their minimal communication overhead [3]. Instantiating an MPC protocol from a ThFHE scheme is not straightforward, and involves multiple steps:

Distributed Key Generation (DKG): a protocol in which the players collaboratively generate a common threshold encryption key ek for a FHE scheme, and where each player also receives a share of the secret key sk.

Input Distribution: players subsequently encrypt their respective inputs using the common threshold encryption key and broadcast the ciphertexts;

Evaluation: players (locally) perform homomorphic computations on the ciphertexts to evaluate the desired function;

Threshold Decryption: players finally jointly execute a threshold decryption protocol using their secret key shares to uncover the computation's output.

Robustness. In the realm of multiparty protocols, an often neglected yet crucial attribute is robustness, specifically referring to the need for a protocol to produce a correct output in a *constant number of rounds* whenever it is executed, even in the presence of malicious behavior. In the context of ThFHE-based MPC, the robust generation of threshold keys is proving challenging, and is our main goal.

1.1 Results

Main Result: the **First Robust Threshold** BFV **Scheme and Robust MPC.** In this work, we construct trBFV, the first robust threshold FHE scheme based on the BFV [6,16] cryptosystem, and propose an MPC protocol as informally stated in Theorem 1 below.

Theorem 1 ((Informal) Robust MPC). *Consider $n = 2t + 1$ players, of which t are maliciously corrupt. There exists a robust protocol in 2 broadcasts + 1 asynchronous P2P rounds that UC implements secure evaluation of any arithmetic circuit.*

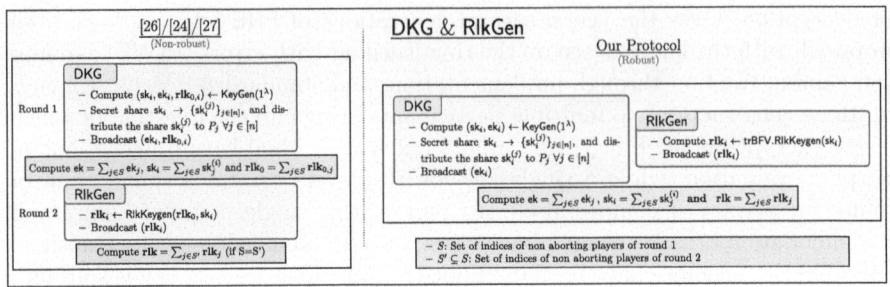

Fig. 1. We present in the left hand side the overall construction of previous DKG&RlkGen protocols [24,26,27]. First, each player P_i runs KeyGen to produce keys $(\mathsf{sk}_i, \mathsf{ek}_i, \mathbf{rlk}_{0,i})$. The secret key sk_i is secret-shared in n shares $\{\mathsf{sk}_i^{(j)}\}_{j=1}^n$, and each $\mathsf{sk}_i^{(j)}$ is distributed to P_j. The last two elements are broadcast and contributions are added together over the set S of indices of non-aborting players to form the common threshold encryption and intermediate relinearization keys ek and $\mathbf{rlk}_0$, as well as a key share sk_i. Then, players run RlkKeygen with their key sk_i and $\mathbf{rlk}_0$ to produce a contribution $\mathbf{rlk}_i$ that is broadcast. Once added together over the set S' of indices of non-aborting players of this second round, players can compute the relinearization key $\mathbf{rlk} = \sum_{j \in S'} \mathbf{rlk}_j$ if $S = S'$. On the right hand side, we present a sketch of our protocol. More specifically, to have robustness, players run in parallel KeyGen and our new relinearization key generation algorithm trBFV.RlkKeygen.

This result follows from our main contribution detailed below.

Main Contribution: Robust Relinearization Key Generation. To evaluate a circuit, players first perform a distributed key generation (DKG) protocol to establish a common threshold encryption key, which basically consists of each player P_i sampling a key pair $(\mathsf{sk}_i, \mathsf{ek}_i)$, using a (n, t)-linear secret sharing scheme $((n, t)$-LSS) to divide sk_i into n shares such that only authorized subsets of $t + 1$ of them can be used to reconstruct the original key, broadcasting its contribution ek_i, and distributing the shares of sk_i to the players. Then, players can set a threshold encryption key $\mathsf{ek} = \sum_{i \in S} \mathsf{ek}_i$ and secret key shares as the sum over the set S of the indices of players that have correctly broadcast a contribution.

To perform homomorphic computation, BFV (along with other RLWE-based FHE schemes such as CKKS [12]) requires the generation of an additional common "relinearization key" $\mathbf{rlk}$. For a secret key sk, it is described for BFV [16] as being of the following form:

$$(1) \qquad \mathbf{rlk} = (\mathsf{sk}^2 w - \mathsf{sk} \cdot \mathbf{r} + \mathbf{e}^{(\mathbf{rlk})}, \mathbf{r})$$

where $\mathbf{r}$ is an uniform random string, $\mathbf{e}^{(\mathbf{rlk})}$ some noise, and w a decomposition basis of dimension some l, i.e. $\mathbf{w} = (w^0, w^1, \ldots, w^{l-1})^T$. Generating this relinearization key in a distributed way proves to be more complex than in the case of the threshold encryption key. Indeed, the presence of the term $\mathsf{sk}^2 w$ introduces a non-linearity. To overcome the challenge posed by the squaring of sk, various RlkGen protocols [24,26,27] for generating $\mathbf{rlk}$, have been proposed. We briefly discuss these RlkGen protocols to emphasize the novelty of our work. Overall, they have the following informal structure:

- In round 1: each player P_i generates a contribution $\mathbf{rlk}_{0,i}$ using its key sk_i.
- In round 2: each player P_i sums together the contributions $\mathbf{rlk}_0 = \sum_{i \in S} \mathbf{rlk}_{0,i}$, where S denotes the set of indices of non-aborting players in the first round. Then, each P_i uses an algorithm RlkKeygen to compute a final contribution $\mathbf{rlk}_i \leftarrow \mathsf{RlkKeygen}(\mathbf{rlk}_0, \mathsf{sk}_i)$ and broadcasts $\mathbf{rlk}_i$.

Finally, the relinearization key is defined as $\mathbf{rlk} = \sum_{i \in S'} \mathbf{rlk}_i$, where S' is the set of indices of non-aborting players in this second round.

However, this generic protocol, illustrated in Fig. 1, has a major drawback, in that it is not robust; if some players take part in some of the rounds, but not all, then no $\mathbf{rlk}$ is generated. Specifically, [24, 26, 27] required S and S' to be equal for RlkGen to output. Otherwise, if the generation were done with non-equal sets S and S', then the resulting $\mathbf{rlk}$ would be incompatible with the ek produced in the first round as $\mathsf{ek} = \sum_{i \in S} \mathsf{ek}_i$.

We overcome this issue by introducing a new trBFV.RlkKeygen algorithm for generating an alternative relinearization key adapted from the multikey FHE scheme of [9], that departs from all previous approaches because it only applies a *linear map* to the secret key sk, *not a squaring*. This allows, as shown in Fig. 1, to design a RlkGen protocol to generate $\mathbf{rlk}$ in only one round that operates *in parallel* of the DKG, and to obtain a robust overall key generation.

Contribution of Independent Interest: Alternative Threshold Decryption Enabling q Power of a Small Prime.
Most previous threshold FHE schemes used the following *mainstream approach* for threshold decryption. To decrypt a ciphertext c, each player P_i did the following:

- First, it used its secret key share sk_i to compute its "decryption share" c_i of c, and added some locally generated *"smudging noise"* $e_{\mathrm{sm},i}$ to prevent leakage of any secret information, before sending the noisy decryption share $\tilde{\mathsf{c}}_i = \mathsf{c}_i + e_{\mathrm{sm},i}$.
- Second, each player used $t+1$ of the received noisy decryption shares to reconstruct the output.

As a result, when the secret sharing was instantiated with Shamir [28], the smudging noises were multiplied by Lagrange coefficients during reconstruction. As explained in [4], this led to the use of a large $n!^2$ scaling factor, in order to clear-out the denominators of the Lagrange coefficients. Overall, this imposed the bit-size of the ciphertext modulus q to be $O(n \log n)$, which resulted in a $n\times$ blowup of the ciphertext length. [4] also required the modulus q to be a prime in order for the multiplied noise to be uniformly distributed modulo q.

A way around both these limitations is proposed in [4] with another threshold decryption protocol based on a $\{0, 1\}$-LSSD scheme [5, 22], which, instead of the Lagrange coefficients used in Shamir, employed binary coefficients to recover the output from the noisy decryption shares. This allowed to remove the extra n in the modulus bit-size, i.e. $\log q = O(\log n)$. However, this also led to a significant

Table 1. Threshold FHE schemes for n players, using modulus q. The last column indicates the size of the shares owned by a player, and the modulus-to-noise ratio refers to the ratio between the modulus and decryption noise of a ciphertext.

	LSS Scheme	Simulation Security	Modulus-to noise ratio	Modulus Size $O(\log q)$	Share Size
[4]	$\{0,1\}$-LSSD	✓	Superpoly	$O(\log n)$	$O(n^{4.2})$
	Shamir			$O(n \cdot \log n)$	$O(1)$
[11]	Shamir	✓	Superpoly	$O(\log n)$	$O(n^{2+o(1)})$
[5]	$\{0,1\}$-LSSD	✗	Poly	$O(\log n)$	$O(n^{4.2})$
Our Scheme	Shamir	✓	Superpoly	$O(n \cdot \log n)$	$O(1)$
	$\{0,1\}$-LSSD	✓	Superpoly	$O(\log n)$	$O(n^{4.2})$
	Shamir with pre-shared noise	✓	Superpoly	$O(\log n)$	$O(1)$

space overhead, as the size of each secret key share is at least $O(n^{4.2})$. Cheon et al. [11] introduced a new scheme denoted TreeSSS, but with each share still of size $O(n^{2+o(1)})$.

Although this mainstream approach could be used in our protocol, we now propose an alternative optional approach for threshold decryption. It enables simultaneously (i) a $n!^3 \times$ smaller total smudging noise, (ii) a modulus q which is possibly a power of a small prime, e.g., 2^e, thereby allowing efficient implementations [10,19], and (iii) secret shares of sizes quasi-independent of n. It is obtained by the novel combination of two existing ingredients. First, players *pre-generate common secret-shared smudging noises* via some distributed protocol. To decrypt c, players use their key shares to perform all-at-once the decryption of c, added with one secret-shared smudging noise that can be obtained in amortized constant overhead. This first ingredient, that allows to remove the $n!^2$ scaling factor, was introduced by [15][1], but was never later used to our knowledge. Second, in order to enable q of small size 2^e, we detail a Shamir sharing over $\mathbb{Z}/2^e\mathbb{Z}$, i.e., embed polynomials into Galois rings extensions [1,17]. Notice that this last ingredient, alone, would *not* have been applicable. Indeed, without the first ingredient, i.e., with the mainstream approach, then it would have been required that q has no factor in common with $n!$. In short, our scheme instantiated with Shamir and a pre-shared noise achieves a modulus size in $O(\log n)$ while maintaining shares of size $O(1)$, unlike related works as shown in Table 1.

Other Threshold Schemes with Smaller Noise But Incompatible with MPC. Some recent works [5,13] addressed an orthogonal size dependency, by replacing the statistical distance used to analyze the noise during the threshold decryption by the Rényi divergence. In more details, the threshold decryption

---

[1] With whom we do not compare ourselves since they do not generate a **rlk** key.

of a ciphertext c allows recovering the plaintext, but also reveals a small *decryption noise* term that depends on the given ciphertext and the secret key. It is precisely to prevent this leakage that some smudging noise is added to the decryption shares. As shown in Table 1, previous works [4,11] required the ratio between the smudging noise and the size of the decryption noise to be superpolynomial in the security parameter. This, in turn, required the RLWE problem to be secure with a superpolynomial modulus-to-noise ratio, which requires larger RLWE parameters. Recently, [5,13] proposed threshold FHE schemes with a polynomial modulus-to-noise ratio. However, the latter do not come without their own drawbacks. Importantly, [5,13] made clear that their schemes are not usable in MPC, i.e., do not offer composability guarantees. On the contrary, our approach produces a threshold decryption functionality in the simulation paradigm, making it usable as a black box in complex protocols.

2   Model

2.1   Notations

All logarithms are in base two. We denote $x \xleftarrow{\$} \mathscr{D}$ the sampling of x according to distribution $\mathscr{D}$. Cardinality of a set X is denoted as $|X|$. For a finite set E, we denote $U(E)$ the uniform distribution on E. The set of positive integers $[1, \ldots, n]$ is denoted $[n]$. For two vectors $\mathbf{u}, \mathbf{v}$ (in bold) we denote $\langle \mathbf{u}, \mathbf{v} \rangle$ the dot product and, for a third vector $\mathbf{w}$, we denote $\mathbf{u} \langle \cdot \cdot \rangle (\mathbf{v}, \mathbf{w}) := (\langle \mathbf{u}, \mathbf{v} \rangle, \langle \mathbf{u}, \mathbf{w} \rangle)$. We denote by λ the security parameter throughout the paper.

We consider a positive integer d, denoted the *lattice dimension*; a monic polynomial f of degree d; $k < q$ positive integers denoted plaintext and ciphertext moduli; and $R := \mathbb{Z}[X]/f(X)$. We denote $R_k = R/(k.R)$ and $R_q = R/(q.R)$ the residue rings of R modulo k and q. We denote $\lceil . \rceil, \lfloor . \rfloor, \lfloor . \rceil$ the rounding to the next, previous, and nearest integer respectively, and $[.]_k$ the reduction of an integer modulo k into R_k. When applied to polynomials or vectors, these operations are performed coefficient-wise. Let $\Delta = \lfloor q/k \rfloor$ be the integer division of q by k. All linear forms are succinctly specified as *linear combinations*, e.g., let $(\overline{x_i})_i$ denote *labels* of some variables $(x_i)_i$, then, $\sum_i l_i \overline{x_i}$ denotes $\{(x_i)_i \rightarrow \sum_i l_i x_i\}$.

2.2   Players and Corruptions

We consider $n = 2t+1$ players $\mathcal{P} = (P_i)_{i \in [n]}$, which are probabilistic polynomial-time (PPT) machines, of public identities. We consider the Universal Composability (UC) model [8] with static corruptions. We consider a PPT machine, denoted as the Environment Env. It fully controls an entity denoted the "adversary" $\mathcal{A}$. At the beginning of the execution, $\mathcal{A}$ may corrupt up to t players of its choice. They behave as arbitrarily instructed by $\mathcal{A}$. We assume that $\mathcal{A}$ corrupts exactly t players, of which we denote the indices by $\mathcal{I} \subset [n]$. The remaining ones are called *honest* and indexed by $\mathcal{H} = [n] \setminus \mathcal{I}$. $\mathcal{A}$ notifies Env of every message received by corrupt players and from (simulated) functionalities. For simplicity, we present our protocol in the *semi-malicious* corruption model of [3], widely adopted since [15].

2.3 Formalizing Eventual Delivery in UC

We now explain the high level idea of the mechanism, denoted fetch-*and*-delay, used to formalize eventual delivery following [14,23]. Every ideal functionality $\mathcal{F}$, when it needs to eventually deliver (ssid, v) to some entity P, engages in the following interaction. It notifies $\mathcal{A}$ of the output id (ssid), initializes a counter $D_{\text{ssid}} \leftarrow 1$, which captures the delivery delay. Upon receiving (delay) from $\mathcal{A}$, it sets $D_{\text{ssid}} \leftarrow D_{\text{ssid}} + 1$. Upon receiving (fetch) from P, it sets $D_{\text{ssid}} \leftarrow D_{\text{ssid}} - 1$, as well as for all other counters related to pending outputs for P. In addition, we specify that it leaks (fetch) to $\mathcal{A}$. It is left implicit that entities fetch as much as they can all. Since $\mathcal{A}$ is PPT, at some point it gets exhausted of pressing the button delay. So, after sufficiently many fetches, the counter drops down to 0. Then $\mathcal{F}$ can deliver (ssid, v) to P.

2.4 Ideal Functionalities

Broadcast with Eventual Termination: BC. We formalize the ideal functionality BC of broadcast, detailed in the full version of this work. It is parametrized by a sender $\mathcal{S}$ and by a set of receivers. It has the following properties: (Termination) all honest receivers eventually output, and (Consistency) any two honest receivers output the same value. Finally, (Validity) if the sender $\mathcal{S}$ is honest and input value x, all honest receivers output the same value x.

(Asynchronous) Authenticated Message Transmitting $\mathcal{F}_{AT}$. We formalize in the full version the ideal functionality of asynchronous *public authenticated* message transmitting with eventual delivery delay, denoted as $\mathcal{F}_{\text{AT}}$. It is parametrized by a sender $\mathcal{S}$ and a receiver R, hence the terminology *authenticated*. It delivers every message sent within a finite delay D, hence the terminology *eventual delivery*, although D can be adaptively increased by $\mathcal{A}$. It leaks the content of every message to $\mathcal{A}$, hence the terminology *public*.

Bulletin Board PKI: bPKI. We formalize the ideal functionality of a bulletin board of public keys, denoted as bPKI. Upon receiving a key pk_i from any player $P_i \in \mathcal{P}$, it stores (P_i, pk_i) and leaks this information to the adversary $\mathcal{A}$. Then, it *waits until it received a public key from every honest player* in $\mathcal{P}$, and sets a timeout. After it elapsed, it sets to $\perp$ the keys of the players which did not give a key, and eventually delivers $\text{pk} \leftarrow (\text{pk}_i)_{i \in [n]}$.

Global Uniform Random String $\overline{\mathcal{G}}_{URS}$. It samples uniformly at random a sequence of bits of length κ, denoted URS, then outputs it to all players.

2.5 Ideal Functionality of MPC $\mathcal{F}_C$

The ideal functionality of MPC that we aim to UC implement, is formalized as $\mathcal{F}_C$ in Fig. 2. It returns to an output learner $\mathcal{L}$ the evaluation of an arithmetic circuit C : $(R_k \cup \{\perp\})^n \to R_k$ over inputs in R_k. For simplicity: C has n input gates, one single output gate, and $\mathcal{F}_C$ expects one single input from each player, and delivers the output to $\mathcal{L}$.

The functionality works as follows. Upon receiving an input m_i from any player P_i, it stores $(P_i, \overline{m_i})^2$ and leaks this information to $\mathcal{A}$. Before $\mathcal{F}_C$ delivers the output, it needs to wait for the inputs to be submitted. However, the adversary $\mathcal{A}$ can choose to never instruct corrupt players to send their inputs. To remedy this, the functionality i) waits until it receives an input from every honest player, ii) sets a timeout T_A, then iii), after it elapsed, sets to $\perp$ the inputs of the (corrupt) players which did not give an input. Once the timeout expires, the output evaluation is delivered following a finite delay chosen by $\mathcal{A}$.

$$\mathcal{F}_C$$

Output format Initialize an empty vector $\mathbf{m} = \{\top\}^n$.

- Initialize outpout$-$available $\leftarrow$ false. //delivery flag.
- When all $m_i \neq \top$, $\forall i \in [n]$, set outpout$-$available $=$ true.

Formalizing timeout for inputs of corrupt players

- Initialize a counter $T_A \leftarrow 1$ // the timeout.
- Upon receiving delay$-$inputs from $\mathcal{A}$, $T_A \leftarrow T_A + 1$.
- Upon receiving fetch from $\mathcal{L}$, $T_A \leftarrow T_A - 1$.
- When $T_A = 0$ for the first time, freeze forever $T_A = 0$. Then, for all $i \in \mathcal{I}$: if $m_i = \top$, then set $m_i \leftarrow \perp$.

Input (Only accessible while outpout$-$available $=$ false) On input (input, $\widetilde{m_i} \in R_k$) from any $P_i \in \mathcal{P}$ for the first time, or possibly from $\mathcal{A}$ if P_i is corrupt, set $m_i \leftarrow \widetilde{m_i}$, then store (input, $\mathcal{S}, m_i$), and *eventually-deliver* (stored, $\overline{m_i}$) to each player $P \in \mathcal{P}$. //eventually-delivers" consists of the fetch-and-delay mechanism explained in Section 2.3.

Formalizing eventual delivery

- Initialize a counter $D_R \leftarrow 0$ // the delivery delay.
- Upon receiving fetch from $\mathcal{L}$, $D_R \leftarrow D_R - 1$.
- When $D_R = 0$ for the first time, if no output was delivered yet to $\mathcal{L}$, wait until outpout$-$available $=$ true, then deliver $y = C(\mathbf{m})$ to $\mathcal{L}$.

Fig. 2. Functionality of secure circuit evaluation. Each m_i is identified by a label $\overline{m_i}$.

3   Cryptographic Ingredients

We now detail the main ingredients needed for the remainder of the paper.

Ring Learning with Errors. Let Ψ_q and $\mathscr{X}_q$ be distributions over R_q. The *decisional*-Ring Learning with Errors (RLWE) [25] assumption with parameter $(R_q, \mathscr{X}_q, \Psi_q)$ can be stated as follows: for a fixed secret sample $s \leftarrow \mathscr{X}_q$, then any

---

[2] Where $\overline{m_i}$ denotes the label of variable m_i.

polynomially long sequence of samples in R_q^2 of the form $(a_i, b_i = s \cdot a_i + e_i)_i$, where $a_i \leftarrow U(R_q)$, and $e_i \leftarrow \Psi_q$, is computationally indistinguishable from a uniform random sequence of elements of R_q^2.

Gadget Decomposition. For later use in Sect. 4, let us define the widely used, e.g., [9,21], *gadget toolkit*:

1. Gadget vector: $\mathbf{g} = (g_0, g_1, ..., g_{l-1}) \in R_q^l$; and integers l and (small) B_g;
2. The gadget decomposition denoted $\mathbf{g}^{-1}(.)$: on input any $x \in R_q$, decomposes it into a vector $\mathbf{u} = (u_0, ..., u_{l-1}) \in R^l$ of (small) coordinates, i.e., $\|u_i\| \leq B_g$ for all $0 \leq i \leq l - 1$, such that $\Sigma_{i=0}^{l-1} u_i.g_i = x \pmod{q}$.

Smudging Lemma [3]. For B_1, B_2 positive integers and $e_1 \in [-B_1, B_1]$ a fixed integer, sample e_2 uniformly at random in $[-B_2, B_2]$. Then the distribution of e_2 is statistically indistinguishable from that of $e_2 + e_1$ if $B_1/B_2 = \text{negl}(\lambda)$.

3.1   BFV [16]

We now describe the BFV cryptosystem, departing from [6,16], by specifying that the key generation algorithm takes a public uniform random string (URS) denoted a as input, whereas in [16] a is instead sampled locally. The reason is that, for our DKG to operate (see Sect. 3.3), some form of additivity will be required between the keys. Let Ψ_q, $\mathscr{B}_{\text{Enc},q}$ and $\mathscr{X}_q$ be distributions over R_q.

- BFV.KeyGen($\text{pp} = (a \in R_q)$): Sample $e^{(\text{ek})} \xleftarrow{\$} \Psi_q$ and $\text{sk} \xleftarrow{\$} \mathscr{X}_q$, and output $\text{ek} \leftarrow (-a \cdot \text{sk} + e^{(\text{ek})}, a) = (b, a)$ and sk.
- BFV.Enc($\text{ek} = (b, a), m \in R_k$): Sample the encryption randomnesses $e_0^{(\text{Enc})} \xleftarrow{\$} \mathscr{B}_{\text{Enc},q}$, $e_1^{(\text{Enc})} \xleftarrow{\$} \Psi_q$, and $u \xleftarrow{\$} \mathscr{X}_q$.
  Output $\mathsf{c} \leftarrow \left(\Delta m + u \cdot b + e_0^{(\text{Enc})}, u \cdot a + e_1^{(\text{Enc})} \right) \in R_q^2$.
- BFV.Dec(sk, c): Given a ciphertext $\mathsf{c} = (\mathsf{c}[0], \mathsf{c}[1]) \in R_q^2$, compute $\mu \leftarrow \mathsf{c}[0] + \mathsf{c}[1] \cdot \text{sk}$. Output $m \leftarrow [\lfloor \frac{k}{q}(\mu) \rceil]_k := \Omega_{\text{Dec}}(\mu) \in R_k$, where Ω_{Dec} denotes a non-linear decoding function.

We defer to Sect. 4 the algorithm used for evaluation, since they depend on the chosen *relinearization key*, of which the choice is our main contribution.

3.2   Linear Secret Sharing, Abstracted-Out as Ideal $\mathcal{F}_{\text{LSS}}$ Functionality

The main ingredient in building a robust threshold FHE scheme is using a (n, t)-linear secret sharing scheme ((n,t)-LSS formally defined in Def. 2 of the full version), that enables to divide a secret s into n shares, with the property that only authorized subsets of $t + 1$ of them can be used to reconstruct the original secret. Interestingly, thanks to the linear property of the sharing, if secrets $m_1, \ldots, m_n$ have been shared, on input some linear form Λ, one can compute

$\Lambda(\{m_i\}_i)$ on the shared inputs. In this section, we abstract this through a functionality $\mathcal{F}_{\mathsf{LSS}}$.

Functionality $\mathcal{F}_{\mathsf{LSS}}$. We specify an ideal functionality for LSS, denoted $\mathcal{F}_{\mathsf{LSS}}$ and detailed in the full version of this work. It is parametrized by i) a set $\mathcal{P}$ of n players, ii) a list $\mathscr{S}$ of entities of the (possibly malicious) senders, where each $\mathcal{S} \in \mathscr{S}$ has a list of inputs: $(x_{\mathcal{S},\alpha})_{\alpha \in X_{\mathcal{S}}}$, identified by input labels $(\overline{x_{\mathcal{S},\alpha}})_{\alpha \in X_{\mathcal{S}}}$. We denote $X_{\mathcal{S}}$ the list of indices α of inputs of sender $\mathcal{S}$. Finally iii), we consider an output learner $\mathcal{L}$.

Setup. Before any sender starts interacting with $\mathcal{F}_{\mathsf{LSS}}$, it needs to wait until (Setup, P) is stored $\forall P \in \mathcal{P}$. However, the adversary $\mathcal{A}$ can choose to never instruct corrupt players to setup. To remedy this, we follow the *fetch-and-delay* mechanism explained in Sect. 2.3 and introduce a timeout $T_{\mathcal{A}}$.

Input. Upon receiving (ready) from the functionality, a sender $\mathcal{S} \in \mathscr{S}$ can then send its inputs $(x_{\mathcal{S},\alpha})_{\alpha \in X_{\mathcal{S}}}$ of labels $(\overline{x_{\mathcal{S},\alpha}})_{\alpha \in X_{\mathcal{S}}}$, after which $\mathcal{F}_{\mathsf{LSS}}$ notifies it to all the players. The former cannot be subsequently updated; once sent, the sender $\mathcal{S}$ is committed to the submitted values.

Opening. Let HOpeners be a set of players, initially empty. Any player P_i can call LCOpen for some linear form Λ, and is then included in HOpeners. When $|\text{HOpeners}| \geq t+1$, and if $\mathcal{F}_{\mathsf{LSS}}$ has stored all the inputs appearing with nonzero coefficient in Λ, then $\mathcal{F}_{\mathsf{LSS}}$ eventually delivers its evaluation. We denote this mechanism a *collective opening*. Now consider the scenario where one isolated honest player would start the LCOpen protocol, i.e. revealing its share of the evaluation. Since it is hard to prevent t corrupt players from also publicly disclosing consistent shares, this results in the evaluation being publicly opened. We qualify such event as an *early opening*. In practice, we give to $\mathcal{A}$ the power to send an (open$-$order) to $\mathcal{F}_{\mathsf{LSS}}$, which triggers an immediate delivery of the evaluation to all players, as soon as one honest player requests (LCOpen).

Implementation of $\mathcal{F}_{\mathsf{LSS}}$. Our main goal is to build a protocol Π_{LSS} that implements $\mathcal{F}_{\mathsf{LSS}}$, i.e. that enables, after an unique round of broadcast, players to have a common view on a set of shared secrets. Subsequently, they can perform the opening of the evaluation of *any* linear map over the shared secrets, using only one step of all-to-all asynchronous peer-to-peer messages. Π_{LSS} is detailed in the full version. Overall it can be outlined as follows.

To send a secret s to $\mathcal{F}_{\mathsf{LSS}}$, i.e., to share it, the first step is to generate a (n,t)-linear secret sharing of s. Let $[s^{(i)} : i \in [n]]$ be the vector of shares obtained. Encrypt each share $s^{(i)}$ under P_i's public key. The n-sized vector of ciphertexts obtained is called a public verifiable secret sharing (PVSS)[3]. To open a linear map Λ over a set of shared secrets $(s_j)_j$: every player P_i decrypts its encrypted shares $(s_j^{(i)})_j$, then evaluates Λ on them. By linearity of the LSS scheme, the result is a partial opening share $z^{(i)}$ of $\Lambda((s_j)_j)$. Then it sends $z^{(i)}$ to all, via

---

[3] The terminology *verifiable*, is because when compiling to fully malicious security, it should be appended NIZKs of knowledge of plaintexts and of a degree t polynomial. State of the art implementations of PVSS can be found in [20].

asynchronous channels. Finally, from any $t+1$ partial opening shares, the desired linear combination $\Lambda((s_j)_j)$ is efficiently reconstructible.

The main technical challenge we face is that we consider efficient homomorphic encryption schemes in which the ciphertext space is a polynomial ring R_q. In turn, this requires an efficient linear secret sharing scheme over polynomial rings. For this, different options exist, that are further detailed in the full version:

1. First, one can consider a class of Linear Secret Sharing Schemes, denoted as $\{0,1\}-\mathsf{LSSD}$, in which the reconstruction coefficients are always binary. We refer to [22] for an example of construction of such a scheme, which leads to a significant space overhead, as each share is now of size $O(n^{4.3})$.

To remove this overhead, one can naturally think of using Shamir [28]. However, this scheme is instantiated over a field $\mathbb{F}$ and involves the computation of Lagrange coefficients, that requires inverting elements of the form $\alpha_i - \alpha_j$, where α_i and α_j are public-points. Working over a field guarantees that all non-zero elements are units, hence that these coefficients exist. Our goal in (2) and (3) below is to sketch a variant of this classical case that works over polynomial rings.

2. Second, we recall the claim known since [17], that it is possible to construct a Shamir scheme over polynomial rings as long as $\alpha_i - \alpha_j$ is invertible, which exists when the prime factor q is of size at least $n+1$. We refer to [24, IV. A] for an example of constructions.

3. Finally, we discuss the full generalization to any q, including the useful case where q is a power $q = p^e$ of a prime, itself possibly small $p \leqslant n$ [10,19]. We detail in the full version $R_{p^e}-$Shamir, a Shamir scheme variant over Galois extensions of polynomial rings, following [1,17].

We prove in the full version that Π_{LSS} does UC-implement $\mathcal{F}_{\mathsf{LSS}}$.

3.3   Distributed Key Generation

Our DKG follows the classical pattern of previous DKGs in one broadcast [7,18]. Provided with a fixed public URS denoted a as input, each player P_i generates a key pair $(\mathsf{ek}_i, \mathsf{sk}_i)$, sends $(\mathsf{input}, \overline{\mathsf{sk}_i}, \mathsf{sk}_i)$ to $\mathcal{F}_{\mathsf{LSS}}$ and broadcasts ek_i. In the second step, players set a threshold key pair without any interaction, as follows. Denote S the set of indices of non-aborting players, i.e., the ones that have broadcast a contribution ek_i and sent an input to $\mathcal{F}_{\mathsf{LSS}}$, then:

$$(2) \qquad (\mathsf{ek} = (b, a) = (-\Sigma_{i \in S}\, a.\, \mathsf{sk}_i + e_i^{(\mathsf{ek})}, a)) \,.$$

Thus, the corresponding secret key is defined as $\mathsf{sk} = \Sigma_{i \in S}\mathsf{sk}_i$. Concretely, each player has a share of sk, consisting in the sum over S of its shares of the sk_i. In our formalism, each contribution is accessible via $\mathcal{F}_{\mathsf{LSS}}$.

Note that since the adversary sees first the contributions ek_i of honest players, before it decides of the contributions of corrupt players, the obtained key pair

$(\mathsf{sk}, \mathsf{ek})$ can be seen as generated by using what [7] formalize as the $\mathsf{BiasKeyGen}$ subroutine. In Sect. 6.2, we will prove that our protocol, as a whole, UC implements MPC. Hence, it can be replaced by the ideal functionality of MPC. Thus the DKG has completely disappeared, and its bias is a no-issue.

4   trBFV, with Robust Relinearization Key Generation

In this section, we introduce a new relinearization key and describe its distributed generation in one single robust round. Along the line, we call trBFV the new robust threshold variant of BFV (presented in Sect. 3.1) obtained with this new ingredient.

In more details, let us recall that in order to perform homomorphic operations, an extra relinearization key denoted $\mathbf{rlk}$ is needed. The homomorphic multiplication of two BFV ciphertexts $c_1, c_2 \in R_q^2$ involves two steps:

(a) The first, denoted *"tensoring"*, produces a *degree two* ciphertext consisting of three elements[4]:

$$(3) \qquad \hat{c} = \left\lfloor \frac{k}{q} c_1 \otimes c_2 \right\rceil = (\hat{c}[0], \hat{c}[1], \hat{c}[2]) \in R_q^3.$$

(b) To reduce the degree back to one, a second step, denoted *relinearization*, must be carried out using $\mathbf{rlk}$ to turn $\hat{c}$ into a "regular" BFV ciphertext $c' = (c'[0], c'[1])$ which can be decrypted as the product of the plaintexts.

As previously discussed in Sect. 1.1, existing protocols for distributed generation of a relinearization key were not robust. In what follows, we detail in Sect. 4.1 our new relinearization key and its robust, distributed generation. Then, we justify in Sect. 4.2 simulatability of our relinearization key generation, before detailing in Sect. 4.3 how to perform homomorphic operations with this new key.

4.1   New Relinearization Key Generation

Our relinearization key generation algorithm heavily leverages the gadget toolkit introduced in Sect. 3. Notably, recall that $\mathbf{g}^{-1} : R_q \to R^l$ is a gadget decomposition corresponding to a gadget vector $\mathbf{g} \in R_q^l$. It also makes use of two uniform random strings, that come in the form of two vectors $(\mathbf{a}, \mathbf{d}_1) \in R_q^{2 \times l}$, of which $a = \mathbf{a}[0]$ is, as described in Sect. 3.1, used to generate encryption keys. As a result, all algorithms that took $a \in R_q$ as input variable, are naturally extended to handle input $\mathbf{a} \in R_q^l$ (and notably KeyGen). We can now define the algorithm $\mathsf{trBFV.RlkKeygen}$ to generate a relinearization key.

- $(\mathbf{d}_0, \mathbf{d}_2) \in R_q^{2 \times l} \leftarrow \mathsf{trBFV.RlkKeygen}(\mathbf{a}, \mathbf{d}_1, \mathsf{sk})$:
    - Sample $r \leftarrow \mathscr{X}_q$.
    - Sample $\mathbf{e}_0^{(\mathbf{rlk})} \leftarrow \Psi_q^l$, and set $\mathbf{d}_0 = -\mathsf{sk} \cdot \mathbf{d}_1 + \mathbf{e}_0^{(\mathbf{rlk})} + r \cdot \mathbf{g}$

---

[4] Where $c_1 \otimes c_2 = (c_1[0] \cdot c_2[0], c_1[0] \cdot c_2[1] + c_1[1] \cdot c_2[0], c_1[1] \cdot c_2[1])$.

– Sample $\mathbf{e}_2^{(\mathrm{rlk})} \leftarrow \Psi_q^l$ and set $\mathbf{d}_2 = r \cdot \mathbf{a} + \mathbf{e}_2^{(\mathrm{rlk})} + \mathsf{sk} \cdot \mathbf{g}$
and set $\mathbf{rlk} = (\mathbf{d}_0, \mathbf{d}_1, \mathbf{d}_2)$.

Interestingly, the overall algorithm to generate **rlk** is linear over the secret key sk, unlike previous ones [24, 26, 27].

Distributed Relinearization Key Generation. To distributively generate a common **rlk**, one can leverage the additional linearity. In short, to build our RlkGen protocol, we let each player P_i compute an additive contribution to the relinearization key $(\mathbf{d}_{0,i}, \mathbf{d}_{2,i}) \leftarrow \mathsf{trBFV.RlkKeygen}(\mathbf{a}, \mathbf{d}_1, \mathsf{sk}_i)$ and broadcast it. From the set S of indices of players who have correctly broadcast their additive contributions to the relinearization key and to the threshold encryption key ek as in Eq. (2), one can then compute:

$$\mathbf{rlk} := (\Sigma_{i \in S} \mathbf{d}_{0,i}, \mathbf{d}_1, \Sigma_{i \in S} \mathbf{d}_{2,i}) \tag{4}$$

4.2 Construction Details and Security

We now justify simulatability of our new **rlk** generation introduced in Sect. 4.1, firstly by giving the reasoning behind its construction, before proving security.

Intuition. The intuitive rationale is that our **rlk** is none other than a particular case of an existing relinearization key! Indeed, the recent work of [9] proposed a n-out-of-n *multi*-key FHE scheme from BFV, and, therefore an algorithm to generate relinearization keys, which operate on multi-key ciphertexts. In this setting, a multi-key ciphertext associated to n players is of the form $\mathbf{c} = (\mathbf{c}_1, \mathbf{c}_2, \ldots, \mathbf{c}_n)$, is decryptable by the concatenated secret key $\mathbf{s} = (\mathsf{sk}_1, \ldots, \mathsf{sk}_n)$, and relinearizable using the concatenated n relinearization keys $\{\mathbf{rlk}_i\}_{i \in [n]}$. Interestingly, we observe that if we only consider the particular single-key case (i.e. $n = 1$), we obtain exactly our **rlk** presented in Sect. 4.1! In the remainder of this section, we discuss this particularization in greater detail.

Detailed Construction Explanation: From Multikey to Single-Key Relinearization Key. Let us slightly abuse future notation and denote RlkKeygen the linear map used in [9] to produce a relinearization key. In our context, the secret key sk comes as a sum $\sum_i \mathsf{sk}_i$ of (secret shared) contributions sk_i from non-aborting players, so we roughly need a robust protocol which generates $\mathbf{rlk} := \mathsf{RlkKeygen}(\mathsf{sk})$. This hints towards the blueprint of our robust distributed solution to generate **rlk**: *in parallel* of linearly secret-sharing its contribution sk_i to the secret key, each player P_i broadcasts the corresponding contribution: $\mathbf{rlk}_i = (\mathbf{d}_{0,i}, \mathbf{d}_{1,i}, \mathbf{d}_{2,i}) = \mathsf{RlkKeygen}(\mathsf{sk}_i)$ to the relinearization key. Then, after it computed the threshold encryption key ek as in Eq. (2), each player sets $\mathbf{rlk} = \sum_{i \in S} \mathbf{rlk}_i$, where S is the *same* set, i.e., of indices of players not aborting in the first round, as the one used to set ek. However, one hurdle remains in that in the linear map RlkKeygen defined in [9], the coefficient of sk_i, denoted $\mathbf{d}_{1,i}$, actually *depends* on the player making the contribution, since $\mathbf{d}_{1,i}$ is sampled by P_i. Hence, this prevents additivity between contributions from different players (in the setting of [9], no additivity was needed).

To solve this, we specify instead that $\mathbf{d}_1$ is in common, and given by an uniform random string (URS). The reason why fixing a common $\mathbf{d}_1$ does actually not degrade the security of the distributed protocol, compared to [9] is that $\mathbf{d}_1$, by definition, appears in clear in the public relinearization key. More particularly, in the proof of Corollary 2, we will show a reduction from the pseudorandomness of our common $\mathbf{rlk}$, into the pseudorandomness of a single-key $\mathbf{rlk}$, with loss only *linear* in n. To give an intuition, a toy model of our reduction is just the well-known reduction from the security of our DKG, into the security of RLWE. In this toy model, what the adversary sees are n samples $(a, \ a \cdot \mathsf{sk}_i + e_i^{(\mathsf{ek})})_{i \in [n]}$, all with the same public uniform randomness a but with *different independently sampled* secrets sk_i. So the idea is that the reduction to RLWE, upon receiving *one* RLWE challenge sample: $(a, \ a \cdot \mathsf{sk}_n + e_n^{(\mathsf{ek})})$, simply generates itself $n - 1$ other challenges: $(a, \ a \cdot \mathsf{sk}_i + e_i^{(\mathsf{ek})})_{i \in [n-1]}$ with the same a, and handles them to our adversary.

Security. In Corollary 2, we prove that, despite our specification of a common $\mathbf{d}_1$, the concatenation of all the honestly generated contributions $(\mathbf{d}_{0,i}, \mathbf{d}_{2,i}) \leftarrow$ trBFV.RlkKeygen$(\mathbf{a}, \mathbf{d}_1, \mathsf{sk}_i)$ to the common relinearization key, as well as the contributions $\mathbf{ek}_i = (\mathbf{b}_i, \mathbf{a})$ to the threshold encryption key, is indistinguishable from a large uniform random string, under the *same* circular security assumption as implicitly made in [9] and detailed in the full version.

Consider a public sampling of a uniform string $(\mathbf{a}, \mathbf{d}_1) \in U(R_q^{l \times 2})$, and a polynomial number M of independent machines. Each of them generates a key pair $(\mathsf{sk}_m, \mathsf{ek}_m)$ by using KeyGen, all using the common public $\mathbf{a}$. Each machine m generates $(\mathbf{d}_{0,m}, \mathbf{d}_{2,m}) \leftarrow$ trBFV.RlkKeygen$(\mathbf{a}, \mathbf{d}_1, \mathsf{sk}_m)$. Then the collection of the public data issued by these machines $\{\mathbf{b}_m, \mathbf{d}_{0,m}, \mathbf{d}_{2,m}\}_{m \in [M]}$, jointly with the public $(\mathbf{a}, \mathbf{d}_1)$, is still indistinguishable from one sample in $U(R_q^{(l \times 3)M} \times R_q^{l \times 2})$.

Corollary 2 (Security with Common Public Randomness). *Consider:*

$$\mathcal{D}_0^M := \Big\{ \big\{ \mathbf{b}_m, \mathbf{d}_{0,m}, \mathbf{d}_{2,m} \big\}_{m \in M}, \mathbf{a}, \mathbf{d}_1 : (\mathbf{a}, \mathbf{d}_1) \leftarrow U(R_q^l)^2, \ and \ \forall m \in [M]:$$

$$\mathsf{sk}_m \leftarrow \mathcal{X}_q, (\mathbf{e}_m^{(\mathsf{ek})}, \mathbf{e}_{0,m}^{(\mathsf{rlk})}, \mathbf{e}_{2,m}^{(\mathsf{rlk})}) \leftarrow (\Psi_q^l)^3, r_m \leftarrow \mathcal{X}_q, \mathbf{b}_m := -\mathbf{a}\,\mathsf{sk}_m + \mathbf{e}_m^{(\mathsf{ek})},$$

$$\mathbf{d}_{0,m} := -\mathsf{sk}_m\,\mathbf{d}_1 + \mathbf{e}_{0,m}^{(\mathsf{rlk})} + r_m\,\mathbf{g}, \ \mathbf{d}_{2,m} := r_m\,\mathbf{a} + \mathbf{e}_{2,m}^{(\mathsf{rlk})} + \mathsf{sk}_m\,\mathbf{g} \Big\}$$

Then the maximum distinguishing advantage $\mathsf{Adv}_{\mathcal{D}_0^M}^\lambda$ between a single sample in $\mathcal{D}_0^M$ and in $U(R_q^{(l \times 3)M} \times R_q^{l \times 2})$, is bounded by $M\mathsf{Adv}_{\mathcal{D}_0}^\lambda$.

Proof. Consider a cascade of oracles $\mathcal{O}_0 := \mathcal{O}_{\mathcal{D}_0^M}, \mathcal{O}_1, \ldots, \mathcal{O}_M$ such that each $\mathcal{O}_i$ returns the first i components of $R_q^{(l \times 3)M}$ in $U(R_q^{(l \times 3)i})$ and the remaining ones as in $\mathcal{D}_0^M$. Then the distinguishing advantage between two consecutive $\mathcal{O}_i$ is at most $\mathsf{Adv}_{\mathcal{D}_0}$, as a straightforward reduction shows (cf Appendix C in the full version). □

4.3   Homomorphic Evaluation of a Circuit

We can now augment the definition presented in Sect. 3.1 with homomorphic operations. Consider two BFV ciphertexts $c_1, c_2 \in R_q^2$ and keys $ek = (b, a)$ and rlk, then we have:

- **(Addition)** $trBFV.Add(c_1, c_2)$: Return $c = c_1 + c_2 \in R_q^2$.
- **(Multiplication)** $trBFV.Mult(c_1, c_2, rlk, b)$: Compute $\hat{c} = \left\lfloor \frac{k}{q} c_1 \otimes c_2 \right\rceil \in R_q^3$ and return $c' \leftarrow Relin(\hat{c}, rlk, b)$ (cf Algorithm 1).
- $trBFV.Eval(C, (c_i \in R_q^2)_{i \in [n]}, rlk, b)$, for a circuit C with n input gates, return the evaluation obtained by applying $trBFV.Add$ and $trBFV.Mult$ gate by gate, with inputs the $(c_i)_{i \in [n]}$.

New Relinearization. We now present our new relinearization algorithm.

Algorithm 1. Relin

Input: $\hat{c} = (\hat{c}[0], \hat{c}[1], \hat{c}[2]) \in R_q^3$, $rlk = [d_0 | d_1 | d_2] \in (R_q^l)^3$, $b \in R_q^l$
Output $c' = (c_0', c_1') \in R_q^2$

1: $c_0' \leftarrow \hat{c}[0]$
2: $c_1' \leftarrow \hat{c}[1]$
3: $c_2' \leftarrow \langle g^{-1}(\hat{c}[2]), b \rangle$
4: $(c_0', c_1') \leftarrow (c_0', c_1') + g^{-1}(c_2') \cdot {\scriptstyle<\cdot>} (d_0, d_1)$
5: $c_1' \leftarrow c_1' + \langle g^{-1}(\hat{c}[2]), d_2 \rangle$

Correctness. Correctness follows from the proof of [9] adapted to our single-key context. In a nutshell, we have:

$$g^{-1}(c_2') {\scriptstyle<\cdot>} (d_0, d_1) {\scriptstyle<\cdot>} (1, sk) \approx r \cdot c_2' \quad \text{and} \quad \langle g^{-1}(\hat{c}[2]), d_2 \rangle \cdot sk \approx -r \cdot c_2' + \hat{c}[2] \cdot sk^2$$

and thus,

$$c_0' + c_1' sk \approx \hat{c}[0] + \hat{c}[1]sk + \hat{c}[2]sk^2$$

We refer to the full version for a complete noise analysis.

5   Threshold Decryption

Recall from Sect. 3.1 that the decryption can be seen as a two steps process: (i) first the interactive opening of a linear map defined for BFV as,

(5) $$\Lambda_{Dec}^c : sk \rightarrow c[0] + c[1] \cdot sk,$$

applied to the (secret shared) secret key sk, with public coefficients equal to the ciphertext c, (ii) followed by the local computation of a non-linear decoding function Ω_{Dec}. However, a direct adaptation from this decryption to the threshold setting is not trivial, when Ω_{Dec} is nontrivial, as the case in fully homomorphic encryption. Indeed, the output μ of (i) allows recovering the plaintext, but also reveals a small *decryption noise* term that depends on the given ciphertext and the secret key, as defined below:

Definition 3 (Decryption noise). *Let* $\mathsf{c} \in \mathscr{C}$, $m \in \mathscr{M}$ *and* $\mathsf{sk} \in \mathscr{X}_q$. *We define the "decryption noise" as* $e^{(\mathsf{Dec})}(\mathsf{c}, \mathsf{sk}, m) := \Lambda^{\mathsf{c}}_{\mathsf{Dec}}(\mathsf{sk}) - \Delta \cdot m$.

Asharov et al. [3] demonstrated that the noisy output μ of (i) reveals too much information about the secret key. Thus, to prevent any information leakage about the secret key, [3] introduced the technique of adding additional noise to μ before it can be reconstructed. This "smudging" noise e_{sm} is, roughly, sampled uniformly in some large enough interval $[-B_{sm}, B_{sm}]$. Now consider an arithmetic circuit C, and denote B_{C} the upper-bound on the decryption noise of a ciphertext after evaluation of circuit C. The choice of B_{sm} is crucial to both the security and correctness of our MPC protocol. This translates into the following two requirements:

(a) First, the output of (i) $\mu = \Lambda^{\mathsf{c}}_{\mathsf{Dec}}(\mathsf{sk})$ must be statistically close enough to the (scaled) plaintext circuit evaluation $\Delta.y$. Then, there should exist some level of noise B_{sm}, so that adding an uniform noise $e_{\mathsf{sm}} \in [-B_{sm}, B_{sm}]$ to both μ and y, makes them indistinguishable, while leaving correct the result: $y = \Omega_{\mathsf{Dec}}(\mu + e_{\mathsf{sm}})$. As stated by the *smudging lemma*, the indistinguishability requirement imposes a level of noise high enough so that $B_{\mathsf{C}}/B_{sm} \leqslant \mathsf{negl}(\lambda)$.
(b) Second, the correctness requirement imposes that B_{C} added with this smudging noise stays small, i.e. we want that:

$$(6) \qquad\qquad B_{\mathsf{C}} + n \cdot B_{sm} \leq \Delta/2,$$

as further explained in Appendix C of the full version.

Below, we give two methods for opening μ added with such noise.

5.1 Mainstream Threshold Decryption Method

The first protocol follows the approach of [3] and has been used in most other works [3,4,24]. Each player P_i locally samples a so-called smudging noise $e_{\mathsf{sm},i} \xleftarrow{\$} [-B_{sm}, B_{sm}]$ uniformly in some interval to be specified, multiplies it by $n!^2$ ([4, Construction 5.11]), then adds it to its decryption share of c, which it sends. The reason for multiplying by $n!^2$ is to clear-out the denominators of the Lagrange coefficients applied at reconstruction (see [4]). Following the previous notation and explanations, the bound B_{sm} is chosen in [4, §5.3.1] such that: $B_{\mathsf{C}}/B_{sm} = \mathsf{negl}(\lambda)$ (for indistinguishability), and such that $B_{\mathsf{C}} + n.n!^3 \cdot B_{sm} < \Delta/2$ (for correctness of Lagrange reconstruction-then-rounding, or $q/4$ instead of $\Delta/2$ in their instantiation with GSW). In a nutshell, this method introduces an overhead of $n.n!^3$ on the ciphertext modulus q. This results in a $n\times$ blowup of the ciphertext length.

5.2   Improved Threshold Decryption Method

To keep the ciphertext size small, the second method, follows a forgotten approach, which we credit to [15]. Players do not anymore blur their opening share
of μ. Instead, they now reconstruct all at once the sum of μ and a common
shared noise e_{sm}, i.e., they open the linear map defined as:

$$(7) \qquad \Lambda^{\mathsf{c}}_{\mathsf{Dec}+sm} : (\mathsf{sk}, e_{\mathsf{sm}}) \to \mathsf{c}[0] + \mathsf{c}[1] \cdot \mathsf{sk} + e_{\mathsf{sm}}$$

The distributed generation of the noise is simply done by adding secret-shared
contributions $e_{\mathsf{sm},i}$, each sampled in $[-B_{sm}, B_{sm}]$. As a result, the correctness
constraint now imposes only $B_{\mathsf{C}} + n.B_{sm} < \Delta/2$ (Eq. 6). Hence, the ciphertext
expansion factor Δ has dependency in n which is only linear, instead of $n.n!^3$
in the previous method. Since the noise can be used only for one threshold
decryption, players must precompute as much noises as many circuits to be subsequently evaluated. We will formalize this simple Distributed Noise Generation
protocol in the MPC protocol presented in Fig. 3. Concretely, each player P_i
secret-shares a contribution $e_{\mathsf{sm},i} \leftarrow [-B_{sm}, B_{sm}]$ in the form of a PVSS in the
broadcast step. Then, players define the common shared smudging noise as the
sum over the contributions of the players which did not abort: $e_{\mathsf{sm}} = \sum_{i \in S} e_{\mathsf{sm},i}$.

6   MPC Protocol

In Fig. 3, we formalize our trBFV scheme as an end-to-end MPC protocol in 2
broadcasts + one asynchronous P2P round, called $\Pi^{\mathcal{F}_{\mathsf{LSS}}}_{\mathsf{MPC}}$, assuming a bulletin
board PKI and an URS. For simplicity, we describe and prove it in the $\mathcal{F}_{\mathsf{LSS}}$-
hybrid model.

6.1   Protocol $\Pi^{\mathcal{F}_{\mathsf{LSS}}}_{\mathsf{MPC}}$ Instantiated from trBFV

We instantiate protocol $\Pi^{\mathcal{F}_{\mathsf{LSS}}}_{\mathsf{MPC}}$ from trBFV. Notably, we use the alternative version of relinearization key generation presented in Sect. 4. Moreover, for security
and correctness, we require Eq. (6); and:

$$(8) \qquad \frac{B_{\mathsf{C}}}{B_{sm}} = \mathrm{negl}(\lambda) \ \text{ and } \ \frac{2dnB}{B_{\mathsf{Enc}}} = \mathrm{negl}(\lambda) \ .$$

where B_{C} is a bound on the noise of a ciphertext after evaluation of circuit
C and B, B_{Enc} bounds on the encryption randomnesses. Note that following
Sect. 5, two possibilities exist for threshold decryption: (i) either by using the
mainstream threshold decryption method (Sect. 5.1), that does not require pre-
shared noises, (ii) or by using the second improved method (Sect. 5.2), in which
players distributively generate a pre-shared noise in parallel with the DKG. We
present the latter in Fig. 3.

Protocol $\Pi_{\mathsf{MPC}}^{\mathcal{F}_{\mathsf{LSS}}}$

Participants: n players $P_1, \ldots, P_n$, each with input m_i.

Bulletin-board PKI setup and URS setup. Each P_i:

- Sends (Setup) to $\mathcal{F}_{\mathsf{LSS}}$ and obtains common URSs $(\mathbf{a}, \mathbf{d}_1) \leftarrow \overline{\mathcal{G}}_{\mathsf{URS}}$.

(1) **Interactive setup in one step of all-to-all broadcasts.**
Upon ready from $\mathcal{F}_{\mathsf{LSS}}$, each P_i:

- *Distributed Keys Generation - broadcasts:*
  - Computes $(\mathsf{sk}_i, (\mathbf{b}_i, \mathbf{a})) \leftarrow \mathsf{BFV.KeyGen}(\mathbf{a})$ and $(\mathbf{d}_{0,i}, \mathbf{d}_{2,i}) \leftarrow \mathsf{trBFV.RlkKeygen}(\mathbf{a}, \mathbf{d}_1, \mathsf{sk}_i)$.
  - Sends $(\mathsf{input}, \overline{\mathsf{sk}_i}, \mathsf{sk}_i)$ to $\mathcal{F}_{\mathsf{LSS}}$ and broadcasts $(\mathbf{b}_i, (\mathbf{d}_{0,i}, \mathbf{d}_{2,i}))$.
- *Distributed Smudging Noises Generation (in parallel of DKG):*
  - Samples $e_{\mathsf{sm},i} \xleftarrow{\$} [-B_{sm}, B_{sm}]$ and sends $(\mathsf{input}, \overline{e_{\mathsf{sm},i}}, e_{\mathsf{sm},i})$ to $\mathcal{F}_{\mathsf{LSS}}$.

(1) **Formation of threshold keys (local):** Each player:

- *Reception of broadcasts:* Initializes an empty list $S \leftarrow \{\}$, and $\forall j \in [n]$, checks if the data received from the broadcast of P_j parses as: $(\mathbf{b}_j, (\mathbf{d}_{0,j}, \mathbf{d}_{2,j}))$, then adds j to S. Also, if the distributed smudging noise generation was activated, it further checks if $\mathcal{F}_{\mathsf{LSS}}$ did notify $(\mathsf{stored}, \overline{e_{\mathsf{sm},j}})$ (else, it does not add j to S).
- *Adding the contributions of non-aborting players:* Computes

$$(9) \qquad \mathbf{b} = \Sigma_{j \in S} \mathbf{b}_j \,,$$

sets the threshold keys: $\mathsf{ek} = (b = \mathbf{b}[0], a = \mathbf{a}[0])$ and $\mathsf{sk} = \Sigma_{i \in S} \mathsf{sk}_i$, and the noise $e_{\mathsf{sm}} = \Sigma_{i \in S} e_{\mathsf{sm},i}$ //accessible through $\mathcal{F}_{\mathsf{LSS}}$, via the labels $\overline{\mathsf{sk}}, \overline{e_{\mathsf{sm}}}$, and:

$$(10) \qquad \mathbf{rlk} = (\Sigma_{j \in S} \mathbf{d}_{0,j}, \mathbf{d}_1, \Sigma_{j \in S} \mathbf{d}_{2,j})$$

(2) **Broadcast of encrypted inputs:** Each P_i:

- Samples $u \xleftarrow{\$} \mathcal{X}_q$, $e_0^{(\mathsf{Enc})} \xleftarrow{\$} \mathcal{B}_{\mathsf{Enc},q}$ and $e_1^{(\mathsf{Enc})} \xleftarrow{\$} \Psi_q$. Computes $\mathbf{c}_i = (\Delta m_i + u \cdot b + e_0^{(\mathsf{Enc})}, u \cdot a + e_1^{(\mathsf{Enc})})$ then broadcasts it.

(2) **Evaluation (local):** Each P_i sets $S_c \subset [n]$ the subset of indices of players from which it received a ciphertext $\mathbf{c}_j$. Then it computes $\mathbf{c} \leftarrow \mathsf{trBFV.Eval}(C, \{\mathbf{c}_j\}_{j \in S_c}, \mathbf{rlk}, b)^a$.

(3) **Threshold Decryption:** Each P_i:

- Given labels $(\overline{\mathsf{sk}}, \overline{e_{sm}})$ and $\mathbf{c}$, sends $(\mathsf{LCOpen}, \Lambda_{\mathsf{Dec}+sm}^{\mathbf{c}}(\overline{\mathsf{sk}}, \overline{e_{sm}}))$ to $\mathcal{F}_{\mathsf{LSS}}$;
- Upon receiving $(\Lambda_{\mathsf{Dec}+sm}^{\mathbf{c}}, \mu)$ from $\mathcal{F}_{\mathsf{LSS}}$, outputs $y := \Omega_{\mathsf{Dec}}(\mu)$.

---

^{a}Without loss of generality, C sets to $\perp$ the non received inputs in $[n] \setminus S_c$.

Fig. 3. MPC Protocol $\Pi_{\mathsf{MPC}}^{\mathcal{F}_{\mathsf{LSS}}}$

312 A. Urban and M. Rambaud

6.2 Proofs of Theorem 1

As Π_{LSS} UC implements $\mathcal{F}_{\mathsf{LSS}}$, the following Theorem 4 implies Theorem 1.

Theorem 4. $\Pi_{\mathsf{MPC}}^{\mathcal{F}_{\mathsf{LSS}}}$ *implemented from* trBFV *UC implements the ideal functionality* $\mathcal{F}_{\mathsf{C}}$ *for any semi-malicious adversary, in the* $(\mathcal{F}_{\mathsf{LSS}}, \mathsf{BC})$*-hybrid model with external resource* $\overline{\mathcal{G}}_{URS}$.

Description of the Simulator Sim *of* $\Pi_{\mathsf{MPC}}^{\mathcal{F}_{\mathsf{LSS}}}$. To prove Theorem 4, we describe a simulator Sim of $\Pi_{\mathsf{MPC}}^{\mathcal{F}_{\mathsf{LSS}}}$, that initiates in its head, a set of n players and may initially receive corruption requests from Env for up to t players, indexed by $\mathcal{I} \subset [n]$. It simulates functionalities $\mathsf{BC}, \mathcal{F}_{\mathsf{LSS}}$ following a correct behavior, apart from the value returned by $\mathcal{F}_{\mathsf{LSS}}$ during the threshold decryption. Upon every output from a simulated functionality to a simulated corrupt player, or, upon every message from a simulated functionality to the simulated $\mathcal{A}$, Sim instantly forwards it to Env, as would have done the actual $\mathcal{A}$.

Intuition. We now convey the main ideas of Sim by describing it via a sequence of incremental changes, starting from a real execution. In the last hybrid, the view of Env is generated solely by interaction with $\mathcal{F}_{\mathsf{C}}$, hence what we are describing is a simulator. The full details about Sim and the proofs are in the full version.

First, in Hybrid_1, we simulate decryption by modifying the behavior of $\mathcal{F}_{\mathsf{LSS}}$ in the threshold decryption. There it, incorrectly, outputs $\mu^{\mathsf{Sim}} := \Delta y + \Sigma_{j \in S} e_{\mathsf{sm},j}$, where $y := C((m_\ell)_{\ell \in S_c})$ is the evaluation of the circuit on the actual inputs. Indistinguishability follows from the "smudging Lemma" (see Sect. 3).

Then, in Hybrid_2, the additive contributions $(\mathbf{b}_i, (\mathbf{d}_{0,i}, \mathbf{d}_{2,i})_{i \in \mathcal{H}}$ of honest players to the keys, are replaced by samples in $U(R_q^{l \times 3})$. Indistinguishability from Hybrid_1 follows from Corollary 2.

Finally, in Hybrid_3, we replace the actual inputs m_ℓ of simulated honest players by $\widetilde{m_\ell} := 0$. Importantly, the behavior of $\mathcal{F}_{\mathsf{LSS}}$ is unchanged, i.e., correct until ③, then outputs $\mu^{\mathsf{Sim}} := \Delta y + \Sigma_{j \in S} e_{\mathsf{sm},j}$, where $y := C((m_\ell)_{\ell \in S_c})$ is still the evaluation of the circuit on the *actual* inputs. Thanks to the modifications so far, we can apply the "IND-CPA under Joint Keys Lemma" detailed in the full version, which adapts the one of [3] in the RLWE setting, and argue that ciphertexts of chosen plaintexts are indistinguishable from random strings.

References

1. Abspoel, M., Cramer, R., Damgård, I., Escudero, D., Yuan, C.: Efficient information-theoretic secure multiparty computation over $z/p^k z$ via galois rings. In: TCC (2019)
2. Albrecht, M., et al.: Homomorphic Encryption Standard (2021)
3. Asharov, G., Jain, A., López-Alt, A., Tromer, E., Vaikuntanathan, V., Wichs, D.: Multiparty computation with low communication, computation and interaction via threshold FHE. In: EUROCRYPT (2012)

4. Boneh, D., et al.: Threshold cryptosystems from threshold fully homomorphic encryption. In: CRYPTO (2018)
5. Boudgoust, K., Scholl, P.: Simple threshold (fully homomorphic) encryption from LWE with polynomial modulus. In: ASIACRYPT (2023)
6. Brakerski, Z.: Fully homomorphic encryption without modulus switching from classical GapSVP. In: Safavi-Naini, R., Canetti, R. (eds.) Advances in Cryptology – CRYPTO (2012)
7. Braun, L., Damgård, I., Orlandi, C.: Secure multiparty computation from threshold encryption based on class groups. In: CRYPTO (2023)
8. Canetti, R.: Universally composable security: a new paradigm for cryptographic protocols. In: FOCS (2001). We refer to eprint 2000/067
9. Chen, H., Dai, W., Kim, M., Song, Y.: Efficient multi-key homomorphic encryption with packed ciphertexts with application to oblivious neural network inference. In: CCS (2019)
10. Chen, H., Han, K.: Homomorphic lower digits removal and improved FHE bootstrapping. In: EUROCRYPT (2018)
11. Cheon, J.H., Cho, W., Kim, J.: Improved universal thresholdizer from threshold fully homomorphic encryption. ePrint 2023/545 (2023)
12. Cheon, J.H., Kim, A., Kim, M., Song, Y.: Homomorphic encryption for arithmetic of approximate numbers. In: ASIACRYPT (2017)
13. Chowdhury, S., et al.: Efficient threshold FHE with application to real-time systems. ePrint 2022/1625 (2022)
14. Coretti, S., Garay, J., Hirt, M., Zikas, V.: Constant-round asynchronous multiparty computation based on one-way functions. In: ASIACRYPT (2016)
15. Dov Gordon, S., Liu, F.H., Shi, E.: Constant-round MPC with fairness and guarantee of output delivery. In: CRYPTO (2015)
16. Fan, J., Vercauteren, F.: Somewhat practical fully homomorphic encryption. IACR ePrint (2012)
17. Fehr, S.: Span programs over rings and how to share a secret from a module. Master's thesis, ETH Zurich (1998)
18. Fouque, P.A., Stern, J.: One round threshold discrete-log key generation without private channels. In: PKC (2001)
19. Geelen, R., Iliashenko, I., Kang, J., Vercauteren, F.: On polynomial functions modulo p^e and faster bootstrapping for homomorphic encryption. In: EUROCRYPT (2023)
20. Gentry, C., Halevi, S., Vadim, L.: Practical non-interactive publicly verifiable secret sharing with thousands of parties. In: EUROCRYPT (2022)
21. Gentry, C., Sahai, A., Waters, B.: Homomorphic encryption from learning with errors: conceptually-simpler, asymptotically-faster, attribute-based. In: CRYPTO (2013)
22. Jain, A., Rasmussen, P.M.R., Sahai, A.: Threshold fully homomorphic encryption. ePrint 2017/257 (2017)
23. Katz, J., Maurer, U., Tackmann, B., Zikas, V.: Universally composable synchronous computation. In: TCC (2011)
24. Kim, E., Jeong, J., Yoon, H., Kim, Y., Cho, J., Cheon, J.H.: How to securely collaborate on data: decentralized threshold he and secure key update. IEEE Access **8**, 191319–191329 (2020)
25. Lyubashevsky, V., Peikert, C., Regev, O.: On ideal lattices and learning with errors over rings. J. ACM **60**(6), 1–35 (2013)

26. Mouchet, C., Troncoso-Pastoriza, J., Bossuat, J.P., Hubaux, J.P.: Multiparty homomorphic encryption from ring-learning-with-errors. PoPETS **2021**(4), 291–311 (2021)
27. Park, J.: Homomorphic encryption for multiple users with less communications. IEEE Access **9**, 135915–135926 (2021)
28. Shamir, A.: How to share a secret. Commun. ACM (1979)

Efficient Blind Rotation in FHEW Using Refined Decomposition and NTT

Ying Liu[1,2], Zhihao Li[3], Ruida Wang[1,2], Xianhui Lu[1,2(✉)],
and Kunpeng Wang[1,2]

[1] Key Laboratory of Cyberspace Security Defense, Institute of Information
Engineering, Chinese Academy of Sciences, Beijing, China
`{liuying,luxianhui}@iie.ac.cn`
[2] School of Cyber Security, University of Chinese Academy of Sciences,
Beijing, China
[3] Ant Group, Beijing, China
`lzh458070@antgroup.com`

Abstract. In this paper, we propose two more efficient implementations for the FHEW scheme. First, for the gate bootstrapping case, we employ approximate gadget decomposition and refined Number Theoretic Transform (NTT) with AVX-512 instructions to improve the efficiency of blind rotation. Compared to the state-of-the-art implementation that uses FFT-based polynomial multiplication, our technique takes 4.7 ms, which is approximately $1.9\times$ faster than TFHEpp and $1.4\times$ faster than TFHE-rs. Furthermore, for the circuit bootstrapping case, we introduce the Residue Number System (RNS) to decompose the larger modulus. Experimental results demonstrate that the RNS decomposition is more efficient than the original numerical decomposition. Our optimized method is more applicable in scenarios involving prime moduli, such as homomorphic trace and automorphism.

Keywords: FHEW · Bootstrapping · Blind Rotation · RNS · NTT · AVX-512

1 Introduction

Fully Homomorphic Encryption (FHE) is a crucial cryptographic primitive that enables computations on encrypted data without requiring decryption. This capability allows for arbitrary operations on ciphertexts. The first FHE scheme was introduced by Gentry in 2009 [13], leveraging the ideal lattice [9] and a novel procedure called bootstrapping. During homomorphic evaluations, noise accumulates with the increasing depth of the circuit. To prevent decryption failure caused by error inflation, bootstrapping is employed to reduce the noise to a manageable level, enabling further evaluations. Since its introduction by Gentry, the efficiency of bootstrapping has been improved significantly, with subsequent works achieving substantial enhancements in both latency and throughput. Nonetheless, bootstrapping remains the primary bottleneck in achieving

ⓒ The Author(s), under exclusive license to Springer Nature Switzerland AG 2025
N. Mouha and N. Nikiforakis (Eds.): ISC 2024, LNCS 15257, pp. 315–334, 2025.
https://doi.org/10.1007/978-3-031-75757-0_16

efficient fully homomorphic encryption. Currently, the homomorphic encryption algorithms supporting the fastest bootstrapping are FHEW [10], TFHE [7], and several outstanding subsequent works based on them, such as [16,21,27], etc. These algorithms have millisecond-level bootstrapping, making them highly efficient for practical applications.

In FHE schemes, particularly in bootstrapping algorithms, homomorphic operations are typically performed over the ring $\mathbb{Z}_Q[x]/f(X)$, where $f(X)$ is a polynomial of degree N. Therefore, polynomial multiplications are core computation units in FHE, significantly affecting overall practical efficiency. To ensure the high efficiency of FHE schemes, current implementations utilize the Number Theoretic Transform (NTT) or the Fast Fourier Transform (FFT) to efficiently compute polynomial multiplications. Compared to traditional polynomial multiplication that has computational complexity of $\mathcal{O}(N^2)$, NTT and FFT reduce the computational complexity to $\mathcal{O}(N \log N)$ by exploiting the cyclicity and symmetry of unit roots. However, while both NTT and FFT have consistent asymptotic complexity theoretically, they exhibit significant performance differences in practical implementations. Specifically, the two most promising public library of TFHE schemes, such as TFHE-rs [28] and TFHEpp [23], both use floating-point operations over Torus and compute polynomial multiplications using FFT. While the state-of-the-art NTT-based FHE library Open-FHE [2] is approximately eight times slower than FFT-based implementations. Clearly, our tests show that a single FFT in TFHEpp takes only around 1.3 µs, while a single NTT in Open-FHE requires about 9.5 µs[1].

The performance gap between NTT-based and FFT-based FHE libraries can be attributed to two primary factors. First, the implementation logic of the Open-FHE library plays a significant role. Open-FHE employs 64-bit data types for storing and computing all data smaller than 2^{64}, aiming for a more generalized implementation. However, this approach proves inefficient for smaller data sizes, both in terms of speed and storage. Second, the inherent algorithmic differences between FFT and NTT also influence performance outcomes. Based on this observation, we aim to determine whether the performance of NTT-based homomorphic encryption libraries can surpass that of FFT-based implementations. Consequently, our motivation is to design a more efficient NTT-based bootstrapping implementation method for homomorphic encryption schemes, reducing the performance gap between existing FFT-based and NTT-based homomorphic encryption libraries.

1.1   Contributions and Technique

In this paper, we focus on improving the bootstrapping efficiency of the FHEW scheme by accelerating blind rotation through the use of finely designed decomposition and optimized NTT techniques.

– **Efficient Gate Bootstrapping using Refined NTT.**

---

[1] All tests are implemented on a computer with an Intel(R) Core i5-11500 @2.70GHz, running Ubuntu 22.04.2 LTS and compiled with clang version 14.0.0.

Given that integers smaller than 32 bits exhibit twice the parallelism in Intel AVX instructions compared to double-precision floating-point numbers, we choose NTT with Intel AVX-512 for gate bootstrapping. To improve computational efficiency, we choose Solinas primes to simplify the modular reductions for the results of adding or subtracting operations. Besides, we use the idea of lazy reduction [26] to reduce the number of modular reductions for the results of additions and subtractions in forward and inverse NTT. Using the above techniques, our implementation reduces the gate bootstrapping time to 4.7 ms at the 128-bit security level, which is about 1.9× faster than TFHEpp [23] and 1.4× faster than TFHE-rs [28].

– **Optimized Circuit Bootstrapping using RNS Decomposition.** Recently, Wang et al. [27] proposed a new circuit bootstrapping framework in Eurocrypt 2024, which sets the ciphertext modulus to be a prime number to facilitate homomorphic trace operations. In this case, the FFT-based polynomial multiplication does not use. In this way, NTT is more suitable to blind rotation process. Technically, we can choose a specific composite number as the modulus for RLWE ciphertexts and then use RNS technique to map the computations onto several rings with Solinas primes smaller than 16 bits. Furthermore, in external product, we can save some NTTs and INTTs using RNS compared with the usage in previous FHE schemes like BFV and BGV [3,17,18], etc. The experimental results show that the circuit bootstrapping using our RNS-based method can achieve a 1.4× speedup compared to using NTT directly over the original ring with the same security level and modulus.

1.2   Related Work

In homomorphic encryption, correctness and efficiency are two central concerns, corresponding respectively to noise management and efficient computation techniques. FHEW and TFHE schemes use the optimized AP [1] and GINX [12] blind rotation methods, respectively, to implement single-message bootstrapping. Their bootstrapping has a very small parameter size compared to other FHE cryptosystems, with the noise size being nearly linear.

Polynomial multiplication is a fundamental operation in homomorphic encryption algorithms. To ensure the efficiency of these algorithms, the NTT is commonly used to accelerate polynomial multiplication. However, when the modulus exceeds the CPU's native type, it needs to be decomposed using RNS and combined with the inverse Chinese Remainder Theorem (ICRT) to recover the result at the end of polynomial multiplication [14]. For a long time, it has been assumed that NTT requires the modulus to be prime. When this is not satisfied, either RNS decomposition to a prime representation or the lifting multiplication method [8] can be used to perform NTT. Subsequently, [19] provided a method for constructing primitive roots for NTT with a composite modulus, where the composite is a product of several NTT-friendly moduli. In 2023, [21] presented the first application in the field of FHE for computing NTT with a composite modulus directly, expanding the range of options for parameter selection.

The RNS technique is widely utilized in homomorphic encryption for decomposing ciphertexts, which not only works in controlling noise but also manages computations with data sizes exceeding native types of CPUs. It is widely applied in the BGV [18], BFV [17], and CKKS [6] schemes, where the moduli commonly exceed one thousand bits, enabling representation of operations using native integer types. In 2023, Guimarães et al. [16] proposed an RNS variant of GSW (Gentry-Sahai-Waters) along with a shrinking operation to reduce ciphertext size and noise. Unlike our motivation of using RNS, their method of packing ciphertexts for amortized bootstrapping increases the noise to at least a square level, necessitating a modulus size Q that exceeds the native CPU types.

1.3 Organization

The structure of this paper is organized as follows. In Sect. 2, we provide important background and techniques used in FHE. In Sect. 3, we introduce the refined NTT and decomposition technique for gate bootstrapping and circuit bootstrapping. In Sect. 4, we provide the parameters, noise analysis and implementation results for gate bootstrapping and bootstrapping. In Sect. 5, we conclude our paper.

2 Preliminaries

2.1 Notation

We use $\mathbb{Z}$ to present the set of integers and denote $\mathbb{R}$ as the set of reals. The ring of integers consisted by the set $\{0, 1, \cdots, Q-1\}$ is denoted as $\mathbb{Z}_Q$. We denote the $2N$-th cyclotomic ring $\mathcal{R} = \mathbb{Z}[X]/(X^N + 1)$, where the positive integer N is a power of 2. Then, its quotient ring is denoted as $\mathcal{R}_Q = \mathcal{R}/Q\mathcal{R}$, which represents the polynomial ring consisting of all polynomials with a degree at most $N - 1$ and coefficients in $\mathbb{Z}_Q$.

In this paper, we present an integer and a vector with a regular lowercase letter (e.g. a) and a bold lowercase letter (e.g. $\mathbf{a}$), respectively. For the polynomial in the ring $\mathcal{R}_Q$, we also use a bold lowercase letter to represent it, such as $\mathbf{a}(X) = a_0 + a_1 X + \cdots + a_{N-1} X^{N-1} \in \mathcal{R}_Q$ with coefficient vector $\mathbf{a} \in \mathbb{Z}_Q^N$. Then, the vectors in the NTT domain are denoted by a symbol with modulus, for example, the coefficient vector $\mathbf{a}$ of polynomial $\mathbf{a}(X) \in \mathcal{R}_Q$ in NTT domain are denoted by $\mathsf{NTT}_Q(\mathbf{a})$. Let $\| \cdot \|_2$ and $\| \cdot \|_\infty$ represents l_2 and l_∞ norms. We use $\mathsf{Err}(\mathsf{ct})$ and $\mathsf{Var}(\mathsf{Err}(\mathsf{ct}))$ to denote the error of ct and the variance of $\mathsf{Err}(\mathsf{ct})$. Let $\lfloor \cdot \rceil$, $\lceil \cdot \rceil$, $\lfloor \cdot \rfloor$ and $[\cdot]_Q$ represents round to nearest integer, round up, round down and the modulo operation with Q, respectively. Let $\langle \cdot \rangle$ and $\odot$ represent inner products and external products, respectively. Besides, the symbol $\odot$ also can represent the matrix Hadmard multiplications and point-wise vector multiplications. We use $\otimes$ represents the tensor product.

2.2   Cryptographic Assumption

Here we introduce the hard problems of learning with errors (LWE) [25] and ring learning with errors (RLWE) [22], which can ensure the security of FHE.

LWE Assumption. For a message $m \in \mathbb{Z}_t$, we define the LWE ciphertext with the secret key $\mathbf{s}$, ciphertext modulus q, plaintext modulus t and dimension n as

$$\mathsf{LWE}^n_{s,q}(m) = (\mathbf{a}, b) = (\mathbf{a}, \langle \mathbf{a}, \mathbf{s} \rangle + \lfloor \frac{q}{t} \cdot m \rceil + e) \in \mathbb{Z}_q^{n+1},$$

where $\mathbf{a}$ is a uniform random vector sampled from $\mathbb{Z}_q^n$ and e is a noise term sampled from Gaussian distribution with parameters σ.

RLWE Assumption. We define the RLWE ciphertext of the message $\mathbf{m} \in \mathcal{R}_t$ with the secret key $\mathbf{s}$, ciphertext modulus Q, plaintext modulus t and ring dimension N as

$$\mathsf{RLWE}^N_{s,Q}(\mathbf{m}) = (\mathbf{a}, \mathbf{b}) = (\mathbf{a}, \mathbf{a} \cdot \mathbf{s} + \lfloor \frac{Q}{t} \cdot \mathbf{m} \rceil + \mathbf{e}) \in \mathcal{R}_Q^2,$$

where $\mathbf{a}$ is a uniform random polynomial in $\mathcal{R}_Q$, with a small noise term $\mathbf{e}$ sampled from error distribution χ.

2.3   Digit Decomposition

For a modulus Q, a decomposition base B, let $\mathbf{g}$ represents a d-dimensional column vector as $\mathbf{g} = (B^0, B^1, \cdots, B^{d-1})^T$, where $d = \lceil \log_2 Q \rceil$. The decomposition function for the polynomial $\mathbf{a} \in \mathcal{R}_Q$ as

$$\mathbf{g}^{-1}(\mathbf{a}) = \left(\sum_{i=0}^{N-1} [a_i]_B, \sum_{i=0}^{N-1} \left[\left\lfloor \frac{a_i}{B^1} \right\rfloor \right]_B, \cdots, \sum_{i=0}^{N-1} \left[\left\lfloor \frac{a_i}{B^{d-1}} \right\rfloor \right]_B \right) \in \mathcal{R}_B^d,$$

where a_i is the i-th coefficient of $\mathbf{a}$. Then, the function $\mathbf{g}^{-1}$ breaks down a polynomial in $\mathcal{R}_Q$ into d polynomials in $\mathcal{R}_B$. Similarly, the polynomial can be recovered utilizing $\langle \mathbf{g}^{-1}(\mathbf{a}) \cdot \mathbf{g} \rangle = \mathbf{a}$.

2.4   RNS Decomposition over Polynomial Rings

The RNS system essentially uses the Chinese Remainder Theorem to break down the modulus Q to several small integers $Q_1, ..., Q_d$, where each Q_i can be stored using 32-bit or 64-bit native integer types. For efficiency, RNS is often used in conjunction with NTT. For a polynomial $\mathbf{a} \in \mathcal{R}_Q$, the coefficient vectors of result polynomials after RNS are

$$\mathbf{g}^{-1}(\mathbf{a}) = (\mathbf{a}_1, \cdots, \mathbf{a}_d) \in \mathbb{Z}_Q^{N \times d},$$

where $\mathbf{a}_i(X) = \mathbf{a}(X) \pmod{Q_i}$ with coefficient vector $\mathbf{a}_i = (a_{i,0}, a_{i,1}, \cdots, a_{i,N-1})$, and its NTT form is denoted as $\mathsf{NTT}_{Q_i}(\mathbf{a}_i)$. So, for two polynomials $\mathbf{a}, \mathbf{b} \in \mathcal{R}_Q$, their multiplication using RNS representation is computed as

$$(\mathsf{NTT}_{Q_1}(\mathbf{a}_1), \cdots, \mathsf{NTT}_{Q_d}(\mathbf{a}_d)) \odot (\mathsf{NTT}_{Q_1}(\mathbf{b}_1), \cdots, \mathsf{NTT}_{Q_d}(\mathbf{b}_d)),$$

which can be recovered using inverse CRT to get the result over $\mathcal{R}_Q$. The gadget vector is

$$\mathbf{g} = \left(Q'_1 \cdot \hat{Q}_1 \cdots Q'_d \cdot \hat{Q}_d \right),$$

where $Q'_i = Q/Q_i, \hat{Q}_i = Q'^{-1}_i \bmod Q_i, i = 1, \cdots, d.$

2.5 Ring GSW Ciphertext and External Product

The traditional GSW ciphertext uses the exact gadget matrix $\mathbf{G}$ to reduce noise [15]. For plaintext $m \in \mathbb{Z}_t$, the RGSW ciphertext is

$$\mathrm{RGSW}_{s,Q}(m) = \begin{pmatrix} \mathbf{a}_0 & \mathbf{a}_0 \cdot \mathbf{s} + \mathbf{e}_0 \\ \cdots & \cdots \\ \mathbf{a}_{2d-1} & \mathbf{a}_{2d-1} \cdot \mathbf{s} + \mathbf{e}_{2d-1} \end{pmatrix} + m \cdot \mathbf{G} \in \mathcal{R}_Q^{2d \times 2},$$

where $\mathbf{a}_i (i = 0, \cdots, 2d-1)$ are $2d$ random polynomials in $\mathcal{R}_Q$, and $\mathbf{s}$ is a secret key of RLWE encryption. The gadget matrix is defined as $\mathbf{G} = \mathbf{I}_2 \bigotimes \mathbf{g} \in \mathcal{R}_Q^{2d \times 2}$. The external product between RLWE ciphertext $\mathrm{RLWE}_{s,Q}(\mu)$ and RGSW ciphertext $\mathrm{RGSW}_{s,Q}(m)$ can be computed as follows using gadget decomposition technique.

$$\begin{aligned}
\mathrm{RLWE}_{s,Q}(\mu) \odot \mathrm{RGSW}_{s,Q}(m) &= \mathbf{G}^{-1}(\mathrm{RLWE}_{s,Q}(\mu)) \odot (\mathrm{RGSW}_{s,Q}(0) + m \cdot \mathbf{G}) \\
&= \mathbf{G}^{-1}(\mathrm{RLWE}_{s,Q}(\mu)) \cdot \mathrm{RGSW}_{s,Q}(0) + m \cdot \mathrm{RLWE}_{s,Q}(\mu) \\
&= \mathrm{RLWE}_{s,Q}(0 + m \cdot \mu) \\
&= \mathrm{RLWE}_{s,Q}(m \cdot \mu)
\end{aligned}$$

2.6 FHEW-Like Bootstrapping with GINX Blind Rotation

The FHEW-like bootstrapping can evaluate gate operations or functions, with blind rotation being the core operation. The FHEW-like bootstrapping can evaluate gate operations or functions, with blind rotation being the core operation. In this paper, we mainly focus on GINX blind rotation, which is more efficient for keys sampled from binary or ternary distributions.

Given an LWE ciphertext $\mathbf{c} = (\mathbf{a}, b) \in \mathbb{Z}_q^{n+1}$ and n RGSW ciphertexts $\mathsf{bsk} = (\mathsf{bsk}_0, \cdots, \mathsf{bsk}_{n-1})$ that encrypt the LWE secret key $\mathbf{s} = (s_0, \cdots, s_{n-1})$, the blind rotation outputs an RLWE ciphertext encrypting $X^{-b+\sum_{i=0}^{n-1} a_i \cdot s_i} \in \mathcal{R}_Q$ with the RLWE secret key $\mathbf{sk}$ and modulus Q. This step requires using the CMux gate as follows:

$$\mathbf{acc} \leftarrow \mathbf{acc} + (X^{a_i} - 1) \cdot (\mathbf{acc} \odot \mathrm{RGSW}_{\mathbf{sk},Q}(s_i)), i = 0, \cdots, n-1.$$

2.7 Montgomery Reduction

The Montgomery Reduction [24] can be efficiently implemented with Intel AVX instructions, as demonstrated in Algorithm 1 as [26]. The operations hi and lo represent the signed high product and low product, respectively. The result of Algorithm 1 can be mapped to $0 \le r < Q$ using shifting and a logical AND operation, i.e., $r + ((r \gg (k-1)) \mathsf{ AND } Q)$.

Algorithm 1. Montgomery Reduction Algorithm with High and Low Multiplication.

Input:

    Two coefficients $x, y \in \mathbb{Z}_Q$, where $-\frac{\beta}{2}Q \leq x \cdot y < \frac{\beta}{2}Q, 0 < Q < \frac{\beta}{2}$.

    Precomputed constant $Q^{-1} \bmod \beta$.

Output:

    $r = x \cdot y \cdot \beta^{-1} \bmod Q$, where $-Q < r < Q$.

1: $m = \mathsf{lo}(x \cdot y) \cdot Q^{-1} \bmod \beta$

2: $t = \lfloor m \cdot Q/\beta \rceil$

3: $r = \mathsf{hi}(x \cdot y) - t$

4: **return** r.

---

3 Improved Blind Rotation Based on NTT

In this section, we present a refined NTT implementation method leveraging the special structure of Solinas primes. We select the appropriate decomposition method to perform blind rotation for computing gate and circuit bootstrapping, taking into account the requirements for correctness and security.

3.1 More Efficient Blind Rotation with Refined NTT

Considering the current implementation disparity between FFT-based and NTT-based homomorphic encryption libraries, we intend to construct more efficient implementations for blind rotation using NTT.

Here, we give the strategy for selecting a modulus to perform NTT efficiently, where the main operations are multiplications, additions, and subtractions over a finite field. Due to the doubling of data size after each multiplication, we employ the Montgomery algorithm to perform modular multiplications. For addition and subtraction, where the data size changes by at most one bit after each operation, we select Solinas primes with form $2^{k_1} \pm 2^{k_2} \pm 1$ to perform NTT. Utilizing Solinas primes for modular additions and subtractions is advantageous, as it permits simpler operations and the application of the lazy reduction technique [26] to reduce the number of modular operations. For Example, the modular reduction with the 29-bit prime number $2^{29} - 2^{18} + 1$ can be performed as illustrated in Algorithm 2. Thus, all primes of the form $2^{k_1} \pm 2^{k_2} \pm 1$ can facilitate modular reductions of addition and subtraction results using simple shift and logic operations, which are simpler compared to Montgomery algorithm.

Lemma 1. *For a signed integer a within 32-bit, Algorithm 2 correctly computes $a \bmod Q$ and the output r satisfies $-2^{31} + 4Q \leq r < 2^{31} - 3Q$.*

Proof. For a signed 32-bit integer a, let the integer t be the quotient and the integer u the remainder of $\frac{a}{2^{29}}$, with $t \in [-4, 3] \cap \mathbb{Z}$ and $u \in [0, 2^{29} - 1] \cap \mathbb{Z}$. Thus one can use t and u to denote a, i.e., $a = t2^{29} + u$. From $Q = 2^{29} - 2^{18} + 1$, we have $2^{29} \equiv 2^{18} - 1 \bmod Q$. Thus with modulus Q there exists

$$a = t2^{29} + u = t\left(2^{18} - 1\right) + u = r \bmod Q.$$

Algorithm 2. Modular algorithms for adding and subtracting when $Q = 2^{29} - 2^{18} + 1$.

Input:
   One coefficient a satisfying $-2^{31} \le a < 2^{31}$.
Output:
   $r = a \bmod Q$, where $-2^{31} + 4Q \le r < 2^{31} - 3Q$.
1: $t = \lfloor \frac{a}{2^{29}} \rfloor$
2: $u = a \bmod 2^{29}$
3: $u = u - t$
4: $t = t \cdot 2^{18}$
5: $r = u + t$
6: **return** r.

Following this, the range of r output by the Algorithm 2 is:

$$-2^{31} + 4Q = -4\left(2^{18} - 1\right) + 0 \le r \le 3\left(2^{18} - 1\right) + 2^{29} - 1 < 2^{31} - 3Q.$$

Based on the output range of Algorithm 2, it is evident that its results can be further added to or subtracted from the outputs of the Montgomery algorithm. This implies that each modular reduction operation with a Solinas modulus can support multiple subsequent addition or subtraction operations before the next modular reduction is needed. Utilizing the special reduction as shown in Algorithm 2 and Montgomery reduction with lazy reduction idea for NTT, the execution time of external products can be reduced dramatically.

3.2   Efficient Approximate Gadget Decomposition for Gate Bootstrapping

The blind rotation focuses on the decomposition technique to control the noise in external products. For example, FHEW [10] uses exact gadget decomposition to guarantee the correctness and security in bootstrapping, which results in only polynomial error growth. TFHE [7] introduces the more advanced approximate gadget decomposition technique to the Torus ring, which can reduce the blocks of decomposition with the same security level as exact decomposition. This reduction in the number of blocks leads to a decrease in the computational complexity of external products in blind rotation. For gate bootstrapping, where a modulus smaller than 32 bits can be used, we utilize approximate decomposition combined with our refined NTT described above.

The approximate gadget decomposition introduces an approximate factor P, satisfying $P \cdot B_g^d < Q$. Specifically, given a modulus Q of length l-bit, we can choose the approximate factor P and the decomposition base B_g such that $l = \log_2 P + d_g \cdot \log_2 B_g$, where the number of decomposition blocks is $d_g = \lfloor \log_{B_g} Q \rfloor + 1$. Correspondingly, the gadget vector is $\mathbf{g}_P = \left(PB_g^0, \cdots, PB_g^{d_g-1}\right) \in \mathbb{Z}_Q^{d_g}$. For a polynomial $\mathbf{a} \in \mathcal{R}_Q$, we denote the decomposition function as $\mathbf{g}_P^{-1}$ as

$$\mathbf{g}_P^{-1}(\mathbf{a}) = (\mathbf{a}_0, \cdots, \mathbf{a}_{d_g-1}) = \left(\left[\lfloor \frac{\mathbf{a}}{PB_g^0} \rceil \right]_{B_g}, \cdots, \left[\lfloor \frac{\mathbf{a}}{PB_g^{d_g-1}} \rceil \right]_{B_g} \right) \in \mathcal{R}_{B_g}^{d_g}.$$

Thus, we can get d_g polynomials $\mathbf{a}_0, \cdots, \mathbf{a}_{d_g-1}$, which minimizes the infinite form of decomposition error $\varepsilon = \mathbf{a} - P \cdot \sum_{i=0}^{d_g-1} \mathbf{a}_i \cdot B_g^i$. To guarantee correctness, the error term must satisfy $\|\varepsilon\|_\infty \le P/2$.

Furthermore, when using the approximate gadget decomposition in external products between RLWE and RGSW ciphertexts, the gadget matrix $\mathbf{G}_P$ can be denoted as $\mathbf{I}_2 \otimes \mathbf{g}_P^T \in \mathbb{Z}_Q^{2d_g \times 2}$. The RGSW ciphertext of $m \in \{0,1\}$ with the form as

$$\mathsf{RGSW}_{\mathbf{sk},Q}(m) = \begin{pmatrix} \mathsf{ct}_0 \\ \vdots \\ \mathsf{ct}_{2d_g-1} \end{pmatrix} + m \cdot \begin{pmatrix} \mathbf{g}_P^T & 0 \\ 0 & \mathbf{g}_P^T \end{pmatrix} \in \mathcal{R}_Q^{2d_g \times 2},$$

where $\mathsf{ct}_i \in \mathsf{RLWE}_{\mathbf{sk},Q}(0)$ are RLWE ciphertexts sampled randomly from $\mathcal{R}_Q$ with noise terms $\mathbf{e}_i'$. The external product using approximate gadget decomposition between $\mathsf{ct} = (\mathbf{a}, \mathbf{b}) \in \mathsf{RLWE}_{\mathbf{sk},Q}(\mu)$ and $\mathsf{CT} \in \mathsf{RGSW}_{\mathbf{sk},Q}(m)$ as

$$\begin{aligned}
\mathsf{ct}_P' &= \mathbf{g}_P^{-1}(\mathsf{RLWE}_{\mathbf{sk},Q}(\mu)) \odot \mathsf{RGSW}_{\mathbf{sk},Q}(m) \\
&= \left(\mathbf{g}_P^{-1}(\mathbf{a}), \mathbf{g}_P^{-1}(\mathbf{b}) \right) \odot (\mathsf{RGSW}_{\mathbf{sk},Q}(0) + m \cdot \mathbf{G}_P) \\
&= \left(\mathbf{g}_P^{-1}(\mathbf{a}), \mathbf{g}_P^{-1}(\mathbf{b}) \right) \cdot \mathsf{RGSW}_{\mathbf{sk},Q}(0) + \mathsf{RLWE}_{\mathbf{sk},Q} \left(m \cdot \mathbf{sk} \cdot (\mathbf{a} + \varepsilon) + m \cdot (\mathbf{b} + \varepsilon) \right) \\
&= \mathsf{RLWE}_{\mathbf{sk},Q}(0 + \sum_{i=0}^{d_g-1} \mathsf{ct}_i' \mathbf{e}_i') + \mathsf{RLWE}_{\mathbf{sk},Q} \left(m \cdot (\mathbf{b} + \mathbf{a} \cdot \mathbf{sk}) + m \cdot \varepsilon + m \cdot \varepsilon \cdot \mathbf{sk} \right) \\
&= \mathsf{RLWE}_{\mathbf{sk},Q}(m \cdot \mu + m \cdot \mathbf{e}_{\mathsf{ct}} + m \cdot \varepsilon + m \cdot \varepsilon \cdot \mathbf{sk} + \sum_{i=0}^{d_g-1} \mathsf{ct}_i' \mathbf{e}_i').
\end{aligned}$$

The term ct_i' is the is the i-th result of the approximate decomposition on ct, and $\mathbf{e}_i'$ is the error term in RGSW ciphertext, $\mathbf{e}_{\mathsf{ct}}$ is the error term in RLWE ciphertext.

Noise Analysis. The error generated by the external product using the approximate gadget decomposition described above is $\mathsf{Err}(\mathsf{ct}_P') = \sum_{i=0}^{d_g-1} \mathsf{ct}_i' \mathbf{e}_i' + \mathbf{sk} \cdot \varepsilon + \varepsilon + \mathbf{e}_{\mathsf{ct}}$. The variance of the result of external product is

$$\mathsf{Var}(\mathsf{Err}(\mathsf{ct}_P')) \le \frac{d_g N Q^2}{12} \cdot \mathsf{Var}(\mathsf{CT}) + \frac{(N+2)P^2}{24} + \mathsf{Var}(\mathsf{ct}).$$

3.3   Efficient RNS Decomposition for Circuit Bootstrapping

In this section, we present the implementation using RNS technique in the GINX blind rotation algorithm for circuit bootstrapping. The aim is to decompose RLWE ciphertexts into smaller components with moduli within 32 bits, thereby enhancing the efficiency of external product computations using AVX-512 to implement highly parallelized NTT.

External Product with RNS. Unlike [10,12], which use digit decomposition and FFT, we opt for combining RNS with NTT to control noise growth and simultaneously enhance the efficiency of external products. The primary advantage of the RNS technique is often seen as decomposing large data, which cannot be represented by a register, into smaller and more manageable sizes, as demonstrated in BFV and BGV [4,11]. However, the additional implementation benefits are frequently overlooked when the modulus is decomposed into smaller sizes. Therefore, for data that can be directly represented within 64 bits, we use RNS to decompose the modulus into several primes not exceeding 32 bits, enabling computations with higher parallelism.

First, we select a composite number that satisfies $Q = \prod_{i=1}^{d_R} Q_i$ as the modulus of an RLWE ciphertext, where $Q_1, \ldots, Q_{d_R}$ are Solinas primes. Thus, we can decompose the RLWE ciphertext over the ring $\mathcal{R}_Q$ into d_R ciphertexts in $\mathcal{R}_{Q_1}, \ldots, \mathcal{R}_{Q_{d_R}}$, respectively, where the external products can be performed using optimized NTT. For simplicity and clarity, we choose $d_R = 2$ for the subsequent description of blind rotation and bootstrapping.

In blind rotation, the results of RNS decomposition cannot be directly used for the external product of RLWE and RGSW ciphertexts. They need to be supplemented based on the number of decomposition moduli d_R. For example, for an RLWE ciphertext $\mathsf{ct} = (\mathbf{a}, \mathbf{b}) \in \mathsf{RLWE}_{\mathsf{sk},Q}(\mu)$, we obtain two ciphertexts after RNS decomposition and supplementation when $d_R = 2$, as

$$
\begin{aligned}
\mathsf{ct}_{Q_1} &= \left([\mathbf{a}]_{Q_1}, \left[[\mathbf{a}]_{Q_2} \right]_{Q_1}, [\mathbf{b}]_{Q_1}, \left[[\mathbf{b}]_{Q_2} \right]_{Q_1} \right) \in \mathcal{R}_{Q_1}^4, \\
\mathsf{ct}_{Q_2} &= \left(\left[[\mathbf{a}]_{Q_1} \right]_{Q_2}, [\mathbf{a}]_{Q_2}, \left[[\mathbf{b}]_{Q_1} \right]_{Q_2}, [\mathbf{b}]_{Q_2} \right) \in \mathcal{R}_{Q_2}^4.
\end{aligned}
\tag{1}
$$

Correspondingly, the RGSW ciphertexts should be stored with moduli Q_1 and Q_2 as $\mathsf{CT}_{Q_1} \in \mathsf{RGSW}_{\mathsf{sk},Q_1}\left([m]_{Q_1} \right)$ and $\mathsf{CT}_{Q_2} \in \mathsf{RGSW}_{\mathsf{sk},Q_2}\left([m]_{Q_2} \right)$, which will be precomputed and stored in NTT form before blind rotation. The two RGSW ciphertexts can be seen as

$$
\mathsf{CT}_{Q_k} = \left[\begin{pmatrix} \mathsf{ct}_0 \\ \mathsf{ct}_1 \\ \mathsf{ct}_2 \\ \mathsf{ct}_3 \end{pmatrix} \right]_{Q_k} + [m]_{Q_k} \cdot \left[\begin{pmatrix} Q_1' \cdot \hat{Q}_1 & 0 \\ Q_2' \cdot \hat{Q}_2 & 0 \\ 0 & Q_1' \cdot \hat{Q}_1 \\ 0 & Q_2' \cdot \hat{Q}_2 \end{pmatrix} \right]_{Q_k} \in \mathcal{R}_{Q_k}^{4 \times 2}, \ k = 1, 2.
$$

Here, $\mathsf{ct}_i \in \mathsf{RLWE}_{\mathsf{sk},Q_k}(0)$ with $i = 0, 1, 2, 3$ are RLWE ciphertexts sampled randomly from $\mathcal{R}_{Q_k}$.

We define the external product between $\mathsf{ct} = (\mathbf{a}, \mathbf{b}) \in \mathsf{RLWE}_{\mathsf{sk},Q}(\mu)$ and $\mathsf{CT} \in \mathsf{RGSW}_{\mathsf{sk},Q}(m)$ over each ring $\mathcal{R}_{Q_k}$ as $\mathsf{ct}_k' = (\mathsf{ct}_{Q_k} \odot \mathsf{CT}_{Q_k}) \bmod Q_k$. Here we present a concise proof of the correctness of the external product with the RNS modulus. For example, in the ring $\mathcal{R}_{Q_1}$, the external product is computed as

$$
\begin{aligned}
\mathsf{ct}'_{Q_1} &= \mathsf{ct}_{Q_1} \odot \mathsf{CT}_{Q_1} \\
&= \mathsf{RLWE}_{\mathbf{sk},Q_1}([\mu]_{Q_1}) \odot \mathsf{RGSW}_{\mathbf{sk},Q_1}([m]_{Q_1}) \\
&= \mathsf{RLWE}_{\mathbf{sk},Q_1}([\mu]_{Q_1}) \cdot \mathsf{RGSW}_{\mathbf{sk},Q_1}(0) + [m]_{Q_1} \cdot \mathsf{RLWE}_{\mathbf{sk},Q_1}([\mu]_{Q_1}) \cdot [\mathbf{G}]_{Q_1} \\
&= \mathsf{RLWE}_{\mathbf{sk},Q_1}(0) + [m]_{Q_1} \cdot \left[\left([\mathbf{a}]_{Q_1} Q'_1 \hat{Q}_1 + [\mathbf{a}]_{Q_2} Q'_2 \hat{Q}_2, \ [\mathbf{b}]_{Q_1} Q'_1 \hat{Q}_1 + [\mathbf{b}]_{Q_2} Q'_2 \hat{Q}_2 \right) \right]_{Q_1} \\
&= \mathsf{RLWE}_{\mathbf{sk},Q_1}(0) + [m]_{Q_1} \cdot \left[\left([\mathbf{a}]_Q, [\mathbf{b}]_Q \right) \right]_{Q_1} \\
&= \mathsf{RLWE}_{\mathbf{sk},Q_1}(0) + [m]_{Q_1} \cdot \mathsf{RLWE}_{\mathbf{sk},Q_1}([\mu]_{Q_1}) \\
&= \mathsf{RLWE}_{\mathbf{sk},Q_1}([m]_{Q_1} \cdot [\mu]_{Q_1})
\end{aligned}
$$

Therefore, we can recover the the external product result $\mathsf{ct}' = \mathsf{ct} \odot \mathsf{CT} \in \mathcal{R}_Q^2$ using the ICRT on $\mathsf{ct}'_{Q_1} \in \mathcal{R}_{Q_1}^2$ and $\mathsf{ct}'_{Q_2} \in \mathcal{R}_{Q_2}^2$ as

$$
\begin{aligned}
\mathsf{ct}' &= \mathsf{ct}'_{Q_1} \cdot Q'_1 \cdot \hat{Q}_1 + \mathsf{ct}'_{Q_2} \cdot Q'_2 \cdot \hat{Q}_2 \\
&= \mathsf{RLWE}_{\mathbf{sk},Q_1}([m]_{Q_1} \cdot [\mu]_{Q_1}) \cdot Q'_1 \cdot \hat{Q}_1 + \mathsf{RLWE}_{\mathbf{sk},Q_2}([m]_{Q_2} \cdot [\mu]_{Q_2}) \cdot Q'_2 \cdot \hat{Q}_2 \\
&= \mathsf{RLWE}_{\mathbf{sk},Q}(m \cdot \mu)
\end{aligned}
$$

Noise Analysis. Unlike approximate decomposition, RNS and ICRT can achieve precise decomposition and reconstruction, avoiding introducing errors during the decomposition process. In the RNS-based external product, the error is $\mathsf{Err}(\mathsf{ct}'_P) = \mathsf{ct}_{Q_1}\mathbf{e}_1 + \mathsf{ct}_{Q_2}\mathbf{e}_2 + e_{\mathsf{ct}}$, where $\mathbf{e}_1$ and $\mathbf{e}_2$ are the error terms in RGSW ciphertext, e_{ct} is the error term in RLWE ciphertext. The variance of the result of external product is

$$
\mathsf{Var}(\mathsf{err}(\mathsf{acc})) \leq \frac{N(Q_1^2 + Q_2^2)}{6} \cdot \mathsf{Var}(\mathsf{err}(\mathsf{CT})) + \mathsf{Var}(\mathsf{err}(\mathsf{ct})). \tag{2}
$$

Efficient GINX Blind Rotation with RNS. When performing iterative RNS-based external products, ciphertexts are needed to switch between coefficient and NTT representations frequently, necessitating careful handling in RNS representation. Intuitively, when the results of the first external product computation ct'_{Q_1} and ct'_{Q_2} are directly input into the next iteration in NTT form, they must be converted back to coefficient representations during the RNS decomposition. After decomposition, we get $\mathsf{ct}_{Q_1} \in \mathcal{R}_{Q_1}^4$ and $\mathsf{ct}_{Q_2} \in \mathcal{R}_{Q_2}^4$, which are then transformed to NTT form before external products performed over the rings $\mathcal{R}_{Q_k}$. The blind rotation requires a total of $12n$ (I)NTTs and $20n$ point multiplications using the RNS modulus Q_k.

In this procedure, we find that there are 4 NTTs can be saved in each iteration of blind rotation after the first CMux gate. For the convenience of describing the algorithm with the idea of saving (I)NTTs, we define two new decomposition functions used on ct'_{Q_1} and ct'_{Q_2} denoted as $\mathbf{g}_{Q_1}^{-1}$ and $\mathbf{g}_{Q_2}^{-1}$, which contains NTT, INTT and RNS operations. For the ciphertexts $\mathsf{ct}'_{Q_1} = (\mathbf{a}_{Q_1}, \mathbf{b}_{Q_1}) \in \mathcal{R}_{Q_1}^2$ and $\mathsf{ct}'_{Q_2} = (\mathbf{a}_{Q_2}, \mathbf{b}_{Q_2}) \in \mathcal{R}_{Q_2}^2$ in NTT form, we have

$$
\mathbf{g}_{Q_1}^{-1}(\mathsf{ct}'_{Q_1}, \mathsf{ct}'_{Q_2}) = (\mathbf{a}_{Q_1}, \mathsf{NTT}_{Q_1}(\mathsf{INTT}_{Q_2}(\mathbf{a}_{Q_2})), \mathbf{b}_{Q_1}, \mathsf{NTT}_{Q_1}(\mathsf{INTT}_{Q_2}(\mathbf{b}_{Q_2}))) \in \mathcal{R}_{Q_1}^4
$$

$$
\mathbf{g}_{Q_2}^{-1}(\mathsf{ct}'_{Q_1}, \mathsf{ct}'_{Q_2}) = (\mathsf{NTT}_{Q_2}(\mathsf{INTT}_{Q_1}(\mathbf{a}_{Q_1})), \mathbf{a}_{Q_2}, \mathsf{NTT}_{Q_2}(\mathsf{INTT}_{Q_1}(\mathbf{b}_{Q_1})), \mathbf{b}_{Q_2}) \in \mathcal{R}_{Q_2}^4.
$$

For the decomposition operation $\mathbf{g}_{Q_k}^{-1}$, ciphertexts with the modulus Q_k can be stored directly because the effect of the continuous NTT and INTT with the same modulus can cancel each other out. This reduces the total number of operations compared to performing the blind rotation directly over each ring in RNS. With this optimization, the procedure for blind rotation is depicted in Fig. 1 in Appendix C. In this context, rectangular boxes denote data in NTT form, while elliptical boxes denote data in their coefficient form. We denote the bootstrapping keys as $\mathsf{bsk}_1 \in \{\mathsf{RGSW}_{\mathbf{sk},Q}(s_i) \bmod Q_1\}$ and $\mathsf{bsk}_2 \in \{\mathsf{RGSW}_{\mathbf{sk},Q}(s_i) \bmod Q_2\}$ for $i = 0, \cdots, n-1$. The whole blind rotation using RNS decomposition is described in the Algorithm 3.

Moreover, from the implementation point of view, two consecutive I(NTT) transformations can be realized using a merged single function. That is, instead of calling two functions of (I)NTT, we can perform $\log_2 N$ levels of GS-butterflies after $\log_2 N$ levels of CT-butterflies directly, which can save a part of the scheduling time in the CPU.

Algorithm 3. Blind Rotation of GINX with RNS Decomposition.

Input:

    An LWE ciphertext $\mathbf{c} = (\mathbf{a}, b) \in \mathsf{LWE}_{\mathbf{s},q}^{n+1}(m)$, where $q|2N$.

    Two sets of bootstrapping key $\mathsf{bsk}_1 \in \{\mathsf{RGSW}_{\mathbf{sk},Q}(s_i) \bmod Q_1\}$, $\mathsf{bsk}_2 \in \{\mathsf{RGSW}_{\mathbf{sk},Q}(s_i) \bmod Q_2\}$ for $i = 0, \cdots, n-1$.

Output:

    An RLWE ciphertext $\mathsf{acc} \in \mathsf{RLWE}_{\mathbf{sk},Q}^N(X^{-b+\sum_{i=0}^{n-1} a_i \cdot s_i})$.

1: for $k = 1$ to 2 do
2:         Set $\mathsf{acc}_k = (0, \mathsf{NTT}_{Q_k}(X^{-b})) \in \mathcal{R}_{Q_k}^2$
3:         Set $\mathsf{ct}_k = (0, 0, \mathsf{NTT}_{Q_k}(X^{-b}), \mathsf{NTT}_{Q_k}(X^{-b})) \in \mathcal{R}_{Q_k}^4$
4:         Set $\mathsf{acc}_k = \mathsf{acc}_k + (\mathsf{ct}_k \odot \mathsf{bsk}_{ki}) \odot (X_{Q_k}^{a_0} - 1) \in \mathcal{R}_{Q_k}^2$
5: end for
6: for $i = 1$ to $n-1$ do
7:         for $k = 1$ to 2 do
8:             $\mathsf{ct}_k = \mathbf{g}_{Q_k}^{-1}(\mathsf{acc}_1, \mathsf{acc}_2) \in \mathcal{R}_{Q_k}^4$
9:             $\mathsf{acc}_k = \mathsf{acc}_k + (\mathsf{ct}_k \odot \mathsf{bsk}_{ki}) \odot (X_{Q_k}^{a_i} - 1) \in \mathcal{R}_{Q_k}^2$
10:       end for
11: end for
12: $\mathsf{acc} = \mathsf{ICRT}(\mathsf{INTT}_{Q_1}(\mathsf{acc}_1), \mathsf{INTT}_{Q_2}(\mathsf{acc}_2))$
13: **return** acc.

Noise Analysis. Here, we present the noise growth for the proposed blind rotation algorithm. Firstly, according to Eq. (2), the variance of noise in the CMux gate is

$$\mathsf{Var}(\mathsf{err}(\mathsf{acc})) \leq \frac{2N(Q_1^2 + Q_2^2)}{6} \cdot \mathsf{Var}(\mathsf{err}(\mathsf{bsk})) + \mathsf{Var}(\mathsf{err}(\mathsf{acc})).$$

In addition, the CMux is perform n times, thus we can get the variance of noise of blind rotation as

$$\mathsf{Var}(\mathsf{err}(\mathsf{acc})) \leq \frac{2nN(Q_1^2 + Q_2^2)}{6} \cdot \mathsf{Var}(\mathsf{err}(\mathsf{bsk})).$$

Computational Complexity Analysis and Comparison. Here we measure the complexity using the number of NTTs/FFTs and point-wise modular multiplications between NTT/FFT vectors. To highlight the advantages of using RNS in NTT-based circuit bootstrapping, we present the theoretical complexity of a blind rotation employing approximate decomposition and NTT. The complexity is categorized according to decomposition methods, including NTT-based approximate decomposition, FFT-based approximate decomposition used in current mainstream libraries, and our NTT-based RNS decomposition. The specific theoretical computational complexities are detailed in Table 1, where the symbol # denotes the number of operations. The subscript in the lower right corner of NTT or FFT indicates the word size used to store the coefficients, denoted by the symbol $\beta = 2^l$. Although RNS-based blind rotation seems to require more (I)NTT transformations, the actual data size involved in the computations is less than half of that in the approximate decomposition. This smaller data size is highly advantageous for NTT implementations, as a decrease in data size results in increased implementation parallelism and speed.

Table 1. The computational complexity comparisons of blind rotation utilizing RNS decomposition and approximate gadget decomposition.

Decomposition Method	Parameter Set	# NTT/FFT	# Modular Multiplication	$\log_2 \beta$
Approximate Decomposition	Ours_appro_53Q_1	$6n \cdot \mathsf{NTT}_{64}$	$10n$	64-bit
	Ours_appro_53Q_2	$4n \cdot \mathsf{NTT}_{64}$	$6n$	64-bit
	TFHEpp_64Q	$10n \cdot \mathsf{FFT}_{64}$	$18n$	64-bit
	TFHE-rs_64Q	$6n \cdot \mathsf{FFT}_{64}$	$10n$	64-bit
RNS Decomposition	Ours_RNS_53Q	$(8n+4) \cdot \mathsf{NTT}_{32}$	$20n$	32-bit
	Ours_RNS_no-reduced	$12n \cdot \mathsf{NTT}_{32}$	$20n$	32-bit

4   Parameters and Implementations

In this section, we give the parameters and implementation results for gate bootstrapping using approximate decomposition and circuit bootstrapping using RNS. Firstly, we give the notation of the parameters to be used for the bootstrapping:

q: Modulus of LWE ciphertext;

n: Lattice dimension of LWE ciphertext;

Q: Modulus of RLWE ciphertext;

N: Ring dimension of RLWE and RGSW ciphertext;

P: The approximate factor in approximate gadget decomposition;

B: The base of digit decomposition in approximate decomposition;

d_g: The length of gadget vector corresponding to the approximate gadget decomposition;

λ: Security level;

σ: Standard deviation of the Gaussian distribution.

4.1 Parameter Sets

Table 2 presents the concrete parameter sets for the FHEW-like bootstrapping using GINX blind rotation with approximate gadget decomposition. We chose to compare with TFHEpp [23] and TFHE-rs [28][2], which are currently the superior implementations in terms of speed. According to the previous analysis, we choose the 32-bit modulus parameter setting for the comparison scheme at 128-bit security level. We selected four sets of parameters for the NTT-based blind rotation, namely *Ours_appro_27Q*, *Ours_appro_31Q*, *Ours_appro_53Q_1* and *Ours_appro_53Q_2*, where *"appro"* means approximate gadget decomposition technique. Specifically, we choose the 27-bit Solinas prime $2^{27} - 2^{21} + 1$, 31-bit prime $2^{31} - 2^{24} + 1$ and 53-bit prime $2^{53} - 2^{34} + 1$ for efficient modular reduction. The parameters *TFHEpp_32Q* and *TFHE-rs_32Q* are the 128-bit security parameter sets provided by the open library TFHEpp [23] and TFHE-rs [28]. Besides, all secret keys are sampled from binary distributions, which are efficient in GINX blind rotation.

Table 3 presents the concrete parameter sets for circuit bootstrapping using GINX blind rotation with approximate gadget decomposition and RNS decomposition. Similarly, we chose to compare with TFHEpp [23] and TFHE-rs [28] using the 64-bit modulus with 128-bit security level. using the 64-bit modulus with 128-bit security level. Concretely, we use *Ours_RNS_53Q* using the method with reducing the number of NTTs as shown in Fig. 1, and *Ours_RNS_53Q_no-reduced* denotes the method using RNS directly without saving (I)NTTs using our function $\mathbf{g}_{Q_k}^{-1}$. For Comparisons, the parameter *TFHEpp_64Q* and *TFHE-rs_64Q* are the 128-bit security parameter sets provided by the open library TFHEpp [23] and TFHE-rs [28]. All secret keys are sampled from binary distributions, which are efficient in GINX blind rotation.

---

[2] TFHE uses the real torus $\mathbb{R}/\mathbb{Z}$ and $\mathcal{R}/\mathbb{Z}$ to describe the ciphertext spaces, thus TFHEpp [23] and TFHE-rs [28] employ different parameter definitions compared with ours. Specifically, we describe the error standard deviation instead of q and Q as it is defined over Torus following [20].

Table 2. Parameter sets for gate bootstrapping with approximate gadget decomposition.

Parameter Set	λ	$\log_2 Q$	N	q	n	d_g	B_g	P	σ
Ours_appro_27Q	128-bit	27	1024	512	512	2	2^7	2^{13}	3.2
Ours_appro_31Q	100-bit	31	1024	512	512	1	2^{15}	2^{16}	3.2
Ours_appro_53Q_1	128-bit	53	2048	1024	512	2	2^{26}	2^{27}	3.2
Ours_appro_53Q_2	128-bit	53	2048	1024	571	1	2^{17}	2^{19}	3.2
TFHEpp_32Q	128-bit	$\sigma = 2^{-25}$	1024	$\sigma = 2^{-13.4}$	636	3	2^6	2^{14}	-
TFHE-rs_32Q	128-bit	$\sigma = 2^{-24.3}$	1024	$\sigma = 2^{-16.2}$	722	3	2^6	2^{14}	-

Table 3. Parameter sets for circuit bootstrapping used in our RNS-based implementation and in FHEpp [23] and TFHE-rs [28].

Parameter Set	λ	$\log_2 Q$	N	q	n	d_g	B_g	P	$\log_2 Q_i$	σ
Ours_RNS_53Q	128-bit	53	2048	1024	571	2	-	-	27	3.2
Ours_RNS_53Q-no-reduced	128-bit	53	2048	1024	571	2	-	-	27	3.2
TFHEpp_64Q	128-bit	$\sigma = 2^{-47}$	2048	$\sigma = 2^{-13.4}$	636	4	2^6	2^{14}	-	-
TFHE-rs_64Q	128-bit	$\sigma = 2^{-24.3}$	2048	$\sigma = 2^{-15.6}$	644	2	2^6	2^{14}	-	-

4.2 Noise Analysis

Here, we evaluate the decryption failure rate for the entire bootstrapping process. Typically, noise increases during blind rotation, modulus switching, and key-switching operations, leading to errors that follow a Gaussian distribution with a standard deviation of

$$\sigma = \sqrt{\frac{q^2}{Q^2} \cdot (\sigma_{ACC}^2 + \sigma_{KS}^2) + \sigma_{MS}^2}.$$

The symbol σ_{ACC}, σ_{KS} and σ_{MS} denotes the standard deviation of the ciphertext after blind rotation, key switching, and modulus switching, respectively. The plaintext modulus t is set to 4 for gate bootstrapping and 2 for circuit bootstrapping. Consequently, we can compute the probability of decryption failure by $1 - \mathsf{erf}\left(\frac{q/2t}{2\sigma}\right)$, where erf is the Gaussian error function. The concrete decryption failure probability with our parameter sets is provided in Table 4.

4.3 Experiment Results of Bootstrapping

In this section, we implement the bootstrapping based on the blind rotation using NTT-based approximate gadget decomposition and RNS decomposition as described above. We also test the bootstrapping in TFHE-rs [28] and TFHEpp [23] with the parameters for the same security level. In order to provide a fair

Table 4. The decryption failure probability for gate bootstrapping and circuit bootstrapping with 128-bit security parameters shown in Table 2 and Table 3.

Parameter Set	Failure Probability
Ours_appro_27Q	2^{-53}
Ours_appro_31Q	2^{-32}
Ours_appro_53Q_1	2^{-40}
Ours_appro_53Q_2	2^{-40}
Ours_RNS_53Q	2^{-40}
TFHEpp_32Q	$2^{-30.5}$
TFHE-rs_32Q	2^{-40}

comparison, both tests are implemented on a computer with an Intel(R) Core i5-11500 @2.70GHz, running Ubuntu 22.04.2 LTS and compiling with clang version 14.0.0.

The implementation results of gate bootstrapping are listed in Table 5. From the implementation results, it is clear that our implementations of gate bootstrapping consume less running time than TFHEpp and TFHE-rs with the same level of security. For parameter sets with 128-bit security, our implementation achieves a speed-up of 1.9× compared to the TFHEpp library [23] and 1.4× compared to the TFHE-rs library [28]. Besides, our gate bootstrapping implementation takes only 3.9 ms with 100-bit security, which can be used in some applications. Moreover, it is evident that the efficiency of the NTT-based bootstrapping using moduli within 32-bit far surpasses that of the implementations within 64-bit. Consequently, when the modulus is less than 32-bit, opting for NTT-based blind rotation enables the most efficient realization.

We implement our optimized blind rotation in circuit bootstrapping, and the running time is presented in Table 6. Specifically, it can be observed that using RNS results in a 1.4× speedup compared to the implementation using approximate decomposition with the same parameter set. Furthermore, as described in Sect. 3.3, our optimized RNS method, which conserves (I)NTT operations, saves approximately 25% in the bootstrapping time when the polynomial ring dimension N is set to 2048. While NTT-based implementations are still less effective than FFT-based ones for circuit bootstrapping, in specific scenarios such as homomorphic trace [5] and automorphisms [16] where only prime moduli are available, FFT algorithms are constrained. However, our NTT-based bootstrapping can be directly applied without any loss in performance.

5   Conclusion

In this paper, we propose more efficient bootstrapping implementations for FHEW/TFHE-like schemes. Using exquisite NTT for gate bootstrapping, we can implement it faster than the state-of-the-art implementation using FFT.

Table 5. Running time for gate bootstrapping.

Parameter Set	Time
Ours_appro_27Q	4.7 ms
Ours_appro_31Q	3.9 ms
Ours_appro_53Q_1	42 ms
Ours_appro_53Q_2	27 ms
TFHEpp_32Q [23]	9 ms
TFHE-rs_32Q [28]	6.8 ms

Table 6. Running time for gate bootstrapping.

Parameter Set	Time
Ours_RNS_53Q	20.2 ms
Ours_RNS_53Q_no-reduced	25 ms
Ours_appro_53Q_1	42 ms
Ours_appro_53Q_2	27 ms
TFHEpp_64Q	22 ms
TFHE-rs_64Q	12.5 ms

For circuit bootstrapping, we propose the implementation using NTT based on RNS, narrowing the efficiency gap between NTT-based and FFT-based homomorphic libraries. Besides, our implementation using NTT is an optimal choice for computational scenarios that FFT is not applicable directly. Overall, our work highlights the advantages of utilizing NTT in FHEW/TFHE-like bootstrapping and can be used in piratical implementations efficiently.

A Modulus Switching

We show the modulus switching algorithm as follows. For the modulus $Q > Q' > t$, the output ciphertext is

$$\mathbf{c}' = \mathsf{ModSwitch}(\mathbf{c})$$

$$= \left(\left\lfloor \frac{\mathbf{a}}{Q} \cdot Q' \right\rceil, \left\lfloor \frac{b}{Q} \cdot Q' \right\rceil \right) \in \mathbb{Z}_{Q'}^{n+1}.$$

We decrypt the ciphertext $\mathbf{c}'$ with the secret key $\mathbf{s}$ to obtain $(\lfloor \frac{Q'}{Q} \cdot b \rceil - \langle \lfloor \frac{Q'}{Q} \cdot \mathbf{a} \rceil, \mathbf{s} \rangle) \bmod Q' = \frac{Q'}{Q} \cdot b - \langle \frac{Q'}{Q} \cdot \mathbf{a}, \mathbf{s} \rangle + \langle \mathbf{r}, \mathbf{s} \rangle + r = \frac{t}{Q'} \cdot m + \frac{Q'}{Q} \cdot e + \langle \mathbf{r}, \mathbf{s} \rangle + r$, where $r \in \mathbb{R}$ and $\mathbf{r} \in \mathbb{R}^n$ are in $[-1/2, 1/2]$. According to [10], the variance error is $\mathsf{Var}(\mathsf{err}(\mathsf{ct}')) \le (\frac{Q'}{Q})^2 \cdot \mathsf{Var}(\mathsf{err}(\mathsf{ct})) + \frac{\|\mathbf{s}\|_2^2 + 1}{12}$.

B Key Switching

The correctness of key switching is described as follows. Let $\mathsf{ksk}_{i,j,v} = (\mathbf{a_k}, \; \mathbf{a_k} \cdot \mathbf{s}' + vs_i B_k + \mathbf{e}_k)$, the key switching step outputs

$$\mathbf{c}' = \mathsf{KeySwitch}(\mathbf{c}, \mathcal{K}) = (0, b) - \sum_{i,j} \mathsf{ksk}_{i,j,a_{i,j}}.$$

We set $\mathbf{a}' = -\sum_{i,j} \mathbf{a}'_{i,j,a_{i,j}}$ and $b' = b - \mathbf{a} \cdot \mathbf{z} + \mathbf{a}' \cdot \mathbf{s} - \sum_{i,j} e_{i,j,a_{i,j}}$. It is easy to see that it is a new LWE ciphertext under the secret key $\mathbf{s}$. In addition, the variance of the noise satisfies $\mathsf{Var}(\mathsf{err}(\mathsf{ct}')) \le Nd_k \cdot \mathsf{Var}(\mathsf{err}(\mathsf{ksk})) + \mathsf{Var}(\mathsf{err}(\mathsf{ct}))$.

C   Blind Rotation Using RNS Directly

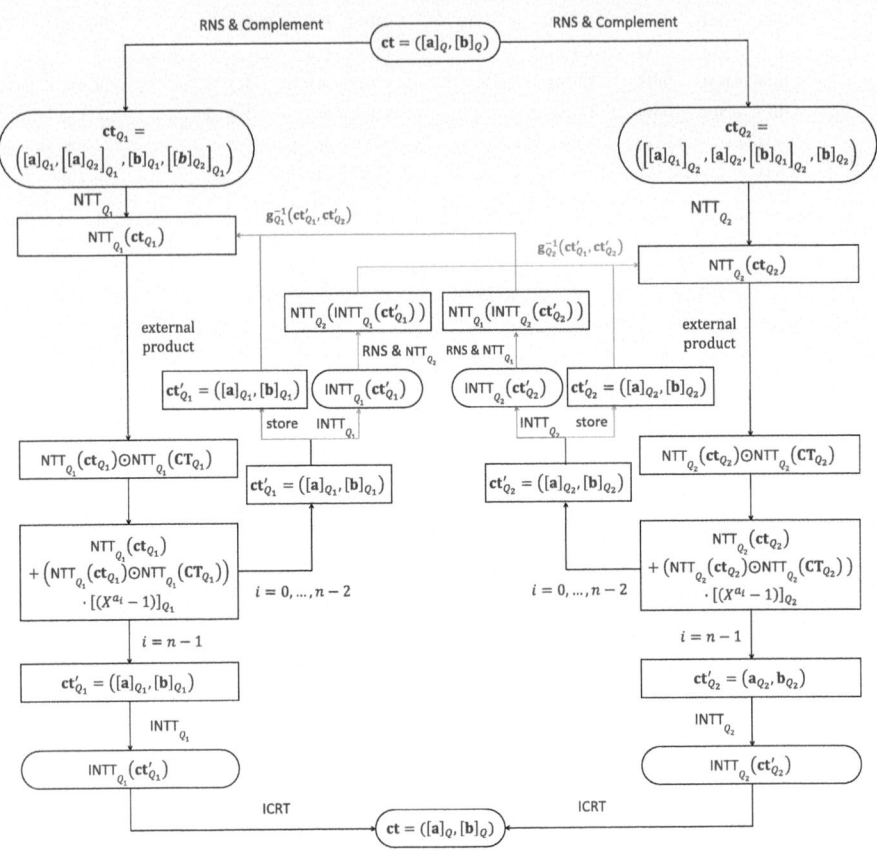

Fig. 1. Blind Rotation using RNS with less NTTs.

References

1. Alperin-Sheriff, J., Peikert, C.: Faster bootstrapping with polynomial error. In: Garay, J.A., Gennaro, R. (eds.) CRYPTO 2014. LNCS, vol. 8616, pp. 297–314. Springer, Heidelberg (2014). https://doi.org/10.1007/978-3-662-44371-2_17
2. Badawi, A.A., et al.: Openfhe: open-source fully homomorphic encryption library. Cryptology ePrint Archive, Paper 2022/915 (2022). https://eprint.iacr.org/2022/915
3. Bajard, J.-C., Eynard, J., Hasan, M.A., Zucca, V.: A full RNS variant of FV like somewhat homomorphic encryption schemes. In: Avanzi, R., Heys, H. (eds.) SAC 2016. LNCS, vol. 10532, pp. 423–442. Springer, Cham (2017). https://doi.org/10.1007/978-3-319-69453-5_23

4. Brakerski, Z., Gentry, C., Vaikuntanathan, V.: (Leveled) fully homomorphic encryption without bootstrapping. ACM Trans. Comput. Theory (TOCT) **6**(3), 1–36 (2014)
5. Chen, H., Dai, W., Kim, M., Song, Y.: Efficient homomorphic conversion between (ring) LWE ciphertexts. In: Sako, K., Tippenhauer, N.O. (eds.) ACNS 2021. LNCS, vol. 12726, pp. 460–479. Springer, Cham (2021). https://doi.org/10.1007/978-3-030-78372-3_18
6. Cheon, J.H., Han, K., Kim, A., Kim, M., Song, Y.: A full RNS variant of approximate homomorphic encryption. In: Cid, C., Jacobson, M., Jr. (eds.) SAC 2018. LNCS, vol. 11349, pp. 347–368. Springer, Cham (2019). https://doi.org/10.1007/978-3-030-10970-7_16
7. Chillotti, I., Gama, N., Georgieva, M., Izabachène, M.: Faster fully homomorphic encryption: bootstrapping in less than 0.1 seconds. In: Cheon, J.H., Takagi, T. (eds.) ASIACRYPT 2016. LNCS, vol. 10031, pp. 3–33. Springer, Heidelberg (2016). https://doi.org/10.1007/978-3-662-53887-6_1
8. Chung, C.M.M., Hwang, V., Kannwischer, M.J., Seiler, G., Shih, C.J., Yang, B.Y.: NTT multiplication for NTT-unfriendly rings: new speed records for saber and NTRU on cortex-M4 and AVX2. IACR Trans. Cryptogr. Hardware Embed. Syst. 159–188 (2021)
9. Ding, J., Lindner, R.: Identifying ideal lattices. Cryptology ePrint Archive (2007)
10. Ducas, L., Micciancio, D.: FHEW: bootstrapping homomorphic encryption in less than a second. In: Oswald, E., Fischlin, M. (eds.) EUROCRYPT 2015. LNCS, vol. 9056, pp. 617–640. Springer, Heidelberg (2015). https://doi.org/10.1007/978-3-662-46800-5_24
11. Fan, J., Vercauteren, F.: Somewhat practical fully homomorphic encryption. Cryptology ePrint Archive (2012)
12. Gama, N., Izabachène, M., Nguyen, P.Q., Xie, X.: Structural lattice reduction: generalized worst-case to average-case reductions and homomorphic cryptosystems. In: Fischlin, M., Coron, J.-S. (eds.) EUROCRYPT 2016. LNCS, vol. 9666, pp. 528–558. Springer, Heidelberg (2016). https://doi.org/10.1007/978-3-662-49896-5_19
13. Gentry, C.: Fully homomorphic encryption using ideal lattices. In: Proceedings of the Forty-First Annual ACM Symposium on Theory of Computing, pp. 169–178 (2009)
14. Gentry, C., Halevi, S., Smart, N.P.: Homomorphic evaluation of the AES circuit. In: Safavi-Naini, R., Canetti, R. (eds.) CRYPTO 2012. LNCS, vol. 7417, pp. 850–867. Springer, Heidelberg (2012). https://doi.org/10.1007/978-3-642-32009-5_49
15. Gentry, C., Sahai, A., Waters, B.: Homomorphic encryption from learning with errors: conceptually-simpler, asymptotically-faster, attribute-based. In: Canetti, R., Garay, J.A. (eds.) CRYPTO 2013. LNCS, vol. 8042, pp. 75–92. Springer, Heidelberg (2013). https://doi.org/10.1007/978-3-642-40041-4_5
16. Guimarães, A., Pereira, H.V., Van Leeuwen, B.: Amortized bootstrapping revisited: simpler, asymptotically-faster, implemented. In: Guo, J., Steinfeld, R. (eds.) ASIACRYPT 2023. LNCS, vol. 14443, pp. 3–35. Springer, Cham (2023). https://doi.org/10.1007/978-981-99-8736-8_1
17. Halevi, S., Polyakov, Y., Shoup, V.: An improved RNS variant of the BFV homomorphic encryption scheme. In: Matsui, M. (ed.) CT-RSA 2019. LNCS, vol. 11405, pp. 83–105. Springer, Cham (2019). https://doi.org/10.1007/978-3-030-12612-4_5
18. Halevi, S., Shoup, V.: Design and implementation of helib: a homomorphic encryption library. Cryptology ePrint Archive (2020)
19. Heinz, D., Pöppelmann, T.: Combined fault and DPA protection for lattice-based cryptography. IEEE Trans. Comput. **72**(4), 1055–1066 (2022)

20. Lee, Y., et al.: Efficient FHEW bootstrapping with small evaluation keys, and applications to threshold homomorphic encryption. In: Hazay, C., Stam, M. (eds.) EUROCRYPT 2023. LNCS, vol. 14006, pp. 227–256. Springer, Cham (2023). https://doi.org/10.1007/978-3-031-30620-4_8

21. Li, Z., et al.: Faster bootstrapping via modulus raising and composite NTT. IACR Trans. Cryptogr. Hardw. Embed. Syst. **2024**(1), 563–591 (2024)

22. Lyubashevsky, V., Peikert, C., Regev, O.: On ideal lattices and learning with errors over rings. In: Gilbert, H. (ed.) EUROCRYPT 2010. LNCS, vol. 6110, pp. 1–23. Springer, Heidelberg (2010). https://doi.org/10.1007/978-3-642-13190-5_1

23. Matsuoka, K.: TFHEpp: pure C++ implementation of TFHE cryptosystem (2020). https://github.com/virtualsecureplatform/TFHEpp

24. Montgomery, P.L.: Modular multiplication without trial division. Math. Comput. **44**(170), 519–521 (1985)

25. Regev, O.: On lattices, learning with errors, random linear codes, and cryptography. J. ACM (JACM) **56**(6), 1–40 (2009)

26. Seiler, G.: Faster AVX2 optimized NTT multiplication for ring-LWE lattice cryptography. Cryptology ePrint Archive (2018)

27. Wang, R., et al.: Circuit bootstrapping: faster and smaller. In: Joye, M., Leander, G. (eds.) EUROCRYPT 2024. LNCS, vol. 14652, pp. 342–372. Springer, Cham (2024). https://doi.org/10.1007/978-3-031-58723-8_12

28. Zama: TFHE-RS: A Pure Rust Implementation of the TFHE Scheme for Boolean and Integer Arithmetics Over Encrypted Data (2022). https://github.com/zama-ai/tfhe-rs

Author Index

N. Mouha and N. Nikiforakis (Eds.): ISC 2024, LNCS 15257, pp. 335–336, 2025.
https://doi.org/10.1007/978-3-031-75757-0

GPSR Compliance

The European Union's (EU) General Product Safety Regulation (GPSR) is a set of rules that requires consumer products to be safe and our obligations to ensure this.

If you have any concerns about our products, you can contact us on ProductSafety@springernature.com

In case Publisher is established outside the EU, the EU authorized representative is:

Springer Nature Customer Service Center GmbH
Europaplatz 3
69115 Heidelberg, Germany

The manufacturer's authorised representative in the EU is Springer
Nature Customer Service Centre GmbH, Europaplatz 3, 69115 Heidelberg,
Germany. If you have any concerns regarding our products, please
contact ProductSafety@springernature.com

Printed and bound by CPI Group (UK) Ltd, Croydon, CR0 4YY

29/04/2026

02099533-0002